Pictorial History of the Civil War

Volume One

D1572808

Benson John Lossing

APPLEWOOD BOOKS
Bedford, Massachusetts

Pictorial History of the Civil War
was originally published in
1866

9781429015820

For a free copy of our current print catalog featuring our bestselling books, write to:

APPLEWOOD BOOKS
P.O. Box 365
Bedford, MA 01730

For more complete listings, visit us on the web at:
awb.com

Prepared for publishing by HP

PICTORIAL HISTORY

OF

THE CIVIL WAR

IN THE

UNITED STATES OF AMERICA.

By BENSON J. LOSSING.

ILLUSTRATED BY MANY HUNDRED ENGRAVINGS ON WOOD, BY LOSSING AND
BARRITT, FROM SKETCHES BY THE AUTHOR AND OTHERS.

VOLUME I.

MANSFIELD, OHIO:

ESTILL & CO., PUBLISHERS.

PREFACE.

HE task of making a record of the events of the late Civil War in our Republic is not a pleasant one for an American citizen. It would be more consonant with his wishes to bury in oblivion all knowledge of those events which compose the materials of the sorrowful story of a strife among his brethren, of terrible energy and woeful operations. But that privilege is denied him. The din of the conflict was heard all over the world, and people of all nations were spectators of the scene. The fact cannot be hidden. It has become a part of the history of the inhabitants of the earth, and will forever occupy a conspicuous place in the annals of mankind. What remains for the American citizen to do, is to see that the *stylus* of history shall make a truthful record.

I imposed upon myself the task of making, so far as my ability and an honest purpose would permit, a correct delineation of the events of the conflict, carefully drawn by the pen and pencil, for the consideration and advantage of posterity. I entitle my work " A History of the Civil War," but I ask for it no higher consideration than that of a faithful CHRONICLE, having the form of history, and aspiring to perform its highest duty, namely : to inspire mankind with a love of justice and a hatred of its opposite, and of every thing that impedes the onward and upward march of humanity.

Taking it for granted that the reader, with the facts plainly set before him, is capable of forming just conclusions, I have confined my labors chiefly to the recording of those facts ; and have only given opinions and speculations concerning their relations, and the evident motives of the chief actors in the drama, sufficient for hints for thought and premises for reasoning, without enlarging

into argument or endeavoring to forestall the judgment. For the
assistance of that judgment, there will be found in the concluding
chapter of this work an outline history of the settlement of our
country ; of the growth of the nation ; of the system of slave-labor,
and its influence upon society ; of the cotton-plant, and its relations
and power ; of immigration from Europe, and its results; and of
the alienation of feeling produced by controversies on the subject
of slavery. These are elements of the great Cause, of which the
civil war was the Effect.

Satisfied that the Rebellion was the work of a few ambitious
men, who for selfish purposes, and without excuse, conspired to
overthrow the Republic, I have given prominence to their sayings
and those of their co-workers and abettors, not with a partisan
spirit, to keep animosities alive (for I would gladly blot their utterances from the memory of man), but that posterity may know, and
profit by the knowledge, how and by whom the people of a group
of States were deceived, and cruelly wronged, and arrayed against
their government, which has been seldom accused, and never convicted, of a single act of injustice or oppression.[1] It seemed just to
the loyal people of the land everywhere to make this record, and
in their name to disclaim these utterances as being any indication
of the spirit and temper of the American people.

The Republic has survived the strife within its bosom, and
it now bears on, in the great procession of nations, its precious
burden of Free Institutions and Democratic Ideas, as nobly and
vigorously as ever. The Union has been preserved, and its broad
mantle of Love and Charity covers all its children with its ample
folds. There should be no more strife—no more alienations ; for
the true interest of each individual of the family is the highest interest of all. If the sorrowful Past may not be forgotten (and it is
best that it should not be forgotten), let the remembrance of it be
a chastening monitor and tutor ; and let all who feel aggrieved be
willing to forgive.

Wishing to secure the advantages of a personal knowledge, by
actual examination, of the principal battle-fields of the war, and the
topography of the regions over which the great armies moved, and
to make sketches of whatever might seem useful as illustrations of
the subject, I did not begin the preparation of this work for the

[1] See speech of Alexander H. Stephens at Milledgeville, Georgia, November 14, 1860, noticed on pages 53 to 57, inclusive, of this volume.

press until the close of the conflict, late in the spring of 1865. Then the proportions of that conflict were known, and its several events were so well comprehended, that it was not a difficult task to give to each act and scene its relative position and due prominence, while compressing the whole narrative into a space so small as to make the chronicle accessible to the great body of my countrymen. I have endeavored to give a popular narrative of the struggle without much criticism, and as free from technical terms and tediousness of detail as possible, leaving the preparation of a scientific and critical history of the war to military experts, who are more competent for the task.

I gladly availed myself of the labors of others with pen and pencil, who kindly permitted me to make use of unpublished materials—such as drawings, photographs, diaries, and letters ; and I am specially indebted to the courtesy of the proprietors of *Harper's Weekly* and *Frank Leslie's Illustrated Newspaper*, whose artists accompanied the great armies throughout the whole struggle, and preserved the lineaments of a thousand objects which were soon swept away by the storms of war. I was accorded free access to all official reports allowed to be made public ; and chiefly from these and the drawings of engineers, the narratives of marches, battles, and sieges were compiled, with accompanying maps and plans. In the work will be found the portraits of the prominent actors, civil and military, of both parties to the conflict ; also views and plans of battle-grounds ; head-quarters of officers ; weapons and ships of war ; forts ; arsenals ; medals of honor, and other gifts of gratitude ; costumes of soldiers ; flags ; banners ; badges ; and a great variety of other objects whereby the eye may be instructed concerning the materials used in the conflict.

The engravings, whilst they embellish the book, have been introduced for the higher purposes of instruction, and are confined to the service of illustrating facts. They have been prepared under my direct supervision ; and great pains have been taken to make them correct delineations of the objects sought to be represented. In each volume will be found a table of contents, and a list of illustrations ; and, at the close of the work, a copious analytical index. There will also be found biographical sketches of the prominent actors in the war, civil and military, arranged in cyclopedia form, and making an important Biographical Dictionary.

I am profoundly grateful to my personal friends, and to my

countrymen of every degree, from the most humble citizen and soldier to statesmen, army and navy officers of every rank, governors, and the President and his cabinet ministers, who kindly aided me in my labors in the collection of materials for this work. It would be a pleasant privilege to mention the name of each, but they are legion, and for obvious reasons it may not be done.

B. J. L.

THE RIDGE, DOVER PLAINS, N. Y.

VOLUME I.

CHAPTER I.

POLITICAL CONVENTIONS IN 1860.

CHAPTER II.

PRELIMINARY REBELLIOUS MOVEMENTS.

CHAPTER III.

ASSEMBLING OF CONGRESS.—THE PRESIDENT'S MESSAGE.

CHAPTER IV.

SEDITIOUS MOVEMENTS IN CONGRESS.—SECESSION IN SOUTH CAROLINA, AND ITS EFFECTS.

CONTENTS.

9

CHAPTER IX.

PROCEEDINGS IN CONGRESS.—DEPARTURE OF CONSPIRATORS.

CHAPTER X.

PEACE MOVEMENTS.—CONVENTION OF CONSPIRATORS AT MONTGOMERY.

CHAPTER XI.

THE MONTGOMERY CONVENTION.—TREASON OF GENERAL TWIGGS.—LINCOLN AND BUCHANAN AT THE CAPITAL.

CHAPTER XII.

THE INAUGURATION OF PRESIDENT LINCOLN, AND THE IDEAS AND POLICY OF THE GOVERNMENT.

CHAPTER XIII.

THE SIEGE AND EVACUATION OF FORT SUMTER.

CHAPTER XIV.

THE GREAT UPRISING OF THE PEOPLE.

CHAPTER XV.

SIEGE OF FORT PICKENS.—DECLARATION OF WAR.—THE VIRGINIA CONSPIRATORS, AND THE PROPOSED CAPTURE OF WASHINGTON CITY.

CHAPTER XVI.

SECESSION OF VIRGINIA AND NORTH CAROLINA DECLARED.—SEIZURE OF HARPER'S FERRY AND GOSPORT NAVY YARD.—THE FIRST TROOPS IN WASHINGTON FOR ITS DEFENSE.

CHAPTER XVII.

EVENTS IN AND NEAR THE NATIONAL CAPITAL.

CHAPTER XVIII.

THE CAPITAL SECURED.—MARYLAND SECESSIONISTS SUBDUED.—CONTRIBUTIONS BY THE PEOPLE.

CHAPTER XIX.

EVENTS IN THE MISSISSIPPI VALLEY.—THE INDIANS.

CHAPTER XX.

COMMENCEMENT OF CIVIL WAR.

CHAPTER XXI.

BEGINNING OF THE WAR IN SOUTHEASTERN VIRGINIA.

CHAPTER XXII.

THE WAR ON THE POTOMAC AND IN WESTERN VIRGINIA.

CHAPTER XXIII.

THE WAR IN MISSOURI.—DOINGS OF THE CONFEDERATE "CONGRESS."—AFFAIRS IN BALTIMORE.—PIRACIES.

CHAPTER XXIV.

THE CALLED SESSION OF CONGRESS.—FOREIGN RELATIONS.—BENEVOLENT ORGANIZATIONS.—THE OPPOSING ARMIES.

CHAPTER XXV.

BATTLE OF BULL'S RUN.

VOLUME I.

THE CIVIL WAR.

CHAPTER I.

N the spring of the year 1861, a civil war was kindled in the United States of America, which has neither a pattern in character nor a precedent in causes recorded in the history of mankind. It appears in the annals of the race as a mighty phenomenon, but not an inexplicable one. Gazers upon it at this moment,ᵃ when its awfully grand and mysterious proportions rather fill the mind with wonder than excite the reason, look for the half-hidden springs of its existence in different directions among the obscurities of theory. There is a general agreement, however, that the terrible war was clearly the fruit of a conspiracy against the nationality of the Republic, and an attempt, in defiance of the laws of Divine Equity, to establish an Empire upon a basis of injustice and a denial of the dearest rights of man. That conspiracy budded when the Constitution of the Republic became the supreme law of the land,[1] and, under the culture of disloyal and ambitious men, after gradual development and long ripening, assumed the form and substance of a rebellion of a few arrogant land and

* 1862.

---

[1] Immediately after the adoption of the National Constitution, and the beginning of the National career, in 1789, the family and State pride of Virginians could not feel contented in a sphere of equality in which that Constitution placed all the States. It still claimed for that Commonwealth a superiority, and a right to political and social domination in the Republic. Disunion was openly and widely talked of in Virginia, as a necessary conservator of State supremacy, during Washington's first term as President of the United States, and became more and more a concrete political dogma. It was because of the prevalence of this dangerous and unpatriotic sentiment in his native State, which was spreading in the Slave-labor States, that Washington gave to his countrymen that magnificent plea for Union—his Farewell Address. According to John Randolph of Roanoke, "the Grand Arsenal of Richmond, Virginia, was built with an eye to putting down the Administration of Mr. Adams (the immediate successor of Washington in the office of President) *with the bayonet*, if it could not be accomplished by other means."—*Speech of Randolph in the House of Representatives*, January, 1817.

slave holders against popular government. It was the rebellion of an OLI-GARCHY against the PEOPLE, with whom the sovereign power is rightfully lodged.

We will not here discuss the subject of the remote and half-hidden springs of the rebellion, which so suddenly took on the hideous dignity of a great civil war. We will deal simply with palpable facts, and leave the disquisition of theories until we shall have those facts arranged in proper order and relations. Then we may, far better than now, comprehend the soul of the great historic phenomenon that so startled the nations, and com-manded the profound attention of the civilized world.

With the choice of Presidential Electors, in the autumn of 1860, the open career of the living conspirators against American Nationality com-menced; and with the nominations of the candidates for the office of Chief Magistrate of the Republic, in the spring and early summer of that year, we will begin our HISTORY OF THE CIVIL WAR.

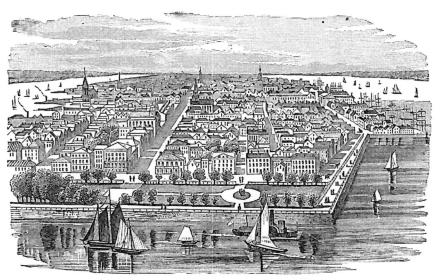

VIEW OF THE CITY OF CHARLESTON, IN 1860.

The two chief political parties into which the voters of the country were divided in 1860, were called, respectively, *Democratic* and *Republican*. These titles really had no intrinsic significance, as indices of principles, when applied to either organization, but were used by the leaders as ensigns are used in war, namely, as rallying-points for the contending ·hosts—familiar in form if not intelligible in character. That year Presidential electors were to be chosen; and, in accordance with a long-established custom, represen-tatives were appointed by the people, to meet in conventions and choose the candidates.

The Democratic party moved first. Its representatives were summoned to assemble in Charleston, a pleasant city of forty thousand inhabitants, and a considerable commercial mart. It is spread over the point of a low sandy cape, at the confluence of the waters of the Ashley and Cooper

Rivers, on the seacoast of South Carolina, and far away from the centers of population and the great forces of the Republic.

The delegates, almost six hundred in number, and representing thirty-two States, assembled on the 23d of April [a] in the great hall of the South Carolina Institute,[1] on Meeting Street, in which three thousand persons might be comfortably seated. The doors were opened at noon. The day was very warm. A refreshing shower had laid the dust at eleven o'clock, and purified the air.

THE SOUTH CAROLINA INSTITUTE.

The delegates rapidly assembled. Favored spectators of both sexes soon filled the galleries. The buzz of conversation was silenced by the voice of Judge David A. Smalley, of Vermont, the Chairman of the National Democratic Committee, who called the Convention to order. Francis B. Flournoy, a citizen of the State of Arkansas, was chosen temporary chairman.—

He took his seat without making a speech, when the Rev. Charles Hanckel, of Charleston, read a prayer, and the Convention proceeded to business.

The session of the first day was occupied in the work of organization. It was evident, from the first hour, that the spirit of the Slave system, which had become the very Nemesis of the nation, was there, full fraught with mischievous intent. It was a spirit potential as Ariel in the creation of elemental strife. For several months, premonitions of a storm, that threatened danger to the integrity of the organization there represented, had been abundant. Violently discordant elements were now in close contact. The clouds rapidly thickened, and before the sun went down on that first day of the session, all felt that a fierce tempest was impending, which might topple from its foundations, laid by Jefferson, the venerable political fabric known as the Democratic Party, which he and his friends had reared sixty years before.

On the morning of the second day of the session, Caleb Cushing, of Massachusetts, was chosen permanent President of the Convention, and a vice-president and secretary for each State were appointed. The choice of President was very satisfactory. Mr. Cushing was a man of much experience in politics and legislation. He was possessed of wide intellectual culture, and was a sagacious observer of men. He was then sixty years of

[a] 1860.

---

[1] This building, in which the famous South Carolina Ordinance of Secession was *signed* (it was *adopted* in St. Andrew's Hall), late in December, 1860, was destroyed by fire in December, 1861. St. Andrew's Hall, in which the conspirators against the Republic who seceded from the Democratic Convention now under consideration assembled, and in which the South Carolina Ordinance of Secession was adopted by the unanimous voice of a Convention, was destroyed at the same time. Everything about the site of these buildings, made infamous in history because of the wicked acts performed in them, yet (1865) exhibits a ghastly picture of desolation.

age; his features expressed great mental and moral energy, and his voice was clear and musical.

On taking the chair, Mr. Cushing addressed the Convention with great vigor. He declared it to be the mission of the Democratic party to "reconcile popular freedom with constituted order," and to maintain "the sacred reserved rights of the Sovereign States." He declared the Republicans to be those who were "laboring to overthrow the Constitution," and "aiming to produce in this country a permanent sectional conspiracy—a traitorous sectional conspiracy of one half of the States of the Union against the other half; those who, impelled by the stupid and half insane spirit of faction and fanaticism, would hurry our land on to revolution and to civil war." He declared it to be the "high and noble part of the Democratic party of the Union to withstand—to strike down and conquer" these "banded enemies of the Constitution."[1] These utterances formed a key-note that harmonized with the feelings of a large body of the delegates, and was a symphony to their action.

CALEB CUSHING.

At the close of the second day the Convention was in fair working order. Some contests for seats were undecided, there being two sets of delegates from New York and Illinois; but the vitally important *Committee on Resolutions*, composed of one delegate from each State, had been appointed without much delay. It was the business of that committee to perform the difficult and delicate task of making a platform of principles for the action of the Convention, and the stand-point of the party during the approaching canvass and election. For this purpose it had been sent to Masonic Hall, at five o'clock in the afternoon; and then and there the electric spark, which kindled the prepared combustibles of civil war into a quick and devouring flame, was elicited by the attrition of radically opposing ideas.

The subject of Slavery, as we have observed, was the troubling spirit of the Convention. It appeared in the open Hall, and it was specially apparent in the room of the Committee on Resolutions. A large number of the delegates from the Slave-labor States had come instructed, and were resolved, to demand from the Convention a candidate and a platform which should promise a guaranty for the speedy and practical recognition, by the General Government and the people, of the system of Slavery as a national and permanent institution. Impelled by this resolution, they had determined to prevent the nomination of Stephen A. Douglas of Illinois (an able statesman, and effective popular orator, then in the full vigor of middle age), who was the most prominent candidate for the suffrages of the Convention. They opposed him because he was so committed to the doctrine of "Popular Sovereignty," as it was called,—that is to say, the doctrine of the right of the people of any Territory of the Republic to decide whether Slavery should

---

[1] *Official Proceedings of the Democratic National Convention, held in 1860, at Charleston and Baltimore*, page 17.

or should not exist within its borders,—that he could not, with honor or consistency, make any further concessions to the Slave interest. This, and the positive committal of the Democratic party to a pro-slavery policy in the administration of the National Government, were the chief business of several delegates in the Convention who were led by such men as John Slidell, of Louisiana, and William L. Yancey, of Alabama, then, and long before, arch-conspirators against the life of the Republic.

In June, 1856, a National Democratic Convention was held at Cincinnati, when James Buchanan was nominated for President of the United States. A platform was then framed, composed of many resolutions and involved declarations of principles, drawn by the hand of Benjamin F. Hallet, of Boston. These embodied the substance of resolutions on the subject of Slavery, drawn up by Benjamin F. Butler, of Massachusetts (afterwards a major-general in the armies of the Republic), and adopted by the Democratic Convention of that State. On the topic of Slavery and State supremacy, the resolutions were clear and explicit. They recognized the doctrine of Popular Sovereignty as "embodying the only sound and safe solution of the Slavery question, upon which the great national idea of the people of this whole country can repose in its determined conservation of the Union, and non-interference of Congress with Slavery in the Territories or in the District of Columbia." This doctrine harmonized with the spirit of popular government; and the platform, of which it was an essential part, was accepted by the Democratic party throughout the Union, as a true exposition of their principles and policy. With this understanding, Mr. Butler, now a member of the Committee on Resolutions sitting in Masonic Hall, on that warm April evening in 1860, proposed as a platform for the Convention and the party the one constructed at Cincinnati four years before, without addition or alteration. He offered a resolution to that effect, when, to the surprise of the representatives of the Free-labor States, the proposition was rejected by a vote of seventeen States (only two of them free) against fifteen States. Recently created Oregon gave the casting vote against it, and, with California, was arrayed on the side of the Slave-labor States.

The majority now proposed an affirmance of the Cincinnati platform, but with additional resolutions, the most vital of which declared that Congress had no power to abolish Slavery in the Territories, and that Territorial Legislatures had no power to abolish Slavery in any Territory, nor to prohibit the introduction of Slavery therein, nor to exclude Slavery therefrom, or to impair or destroy the right of property in slaves by any legislation whatever. This resolution was a positive rejection of the doctrine of Popular Sovereignty. The minority of the committee, composed wholly of delegates from the Free-labor States, and representing a majority of the Presidential electors (one hundred and seventy-two against one hundred and twenty-seven), were amazed because of the bad faith and arrogant assumptions of their Southern brethren. It was clearly seen that the latter were united, evidently by pre-concert, in a determination to demand from the people of the Free-labor States further and most offensive concessions to their greed for political domination.

The manhood of the minority was evoked, and they resolved that the limit of concession was reached, and that they would yield to no further demands. They at once proposed an affirmance of the Cincinnati platform in letter and spirit, at the same time expressing, by resolution, a willingness to abide by any decision of the Supreme Court of the United States on questions of constitutional law. They offered a word for conciliation by denouncing, in another resolution, the acts of certain State Legislatures known as Personal Liberty Laws, as "hostile in character, subversive of the Constitution, and revolutionary in their effects." Mr. Butler was opposed to making even this concession, and adhered to his proposition for a simple affirmance of the Cincinnati platform.

The labors of the Committee resulted, on the evening of the fourth day of the session, in the production of three reports, and on the following morning these were submitted to the Convention: the majority report by William W. Avery, of North Carolina; the minority report, drawn by H. B. Payne, of Ohio, and a resolution for the affirmance of the Cincinnati platform without alteration, by B. F. Butler.

Mr. Avery opened debate on the subject, by frankly assuring the Convention that if the doctrine of Popular Sovereignty should be adopted as the doctrine of the Democratic party, the members of the Convention from the Slave-labor States, and their constituents, would consider it as dangerous and subversive of their rights, as the adoption of the principle of Congressional interference or prohibition. From that time until Monday, the 30th of April,[a] the debate was continued, in the midst of much   [a] 1860. confusion and disorder in the Convention. The streets of Charleston in the pleasant evenings resounded with music, the speeches of politicians, and the huzzas of the multitude. Society there was in a bubble of excitement, and the final vote of the Convention on the resolutions was awaited with the most lively interest. The hour for that decision at length arrived.   [b] April, It was on the morning of the 30th.[b] The Hall was densely   1860. crowded. A vote was first taken on Butler's resolution. It was rejected by a decisive majority. The minority report—the Douglas platform—which had been slightly modified, was now offered by B. M. Samuels, of Iowa. It was adopted by a handsome majority. In the Convention now, as in the Committee, the voices of Oregon and California, Free-labor States, were with those of the Slave-labor States.

Preconcerted rebellion now lifted its head defiantly. The spirit manifested in the resolutions, speeches, and deportment of the representatives of the Slave interest, now assumed tangible form, in action. L. P. Walker, who was afterward one of the most active insurgents against the National Government, as the so-called Secretary of War of Jefferson Davis, led the way. He spoke for the delegates from Alabama, who had been instructed by the convention that appointed them not to acquiesce in or submit to any Popular Sovereignty platform, and, in the event of such being adopted, to withdraw from the Convention. That contingency had now occurred, and the Alabama delegates formally withdrew, in accordance with a previous arrangement. They were followed by all the delegates from Mississippi, all but two from Louisiana, all from Florida and Texas, three from Arkansas, and all from South Carolina. On the following morning, twenty-six of the thirty-four Georgia delegates withdrew; and Senator Bayard and Representative Whiteley, delegates from Delaware, also left the Convention and joined the seceders, who had repaired to St. Andrew's Hall the previous evening for consultation.

The disruption of the Democratic party represented in Convention was now complete. The wedge of Slavery had split it beyond restoration. The event had been amply provided for in secret; and when D. C. Glenn, of Mississippi, in announcing the withdrawal of the delegates from that State, said, " I tell Southern men here, and, for them, I tell the North, that in less than sixty days you will find a united South standing side by side with us," there was long and vehement cheering, especially from the South Carolinians, who were joyous over the result. Charleston, that night, was the scene of unbounded pleasurable excitement.

So the arrogant representatives of the Slave interest, in contempt of the democratic principle of acquiescence in the fairly expressed will of the majority, which lies at the foundation of all order in popular government, and with an eye single to the accomplishment of an intensely selfish end, began a rebellion, first against the dominant party then in possession of the National Government, and secondly against that Government itself, which resulted in a bloody civil war, and the utter destruction of the vast and cherished interest, for the conservation of which they cast down the gauntlet defiantly and invited the arbitrament of the sword.

At twilight, on the eighth day of the session of the Convention,[a] [a] May, 1860. when the excitement occasioned by the withdrawal of many delegates had somewhat subsided, that body proceeded to ballot for a candidate for the Presidency of the Republic. At least two hundred votes were necessary to a choice. Stephen A. Douglas led off with at least fifty less than the requisite number. There was very little variation as the voting went on. Finally, on the tenth day, when fifty-seven ballotings had been taken with no prospect of a change, it was agreed to adjourn the Convention, to meet in the city of Baltimore, in Maryland, on the eighteenth day of June following. It was also resolved to invite the Democracy of the several States to make provision for supplying all vacancies in their respective delegations to the Convention when it should reassemble.

The seceding delegates partially organized a convention at St. Andrew's Hall, on the evening after their withdrawal from the regular body. On the following day, at

ST. ANDREW'S HALL.[1]

noon, they assembled at Military Hall, when they chose James A. Bayard, of Delaware, to be their president. They declared themselves, by resolution offered by Mr. Yancey, to be entitled to the style of the

---

[1] In this building, as we have observed, the Secession Convention of South Carolina politicians was assembled when it passed the Ordinance of Secession, on the 20th of December, 1860.

" Constitutional Convention," and sneeringly called those whom they had abandoned, the " Rump Convention." On the second day of their session they met in the Theater.[1] The dress circle was crowded with the women of Charleston. They had hitherto filled the galleries of the Institute Hall. Their sympathies were with the seceders, and they now followed them.

President Bayard, a dignified, courtly gentleman, sat near the foot-lights of the stage. The painted scene behind him was that of the Borgia Palace,[2] around which clustered associations of great crimes. The actors on this occasion, contrary to precedent, occupied the pit, or parquette; and there they performed only the first act of a drama to which the whole civilized world became amazed spectators. They adopted the report of the majority, offered by Mr. Avery in the regular Convention, as their platform of principles, but went no further then. They refrained from nominating a candidate for the Presidency of the Republic, and refused to listen to a proposition to send forth an address to the people. Their appointed work for the present was finished. They had accomplished the positive disruption of the Democratic party, which, as a Southern historian of the war says, had become " demoralized" on " the Slavery question," and were " unreliable and rotten,"[3] because they held independent views on that great topic of national discussion. The paralysis or destruction of that party would give the Presidency to a Republican candidate, and then the conspirators would have a wished-for pretext for rebellion.[4] The seceders were confident that their work had been effectually performed, and their desired object attained. They well knew that their class held such absolute political control in the Slave-labor States, that the great mass of their constituency would applaud their action and follow their lead. Reposing upon this knowledge, they could afford to wait for further developments; so, on the evening of the 3d of May,[a] they adjourned to meet in the city of Richmond, in Virginia, on the second Monday of June following, for further action. To that Convention they invited the Democracy of the country who might sympathize with their movement and their platform to send representatives. • 1860.

The seceders reassembled in Metropolitan Hall (on Franklin Street, near Governor), in Richmond, at the appointed time, namely, on Monday, the 11th day of June. In the mean time some of the leading Southern Congressmen, among whom were Robert Toombs, of Georgia, and other conspirators, had issued an address from Washington City, urging that the Richmond Convention should refrain from all important action, and adjourn to Baltimore, and there, re-entering the regular Convention, if possible defeat the nomination of Mr. Douglas, and thus, as they said, with well-feigned honesty of expression, " make a final effort to preserve the harmony and unity of the Democratic party." The consequence was, that the Convention at Richmond

[1] This was the fourth place in which the conspirators met in the course of forty-eight hours. All of these public buildings are now (1865) in ruins.

[2] *History of the National Political Conventions in* 1860: by M. Halstead, an Eye-witness, page 100.

[3] *First Year of the War:* by Edward A. Pollard. Richmond, 1862, page 28.

[4] When, in 1832 and 1833, Calhoun and his associates in South Carolina attempted to strike a deadly blow at our nationality, they made a protective tariff, which they called an oppression of the cotton-growing States, the pretext. In May, 1833, President Jackson, in a letter to the Rev. A. J. Crawford, of Georgia, after speaking of the trouble he had endured on account of the Nullifiers, said, " The Tariff was only the *pretext*, and Disunion and a Southern Confederacy the real object. *The next pretext will be the Negro or Slavery question.*"

was respectable in talent, but small in numbers, and wicked in conception and design.

On motion of a son of John C. Calhoun, who was chairman of the Committee on Organization, John Irwin, of Alabama, was chosen president of the Convention. It then proceeded to action, under a little embarrassment at first. There were delegates from the city of New York begging for admission to seats.[1] They were finally treated with courteous contempt, by being simply admitted to the floor of the Convention as tolerated "commissioners," and were regarded by some as spies. In this matter, as in others, the proceedings were cautiously

METROPOLITAN HALL.[2]

managed. The leaders allowed no definite action. An expression of opinion concerning the platforms offered at Charleston was suppressed; and on the second day of the session, while a "Colonel Baldwin," of the New York "commissioners," smarting under the lash of W. L. Barry, of Mississippi, who charged him with "abusing the courtesy of the Convention" by talking of the "horrors of disunion," was asking forgiveness in an abject manner,[3] the Convention adjourned, to meet at the same place on the 21st of the month.* Most of the delegates then hastened to Baltimore, pursuant to the plan of the Congressional conspirators, while the South *June, 1860. Carolina delegation, who assumed to be special managers of the treasonable drama, remained in Richmond, awaiting further developments of the plot.

The adjourned Democratic National Convention reassembled in the Front Street Theater, on Front Street, opposite Low Street, in Baltimore, on Monday, the 18th day of June. The parquette and stage were occupied by the delegates, and the dress circle was filled by spectators—a large portion of whom were women. The delicate and difficult question concerning the admission to seats in the Convention of representatives of States whose delegates had withdrawn from that body, was the first to present it-

---

1 These delegates appear to have been representatives of an association of some kind in the city of New York, who sympathized with the Secessionists. They exhibited, as credentials, a certificate of the "Trustees of the National Democratic Hall" in New York, signed by "Samuel B. Williams, *Chairman*, M. Dudley Bean, *Secretary* of the Trustees." It was also signed by William Beach Lawrence, *Chairman*, and James B. Bensel, *Secretary*, of an Executive Committee; and Thaddeus P. Mott, *Chairman*, and J. Lawrence, *Secretary* of the Association, whatever it was. These certified that Gideon J. Tucker and Dr. Charles Edward Lewis Stuart had been appointed "delegates at large from the Association;" and that Colonel Baldwin, Isaac Lawrence, James B. Bensel, and James Villiers, had been appointed *Delegates*, and N. Drake Parsons, James S. Selby, M. Dudley Bean, and A. W. Gilbert, *Alternatives*, "to represent the Association at the Richmond Convention for the nomination of President and Vice-president," &c.

2 This building was formerly occupied as a Presbyterian Church, and known as that of Dr. Plummer's.

3 Halstead's *History of the National Political Conventions in* 1860, page 158.

self. Mr. Cushing, again in the chair, refused to make any decision, and referred the whole matter to the Convention. It was claimed, that the seceding delegates had a right to re-enter the Convention if they chose to do so. This right was denied, and the language of the resolution respecting the adjournment at Charleston, by which the States represented by the seceders were called upon to " fill vacancies," was referred to as an expression of the Convention, if fairly interpreted, against the right of the seceders to return.

FRONT STREET THEATER, IN BALTIMORE, IN 1860.

It was proposed, also, that no delegate should be admitted to a seat, unless he would pledge himself to abide by the action of a majority of the Convention, and support its nominations. Debate speedily ensued. It was hot and acrimonious during, at least, six hours on that first day of the session ; and in the evening there were two mass meetings of the Democracy in the streets of Baltimore, at which vehement speeches were heard for three hours, by tens of thousands of people, citizens and strangers.

On the following morning, the subject of contesting delegations was referred to the committee on credentials. They could not agree ; *a June 21, 1860.* and on the fourth day of the session[a] two reports were submitted, the majority report recommending the admission of Douglas delegates (in place of seceders) from Louisiana and Alabama, and parts of the delegations from other States. The minority report was against the admission of the new delegates. These reports were discussed with great warmth, which sometimes reached the point of fierce personal quarrels. The proslavery men gave free scope to the expression of their opinions and feelings ; and one of them, a mercantile dealer in slaves, from Georgia, named Gaulden, advocated the reopening of the Slave-trade, and thought he should live to see the day when the doctrines which he advocated would be " the doctrines of Massachusetts and of the North." He spoke in language shocking to every right-minded man ; yet, while he disgusted a great majority of his hearers, he elicited the applause of many.

Finally, on Friday, the 22d, the majority report was adopted, and the places of most of the seceders were filled by Douglas men. Again there was rebellion against the fairly expressed will of the majority. The whole or a part of the delegations from Virginia, North Carolina, Tennessee, Maryland, California, Delaware, and Missouri, withdrew. That night was a gloomy one for those who earnestly desired the unity of the Democratic party. On the following morning, their hopes were utterly blasted when Mr. Cushing, the President of the Convention, and a majority of the Massachusetts delegation, also withdrew. " We put our withdrawal before you," said Mr. Butler, of that delegation, " upon the simple ground, among others, that there has been a withdrawal, in part, of a majority of the States, and, further (and that, perhaps, more personal to myself), upon the ground that

I will not sit in a Convention where the African Slave-trade—which is piracy by the laws of my country—is approvingly advocated."

On the retirement of Mr. Cushing, Governor David Tod, of Ohio, one of the vice-presidents, took the chair, and the Convention proceeded to ballot for a Presidential candidate. A considerable number of Southern delegates, who were satisfied with the Cincinnati platform, remained in the Convention, and, as their respective States were called, some of them made brief speeches. One of these was Mr. Flournoy, of Arkansas, the temporary Chairman of the Convention at Charleston. "I am a Southern man," he said, "born and reared amid the institution of Slavery. I first learned to whirl the top and bounce the ball with the young African. Everything I own on earth is the result of slave-labor. The bread that feeds my wife and little ones is produced by the labor of slaves. They live on my plantation with every feeling of kindness, as between master and slave. Sir, if I could see that there is anything intended in our platform unfriendly to the institution of Slavery—if I could see that we did not get every constitutional right we are entitled to, I would be the last on earth to submit in this Union; I would myself apply the torch to the magazine, and blow it into atoms, before I would submit to wrong. But I feel that in the doctrines of non-intervention and popular sovereignty is enough to protect the interests of the South."

This speech had a powerful effect upon delegates from the Free-labor States, in favor of Mr. Douglas; and of one hundred and ninety-four and a half votes cast, on the second ballot, he received one hundred and eighty-one and a half, when he was declared duly nominated for the Presidency.

James Fitzpatrick, of Alabama, was nominated for Vice-president. Two days afterward, Fitzpatrick declined the nomination, when the National Committee substituted Herschel V. Johnson, of Georgia.[1] On the evening of the 23d, the Convention made a final adjournment.

The seceders, new and old, assembled at noon on Saturday, the 23d, in the Maryland Institute Hall, situate on Baltimore Street and Marsh Market Space, a room more than three hundred feet in length

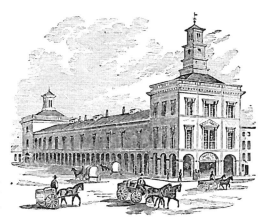

THE MARYLAND INSTITUTE IN 1860.

and seventy in breadth, with a gallery extending entirely around. It was capable of seating five thousand people; and it was almost full when the Convention was permanently organized by the appointment of Mr. Cushing to preside. That gentleman was greeted, when he ascended the platform,

---

[1] The National Committee assembled at the National Hotel, in Washington City, on the 25th of June. In it all the States were represented, excepting Delaware, South Carolina, Mississippi, and Oregon.

with the most vociferous applause, and other demonstrations of satisfaction. On taking the chair, he declared that the body then assembled formed the true *National Democratic Convention*, composed, as it was, of delegates duly accredited thereto from more than twenty States. The Convention then proceeded to business with the greatest harmony. They resolved, that the delegates to the Richmond Convention should be requested to unite with their brethren of the *National Democratic Convention*, then assembled, on the same platform of principles with themselves, if they felt authorized to do so. They took seats accordingly. Mr. Avery, of North Carolina, offered the majority report, which he had submitted in Convention at Charleston, and it was adopted without dissent, as the platform of principles of the sitting Convention, and of the party it represented.

After some further business, the Convention proceeded to the nomination of candidates for the Presidency and Vice-presidency, when George B. Loring, of Massachusetts, arose and said : " We have seen the statesmen of Mississippi coming into our own borders and fearlessly defending their principles, ay, and bringing the sectionalism of the North at their feet by their gallantry.[1] We have admiration for this courage, and I trust to live by it and be governed by it. Among all these men to whom we have been led to listen, and whom we admire and respect, there is one standing pre-eminently before this country—a young and gallant son of the South." He then named John C. Breckinridge, of Kentucky, as a nominee for the Presidency.[2] Vehement applause followed. A vote by States was taken, and Breckinridge received eighty-one ballots against twenty-four for Daniel S. Dickinson, of New York. The latter candidate was withdrawn, and the nomination of Breckinridge was declared. Joseph Lane, of Oregon, was nominated for the Vice-presidency; and after a session of only a few hours, the business was ended and the Convention adjourned.[a]

a June 23, 1860.

The South Carolina delegation, who remained in Richmond, formally assembled at Metropolitan Hall on the 21st, according to appointment, and adjourned from day to day until the evening of the 26th, when Mr. Yancey and many others arrived from Baltimore. The Convention then organized for business, which was soon dispatched. The platform and candidates offered to the party by the seceders' Convention at Baltimore were adopted by unanimous vote, with great cheering by the delegates and the crowd who filled the galleries. Then the Convention adjourned.

So ended the Conventions of the divided Democratic party, in the early

---

[1] One of these was Jefferson Davis. In a speech in Faneuil Hall, on the 11th of October, 1858, while denouncing the Abolitionists as disunionists, he said, pointing to the portraits of the elder Adams and others, on the walls:—" If those voices, which breathed the first instincts into the Colony of Massachusetts, and into the other colonies of the United States, to proclaim community—independence—and to assert it against the powerful mother country ; if those voices live here still, how must they feel who come here to preach treason to the Constitution, and assail the Union it ordained and established ? It would seem that their criminal hearts would fear that those voices, so long slumbering, would break their silence; that those forms which look down from these walls, behind and around, would come forth, to drive from this sacred temple these fanatical men—who deserve it more than did the changers of money and those who sold doves in the temple of the living God." At that very time, that bold, bad man was doubtless plotting " treason to the Constitution," and preparing to " assail the Union it ordained and established "—a proper subject for his own denunciations.

[2] Mr. Breckinridge was then Vice-president of the United States under President Buchanan, and subsequent events show that he was a co-worker with Davis and others against the Government. He joined the insurgents, and, during a portion of the civil war that ensued, he was the so-called " Secretary of War " of Jefferson Davis.

summer-time of 1860. The respective friends of the opposing candidates of that party (STEPHEN A. DOUGLAS and JOHN C. BRECKINRIDGE) went into the canvass with great bitterness of feeling, such as family quarrels usually exhibit.

Six days after the adjournment of the *Democratic* Conventions at Charleston, representatives of a new political organization, not more than six months old, met in Convention at Baltimore.[a] They styled themselves the *National Constitutional Union Party*, composed almost wholly of members of the old *Whig* party and a waning organization known as the *American*, or *Know-nothing* party. They assembled in the First Presbyterian Meeting-house (known as the Two-steeple Church), ·on Fayette Street, between Calvert and North Streets, which has since been demolished, and its place occupied by the United States Court-house. Its interior was well decorated with National emblems. Back of the president's chair was a full-length portrait of Washington, with large American flags, over which hovered an eagle; and the galleries, which were crowded with spectators, were festooned with numerous Union banners.

[a] May 9, 1860.

THE FIRST PRESBYTERIAN CHURCH, BALTIMORE, IN 1860.

The venerable John J. Crittenden, of Kentucky, Chairman of the National Constitutional Union Committee, called the Convention to order, and on his nomination, Washington Hunt, once Governor of the State of New York, and distinguished for talent, culture, and great urbanity of manner, was chosen temporary president of the Convention. Credentials of delegates were called for, when it was found that almost one-third of all the States were unrepresented.[1]

Toward evening, after a recess, Governor Hunt was elected permanent President. When the subject of a platform was proposed, Leslie Coombs, of Kentucky, an ardent follower and admirer of Henry Clay, took the floor, and put the Convention in the best of humor by a characteristic little speech. He declared that he had constructed three platforms: one for the "harmonious Democracy, who had agreed so beautifully, at Charleston;" another for the Republicans, about to assemble at Chicago; and a third for the party then around him. For the first, he proposed the Kentucky and Virginia Resolutions of 1798, which seemed to give license for the secession

---

[1] The States not represented were California, Florida, Iowa, Louisiana, Michigan, New Hampshire, Rhode Island, Oregon, South Carolina, and Wisconsin—ten in all.

of States, and disunion; for the second, the Blue-Laws of Connecticut; and for the third, the Constitution of the United States—"the Constitution as it is, and the Union under it, now and forever." The last sentence touched a sympathetic chord in the Convention, of marvelous sensitiveness. The suggestion was received with the most enthusiastic demonstrations of delight; and on the second day of the session, Joseph R. Ingersoll, Chairman of the Committee on Platform, reported resolutions, which repudiated all creeds formed for a temporary purpose, as "calculated to mislead and deceive the people," and recommended, as a foundation for the party to plant itself upon in the coming contest, that which was defined by the words:—THE CONSTITUTION OF THE COUNTRY, THE UNION OF THE STATES, AND THE EN-

WASHINGTON HUNT.

FORCEMENT OF THE LAWS. This platform was adopted unanimously.

The Convention now proceeded to vote for candidates for the offices of President and Vice-president, when two hundred and fifty-four votes were cast; and on the second ballot, John Bell, of Tennessee, an eminent politician, then past sixty-three years of age, was nominated for the Presidency.[1] The renowned scholar, statesman, and diplomat, the late Edward Everett, of Massachusetts, was selected for the office of Vice-president. In the canvass that followed, the adherents of these gentlemen were popularly known as the *Bell-Everett* party.

The greatest harmony prevailed in this Convention. Not a word was said about "Americanism," or other old party issues, nor was there a whisper on the subject of Slavery, excepting an ejaculation of Neil S. Brown, of Tennessee, who thanked God that he had at last found a Convention in which the "nigger" was not the sole subject of consideration. The great topic for speech was the *Constitution*, which they thought would be imperiled by the election of either Douglas, Breckinridge, or the nominee of the Republican party, whoever he might be. The Convention adjourned on the second day of the session, and that night a ratification meeting was held in Monument Square, in Baltimore, whereat speakers and musicians were abundant. The spacious platform, erected in the Square, was spanned by an immense arch, on which were inscribed the words—"THE UNION, THE CONSTITUTION, AND THE ENFORCEMENT OF THE LAWS."

Six days after the adjournment of the *National Constitutional Union* Convention, the representatives of the Republican party assembled in large numbers at Chicago, Illinois—a city of more than one hundred thousand souls, on the verge of a prairie on the western shore of Lake Michigan, where, in '1830, there were only a small fort, and a few scattered houses of traders—a city

---

[1] When the Rebellion broke out, in the spring of 1861, Mr. Bell was one of the earliest, if not the very first, of the professed Unionists of distinction who joined the enemies of his country in their attempt to overthrow the Constitution and destroy the nationality of the Republic.

illustrious as one of the wonders of the growth of our Republic. All of the Free-labor States were fully represented, and there were delegates from several of the Slave-labor States. An immense building of boards, called a

WIGWAM AT CHICAGO, IN 1860.

Wigwam, had been erected by the Republicans of Chicago, at an expense of seven thousand dollars, for the special use of the Convention. It was tastefully decorated within, and was spacious enough to hold ten thousand persons. A rustic seat, made of a huge knot of a tree, was prepared for the use of the President of the Convention; and everything about the affair was rough and

PRESIDENT'S CHAIR.

rural in appearance. The Convention met in the Wigwam, on the 16th day of May. Not more than one-third of the vast gathering of people could enter the building. E. D. Morgan, of New York, Chairman of the National Republican Exec-

utive Committee, called the Convention to order, and David Wilmot, of Pennsylvania, was chosen temporary chairman. In due time, George Ashmun, of Massachusetts, was chosen permanent President. It was a wise choice. His voice could be heard above any clamor that might be raised in the assembly, and he was remarkable for coolness, clearness of judgment, and executive ability. He was presented with a gavel made of a piece of the oak timber of Perry's flag-ship, *Lawrence ;* and with this emblem of authority, inscribed with the words, "*Don't give up the ship !*" he called the Convention to order, and invited the delegates to business. A committee on resolutions, composed of one delegate from each State represented, was appointed, and on the following morning[a] it submitted to the Convention a platform of principles, in the form of seventeen resolutions.

[a] May 17, 1860.

After affirming that the maintenance of the principles promulgated in the Declaration of Independence, and embodied in the National Constitution, is essential to the preservation of our republican institutions ; congratulating the country that no Republican member of Congress had uttered or countenanced any threats of disunion, " so often made by Democratic members without rebuke, and with applause from their political associates," and denouncing such threats as " an avowal of contemplated treason," the resolutions made explicit declarations upon the topic of Slavery, so largely occupying public attention. In a few paragraphs, they declared that each State had the absolute right of control in the management of its own domestic concerns; that the new dogma that the Constitution, of its own force, carries Slavery into any or all of the Territories of the United States, was a dangerous political heresy, revolutionary in its tendency, and subversive of the peace and harmony of the country; that the normal condition of all the territory of the United States is that of freedom, and that neither Congress, nor a Territorial legislature, nor any individuals, have authority to give legal existence to Slavery in any Territory of the United States; and that the reopening of the African Slave-trade, then recently commenced in the Southern States, under the cover of our national flag, aided by perversions of judicial power, was a crime against humanity, and a burning shame to our country and age.

GEORGE ASHMUN.

This platform was adopted at six o'clock in the evening, by unanimous vote; when the Convention adjourned until next morning, without taking a ballot for candidates for the Presidency and Vice-presidency. When the vote on the platform was announced, the scene that ensued, says an eye-witness, was of the "most astounding character. All the thousands of men in that enormous Wigwam commenced swinging their hats, and cheering with immense enthusiasm, and the other thousands of ladies waved their handkerchiefs and clapped their hands. Such a spectacle as was witnessed for some minutes has never before been witnessed at a convention. As the great assemblage poured through the streets after adjournment, it seemed to electrify the city. The agitation of the masses that packed the hotels and thronged the streets, certainly forty thousand strong, was such as made the little excitement at Charleston seem insignificant."[1]

May 19, 1860.   On the morning of the third day of the session,[a] the Convention was opened with prayer, by the Rev. Mr. Green, of Chicago, who expressed a desire that the evils which then invested the body politic should be wholly eradicated from the system, and that the pen of the historian might trace an intimate connection between that "glorious consummation and the transactions of the Convention." Then that body proceeded to the choice of a Presidential candidate, and on the third ballot Abraham Lincoln, of Illinois, was nominated. The announcement of the result caused the most uproarious applause; and, from the common center at Chicago, the electric messengers flew with the intelligence, almost as quick as thought, to every part of the vast Republic, eastward of the Rocky Mountains, before sunset. The Convention took a recess, and in the evening nominated Hannibal Hamlin, of Maine, for Vice-president. Their labors

---

[1] Halstead's *History of the National Political Conventions in* 1860, page 139.

were now done, and, after a brief speech by their presiding officer, the Convention adjourned, with nine cheers for the ticket.

Mr. Lincoln, the nominee, was at his home in Springfield, Illinois, at this time. He had been in the telegraph-office during the first and second baliotings, when he left, went to the office of the *State Journal*, and was conversing with friends when the third balloting occurred. The result was known at Springfield a few minutes after the voting was finished. The superintendent of the telegraph there wrote on a scrap of paper, "Mr. Lincoln, you are nominated," and sent a boy with it to the nominee. Mr. Lincoln read it to his friends, and, while they huzzaed lustily, he looked at it in silence. Then, putting it quietly in his pocket, he bade them "good evening," and went home.[1]

On the following day, a committee, appointed by the Convention, with President Ashmun at their head, waited upon Mr. Lincoln, and formally communicated to him, orally, and by an official letter, the fact of his nomination. He received the message with great modesty and gravity, and promised to respond to it in writing. This he did three days afterward,[a] in which, after accepting the nomination, he said:— ^{a May 23, 1860.} "The declaration of principles and sentiments which accompanies your letter, meets my approval, and it shall be my care not to violate it, or disregard it in any part. Imploring the assistance of Divine Providence, and with due regard to the views and feelings of all who were represented in the Convention, to the rights of all the States and Territories and people of the nation, to the inviolability of the Constitution, and the perpetual union, harmony, and prosperity of all, I am most happy to co-operate for the practical success of the principles declared by the Convention."

In the beautiful month of June, when Nature, in the temperate zone, is most wealthy in flowers and foliage and the songs of birds, and there is every thing in her aspect to inspire delight, and harmony, and good-will, one of the most important political campaigns noted in history was opened with intense vigor, and the most uncompromising and relentless hostility of parties. There were four of these parties in the field of contest, namely :—

1. The *Republican*, who declared freedom to be the normal condition of all territory, and that Slavery can exist only by authority of municipal law. Of this party, Abraham Lincoln was the standard-bearer.

2. The wing of the Democratic party led by John C. Breckinridge, who declared that no power existed that might lawfully control Slavery in the Territories; that it existed in any Territory, in full force, whenever a slaveholder and his slaves entered it; and that it was the duty of the National Government to protect it there.

3. The wing of the Democratic party led by Stephen A. Douglas, whose platform of principles assumed not to know positively whether slavery might or might not have lawful existence in the Territories, without the action of the inhabitants thereof, but expressed a willingness to abide by the decisions of the Supreme Court in all cases.

4. The *National Constitutional Union* party, led by John Bell, who

---

[1] "There is a little woman down at our house," said Mr. Lincoln, in allusion to his wife, as he left the room, "who would like to hear this—I'll go down and tell her."

declined,to express any opinion upon any subject, but pointed to the National Constitution, without note or comment, as their political guide.

The politicians of only the two parties first named seemed to have positive convictions, as units, on the great subject which had so long agitated the nation, and they took issue squarely, definitely, and defiantly. A large portion of the Douglas party were also inclined to disregard the resolution which bound them to absolute submission to the decisions of the Supreme Court, and to stand firmly upon a pure "Popular Sovereignty" Platform, which that resolution had eviscerated, for they regarded a late decision of the majority of that court, in the case of Dred Scott,[1] as sufficiently indicative of its opposition to the great doctrine of that platform. All parties were agreed in earnest professions of love for the Union and the Constitution; and, with such avowals emblazoned on their standards, they went into the fight, each doubtful of success, and all conscious that a national crisis was at hand. There was a vague presentiment before the minds of reflecting men everywhere, that the time when the practical answer to the great question—What shall be the policy of the Nation concerning Slavery?—could no longer be postponed.

The conflict was desperate from July to November, and grew more intense as it approached its culmination at the polls. The Republicans and Douglas Democrats were denounced by their opponents as Abolitionists—treasonably sectional, and practically hostile to the perpetuation of the Union. The Breckinridge party, identified as it unfortunately was with avowed disunionists—men who for long years had been in the habit of threatening to attempt the dissolution of the Union by the process of secession, whenever the revelations of the Census or other causes should convince them that the domination of the Slave interest in the National Government had ceased forever—men who rejoiced when they saw, in the absolute disruption of the Democratic party at Charleston and Baltimore, a prospect for the election of the Republican candidate, which might serve them as a pretext for rebellion—men who afterward became leaders in the great insurrection against the National Government—was charged with complicity in disunion schemes. In speeches, newspapers, and in social gatherings, these charges were iterated and reiterated; and yet there were but few persons in the Free-labor States who really believed that there were men mad enough and wicked enough to raise the arm of resistance to the authority of the Supreme Government, founded on the National Constitution.

But the election of Mr. Lincoln, which was the result of the great political conflict in the summer and autumn of 1860, soon revealed the existence of a well-organized conspiracy against the life of the Republic, widespread, powerful, and intensely malignant. The leading conspirators were few, and nearly all of them were then, or had been, connected with the

---

[1] Dred Scott had been a slave in Missouri, but claimed to be a freeman on account of involuntary residence in a free State. The case did not require a decision concerning the right of a negro to citizenship; but the Chief-Justice took the occasion to give what is called an extra-judicial opinion. He decided that a freed negro slave, or a descendant of a slave, could not become a citizen of the Republic. He asserted, in that connection, that the language of the Declaration of Independence showed that the negroes were not included in the beneficent meaning of that instrument, when it said, "*all* men are created equal," and that they were regarded "as so far inferior, that they had no rights which the white man was bound to respect."

National Government, some as legislators, and others as cabinet ministers. They were not so numerous at first, according to a loyal Tennessean (Horace Maynard), who knew them well, "as the figures on a chess-board," but became wonderfully productive of their kind. "There are those," he said, in a speech in Congress, "within reach of my voice, who also know them, and can testify to their utter perfidy; who have been the victims of their want of principle, and whose self-respect has suffered from their insolent and overbearing demeanor. No Northern man was ever admitted to their confidence, and no Southern man, unless it became necessary to keep up their numbers; and then, not till he was thoroughly known by them, and known to be thoroughly corrupt. They, like a certain school of ancient philosophers, had two sets of principles or doctrines—one for outsiders, the other for themselves; the one was 'Democratic principles' for the Democratic party, the other was their own and without a name. Some Northern men and many Southern men were, after a fashion, petted and patronized by them, as a gentleman throws from his table a bone, or a choice bit, to a favorite dog; and they imagined they were conferring a great favor thereby, which could be requited only by the abject servility of the dog. To hesitate, to doubt, to hold back, to stop, was to call down a storm of wrath that few men had the nerve to encounter, and still fewer the strength to withstand. Not only in political circles, but in social life, their rule was inexorable, their tyranny absolute. God be thanked for the brave men who had the courage to meet them and bid them defiance, first at Charleston, in April, 1860, and then at Baltimore, in June! To them is due the credit of declaring war against this intolerable despotism." The truthfulness of this picture will be fully apparent in future pages.

CHAPTER II.

PRELIMINARY REBELLIOUS MOVEMENTS.

HE choice of Presidential electors, by ballot, occurred on the 6th of November, 1860. They were three hundred and three in number, and, when assembled in Electoral College,[1] one hundred and eighty of them voted for Mr. Lincoln, giving him fifty-seven electoral votes more than all of his opponents received.[2] Of the popular votes, numbering 4,680,193, he received 1,866,452. Although he had a large majority over each candidate, he received 979,163 less than did all of his opponents.[3] This fact, and the circumstance that in nine Slave-labor States there was no Republican electoral ticket, gave factitious vigor to the plausible cry, which was immediately raised by the conspirators and their friends, that the President elect would be a usurper when in office, because he had not received a majority of the aggregate vote of the people; that he would be a sectional ruler, and, of necessity, a tyrant; and that his antecedents, the principles of the Republican platform, and the fanaticism of his supporters, pledged him to wage relentless war upon the system of Slavery, and the rights of the Slave-labor States.

It was not denied that Mr. Lincoln had been elected in accordance with the letter and spirit of the National Constitution,[4] and that it was the fault of the politicians in the nine States that there were no electoral tickets therein.[5] Many of these politicians began at once, with intense zeal, which often amounted to ferocity, to put in motion a system of terrorism, in which the hangman's rope, the incendiary's torch, and the slave-hunter's blood-hound, formed prominent features. It was often perilous to his life and property, for a man below North Carolina and Tennessee to express a desire for Mr. Lincoln's election. The promise of a United States Senator from North Carolina (Clingman), that Union men would be hushed by "the swift attention of vigilance committees," was speedily fulfilled.

It was not denied that the election had been fairly and legally conducted, or that the Republican platform pledged the nominee and his supporters to absolute non-interference with the rights and domestic policy of the States. That platform expressly declared, that "the maintenance, inviolate, of the rights of the States, and especially the right of each State to order and con-

---

[1] See Article XII. of the Amendments to the Constitution.

[2] Bell received 39, Douglas 12, and Breckinridge 72.

[3] He received 491,295 over Douglas, 1,018,499 over Breckinridge, and 1,275,821 over Bell. The votes for the four candidates, respectively, were : For Lincoln, 1,866,452 ; for Bell, 590,631 ; for Douglas, 1,375,144 ; and for Breckinridge, 847,953.

[4] See Article XII. of the Amendments to the Constitution.

[5] These were North Carolina, Georgia, Alabama, Mississippi, Tennessee, Louisiana, Arkansas, Florida, and Texas. The electors of South Carolina were chosen by the State Legislature.

trol its own domestic institutions according to its own judgment, is essential to that balance of power on which the perfection and endurance of our political fabric depend." But these and other facts, essential to a correct understanding of the issue, were studiously concealed from the people, or so adroitly shrouded in sophistry that they were kept far away from popular cognizance.

During the canvass preceding the election, the conspirators, and the politicians in their train, employed all the means in their power to excite intensely every blinding passion of the slaveholders and the masses of the people. They appealed to their fears, their prejudices, their local patriotism, and their greed. They asserted, with all the solemn seeming of sober truth, that the people of the Free-labor States, grown rich and powerful through robbery of the people of the Slave-labor States, by means of tariff laws and other governmental measures, and by immigration from foreign lands, had elected a sectional President for the purpose of carrying out a long-cherished scheme of ambition, namely, the political and social subjugation of the inhabitants of the Slave-labor States; the subversion of their system of labor; the elevation of the negro to social equality with the white man; and the destruction of Slavery, upon which, they alleged, had rested in the past, and must forever rest in the future, all substantial prosperity in the cotton-growing States. They held the Republican party responsible for John Brown's acts at Harper's Ferry,[1] and declared that his raid was the forerunner of a general and destructive invasion of the Slave-labor States by "the fanatical hordes of the North." They cited the publications and speeches of the Abolitionists of the North during the past thirty years; the legislation in the same section unfriendly to slavery; and the more recent utterances of leading members of the Republican party, in which it had been declared that "there is an irrepressible conflict between freedom and slavery"—"the Republic cannot exist half slave and half free"—"freedom is the normal condition of all territory," &c.; they cited these with force, as proofs of long and earnest preparation for a now impending war upon "the South" and its institutions. They pictured, in high coloring, the dreadful paralysis of all the industry and commerce of "the South," and the utter extinguishment of all hopes of future advancement in art, science, literature, and the development of the yet hidden resources in the region below the Susquehanna, the Potomac, and the Ohio, as a consequence of the domination in the National Government of their "bitter enemies," as they unjustly termed the people of the Free-labor States.[2]

In this unholy work, the press and the pulpit became powerful auxili-

[1] For the purpose of liberating the slaves of Virginia, John Brown, an enthusiast, with a few followers, seized Harper's Ferry, at the confluence of the Potomac and Shenandoah Rivers, in October, 1859, as a base of operations. He failed. He was arrested by National and Virginia troops, and was hanged, in December following, by the authorities of Virginia.

[2] This false teaching was not new. It was begun by John C. Calhoun, and had been kept up ever since. It was so in Madison's later days. In a letter to Henry Clay, cited by Dr. Sargeant, in his admirable pamphlet, entitled, *England, the United States, and the Southern Confederacy*, that statesman and patriot said:—" It is painful to see the unceasing efforts made to alarm the South, by imputations against the North of unconstitutional designs on the subject of Slavery." Madison and Clay were both slaveholders. Again, the former wrote: "The inculcated impression of a permanent incompatibility of interests between the North and the South *may put it in the power of popular leaders, aspiring to the highest stations*, to unite the South on some critical occasion. In pursuing this course, the first and most obvious step is nullification, the next secession, and the last, a final separation."

aries. The former was widely controlled by politicians of the small ruling class in the Slave-labor States, and was almost everywhere subservient to their will in the promulgation of false teachings. There were exceptions, however—

W. G. BROWNLOW.

noble exceptions; and there were those among influential newspaper conductors, like the heroic "Parson Brownlow," of Knoxville, East Tennessee, now (1865) Governor of that State, who could never be brought to bend the knee a single line to Baal nor to Moloch; but stood bravely erect until consumed, as it were, at the stake of martyrdom.[1]

So with the pulpit. It was extensively occupied by men identified socially and pecuniarily with the slave system. These men, with the awful dignity of ambassadors of Christ—vicegerents of the Almighty—declared Slavery to be a "divine institution," and that the fanatics of the Free-labor States who denounced it as wrong and sinful were infidels, and deserved the fate of heretics. They joined their potential voices with those of the politicians, in the cry for resistance to expected wrong and oppression;[2] and thousands upon thousands of men and women, regarding them as oracles of wisdom and truth, followed them reverentially in the broad highway of open treason.[3]

---

[1] For an account of Dr. Brownlow's sufferings at the beginning of the war, see his work, entitled, *Sketches of the Rise, Progress, and Decline of Secession ; with a Narrative of Personal Adventures among the Rebels.* G. W. Childs. 1862.

[2] See *The Church and the Rebellion*, by R. L. Stanton, D. D., of Kentucky.

[3] The change in the sentiments of the clergy in the Slave-labor States, during the twenty-five years preceding the war, was most remarkable. We will notice only two or three instances in a single religious body, namely, the Presbyterians. In 1835, the representatives of that denomination in South Carolina and Georgia, in Convention assembled, made an official report against the perpetuation of the system of Slavery. "We cannot go into detail," they said; "it is unnecessary. We make our appeal to universal experience. We are chained to a putrid carcass. It sickens and destroys us. We have a millstone about the neck of our society to sink us deep in the sea of vice. Our children are corrupted from their infancy, nor can we prevent it." &c.

In November, 1860, one of the most eminent Doctors of Divinity in the Presbyterian Church said, in his pulpit in New Orleans, after speaking of the character of the South:—"The particular trust assigned to such a people becomes the pledge of the Divine protection, and their fidelity to it determines the fate by which it is finally overtaken. What that trust is, must be ascertained from the necessities of their position, the institutions which are the outgrowth of their principles, and the conflicts through which they preserve their identity and independence. If then the South is such a people, what, at this juncture, is their providential trust? I answer, that it is *to conserve and to perpetuate the institution of domestic Slavery as now existing.*" Again: "I simply say, that for us, as now situated, the duty is plain of conserving and transmitting the system of Slavery, with the freest scope for its natural development and extension." Again: "Need I pause to show how this system is interwoven with our entire social fabric? That these slaves form parts of our households, even as our children; and that, too, through a relationship recognized and sanctioned in the Scriptures of God, even as the other? Must I pause to show how it has fashioned our modes of life, and determined all our habits of thought and feeling, and molded the very type of our civilization? How then can the hand of violence be laid upon it, without involving our existence?"—*The South, her Peril and her Duty : a Thanksgiving Discourse,* Nov. 29, 1860, by Rev. B. M. Palmer, D. D.

Ten or fifteen years before the war, an eminent Doctor of Divinity of the Presbyterian Church, in Charleston, South Carolina, put forth two pamphlets, in which he sought to claim for that denomination the glory of the authorship of the Declaration of Independence, alleging that its form and substance were fashioned after the bands and covenants of the church in Scotland. "Presbyterianism," he says exultingly, in praising the Declaration of Independence as almost divine in origin and character, "has proved itself to be the pillar and ground of truth, amid error and defection. It has formed empires, in the spirit of Freedom and Liberty, and has given birth to declarations and achievements which *are the wonder of the present, and will*

The "common people"—the non-slaveholders and the small slaveholders—whom the ruling class desired to reduce to vassalage,[1] but to whom they now looked for physical aid in the war which their madness might kindle, were blinded, confused, and alarmed. They were assured that the independence of the South would bring riches and honor to every household. They were deluded with promises of free trade, that would bring the luxuries of the world to their dwellings. They were promised the long-desired reopening of the African Slave-trade, which would make slaves so cheap that every man might become an owner of many, and take his position in the

---

be the admiration of every future age." On the 21st of November, 1860, the same Doctor of Divinity said, from the pulpit of the Second Presbyterian Church in Charleston, after stating that he stood there " in God's name and stead, to point out the cause of His anger:"—"Now, to me, pondering long and profoundly upon the course of events, the evil and bitter root of all our evils is to be found in the infidel, atheistic, French Revolution, Red Republican principle, embodied as an axiomatic seminal principle—not in the Constitution, but in the Declaration of Independence. That seminal principle is this:—'We hold these truths to be self-evident: that all men are created equal; that they are endowed by their Creator with certain inalienable rights; that among these are life, liberty, and the pursuit of happiness.'—*The Sin and the Cure*, by Rev. Thomas Smyth, D. D.

Doctor James H. Thornwell, President of a Theological Seminary at Columbia, S. C., one of the most eminent scholars and theologians in the South, and who was known in that State as "The Calhoun of the Church," was ever foremost in the defense of Slavery as a divine institution. He even went so far as to assert his conviction that the horrible African Slave-trade was "the most worthy of all Missionary Societies." Clergymen of every religious denomination in the Slave-labor States were involved in the crime of rebellion, for the sake of perpetuating human Slavery. Their speeches, and sermons, and recorded acts are full of evidence that the Church, in the broad meaning of that term, had become horribly corrupted by the Slave system, and made a willing instrument of the conspirators. It is related by the Rev. Dr. Stanton (*The Church and the Rebellion*, p. 163), that Robert Toombs, of Georgia, an arch-conspirator, went early to New Orleans, to stir up the people to revolt. The Union sentiment was too strong for him, and he was about to leave, when it was suggested that the Rev. Dr. Palmer might be induced to preach a new gospel, whose chief tenet should be the righteousness of Slavery. He seems to have been very ready to do so, and the Fast-day Sermon of Dr. Palmer, above alluded to, with all its terrible results, was a part of the fruits of the mission of Toombs to New Orleans, in the autumn of 1860.

Dr. Palmer's discourse was seditious throughout. It was printed, and circulated by thousands all over the Slave-labor States, with direful effect. In the summer of 1865, after the war was ended, Dr. Palmer entered the same pulpit, and " frankly told his people," says a New Orleans correspondent of the *Boston Post*, "that they had all been wrong, and he ' the chief of sinners;' that they had been proud and haughty, disobedient, rebellious; that he himself had been humbled before God, and received merited chastisement; that they had all been taught a good lesson of obedience to civil authority, and he hoped it would be filially received by them as the children of Christ, and laid up in their heart of hearts."

For a complete history of the change in the sentiments of Christians of all denominations in the Slave-labor States, and the relations of the clergy to the conspirators, see a volume entitled *The Church and the Rebellion*, by R. L. Stanton, D. D., of Kentucky.

[1] Of the 12,000,000 of inhabitants in the Slave-labor States, at the beginning of the war, the ruling class—those in whom resided, in a remarkable degree, the political power of the States—numbered about 1,000,000. Of these, the large land and slave holders, whose influence in the body of the million named was almost supreme, numbered less than 200,000. "In 1850," says Edward Atkinson, in the *Continental Monthly* for March, 1862, page 252, "there were in all the Southern States less than 170,000 men owning more than five slaves each, and they owned 2,800,000 out of 3,300,000." The production of the great staple, cotton, which was regarded as king of kings in an earthly sense, was in the hands of less than 100,000 men.

The remaining 11,000,000 of inhabitants in the Slave-labor States consisted of 6,000,000 of small slaveholders and non-slaveholders, mechanics, and laboring men; 4,000,000 of negro slaves, and 1,000,000 known in those regions by the common name of " poor white trash," a degraded population scattered over the whole surface of these States. The foregoing figures are only proximately exact, but may be relied on as a truthful statement of statistics, in round numbers.

For several years preceding the rebellion, many of the leading publicists in the Slave-labor States openly advocated a form of government radically opposed to that of our Republic. Their chief vehicle of communication with the small ruling class in those States was *De Bow's Review*, a magazine of much pretension and of acknowledged authority. The following brief paragraphs from the pages of that periodical, selected from a thousand of like tenor, will serve to illustrate the truth of the assertion in the text, that the vassalage of the " common people," in the new empire which long-contemplated revolt was to establish, was intended:—

" The right to govern resides in a very small minority; the duty to obey is inherent in the great mass of mankind."

" There is nothing to which the South [the ruling class] entertains so great a dislike as of universal suffrage. Wherever foreigners settle together in large numbers, there universal suffrage will exist. They understand and admire the leveling democracy of the North, but cannot appreciate the aristocratic feeling of a privileged class, so universal at the South."

" The real civilization of a country is in its aristocracy. The masses are molded into soldiers and artisans by intellect, just as matter and the elements of nature are made into telegraphs and steam-engines. The poor,

social scale, with the great proprietors of lands and sinews.[1] Every avenue through which truth might find its way to the popular understanding was quickly closed, and the people had no detecter of its counterfeits. "Perhaps there never was a people," wrote a Southern Unionist, in the third year of the war, "more bewitched, beguiled, and befooled than we were when we drifted into this rebellion."[2]

Commenting on these actions of the politicians, President Lincoln said :— "At the beginning, they knew they would never raise their treason to any respectable magnitude by any name which implies violation of law. They knew their people possessed as much moral sense, as much of devotion to law and order, and as much pride in, and reverence for, the history and Government of their common country, as any other civilized and patriotic people. They knew they would make no advancement directly in the teeth of these strong and noble sentiments. Accordingly, they commenced by an insidious debauching of the public mind. They invented an ingenious sophism, which, if conceded, was followed by perfectly logical steps, through all the incidents, to the complete destruction of the Union. The sophism itself is, that any State of the Union may, consistently with the National Constitution, and therefore lawfully and peacefully, withdraw from the Union, without the consent of the Union, or of any other State. The little disguise that the supposed right is to be exercised only for just cause, themselves to be the judges of its justice, is too thin to merit any notice. With rebellion thus sugarcoated, they have been drugging the public mind of their section for more than thirty years, until, at length, they have brought many good men to a willingness to take up arms against the Government, the day after some assemblage of men have enacted the farcical pretense of taking their State out of the Union, who could have been brought to no such thing the day before."[3]

---

who labor all day, are too tired at night to study books. If you make them learned, they soon forget all that is necessary in the common transactions of life. To make an aristocrat in the future, *we must sacrifice a thousand paupers.* Yet we would by all means make them—make them permanent, too, by laws of entail and primogeniture. An aristocracy is patriarchal, parental, and representative. The feudal barons of England were, next to the fathers, the most perfect representative government. The king and barons represented everybody, because *everybody belonged to them.*"

And when the war broke out, a writer in the *Review* said, with truth and candor:—"The real contest of to-day is not simply between the North and South; but to determine whether for ages to come our Government shall partake more of the form of monarchies or of more liberal forms."

[1] There is ample evidence on record to show that Yancey, Davis, Stephens, and other leaders in the great rebellion were advocates of the foreign Slave-trade. Southern newspapers advocated it. The *True Southron*, of Mississippi, suggested the "propriety of stimulating the zeal of the pulpit by founding a prize *for the best sermon in favor of free trade in negroes.*" For the purpose of practically opening the horrible traffic, an "African Labor-supply Association" was formed, of which De Bow, editor of the principal organ of the oligarchy, was made president. Southern legislatures discussed the question. John Slidell, in the United States Senate, urged the propriety of withdrawing American cruisers from the coast of Africa, that the slavers might not be molested ; and the administration of Mr. Buchanan was made to favor this scheme of the great cotton-planters, by protesting against the visitation of suspected slave-bearing vessels, carrying the American flag, by British cruisers.

[2] *New York Daily Times*, June 4, 1864.

[3] Message to Congress, July 4, 1861. Mr. Carpenter, the artist who painted the picture of *The Signing of the Emancipation Proclamation*, relates the following anecdote concerning the last sentence in the above quotation from the Message :—"Mr. De Frees, the Government printer, told me that when the Message was being printed, he was a good deal disturbed by the use of the term 'sugar-coated,' and finally went to the President about it. Their relations to each other being of the most intimate character, he told Mr. Lincoln frankly that he ought to remember that a message to Congress was a different affair from a speech at a mass meeting in Illinois—that the messages became a part of history, and should be written accordingly. 'What is the matter now?' inquired the President. 'Why,' said Mr. De Frees, 'you have used an undignified expression in the Message;' and then reading the paragraph aloud, he added, ' I would alter the structure of that, if I were you.' 'De Frees,' replied Mr. Lincoln, ' that word expresses precisely my idea, and I am not going to change it. The time will never come, in this country, when the people won't know exactly what *sugar coated* means!' "

During the summer and early autumn of 1860, William L. Yancey, one of the most active and influential of the conspirators, with other disunionists, made a pilgrimage through the Free-labor States, for the purpose of vindicating the claims put forth by the extremists of the South, concerning State supremacy and the unrestricted extension of Slavery. They were listened to patiently by thousands at public meetings; were hospitably treated everywhere; received assurances of sympathy from vast numbers of men who regarded the agitation of the Slavery question, by the Abolitionists, as mischievous, unfriendly, and dangerous to the peace of the Union; and then they went back, with treason in their hearts and falsehoods upon their lips, to deceive and arouse into rebellion the masses of the Southern people, who regarded them as oracles. Like an incarnation of Discord, Yancey cried, substantially as he had written two years before:—" Organize committees all over the Cotton States; fire the Southern heart; instruct the Southern mind; give courage to each other; and at the proper moment, by one organized, concerted action, precipitate the Cotton States into revolution."[1]

WILLIAM L. YANCEY.

This advice was instantly followed when the election of Mr. Lincoln was assured by the decision of the ballot-box, on the 6th of November. Indeed, before that decision was made, South Carolina conspirators—disciples and political successors of John C. Calhoun[2]—met at the house of James

[1] Letter to James Slaughter, June 15, 1858.

[2] John Caldwell Calhoun, of South Carolina, always appears in history as the central figure of a group of politicians who, almost forty years ago, adopting the disunion theories put forth by a few Virginians, like John Taylor, of Caroline, and used by Jefferson and his friends for the temporary purpose of securing a political party victory at the close of the last century, began, in more modern times, the work of destroying the nationality of the Republic. With amazing intellectual vigor and acumen, Mr. Calhoun crystallized the crude elements of opposition to that nationality, found in so great abundance, as we have observed, in Virginia, during Washington's Administration, that it drew from him his great plea for union in his Farewell Address to his countrymen. Calhoun reduced these elements to compact form, and, by the consummate use of the most subtle sophistry, of which he was complete master, he instilled the most dangerous disintegrating poison, known as the doctrine of Supreme State Sovereignty, into the public mind of the Slave-labor States, for the purpose of meeting a contingency which he contemplated as early as the year 1812. The now [1865] venerable Rear-admiral Stewart, in a letter to George W. Childs, of Philadelphia, relates a conversation between himself and Mr. Calhoun, in Washington City, in the winter of 1812:—" You in the South," said Stewart, " are decidedly the aristocratic portion of this Union; you are so, in holding persons in perpetual slavery; you are so, in every domestic quality; so in every habit of your lives, modes of living, and action. You neither work with your hands, head, nor any machinery, but live and have your being,,not in accordance with the will of your Creator, but by the sweat of slavery; and yet you assume all the attributes, professions, and advantages of Democracy." Mr. Calhoun replied:—" I admit your conclusions in respect to us Southerners. That we are essentially aristocratic, I cannot deny. But we can, and do, yield much to Democracy. *This is our sectional policy.* We are, from necessity, thrown upon and solemnly wedded to that party, however it may occasionally clash with our feelings, for the conservation of our interests. It is through our affiliation with that party, in the Middle and Western States, that we hold power. *But when we cease thus to control this nation, through a disjointed Democracy, or any material obstacle in that party shall tend to throw us out of that rule and control, we shall resort to a dissolution of the Union. The compromises of the Constitution, under the circumstances, were sufficient for our fathers; but under the altered condition of our country, from that period, leave to the South no resource but dissolution."*

This avowal of Mr. Calhoun, then a leading Democratic member of Congress, that the politicians of the South were determined to rule the Republic, or ruin it, was made forty-eight years before the great rebellion occurred. Under the lead of Calhoun, the politicians of South Carolina attempted a rebellion about thirty years before, but failed.

42 SECRET MEETINGS OF THE CONSPIRATORS.

H. Hammond (son of a New England schoolmaster, and an extensive land and slave holder, near the banks of the Savannah River), to consult upon a plan of treasonable operations. Hammond was then a member of the United States Senate, pledged by solemn oath to see that the Republic received no hurt; and yet, under his roof, he met in conclave a band of men, like himself sworn to be defenders of his native land, from foes without and foes within, to plot schemes for the ruin of that country. At his table, and in secret session in his library, sat William H. Gist, then Governor of South Carolina; ex-governor James H. Adams; James L. Orr, once Speaker of the National House of Representatives; the entire Congressional Delegation of South Carolina,[1] excepting William Porcher Miles (who was compelled by sickness to be absent), and several other prominent men of that State. Then and there the plan for the overt act of rebellion, performed by South Carolinians in Convention at Charleston, sixty

JOHN CALDWELL CALHOUN.

days later, seems to have been arranged. They were assured that their well-managed sundering of the Democratic party at Charleston, in April,[2] would result in the election of Mr. Lincoln, and that the pretext for rebellion, so long and anxiously waited for, would be presented within a fortnight from that time.

This meeting was followed by similar cabals in the other cotton-growing States; and, in Virginia, that ever-restless mischief-maker, ex-governor Henry A. Wise, with R. M. T. Hunter, John Tyler, James M. Mason, the author of the Fugitive Slave Law of 1850, who had been his co-plotter against the life of the Republic four years before,[3] and other leading politicians in that State, were exceedingly active in arranging plans for that Commonwealth to join her Southern sisters in the work of treason. Wise, who assumed to be their orator on all occasions, had openly declared, that

---

[1] These were John McQueen, Lawrence M. Keitt, Milledge L. Bonham, John D. Ashmore, and William W. Boyce, of the House of Representatives, and Senators James H. Hammond and James Chesnut, Jr.

[2] See page 23.

[3] In response to an invitation from Wise, a convention of Governors of Slave-labor States was secretly held at Raleigh, North Carolina, of which Jefferson Davis, then the Secretary of War, was fully cognizant. The object was to devise a scheme of rebellion at that time, in the event of the election of Colonel John C. Frémont, the Republican candidate for the Presidency. Wise afterward boasted that, had Frémont been elected, he should have marched, at the head of twenty thousand men, to Washington, taken possession of the Capitol, and prevented the inauguration of the President elect. Frémont's defeat postponed overt acts of treason by the conspirators.—*The American Conflict:* by Horace Greeley, i. 329. Senator Mason, writing to Jeff. Davis on the 30th of September, said:—"I have a letter from Wise, of the 27th, full of spirit. He says the governments of North Carolina, South Carolina, and Louisiana have already agreed to the *rendezvous* at Raleigh, and others will—this in your *most private ear.* He says further, that he had officially requested you to exchange with Virginia, on fair terms of difference, percussion for flint muskets. I don't know the usage or power of the Department in such cases; but, if it can be done, even by liberal construction, I hope you will accede. Was there not an appropriation at the last session for converting flint into percussion arms? If so, would it not furnish good reason for extending such facilities to the States? Virginia probably has more arms than the other Southern States, and would divide, in case of need. In a letter, yesterday, to a committee in South Carolina, I gave it as my judgment, in the event of Frémont's election, the South should not pause, but proceed at once to 'immediate, absolute, and eternal separation' So I am a candidate for the first halter."

if Lincoln was elected, he "would not remain in the Union one hour." He applauded, as hopeful words for his class, the declaration of Howell Cobb (then President Buchanan's Secretary of the Treasury), at a public gathering in the city of New York, that, in the event of Mr. Lincoln's election, secession would have the "sympathy and co-operation of the Administration," and that he "did not believe another Congress of the United States would meet." He hailed with delight, as chivalrous to the last degree, the assurances of Lawrence M. Keitt, of the House of Representatives, in a public speech, at Washington, that President Buchanan was "pledged to secession, and would be held to it ;" that "South Carolina would shatter the accursed Union," and that, if she could not accomplish it otherwise, "she would throw her arms round the pillars of the Constitution, and involve all the States in a common ruin." He listened with peculiar pleasure to the declaration of Robert Barnwell Rhett, also of South Carolina, that "all true statesmanship in the

HENRY A. WISE.

South consists in forming combinations and shaping events, so as to bring about, as speedily as possible, a dissolution of the present Union, and a Southern Confederacy."—"Rather than submit one moment to Black Republican rule," Wise wrote to an old friend of his father, in the North, "I would fight to the last drop of blood to resist its fanatical oppression. Our minds are made up. *The South will not wait until the 4th of March. We will be well under arms before then*, or our safety must be guaranteed."[1]

Everywhere the conspirators and their followers and agents were sleepless in vigilance and tireless in energy. Hundreds of telegraphic messages, volumes of letters, and scores of couriers, went from plantation to plantation, from village to village, from city to city, and from State to State, wherever the Slave power held sway, stirring up the people to revolt; whilst prominent individuals and public bodies hastened, on hearing of the result of the election, to swell the grand chorus of treasonable speech, led by the dozen—they were but a little more in number—of the chief conspirators.[2]

Three, if not four, of these chief conspirators were President Buchanan's cabinet ministers and constitutional advisers. The three were Howell Cobb, of Georgia, Secretary of the Treasury ; John B. Floyd, of Virginia, Secretary of War ; and Jacob Thompson, of Mississippi, Secretary of the Interior. William H. Trescot, of South Carolina, who for many years had

[1] Autograph letter to Josiah Williams, of Poughkeepsie, N. Y., dated "Rolleston, near Norfolk, Va., December 24, 1860." Governor Wise, it will be remembered, was chiefly instrumental in procuring the execution of John Brown for treason, less than a year before. Four years later, his estate of "Rolleston, near Norfolk," was occupied as a camp for freed negroes; and, in his mansion, a daughter of John Brown was teaching slaves' children how to read and write the English language.

[2] See the remarks of Horace Maynard, on page 35.

been plotting against the life of the nation, was then Assistant Secretary of State, and their confederate in crime. These men, while in office, and pledged by solemn oaths to support the National Constitution and laws, were for months plotting schemes for the destruction of the former and defiance of the latter.

HOWELL COBB.

a December 6, 1860.

From his official desk at Washington, Cobb wrote*a* an inflammatory address to the people of Georgia, in which he said, in conclusion :—" On the 4th of March, 1861, the Federal Government will pass into the hands of the Abolitionists. It will then cease to have the slightest claim either upon your confidence or your loyalty ; and, in my honest judgment, each. hour that Georgia remains thereafter a member of the Union will be an hour of degradation, to be followed by certain and speedy ruin. I entertain no doubt either of your right or duty to secede from the Union. Arouse, then, all your manhood for the great work before you, and be prepared, on that day, to announce and maintain your independence of the Union, for you will never again have equality and justice in it. Identified with you in heart, feeling, and interest, I return to share in whatever destiny the future has in store for our State and ourselves." Two days afterward,*b* Cobb resigned his office,[1] hastened to Georgia, and afterward took up arms against his country.[2]

b December 8, 1860.

---

[1] In his letter to Mr. Buchanan, resigning his office, Mr. Cobb frankly informed him that duty to his State required him to sever his connection with the National Government, and lend his powers for the good of his own people. "I have prepared," he said, "and must now issue to them an address, which contains the calm and solemn convictions of my heart and judgment." As his views would, if he remained in the Cabinet, expose himself to suspicion, and put the President in a false position, he thought it proper to resign. In this, Mr. Cobb was more honest and honorable than his traitorous associates in the Cabinet, who remained almost a month longer.

[2] Cobb's plans had been matured before the election of Mr. Lincoln. So early as the 1st of November, 1860, Trescott, the Assistant Secretary of State, wrote to the editor of the *Charleston Mercury*, as follows:—

"WASHINGTON, Nov. 1, 1860.

"DEAR RHETT: I received your letter this morning. As to my views or opinions of the Administration, I can, of course, say nothing. As to Mr. Cobb's views, he is willing that I should communicate them to you, in order that they may aid you in forming your own judgment; but, you will understand that this is confidential —that is, neither Mr. Cobb nor myself must be quoted as the source of your information. I will not dwell on this, as you will, on a moment's reflection, see the embarrassment which might be produced by any *authorized* statement of his opinions. I will only add, by way of preface, that after the very fullest and freest conversations with him, I feel sure of his earnestness, singleness of purpose, and resolution in the whole matter.

"Mr. Cobb believes that the time is come for resistance; that upon the election of Lincoln, Georgia ought to secede from the Union, and that she will do so. That Georgia and every other State should, as far as secession, act for herself, resuming her delegated powers, and thus put herself in position to consult with other sovereign States who take the same ground. After the secession is effected, then will be the time to consult. But he is of opinion, most strongly, that whatever action is resolved on, should be consummated on the 4th of March, not before. That while the action determined on should be decisive and irrevocable, its initial point should be the 4th of March. If a Southern convention is held, it must be of delegates empowered to *act*, whose action is at once binding on the States they represent.

"But he desires me to impress upon you his conviction, that any attempt to precipitate the actual issue upon this Administration will be most mischievous—calculated to produce differences of opinion and destroy

Floyd's treachery consisted more in secret, efficient action than in open words. As we shall observe presently, he had used the power of his official station to strip the arsenals of the Free-labor States of arms and ammunition, and to crowd those of the Slave-labor States with these materials of war; while Thompson, for more than ten years an avowed disunionist, was now plotting treason, it seems, by night and by day. He wrote from his official desk at Washington, as early as the 20th of November:—"My allegiance is due to Mis-

sissippi[1] and her destiny. I believe she ought to resist, and to the bitter end, Black Republican rule. . . . As long as I am here, I shall shield and protect the South. Whenever it shall come to pass that I think I can do no further good here, I shall return to my home. Buchanan is the truest friend to the South I have ever known in the North. He is a jewel of a man." After speaking of the intended secession of Mississippi, he said:— "I want the co-operation of the Southern States. I wish to do all I can to secure their sympathy and co-operation. A confederacy of the Southern States will be

JACOB THOMPSON.

strong enough to command the respect of the world, and the love and confidence of our people at home. South Carolina will go. I consider Georgia and Florida as certain. Alabama probable. Then Mississippi must go. But I want Louisiana, Texas, Arkansas, Tennessee, North Carolina, Virginia; and Maryland will not stay behind long. . . . As soon as our mechanics, our merchants, our lawyers, our editors, look this matter in the face, and calculate the consequences, they will see their in-

---

unanimity. *He thinks it of great importance that the cotton crop should go forward at once, and that the money should be in the hands of the people, that the cry of popular distress shall not be heard at the outset of this move.**

"My own opinion is. that it would be well to have a discreet man, one who knows the value of silence, who can listen wisely, present in Milledgeville, at the meeting of the State Legislature, as there will be there an outside gathering of the very ablest men of that State.

"And the next point, that you should, at the earliest possible day of the session of our own legislature, elect a man as governor, whose name and character will conciliate as well as give confidence to all the men of the State. If we do act, I really think this half the battle; a man upon whose temper the State can rely.

"I say nothing about a convention, as I understand, on all hands, that that is a fixed fact, and I have confined myself to answering your question. I will be much obliged to you if you will write me soon and fully from Columbia. It is impossible to write to you, with the constant interruption of the office, and as you want Cobb's opinions, not mine, I send this to you. Yours, W. H. T."

The original of the above letter is in my possession.

[1] Ten years before, this man, then engaged in treasonable schemes, dating his letter at Washington, "House of Representatives, September 2, 1850," wrote to General Quitman, then Governor of Mississippi, on whom the mantle of Calhoun, as chief conspirator against American Nationality, had worthily fallen, saying:—"When the President of the United States commands me to do one act, and the Executive of Mississippi commands me to do another thing, inconsistent with the first order, I obey the Governor of my State. To Mississippi I owe *allegiance*, and, because she commands me, I owe obedience to the United States."—*Life and Correspondence of John A. Quitman:* by J. F. H. Claiborne, ii. 63. This is the pure doctrine of Supreme State Sovereignty, on which the conspirators founded their justification for the so-called secession of the States from the Union.

---

* The iniquity of this recommendation of Cobb is made apparent by the fact, that it was a common practice for the planter to receive pay for his crop in advance. The crop now to "go forward" was already paid for. The money to be received, on its delivery, was for the next year's crop, which would never be delivered. Here was a proposition for a scheme to swindle Northern men to the amount of many millions of dollars.

terest so strong in the movement, I fear they will be violent beyond control." The seizure of the Government, before Mr. Lincoln's inauguration, was a part of the plan of operations. " The successful, unrestricted installation of Lincoln," wrote this viper, nestled in the warm bosom of the Republic, " is the beginning of the end of Slavery."[1] Thompson afterward took up arms against the Republic, plotted the blackest crimes against the people of his country while finding an asylum in Canada, and was finally charged with complicity in the murder of President Lincoln. Floyd, indicted for enormous frauds on the Government while in office, perished ignobly, after wearing the insignia of a brigadier-general among the insurgent enemies of his country.

The Governors and Legislatures of several of the Slave-labor States took early action against the National Government. The South Carolina politicians moved first. They were traditionally rebellious, gloried in their turbulence, and were jealous of any leadership or priority of action in the great drama of Treason about to be opened.

Governor Gist called the South Carolina Legislature to meet in extraordinary session, in the old State House at Columbia, on Monday, the 5th of November, for the purpose of choosing, on the following day, Presidential electors.[2] In his message to both Houses, he recommended the authorization of a convention of the people, to consider the expediency of withdrawing the State from the Union, in the event of Lincoln's election. He expressed a desire that such withdrawal should be accomplished. " The indications from many of the Southern States," he said, " justify the conclusion that the seces-

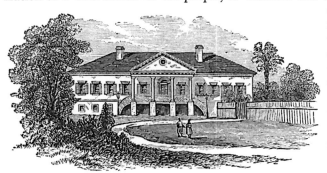

THE OLD STATE HOUSE AT COLUMBIA.

sion of South Carolina will be immediately followed, if not adopted simultaneously, by them, and ultimately by the entire South. . . . The State has, by great unanimity, declared that she has the right peaceably to secede,[3] and no power on earth can rightfully prevent it. If, in the exercise of arbitrary power, and forgetful of the lessons of history, the Government of the United States should attempt coercion, it will become our solemn duty to meet force by force; and, whatever may be the decision of the conven-

---

[1] Letter to Mr. Peterson, of Mississippi. It fell into the hands of United States troops while in that region, in 1863.

[2] In South Carolina, political power had always been as far removed from the people as possible. The Governor of the State and the Presidential electors were, by a provision of the State Constitution, chosen by the Legislature, and not directly by the people.

[3] In 1852, a State Convention in South Carolina reiterated the sentiments of the Nullification Convention twenty years before, and declared that the State had a "right to secede from the Confederacy whenever the occasion should arise justifying her, in her judgment, in taking that step." The Convention informed the world that the State forbore the immediate exercise of that right from considerations of expediency only.

tion representing the sovereignty of the State, and amenable to no earthly tribunal, it shall, during the remainder of my administration, be carried out to the letter, regardless of any hazard that may surround its execution." He recommended the immediate arming, "with the most efficient weapons of modern warfare," every white man in the State between the ages of eighteen and forty-five, and placing the whole military force of the Commonwealth "in a position to be used at the shortest notice, and with the greatest efficiency." He also recommended the immediate acceptance of ten thousand volunteers, to be officered and drilled, and held in readiness to be called upon at the shortest notice.

These recommendations to prepare for revolt were made on the day before the election of Mr. Lincoln. They met with a hearty response. On that evening, prominent South Carolinians, who were in attendance, were serenaded and made speeches. One of these was James Chesnut, Jr., a member of the United States Senate. He told the crowd of listeners that he had no doubt of the election of Mr. Lincoln on the morrow, and that then they had arrived "at the initial point of a new departure. We have two ways before us," he said, "in one of which, whether we will or not, we must tread. . . . In both lie dangers, difficulties, and troubles, which no human foresight can foreshadow or perceive; but they are not equal in magnitude. One is beset with humiliation, dishonor, *émeutes*, rebellions—with submission, in the beginning, to all, and at all times, and confiscation and slavery in the end. The other, it is true, has its difficulties and trials, but no disgrace. Hope, duty, and honor shine along the path." "The Black Republicans," he said, "claim the dogmas of the Declaration of Independence as part of the Constitution, and that it is their right and duty to so administer the Government as to give full effect to them. The people now must choose whether they will be governed by enemies or govern themselves. For myself, I would unfurl the Palmetto flag, fling it to the breeze, and, with the spirit of a brave man, determine to live and die as becomes our glorious ancestry, and ring the clarion notes of defiance in the ears of an insolent foe." He spoke of the undoubted right of South Carolina to withdraw from the Union, and recommended its immediate action in that direction, saying, "the other Southern States will flock to our standard." His speech was received with vehement applause, and met with greetings of satisfaction throughout the State.

In a similar manner, W. W. Boyce, who had been a member of Congress since 1853, responded to a serenade on the following evening,[a] from the balcony of the Congaree House. "In my opinion," he said, "the South ought not to submit. If you intend to resist, the way to resist in earnest is to act; the way to enact revolution is to stare it in the face. I think the only policy for us is to arm as soon as we receive authentic intelligence of the election of Lincoln. It is for South Carolina, in the quickest manner, and by the most direct means, to withdraw from the Union. Then we will not submit, whether the other Southern States will act with us or with our enemies. . . . When an ancient philosopher wished to inaugurate a revolution, his motto was: To dare! To dare!" From that moment, he was zealously engaged in efforts to destroy his Government.

[a] November 6, 1860.

From the same balcony Edmund Ruffin, of Virginia, a white-haired old man, made a speech to the excited people. He was well known as a political and agricultural writer, and a warm personal friend and admirer of John C. Calhoun and his principles. He had made it an important part of the business of his life to applaud the system of Slavery, and to create in the Slave-labor States a hatred of the people of the Free-labor States. He soon afterward acquired the unenviable distinction of having raised the first spade-full of earth in the construction of military works for the assault on Fort Sumter, and also of having fired the first shot at that fortification.[1] He had now hastened from his home in Virginia to Columbia, to urge the importance of immediate secession. "I have studied the question now before the country," he said, "for years. It has been the one great idea of my life. The defense of the South, I verily believe, is only to be secured through the lead of South Carolina. Old as I am, I have come here to join her in that

lead. I wish Virginia was as ready as South Carolina, but, unfortunately, she is not. But the first drop of blood spilled on the soil of South Carolina will bring Virginia and every other Southern State to her side."

It had been agreed that revolutionary movements should commence immediately after the fact should be made known that Mr. Lincoln was elected. Accordingly, on the evening of the 7th,[a] a dispatch went up to Columbia from Charleston, saying that many of the National officers had resigned. That morning,

EDMUND RUFFIN.

[a] November, 1860.

the United States District Court had assembled in Charleston, over which one of the leaders of rebellion, Judge A. G. Magrath, presided. The Grand Jury, according to instructions, declined to make any presentments. They said that the action of the ballot-box on the previous day had destroyed all hopes of a permanent confederacy of the "Sovereign States," and that the public mind was constrained to "rise above the consideration of details in the administration of law and justice, up to the vast and solemn issues that have been forced upon us—issues which involve the existence of the Government of which this Court is the organ." They therefore declined to act. This solemn judicial farce was perfected by the formal resignation of Judge Magrath. With ludicrous gravity, he said to the jurors:—"For the last time I have, as Judge of the United

[1] Ruffin was in Richmond at the close of the following summer, and visited the National prisoners who were captured at the battle of Bull's Run in July. He told them that he was then a resident of Charleston, in South Carolina, and boasted that he was the person who fired the first shot at Sumter. Mr. Ely, member of Congress, who was among the prisoners, speaks of him in his *Journal*, kept while in confinement in Richmond, as "a patriarchal citizen, whose long locks extended over his shoulders, whitened by the snows of more than seventy winters." Ruffin did not appear prominently in the war that ensued. He survived the conflict, in which he lost all of his property. On Saturday, the 17th of June, 1865, he committed suicide by blowing off the top of his head with a gun, at the residence of his son, near Danville, in Virginia. He left a note, in which he said:—"I cannot survive the liberties of my country." The wretched man was then almost eighty years of age.

States, administered the laws of the United States within the limits of South Carolina. So far as I am concerned, the Temple of Justice, raised under the Constitution of the United States, is now closed." He then laid aside his gown, and retired.

The Collector of Customs at Charleston, C. J. Colcock, and James Conner, the United States District Attorney, resigned at the same time; and B. C. Pressley, the National Sub-treasurer, also announced his determination to resign, as soon as he could with due respect to President Buchanan. Although a convention to make a formal declaration of the withdrawal of the State from the Union had not yet been authorized, the conspirators and their political instruments throughout South Carolina now acted as if disunion had been actually accomplished.

A. G. MAGRATH.

On the morning of the 7th,[a] when the telegraph had flashed intelligence of Lincoln's election over the length and breadth of the land, and bore tidings of great joy elsewhere because of the auspicious

a November, 1860.

event, the enthusiasm of the rebellious people in Charleston was unbounded and irrepressible. The conspirators and their friends greeted each other with signs of the greatest exultation. They grasped each other's hands, and some of them cordially embraced, in the ecstasy of their pleasure. The Palmetto flag was everywhere unfurled; and from the crowded streets went up cheer after cheer for a Southern Confederacy. All day the enthusiasm was kept up by speeches, harangues, and the booming of cannon; and, at evening, the city was illu-

PALMETTO FLAG.

minated by bonfires. The wished-for pretext for insurrection was at hand, and the master spirits of treason were everywhere jubilant. Their work, begun so hopefully in the Convention at Charleston, in April, was now wellnigh finished in November. The germ of revolution then planted had expanded, and budded, and blossomed, and now promised abundant fruit.

There was intense excitement at Columbia, on the morning after the election. Governor Gist was the recipient of many messages by telegraph:— "The Governor and Council are in session," said one from Raleigh, North Carolina. "The people are very much excited. North Carolina is ready to secede."—"Large numbers of Bell men," said another, from Montgomery, Alabama, "headed by T. H. Watts,[1] have declared for secession, since the announcement of Lincoln's election. The State will undoubtedly secede." —"The hour for action has come," said a message from Milledgeville, Geor-

---

[1] Thomas H. Watts was a "Bell-Everett" elector, but espoused the cause of the conspirators at the very beginning of their open career. He was elected Governor of Alabama in 1863, and used his official power to its utmost in favor of the rebellion.

gia. "This State is ready to assert her rights and independence. The leading men are eager for the business."—"There is a great deal of excitement here," said a dispatch from Washington City; "several extreme Southern men, in office, have donned the Palmetto cockade,[1] and declared themselves ready to march South."—"If your State secedes," said another, from Richmond, Virginia, "we will send you troops of volunteers to aid you."—"Placards are posted about the city," said a message from New Orleans, "calling a convention of those favorable to the organization of a corps of *Minute-men*. The Governor is all right."—"Be firm," said a second dispatch from Washington; "a large quantity of arms will be shipped South from the Arsenal here, to-morrow. The President is perplexed.

SECESSION COCKADE.

His feelings are with the South, but he is afraid to assist them openly."—"The bark *James Gray*, owned by Cushing's Boston line, lying at our wharves," said a message from Charleston, "has hoisted the Palmetto flag, and fired a salute of fifteen guns, under direction of her owner. The *Minute-men* throng the streets with Palmetto cockades in their hats. There is great rejoicing here."

Stimulated by these indications of sympathy, the South Carolina Legislature took bold and vigorous action. Joint resolutions were offered in both Houses, providing for the calling of a State Convention at an early day, for the purpose of formally declaring the withdrawal of the State from the Union. These, generally, contemplated immediate separate State action, before the excitement caused by the election should subside, and the heads of the people should become cool and capable of sober reflection. But there were able men in that Legislature, who foresaw the perils which a single State, cut loose from her moorings during a terrible storm of passion, would have to encounter, and pleaded eloquently for the exercise of reason and prudence. They were as zealous as their colleagues for ultimate secession, but regarded the co-operation of at least the other Cotton-growing States as essential to success. "If the State, in her sovereign capacity, determines that secession will produce the co-operation which we have so earnestly sought," said Mr. McGowan, of Abbeville, "then it shall have my hearty approbation. . . . If South Carolina, in Convention assembled, deliberately secedes—separate and alone, and, without hope of co-operation, decides to cut loose from her moorings, surrounded as she is by Southern sisters in like circumstances—I will be one of her crew, and, in common with every true son of hers, will endeavor, with all the power that God has given me, to

> ' Spread all her canvas to the breeze,
> Set every threadbare sail,
> And give her to the God of storms,
> The lightning and the gale.' "

But these cautious men were overborne by the fiery zealots. One of these (Mullins, from Marion), in his eagerness to hurry the State out of the Union, revealed not only the fact that the heads and hearts of the great mass of the people of South Carolina were not in unison with the desperate

---

[1] Made of blue silk ribbon, with a button in the center, bearing the image of a Palmetto-tree.

politicians who were exciting them to revolt, but another fact, afterward made clear—that months before Mr. Lincoln's election, emissaries of the conspirators had been sent to Europe, to prepare the way for aid and recognition of the contemplated Southern Confederacy by foreign powers. "If we wait for co-operation," he said, "*Slavery and State Rights will be abandoned, State Sovereignty and the cause of the South lost forever;* and we would be subjected to a dominion, the parallel to which is that of the poor Indian under the British East India Company. When we have pledged ourselves to take the State out of the Union, and place it on record, then I am willing to send a commissioner to Georgia, or any other Southern State, to announce our determination, and to submit the question whether they will join us or not. We have it from high authority, that the representative of one of the imperial powers of Europe, in view of the prospective separation of one or more of the Southern States from the present Confederacy, has made propositions in advance for the establishment of such relations between it and the government about to be established in this State, as will insure to that power such a supply of cotton for the future as their increasing demand for that article will require."[1]

Led by Robert Barnwell Rhett, Senior, the extremists in the South Carolina Legislature held sway in that body, and on the 9th of November a bill calling a convention for the purpose of secession passed the Senate, and was concurred in by the House on the 12th. It provided for the election of delegates on the 6th of December, to meet in convention on the 17th of that month. This accomplished, Messrs. Chesnut and Hammond formally offered the resignation of their seats in the Senate of the United States. The offer was accepted with great applause, as the beginning of the dissolution of the Union.

Georgia was the first to follow the bad example of South Carolina. Its Legislature was convened on the 7th of November. Robert Toombs and Alfred Iverson, then United States Senators, and others, had been laboring with intense zeal, during the Presidential canvass, to arouse the people to revolt when the leaders should give the signal. Many influential men were co-workers with them. It was exceedingly difficult to seduce the people of that State from their affection for the Union. They succeeded, however, in producing a general ferment and unrest throughout the State; and, by falsehoods, impassioned addresses, and, in some cases, intimations of impending wrath for Union men, they confused, distracted, and divided the people. Toombs, like Rhett, was anxious for the immediate and separate secession of his State.

By the time the Legislature met, which was on the day after the Presidential election,[*] there had been created quite a strong disunion   * November 7. feeling throughout the State. It permeated the woof of society, and was prominent in the whole social fabric. The Legislature was divided in sentiment; and a majority of them did not coincide with the Speaker, who, in opening the session, declared that the triumph of the Republican party would lead to a nullification of the Fugitive Slave Law; the exclusion of Slavery from the Territories; the non-admission of any more Slave States

---

[1] This matter is elucidated in another portion of this work.

into the Union; the abolition of Slavery in the District of Columbia; the desecration of the Church, by the installation therein of an " Anti-slavery God ;" the dissolution of every bond of union between the North and the South, and a practical application of the theory that the Republic could not exist, half slave and half free. These predictions of the Speaker, through the operations of war, were fulfilled to the letter. They are now History.

Governor Joseph E. Brown's message to the Legislature of Georgia was long, temperate in language, but very hostile toward the people of the North. After reviewing, at great length, the legislation in several of the Northern States concerning the Fugitive Slave Law, he urged the enactment, as a retaliatory measure, of a law making it a penal offense to introduce any goods, wares, or merchandise into Georgia from any of those States. " In my opinion," he said, " the time for bold, decided action, has arrived." He was opposed to secession as a remedy for existing evils, and did not like the project of a Southern Convention of States looking to that end, which had been proposed ; yet, he recommended the appropriation of a million of dollars for the purpose of arming the State.

The Legislature discussed the exciting topics presented to them with calmness. It was generally agreed that the State could not remain within the Union excepting on certain conditions, such as the repeal of the Personal Liberty Laws existing in some of the Free-labor States, and the enactment of laws by Congress for the protection of Slave property in the Territories. By a heavy majority they voted that a " Sovereign State " of the Union had a right to secede from it, adopting as their own the doctrine put forth by the Governor in his message, that the States of the Union are not subordinate to the National Government; were not created by it, and do not belong to it; that *they* created the National Government; from them it derives its powers ; to them it is responsible, and, when it abuses the trust reposed in it, they, as equal sovereigns, have a right to resume the powers respectively delegated to it by them.

This is the sum and substance of the doctrine of State supremacy, as defined and inculcated by Calhoun and his followers, for the evident purpose of weakening the attachment of the people to the Union, and so dwarfing their patriotism that narrow State pride should take the place of the lofty sentiment of nationality, and predispose them to acquiescence in the scheme for forming a " Southern Confederacy," to be composed of the Slave-labor States. That definition of the character of our Government has no real foundation in truth, discoverable in the teachings or actions of the founders of the Republic who framed the National Constitution, nor in the revealments of history.[1] It defines, with proximate accuracy, the char-

---

[1] Let us here consider two or three expressions of those founders :—

" I hold it for a fundamental point, that an individual independence of the States is utterly irreconcilable with the idea of an aggregate sovereignty."—*Letter to Edmund Randolph*, April 8, 1787, by James Madison.

"The Swiss Cantons have scarce any union at all, and have been more than once at war with one another. How, then, are all these evils to be avoided? Only by such a complete sovereignty in the General Government as will turn all the strong principles and passions above mentioned on its side."—*Speech by Alexander Hamilton in the Constitutional Convention*, June 18, 1787.

" A thirst for power, and the bantling—I had like to have said the MONSTER—sovereignty, which have taken such fast hold of the States individually. will, when joined by the many whose personal consequence in the line of State politics will, in a manner, be annihilated, form a strong phalanx against it."—*Letter of Washington to John Jay*, March 10, 1787, on proposed changes in the fundamental laws of the land.—*Life of Jay*, i. 259.

See also, *Two Lectures on the Constitution of the United States*, by Francis Lieber, LL. D.

acter of the Government under the old Confederation, which existed for
eight or ten years before the National Constitution became the supreme law
of the land ; but it is clearly erroneous as applied to the Government which
was founded on that Constitution in 1789. Instead of the National Government being a creation of the States, as States, it is a creation of the *people*
of the original thirteen States existing when the present Government was
formed, and is the political creator of every State since admitted into the
Union, first as a Territory, and then as a State, solely by the exercise of its
potential will expressed by the general Congress. Without the consent of
Congress, under the provisions of the Constitution, no State can enter the
Union.[1] This subject has received the attention due to its importance in
another portion of this work. It is introduced here incidentally, to mark
the line of difference between Unionists and Secessionists at the beginning
of the great struggle—between those who hold that our Republic is a unit
or consolidated nation, composed of distinct commonwealths, and those who
hold that it is only a league of Sovereign States, whose existence may be
ended by the withdrawal, at its own pleasure, of any member of the league.
We will only add, that the leaders in the great rebellion found their full
justification in the doctrine of the supremacy of the States, which, if it be
the true interpretation of our system of government, makes secession and
consequent disunion lawful.

Whilst the Georgia Legislature was considering the great questions of
the day, and Robert Toombs and other conspirators were urging them to
treasonable action, Alexander H. Stephens, a leading man in intellect and
personal character in that State, and for a long time its representative in Congress, addressed a large concourse of people," in " November 14, 1860.
the Assembly Chamber at Milledgeville. Toombs had harangued
them on the previous evening, with his accustomed arrogance of manner
and insolence of speech. He denounced the National Government as a
curse, and made many false charges concerning its partiality to Northern
interests, to the injury of Southern interests. He also urged the Legislature
to act on the subject of Secession, independent of the people. He was
"afraid of conventions," he said; that is to say, he was afraid to trust the
people. His language was violent and seditious in the extreme.[2] He demanded unquestioning acquiescence in his secession schemes, and, with the
bravado characteristic of a nature lacking true courage, he said :—"I ask you
to give me the sword; for, if you do not give it to me, as God lives, I will
take it myself,"—and much more of like tenor. It may not be amiss to say,
in this connection, that, during the war that ensued, Toombs was made a
brigadier-general in the armies of the conspirators, and, acting in accordance
with the maxim, that "Prudence is the better part of valor," was never

[1] See Section 3, Article IV. of the National Constitution.
[2] After telling the people that after the 4th of March ensuing, the National Government, which had from
the beginning been controlled by men from the Slave-labor States, would be in the hands of the majority composing the population of the Free-labor States, he said:—" Withdraw your sons from the Army, from the Navy,
and every department of the Federal public service. Keep your own taxes in your own coffers. Buy arms
with them, and throw the bloody spear into this den of incendiaries and assassins, and let God defend the
right. ... Twenty years of labor, and toils, and taxes, all expended upon preparation, would not make up
for the advantage your enemies would gain if the rising sun on the 5th of March should find you in the Union.
Then strike while it is yet time!"

known to remain a moment longer than he was compelled to in a place of danger to himself.

Stephens's matter and manner were the reverse of all this. He was calm, cool, dignified, dispassionate, and solemn, but apparently earnest. "My object," he said, "is not to stir up strife, but to allay it; not to appeal to your passions, but to your reason." With the fervor which patriotic impulses inspire, and the apparent candor as well as sagacity of a philosopher, he commented on the election just ended, its significance, and its probable bearing upon the future history of the country, and especially of the Slave-labor States. "Let us reason together," he said. "Shall the people of the South secede from the Union in consequence of the election of Mr. Lincoln to the Presidency of the United States? My countrymen, I tell you frankly, candidly, and earnestly, that I do not think that they ought. In my judgment, the election of no man, constitutionally chosen, to that high office, is sufficient cause for any State to separate from the Union. It ought to stand by and aid still in maintaining the Constitution of the country. To make a point of resistance to the Government, to withdraw from it, because a man has been constitutionally elected, puts us in the wrong. We are pledged to maintain the Constitution. Many of us have sworn to support it. Can we, therefore, for the mere election of a man to the Presidency, and that, too, in accordance with the prescribed forms of the Constitution, make a point of resistance to the Government, by withdrawing from it, without becoming the breakers of that sacred instrument ourselves? Would we not be in the wrong? Whatever fate is to befall this country, let it never be laid to the charge of the people of the South, and especially to the people of Georgia, that we were untrue to our national engagements. Let the fault and the wrong rest upon others. If all our hopes are to be blasted—if the Republic is to go down—let us be found to the last moment standing on the deck, with the Constitution of the United States waving over our heads. Let the fanatics of the North break the Constitution, if that is their fell purpose. Let the responsibility be upon them. I shall speak presently more of their acts; but let not the South—let us not be the ones to commit the aggression. We went into the election with this people. The result was different from what we wished; but the election has been constitutionally held. Were we to make a point of resistance to the Government, and go out of the Union on that account, the record would be made up hereafter against us."

Mr. Stephens then showed, that with a majority of the United States Senate and of the Supreme Court politically opposed to him, the new President would be powerless to do evil to the Slave system. "Why, then," he asked, "should we disrupt the ties of this Union when his hands are tied, and he can do nothing against us?" "My countrymen," he continued, "I am not one of those who believe this Union has been a curse, up to this time. True men, men of integrity, entertain different views from me on this subject. I do not question their right to do so; I would not impugn their motives in so doing. Nor will I undertake to say that this Government of our fathers is perfect. There is nothing perfect in this world, of a human origin—nothing connected with human nature, from man himself to any of his works. . . . But that this Government of our fathers, with all its defects, comes nearer the objects of all good governments than any other on the face of the earth, is my settled conviction. . . . Where will you go, following the sun in its circuit round our globe, to find a government that better protects the liberties of the people, and secures to them the blessings we enjoy? I think that one of the evils that beset us is a surfeit of liberty, an exuberance of priceless blessings for which we are ungrateful."

Mr. Stephens then proceeded to expose the misstatements and dissipate the fallacies uttered by Toombs the previous evening, and was frequently applauded. Toombs was present, and felt the scourge most keenly. With ill-concealed rage and disappointment, he frequently interrupted the speaker, sometimes with tones of anger, and sometimes with those of scorn. These did not disturb the equanimity of his competitor in the least. With perfect coolness, courtesy, and even gentleness, he went forward in his work of apparently endeavoring to stay the rising tide of revolution against the Government he professed to love so well, defending its claim to justice and beneficence. "The great difference between our country and all others, such as France, and England, and Ireland, is," he said, "that here there is popular sovereignty, while there sovereignty is exercised

ROBERT TOOMBS.

by kings and favored classes. This principle of popular sovereignty, however much derided lately, is the foundation of our institutions. Constitutions are but the channels through which the popular will may be expressed. Our Constitution came from the people. They made it, and they alone may rightfully unmake it." . . . "I believe in the power of the people to govern themselves, when wisdom prevails and passion is silent. Look at what has already been done by them for their advancement in all that ennobles man. There is nothing like it in the history of the world. Look abroad from one extent of the country to the other; contemplate our greatness. We are now among the first nations of the earth. Shall it be said, then, that our institutions, founded upon principles of self-government, are a failure? Thus far, our Government is a noble example, worthy of imitation. The gentleman (Mr. Cobb),[1] the other night, said it had proven a failure. A failure in what? In growth? Look at our expanse in national power. Look at our population, and increase in all that makes a people great. A failure? Why, we are the admiration of the civilized world, and present to it the brightest hopes of mankind." With an appropriateness, armed with a peculiar sting for both Toombs and Cobb, and for other demagogues, he added:—"*Some of our public men have failed in their aspirations; that is true, and from that comes a great part of our troubles.*" As soon as prolonged applause ended, Mr. Stephens said:—"No, there is no failure of this Government yet. We have made great advancement under the Constitu-

---

[1] T. R. R. Cobb.

tion, and I cannot but hope that we shall advance higher still.   Let us be
true to our cause."[1]

Mr. Stephens's speech made a powerful impression throughout the Republic, and many men in the North expressed a wish that Mr. Lincoln might
invite him to a seat in his cabinet, as a concession to the South.   The true
friends of the Government everywhere hoped that it might do its proposed
work of allaying the storm of passion, then increasing in violence in the
Slave-labor States every hour.   That storm had been long gathering.   Its
elements were marked by intense potency, and it had now burst upon the
land with such force that no human work or agency could withstand its
blind fury.   It was sweeping onward, roaring with the most vehement rage,
like a tropical tornado, making every thing bend to its strength.   Mr.
Stephens himself was lifted by it from the rock of the Constitution, on

ALEXANDER H. STEPHENS.

which he had so ostentatiously planted
his feet at this time, and within ninety
days he was riding proudly upon the
wings of the tempest, as the second actor
in a Confederacy of rebellious men, banded
for the avowed purpose of destroying
that Constitution, and laying in hopeless
ruins the glorious Republic which rested
upon it, and which he now professed so
ardently to love and admire!   He did,
indeed, seem to try hard to resist the
storm for several weeks; and, during
that time, told his countrymen some sober
truths concerning the control of the National Government by the Slave interest
from its beginning, which should have
made the cheeks of every conspirator crimson with shame, because of his
mean defiance of every principle of honor and true manhood—his wickedness without excuse.

In the State Convention of Georgia, early in January, 1861, Mr. Stephens
said:—"I must declare here, as I have often done before, and which has been
repeated by the greatest and wisest of statesmen and patriots in this and
other lands, that it is the best and freest Government, the most equal in its
rights, the most just in its decisions, the most lenient in its measures, and the
most inspiring in its principles to elevate the race of men, that the sun of
heaven ever shone upon.   Now, for you to attempt to overthrow such a

[1] In a private letter, written eleven days after this speech (dated "Crawfordsville, Ga., Nov. 25, 1860"), Mr.
Stephens revealed the fact that in him the patriot was yet subservient to the politician—that his aspirations
were really more sectional than national.   He avowed that his attachment to Georgia was supreme, and that
the chief object of his speech at Milledgeville, on the 14th, was not so much for the preservation of the Union
as the security of unity of action in his State.   "The great and leading object aimed at by me, in Milledgeville,"
he said, "was *to produce harmony on a right line of policy*.   If the worst comes to the worst, as it may, and
our State has to quit the Union, it is of the utmost importance that all our people should be united cordially in
this course."   After expressing a desire that the rights of Georgia might be secured "in the Union," he said:—
"If, after making an effort, we shall fail, then all our people will be united in making or adopting the last resort,
the *ultima ratio regum* "—the last argument of kings—the force of arms.   He then predicted, that when the
Union should be dissevered, "at the North, anarchy will ensue," yet he was doubtful whether the South would
be any better off.

Government as this, under which we have lived for more than three-quarters
of a century—in which we have gained our wealth, our standing as a nation,
our domestic safety, while the elements of peril are around, with peace and
tranquillity, accompanied with unbounded prosperity and rights unassailed—is
the hight of madness, folly, and wickedness, to which I can neither lend my
sanction nor my vote."[1]   A month later, he was Vice-President of a Confederacy of traitors to that Government!   Indeed, in the first speech here
cited he had provided himself with means for escape, should there be an
occasion, growing out of a perhaps foreshadowed necessity, by declaring:—
"Should Georgia determine to go out of the Union, I speak for one, though
my views might not agree with them, whatever the result may be, I shall
bow to the will of the people of my State.[2]   Their cause is my cause, and
their destiny is my destiny; and I trust this will be the ultimate course of

---

[1] In this speech, Mr. Stephens said, truly, that the Slave-labor States had always received from the National
Government all they had ever asked. When they demanded it, the Slave-trade was allowed, by a special provision in the Constitution, for twenty years. When they asked for a three-fifths representation in Congress for
their slaves, it was granted. When they asked for the return of fugitive slaves, a provision of the Constitution
and special laws were made for that purpose. When they asked for more territory, they received Louisiana,
Florida, and Texas. "We have always had the control of the General Government," he said, "and can yet, if
we remain in it, and are as united as we have been. We have had a majority of the Presidents chosen from the
South, as well as the control and management of most of those chosen from the North. We have had sixty years
of Southern Presidents to their twenty-four, thus controlling the Executive Department. So of the judges of
the Supreme Court; there have been eighteen from the South, and but eleven from the North. Although nearly
four-fifths of the judicial business has arisen in the Free States, yet a majority of the Court has always been from
the South. This we have received, *so as to guard against any interpretation unfavorable to us.* In like manner we have been equally watchful to guard our interests in the Legislative branch of the Government. In
choosing the Presidents of the Senate, *pro tempore,* we have had twenty-four to their eleven. Speakers of the
House, we have had twenty-three and they twelve. While the majority of the Representatives, from their
greater population, have always been from the North, yet we have generally secured the Speaker, because he, to
a great extent, shapes and controls the legislation of the country. Nor have we had any less control in every
other department of the General Government. Attorney-generals we have had fourteen, while the North have
had but five. Foreign Ministers we have had eighty-six, and they but fifty-four." He then went on to show that
while three-fourths of the business demanding diplomatic agents abroad was from the Free-labor States, his
section had had the principal Embassies; that a vast majority of higher officers of the Army and Navy were
from the South, while a larger portion of the soldiers and sailors were drawn from the North; and that two-
thirds of the clerks in the Departments at Washington had been taken from the Slave-labor States, while they had
only about one-third of the white population. During the same time, over three-fourths of the revenue collected
for the support of the Government was uniformly raised from the North. . . . The expense for the transportation of the mails in the Free-labor States was, by the Report of the Postmaster-general for 1860, a little over
$13,000,000, while the income was $19,000,000. But in the Slave-labor States, the cost of the transportation of
the mails was $14,716,000, while the revenue from the same was $8,001,026; leaving a deficit of $6,704,974.
In view of all this, Mr. Stephens might well ask, as he did, "For what purpose will you break up this Union
—this American Government, established by our common ancestry, cemented and built up by their sweat and
blood, and founded on the broad principles of *Right, Justice,* and *Humanity!*"

[2] In contrast with this subserviency to the idea of State supremacy, and with more enlarged views of the
duty of American citizens, Henry Clay, as much interested in Slavery as Mr. Stephens, once said on the floor
of Congress, in rebuke of disunion sentiments:—"If Kentucky, to-morrow, unfurls the banner of resistance,
I never will fight under that banner; I owe a *paramount* allegiance to the whole Union—a subordinate one to
my own State." A writer in the New York *Evening Post* ("W. L. P."), of February 8th, 1865, in a long poem,
called "Aleck and Abe," thus alludes to Stephens's defection, which some have attributed to "coercion:"

"But by and by, our doleful friend	Screamed Yancey, 'You shall eat those words,
Received a rousing start,	As sure as I am I.'
As Yancey waved his lucifers	And, sooth, he did it in a twink,
To 'fire the Southern heart.'	With many a wry grimace;
'Hold, there!' shrieked Aleck, in dismay;	As Jeff. and Toombs stood by, and shook
'Was ever wretch so rash?	A halter in his face.
If you ignite that magazine,	And when the words were all devoured,
You'll blow us all to smash!'	With right hand on his breast,
Outspoke the Fire-fiend of the South:	He whimpered, 'Pray, forgive me, friends;
'Not so, by grandest odds—	Indeed, I did but jest.
If I let off this magazine	And now I've had my little joke,
We all become as gods!'	And you your natural "swear;"
'You lie,' cried Aleck, 'in your throat;	I'm all agog to back your aims—
And more, you *know* you lie!'	What's first to do or dare?' " .

all.   Let us call a convention of the people; let all these matters be submitted
to it; and when the will of a majority of the people has thus been expressed,
the whole State will present one unanimous voice in favor of whatever may
be demanded."

Influences more powerful than any Mr. Stephens could command were at
work upon the public mind.   Only two days before his speech
[a] November 12, was pronounced, a Military Convention was held at Milledge-
1860.   ville,[a] which was addressed by the Governor of the State, in very
incendiary language.   He affirmed the *right* of secession, and also the duty
of all the Southern States to sustain the action of the South Carolina Legislature.   "I would like," he said "to see Federal troops dare attempt the
coercion of a seceding Southern State.   For every Georgian who should fall
in a conflict thus incited, the lives of two Federal soldiers should expiate the
outrage on State Sovereignty."   These were brave words in the absence of
all danger.   When that danger was nigh—when "Federal sol-
[b] November, diers" under Sherman, just four years later,[b] were marching
1864.   through Georgia, in triumphant vindication of the National au-

thority, Governor Brown and many members of the Legislature were trembling fugitives from that very capitol where Toombs,
and Cobb, and Iverson, and Benning, and
Brown himself, had fulminated their foolish
threats.

The Military Convention, by a heavy
majority, voted in favor of secession; and
this action had great weight with the
Legislature and the people.   On
[c] November 13. the following day,[c] the Legislature voted an appropriation of a million
of dollars for arming and equipping the
militia of the State; and on the 7th of
December, an act, calling a convention of

OSEPH E. BROWN.

[d] 1861.   the people, was passed, which provided for the election of delegates on the 2d of January,[d] and their assemblage on the 16th.
The preamble to the bill declared that, in the judgment of that Assembly, the
"present crisis in National affairs demands resistance," and that "it is the
privilege of the people to determine the mode, measure, and time of such
resistance."   Power to do this was given to the Convention by the act.

On the 14th of December, a large meeting of the members of the Legislature assembled in the Senate Chamber, and agreed to an address to the
people of South Carolina, Alabama, Mississippi, and Florida, urging upon them
the importance of co-operation, rather than separate State action, in the matter
of secession.   "Our people must be united," they said; "our common interests
must be preserved."   The address was signed by fifty-two members of the
Legislature.   It was so offensive to the Hotspurs of the South Carolina State
Convention, that that body refused to receive it.   We shall again refer to
the action of the Georgia Legislature.

The Legislature of Mississippi assembled at Jackson early in November,
and adjourned on the 30th.   The special object of the session was to make

preparations for the secession of the State. An act was passed, providing for a Convention, to be held on the 7th of January; and the 20th of December was the day appointed by it for the election of delegates thereto. The Governor (John J. Pettus) was authorized to appoint commissioners to visit each of the Slave-labor States, for the purpose of officially informing the governors or legislatures thereof, that the State of Mississippi had called a Convention, "to consider the present threatening relations of the Northern and Southern sections of the Confederacy, aggravated by the recent election of a President upon principles of hostility to the States of the South; and to express the earnest hope of Mississippi, that those States will co-operate with her in the adoption of efficient measures for their common defense and safety." A portion of the Legislature was for immediate separation and secession. The press of the State was divided in sentiment, and so were the people, while their representatives in Congress were active traitors to their government. One of these (Lucius Quintius Curtius Lamar, a native of Georgia, who remained in Congress until the 12th of January, 1861, and was afterward sent to the Russian Court, as a diplomatic agent of the conspirators), submitted to the people of Mississippi, before the close of November, 1860, a plan for a "Southern Confederacy." After reciting the ordinance by which Mississippi was created a State of the Union, and proposing her formal withdrawal therefrom, the plan proposed that the

LUCIUS Q. C. LAMAR.

State of Mississippi should "consent to form a Federal Union" with all the Slave-labor States, the Territory of New Mexico, and the Indian Territory west of Arkansas, "under the name and style of the United States of America, and according to the tenor and effect of the Constitution of the United States," with slight exceptions. It proposed to continue in force all laws and treaties of the United States, so far as they applied to Mississippi, until the new Confederation should be organized, and that all regulations, contracts, and engagements made by the old Government should remain in force. It provided that the Governor of Mississippi should perform the functions of President of the new United States, within the limits of that State, and that all public officers should remain in place until the new government should be established. It was also provided that the accession of nine States should give effect to the proposed ordinance of confederation; and that, when such accession should occur, it should be the duty of the Governor to order an election of Congressmen and Presidential Electors. This scheme, like a score of others put forth by disloyal men, ambitious to appear in history as the founders of a new empire, soon found its appropriate place in the tomb of forgotten things.

The southern portion of Alabama was strongly in favor of secession, while the northern portion was as strongly in favor of Union. The Governor (Andrew B. Moore) sympathized with the secessionists, and, with Yancey

and others, stirred up the people to revolt. He had been active in procuring
the passage of joint resolutions by the Legislature of that State,
^a February 24, long before the Presidential election,^a which provided, in the
1860　　　 event of the election of the Republican candidate, for a conven-
tion to consider what should be done; in other words, to declare the secession of the State from the Union, in accordance with the long and well-
devised plan of the conspirators. So early as October, Herschell V. Johnston, the candidate for Vice-President on the Douglas ticket,
^b October 24. declared, in a speech in the Cooper Institute, New York,^b that
Alabama was ripe for revolt, in the event of Mr. Lincoln's elec-
tion—" pledged," he said, " to withdraw from the Union, and has appropriated two hundred thousand dollars for military contingencies."[1] In an
address to the people of the State, early in November, the Governor declared
that, in his opinion, " the only hope and future security for Alabama and
other Slaveholding States, is in secession from the Union." On the 6th of
December he issued a proclamation, assuring the people that the contingency
contemplated by the Legislature had occurred, namely the election of Mr.
Lincoln, and, by the authority given him by that body, he ordered delegates
to be chosen on the 24th of December, to meet in convention on
^c 1861. the 7th of January.^c Five days before that election, the Alabama
Conference of the " Methodist Church South," a very large and
most influential body, sitting at Montgomery, resolved that they believed
" African Slavery, as it existed in the Southern States of the Republic,
to be a wise, humane, and righteous institution, approved of God, and calculated to promote, to the highest possible degree, the welfare of the slave;[2]
that the election of a sectional President of the United States was evidence
of the hostility of the majority to the people of ' the South,' and which,
in fact, if not in form, dissolves the compact of Union between the States,
and drives the aggrieved party to assert their independence;" and therefore
they said, " our hearts are with the South, and should they ever need our
hands to assist in achieving our independence, we shall not be found wanting in the hour of danger."[3]

Florida, the most dependent upon the Union for its prosperity of all the
States, and the recipient of most generous favors from the National Government, was, by the action of its treasonable politicians, and especially by its
representatives in Congress, made the theater of some of the earliest and
most active measures for the destruction of the Republic. Its Legislature
met at Tallahassee on the 26th of November, and its Governor, Madison S.
Perry, in his message at the opening of the session, declared that the

<hr/>

[1] Report of Johnson's speech, in the New York *World*, October 25, 1860.
[2] See Note 3, page 38.
[3] In the first act of the melodrama of the rebellion, there were some broad farces. One of these is seen
in the action of the Grand Jury of the United States for the Middle District of Alabama. That body made the
following presentment at the December Term, 1860:—
" That the several States of Massachusetts, New Hampshire, Vermont, New York, Ohio, and others, have
nullified, by acts of their several Legislatures, several laws enacted by the Congress of the Confederation for
the protection of persons and property ; and that for many years said States have occupied an attitude of hostility to the interests of the people of the said Middle District of Alabama. And the said Federal Government,
having failed to execute its enactments for the protection of the property and interests of said Middle District,
and this court having no jurisdiction in the premises, this Grand Jury do present the said Government as worthless, impotent, and a *nuisance.*　　　　　　　　　　　　　　C. G. GUNTHER, *Foreman,*
　　　　　　　　　　　　　　　　　　　　　　　　　　　　　　and nineteen others."

"domestic peace and future prosperity" of the State depended upon "secession from their faithless and perjured confederates." He alluded to the argument of some, that no action should be taken until they knew whether the policy of the new Administration would be hostile to their interests or not; and, with the gravity of the most earnest disciple of Calhoun, he flippantly said :—"My countrymen, if we wait for an overt act of the Federal Government, our fate will be that of the white inhabitants of St. Domingo. Why wait?" he asked. "What is this Government? It is but the trustee, the common agent of all the States, appointed by them to manage their affairs, according to a written constitution, or power of attorney. Should the Sovereign States then—the principals and the partners in the association —for a moment tolerate the idea that their action must be graduated by the will of their agent? The idea is preposterous." This was but another mode of expressing the doctrine of State Supremacy.

Louisiana was rather slow to move in the direction of treason. Her worst enemy, John Slidell, then misrepresenting her in the Senate of the United States, had been engaged for years in corrupting the patriotism of her sons, and had been aided in his task by Judah P. Benjamin, a Hebrew unworthy of his race, and others of less note. Slidell was universally detested by right-minded men for his political dishonesty,[1] his unholy ambition, his lust for aristocratic rank and power, and his enmity to republican institutions. He had tried in vain, during the summer and autumn of 1860, to engage many of the leading men in Louisiana in treasonable schemes. With others, such as Thomas O. Moore (the Governor of the State), and a few men in authority, he was more successful. Among the leading newspapers of the State, the New Orleans *Delta* was the only open advocate of hostility and resistance to the National Government, after the Presidential election.

Governor Moore called an extraordinary session of the Legislature, to meet at Baton Rouge on the 10th of December, giving as a reason the election of Mr. Lincoln by a party hostile to "the people and institutions of the South." In his message he said, he did not think it comported "with the honor and self-respect of Louisiana, as a Slaveholding State, to live under the government of a Black Republican President," although he did not dispute the fact that he had been elected by due form of law. "The question," he said, "rises high above ordinary political considerations. It involves our present honor, and our future existence as a free and independent people." He asserted the right of a State to secede; and hoped that, if any attempt should be made by the National authority "to coerce a Sovereign State, and compel her to submission to an authority she had ceased to recognize," Louisiana would "assist her sister States with the same alacrity and courage that the Colonies assisted each other in their struggle against the despotism of the Old

---

[1] A single incident in the political career of Slidell illustrates not only the dishonesty of his character, but the facilities which are frequently offered for politicians to cheat the people. Slidell had resolved to become a member of Congress. He was rich, but was, personally, too unpopular to expect votes enough to elect him. He resorted to fraud. None but freeholders might vote in Louisiana. Slidell bought, at Government price (one dollar and twenty-five cents an acre), one hundred and eighty-eight acres of land, and deeded it, in small parcels, to four thousand eight hundred and eight of the most degraded population of New Orleans. They went to his district (Plaquemine), where their land lay, and, in a body, gave him their votes for Congress, and elected him! That was in 1842.

World. If I am not mistaken in public opinion," he said, "the Convention, if assembled, will decide that Louisiana will not submit to the Presidency of Mr. Lincoln." The Legislature passed an act providing for a State Convention, to assemble on the 22d of January; and another, appropriating five hundred thousand dollars for military purposes. They listened to a commissioner from Mississippi (Wirt Adams), but refused to authorize the Governor to appoint like agents to visit the Slave-labor States. They gave him authority to correspond with the governors of those States upon the great ᵃ1861. topic of the day, and adjourned on the 13th, to meet again on the 23d of January.ᵃ

Texas, under the leadership of its venerable Governor, Samuel Houston, and the influence of a strong Union feeling, held back, when invited by conspirators to plunge into secession. So did Arkansas, Missouri, Kentucky, Tennessee, Virginia, Maryland, and Delaware, all Slave-labor States. The Governor of Tennessee, Isham G. Harris, who was a traitor at heart, and had corresponded extensively with the disunionists of the Cotton-growing States, made great but unsuccessful exertions to link the fortunes of his State with those of South Carolina in the secession movement.

North Carolina took early but cautious action. The most open and influential secessionists in that State were Thomas L. Clingman, then a member of the United States Senate, and John W. Ellis, the Governor of the Commonwealth. They made great efforts to arouse the people of the State to revolt, but failed. The Union sentiment, and the respect for law and the principles of republican government were so deeply implanted in the nature and the habits of the people, that they could not be easily seduced from their allegiance to the National Government. The Legislature met on the 19th of November. An act was passed providing for a Convention, but directing that "no ordinance of said Convention, dissolving the connection of the State of North Carolina with the Federal Government, or connecting it with any other, shall have any force or validity until it shall have been submitted to and ratified by a majority of the qualified voters of the State for members of the General Assembly, to whom it shall be submitted for their approval or rejection;" and that it should be "advertised for at least thirty days in the newspapers of the State, before the people should be called upon to vote on the same."

Such is a brief outline of the preparations for the marshaling of the cohorts of rebellion in the Slave-labor States; for a vigorous assault, not only upon the Republic, but upon the advancing civilization of the age, and the rights of man—upon the cherished institutions of good and free government inherited from the patriots of the old War for Independence, and the hopes of aspirants for freedom throughout the world.

It is evident, in even this shadowy picture, which reveals similarity of expressions and actions in the movements of the opponents of the Government in widely separated portions of the Slave-labor States, that there had been long and thorough preparation for the revolt. This will become more manifest as we proceed in our inquiry; and when, at the close of this work, we shall consider the history of political parties at the beginning of our national career, and the gradual development of radical differences of social and political opinions in sections of the Republic remote from each other, we shall perceive that rebellion and civil war were logical results of the increasing activity of potential antagonisms, controlled and energized by selfish men for selfish purposes.[1]

---

[1] The contemplation of disunion, as an emollient for irritated State pride, had been a habit of thought in Virginia and the more Southern Slave-labor States from the beginning of the Government. Whenever the imperious will of a certain class of politicians in those States was offended by a public policy opposed to its wishes, they were in the habit of speaking of the dissolution of the Union as their remedy for the provocation. They threatened to dissolve the Union in 1795, if Jay's Treaty with Great Britain should be ratified by the United States Senate; and the famous Kentucky and Virginia Resolutions of 1798, in which the doctrine of State Supremacy was broadly inculcated, familiarized the popular mind with the idea that the National Government was only the agent of the States, and might be dismissed by them at any time.

The more concrete and perfect form of these sentiments, embodied in deliberate intentions, was exhibited by John C. Calhoun, as we have observed (note 2, page 41), in 1812. Disloyalty was strongly manifested during the discussions of the Slavery question before the adoption of the Missouri Compromise, in 1820. After the Tariff Act, so obnoxious to the Cotton-growers, became a law, in 1828, the dissolution of the Union was loudly talked of by the politicians of the Calhoun school. "The memorable scenes of our Revolution have again to be acted over," said the *Milledgeville* (Georgia) *Journal;* and the citizens of St. John's Parish, in South Carolina, said, in Convention:—"We have sworn that Congress shall, at our demand, repeal the tariff. If she does not, our State Legislature will dissolve our connection with the Union, and we will take our stand among the nations; and it behooves every true Carolinian ' to stand by his arms,' and to keep the halls of our Legislature pure from foreign intruders."

When, in the autumn of 1832, the famous Nullification Ordinance was passed by the South Carolina Convention, so certain were the mad politicians that composed it of positive success, that they caused a medal to be struck with this inscription:—"JOHN C. CALHOUN, FIRST PRESIDENT OF THE SOUTHERN CONFEDERACY!" Their wicked scheme failed, and Calhoun and his followers went deliberately at work to excite the bitterest sectional strife, by the publication, in the name of Duff Green, as editor and proprietor, of the *United States Telegraph*, at Washington City. At about the same time (1836), a novel was written by Beverly Tucker, of Virginia, called *The Partisan Leader*, in which the doctrine of State Supremacy and the most insidious sectionalism were inculcated in the seductive form of a tale, calculated, as it was intended, to corrupt the patriotism of the Southern people, and prepare them for revolution. This was printed by Duff Green, the manager of Calhoun's organ, and widely circulated in the South.

Finally, "Southern Rights Associations" were formed, having for their object the dissolution of the Union. Concerning this movement, Muscoe R. H. Garnett, who was a Member of Congress from Virginia when the late civil war broke out, wrote to Wm. H. Trescot (afterward Assistant Secretary of State under Mr. Buchanan), in May, 1851, when great preparations were made by the oligarchy for a revolt, saying:—"I would be especially glad to be in Charleston next week, and witness your Convention of delegates from the Southern Rights Associations. The condition of things in your State deeply interests me; her wise foresight and manly independence have placed her at the head of the South, to whom alone true-hearted men can look with any hope or pleasure. Momentous are the consequences which depend upon your action." Garnett mourned over the action of Virginia, in hesitating to go with the revolution. "I do not believe," he said, "that the course of the Legislature is a fair expression of the popular feeling. In the east, at least, the great majority believe in the right of secession, and feel the deepest sympathy with Carolina in opposition to measures which they regard as she does. But the west—Western Virginia—here is the rub! *Only sixty thousand slaves to four hundred and ninety-four thousand whites!* When I consider this fact, and the kind of argument which we have heard in this body, I cannot but regard with the greatest fear the question, whether Virginia would assist Carolina in such an issue. I must acknowledge, my dear Sir, that I look to the future with almost as much apprehension as hope. *You will object to the term Democrat. Democracy, in its original philosophical sense, is indeed incompatible with Slavery, and the whole system of Southern society.* Yet, if we look back, what change will you find made in any of our State Constitutions, or in our legislation, in its general course, for the last fifty years, which was not in the direction of Democracy? Do not its principles and theories become daily more fixed in our practice?—I had almost said, in the opinions of our people, did I not remember with pleasure the great improvement of opinion in regard to the abstract question of Slavery. And if such is the case, what have we to hope for the future? I do not hesitate to say, that if the question is raised between Carolina and the Federal Government, and the latter prevails, the last hope of Republican Government, and, I fear, of Southern civilization, is gone. Russia will then be a better Government than ours."

See pages 92 and 93 of this volume.

CHAPTER III.

ASSEMBLING OF CONGRESS.—THE PRESIDENT'S MESSAGE.

HILST the Cotton-growing States were in a blaze of excitement, and the Slave-labor States north of them were surging, and almost insurgent, with conflicting opinions and perplexing doubts and fears, and the Free-labor States were looking on in amazement at the madness of their colleagues, who were preparing to resist the power of the Constitution and laws of the land, the Thirty-Sixth Congress assembled at Washington City. It began its second and last session at the Capitol, on Monday, the 3d of December, 1860. It was on a bright and beautiful morning; and as the eye looked out from the western front of the Capitol upon the city below, the winding Potomac and the misty hights of Arlington beyond, it beheld a picture of repose, strongly contrasting with the spirits of men then assembling in the halls of Congress.

Never, since the birth of the Nation—more than seventy years before—had the people looked with more solemn interest upon the assembling of the National Legislature than at this time. The hoarse cry of Disunion, which had so often been used in and out of Congress by the representatives of the Slave interest, as a bugbear to frighten men of the Free-labor States into compliance with their demands, now had deep significance. Its tone was terribly earnest and defiant, and action was everywhere seen in support of words. It was evident that a crisis in the history of the Republic was present, with demands for forbearance, patience, wisdom, and sound statesmanship, in an eminent degree, to save the nation from dreadful calamities, if not from absolute ruin. Therefore with the deepest anxiety the people, in all parts of the Republic, listened to hear the voice of the President in his Annual Message to Congress, which, it was supposed, would indicate, with clearness and precision, the line of policy which the Government intended to pursue.

JOHN C. BRECKINRIDGE.

Both Houses of Congress convened at noon on the 3d of December. The Senate, with Mr. Breckinridge, the Vice-President, in the chair, was opened by a prayer by the Rev. P. D. Gurley, D. D., the Chaplain of that House, who fervently prayed that all the rulers and the people might be delivered from "erroneous judgments, from misleading influences, and from the sway of evil passions." The House of Representatives, with William Pennington, the Speaker, in the chair, was opened with prayer by its Chaplain, the Rev. Thomas H. Stockton, who fervently thanked God for the " blessings we have enjoyed within this Union—natural blessings, civil blessings, spiritual blessings, social blessings, all kinds of blessings—such blessings as were never enjoyed by any other people since the world began."

Committees were appointed by each House to inform the President of its organization, and readiness to receive any communication from him. These reported that he would send in to them a written message at noon on Tuesday.[1] At the appointed hour, the President's private Secretary, A. J. Glossbrenner, appeared below the bar of the Senate, and announced that he was there by direction of the Chief Magistrate, "to deliver to the Senate a message in writing." The House of Representatives also received it. It was read to both Houses, and then its parts were referred to appropriate committees, in the usual manner.

The telegraph carried the President's Message quickly to every part of the land. The people sat down to read it with eagerness, and arose from its perusal with brows saddened with the gravest disappointment. This feeling was universal. The Message was full of evidences of faint-heartedness and indecision in points where courage and positive convictions should have been apparent in its treatment of the great topic then filling all hearts and minds, and bore painful indications that its author was involved in some perilous dilemma into which he had fallen, and was anxiously seeking a way of escape. The method chosen was most unwise and unfortunate. It recoiled fearfully upon the public character of the venerable President; and, in the estimation of thoughtful men, a reputation gained by many important and useful public services, during a long and active life, was laid in ruins.

In the second paragraph of his Message, the President began the consideration of the troubles which then beset the nation. After recounting some of the blessings then enjoyed by the people, he asked, " Why is it, then, that discontent now so extensively prevails, and the Union of the States, which is the source of all these blessings, is threatened with destruction?" He answered his own question, by alleging, in contradiction of the solemn assurances of leaders in the rising revolt to the contrary, that "the long-

JAMES BUCHANAN.

continued and intemperate interference of the Northern people with the question of Slavery in the Southern States"[2] had produced these estrangements and

---

[1] During the administrations of George Washington and John Adams, the message or speech of the President, at the opening of each session of Congress, was read to them by the Chief Magistrate in person. Mr. Jefferson abandoned this practice when he came into office, because it seemed to be a too near imitation of the practice of the monarchs of England in thus opening the sessions of Parliament in person.

[2] Senator Hammond, of South Carolina, and others, publicly declared, long before the rebellion broke out, that the discussion of the subject of Slavery at the North had been very useful. After speaking of the great

troubles. He alleged that the immediate peril did not arise so much
from the claims on the part of Congress, or of the Territorial Legislatures,
to exclude Slavery from the Territories, or the enactment of Personal Liberty
Laws by some of the Northern States, "as from the fact of the incessant
and violent agitation of the Slavery question throughout the North, for the
last quarter of a century." This agitation, he alleged, had "inspired the
slaves with vague notions of freedom," and hence "a sense of security no
longer exists around the family altar." Then, with substantial repetition of
the words of John Randolph on the floor of Congress, fifty years before,[1]
he said:—"This feeling of peace at home has given place to apprehensions
of servile insurrection. Many a matron throughout the South retires at night
in dread of what may befall herself and her children before the morning."[2]
This state of things, he intimated, was a sufficient excuse, if continued, for
the lifting of a fratricidal hand. "Should this apprehension of domestic
danger," he said, "whether real or imaginary, extend and intensify itself,
until it shall pervade the masses of the Southern people, then disunion will
become inevitable. Self-preservation is the first law of nature. . . . And no
political Union, however fraught with blessings and benefits in all other respects, can long continue, if the necessary consequence be to render the
homes and the firesides of nearly half the parties to it habitually and hope-

---

value of Slavery to the Cotton-growing States, Mr. Hammond observed:—"Such has been for us the happy results of the Abolition discussion. So far our gain has been immense from this contest, savage and malignant as
it has been. Nay, we have solved already the question of Emancipation, by this re-examination and exposition
of the false theories of religion, philanthropy, and political economy, which embarrassed the fathers in their day.
. . . At the North, and in Europe, they cried havoc, and let loose upon us all the dogs of war. And how stands
it now? Why, in this very quarter of a century, our slaves have doubled in numbers, and each slave has more
than doubled in value."—*Speech at Barnwell Court House*, Oct. 27, 1858.
        In July 1859, Alexander H. Stephens, in a speech in Georgia, said he was not one of those who believed that
the South had sustained any injury by those agitations. "So far," he said, "from the institution of African
Slavery in our section being weakened or rendered less secure by the discussion, my deliberate judgment is, that
it has been greatly strengthened and fortified."
        Senator R. M. T. Hunter, of Virginia, said, in 1860:—"In many respects, the results of that discussion have
not been adverse to us."
        Earl Russell said, in a letter to Lord Lyons, in May, 1861, "that one of the Confederate Commissioners told
him, that the principal of the causes which led to secession was not Slavery, but the very high price which, for
the sake of protecting the Northern manufacturers, the South were obliged to pay for the manufactured goods
which they required."
        George Fitzhugh, a leading publicist of Virginia, in an article in *De Bow's Review* (the acknowledged organ
of the Slave interest) for February, 1861, commenting on the Message, said:—"It is a gross mistake to suppose
that Abolition is the cause of dissolution between the North and the South. The Cavaliers, Jacobites, and the
Huguenots, who settled the South, naturally hate, contemn, and despise the Puritans, who settled the North.
The former are master races—the latter a slave race, the descendants of the Saxon serfs."
        The Charleston *Mercury*, the chief organ of the conspirators in South Carolina, scorning the assertion that
any thing so harmless as the "Abolition twaddle" had caused any sectional feeling, declared substantially that
it was an abiding consciousness of the degradation of the "Chivalric Southrons" being placed on an equality in
government with the "boors of the North," that made "Southern gentlemen" desire disunion. It said,
haughtily, "We are the most aristocratic people in the world. Pride of caste, and color, and privilege makes
every man an aristocrat in feeling. Aristocracy is the only safeguard of liberty."
        These testimonies against the President's assertions might be multiplied by scores.
        [1] "I speak from facts," said Randolph, in 1811, "when I say that the night-bell never tolls for fire in Rich-
mond, that the frightened mother does not hug her infant the more closely to her bosom, not knowing what may
have happened. I have myself witnessed some of the alarms in the capital of Virginia." This was a quarter
of a century before there was any "violent agitation of the Slavery question throughout the North."
        [2] George Fitzhugh, in the article in *De Bow's Review* just alluded to, pronounced this statement a "gross
and silly libel," "which could only have proceeded from a nerveless, apprehensive, tremulous old man. Our
women," he continued, "are far in advance of our men in their zeal for disunion. They fear not war, for
every one of them feels confident that when their sons or husbands are called to the field, they will have a faithful body-guard in their domestic servants. Slaves are the only body-guard to be relied on. Bonaparte knew it,
and kept his Mohammedan slave sleeping at his door." The same writer added, that it was "they [the women]
and the clergy who lead and direct the disunion movement."

lessly insecure. Sooner or later, the bonds of such a union must be severed." He then referred to the efforts used by the Abolitionists, through "pictorial handbills and inflammatory appeals," in 1835, calculated to stir up the slaves to insurrection and servile war, and said: " This agitation has ever since been continued by the public press, by the proceedings of State and County Conventions, and by Abolition sermons and lectures. The time of Congress has been occupied in violent speeches on this never-ending subject; and appeals, in pamphlet and other forms, indorsed by distinguished names, have been sent forth from this central point, and spread broadcast over the Union."

"How easy it would be," the President said, " for the American people to settle the Slavery question forever, and to restore peace and harmony for this distracted country. They, and they alone, can do it. All that is necessary to accomplish the object, and all for which the Slave States have 'ever contended, is, to be let alone, and permitted to manage their domestic institutions in their own way. As Sovereign States, they, and they alone, are responsible before God and the world for the Slavery existing among them. For this the people of the North are not more responsible, and have no more right to interfere, than with similar institutions in Russia or Brazil. Upon their good sense and patriotic forbearance I confess I greatly rely."

Having said so much that might be pleasant for the ears of the people of the Slave-labor States, Mr. Buchanan proceeded to argue that the election of a President obnoxious to the inhabitants of one section of the Republic afforded no excuse for the offended ones to rebel. " Reason, justice, a regard for the Constitution," he said, " all require that we shall wait for some overt and dangerous act on the part of the President elect before resorting to such a remedy." He also argued, as Stephens had done before him, that the hands of the new President would be tied by a majority against him in Congress, and on the bench of the Supreme Court of the United States. He then touched upon the provocations endured by the " Southern States " in connection with the subject of Slavery in the Territories, and the Fugitive Slave Law ; and expressed a hope that the State Legislatures would repeal any unconstitutional and obnoxious enactments on their statute-books—in other words, their Personal Liberty Acts—so offensive to the people of the Slave-labor States and the plain commands of the Constitution ; and that the President elect would feel it to be his duty, as Mr. Buchanan had done, to act vigorously in executing the Fugitive Slave Law " against the conflicting enactments of State Legislatures." " The Southern States," he said, " standing on the basis of the Constitution, have a right to demand this act of justice from the States of the North. Should it be refused," he continued, as he warmed with zealous sympathy for the oppressed people of the Slave-labor States, " then the Constitution, to which all the States are parties, will have been willfully violated by one portion of them, in a provision essential to the domestic security and happiness of the remainder. In that event, the injured States, after having first used all peaceful and constitutional means to obtain redress, *would be justified in revolutionary resistance to the Government of the Union.*"

Let us look a moment at this Fugitive Slave Law and those Personal Liberty Laws, the non-execution of the one by the President, and the non-repeal of the others by the State Legislatures who enacted them, would, in the opinion of Mr. Buchanan, be a sufficient justification of the people of the Slave-labor States in "revolutionary resistance to the Government of the Union." Knowledge concerning them is essential to a proper understanding of the early history of the rebellion.

In the year 1850, an act was passed by the National Congress, under the provisions of the third clause, second section, and fourth Article of the Constitution, providing for the rendition of slaves who might escape from bondage into the Free-labor States. The sixth section of that law provided that the master of a fugitive slave, or his agent, might go into any State or Territory of the Republic, and, with or without legal warrant there obtained, seize such fugitive, and take him forthwith before any judge or commissioner whose duty it should be to hear and determine the case. On satisfactory proof being furnished him, such as the affidavit in writing, or other acceptable testimony, by the pursuing owner or agent, that the arrested person "owes labor" to the party that had arrested him, or to his principal, it was made the duty of said judge or commissioner to use the power of his office to assist the claimant in taking the fugitive back into bondage. It was further provided, that in no trial or hearing under the act, *should the testimony of such alleged fugitive be admitted in evidence ;* and that the parties claiming the fugitive should not be molested in their work of carrying the person back "by any process issued by any court, judge, magistrate, or other person whomsoever."

The last clause of the act was so offensive to every sentiment of humanity and justice, and so repugnant to the feelings of the people in the Free-labor States, that while respect for law, so deeply interwoven in the texture of American society, caused a general acquiescence in the requirements of the statute, there was rebellion against it in every Christian heart. It was plainly seen that, under that law, free negroes might, by the perjury of kidnappers, and the denial of the common right to defense allowed to the vilest criminal, be carried away into hopeless slavery, beyond the reach of pity, mercy, or law. This perception of possible wrong caused the Legislatures of several of the Free-labor States to pass laws for the protection of free colored citizens within their borders, made so by the circumstance of birth or existing laws.[1]

In the framing of laws consonant with the public sentiment against the Fugitive Slave Law, some of the Legislatures perhaps transcended the constitutional limits, and enacted statutes in direct contravention of the National law. Others were strictly within the limits of constitutional requirements ; and all might be speedily made inoperative by a decision of the Supreme Court of the United States, a majority of whose nine judges were slaveholders, and decidedly in sympathy with that class. Up to the time of the delivery of the President's Message, not a single case had been adjudicated under a Personal Liberty Law in any State, and their practical hostility to the interests of the slaveholders was as unreal as the tyranny and oppression of

---

[1] The law in Maine provided, that no public officer of the State should arrest or detain (or aid in so doing) in any prison or building belonging to the State, or county or town in it, any person, on account of a claim on him as a fugitive slave. This was to leave the whole business of arrests to United States officers.

The law in New Hampshire provided, that any slave brought into the State, by or with the consent of the master, should be free; and declared that the attempt to hold any person as a slave within the State was a

the President elect, neither of them having had occasion to act. They were made one of the several pretexts sought by the conspirators for rebellion; and yet some of the bolder ones, who did not care for a pretext, denied that opposition to the Fugitive Slave Law was a grievance to be complained of. "The secession of South Carolina," said Robert Barnwell Rhett (the most malignant and unscrupulous of the conspirators in that State), in the Secession Convention, "is not an event of a day. It is not any thing produced by Mr. Lincoln's election, or by the non-execution of the Fugitive Slave Law. It is a matter which has been gathering head for thirty years. . . . In regard to the Fugitive Slave Law, I myself doubted its constitutionality, and doubted it on the floor of the Senate, when I was a member of that body.[a] *The States, acting in their sovereign capacity, should be responsible for the rendition of fugitive slaves.* That was our best security."—"It is no spasmodic effort," said Francis S. Parker, another member of the Convention, "that has come suddenly upon us; it has been gradually culminating for a long period of thirty years." —"As my friend (Mr. Parker) has said," spoke John A. Inglis, another member of the Convention, "most of us have had this matter under consideration for the last twenty years." And Lawrence M. Keitt, the supporter of Preston S. Brooks, when he brutally assailed Senator Sumner in the Senate Chamber, in 1856, who was also a member of the Secession Convention, said:—"I have been engaged in

[a] 1850-1851.

LAWRENCE M KEITT.

this movement ever since I entered political life." Let us return to the Message.

Having informed the conspirators that they had many grievances, and that, under certain contingencies, the people of the Slave-labor States might be justified in rebellion, the President proceeded to consider the right of secession and the relative powers of the National Government. This was the topic to which the attention of the people was most anxiously turned.

---

felony, unless done by United States officers in the execution of legal process. This was to relieve the people from the duty of becoming slave-catchers by command of United States officers.

The law in Vermont provided, that no court, justice of the peace, or magistrate, should take cognizance of any certificate, warrant, or process, under the Fugitive Slave Law, and that no person should assist in the removal of an alleged fugitive slave from the State, excepting United States officers. It also ordered that the privilege of the writ of *habeas corpus*, and a trial of facts by a jury, should be given to the alleged fugitive, with the State's Attorney as counsel; and also that any person coming into the State a slave, shall be forever free. This was a nullification of the Fugitive Slave Law.

The law in Massachusetts provided for trials by jury of alleged fugitive slaves, who might have the services of any attorney. It forbade the issuing of any process, under the Fugitive Slave Law, by any legal officer in the State, or "to do any official act in furtherance of the execution of the Fugitive Slave Law of 1793, or that of 1850." It forbade the use of any prisons in the State for the same purpose. All public officers were forbidden to arrest, or assist in arresting, any alleged fugitive slave. And no officer of the State, acting as United States commissioner, was allowed to issue any warrant, excepting for the summoning of witnesses, nor allowed to hear and try any cause under the Fugitive Slave Law. This was a virtual nullification of the Fugitive Slave Law.

The law in Connecticut was made only to prevent the kidnapping of free persons of color within its borders, by imposing a heavy penalty upon those who should arrest, or cause to be arrested, any free colored person, with intent to reduce him or her to slavery.

What will the President do in the event of open rebellion? was the momentous question on every lip. It greatly exercised the mind of the President himself, and he turned to his legal adviser, Jeremiah S. Black, the Attorney-General of the Republic, for advice. This was given him, in liberal measure, on the 20th of November. It was conveyed in no less than three thousand words.

Assuming that States, as States, might rebel, the Attorney-General's argument gave much "aid and comfort" to the conspirators. After speaking of occasions when the President, as commander-in-chief of all the military forces of the Republic, might properly use them in support of the laws of the land, he supposed the case of a State in which all the National officers, including judges, district attorneys, and marshals, affected by the delirium of rebellious fever, should resign

JEREMIAH S. BLACK.

their places—a part of the programme of revolution in South Carolina already adopted, and which was carried out a month later. What then should be done? It was clearly the duty of the President to fill the offices with other men. "But," he said, "we can easily conceive how it might become altogether impossible." Indeed, this contingency had been contemplated by the conspirators, and provided for by prospective vigilance committees. "Then," he continued, "there would be no courts to issue judicial process, and no ministerial officers to execute it." What then? Why, the State has virtually disappeared as a part of the Republic; and the power of the Supreme Government being only auxiliary to State life and force, National troops would certainly "be out of place, and their use wholly illegal. If they are sent to aid the courts and marshals, there must be courts and marshals to be aided. Without the exercise of those functions which belong exclusively to the civil service, the laws cannot be executed in any event, no

---

The law in Rhode Island forbade the carrying away of any person by force out of the State; and provided that no public officer should officially aid the execution of the Fugitive Slave Law, and denied the use of the jails for that purpose.

New York took no action on the subject; neither did New Jersey or Pennsylvania. Their statute-books had laws already therein relating to slavery.

The law in Michigan secured to the person arrested the privilege of the writ of *habeas corpus*, a trial by jury, and the employment of the State's Attorney as counsel for the prisoners. It denied the use of the jails of the State for the purposes contemplated in the Fugitive Slave Law, and imposed a heavy penalty for the arrest of a free colored person as an alleged fugitive slave.

The law in Wisconsin was substantially the same as that in Michigan, with an additional clause for the protection of its citizens from any penalties incurred by a refusal to aid or obey the Fugitive Slave Law.

Iowa, Ohio, Illinois, Minnesota, California, and Oregon, made no laws on the subject.

It is worthy of note, in this connection, that the *statute-books of every Slave-labor State in the Union contained, at that time, Personal Liberty Acts, all of them as much in opposition to the letter and spirit of the Fugitive Slave Law of* 1850 *as any act passed by the Legislatures of Free-labor States.* Some of them had penalties more severe. All of them provided for the use of law by the alleged slave; most of them gave him a trial by jury; and those of North Carolina and Texas punished the stealer and seller of a free negro with DEATH. The spirit and object of all were expressed in the preamble to the law in Georgia, as follows:— "Whereas free persons of color are liable to be taken and held fraudulently and illegally in a state of slavery by wicked white men, and to be secretly removed whenever an effort may be made to redress their grievances, so that due inquiry may not be had into the circumstances of the detention of the same, and their right of freedom," *et cætera,* "Be it enacted," &c.

matter what may be the physical strength which the Government has at its command. Under such circumstances, to send a military force into any State, with orders to act against the people, would be simply making war upon them."

The Attorney-General limited the exercise of the powers of the Executive, in the matter in question, to a simple protection of the public property. If he could not collect the revenue on account of insurrection, he had no warrant for the use of military force. Congress might vote him the power, yet he doubted the ability of that body to find constitutional permission to do so. It seemed to him, that an attempt to force the people of a State into submission to the laws of the Republic, and to desist from attempts to destroy it, would be making war upon them, by which they would be converted into alien enemies, and "would be compelled to act accordingly." If Congress should sanction such an attempt to uphold the authority of the National Government, he wished to know whether all of the States would "not be absolved from their Federal obligations? Is any portion of the people," he asked, "bound to contribute their money or their blood to carry on a contest like this?" The Attorney-General virtually counseled the President to suffer this glorious concrete Republic to become disintegrated by the fires of faction, or the blows of actual rebellion, rather than to use force, legitimately at his service, for the preservation of its integrity.

The vital weakness in the arguments of the conspirators, and of those who adopted their peculiar political views, appears at all times in the erroneous assumption, as premises, that *States*, as such, had seceded, and that the National Government, if it should take action against rebellious movements, must of necessity war against a "Sovereign State." The undeniable fact opposed to this argument was, that no *State*, as such, had seceded, or could secede ; that the secession of certain States had been declared only by certain *politicians* in those States, who were usurpers, as we shall observe hereafter, of the rights and sovereignty which belonged only to the *people ;* that only certain persons in certain States were in rebellion, and that the Government could only act against those certain persons in certain States as individuals collectively rebellious, like a mob in a city. Therefore, there could be no such thing as the "coercion of a State." That which the conspirators and the politicians so adroitly and effectively exhibited as "coercion" was an unsubstantial phantom, created by the subtle alchemy of sophistry, for an ignoble purpose—an invention of disloyal metaphysicians in the Slave-labor States, bearing, to undisciplined and unreasoning minds, the semblance of truth and reality. If we shall keep this fact in mind clearly, as we proceed in our consideration of the events of the civil war, we shall perceive the wisdom, righteousness, and dignity of the National Government, and the opposing qualities in its enemies, from the beginning to the end of the troubles.

The President followed the counsel of his legal adviser in the preparation of that part of his Message which related to anticipated insurrection. But before yielding wholly to that counsel, he said, in discussing the doctrine of the right of a State to secede :—" In order to justify secession as a constitutional remedy, it must be on the principle that the Federal Government is a mere voluntary association of States, to be dissolved at pleasure by any one of the contracting parties.[1] If this be so, the Confederacy is a rope of sand, to be penetrated and dissolved by the first adverse wave of public opinion in any of the States. In this manner our thirty-three States may resolve themselves into so many petty, jarring, and hostile republics, each one retiring from the Union without responsibility, whenever any sudden excitement might impel them to such a course. By this process, a Union might be entirely broken into fragments in a few weeks, which cost our fathers many years of toil, privation, and blood to establish."

In these wise, truthful, and statesmanlike sentences the President cast off the restraints of the meshes of political and personal difficulty in which he was evidently entangled ; and by so doing he gave unpardonable offense to the conspirators. With the freedom of will and judgment which that momentary relief gave him, and with a lofty conception of the dignity of the Republic and his own position, he continued :—" This Government is a great and powerful Government, invested with all the attributes of sovereignty over the special subjects to which its authority extends. Its framers never intended to implant in its bosom the seeds of its own destruction, nor were they, at its creation, guilty of the absurdity of providing for its own dissolution. It was not intended by its framers to be the baseless fabric of a vision, which, at the touch of the enchanter, would vanish into thin air ; but a substantial and mighty fabric, capable of resisting the slow decay of time, and of defying the storms of ages. Indeed, well may the zealous patriots of that day have indulged fears that a government of such high powers might violate the reserved rights of the States, and wisely did they adopt the rule of a strict construction of these powers to prevent danger. But they did not fear, nor had they any reason to imagine, that the Constitution would ever be so interpreted as to enable any State, by her own act, and without the consent of her sister States, to discharge her people from all or any of their Federal obligations."

These were brave words, and the President had constitutional and popular power to follow them with corresponding brave actions. But a sense of restraint seems to have paralyzed his will, and while he declared that the forts and other public property must be protected, he yielded every thing to the conspirators by saying, in their own phraseology, that there was no power known to the Constitution to compel a " seceding State " to return to its allegiance. He saw no way in which a " subjugated State " could be governed afterward ; and even if the National Government had the power to compel the obedience of a State, " would it be wise to exercise it, under the circumstances ?" he asked. In the fraternal conflict that would ensue, a vast amount of blood and treasure would be expended, rendering future reconciliation impossible. He declared that the States were colleagues of one another ; and if some of them, he said, " should conquer the rest, and hold them as subjugated provinces, it would totally destroy the whole theory upon which they are now connected. If this view of the subject be as correct as I think it is," he said, " then the Union must utterly perish at the moment

---

[1] This, as we have observed, is the vital principle involved in the doctrine of Supreme State Sovereignty, and the corner-stone of the foundation on which the great rebellion rested for justification. Against this corner-stone the President hurled the conclusions in this paragraph.

when Congress shall arm one part of the people against another, for any purpose beyond that of merely protecting the General Government in the exercise of its proper constitutional functions. . . . Congress possesses many means of preserving it by conciliation; but the sword was not placed in their hands to preserve it by force."

Having declared that secession was a crime, and the doctrine of State Supremacy a heresy dangerous to the nationality of the Republic, but that both might be indulged in to the fullest extent with impunity, because the Government, as an executive force, was constitutionally and utterly impotent to protect the nation against rebellious hands uplifted to destroy it—in other words, that the hands of wicked assassins were ready with strength to crush out the National life, but the Republic possessed no power, excepting that of moral suasion, to protect and preserve that life—the President proposed to conciliate its enemies, by allowing them to infuse deadly poison into the blood of their intended victim, which would slowly but as surely accomplish their purpose, in time. To do this, he proposed an "explanatory amendment" to the Constitution, on the subject of Slavery, which should give to the conspirators every thing which they had demanded, namely, the elevation of the Slave system to the dignity of a national institution, and thus sap the very foundations of our free government. This amendment was to consist of an express recognition of the right of property in slaves, in the States where it then existed or might thereafter exist; of the recognition of the duty of the National Government to protect that right in all the Territories throughout their Territorial existence; the recognition of the right of the Slave-owner to every privilege and advantage given him in the Fugitive Slave Law of 1850; and a declaration that all the State laws impairing or defeating that law were violations of the Constitution, and consequently null and void.

This Message, so indecisive, and, in many respects, inconsistent, alarmed the people. They felt themselves, in a measure, adrift upon a sea of troubles without a competent pilot, a compass, or a pole-star. As we have observed, it pleased nobody. In the Chamber of the United States Senate, when a motion for its reference was made, it was spoken lightly of by the friends and foes of the Union. Clingman, of North Carolina, who, misrepresenting the sentiment of his State, was the first to sound the trumpet of disunion in that hall, at this time declared that it fell short of stating the case that was before the country. Wigfall, of Texas, said he could not understand it; and, at a later period,[a] Jefferson Davis, of Mississippi, said in the [a] January 10, 1861.
Senate, that it "had all the characteristics of a diplomatic paper, for diplomacy is said to abhor certainty, as nature abhors a vacuum; and it is not within the power of man to reach any fixed conclusion from that Message. When the country was agitated, when opinions were being formed, when we are drifting beyond the power ever to return, this was not what we had a right to expect from a Chief Magistrate. One policy or the other he ought to have taken." "He should have taken the position," he said, either of a "Federalist, that every State is subordinate to the Federal Government," and he was bound to enforce its authority; or as a State Rights Democrat, which he professed to be, holding that "the Constitution gave no power to the Federal Government to coerce a State." He said, truly, "That the

President should have brought his opinion to one conclusion or another, and, to-day, our country would have been safer than it is."

Senator Hale, of New Hampshire, said that, if he understood the Message on the subject of secession, it was this:—" South Carolina has just cause for seceding from the Union; that is the first proposition. The second is, that she has no right to secede. The third is, that we have no right to prevent her from seceding. He goes on to represent this as a great and powerful country, and that no State has a right to secede from it; but the power of the country, if I understand the President, consists in what Dickens makes the English constitution to be—a power to do nothing at all. Now, I think it was incumbent on the President of the United States to point out definitely and recommend to Congress some rule of action, and to tell us what he re-

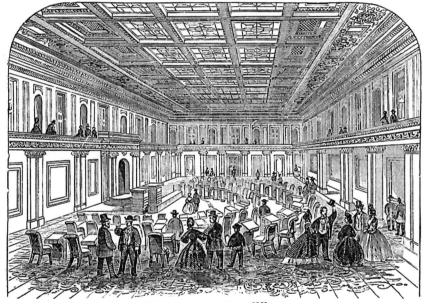

THE SENATE CHAMBER IN 1860.

commended us to do. But, in my judgment, he has entirely avoided it. He has failed to look the thing in the face. He has acted like the ostrich, which hides her head, and thereby thinks to escape danger."

So thought the people. They saw great dangers, but could not comprehend the fearful proportions of those dangers. Had they done so, they would almost have despaired. They watched with intense interest the rising waves of rebellion in the Slave-labor States, and heard with alarm the roaring of their surges in the halls of Congress. Their thoughts often wandered back to an earlier period in their history, when a Chief Magistrate had the courage to check by a menace, and would have crushed by the force of arms, if it had been necessary, the foul serpent of rebellion, that appeared a generation before as a petted monster, among the politicians of South Carolina, and was exhibited to the people whenever Calhoun waved the sorcerer's wand. In the contrast between Jackson and Buchanan, which that retrospect exhibited, they saw cause for gloomy forebodings.

Patriotic men wrote earnest letters to their representatives in Congress, asking them to be firm, yet conciliatory; and clergymen of every degree and religious denomination—Shepherds of the Church of Christ, the Prince of Peace—exhorted their flocks to be firm in faith, patient in hope, careful in conduct, and trustful in God. "This is no time for noisy disputants to lead us," wrote Bishop Lay, at Fort Smith, Arkansas. "We should ask counsel of the experienced, the sober, the God-fearing men among us. We may follow peace, and yet guard our country's rights; nor should we, in concern for our own, forget the rights and duties of others."[1]—"In our public congregations, in our family worship, in each heart's private prayers," wrote Bishop McIlvaine, of Ohio, "I solemnly feel that it is a time for all to beseech God to have mercy upon our country—not to deal with us according to our sins—not to leave us to our own wisdom and might—to take the counsels of our senators and legislators, and all in authority, into His own guidance and government."[2]—"These evils are the punishment of sin," wrote Bishop McFarland, of Hartford, Connecticut, to the clergy of his diocese, "and are to be averted only by appeasing the anger of Heaven. You will, therefore, request your congregation to unite in fervent prayers for the preservation of the Union and the peace of the country. For this intention, we exhort them to say, each day, at least one 'Our Father' and one 'Hail Mary;' to observe with great strictness the Fast-days of this holy season; to prepare themselves for the worthy reception of the Sacraments of Penance and the Holy Eucharist, at or before Christmas; to give alms generally to the poor, and to turn their whole hearts in all humility to God."[3] More than forty leading clergymen of various denominations in New York, New Jersey, and Pennsylvania united in sending forth[a] a circular letter, in the [a January 1, 1861.] form of an appeal to the churches, in which they said:—"We cannot doubt that a spirit of candor and forbearance, such as our religion prompts, and the exigencies of the times demand, would render the speedy adjustment of our difficulties possible, consistently with every constitutional right. Unswerving fealty to the Constitution justly interpreted, and a prompt return to its spirit and requirements wherever there may have been divergence from either, would seem to be the first duty of citizens and legislators. It is our firm, and, we think, intelligent conviction, that only a very inconsiderable fraction of the people of the North will hesitate in the discharge of their constitutional obligations; and that whatever enactments are found to be in conflict therewith will be annulled." They urged the necessity of a more candid and temperate discussion, on the part of the press and the pulpit, of moral and political questions—a greater regard "for the rights and feelings of men."

So early as the close of October,[b] that venerable soldier, Lieu- [b October 30, 1860.] tenant-General Winfield Scott, the General-in-chief of the armies of the Republic, perceiving the gathering cloud betokening a storm, spoke

---

[1] Pastoral Letter of Bishop Henry C. Lay, December 6, 1860.
[2] Pastoral Letter to the Clergy and Laity of the Diocese of Ohio, December 7, 1860.
[3] Pastoral Letter to the Roman Catholic Clergy of the Diocese of Hartford, December 14, 1860.

words of warning to the President and Secretary of War. He was evidently ignorant of the perplexities of the former and the wickedness of the latter, or he would never have wasted words, as he did, in saying: "From a knowledge of our Southern population, it is my solemn conviction that there is some danger of an early act of rashness preliminary to secession, namely, the seizure of some or all of the Southern forts," which he named. "In my opinion," he said, "all these works should be immediately so garrisoned as to make any attempt to take any one of them, by surprise or *coup de main*, ridiculous." . . . "It is the opinion that instructions should be given at once to the commanders of the Barancas [Pensacola], Forts Moultrie and Monroe, to be on their guard against surprises."

Another veteran warrior, who had been Scott's companion in arms for fifty years, full of patriotic zeal, and with a keen perception of danger, after reading the President's message wrote a letter remarkable for its good sense, foresight, and wisdom. That soldier was Major-General John Ellis Wool, then commander of the Eastern Department, which included the whole country eastward of the Mississippi River. He wrote to the venerable General Lewis Cass (also his companion-in-arms in the War of 1812), Buchanan's

Secretary of State, on the 6th of December, saying:—"South Carolina says she intends to leave the Union. Her representatives in Congress say she has already left the Union. It seems she is neither to be conciliated nor comforted. I command the Eastern Department, which includes South Carolina, Georgia, Alabama, and Mississippi. You know me well. I have ever been a firm, decided, faithful, and devoted friend of my country. If I can aid the President to preserve the Union, I hope he will command my services. *It will never do for him or you to leave Washington*

LEWIS CASS.

without every star in this Union in its place. Therefore, no time should be lost in adopting measures to defeat those who are conspiring against the Union. Hesitation or delay may be no less fatal to the Union than to the President, or your own high standing as a statesman."

This patriotic soldier then urged upon the Government the absolute necessity of sending re-enforcements to the forts in Charleston harbor; and he spurned the excuse for not doing so, urged by some, that such a step would serve to increase the excitement among the people of South Carolina. "That is nonsense," he said, "when the people are as much excited as they can be, and the leaders are determined to execute their long-meditated purpose of separating the State from the Union. Do not leave the forts in the harbor in a condition to induce the attempt to take possession of them. It might easily be done at this time. If South Carolina should take them, it might, as she anticipates, induce other States to join her. The Union can be preserved, but it requires firm, decided, prompt, energetic action on the part of the President. He has only to exert the power conferred on him by the Constitution and laws of Congress, and all will be safe, and he will prevent a civil war, which never fails to call forth all the baser passions of the human heart. If a separation should take place, be assured, blood would flow in torrents. Let me conjure you to save the Union, and thereby avoid the desolating example of Mexico. . . . Think of these things, my dear General, and save the country, and save the prosperous South from pestilence, famine, and desolation. Peaceable secession is not to be thought of. Even if it should take place in three months, we would have a bloody war on our hands."

The patriotic Cass was powerless. Fully convinced by recent developments that the Cabinet was filled with traitors, bent upon the destruction of the Republic, and utterly unable, with his single hand and voice, to restrain or persuade them, he resigned the seals of his office on the 12th of December, and retired to private life.[1] The President, too, conscious of his own impotence—conscious that the Government was in the hands of its enemies—and despairing of the salvation of the Union by human agency, issued a Proclamation on the 14th of December, recommending the observance of the 4th day of January following as a day for humiliation, fasting, and prayer, throughout the Republic. " The Union of the States," he said, " is at the present moment threatened with alarming and immediate danger ; panic and distress, of a fearful character, prevail throughout the land ; our laboring population are without employment, and, consequently, deprived of the means of earning their bread ; indeed, hope seems to have deserted the minds of men. All classes are in a state of confusion and dismay, and the wisest counsels of our best and purest men are wholly disregarded. In this, the hour of our calamity and peril, to whom shall we resort for relief but to the God of our Fathers ? His omnipotent arm only can save us from the awful effects of our own crimes and follies—our own ingratitude and guilt toward our Heavenly Father." He then recommended a union of the people in bowing in humility before God, and said, in words not only of faith, but of remarkable prophecy :—" An Omnipotent Providence may overrule existing evils for permanent good."[2]

SEAL OF THE STATE DEPARTMENT.

---

[1] He was succeeded by Jeremiah S. Black, Buchanan's Attorney-General. Two days before, as we have observed on page 44, Howell Cobb left the office of Secretary of the Treasury, because his "duty to Georgia required it," and was succeeded by Philip F. Thomas, of Maryland. Cobb's letter of resignation was dated the 8th, but he did not leave office until the 10th.

[2] The Proclamation, in sentiment and expression, was all that Christian men could ask, of its kind; but lovers of righteousness thought that a better formula might have been framed, considering the social condition of the nation, after pondering the following words in the fifty-eighth chapter of Isaiah, beginning at the third verse:—

"Wherefore have we fasted, say they, and thou seest not ? Wherefore have we afflicted our soul, and thou takest no knowledge ? Behold, in the day of your fast you find pleasure, and exact all your labors. Behold, ye fast for strife and debate, and to smite with the fist of wickedness: ye shall not fast as ye do this day, to make your voice to be heard on high. Is it such a fast that I have chosen ? a day for a man to afflict his soul ? is it to bow down his head as a bulrush, and to spread sackcloth and ashes under him ? Wilt thou call this a fast, and an acceptable day to the Lord ? Is not this the fast that I have chosen ? to loose the bands of wickedness,

In the mean time, the halls of Congress had become theaters wherein treason was openly and defiantly displayed, especially in the Senate Chamber, where, as we have observed, Senator Clingman, of North Carolina, who afterward became a brigadier-general in the Confederate army, had first sounded the trumpet-note of revolt. The occasion was the discussion of his

THOMAS L. CLINGMAN.

own motion to print the President's Message. Adopting the false assumption as true, that the people of the Free-labor States had resolved, because they formed a constitutional majority, to oppress and despoil of their rights the people of the Slave-labor States, and had elected a President "because he was known to be a dangerous man" to the latter section, he boldly announced the determination of the South—that is to say, the politicians, like himself, of the Slave-labor States—to submit no longer to the authority of the National Government. To his political opponents, on the other side of the House,

he said:—"I tell those gentlemen, in perfect frankness, that, in my judgment, not only will a number of States secede in the next sixty days, but some of the other States are holding on merely to see if proper guaranties can be obtained. We have in North Carolina only two considerable parties. The absolute submissionists are too small to be called a party." He falsely alleged that the great "mass of the people consist of those who are for immediate action," and then threatened, that unless ample guaranties should be given, by amendments of the Constitution, for the protection of the rights of the South in regard to Slavery, they would see "most of the Southern States in motion at an early day. I will not undertake to advise," he said; "but I say that, unless some comprehensive plan of some kind be adopted, which shall be perfectly satisfactory, in my judgment, the wisest thing this Congress can do would be to divide the public property fairly, and apportion the public debt. I say, Sir—and events in the course of a few months will determine whether I am right or not—in my judgment, unless decisive constitutional guaranties are obtained at an early day, it will be best for all sections that a peaceable division of the public property should take place."

After thus demanding "guaranties" or concessions, Mr. Clingman broadly intimated that no concessions would satisfy the South ; and, after drawing a picture of the advantages to be derived from secession by the people of the Slave-labor States, he protested against waiting for an overt act of offense on the part of the President elect. He wanted no further parley with the people of the Free-labor States. "They wish," he said "to have an opportunity, by circulating things like Helper's book,[1] of arraying the non-slaveholders

---

to undo the heavy burdens, and to let the oppressed go free, and that ye break every yoke? Is it not to deal thy bread to the hungry, and that thou bring the poor that are cast out to thy house? When thou seest the naked, that thou cover him ; and that thou hide not thyself from thine own flesh? . . . Then shalt thou call, and the Lord shall answer ; thou shalt cry, and he shall say, Here I am."

[1] In 1859, a volume was published, entitled The Impending Crisis of the South, by Hinton Rowan Helper, a North Carolinian. It was an appeal to the great mass of the people in the Slave-labor States, to break loose

and poor men against the wealthy. I have no doubt that would be their leading policy, and they would be very quiet about it. They want to get up that sort of 'free debate' which has been put into practice in Texas, according to the Senator from New York [Mr. Seward], for he is reported to have said, in one of his speeches in the Northwest, alluding to recent disturbances, to burnings and poisonings there, that Texas was 'excited by free debate.' Well, Sir," continued Clingman, with peculiar emphasis, "a Senator from Texas' told me, the other day, that *a good many of those 'debaters' were hanging up by the trees in that country!*"

When Clingman ceased speaking, the venerable John Jay Crittenden, of Kentucky, tottering with physical infirmities and the burden of seventy-five years—the Nestor of Congress—instantly arose and mildly rebuked the Senator, while his seditious words were yet ringing in the ears of his amazed peers. "I rise here," he said, "to express the hope, and that alone, that the bad example of the gentleman will not be followed." He spoke feelingly of costly sacrifices made for the establishment of the Union; of its blessings and promises; and hoped that "there was not a Senator present who was not willing to yield and compromise much for the sake of the Government and the Union."

Mr. Crittenden's mild rebuke, and earnest appeal to the patriotism of the Senate, was met by more scornful and violent harangues from other Senators, in which the speakers seemed to emulate each other in the utterance of seditious sentiments. Clingman, more courteous than most of his compeers, said, "I think one of the wisest remarks that Mr. Calhoun ever made was, that the Union could not be saved by eulogies upon it." Senators Alfred Iverson, of Georgia, Albert G. Brown, of Mississippi, and Louis T. Wigfall, of Texas, followed. They had been stirred with anger by stinging words from Senator Hale, of New Hampshire, who replied to some of Clingman's remarks:—"If the issue which is presented is, that the constitutional will of the public opinion of this country, expressed through the forms of the Constitution, will not be submitted to, and war is the alternative, let it come in any form or in any shape. The Union is dissolved, and it cannot be held together as a Union, if that is the alternative upon which we go into an election. If it is pre-announced and determined that the voice of the majority, expressed through the regular and constitutional forms of the Constitution, will not be submitted to, then, Sir, this is not a Union of equals; it is a Union of a dictatorial oligarchy on the one side, and a herd of slaves and cowards on the other. That is it, Sir; nothing more; nothing less."

The conspirators were not accustomed to hear such defiant words from their opponents. They indicated a spirit of resistance to their demands —powerful, resolute, and unyielding. They were astonished and enraged. They felt compelled to cast off all disguises and cease circumlocution. Hale had said, "The plain, true way, is, to look this thing in the face—see where we are." The conspirators now thought so too, and accepted the challenge. Senators Iverson and Wigfall, the most outspoken of the disloyalists present,

---

from their social and political vassalage to the large land and slave owners, and to aid in freeing the Republic of slavery.

¹ The Senators from Texas were John Hemphill and Louis T. Wigfall.

revealed to the country, in bold outlines, the plans and intentions of the plotters against the life of the nation, in speeches marked by a superciliousness of tone and manner exceedingly offensive at that time, but perfectly ridiculous when viewed in the light of history to-day. They evidently felt confident of success in all their treasonable undertakings. They knew how well their people were prepared for military operations, by means of the teachings of their State military schools for years, their drillings during the past year, and the wealth of the arsenals in the Slave-labor States, made so by the impoverishment of those of the North, by the Secretary of War. They had arranged deep plans, which were afterward carried out, for the subjugation of the *people* of the Slave-labor States to their will; and they felt well assured that the great party in the Free-labor States which had been in political sympathy with them would keep the sword of the Republic in its scabbard, while commerce, ever sensitive to the least disturbance of its peace and quiet, would join hands with the politicians in keeping bound in triple chains the fierce dogs of war.

Senator Iverson, a man over sixty years of age, and a member of the Military Committee of the Senate, startled that body by his boldness in seditious speech. He admitted that a State had no constitutional right to secede, but he claimed for all the right of revolution. He then announced that the Slave-labor States intended to revolt. "We intend to go out of this Union," he said. "I speak what I believe, that, before the 4th of March, five of the Southern States, at least, will have declared their independence. . . . Although there is a clog in the way of the lone-star State of Texas, in the person of her Governor (Houston), who will not consent to call her Legislature together, and give the people of that State an opportunity to act, yet the public sentiment there is so decided in favor of this movement, that even the Governor will be overridden; and if he does not yield to public sentiment, some Texan Brutus

will arise to rid his country of the hoary-headed incubus that stands between the people and their sovereign will. We intend to go out peaceably, if we can; forcibly, if we must. I do not believe there is going to be war. . . . If five or eight States go out of this Union, I would like to see the man who would propose a declaration of war against them, or attempt to force them into obedience to the Federal Government at the point of the bayonet or the sword. . . . We shall, in the next twelve months, have a Confederacy of the Southern States, and a government, inaugurated · and in successful operation, which, in my opinion, will be a

ALFRED IVERSON.

government of the greatest prosperity and power that the world has ever seen. There will be no war, in my opinion. . . . The fifteen Slave States, or the five of them now moving, banded together in one government, and united as they are soon to be, would defy the world in arms, much less the Northern States of this Confederacy. Fighting on our own soil, in defense of our own sacred rights and honor, we could not be conquered, even by the combined forces of all the other States; and sagacious, sensible men in the

Northern States would understand that too well to make the effort." He said that if they were allowed to go in peace, they would condescend to consider the Free-labor States as "a favored nation, and give them all the advantages of commercial and amicable treaties." He referred to the hostile feeling in the Senate as a type of that of the sections. "You sit, upon your side," he said, "silent and gloomy. We sit, upon ours, with knit brows and portentous scowls;" and added, wickedly or ignorantly, "I believe that the Northern people hate the South worse than ever the English people hated France; and I can tell my brethren over there, that there is no love lost upon the part of the South." He concluded with angry voice and gesture, saying, "I do not believe there will be any war; but if war is to come, let it come. We will meet the Senator from New Hampshire, and all the myrmidons of Abolitionism and Black Republicanism everywhere, upon our own soil; and, in the language of a distinguished member from Ohio in relation to the Mexican War, we will ' welcome you with bloody hands to hospitable graves.' "

Senator Jefferson Davis followed with a few words, soft, but significant of treason in his purpose. "I am here," he said, "to perform the functions of a Senator of the United States. Before a declaration of war is made against the State of which I am a citizen, I expect to be out of this Chamber; that when that declaration of war is made, the State of which I am a citizen will be found ready and quite willing to meet it. While we remain here, *acting as embassadors of Sovereign States*, at least under the form of friendship, held together by an alliance as close as it is possible for Sovereign States to stand to each other, threats from one to the other seem to be wholly inappropriate."

Wigfall, of Texas, a truculent debater, of ability and ready speech, of whom it might have been truthfully said, in Shakspeare's words :—

> "Here's a large mouth, indeed,
> That spits forth death, and mountains, rocks, and seas;
> Talks as familiarly of roaring lions
> As maids of thirteen do of puppy-dogs,"

did not seem to agree with the cautious, wily, and polished Mississippi Senator. After declaring that State after State would soon leave the Union, and that, so far as he was concerned, he chose not to give a "reason for the high sovereign act," he said, "Now, Sir, I admit that a constitutional majority has a right to govern. . . . . . If we proposed to remain in this Union, we should undoubtedly submit to the inauguration of any man who was elected by a constitutional majority. We propose nothing of that sort. We simply say that a man who is distasteful to us has been elected, and we choose to consider that as a sufficient ground for leaving the Union, and we intend to leave the Union.

LOUIS T. WIGFALL.

Then, if you desire it," he said, with a half sneering, half defiant tone, "bring us back. When you undertake that, and have accomplished it, you may be like the man who purchased the elephant—you will find it rather difficult to decide what you will do with the animal."

Some days later, the same speaker, in a few sentences, revealed the main-spring of the hopes of success in their treasonable work, entertained by the ·conspirators.   It was the *cotton crop* of the planting coast States, upon which England, France, and the States north of the Potomac, chiefly de-pended for the supply of their mills.   For fifty years the orators and pub-licists of the Cotton-growing States had proclaimed the power of cotton in the preservation of peace between the United States and Great Britain, because of the commanding influence of the commercial and manufacturing interests in the politics of the latter country, to which American cotton had become almost an indispensable commodity.   It had, indeed, become a power, both social and political, yet not so absolutely omnipotent as the conspirators believed it to be.   So palpable was its commercial importance, however, and so evident was it that the mills of Europe, and those of the Free-labor States in America, with their five millions of spindles, were, and must continue to be, mostly dependent upon the product of only an inconsiderable portion of ten of the States of our Republic, that its puissance was generally conceded. In the Senate of the United States, in March, 1858, Senator Hammond, of South Carolina, said, exultingly:—"You dare not make war upon Cotton. No power on earth dares to make war upon it.   Cotton is KING.   Until lately the Bank of England was king; but she tried to put her screws, as usual, the Fall before last, on the cotton crop, and was utterly vanquished. The last power has been conquered.   Who can doubt, that has looked at recent events, that Cotton is supreme?"

Cotton is KING! shouted the great land and slave holders of the Gulf States, whose fields were hoary with his bounteous gifts, when they thought of rebellion, and revolution, and independent empire; for they believed that his scepter had made England and France their dependents, and that they must necessarily be the allies of the cotton-growers, in the event of war.

Cotton is KING! echoed back submissively the spindles of Old and New England.

" Old Cotton will pleasantly reign
When other kings painfully fall,
And ever and ever remain
The mightiest monarch of all,"

sang an American bard[1] years before; and now, a Senator (Wigfall) of the Republic, with words of treason falling from his lips, like jagged hail, in the very sanctuary where loyalty should be adored exclaimed:—"I say that Cotton is KING, and that he waves his scepter, not only over these thirty-three States, but over the Island of Great Britain and over Continental Europe; and that there is no crowned head upon that island, or upon the continent, that does not bend the knee in fealty, and acknowledge allegiance to that monarch.   There are five millions of people in Great Britain who live upon cotton.   You may make a short crop of grain, and it will never affect them; but you may cram their granaries to bursting; you may cram them

---

[1] The late George P. Morris, whose son, Brigadier-General William H. Morris, gallantly fought some of the Cotton-lords and their followers on the Peninsula, in the "Wilderness," and in the open fields of Spottsylvania, in Virginia, where he was wounded.

until the corn actually is lifting the shingles from the roofs of their barns, and exhaust the supply of cotton for one week, and all England is starving." Then referring to threats of war, and expectations of negro insurrections that might follow, Wigfall said :—" I tell you, Senators, that next year you will see the negroes working as quietly and contentedly as if their masters were not leaving that country for a foreign land, as they did, a few years ago, when they were called upon to visit the Republic of Mexico." The cotton crop, he said, was worth two hundred and fifty millions of dollars a year, and would never be less. That amount, the people of the new Confederacy would export, and it would bring the same amount of imports into the country,

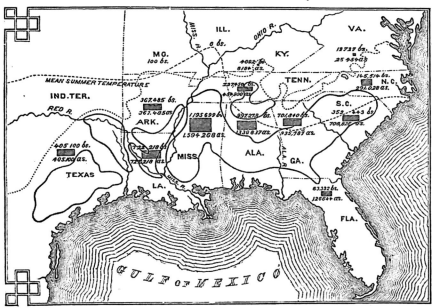

THE COTTON "KINGDOM" IN THE UNITED STATES.

"not through Boston, and New York, and Philadelphia," but through their own ports. "What tariff we shall adopt as a war tariff," he said, "I expect to discuss in a few months later, in another chamber. I tell you that *Cotton is King!*"[1]

---

[1] The production of cotton for commerce has hitherto been confined to a portion of ten States, as indicated on the accompanying map, the northern limit of the profitable culture of the plant being, it is said, the northern boundary of Arkansas, Tennessee, and North Carolina. The entire area of the ten Cotton-producing States, in 1860, was 666,196 square miles, of which only 10,888 square miles were devoted to the cotton culture in that year. On those 10,888 square miles, 4,675,770 bales of cotton, weighing 400 pounds each, were raised in 1859–60. Of this amount Great Britain took 2,019,252 bales, or more than one-third of the entire crop; France took 450,696 bales, and the States north of the Potomac took 760,218 bales.

The accompanying map is a reduced copy of a part of one, prefixed to a *Report to the Boston Board of Trade on the Cotton Manufacture of* 1862, by Edward Atkinson. The solid black lines inclose the principal cotton regions in the ten States alluded to. The limit of cotton culture in 1860 is indicated by a dotted line, thus .... The isothermal line of mean summer temperature is shown by dotted lines, thus - - - - - -

It was the continual boast of the politicians in the Cotton-producing States, that the money value of their staple was greater than that of all the other agricultural productions of the whole country. This assertion went from lip to lip, uncontradicted, and fixed the impression on the public mind that Cotton really was King. Every census contradicted it, but the people in the Slave-labor States were allowed to know very little about the

How utterly fallacious were all the promises, hopes, and expectations founded upon the assumption that Cotton was KING, will be seen hereafter.

It was plain to some of the least discerning, that the whole scheme of revolt had been deliberately planned long before the assembling of Congress, and that the talk about guaranties, and concessions, and compromises, on the part of the conspirators, was sheer hypocrisy, intended to deceive their constituents, and to lull the suspicions of the loyal people of the Republic. " You talk about concessions," exclaimed the out-spoken Iverson. " You talk about repealing the Personal Liberty Bills, as a concession to the South ! Repeal them all to-morrow, Sir, and it would not stop the progress of this revolution. . . . It is the existence and the action of the public sentiment of the Northern States that are opposed to this institution of Slavery, and are determined to break it down—to use all the power of the Federal Government, as well as every other power in their hands, to bring about its ultimate and speedy extinction.   That is what we apprehend, and what, *in part*, moves us to look for security and protection in secession and a Southern Confed-

ª December 13, 1860.

eracy."—" Before this day next week," said Wigfall,ª " I hazard the assertion that South Carolina, in convention assembled, will have revoked the ratification of the treaty which makes her one of these United States.   Having revoked that ratification, she will adopt an amendment to her constitution, by which she will have vested in the government of South Carolina all those powers which she, conjointly with the other States, had previously exercised through this foreign department; and in the government of South Carolina will be vested the right to declare war, to conclude peace, to make treaties, to enter into alliances, and to do all other matters and things which Sovereign States may of right do.   When that is done, a minister plenipotentiary and envoy extraordinary will be sent to present his credentials; and when they are denied, or refused to be recognized by this Government, I say to you, that the sovereignty of her soil will be asserted, and it will be maintained at the point of the bayonet." ' Then, referring to a threat that " seceding States would be coerced into submission," he expressed a hope that such Democrats as Vallandigham, and Richardson, and Logan, and Cox, and McClernand, and Pugh, of Ohio—members of the House of Representatives—would stand by the Slave power in this matter, and pre-

census.   That of 1860 shows that the wheat crop alone (raised mostly in the Free-labor States), in that year, far exceeded in value, at the current price, that of the entire cotton crop.   The aggregate value of the cotton was $183,000,000, and that of wheat was $240,000,000, or $57,000,000 greater.   The aggregate value of the wheat, corn, hay, and oats crops alone, that year, was over $1,100,000,000.   As an article of export, cotton was largely in excess of any other item of agricultural production.   The total value of these productions of the United States exported to foreign countries, for the year ending the 30th of June, 1859, was $222,909,718.   That of cotton was $161,434,923, or sixty-two and a half millions of dollars less than that of other agricultural exports.   The value of the cotton crop was not an eighth part of that of the whole agricultural products of the country; and yet, politicians, in order to deceive the Southern people with false notions of their strength and independence, and the absolute sovereignty of Cotton, declared it to be greater than all others.   When the trial came, and the claim of Cotton to kingship was tested, the result justified the poet in writing, that—

> " *Cotton* and *Corn* were mighty Kings,
>   Who differed at times on certain things,
>   To the country's dire confusion:
>   *Corn* was peaceable, mild, and just,
>   But *Cotton* was fond of saying, You must;'
> So, after he'd boasted, and bullied, and cussed,
>   He got up a Revolution.
> But, in course of time, the bubble is bursted,
> And *Corn* is King, and *Cotton* is—worsted."

vent the erection of (what he was pleased to call the armed power of the United States) "a military despotism." "The edifice is not yet completed," he said. "South Carolina, thank God! has laid her hands upon one of the pillars, and she will shake it until it totters first, and then topples. She will destroy that edifice, though she perish amid the ruins."

Such were some of the ravings of conspirators in the Senate of the Republic, who possessed only the "guinea stamp" of statesmen. They were counterfeit coin, made of the basest metal, and lacking every ingredient of true statesmanship. They had been palmed off upon the confiding inhabitants of the Southern States by the arrogant Slave interest, as men fitted for the high and holy work of legislating for a free people. They were mere demagogues—instruments chosen for their known usefulness as such, to an interest which had resolved to rule the Republic with relentless rigor, and crush out from its political and social systems every element of Democracy, or to lay that Republic in ruins.

It will forever appear incredible—an inconsistent tale of romance—that these men should have thus played the traitor, undisturbed by competent authority, upon the very proscenium of the great theater of National legislation, with the Chief Magistrate of the Republic and his constitutional advisers sitting quietly as a part of the audience, while holding in their hands the lightning of the sovereign power of the people, which might, at their bidding, have consumed in a moment those enemies of the Constitution and violators of the law. Why were they permitted thus to play the traitor, undisturbed? Perhaps only at the Great Assize will the question be answered.

CHAPTER IV.

SEDITIOUS MOVEMENTS IN CONGRESS.—SECESSION IN SOUTH CAROLINA, AND
ITS EFFECTS.

HILST Treason was rampant and defiant in the Senate Chamber, it was equally determined, but less demonstrative at first, in the hall of the House of Representatives. It first gave utterance there when Alexander R. Boteler, of Virginia, proposed, by resolution, to refer so much of the President's Message as "related to the present perilous condition of the country," to a select committee, consisting of one from each State (thirty-three), with power to report at any time. This resolution was adopted by a vote of one hundred and forty-five to thirty-eight. During the voting, many members from the Slave-labor States exhibited their treasonable purposes, some by a few words, and all by a refusal to vote. "I do not vote," said Singleton, of Mississippi, "because I have not been sent here to make any compromises or patch up existing difficulties. The subject will be decided by a convention of the people of my State." Hawkins, of Florida, said:— "The day of compromise has passed. I am opposed, and so is my State, to all and every compromise. I shall not vote." Clopton, of Alabama, considered secession as the only remedy for existing evils, and would not sanction any temporizing policy. Pugh, of Alabama, said:—"As my State intends following South Carolina out of the Union, by the 10th of January next, I pay no attention to any action taken in this body."

No less than fifty-two members from the Slave-labor States refused to vote on this occasion. These comprised all of the South Carolina delegation, and most of those from Florida, Alabama, Mississippi, and Georgia. By this action, they virtually avowed their determination to thwart all legislation in the direction of compromise· or conciliation. And when Mr. Morris, a Democrat from Illinois, offered a resolution,[a] that the House of Representatives were "unalterably and immovably attached to the Union of the States," these men opposed it, and stayed the further consideration of it that day by carrying a motion to adjourn. It was clearly apparent that they had resolved on disunion, and that nothing in the way of concession would be accepted.

[a] December 4, 1860.

The appointment of the Select Committee of Thirty-three was made by the Speaker,[1] and it became the recipient, by reference, of ·a large

---

[1] The Committee consisted of the following persons:—Thomas Corwin, of Ohio; John S. Millson, of Virginia; Charles Francis Adams, of Massachusetts; W. Winslow, of North Carolina; James Humphreys, of New York; Wm. W. Boyce, of South Carolina; James H. Campbell, of Pennsylvania; Peter E. Love, of Georgia; Orris S. Ferry, of Connecticut; Henry Winter Davis, of Maryland; C. Robinson, of Rhode Island; W. G.

number of resolutions, suggestions, and propositions offered in the House for the amendment of the National Constitution, most of them looking to concessions to the demands of the Slave interest; for there was such an earnest desire for the preservation of peace, that the people of the Free-labor States were ready to make every reasonable sacrifice for its sake. The most important of these conciliatory suggestions were made by Representatives John Cochrane and Daniel E. Sickles, of New York; Thomas C. Hindman, of Arkansas; Clement L. Vallandigham, of Ohio; and John W. Noell, of Missouri.

Mr. Cochrane, who was afterward a general in the National Army, fighting the Slave interest in rebellion, and also a candidate of the "Radical Abolitionists" for the office of Vice-President of the United States, proposed the

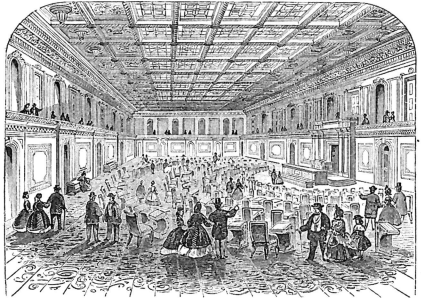

HALL OF THE HOUSE OF REPRESENTATIVES.

acceptance of the decision of the Supreme Court, in the case of Dred Scott, that the descendant of a slave could not be a citizen of the United States,[1] as the settled policy of the Government toward the inhabitants of the country, of African origin. He also proposed that neither Congress nor the people of any Territory should interfere with Slavery therein, while it remained a

Whiteley, of Delaware; M. W. Tappen, of New Hampshire; John L. N. Stratton, of New Jersey; F. M. Bristow, of Kentucky; J. S. Morrill, of Vermont; T. A. R. Nelson, of Tennessee; Wm. McKee Dunn, of Indiana; Miles Taylor, of Louisiana; Reuben Davis, of Mississippi; William Kellogg, of Illinois; George S. Houston, of Alabama; F. H. Morse, of Maine; John S. Phelps, of Missouri; Albert Rust, of Arkansas; William A. Howard, of Michigan; George S. Hawkins, of Florida; A. J. Hamilton, of Texas; C. C. Washburn, of Wisconsin; S. R. Curtis, of Iowa; John C. Burch, of California; William Winslow, of Minnesota; and Lansing Stout, of Oregon. The Speaker, in framing this Committee, chose conservative men of the Free-labor States. Those holding extreme anti-slavery views were excluded. Mr. Pennington shared in the feeling throughout the Free-labor States, that conciliation was desirable, and that every concession, consistent with right, should be made to the malcontents.

[1] See Note 1, page 34.

Territory ; that the Missouri Compromise, as to the limits of Slavery, should be revived ; that Congress should not have power to abolish the inter-State Slave-trade; that the Fugitive Slave Law should be reaffirmed ; that slave-holders might pass unmolested with their slaves through any Free-labor State, and that all nullifying laws of State Legislatures should be inoperative; also, a declaration that the Constitution was an article of agreement between Sovereign States, and that an attempt of the National Government to coerce a Sovereign State into obedience to it would be levying war upon a substantial power, and would precipitate a dissolution of the Union.[1]

Mr. Sickles, who afterward fought the secessionists in arms, as a commanding general, and lost a leg in the fray, proposed an amendment declaring that when a State, in the exercise of its sovereignty, should secede, the Government of the United States should appoint commissioners to confer with duly appointed agents of such State, and agree upon the disposition of the public property and territory belonging to the United States lying within it, and upon the proportion of the public debt to be assumed and paid by that State ; also authorizing the President, when all should be settled, to proclaim the withdrawal of such State from the Union. This was substantially Clingman's proposition, when he made his seditious speech in the Senate a fortnight before.[2]

Mr. Hindman, afterward a general in the armies of the conspirators arrayed against the Republic, proposed an amendment that should guarantee the express recognition of slavery wherever it existed ; no interference with the inter-State or domestic Slave-trade, from which Virginia was receiving a large annual income ; to give free scope for slaveholders with their slaves while traveling in Free-labor States; to prohibit to any State the right of representation in the Congress whose Legislature should pass laws impairing the obligations of the Fugitive Slave Law ; to give the Slave-labor States a negative upon all acts of the Congress concerning Slavery; to make these, and all other provisions of the Constitution relating to Slavery, unamendable ; and to grant to the several States authority to appoint all National officers within their respective limits.[3]

Mr. Vallandigham, who was afterward convicted of, and punished for, alleged treasonable acts,[4] submitted a proposition for a change in the National Constitution, providing for a division of the Republic into four sections, to be called, respectively, *The North, The West, The Pacific,* and *The South.*[5] His proposition, says a late writer, " was the fullest and most logical embodiment yet made of Mr. Calhoun's subtle device for enabling a minority to

[1] Proceedings of Congress, December 12, 17, and 24, 1860, reported in the *Congressional Globe.*
[2] Proceedings of Congress, December 17, 1860, reported in the *Congressional Globe.*
[3] Proceedings of Congress, December 12, 1860, reported in the *Congressional Globe.*
[4] See Report of his Trial, published by Rickey & Carroll: Cincinnati, Ohio, 1863.
[5] Proceedings of Congress, Feb. 7, 1861, reported in *Congressional Globe.* Mr. Vallandigham proposed the following grouping of States in the four sections:—*The North,* Maine, New Hampshire, Vermont, Massachusetts, Rhode Island, Connecticut, New York, New Jersey, and Pennsylvania. *The West,* Ohio, Indiana, Illinois, Michigan, Wisconsin, Minnesota, Iowa, and Kansas. *The Pacific,* Oregon and California. *The South,* Delaware, Maryland, Virginia, North Carolina, South Carolina, Georgia, Florida, Alabama, Mississippi, Louisiana, Texas, Arkansas, Tennessee, Kentucky, and Missouri. These were all Slave-labor States.

This scheme for dividing the States, and the accompanying propositions concerning the election of President and Congressmen, was admirably adapted to the uses of the conspirators, for it would make the voice of three hundred thousand slaveholders as potential, politically, as that of twenty millions of non-slaveholders. It was advocated in Congress so late as January, 1863.

obstruct and baffle the majority under a political system preserving the forms of a republic."[1]

Mr. Noell proposed to instruct the Committee to inquire and report as to the expediency of abolishing the office of President of the United States, and establishing, in lieu thereof, an Executive Council of three.members, to be elected by districts composed of contiguous States, as nearly as possible, and each member to be invested with a veto power. He wished the Committee also to inquire whether the equilibrium between the Free-labor and Slave-labor States might not be restored and preserved, particularly by a voluntary division on the part of some of the latter States into two or more States.[2]

There were other propositions for conciliation and the preservation of the Union presented, some similar and some quite dissimilar to those already mentioned; and it was evident to the people at large that the Republic would not be saved by the wisdom of their representatives alone. There seemed to be a general desire among patriots to concede every thing but honor and the best interests of the country for the preservation of the Union, while the conspirators, having trampled both honor and patriotism under their feet, would yield nothing, and even presented their requisitions in such questionable shapes, that they might interpret them, at the critical moment of final decision, as their interests should dictate.

The result of the labors of the Committee of Thirty-three, and the action on measures proposed outside of that Committee, will be considered hereafter.

In the Senate there was a like desire, on the part of many of the members from the Free-labor and the Border Slave-labor States, for conciliation, and a disposition to compromise much for the sake of fraternal good-will and peace. On motion of Lazarus W. Powell, of Kentucky, a Committee of Thirteen was appointed by Vice-President Breckinridge, to consider the condition of the country, and report some plan, by amendments of the National Constitution or otherwise, for its pacification.[3] On the same day, the venerable John J. Crittenden offered to the Senate a series of amendments of the Constitution, and Joint Resolutions, for the protection of Slavery and the interests of the slaveholders, which, embodied, are known in history as the *Crittenden Compromise.* The amendments proposed were substantially as follows :—

I. To re-establish, as a boundary between Free and Slave-labor States forever, the parallel of 36° 30′ north latitude, running from the southern boundary of Missouri to the Pacific Ocean, and known as the Missouri Compromise line. North of that line there should be no Slavery ; south of it, the system might flourish, and all interference with it by the Congress should be forbidden. Not only this, but the Congress, by law, should protect this "property" of the slave-owners from interference "by all the departments of

---

[1] *The American Conflict*, by Horace Greeley, i, 384.
[2] Proceedings of Congress, December 12, 1860, reported in *Congressional Globe*.
[3] This Committee consisted of L. W. Powell and John J. Crittenden, of Kentucky; William H. Seward, of New York; J. Collamer, of Vermont; William Bigler, of Pennsylvania; R. M. T. Hunter, of Virginia; Robert Toombs, of Georgia; Jefferson Davis, of Mississippi; H. M. Rice, of Minnesota; Stephen A. Douglas, of Illinois; Benjamin Wade, of Ohio; J. R. Doolittle, of Wisconsin. and J. W. Grimes, of Iowa. The Committee was composed of eight Democrats and five Republicans.

the Territorial government, during its continuance as such. That such Territory should, when legally qualified, be admitted into the Union as a State, with or without Slavery, as its constitution should determine."

II. That the Congress should not abolish slavery in places under its jurisdiction when such places should be within the limits of Slave-labor States, or wherein Slavery might thereafter be established.

III. That the Congress should have no power to abolish Slavery in the District of Columbia, so long as it should exist in the adjoining States of

JOHN JAY CRITTENDEN.

Maryland and Virginia, nor without the consent of the inhabitants thereof, nor without just compensation made to the owners of slaves who should not consent to the abolishment. That the Congress should not prevent Government officers, sojourning in the District on business, bringing their slaves with them, and taking them with them when they should depart.

IV. That Congress should have no power to prohibit or hinder the transportation of slaves from one State to another, or into Territories where Slavery should be allowed.

V. That the National Government should pay to the owner of a fugitive slave, who might be rescued from the officers of the law when attempting to take him back to bondage, the full value of such "property" so detained and lost; and that the amount should be refunded by the county in which the rescue might occur, that municipality having the power to sue for and recover the amount from the individual actors in the offense.

VI. That no future amendments of the Constitution should be made that might have an effect on the five preceding amendments, or on sections of the Constitution on the subject, already existing; nor should any amendment be made that should give to the Congress the right to abolish or interfere with Slavery in any of the States where it existed by law, or might hereafter be allowed.

In addition to these amendments of the Constitution, Mr. Crittenden offered four resolutions, declaring substantially as follows:—1. That the Fugitive Slave Act was constitutional, and must be enforced, and that laws ought to be made for the punishment of those who should interfere with its due execution. 2. That all State laws [Personal Liberty Acts] which impeded the execution of the Fugitive Slave Act were null and void; that such laws had been mischievous in producing discord and commotion, and therefore the Congress should respectfully and earnestly recommend the repeal of them, or, by legislation, make them harmless. 3. This resolution referred to the fees of commissioners acting under the Fugitive Slave Law, and the modification of the section which required all citizens, when called upon, to aid the owner in catching his runaway property. 4. This resolution declared that strong measures ought to be adopted by the Congress for the suppression of the African Slave-trade.

The results of the labors of the Committee of Thirteen, who acted upon the Crittenden Compromise and other measures, will be considered hereafter. Let us now, for a while, leave the halls of legislation, and become spectators of the movements in South Carolina, preparatory to the open revolt that occurred in that State early in 1861.

The rebellious movement in South Carolina was under the control of a few sagacious and unscrupulous men, who were the self-constituted leaders of the people. They were men who hated democracy and a republican form of government—men who yearned for the pomps of royalty and the privileges of an hereditary aristocracy; and who had persuaded themselves and the common people around them that they were superior to all others on the continent, and patterns of gentility, refinement, grace, and every character-istic in the highest ideal of chivalry. "More than once," said one of her orators, and an early conspirator, " has the calm self-respect of old Carolina breeding been caricatured by the consequential insolence of vulgar imita-tion."[1] And this was the common tone of thought among them. They cherished regret that their fathers were so unwise as to break the political connection with Great Britain. "Their admiration," says a correspondent of the London *Times*, writing from Charleston at the close of April, 1861, "for monarchical institutions on the English model, for privileged classes, and for a landed aristocracy and gentry, is undisguised and apparently genu-ine. Many are they who say, ' We would go back to-morrow, if we could.' An intense affection for the British connection, a love of British habits and customs, a respect for British sentiment, law, authority, order, civilization, and literature, pre-eminently distinguish the inhabitants of this State, who, glorying in their descent from ancient families on the three islands, whose fortunes they still follow, and with whose members they maintain, not unfre-quently, familiar relations, regard with an aversion which it is impossible to give an idea of to one who has not seen its manifestations, the people of New England and the population of the Northern States, whom they regard as tainted beyond cure by the venom of Puritanism."[2] They were ready for any thing rather than continue a union with the North, with whom they declared it was ." an insufferable degradation to live as equals. " They were arro-gantly boastful of their honor, their courage, their invincibility, and their ever-willingness to die in defense of their rights and their " sacred soil." How well the conduct of these men—these betrayers of the people—justified their boastings, let the history of the Civil War determine.

In this overweening pride, this arrogant self-conceit, this desire for class privileges and every anti-republican condition for the favored few at the

---

[1] William H. Trescot, Assistant Secretary of State under President Buchanan, in an Oration before the South Carolina Historical Society, in 1859. Mr. Trescot was a member of an association of South Carolinians, in 1850, whose avowed object was the destruction of the Republic by disunion.

[2] Letter of William H. Russell, LL.D., dated Charleston, April 30, 1861. Mr. Russell was sent over by the proprietors of the London *Times*, at the breaking out of the insurrection, as a special war correspondent of that paper. He landed in New York and proceeded southward. He mingled freely with the ruling class there, among whom he heard, he says, but one voice concerning their aspirations for an eternal separation from democ-racy. "Shades of George III., of North, of Johnston," he exclaims; "of all who contended against the great rebellion which tore these colonies from England, can you hear the chorus which rings through the State of Marion, Sumter, and Pinckney, and not clap your ghostly hands in triumph? That voice says, ' If we could only get one of the royal race of England to rule over us, we should be content.' That sentiment, varied a hundred ways, has been repeated to me over and over again."

expense of the great mass of the people around them, which for a generation
had appeared in the deportment, the public speeches, the legislation, and the
literature of the oligarchy of South Carolina, we may look for a solution and
explanation of that insanity which made them emulous of all others in the mad
race toward destruction which their wicked revolt brought upon them.

Ever since the failure of their crazy scheme of disunion in 1832–'3, in
which John C. Calhoun was the chief actor as well as instigator, the politicians of that State—survivors of that failure, and their children, trained to
seditious acts—had been restive under the restraints of the National Constitution, and had been seeking an occasion to strike a deadly blow at the life of
the Republic, either alone, or in concert with the politicians of other Slave-
labor States. Strong efforts were made in that direction in 1850, when the
National Congress mortally offended the Slave interest by discussing the admission of California into the Union as a Free-labor State. Then the Legislature of South Carolina openly deliberated on the expediency of a "Southern
Congress," for the initiation of immediate measures looking to disunion as an
end. There were utterances, in the course of that discussion, calculated to
"fire the Southern heart," as they were intended to do. The debaters spoke
vaguely of wrongs suffered and endured by South Carolina, but very clearly
of the remedy, which was *secession*. "The remedy," said W. S. Lyles, "is
the union of the South and a Southern Confederacy. The friends of the
Southern movement in the other States look to the action of South Carolina;
and I would make the issue in a reasonable time, and the only way to do so
is by secession. There will be no concert among the Southern States until a
blow is struck." F. D. Richardson said:—"We must not consider what we
have borne, but what we must bear hereafter. There is no remedy for these
evils in the Government; we have no alternative but to come out of the Government." John S. Preston was afraid of the people, and opposed a convention. He thought popular conventions "dangerous things, except when the
necessities of the country absolutely demand them." He opposed them, he
said, "simply and entirely with the view of hastening the dissolution of the
Union." For the same reason, Lawrence M. Keitt favored a convention. "I
think," he said, "it will bring about a more speedy dissolution of the
Union."[1]

The passage of the Compromise Act[2] in September, 1850, silenced the

[1] At this time the Union men of the State took measures for counteracting the madness of the disunionists.
They celebrated the 4th of July by a mass meeting at Greenville, South Carolina. Many distinguished citizens
were invited to attend, or to give their views at length on the great topic of the Union. Among these was
Francis Lieber, LL.D., Professor of History and Political Economy in the South Carolina College at Columbia.
He sent an address to his fellow-citizens of the State, which was a powerful plea for the Union and against
secession. He warned them that secession would lead to war. "No country," he said, "has ever broken up or
can ever break up in peace, and without a struggle commensurate to its own magnitude." He asked, "Will any
one who desires secession for the sake of bringing about a Southern Confederacy, honestly aver that he would
insist upon a provision in the new constitution securing the full right of secession whenever it may be desired
by any member of the expected Confederacy?" This significant question was answered in the affirmative, ten
years later, by the madmen at Montgomery, who formed such "Confederacy" and "new constitution;" and before the rebellion that ensued was crushed, the "Confederacy" was in the throes of dissolution, caused by the
practical assertion of the "right of secession."

[2] In February, 1850, the representatives of California in Congress asked for the admission of the Territory as
a Free-labor State, the inhabitants having formed a State constitution in which Slavery was prohibited. This was
in accordance with the doctrine of Popular Sovereignty, accepted by the Slave power as right at that time, and
for some years afterward; and yet that power now declared that, if California should be admitted as a Free-labor
State, the Slave-labor States should leave the Union. To allay this feeling, Henry Clay proposed a compromise-

·conspirators for a while ; but when, in 1856, John C. Frémont, an opponent of Slavery, was nominated for the Presidency by the newly formed Republican party, they had another pretext for a display of their boasted disloyalty to the Union. One of their number, named Brooks, with his hands stained, as it were, with the blood of a Senator whom he had struck to the floor in the Senate Chamber at Washington with a bludgeon, with murderous intent (and who, for this so-called " chivalrous act," was rewarded by his compeers with the present of a gold-headed cane, and re-election to Congress), said, in an harangue before an excited populace, " I tell you that the only mode which I think available for meeting the issue is just to tear in twain the Constitution of the United States, trample it under-foot, and form a Southern Confederacy, every State of which shall be a Slave-holding State. . . . I have been a disunionist from the time I could think. If I were commander of an army, I never would post a sentinel who would not swear that slavery was right. . . . If Frémont be elected President of the United States, I am for the people in their majesty rising above the laws and leaders, taking the power into their own hands, going by concert, or not by concert, and laying the strong arm of Southern freemen upon the treasury and archives of the Government." This is a favorable specimen of speeches made to excited crowds all over South Carolina and the Cotton-growing States at that time.

The restless spirits of South Carolina were quieted, for a while, by the election of Buchanan, in the autumn of 1856. They were disappointed, because they seemed compelled to wait for another pretext for rebellion. But they did not wait. They conferred secretly, on the subject of disunion, with politicians in other Slave-labor States, and finally took open action in the old State House at Columbia. The lower House of the South Carolina Legislature, on the 30th of November, 1859, resolved that the " Commonwealth was ready to enter, together with other Slaveholding States, or such as desire prompt action, into the formation of a Southern Confederacy." At the request of the Legislature, the Governor of the State sent a copy of this resolution to the Governors of the other Slave-labor States; and in January following,[a] ᵃ 1860. C. G. Memminger, one of the arch-conspirators of South Carolina, appeared before the General Assembly of

CHARLES G. MEMMINGER.

Virginia as a special commissioner from his State. His object was to enlist the representatives of Virginia in a scheme of disunion, whilst, with the degrading hypocrisy which has ever characterized the leaders in the Great Rebellion, he professed zealous attachment to the Union. He proposed, in the name of South Carolina, a

and as an offset for the admission of California as a Free-labor State, the infamous Fugitive Slave Law, which no man not interested in slavery ever advocated as right in principle, became a law of the land, with some other concessions in that direction.

convention of the Slave-labor States, to consider their grievances, and to
" take action for their defense." He reminded the Virginians of the coincidence of the people of the two States in long cherishing sentiments of disunior.
He pointed to their public acts relative to meditated revolt, under certaih
contingencies.[1] He reminded them of the dangers which had just menaced
their State by the raid of John Brown and twenty men, at Harper's Ferry,
of the " implacable condition of Northern opinion" concerning Slavery;
and the rapid increase of Abolition sentiment in the Free-labor States.
He reminded them that "the South" had a right to demand the repeal
of all laws hurtful to Slavery; the " disbanding of every society which
was agitating the Northern mind against Southern institutions;" and
the " surrender of the power to amend the Constitution in regard to Slavery,"
after it should be amended so as to nationalize the system. He made an
able plea, and closed by saying:—" I have delivered into the keeping of
Virginia the cause of the South." But the politicians of Virginia, who, like
those of South Carolina, had usurped the powers of the people, were averse
to the establishment of a Southern Confederacy in which there was to be
free trade in slaves brought from Africa; for that free trade would destroy
the inter-State trade in slaves, from which the oligarchy of Virginia were
receiving an annual income of from twelve millions to twenty millions of
dollars.[2] The Virginia Legislature, which Mr. Memminger said he found
" extremely difficult to see through,"[3] consequently hesitated.

There was also another reason for hesitation, which one of Virginia's
ablest, most patriotic, and Union-loving men unhesitatingly avowed to a
friend, who wished to enlist him in the revolutionary scheme of South Carolina :—" If a new Confederacy should be formed," he said, "I could not go
with you, for I should use whatever influence I might be able to exert against
entering into one with South Carolina, that has been a common brawler and
disturber of the peace for the last thirty years, and who would give no
security that I would be willing to accept, that she would not be as faithless

---

[1] See resolutions of the General Assembly of Virginia, in March, 1847, concerning the measure known as
the *Wilmot Proviso*, in relation to Slavery in the region just taken from Mexico.

[2] When, as we shall hereafter observe, Virginia hesitated to join the Southern Confederacy, formed at
Montgomery, Alabama, in February, 1861, the threat was held out that there should be a clause in the Constitution of the Confederacy prohibiting the importation of slaves from any State not in union with them. The
threatened loss of this immense revenue was the most powerful argument used by Virginia politicians in favor
of uniting the fortunes of that State with those of the Cotton-growing States. The Richmond papers shamelessly advocated the union of Virginia with these States in the revolt, on the ground, almost solely, that she
would otherwise lose the chief source of income for " seventy thousand families of the State," arising from the
sale of boys and girls, men and women. According to a report before me, five thousand slaves were sent South
from Richmond, Virginia, over the Petersburg Road, five thousand over the Tennessee Road, and two thousand
by other channels, during the year 1860, valued at one thousand dollars each. "Twelve millions of dollars have
been received in cash by the State," said the report.

[3] Mr. Memminger, in an autograph letter before me, written to R. B. Rhett, Jr., editor of *The Charleston
Mercury*, and dated "Richmond, Va., January 28, 1860," revealed some of the difficulties in the way of the
success of his treasonable mission. He says:—

" It is extremely difficult to see through the Virginia Legislature. The Democratic party is not a unit, and
the Whigs hope to cleave it with their wedge, whenever dissensions arise. Governor Wise seems to me to be
really with us, as well as Mr. Hunter, but he seems to think it necessary to throw out tubs to the Union whale.
The effect here of Federal politics is most unfortunate. It makes this great State comparatively powerless. I
am making but little progress, as every thing proceeds here very slowly. They have got into a tangle about
committees, which has excited considerable feeling to-day, and may embarrass the result. But still I hope that
the result will be favorable. *I see no men, however, who would take the position of leaders in a Revolution*

" As soon as I can get a printed copy of my Address, I will send it to you.

" Yours very truly,   C. G. MEMMINGER."

to the next compact as she has been to this which she is now endeavoring to avoid."[1] We may also add the important fact that the great mass of the people, especially of Western Virginia, were too thoroughly loyal to follow the leadings of the politicians into revolutionary ways.

Almost a year rolled away, and the same man (Memminger) [a] stood up before a large congregation of citizens in Charleston,[a] and, in a speech which perfectly exhibited the power of the *politicians* over the *people* of South Carolina, foreshadowed, in distinct outline, the course of revolutionary events in the near future. He foretold the exact day when an ordinance of secession would be passed in the coming State Convention; that Commissioners would be sent to Washington to treat on the terms of separation; that the demand would be made for the surrender of the forts in Charleston harbor into the hands of insurgents, and if surrender should be refused, armed South Carolinians would take them. He spoke of the weakness of the National Government with Buchanan at its head, and the consequently auspicious time for them then to strike the murderous blow at the life of the Republic. He exhorted the people to be prepared for revolution, for it was surely at hand. He knew how plastic would be the material of the Legislature and the coming Convention in the hands of the few leaders like himself, and that these leaders had power to accomplish the fulfillment of their own prophecies concerning the course of events under their control.

Memminger was one of the managers of a league of conspirators in Charleston known as " The 1860 Association," formed in September previous, for the avowed purpose of maddening the people, and forcing them into acquiescence in the revolutionary scheme of the conspirators. As early as the 19th of November, Robert N. Gourdin, " Chairman of the Executive Committee " of the Association, in a circular letter said :—" The North is preparing to soothe and conciliate the South, by disclaimers and overtures. The success of this policy would be disastrous to the cause of Southern union and independence, and it is necessary to resist and defeat it. The Association is preparing pamphlets for this special object." As we shall observe hereafter, all of the time and labor spent in Congress in endeavors to conciliate the Slave-power was wasted. There was a predetermination to accept of nothing as satisfactory.[2]

South Carolina was then in a blaze of excitement. The Legislature, which, in special session, had provided for a Convention and the arming of the State, had adjourned on the 13th of November. The members were honored that evening by a great torch-light procession in the streets of Columbia. The old banner of the Union was taken down from the State House and the Palmetto Flag was unfurled in its place; and it was boastfully declared that the old ensign—the " detested rag of the Union "—should never again float in the free air of South Carolina.

[a] November 30, 1860.

---

[1] Letter of John Minor Botts to " II. B. M., Esq.," of Staunton, dated November 27, 1860.

[2] See Chapter IX. In the circular referred to, Gourdin stated the principal objects of the Association to be the interchange of views to " prepare the Slave States to meet the impending crisis;" to prepare, print, and circulate tracts and pamphlets designed to awaken the people " to a sense of danger," and to aid the Legislature in promptly establishing " an effective military organization." The object of this circular was to beg for money to carry on the work of the Association. He stated that one hundred and sixty thousand pamphlets had already been distributed, and yet there was a good demand for them.

Already Robert Barnwell Rhett, appropriately called the "Father of South Carolina secession," had sounded the tocsin. He was an arrogant demagogue, whose family name was Smith, and whose lineal root was to be found in obscurity, among the sand-hills near the mouth of the Cape Fear River, in North Carolina. He made his residence at Beaufort, South Carolina, when he dropped the name of Smith and took that of Rhett—a name honorable in the early history of that State.[1] He succeeded in taking position among respectable men in South Carolina. With vulgar instinct

he spurned the "common people," boasted of "superior blood," and by the force of social influence, and much natural talent for oratory and intrigue, with the aid of the *Charleston Mercury*, edited by his equally disloyal son, he did more than any other man since the days of Hamilton, and Hayne, and Calhoun, to bring the miseries of civil war upon the State that gave him shelter and honor. From the moment of the disruption of the Charleston Convention of Democrats, in April, 1860,[2] he had been an active traitor in deeds and words; and so early as the 12th of November, the day before the South Carolina

ROBERT BARNWELL RHETT.

Legislature adjourned, he declared in Institute Hall,[3] in Charleston, that the Union was dissolved, and that henceforth there would be deliverance, and peace, and liberty for South Carolina. "The long weary night of our humiliation, oppression, and danger," he said, "is passing away, and the glorious dawn of a Southern Confederacy breaks on our view." Alluding to the people of the North, he said, "Swollen with insolence and steeped in ignorance, selfishness, and fanaticism, they will never understand their dependence on the South until the Union is dissolved, and they are left naked to their own resources." Then the poor madman, with ludicrous gravity, began to prophesy. "Then, and not till then," he said, "will they realize what a blessing the Almighty conferred upon them when he placed them in union with the South; and they will curse, in the bitterness of penitence and suffering, the dark day on which they compelled us to dissolve it with them. Upon a dissolution of the Union, their whole system of commerce and manufactures will be paralyzed or overthrown—their banks will suspend specie payments—their stocks and real estate will fall in price, and confusion and distress will pervade the North. Broad processions will walk the streets of their great cities; mobs will break into their palaces, and society there will be resolved into its original chaos." He then went on to say, that there would be great difficulty in limiting the Southern Confederacy. "Many of the Free States," he said, "will desire to join us." He proposed to let them in, on condition that "the Southern Confederacy should be a Slaveholding Confederacy;"[4] that taxation should be light, and that the forts in Charleston

---

[1] Note to article on "Beaufort District," by Frederic Kidder, in the *Continental Monthly*, 1862.
[2] See page 19.   [3] See page 19.
[4] Anxious to secure European good-will, the leaders in the great revolt, when it assumed the form of civil war, tried to hide this fact—this great object of the Rebellion—but there were some too honest or too

harbor should "never be surrendered to any power on earth." Such was the language of a "leading statesman" of South Carolina, whom the people were required to venerate as an oracle of wisdom.

Rhett gave the key-note. Men went out at once, as missionaries of treason, all over South Carolina, and motley crowds of men, women, and children—Caucasian and African—listened, in excited groups, at cross-roads, court-houses, and other usual gathering-places. The burden of every speech was the wrongs suffered by South Carolina, in the Union; her right and her duty to leave it; her power to "defy the world in arms;" and the glory that would illumine her whole domain in that near future, when her independence of the thralls of the "detested Constitution" should be secured. "Statesmen," released from service in the Legislature, joined in this missionary work. To the slaveholders one said, in a speech in Charleston:— "Three thousand millions of property is involved in this question, and if you say at the ballot-box that South Carolina shall not secede, you put into the sacrifice three thousand millions of your property. . . . The Union is a dead carcass, stinking in the nostrils of the South. . . . Ay, my friends, a few weeks more, and you will see floating from the fortifications the ensign that now bears the Palmetto, the emblem of a Southern Confederacy." The *Charleston Mercury*, conducted, as we have observed, by a son of R. B. Rhett, called upon all natives of South Carolina in the Army or Navy of the United States to throw up their commissions, and join in the revolt. "The mother looks to her sons," said this fiery organ of treason, "to protect her from outrage. . . . She is sick of the Union — disgusted with it, upon any terms within the range of the widest possibility." The call was responded to by the resignations of many commissions held by South Carolinians; and the conspirators, unable to comprehend a supreme love for the Union, boasted that not a son of that State would prove loyal to the old flag.[2] They were amazed when patriots like Commodore Shubrick refused to do the bidding of traitors.

THE PALMETTO.[1]

---

reckless to keep it back. At the end of almost four years of war, the *Charleston Mercury*, the leading organ of rebellion from the beginning, declared [February, 1864]: "South Carolina entered into this struggle *for no other purpose than to maintain the institution of Slavery.* Southern independence has no other object or meaning. . . . Independence and Slavery must stand together or fall together."

[1] The tree of the palm family, known as the *Cabbage Palmetto*, grows near the shores of South Carolina and Georgia, in great perfection. It is confined to the neighborhood of salt water. Its timber is very valuable in all submarine constructions. Its unexpanded young leaves form a most delicious vegetable for the table. Its perfect leaves are used in the manufacture of hats, mats, baskets, &c. The foliage forms a broad tuft at the upper part of the stem. It is the chief figure on the seal of South Carolina, and has ever been an emblem of the State.

[2] One of those who abandoned the flag was Lieutenant J. R. Hamilton, of the Navy, who, on the 14th of January, 1861, issued a circular letter from Fort Moultrie to his fellow-officers in that branch of the service,

On the 16th of November, the Chancellor (Dunkin) of South Carolina closed his court, and expressed a hope that when the members should reassemble, it would be "as a court in an independent State, and that State a member of a Southern Confederacy." The next day was a gala one in Charleston. A pine "liberty-pole," ninety feet in height, was erected, and a Palmetto flag was unfurled from its top—a white flag, with a green Palmetto-tree in the middle, and the motto of South Carolina:—ANIMIS OPIBUSQUE PARATI; that is, "Prepared in mind and resources—ready to give life and property." It was greeted with the roar of cannon a hundred times repeated, and the "Marseillaise Hymn" by a band. This was followed by the "Miserere" from "Il Trovatore," played as a requiem for the departed Union. Full twenty thousand people, it is said, participated in this "inauguration of revolution;" and the Rev. C. P. Gadsden invoked the blessing of God upon their acts. These ceremonies were followed by speeches (some from Northern men, in Charleston on business), in which the people were addressed as "Citizens of the Southern Republic;" and processions filled the streets, bearing from square to square many banners with significant inscriptions.[1] No Union flag was seen upon any ship in the harbor, for vigilance committees, assuming police powers, had already been formed in Charleston and other places, as a part of the system of coercion put in practice against Union men in the Slave-labor States immediately after Lincoln's election.[3]

These vigilance associations were in active operation by the close of November, and before the ordinance of secession had been decreed by the Convention, large numbers of persons from the North had been arraigned by them, and banished from the State, after much suffering, on suspicion of being unfriendly to the schemes of the conspirators. In some cases, where men were accused of being actual Abolitionists, they were stripped, and covered with tar and feathers. These committees, with the power to torture, soon made the expressed sentiment of South Carolina "unanimous in favor of secession;" and the organ of the conspirators—the *Mercury*—was justified in assuring the South Carolinians in the employment of the United States Government, when calling them home, that "they need have no more doubt of South Carolina's going out of the

STREET FLAG-
STAFF.[2]

---

calling upon them to follow his example. It was a characteristic production. After talking much of "honor," he thus counseled his friends to engage in plundering the Government:—"What the South most asks of you now is, to bring with you every ship and man you can, that we may use them against the oppressors of our liberties, and the enemies of our aggravated but united people." At that time, thirty-six naval officers, born in Slave-labor States, had resigned.

[1] On these banners were the words:—"South Carolina goes it alone;" "God, Liberty, and the State;" "South Carolina wants no *Stripes*;" "Stand to your arms, Palmetto Boys;" "Huzza for a Southern Confederacy;" "Now or never, strike for Independence;" "Good-by, Yankee Doodle;" "Death to all Abolitionists;" "Let us bury the Union's dead carcass," &c.

[2] In this little sketch is seen the spire of the Roman Catholic Cathedral of St. John and St. Finbar, mentioned at near the close of Chapter XIII. of this volume.

[3] Orville J. Victor, in the first volume (page 47) of his *History of the Southern Rebellion and War for the Union*, cites the resolutions of the citizens of Lexington District, South Carolina, in forming a vigilance asso-

Union than of the world's turning round. *Every man that goes to the Convention will be a pledged man,*" it said, "pledged for immediate separate State secession, *in any event whatever.*" This was before the members of the proposed convention had been chosen. The *Southern Presbyterian,* a theological work of wide and powerful influence, published at Columbia, said, on the 15th of December, "It is well known that the members of the Convention have been elected with the understanding and expectation that they will dissolve the relations of South Carolina with the Federal Union, immediately and unconditionally. This is a foregone conclusion in South Carolina. It is a matter for devout thankfulness that the Convention will embody the very highest wisdom and character of the State: *private gentlemen, judges of her highest legal tribunals, and ministers of the Gospel.* . . . Before we issue another number of this paper the deed may be done—the Union may be dissolved—we may have ceased to be in the United States." One of the most distinguished literary men of the South (William Gilmore Simms), in a letter to the author, dated December 13,[a] said: "In ten days   • 1860. more, South Carolina will have certainly seceded; and in reasonable interval after that event, if the forts in our harbor are not surrendered to the State, they will be taken." With equal confidence and precision all the politicians spoke in the ears of the people, and only a few men, like the noble and venerable J. L. Pettigru of Charleston, gladly doubted the success of the kindling revolt, and dared to say so. The conspirators had settled the question beforehand; the *people* had nothing to do with it, excepting as instruments employed to give to the work of these men the appearance of its having been done "according to due forms of law."

The Legislature of South Carolina met in regular session on the 26th of November; and on the 10th of December it chose Francis W. Pickens to be Governor of the State. That body was greeted with the most cheering news of the spreading of secession sentiments, like a fierce conflagration, all over the Slave-labor States; and Governor Gist, in his farewell message, intended as much for the Convention as the Legislature, stimulated it to revolutionary action. He urged the necessity of quickly arranged and efficient measures on the part of South Carolina. He was afraid of the return of calm thought to the minds of the people. "The delay of the Convention," he said, "for a single week to pass the Ordinance of Secession will have a blighting and chilling influence upon the other States. He hoped that, by the 28th of December, "no flag but the Palmetto would float over any part of South Carolina." Pickens, who had been a member of the   ♭ 1835-1845. National Congress ten consecutive years,[b] and minister to the Russian Court by Buchanan's appointment, was a worthy successor of Gist;

ciation, as a fair example of the power conferred upon these self-constituted guardians of "Southern Rights." They provided for monthly meetings of the officers, who should have full power to decide all cases that might be brought before them, which decisions should be "final and conclusive;" that the president should appoint as many captains of patrol of five men as he might think necessary; that the patrol companies should have power to arrest all suspicious white persons, and bring them before the Executive Committee for trial; that they stood pledged to "put down all negro preachings, prayer-meetings, and all congregations of negroes that may be considered unlawful by the patrol companies;" that these companies should have the power to correct and punish all slaves, free negroes, mulattoes, and mestizoes, as they may deem proper; that they should give special passes; that every person should be requested to sign the resolutions, and thus sanction them: that all who refuse to do duty, when called upon, should be reported; and that all peddlers should be prohibited from passing through the country, unless duly authorized to do so.

and he entered into the schemes of the conspirators with all the powers that he possessed.

The members of the Convention were chosen on the 3d of December.

DAVID F. JAMISON.

Not one had been nominated who was opposed to secession; and when, on the 17th,[a] they assembled in the Baptist Church at Columbia, they were all of one mind in relation to the main question. David F. Jamison, a delegate from Barnwell District, was chosen temporary chairman. He made a brief speech, in which he counseled the members to beware of outside pressure, and disputations among themselves. He trusted that the door was now forever closed "from any further connection with our Northern confederates;" and then, either ignorantly or wickedly, asserted that "*every* Northern State" had trampled the Constitution under foot, "by placing on their books statutes nullifying the laws for the recovery of fugitive slaves!"[1] He concluded by saying that he could offer them nothing better, in inaugurating such a movement, than the words of Danton at the commencement of the French Revolution: "To dare! and again to dare! and without end to dare!"

A difficulty now presented itself. A motion was made, by Charles G. Memminger, to receive the credentials and swear in the members. It was suggested that the Constitution of South Carolina provided that they should, on such an occasion, take an oath to support the Constitution of the United States. "But we have come here," said ex-Governor Adams, the discoverer of this lion in the way, "to break down a government, not to take an oath to support it." The difficulty was a slight one, in the opinion of lawless men. What did they care for *any* constitutions? There was, to them, no sanctity in oaths; and so they formed their Convention without oaths, in defiance of the Constitution of South Carolina. They elected their temporary chairman permanent President of their body, and appointed B. F. Arthur the clerk. They well knew that the Constitution of South Carolina declared their Convention, when organized, to be an unlawful assemblage, and that their acts could have no legal effect. If secession had been lawful, the ordinances of those usurpers were never legally binding upon a soul on the earth.

If these men had no respect for written constitutions, they had for the unwritten and inexorable laws of being, and heeded their menaces. They were about to proceed in their revolutionary schemes, after the Rev. Mr. Breaker had invoked the blessings of the Almighty upon their proposed work, when intelligence came that the small-pox was raging as an epidemic in Columbia. Men who were professedly ready to die for the cause turned pale at the message, and proposed an immediate flight, by railway, to Charleston. William Porcher Miles, just from his abandoned seat in Con-

---

[1] See a refutation of this misstatement in note 1, page 68, concerning Personal Liberty Laws.

[a] December, 1860.

gress, who feared public ridicule more than the contagion, begged them not to flee. "We shall be sneered at," he said. "It will be asked on all sides, 'Is this the chivalry of South Carolina?' They are prepared to face the world, but they run away from small-pox." He was afraid of an hour's delay in their treasonable work. He said that the last thing urged upon him by Congressmen from the Cotton-producing States, when he left Washington, was to take South Carolina out of the Union instantly. "Now, Sir," he said, "when the news reaches Washington that we have met here, that a panic arose about a few cases of small-pox in the city, and that we forthwith scampered off to Charleston, the effect would be a little ludicrous." The "chivalry of South Carolina" did "scamper off to Charleston" the next morning,[a] where they were received with military honors, and at four o'clock in the afternoon re-assembled in Institute Hall.

[a] December 18, 1860.

At the evening session in Columbia, before their flight, John A. Elmore, of Alabama, and Charles E. Hooker, of Mississippi, were introduced to the Convention as commissioners from their respective States. They successively addressed the Convention in favor of the immediate and unconditional secession of the State; and so anxious was Governor Moore, of Alabama, that South Carolina should not delay a moment, for fear of the people, that he telegraphed to Elmore as follows:—"Tell the Convention to listen to no proposition of compromise or delay."[1]

WILLIAM PORCHER MILES.

On assembling at Charleston, the Convention proceeded at once to business. They appointed[b] one Committee to draft an ordinance of secession;[2] another to prepare an address to the people of the Southern States;[3] another to draft a declaration of the causes that impelled and justified the secession of South Carolina;[4] and five others, consisting of thirteen persons each, and entitled, respectively, "Committee on the Message of the President of the United States, relating to property;" "Committee on Relations with the Slaveholding States of North America;" "Committee on Foreign Relations;" "Committee on Commercial Relations and Postal Arrangements;" and "Committee on the Constitution of this State."

[b] December 18.

Judge Magrath moved to refer to a committee of thirteen so much of President Buchanan's Message as related to the property of the United States within the limits of South Carolina, and instruct them to report "of what such property consists, how acquired, and whether the purpose for which it was so acquired can be enjoyed by the United States after the State of South

[1] The American Annual Cyclopedia, 1861, page 649.

[2] This committee was composed of John A. Inglis, Robert Barnwell Rhett, James Chesnut, Jr., James L. Orr, Maxey Gregg, Benjamin Faneuil Duncan, and W. Ferguson Hutson.

[3] This committee was composed of Robert Barnwell Rhett, John Alfred Calhoun, W. P. Finley, Isaac D. Wilson, W. F De Saussure, Langdon Cheves, and Merrick E. Carn.

[4] This committee was composed of C. G. Memminger, F. H. Wardlaw, R. W. Barnwell, J. P. Richardson, B. H. Rutledge, J. E. Jenkins, and P. E. Duncan.

Carolina shall have seceded, consistently with the dignity and safety of the State; also, the value of the property of the United States not in South Carolina, and the value of the share thereof to which South Carolina would be entitled upon an equitable division thereof among the United States." The President, he said, had affirmed it to be his high duty to protect the national property in South Carolina, and to enforce the laws of the nation within its borders. "He says he has no constitutional powers," said Magrath, "to coerce South Carolina, while, at the same time, he denies to her the right of secession." He was afraid that an attempt would be made to coerce the Commonwealth, under the pretext of protecting the property of the United States within its limits, and he wanted to test, at the very threshold of their deliberations, the accuracy of the President's logic.

This brought out William Porcher Miles, who assured the Convention that they had nothing to fear from any hostile action on the part of President Buchanan. There was not the least danger of his sending any re-enforcements to the forts in Charleston harbor. He (Miles) and some of his colleagues, he said, had conversed with the President[a] on the subject, and had orally and in writing admonished him, that if he should attempt to send a solitary soldier to those forts, the instant the intelligence reached South Carolina, the people would forcibly storm and capture them. They assured him that they would take good care to give that information to the people, and that they had sources of information at Washington (the traitorous Secretary of War?) which made it impossible for an order for the sending of re-enforcements to be issued, without their knowing it. They further said to the President, that "a bloody result would follow the sending of troops to those forts;" and at his request they assured him, in writing, that in their opinion there would be no movement toward seizing them by South Carolinians before an offer should be made, by an accredited representative, to negotiate "for an amicable arrangement of all matters between the State and Federal Governments; provided, that no re-enforcements should be sent into those forts." There was, he said, "a tacit, if not an actual agreement," between the President and the South Carolina delegation in Congress,[1] that the relative military condition should remain the same, while each party forbore hostile movements. This statement of Miles satisfied the Convention that they might play treason to their hearts' content until the 4th of March; provided, they kept violent hands off the property of the United States. The President, as we shall observe hereafter, denied that he ever gave such pledge, and pronounced the accusation untrue, as it undoubtedly was.

[a] December 9, 1860.

After resolutions were offered and referred, which proposed a Provisional Government for the Slave-labor States that might secede, on the basis of the National Constitution; also, to send Commissioners to Washington to negotiate for the cession of the property of the United States within the limits of South Carolina; and the election of five delegates, to meet others from Slave-labor States, for the purpose of forming a Southern Con-

[1] The written communications to the President were signed by the following named persons, then Representatives in Congress from South Carolina:—John McQueen, William Porcher Miles, M. L. Bonham, W. W. Boyce, and Lawrence M. Keitt.

federacy, the Committee appointed to prepare an ordinance of secession reported. This was on the 20th of December. Their report, submitted by Mr. Inglis, was very brief, and embodied the draft of an ordinance, in the following words:—

"WE, THE PEOPLE OF THE STATE OF SOUTH CAROLINA, IN CONVENTION ASSEMBLED, DO DECLARE AND ORDAIN, AND IT IS HEREBY DECLARED AND ORDAINED, THAT THE ORDINANCE ADOPTED BY US IN CONVENTION, ON THE TWENTY-THIRD DAY OF MAY, IN THE YEAR OF OUR LORD ONE THOUSAND SEVEN HUNDRED AND EIGHTY-EIGHT, WHEREBY THE CONSTITUTION OF THE UNITED STATES WAS RATIFIED, AND ALSO ALL ACTS AND PARTS OF ACTS OF THE GENERAL ASSEMBLY OF THE STATE, RATIFYING AMENDMENTS OF THE SAID CONSTITUTION, ARE HEREBY REPEALED, AND THE UNION NOW SUBSISTING BETWEEN SOUTH CAROLINA AND OTHER STATES, UNDER THE NAME OF THE UNITED STATES OF AMERICA, IS HEREBY DISSOLVED."

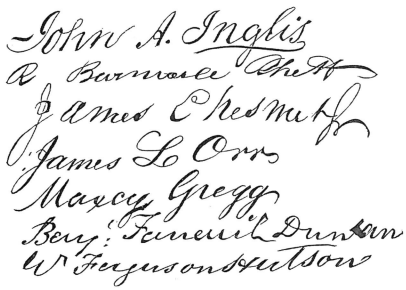

SIGNATURES OF THE COMMITTEE ON SECESSION ORDINANCE.

This ordinance was immediately adopted by the unanimous voice of the Convention. The hour when the important event occurred was a quarter before one o'clock. The number of votes was one hundred and sixty-nine. W. F. De Saussure immediately moved that the Convention should march in procession from St. Andrew's Hall,[1] where they had held their sessions since the 19th, to Institute Hall, and there, at seven o'clock in the evening, in the presence of the constituted authorities of the State and of the people, sign the ordinance. The Governor, both branches of the Legislature, and several clergymen were specially invited to be present at the solemn act—"the great act of deliverance and Liberty."

The cry at once went out:—"*The Union is dissolved! The Union is dissolved!*" An immense crowd in front of the Hall caught up the words with the wildest enthusiasm, and they went from lip to lip, until the whole city was alive with emotion. A placard printed at the *Mercury* office, half an hour after the vote was taken, bearing a copy of the ordinance, and the words, in large letters, THE UNION IS DISSOLVED ! was scattered broad-cast over the town, and diffused universal joy. Groups gathered in many places to hear it read ; and from each went up shout after shout, which attested the popular satisfaction. All business was suspended. The streets of Charleston were filled with excited people huzzaing for a Southern Confederacy, and several women made a public display of their so-called patriotism, by appearing on the crowded side-walks with "secession bonnets,"[1] the invention of a Northern milliner in Charleston. Small Palmetto flags, with a lone star on each, fluttered with white handkerchiefs out of many a window, and large

CALHOUN'S TOMB IN ST. PHILIP'S CHURCH-YARD.

ones waved over every public and many private buildings. The bells of the churches rang out merry peals ; and these demonstrations of delight were accompanied by the roar of cannon. Some enthusiastic young men went to the church-yard where the remains of John C. Calhoun reposed, and there, with singular appropriateness, they formed a circle around his tomb, and made a solemn vow to devote their "lives, their fortunes, and their sacred honor" to the "cause of South Carolina independence."[2] And Paul H. Hayne, author of "The Temptations of Venus" and other poems, inspired by the occasion, produced, before he slept that night, a "Song of Deliverance," in which is the following allusion to South Carolina and her position :—

> " See ! see ! they quail and cry !
> The dogs of Rapine fly,
> Struck by the terror of her mien, her glance of lightning fire !
> And the mongrel, hurrying pack
> In whimpering fear fall back,
> With the sting of baffled hatred hot, and the rage of false desire.
> O, glorious Mother Land !
> In thy presence, stern and grand,
> Unnumbered fading hopes rebloom, and faltering hearts grow brave,
> And a consentaneous shout
> To the answering heavens rings out—
> ' Off with the livery of disgrace, the baldric of the Slave !' "

---

[1] This bonnet was composed of white and black Georgia cotton, the streamers ornamented with Palmetto-trees and a lone star, embroidered with gold thread, while the plumes were formed of white and black worsted.

[2] At one time, during the civil war, when it was believed that the National troops would take possession of Charleston, three of Mr. Calhoun's friends, professing to have fears that the invaders might, in their anger and zeal, desecrate his tomb, and scatter his remains to the winds, removed them to a place of greater safety. They were replaced after the war. The recumbent slab over the grave, which bears the single word "CALHOUN," was much broken by his admirers, who carried away small pieces as relics and mementos.

The telegraph instantly sent its swift messages with the intelligence to every accessible part of the Republic; and within twenty-four hours after the passage of the ordinance, the nation was profoundly moved by this open revolutionary act. Three days afterward, a railway train came in from Savannah with twenty delegates from an organization there, known as the "Sons of the South." They represented, they said, "three hundred and fifty gentlemen in Georgia," and were authorized to offer their services to the Governor of South Carolina, to aid in "maintaining her noble and independent position." They brought with them the banner of their association, which was white, with the device of a Palmetto-tree, having its trunk entwined by a rattle-snake; also, five stars and a crescent, and the words, "SEPARATE STATE ACTION."

At a quarter before four o'clock the Convention took a recess, and while leaving St. Andrew's Hall and going in irregular procession through Broad Street, to dinner, they were cheered by the populace, and the chimes of St. Michael's Protestant Episcopal Church[1] pealed forth "Auld Lang Syne" and other airs. At seven o'clock they re-assembled in the great hall of the South Carolina Institute,[2] afterward known as "Secession Hall," for the purpose of signing the ordinance, which, in the mean time, had been engrossed on a sheet of parchment twenty-five by thirty-three inches in size, with the great seal of South Carolina attached. The Governor and his Council, and both branches of the Legislature were present,

SEAL OF SOUTH CAROLINA.

and the remainder of the hall not occupied by the Convention and those State officials, was crowded densely with the men and women of Charleston. Back of the President's chair was suspended a banner, a copy of which, in miniature, is given on the next page.[3] It was a significant object for the contemplation of the excited multitude. On each side of the platform on which sat the President stood a real Palmetto-tree, that had been brought in for the occasion.

[1] St. Michael's is one of the oldest, if not the oldest Church in Charleston, and the bells chimed for the unholy purpose mentioned in the text have interesting historical associations. When an attack on Charleston was expected, in 1776, the church spire, which was white, and was visible from some distance at sea, was painted black, that the enemy might not see it as a beacon. It was a mistake, for it was then more prominent than ever against a light gray sky. When the British finally took possession of the city, in the spring of 1780, the bells of St. Michael's were sent to London as spoils of victory. The merchants of that city purchased them, and returned them to the church, where they chimed and chimed, until the conspirators now believed they had sounded the death-knell of the Union, which its vestry, in 1776, zealously assisted to create. St. Michael's spire was the target for General Gillmore's great cannon, called "The Swamp Angel," during his long siege of Charleston, in the latter years of the civil war. It was afterward found that a shell from the " Angel" had gone through the church, and, striking the tablet of the Commandments on the wall, effaced every one of them but these:— "Thou shalt not steal." "Thou shalt not commit adultery." So declared a writer in the New York *Independent*, who professed to have been an eye-witness of the effects of the shell.

[2] See page 19.

[3] This banner is composed of cotton cloth, with devices painted in water-colors, by a Charleston artist named Alexander. The base of the design is a mass of broken and disordered blocks of stone, on each of which are the name and arms of a Free-labor State. Rising from this mass are seen two columns of perfect and symmetrical blocks of stone, connected by an arch of the same material, on each of which, fifteen in number, are seen the name and coat-of-arms of a Slave-labor State. South Carolina forms the key-stone of the arch, on which stands Powers' statue of Calhoun leaning upon the trunk of a Palmetto-tree, and displaying, to spectators, a scroll, on

The ceremony of signing the ordmance commenced at the appointed hour. "The scene was one profoundly grand and impressive," said the *Charleston Mercury*, the next morning. "There were a people assembled

BANNER OF THE SOUTH CAROLINA CONVENTION.

through their highest representatives—men, most of them, upon whose heads the snows of sixty winters had been shed—patriarchs in age—dignitaries of the land—the high-priests of the Church of Christ—reverend statesmen—

which are the words, "Truth, Justice, and the Constitution." On one side of Calhoun is an allegorical figure of *Faith*, and, on the other side, of *Hope*. Beyond each of these is the figure of a North American Indian armed with a rifle. In the space formed by the two columns and the arch, is the device on the seal and flag of South Carolina, namely, a Palmetto-tree with a rattlesnake coiled around its trunk, and at its base a park of cannon, and some emblems of the State commerce. On a scroll fluttering from the body of the tree are the words,

and the wise judges of the law. In the midst of deep silence, an old man, with bowed form and hair as white as snow, the Rev. Dr. Bachman, advanced forward with upraised hands, in prayer to Almighty God for His blessing and favor on this great act of His people about to be consummated. The whole assembly at once rose to its feet, and, with hats off, listened to the touching and eloquent appeal to the All-wise Disposer of events."

At the conclusion of the ceremonies, when the signatures had all been affixed by the members, whose names were called in the order of their districts,[1] the President of the Convention (Jamison) stepped forward, exhibited

---

"Southern Republic." Over the whole design, on the segment of a circle, are fifteen stars, the then number of Slave-labor States. Underneath all, in large letters, are the words, BUILT FROM THE RUINS.

This picture, painted for the South Carolina Convention, and under the direction of its leaders, is a remarkable testimony concerning the real intentions of the conspirators at the beginning, which they continually attempted to conceal beneath the mantle of hypocrisy. It was designed and painted before any ordinance of secession had been adopted, or any convention for the purpose had been held in any State excepting South Carolina, and yet it foreshadows their grand plan, well understood by the conspirators in all of the Slave-labor States, *to lay the Republic in ruins, and upon those ruins to construct an empire whose " corner-stone " should be NEGRO LABORERS IN PERPETUAL AND HOPELESS SLAVERY.* It was their intention to cast down and break in pieces the Free-labor States, and build the new structure wholly of Slave-labor States, most of which were known to be, at that time, hostile to the disunion schemes of the South Carolina politicians. The egotism and arrogance of these politicians are most conspicuously shown in making South Carolina not only the key-stone of the arch, with its revered Calhoun as the surmounting figure—in heraldic language, the symbolizing *crest* of the device—but in giving as the prominent feature of the affair the palmetto, snake, &c., which are the chosen insignia of the power of the State. It said plainly to the fifteen Slave-labor States, "South Carolina is to be the head and heart of the new Confederacy ; the Dictator and Umpire." The banner was intended as a menace and a prophecy. How the events of four succeeding years rebuked the arrogant false prophets ! Most of the Slave-labor States were in ruins, and South Carolina, that was to be the key-stone of the new and magnificent structure, was the weakest and most absolutely ruined of all. This banner is now (1865) in the possession of John S. H. Fogg, M. D., of Boston. It was presented by the painter to John F. Kennard, of Charleston, who, after the attack on Fort Sumter, in April, 1861, sent it to Dr. Fogg, by the hands of Mrs. Fogg, who was then visiting in Charleston. I am indebted to Dr. Fogg for a sketch of the banner, kindly made for my use by J. M. Church, of Boston.

[1] The signatures were written in five columns, and in the following order:—

"D. F. JAMISON, Delegate from Barnwell, and President of the Convention.

Thomas Chiles Perrin.	R. G. M. Dunovant.	A. W. Bethea.	John M. Shingler.	R. H. Rutledge.
Edward Noble.	James Parsons Carroll.	E. W. Goodwin.	Daniel Du Pré.	Edward M'Crady.
J. H. Wilson.	William Gregg.	William D. Johnson.	A. Mazyck.	Francis I. Porcher.
Thos. Thomson.	Andrew J. Hammond.	A'ex. M'Leod.	William Cain.	T. L. Gourdin.
David Lewis Wardlaw.	James Tompkins.	John P. Kinard.	P. G. Snowden.	John S. Palmer.
John Alfred Calhoun.	James C. Smyly.	Robert Moorman.	George W. Seabrook.	John L. Nowell.
John Izard Middleton.	John Hugh Means.	Joseph Caldwell.	John Jenkins.	John S. O'Hear.
Benjamin E. Sessions.	William Strother Lyles.	Simon Fair.	R. G. Davant.	John G. Landrum.
J. N. Whitner.	Henry Campbell Davis.	Thomas Worth Glover.	E. M. Seabrook.	B. B. Foster.
James L. Orr.	John Buchanan.	Lawrence M. Keitt.	John J. Wannamaker.	Benjamin F. Kilgore.
J. P. Reed.	James C. Furman.	Donald Rowe Barton.	Elias B. Scott.	James H. Carlisle.
R. S. Simpson.	P. E. Duncan.	William Hunter.	Jos. E. Jenkins.	Simpson Bobo.
Benjamin Franklin Mauldin.	W. K. Easley.	Andrew F. Luis.	Langdon Cheves.	William Curtis.
Lewis Malone Ayer, Jr.	James Harrison.	Rob't A. Thompson.	Georde Rhodes.	H. D. Green.
W. Peronneau Finley.	W. H. Campbell.	William S. Grisham.	A. G. Magrath.	Mathew P. Mayes.
I. I. Brabham.	T. J. Withers.	John Maxwell.	Wm. Porcher Miles.	Thomas Reese English, Sr.
Benjamin W. Lawton.	James Chesnut, Jr.	John E. Frampton.	John Townsend.	Albertus Chambers Spain.
John McKee.	Joseph Brevard Kershaw.	W. Ferguson Hutson.	Robert N. Gourdin.	J. M. Gadberry.
Thomas W. Noon.	Thomas W. Beaty.	W. F. De Saussure.	H. W. Conner.	J. S. Sims.
Richard Woods.	William I. Ellis.	William Hopkins.	Theodore D. Wagner.	Wm. H. Gist.
A. Q. Dunovant.	R. L. Crawford.	James H. Adams.	R. Barnwell Rhett.	James Jefferies.
John A. Inglis.	W. C. Caruthers.	Maxcy Gregg.	C. G. Memminger.	Anthony W. Dozier.
Henry McIver.	D. P. Robinson.	John H. Kinsler.	Gabriel Manigault.	John G. Pressley.
Stephen Jackson.	H. E. Young.	Ephraim M. Clark.	John Julius Pringle Smith.	R. C. Logan.
W. Pinckney Shingler.	H. W. Garlington.	Alex. H. Brown.	Isaac W. Hayne.	Francis S. Parker.
Peter P. Bonneau.	John D. Williams.	E. S. P. Bellinger.	Jn. H. Honour.	Benj. Faneuil Duncan.
John P. Richardson.	W. D. Watts.	Merrick E. Carn.	Richard De Treville.	Sam'l Taylor Atkinson.
John L. Manning.	Thos. Wier.	E. R. Henderson.	Thomas M. Hanckel.	Alex. M. Forster.
John I. Ingram.	H. I. Caughman.	Peter Stokes.	A. W. Burnet.	Wm. Blackburn Wilson.
Edgar W. Charles.	John C. Geiger.	Daniel Find.	Thomas Y. Simons.	Robert T. Allison.
Julius A. Dargan.	Paul Quattlebaum.	David C. Appleby.	Artemas T. Darby.	Samuel Rainey.
Isaac D. Wilson.	W. B. Rowell.	R. W. Barnwell.	L. W. Spratt.	A. Baxter Springs.
John M. Timmons.	Chesley D. Evans.	Jos. Dan'l Pope.	Williams Middleton.	A. L Barron.
Francis Hugh Wardlaw.	Wm. W. Harllee.	C. P. Brown.	F. D. Richardson.	

" Attest, BENJAMIN F. ARTHUR, Clerk of the Convention."

the instrument to the people, read it, and then said, "The Ordinance of Secession has been signed and ratified, and I proclaim the State of South Carolina an Independent Commonwealth." He then handed it to the Secretary of State, to be placed for preservation in the archives of South Carolina, at Columbia. A great shout of exultation went up from the multitude, and at a little after nine o'clock the Convention adjourned until the next day. The audience then despoiled the two Palmetto-trees at the platform of their foliage, every leaf of which was borne away as a memorial of the occasion.

The question immediately arose in the Convention, after the passage of the Ordinance of Secession, "How does this affect the public officers in this State?" It was an important question. There was no precedent on record. All felt that the question must be immediately answered, or there would be chaos. An ordinance was offered which provided for the continuance in office, and the discharge of the duties of their respective stations, of collectors of customs, postmasters, and other officers of the United States Government within the limits of South Carolina, as agents of that State alone, until the Legislature, or other competent body, should provide otherwise. This elicited debate. Judge Magrath wished immediate action, for, to his understanding, there was then no collector of a port or a postmaster in all South Carolina. The authority of every officer in that State, appointed by the National Government, was extinguished by the Ordinance of Secession; and he was for making provisional arrangements for carrying on government in the lone Commonwealth.

Mr. Gregg believed that, with the passage of the Ordinance of Secession, all the laws of Congress, in South Carolina, fell to the ground instantly. "There is now," he said, "no law on the subject of the collection of duties in South Carolina, now that we have *accomplished the work of forty years.*" —"The Congress of the United States is no longer our Government," said Mr. Hayne. "The Legislature," he contended, "was competent to declare "what laws of the United States should be continued, and what not."—"All the revenue and postal laws," repeated Mr. Gregg, "fell to the ground on the passage of the Ordinance of Secession." Mr. Cheves declared, to avoid inconvenience to the people, temporary arrangements must be adopted for carrying on the Government. "An immense chasm," he said, "has been made in law." Mr. Miles said that they must prevent confusion and anarchy in the derangement of governmental affairs, and that "things must for the present remain *in statu quo*, or confusion will arise."

Mr. Mazyck agreed with Cheves and others, that the duties of collectors and postmasters in South Carolina were extinguished. He was favorable to an abandonment of a public postal system altogether, and giving the business into private hands. Mr. Calhoun said, "We have pulled the temple down that has been built for three-quarters of a century. We must now clear the rubbish away, and construct another. We are now houseless and homeless. We must secure ourselves from storms." Chancellor Dunkin said, that the functions of all officers might "go on as before. There is nothing in the ordinance to affect the dignity, honor, or welfare of the State of South Carolina. We must keep the wheels of government in motion." He thought the ordinance had not entirely "abrogated the Constitution of the United

States," and noted the fact, that the gold and silver of the National Government was the legal tender in South Carolina.

And so the argument went on. Barnwell was for sacrificing postal conveniences rather than seem to have any connection with the United States. "There never was any thing purchased," he said, "worth having, unless at the cost of sacrifice." Rhett said:—"This great revolution must go on with as little change as possible," and thought the best plan was to use the United States officers then in place. "By making the Federal agents ours," he said, "the machinery will move on." This was finally the arrangement, substantially.

On the 21st,[a] the Convention appointed Robert W. Barnwell, James H. Adams, and James L. Orr, Commissioners to proceed to Washington, to treat for the possession of the National property within the limits of South Carolina. On the same day, the Committee appointed to prepare an "Address of the people of South Carolina to the people of the Slaveholding States," made a report. It was drawn by the

[a] December, 1860.

SIGNATURES OF THE COMMITTEE ON ADDRESS TO THE SLAVE-LABOR STATES.

chairman, R. B. Rhett, and bore in every sentence indications of the characteristics of that conspirator. It was remarkable for a reckless disregard of truth in its assertions, and its deceptive and often puerile logic. It did not, in a single paragraph, rise above the dignity of a partisan harangue. It professed to review the alleged grievances suffered by South Carolina in the Union, but it actually stated not one that might be perceived by the eye of truth. The fact that her politicians had twice placed her in an attitude of hostility to the National Government, to whose fostering care and protection she was indebted for her prosperity and respectability, was shamelessly and ostentatiously paraded; and it was asserted that the Government of the United States was no longer a "Government of Confederated Republics, but of a consolidated Democracy;" that the Constitution was but an experiment, and as such had failed; that the relations of "the South to the North" were such as were those of the Colonies to Great Britain, at the breaking out of the Revolution; and so on, sentence after sentence of like tenor, at the same time appealing to the self-esteem of the Southern people by saying : " Whilst constituting a portion of the United States, it has been *your* statesmanship which has guided it in its mighty strides to power and expansion. In the field, as in the Cabinet, *you* have led the way to its renown and grandeur." The Address, no doubt, served its intended purpose, namely, to deceive the uninformed, to inflame the public mind in the Slave-labor States, and to hasten the ripening of the rebellion.[1]

More dignified, but not less reckless in sweeping, unsupported assertions, was the " Declaration of the Causes which justify the Secession of South Carolina from the Federal Government," drawn up and reported by Charles G. Memminger, who was afterward the financial agent of the confederated conspirators. After taking a glance at the history of the Union down to the ratification of the National Constitution by the people of South Carolina, he proceeded in his difficult task of searching for grievances inflicted by the National Government upon the people of that State. He was entirely unsuccessful. It was painfully apparent, that a once honest but now corrupt man was trying to deceive himself and others into the belief that a great crime was a commendable virtue. He complained of the refusal of the people of the North to regard with favor the system of slavery in the South, and also of their exercise of the freedom of speech on the subject. He complained of their refusal to believe that a decision of the Supreme Court of the United States can reverse the judgment and decrees of the Almighty, as recognized by the wisest men in all time; and he pointed to the actions of some of the States northward of the Potomac hostile to the Fugitive Slave Law of 1850, as the strongest evidence, among others, of " a sectional combination for the subversion of the Constitution." But in no word in that " Declaration" was the National Government, whose authority and protection he and his followers in crime were defying and discarding, charged with the slightest actual wrong-doing. The debate which this " Declaration" elicited, revealed quite a diversity of opinion concerning the real cause of, or the real pretext for, secession. In that debate, several members made the statements quoted on page 69 of this volume.

Memminger's manifesto, which was concluded with a ludicrous appropriation of the closing words of the great Declaration of Independence by the Fathers, in 1776, viewed in the light of truth and soberness, appears in itself a solemn protest against the wicked actions of the conspirators at that time, and ever afterward. It also presents a fair specimen of that counter-

---

[1] " South Carolina desires no destiny separate from yours," said the Address, in conclusion. " To be one of a great SLAVEHOLDING CONFEDERACY—stretching its arms over territory larger than any power in Europe possesses—with a population four times greater than that of the whole United States when they achieved their independence of the British Empire—with productions which make our existence more important to the world than that of any other people inhabiting it—with common institutions to defend, and common dangers to encounter, we ask your sympathy and confederation. . . . All we demand of other people is to be let alone to work out our own high destinies. United together, and we must be the most independent, as we are the most important, among the nations of the world. United together, and we require no other instrument to conquer peace than our beneficent productions. United together, and we must be a great, free, and prosperous people, *whose renown must spread throughout the civilized world, and pass down, we trust, to the remotest ages. We ask you to join us in forming a Confederacy of Slaveholding States.*"

feit statesmanship which for years was palmed off on the confiding people of the Slave-labor States as genuine.[1]

On the same day when the "Declaration" was adopted, Governor Pickens issued a proclamation declaring to the world that "South Carolina is, and has a right to be, a separate, sovereign, free, and independent State, and, as such, has a right to levy war, to conclude peace, to negotiate treaties, leagues, or covenants, and to do all acts whatever that rightfully appertain to a free and independent State." He declared the proclamation to be given under his hand, on the 24th of December, 1860, "and in the eighty-fifth year of the sovereignty and independence of South Carolina."[2]

SOUTH CAROLINA MEDAL.

With perfect consistency, the Charleston papers now published intelligence from all the other States of the Union as "Foreign News." In various ways, the world was given to understand that South Carolina was a first-class Power among the nations of the earth, whose smiles would be blessings, but whose frowns would be calamitous; and a small medal was struck in commemoration of the great act of separation, which was adorned with appropriate devices and inscriptions.[3]

On the day when the Ordinance of Secession was passed, the Convention adopted a banner for the new empire. It was composed of red and blue silk, the former being the ground of the standard, and the latter, in the form of a cross, bearing fifteen stars. The largest star was for South Carolina. On the red field were a silver Palmetto and Crescent.[4] The introduction of the Crescent

[1] The *Augusta* (Georgia) *Chronicle and Sentinel*, a leading newspaper in the South, said, twelve days after the Ordinance of Secession was passed in the South Carolina Convention:—"It is a sad thing to observe, that those who are determined on immediate secession have not the coolness, the capacity, or the nerve, to propose something after that. . . . No statesmanship has ever been exhibited yet, so far as we know, by those who will dissolve the Union."—*January* 1, 1861.

[2] The London *Morning Star*, commenting on this declaration of the "Sovereignty" of South Carolina, said:— "A nationality! Was there ever, since the world began, a nation constituted of such materials—a commonwealth founded on such bases? The greatest empire of antiquity is said to have grown up from a group of huts, built in a convenient location by fugitive slaves and robber huntsmen. But history nowhere chronicles the establishment of a community of slaveholders solely upon the alleged right of maintaining and enlarging their property in man. Paganism at least protected the Old World from so monstrous a scandal upon free commonwealths, by shutting out the idea of a common humanity, and of individual rights derivable from inalienable duties. . . . They are not content to be left in undisturbed possession of the human beings they have, bought or bred. They demand that the law and government of a confederacy embracing States twice as populous as their own shall consecrate slavery forever; that in none of these States shall there be any hiding-place for the fugitive; nay, no platform on which the abstract rights of the slave may be asserted. It is not on account of abolition that they separate from the Union, but of Abolitionism. In the vulgar but expressive phraseology invented by themselves, they not only claim the right to 'wallop their own niggers,' but that all their neighbors shall for them turn slave-catchers and scourgers. They would make the vast territory of the Union one great slave-field, and put in the hand of every freeman a fetter and a whip for himself as well as for the negro. Such audacity of folly and wickedness revolts the common sense of mankind. For the sake of interests dear to all humanity, we pray the Northern States to let these madmen go, rather than restrain or chastise them with the sword. But the burlesquers of the grand drama of American independence excite only scorn, and their blasphemous appeals to Divine and human sympathy can bring down only the rebuke of universal hatred and contempt."

[3] The engraving is the exact size of the medal. On one side is a Palmetto-tree; a group of barrels and bales of cotton; a cannon and heap of balls; the date 1860; a radiation of light from behind the Palmetto and its accompaniments, and fifteen stars, with the words, "NO SUBMISSION TO THE NORTH." On the other side is a group of Southern productions of the earth, and over and around them the words, "THE WEALTH OF THE SOUTH —RICE, TOBACCO, SUGAR, AND COTTON."

[4] The *Crescent* was placed in the South Carolina flag in 1775, under the following circumstances:—The Provincial Council had taken measures to fortify Charleston, after the Royal Governor was driven away. "As there

or New Moon on the standard was considered even by thinking South Carolinians, as singularly appropriate, for those who there inaugurated the rebellion  were certainly afflicted with *lunacy*, "a species of insanity or madness," says the lexicon, "which is broken by intervals of reason, formerly supposed to be influenced by the changes of the *Moon*." It is related of the late Judge Pettigru, of Charleston, who resisted the madness of the secessionists while he lived, that on being asked by a stranger in the streets of his city the right direction to the Lunatic Asylum, he pointed to the east, the west, the north, and the south, and said, "It is there, and there, and there, and there—

BANNER OF SOUTH CAROLINA.   the whole State is a lunatic asylum."

On the 26th, the Convention agreed to send a commissioner to each Slave-labor State that might hold a convention, to bear to them a copy of the South Carolina Ordinance of Secession;[1] to ask their co-operation; to propose the National Constitution just abandoned as a basis for a provisional government; and to invite the seceding States to meet South Carolina in convention at Montgomery, Alabama, on the 13th of February, 1861, for the purpose of forming a Southern Confederacy. They also made provision[a] for continuing commercial operations, by using the United States officers and revenue laws, but changing the style of all papers to the name of "South Carolina," and ordering all duties to be paid into the State treasury. On the following day, the Governor was authorized to receive embassadors, ministers, consuls, &c., from foreign countries, and to appoint the same officers to represent South Carolina abroad. It was also decreed, that all citizens of the United States who were living within the limits of South Carolina at the time of the passage of the Ordinance of Secession should be considered citizens of the new "nation."

* December 26, 1860.

On the 29th, the Convention, which assumed supreme dignity in the State, transferred to the Legislature the powers lately vested in Congress, excepting during the session of the Convention. The judicial powers of the United States were vested in the State Courts; and Governor Pickens, who had organized his cabinet, assumed the exalted position of the Chief Magistrate of an independent nation. His constitutional advisers consisted of A. G. Magrath, Secretary of State; D. F. Jamison, Secretary of War; C. G. Memminger, Secretary of the Treasury; W. W. Harllee, Postmaster-General; and A. C. Garlington, Secretary of the Interior. After making provision for

---

was no national flag at the time," says General Moultrie, in his Memoirs, "I was desired by the Council of Safety to have one made, upon which, as the State troops were clothed in blue, and the fort [Johnson, on James Island] was garrisoned by the First and Second Regiments, who wore a silver crescent on the front of their caps, I had a large blue flag made, with a crescent in the dexter corner, to be in uniform with the troops. This was the first American flag displayed in the South." See Lossing's *Pictorial Field-book of the Revolution,* ii. 545.

[1] When this question was before the Convention, a member (Mr. Dargan) proposed to send a copy of the ordinance, with the "Declaration of Causes, &c.," to all the States of the Union; and, when it was objected to, he said that a statement of reasons is required, as well as the ordinance. "Courtesy to our late Confederates," he said, "whether enemies or not, calls for the reasons that have actuated us. It is not true, in point of fact, that *all* the Northern people are hostile to the rights of the South. *We have a Spartan band in every Northern State.* It is due to them that they should know the reasons which influence us." The proposition was not agreed to.

The following are the names of the Commissioners appointed to visit other Slave-labor States:—To

military operations, and transacting some other business, chiefly in secret session, the Convention adjourned, on the 5th of January, 1861, subject to the call of the President. They had ordered the table, President's chair, inkstand, and other things used at the ceremony of signing the Ordinance of Secession, to be placed in the State House at Columbia, for preservation.

The Legislature of South Carolina, which had been in session during the sitting of the Convention, but almost idle, now took measures for putting the State in a strongly defensive attitude. A loan of four hundred thousand dollars was authorized, which was immediately taken by the banks of the State, they having been permitted, by legislative decree, to suspend specie payments.[1] A call for volunteers was made, and also provisions for a draft, if it should be necessary. Little else was done during the session but preparations for making the revolutionary movement a success.

Thus the South Carolina politicians rebelled, and prepared to resist the authority of their Government by force of arms. When intelligence of the passage of their Ordinance of Secession went over the country, it produced, as we have observed, a profound sensation. That action was greeted with delight by disunionists in most of the Slave-labor States. A hundred guns were fired both at Montgomery and Mobile, by order of the Governor (Moore) of Alabama, in honor of the event. In the latter city there was also a military parade. Bells were rung and oratory was heard. At Macon, Georgia, bells rang, bonfires blazed, cannon thundered, processions moved, and the main street of the city was illuminated. A hundred guns were fired at Pensacola. The same number were discharged in New Orleans, where the Pelican flag[2] was unfurled, speeches were made to the populace, and no other airs were played in the streets but polkas and the Marseillaise Hymn. At Wilmington, in North Carolina, one hundred guns were fired. In Portsmouth, Virginia, fifteen were fired, being the then number of the Slave-labor States; and at Norfolk, the Palmetto flag was outspread from the top of a pole a hundred feet in hight. A banner with the same device was displayed over the custom-house at Richmond. An attempt was made to fire fifteen guns in Baltimore, when the loyal people there prevented it. On the 22d, a jubilant meeting at Memphis, Tennessee, "ratified" the ordinance. Fifteen guns were fired, and the office of the *Avalanche*, then an organ of the conspirators in that region, was illuminated. At the same time, the politicians of several of the Slave-labor States, as we shall observe presently, were rapidly placing the people in the position of active co-operation with those of South Carolina. Those who did not choose to follow the lead of South Carolina were treated with amazing insolence by the usurpers in that State, and were scorned as unworthy of association with the Palmetto Chivalry.

The news was received with far different feelings in the Free-labor States,

---

Alabama, A. P. Calhoun; to Georgia, James L. Orr; to Florida, L. W. Spratt; to Mississippi, M. L. Bonham; to Louisiana, J. L. Manning; to Arkansas, A. C. Spain; to Texas, J. B. Kershaw; to Virginia, John S. Preston.

[1] According to the returns made to the Controller-general of South Carolina, for the month of December, 1860, the number of banks in that State was only twenty, with an aggregate capital of about fifteen millions of dollars, and a circulation of about seven millions of dollars. They had only one million three hundred and fifty-five thousand dollars in specie.

[2] On the great seal of Louisiana is the device of a Pelican, hovering over a nest of young ones in the attitude of protectron, at the same time feeding them. The same device was on the Louisiana flag. It was designed to symbolize the parental care of the National Government, and it appeared out of place in the hands of men banded to destroy that government.

where reason and not passion ruled the people. The leaders of the Breckin-ridge Democrats,[1] who were more intimately affiliated, as partisans, with the politicians in the Slave-labor States than others, were eager to suppress all discussion of the Slavery question at the North, and were willing to give Slavery free scope by the repeal of all Personal Liberty Laws, the rigid execu-tion of the Fugitive Slave Act, and an amendment of the Constitution, so as to secure the right of property in slaves everywhere. The Douglas Democrats[2] adhered to the doctrine of Popular Sovereignty, but were willing to make liberal concessions to the Slave interest by the repeal of Personal Liberty laws and the rigid execution of the Fugitive Slave Act. The Republicans[3] adhered to their opposition to Slavery, yet favored conciliatory measures, as shadowed by one of their chief leaders;[4] while a few corrupt politicians, whose love of party and its honors and emoluments was far greater than love of country, openly defended the course of the traitors, and advocated seces-sion as not only a constitutional right, but as expedient. But while there was a general desire to conciliate the madmen of the South, the great mass of the people in the Free-labor States, comprising the bulk of all parties, were firmly attached to the Union, and resolutely determined to maintain the National integrity at all hazards. Union meetings were held, and Union sentiments were expressed with a vehemence and power which alarmed the more discreet leaders in the South.

The men of the North had watched the rising rebellion, first with incre-dulity and then with amazement; but when it assumed tangible form and substance—when it became a reality, aggressive and implacable—they prepared to meet it with calmness and firmness. They deprecated all inflam-matory proceedings like the commemoration, in Boston, of the a December 3. execution of John Brown,[a][5] and were anxious to be exactly just toward their brethren in the Slave-labor States: yet they were ready and willing to oppose force to force, morally and physically, when the insurgents should attack the bulwarks of the Republic.

The conservative influence of commerce and manufactures was a power-ful restraint upon the passions of the indignant people of the North, when they perceived the utter faithlessness of the Southern leaders, not only in their political, but in their business relations. The South was an immense debtor to the North for merchandise purchased on long credits,[6] and it was very soon apparent, from the recommendations of the leaders in the Slave-labor States, that a scheme was on foot for the repudiation of all debts due to merchants and manufacturers in the Free-labor States. So early as the day of the Presidential election, it was evident to sagacious men that a

---

[1] See page 33.   [2] See page 33.   [3] See page 33.

[4] In a speech at Auburn, New York (his home), on the 20th of November, 1860, Mr. Seward counseled moderation and conciliation. He begged them to be patient and kind toward their erring brethren. "We are all fellow-citizens, Americans, brethren," he said. "It is a trial of issues by the forces only of reason."

[5] Quite a number of citizens of Boston, and some from other places, assembled in Tremont Temple, in that city, on the 3d of December, 1860, to celebrate the anniversary of the execution of John Brown, in Virginia, the year before. A larger number of inhabitants, led by a man named Fay, also assembled there, took posses-sion of the Temple, organized a meeting, denounced the acts of John Brown as "bloody and tyrannical," and his sympathizers as disturbers of the public peace; and then, according to a published account, expelled from the hall "the Abolitionists and negroes by sheer force."

[6] More than two hundred millions of dollars were due to the Northern merchants and manufacturers by Southerners.

monetary crisis was impending, and then commenced business restrictions and the withdrawal of capital from investment. Manufacturers and importers became anxious to get rid of their stocks on hand, and the markets, in commercial centers, were soon crowded.

By the middle of November, remittances from the South had almost entirely ceased, partly on account of the dishonesty of a large class who had resolved not to pay, partly because of the absolute inability of others to do so, and partly because of the high rates of exchange on the Northern commercial cities and the depreciation of Southern bank-notes, the Legislatures of several States having authorized the banks to suspend specie payments. The consequence was the subjection of large business houses, and, indeed, whole communities in the North, to great financial straits. Added to this was the sad condition of the National exchequer, and consequent distrust of Government paper. Howell Cobb, the treacherous Secretary of the Treasury, who found the coffers of the Government so overflowing when they came into his custody, in 1857, that the treasury notes next due were bought in, had so adroitly managed his scheme for the paralysis of this strong arm of the Republic, for the benefit of the conspirators, that it was empty in the summer of 1860; and in the autumn of that year he was in the market as a borrower of money to carry on the ordinary operations of the Government and to pay the interest on its loans. His management had created such distrust in financial circles, that he was compelled to pay ruinous premiums at a time when money was never more abundant in the country. Even bids on this loan were not all paid in; and early in December he left the treasury greatly embarrassed, to the delight of his fellow-conspirators.

The cereal crop of the West had filled the granaries to repletion, and operators were pushing heavy quantities to the sea-board cities for exportation; while the cotton-growers, anticipating great trouble ahead, were in equal haste to press the heavy crop of their staple on the market.[1] But capital had hidden in fear of danger, and could not be found to assist in the movement of these materials of national wealth. Doubt and uncertainty everywhere prevailed, and a desolating panic seemed inevitable.

Fortunately for the Republic and the cause of free government, the country was never really so rich as at that moment. Never were the people generally in such easy circumstances. The banks in the North were in a very healthy condition. The exports had greatly exceeded the imports. The exportation of cotton and grain had been very large, and the tide of trade and exchange was running so heavily in our favor toward the close of November, that coin soon came flowing into the country from Europe in immense volume. The pressure on the market, in the mean time, of unsalable foreign exchange, was so great, and the wants of commission merchants had become so pressing, that the banks of New York City, to give relief, purchased two millions five hundred thousand dollars of foreign exchange, upon which gold might be realized in thirty days. They also resolved upon a liberal line of discounts, by a consolidated fund arrangement with the Clearing-house, and thus they set loose ten millions of dollars, and saved many first-class mercantile houses from failure. General John A. Dix, of New York, soon afterward[a] succeeded Cobb as Secretary of the Treasury, and confidence in its management and soundness was restored. The portentous clouds of a commercial panic were dispersing when South Carolinians declared the Union to be dissolved, and there was an equipoise in the mind of the people of the Free-labor States, in view of their financial condition, which made them strong and hopeful.

[a] January 11, 1861.

While, as we have observed, all, and especially heavy merchants and manufacturers, deprecated national disturbance, and were willing to make costly sacrifices for the sake of peace and quiet, there were seen in the North great calmness, firmness, and steadiness among the masses of the people, which indicated confidence in their material and moral strength, and a consciousness of having done no wrong to the constituents of their turbulent maligners, the politicians of the South. They were sensible of the existence of sufficient virtue to save the Republic, and they resolved to plant their feet firmly on the Constitution, and fight manfully against the banded enemies of our nationality.

The people, after the opening of Congress, had no hope of aid in the impending struggle from the Chief Magistrate of the nation, then sitting in the chair of Washington and Jackson; but their hearts were amazingly strengthened by the oracular utterances of the accredited organ of the President elect, when it said:—"If South Carolina does not obstruct the collection of the revenues at her ports, nor violate another Federal law, there will be no trouble, and she will not be out of the Union. If she violates the law, then comes the tug of war. The President of the United States, in such an emergency, has a plain duty to perform. Mr. Buchanan may shirk it, or the emergency may not exist during his administration. If not, then the Union will last through his term of office. If the overt act, on the part of South Carolina, takes place on or after the 4th day of March, 1861, then the duty of executing the laws will devolve upon Mr. Lincoln."[1]

---

[1] The *Journal*, published at Springfield, Illinois, the home of the President elect.

CHAPTER V.

EVENTS IN CHARLESTON AND CHARLESTON HARBOR IN DECEMBER, 1860. — THE
CONSPIRATORS ENCOURAGED BY THE GOVERNMENT POLICY.

VENTS that occurred in the harbor of Charleston during the latter part of December, 1860, were quite as exciting as those in the city of Charleston. There are four military works there belonging to the National Government, namely, Castle Pinckney, Fort Moultrie, Fort Sumter, and Fort Johnson.

Castle Pinckney is situated upon the southern extremity of marshy land known as Shute's Folly Island, and is near the city. It presents a circular front on the harbor side, as seen in the engraving. It is not strong, and was never considered very valuable as a defensive work. At the time in question it had about fifteen guns mounted *en barbette*, or on the parapet; and some columbiads, and a small supply of powder, shot, and shell, was within its walls, but no garrison to use them.

CASTLE PINCKNEY.

Fort Moultrie is on Sullivan's Island, between three and four miles from Charleston, near the site of the famous little palmetto-log fort of that name, which defied the British fleet in 1776. At the time we are considering, it was in reality only a large inclosed water-battery, constructed with an outer and inner wall of brick, capped with stone, and filled between with sand, and presenting a solid mass about sixteen feet in thickness. It was built with salient and re-entering angles on all sides, having a front on the southeast, or water side, of about three hundred feet, and a mean depth of about two hundred and forty feet. During the autumn, about one hundred and seventy men had been employed by the post com-

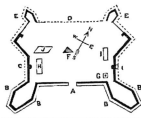

PLAN OF FORT MOULTRIE IN DECEMBER, 1860.[1]

---

[1] *Explanation of the Diagram.*—A, gate and draw-bridge; B, B, B, B, abutments commanding the gate and approaches; C, C, old sally-ports; D, moat; E, E, bastionettes commanding moat; F, furnace for heating shot; G, powder-magazine; H, barracks; I, officers' quarters; J, kitchen, storehouses, &c.

mander, Colonel John L. Gardner, of the First Regiment of Artillery, in repairing, making additions, and generally strengthening the fort. It was the only one of the four that was garrisoned.

SOUTH VIEW OF FORT MOULTRIE.

Fort Sumter, then the largest and by far the best of the strongholds, stands in the middle of the entrance to Charleston Harbor proper, on the southwestern edge of the ship-channel, and nearly three and a half miles from the city. It was a work of solid brick and concrete masonry, a truncated pentagonal in form, and built upon an artificial island resting on a mud-bank. The island was constructed of chips from New England granite-quarries,

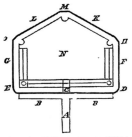

PLAN OF FORT SUMTER IN 1860.[1]

carried there during a period of ten consecutive years, at the cost of half a million of dollars. The fort itself cost another half million. The walls were sixty feet in hight, and from eight to twelve feet in thickness, the weakest part being on the south or Morris Island side. It was pierced for three tiers of guns on the north, east, and west sides. The two lower tiers were under bomb-proof casemates. The first was designed for 42-pounder Paixhans, and the second for 8 and 10-inch Columbiads. The third tier was open, so that the ordnance, to consist of mortars and 24-pounder guns, would be *en barbette*, or nearly so, there being embrasures. Its complement of heavy guns was one hundred and forty, but only seventy-five were now in the work. For some time a large number of men had been employed in mounting ordnance there, and otherwise putting the fort in order for defense, yet there was no regular garrison to man it.

Fort Johnson, on James Island, directly West from Fort Sumter, was of but little account then as a fortification. It was a relic of the old war for Independence.

In October, 1860, Colonel Gardner was removed from the command in Charleston Harbor, by Floyd, for attempting to increase his supply of ammunition,[2] and Major Robert Anderson, a native of Kentucky, and a meritorious officer in the war with Mexico, was appointed to succeed him in November. He arrived there on the 20th, and assumed the command. He was convinced, from the tone of conversation and feeling in Charleston, and the military drills continually going on there, with other preparations of like nature, that the conspirators had resolved to inaugurate a revolution. "That there is a settled determination," he said, in a letter to Adjutant-General Cooper, on the 23d of November, "to leave the Union and to obtain possession of this

---

[1] *Explanation of the Diagram.*—*A*, wharf; *B, B*, esplanade; *C*, sally-port; *D*, right gorge angle; *E*, left gorge angle; *F*, right flank; *G*, left flank; *H*, right shoulder angle; *I*, left shoulder angle; *K*, right face; *L*, left face; *M*, salient; *N*, parade.

[2] *History of the War for the Preservation of the Union:* by Lorenzo H. Whiting, i. 145.

work [Moultrie], is apparent to all." In that letter, which subsequent events converted into a most important historical document, he announced to the Government the weakness of the forts in Charleston harbor, and urged it to take immediate and effective measures for strengthening them. He told the Secretary of War that Fort Moultrie was so weak as to invite an attack, then openly threatened, for the garrison was only between fifty and sixty in number, and had a line of ramparts to defend, fifteen hundred feet in length. "Fort Sumter and Castle Pinckney," he said, "must be garrisoned immediately, if the Government determines to keep command of this harbor." Sumter, he said, was supplied with forty thousand pounds of cannon-powder and ammunition sufficient for one tier of guns, but was lying at the mercy of insurgents. Should they take pos-

session of it, its guns would command Fort Moultrie, and soon drive out its occupants. Sumter was the key to the harbor; and Castle Pinckney was so near the city, and utterly undefended, that the Charlestonians considered it already in their possession. He informed the Government that two heavy mortars had been taken to the Arsenal in Charleston, several months before, with the professed design of having them repaired, but they had never been returned; and that Captain Foster had actually been requested, by the adjutant of a South Carolina regiment, to show him the roll of his workmen on the fort, that

ROBERT ANDERSON.

they might be enrolled by the State authorities for military duty, as they were organizing and drilling men in Charleston and elsewhere.

"The clouds are threatening," wrote the patriotic Anderson, "and the storm may burst upon us at any moment. I need not say to you how anxious I am, indeed determined, as far as honor will permit, to avoid collision with the citizens of South Carolina. Nothing will, however, be better calculated to prevent bloodshed, than our being found in such an attitude that it would be madness and folly to attack us. I do, then," he repeated, "most earnestly entreat that a re-enforcement be immediately sent to this garrison, and that at least two companies be sent to Fort Sumter and Castle Pinckney; half a company, under a judicious commander, sufficing, I think, for the latter work. I feel the full responsibility of making the above suggestions, because I firmly believe that, as soon as the people of South Carolina learn that I have demanded re-enforcements, and that they have been ordered, they will occupy Castle Pinckney and attack this fort." If these precautionary measures should be taken, he said, "I shall feel that, by the blessing of God, there may be a hope that no blood will be shed, and that South Carolina will attempt to obtain possession of the forts in the harbor by diplomacy, and not by arms. If we neglect, however, to strengthen ourselves, she will, unless these works are surrendered on her first demand, most assuredly attack them immediately. I will thank the Department to give me special instructions, as my position here is rather politico-military than a military one. . . . Unless otherwise directed, I shall make future communications through the regular channels;"[1] that is, through Lieutenant-General Scott, the general-in-chief.

Major Anderson did not suspect, that in addressing the chief of the War Department of his Government through the Adjutant-General, he was assailing ears deafened to such patriotic appeals by rank treason, and that he was laying before confederates of South Carolina politicians information of the weakness of national forts, that would give them pleasure rather than pain. Yet it was so. Adjutant-General Samuel Cooper, a native of the State of

 New York, had married a sister of Senator Mason, one of the arch-conspirators of Virginia, and was doubtless fully informed of the plans of the public enemies; for on the 3d of March, 1861, a little more than three months later, he left his office at Washington, hastened to Montgomery, Alabama, the head-quarters of the confederated conspirators, and was by them made adjutant-general of the insurgent forces, then preparing for the revolt. John B. Floyd, the Secretary of War, was, at the very time we are considering, stripping the arsenals of the North of guns and ammunition, and transferring them to the South, for the use

SAMUEL COOPER.

of the conspirators. Let us look at the testimony of official records on this point.

From the beginning of the session, there was evident alarm among the conspirators in Congress whenever there was any intimation that official inquiry would be made concerning the condition of forts and arsenals in the Slave-labor States. When, on the 20th of December, Mr. Clark, of New Hampshire, called up a resolution he had offered in the Senate, asking the President for information concerning the condition of the forts and arsenals at Charleston, and their relation to the National Government and citizens of South Carolina, and for the official correspondence on the subject, Hunter and Mason of Virginia, Davis of Mississippi, Saulsbury of Delaware, and others, vehemently opposed it, on the pretext that such action would tend to increase the excitement in the public mind. On that occasion, Davis made a peculiar exhibition of his dishonesty and flimsy sophistry. He said such an inquiry would inflame the public mind, and result in an "irreparable injury to the public peace and future hopes of those who look forward to an amicable solution of existing difficulties." He (the President) had no power to increase the garrison at Fort Moultrie, and, if he had, the act would be unwise. He had heard that the troops in Fort Moultrie were hostile to the city of Charleston. If so, they ought to be removed. He hoped there would be no collision. He hoped the troops would simply hold the fort until peaceably transferred to other duty; "but if there is danger," he said, "permit me here to say that it is because there are troops in it, not because the garrison is too weak. Who hears of any danger of the seizure of forts where there is no garrison?

---

[1] Major Anderson's MS. Letter-book.

There stand Forts Pulaski and Jackson, at the mouth of the Savannah River. Who hears of any apprehension lest Georgia should seize them? There are Castle Pinckney and Fort Sumter in Charleston harbor. Who hears of any danger to them? The whole danger then, Mr. President, arises from the presence of United States troops." Such was the lullaby with which this arch-conspirator attempted to quiet the just suspicions of the people, that all the public property in the Slave-labor States was in danger of seizure by disloyal men. There is ample proof that at that very time Davis and his confederates had planned the seizure of all the forts and arsenals in those States.

On the 31st of December, Mr. Wilson, of Massachusetts, offered a resolution in the Senate, asking the Secretary of War to give to that body information concerning the disposition of arms manufactured in the national armories or purchased for the use of the Government during the past year. A loyal man (Mr. Holt) was now at the head of the War Department, and correct information was looked for.

Finally, a report of the Committee on Military Affairs, of the House of Representatives, revealed some startling facts. According to that report, so early as the 29th of December, 1859, Secretary Floyd had ordered the transfer of sixty-five thousand percussion muskets, forty thousand muskets altered to percussion, and ten thousand percussion rifles, from the armory at Springfield in Massachusetts, and the arsenals at Watervliet in New York, and Watertown in Massachusetts, to the arsenals at Fayetteville in North Carolina, Charleston in South Carolina, Augusta in Georgia, Mount Vernon in Alabama, and Baton Rouge in Louisiana; and these were distributed during the spring of 1860.[1]

Eleven days after the issuance of the above order by Floyd, Jefferson Davis introduced[a] into the National Senate a bill "to authorize the sale of public arms to the several States and Territories, and to regulate the appointment of Superintendents of the National Armories." This proposition appeared, to the common observer, to be a very harmless affair. Davis reported it from the Military Committee of the Senate without amendment,[b] and called it up on the 21st of February, saying, in the blandest manner, "I should like the Senate to take up a little bill which *I hope will excite no discussion.* It is the bill to authorize the States to purchase arms from the national armories. *There are a number of volunteer companies wanting to purchase arms,* but the States have not a sufficient supply." There were vigilant men who thought they discovered a treacherous cat under this heap of innocent meal; and, on the 23d of February, when the bill was the special order for the day, Senator Fessenden, of Maine, asked for an explanation of

[a] January 9, 1860.

[b] January 18.

---

[1] The distribution was as follows:—

	PERCUSSION MUSKETS.	ALTERED MUSKETS.	RIFLES.
To Charleston Arsenal	9,280	5,720	2,000
To Fayetteville Arsenal	15,480	9,520	2,000
To Augusta Arsenal	12,380	7,620	2,000
To Mount Vernon Arsenal	9,280	5,720	2,000
To Baton Rouge Arsenal	18,580	11,420	2,000
Totals	65,000	40,000	10,000

the reasons for such action. Davis said that the Secretary of War had recommended an increase of the appropriation for arming the militia of the country, and he thought it best for volunteers to have arms made by the Government, so that, in case of war, the weapons would all be uniform. Fessenden offered an amendment, that would deprive the bill of its power to do mischief, but it was lost. The bill was *a* March 26, 1860. finally adopted by the Senate,[a] by a strict party vote, twenty-nine supporters of the Administration voting in the affirmative, and eighteen of the opposition voting in the negative. During the debate, Davis took the high State Supremacy ground, that the *militia of the States were not a part of the militia of the United States.* The bill was smothered in the House of Representatives.

The conspirators were not to be foiled. By a stretch of authority given in the law of March 3, 1825, authorizing the Secretary of War to sell arms, ammunition, and other military stores, which should be found unsuitable for the public service, Floyd sold to States and individuals over thirty-one thousand muskets, altered from flint to percussion, for two dollars and fifty cents each.[1] On the very day when Major Anderson dispatched his *b* November 24. letter above cited to the Adjutant-General,[b] Floyd sold ten thousand of these muskets to G. B. Lamar, of Georgia; and only eight days before,[c] he sold five thousand of them to the State of Vir- *c* November 16. ginia. With a knowledge of these facts, the *Mobile Advertiser*, one of the principal organs of the conspirators in Alabama, said, exultingly:— "During the past year, one hundred and thirty-five thousand four hundred and thirty muskets have been quietly transferred from the Northern arsenal at Springfield alone to those in the Southern States. We are much obliged to Secretary Floyd for the foresight he has thus displayed, *in disarming the North and equipping the South for this emergency.*[2] There is no telling the quantity of arms and munitions which were sent South from other arsenals. There is no doubt but that every man in the South who can carry a gun can now be supplied from private or public sources. The Springfield contribution alone would arm all the militia-men of Alabama and Mississippi." A Virginia historian of the war makes a similar boast, and says:—"Adding to these the number of arms distributed by the Federal Government to the States in preceding years of our history, and those purchased by the States and citizens, it was safely estimated that the South entered upon the war with one hundred and fifty thousand small arms of the most approved modern pattern, and the best in the world."[3] General Scott afterward asserted[4] that "Rhode Island,

---

[1] The Committee on Military Affairs of the House of Representatives, in their report on this subject, on the 18th of February, 1861, said that, in their judgment, it would require "a very liberal construction of the law to bring these sales within its provisions."

[2] Ex-President Buchanan generously assumed, in a degree, the responsibility of these acts. In a letter to the *National Intelligencer*, dated, "Wheatland, near Lancaster, October 28, 1862," in reply to some statements of General Scott, in relation to the refusal to re-enforce the forts on the Southern coast, according to his recommendation, in the autumn of 1860, Mr. Buchanan said:—"This refusal is attributed, without the least cause, to the influence of Governor Floyd. All my Cabinet must bear me witness that I was President myself, responsible for all the acts of the Administration; and certain it is, that during the last six months previous to the 29th of December, 1860, the day on which he resigned his office, after my request, he exercised less influence on the Administration than any other member of the Cabinet."

[3] *The First Year of the War:* by Edward A. Pollard, page 67. Pollard was in public employment at Washington during Buchanan's Administration, and was in the secret councils of the conspirators.

[4] Letter on the early history of the rebellion, December 2, 1862.

Delaware, and Texas had not drawn, at the close of 1860, their annual quotas of arms, and Massachusetts, Tennessee, and Kentucky only in part; while Virginia, South Carolina, Georgia, Florida, Alabama, Louisiana, Mississippi, and Kansas were, *by order of the Secretary of War, supplied with their quotas for* 1861 *in advance*, and Pennsylvania and Maryland in part." This advance of arms to the eight Southern States was in addition to the transfer, at about the same time, of one hundred and fifteen thousand muskets to Southern arsenals by the same Secretary of War.

RODMAN COLUMBIAD.

Not content with thus supplying the Slave-labor States with small arms, that traitorous minister attempted to give them heavy guns only a few days before he left his office. On the 20th of December, he ordered forty columbiads[1] and four 32-pounders to be sent immediately from the arsenal at Pittsburg, Pennsylvania, to the unfinished fort on Ship Island, off the coast of Mississippi; and seventy-one columbiads and seven 32-pounders to be sent from the same arsenal to the embryo fort at Galveston, which would not be ready for its armament in less than five years. This bold attempt of the conspirator to furnish the enemies of the Government with heavy ordnance was frustrated by the vigilance and prompt action of the people of Pittsburg. When the fact became known that Quartermaster Taliaferro (a Virginian) was about to send these guns from the arsenal, an immense meeting of the citizens, called by the Mayor, was held, and the guns were retained. The conspirators, in Congress and out of it, denounced this exhibition of "mob law" bitterly. Floyd soon afterward fled to Virginia, and his successor, Joseph Holt, countermanded the order.

It was to that faithless minister (Floyd) and his plastic implement of treason, Adjutant-General Cooper, that Major Anderson addressed his earnest letter, pleading for power to protect the property of the Republic in Charleston harbor, and to preserve the integrity of the nation. The reply was precisely as might be expected from such men. It was contained in less than a dozen lines, by which permission was given him to send a few workmen to repair Castle Pinckney; and he was instructed that when, thereafter, he had any communication to make for the information of the Department, it must be addressed to the Adjutant-General's office, or to the Secretary of War.[2] They discovered in Anderson too true a patriot for their use, and they were

---

[1] A columbiad is an American cannon, of very large caliber, invented by Colonel George Bomford, of New York, who was in the Ordnance Department in the War of 1812. These guns were used in that war, chiefly as bomb-cannon. They were introduced into the French service, with slight modifications, by General Paixhan, and are known as Paixhan guns. Those of the old pattern were chambered, but they are now cast without, and are otherwise greatly improved. The 10-inch columbiad weighs fifteen thousand four hundred pounds, and is one hundred and twenty-six inches in length. The immense columbiad of 15-inch caliber, represented in the engraving, and of which more will be said hereafter, was invented by Captain T. J. Rodman, of the Ordnance Corps. These, unlike most other cannon, are cast hollow. The original inventor of the Columbiad (Bomford) died in Boston, in the spring of 1848.

[2] Anderson's MS. Letter-book.

unwilling to have his earnest pleading go to the ears of General Scott, to whom it was the duty of all subordinate officers to report.

Notwithstanding the apathy, as it seemed, at Washington, and the assurances sent from there that there was no danger, so long as he acted prudently, Major Anderson continued to urge the necessity of re-enforcements. He was convinced that every able-bodied man in South Carolina would be called into the military service of the State, if necessary, for the seizure of the forts. He knew that there were nightly military drills in Charleston; and he was positively assured that the South Carolinians regarded the forts as their property. He saw whole columns of the Charleston journals made pictorial by the insignias of various military companies attached to orders for

WASHINGTON LIGHT INFANTRY.

meetings, day after day, such as the "Washington Light Artillery," the "Palmetto Guard," the "Carolina Light Infantry," the "Moultrie Guards," the "Marion Artillery," the "Charleston Riflemen," the "Meagher Guard" of Irishmen, and the "German Riflemen."[1] He read the general orders of R. G. M. Dunovant, the Adjutant and Inspector-General of the State, requiring colonels commanding regiments to "report forthwith the number, kind, and condition of all public arms in possession of the Volunteer Corps composing the several commands," and the appointment of nine aides-de-camp to Governor Pickens.

PALMETTO GUARD.

These were signs of approaching hostilities that the dullest mind might comprehend; and, in addition, Anderson had the frank avowals of men in power. Floyd had summoned Colonel Huger, of Charleston, to Washington, for the real purpose, no doubt, of arranging more perfect plans for the seizure of the forts, for that officer was afterward an active general in the military service of the conspirators. Anderson was directed by the Secretary to confer with Huger before his departure, and in that interview the Colonel, the Mayor

---

[1] More than a column of the *Mercury* of December 21, now before the writer, was filled with these notices and devices. A few of the latter are given on this and the next page, as mementoes of the time. The "Washington Light Infantry" was an old company, and bore the Eutaw flag of the Revolution. The "Charleston Riflemen" was an old company, organized in 1806. The insignia of the "Marion Artillery" was a copy of White's picture of Marion dining the British officer. That of the "Meagher Guard" appears to have been made for the occasion—a rude wood-cut, with the words *Independence or Death*. The title of this company was given in honor of the Irish exile, Thomas F. Meagher, whose honorable course, in serving his adopted country gallantly as a brigadier-general during the civil war that followed, was a fitting rebuke to these unworthy sons of Ireland, who had fled from oppression, and were now ready to fight for an ignoble oligarchy, who were enemies of human freedom and enlightenment. So were the Germans of South Carolina rebuked by Sigel and thousands of their countrymen, who fought in the National armies for those democratic principles which for years had burned intensely in the bosoms of their countrymen in Father-land.

(Macbeth), and other leading citizens of Charleston assured him that the forts "must be theirs, after secession."[1] All this he reported promptly to the Government, and was mocked by renewed assurances of the safety of the forts from attack, and the wisdom of the policy of not adding to the military force in Charleston harbor, for fear of increasing and intensifying the excitement of the South Carolinians. He was even instructed to deliver over to the authorities of South Carolina " any of Captain Foster's workmen," should a demand be made for them, "on the ground of their being enrolled into the service of the State."[2] These men, intimately acquainted with every detail of knowledge concerning the forts, would be of infinite service to the conspirators.

CHARLESTON RIFLEMEN.

feeble resources, he discovered that many men under his command had been tampered with by the conspirators. This fact he promptly communicated to the Government, saying:—"Captain Foster informed me yesterday that he found that fifty

Whilst Anderson was thus left to rely on his own men of his Fort Sumter force, whom he thought were perfectly reliable, will not fight if an armed force approaches the work; and I fear that the same may be anticipated of the Castle Pinckney force."[3] And thus he continued reporting almost daily the condition of the fortifications and of his forces, the movements of the South Carolinians, and the almost hourly accumulation of evidence that the seizure of Fort Sumter would be soon attempted. That stronghold lost, all would be lost. But his appeals for men and arms were in vain. His warnings were purposely unheeded. The burden of responses to his letters was :—Be prudent; be kind: do nothing to excite the South Carolinians. It will not do to send you re-enforcements, for that might bring on hostilities. At the same time, he was instructed " to hold possession of the forts, and, if attacked, to defend himself to the last extremity."[4]

Time after time, from October 29th until the close of December, General Scott urged ·the Government to re-enforce the forts on the coasts of the Slave-labor States. He laid before the President facts showing their nakedness (the Secretary of War having denuded the whole Atlantic coast of troops, and sent them to Texas, and the Territories north of it), and that they

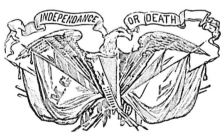

MEAGHER GUARD.

were completely at the mercy of insurgents. On the 31st of October he asked permission to admonish the commanders of Southern forts to be on the

[1] Letter to Adjutant-General Cooper, December 6, 1860: Anderson's MS. Letter-book.
[2] Adjutant-General Cooper to Major Anderson, December 14, 1860: Anderson's MS. Letter-book.
[3] Letter dated December 6, 1860: MS. Letter-book.
[4] Copy of a memorandum of verbal instructions from the Secretary of War, signed "D. C. Buell, Assistant Adjutant-General." This officer (afterward a major-general in command in Kentucky and Tennessee) was sent to Major Anderson with verbal instructions from his Government, and, after his arrival at Fort Moultrie, he

alert against surprise or sudden assault; but even this was not given by the President before January 3, 1861, when it was too late.[1] He went to Washington City on the 12th of December, and on the following day begged the Secretary of War to re-enforce the Southern forts. The Secretary did not coincide in his views. He then asked Floyd to procure for him an early interview with the President. That interview occurred on the 15th, when the subject of secession and the strengthening of the forts was freely discussed. In reply to Scott's suggestion to send re-enforcements immediately to Charleston harbor, the President said the time for such measures had not arrived. He expected the Convention of South Carolinians, who would assemble on the 17th, would send commissioners to him, to negotiate with him and Congress respecting the secession of the State, and the property of the United States within its limits, and that, if Congress should decide against secession, then he would send a re-enforcement, and order Major Anderson to hold the forts against attack.[2]

The last sentence gave Floyd a new idea of a method to aid the conspiracy. The Virginia traitors (of whom he was the chief, in efficient action), at that time, contemplated the seizure of the immense Fortress Monroe at Hampton Roads, which guarded the great Navy Yard at Norfolk, and would be of vast importance to the conspirators in executing the scheme entertained by Wise and others, of seizing the National Capital before Lincoln's inauguration, and taking possession of the Government. Floyd would gladly weaken the garrison of Fortress Monroe for that purpose, at the expense of the Charleston forts; and he now said quickly, and with great animation, "We have a vessel-of-war (the *Brooklyn*) held in readiness at Norfolk, and I will send three hundred men in her, from Fort Monroe to Charleston." Scott replied that so many men could not be spared from Fortress Monroe, but might be taken from New York.[3] No doubt it was Floyd's intention, had the President ordered re-enforcements to Charleston, to take them from the already small garrison in Fortress Monroe.[4]

---

committed them to writing. They were afterwards modified by the Secretary of War, so as to more closely restrict Major Anderson. Buell arrived at Fort Moultrie on the 11th of December.

The wife of one of the officers of the garrison wrote as follows, at this time:—"I feel very indignant. I can hardly stand the way in which this weak little garrison is treated by the head of the Government. Troops and proper accommodations are positively refused, and yet the commander has orders to hold and defend the fort. Was ever such a sacrifice—an intentional one—known? The Secretary has sent several officers, at different times, to inspect here, as if that helped. It is a mere sham, to make believe he will do something. In the mean time a crisis is very near. I am to go to Charleston the first of the week. I will not go farther, if I can help it. Within a few days, we hear—and from so many sources, that we cannot doubt it—that the Charlestonians are erecting two batteries, one just opposite to us, at a little village—Mount Pleasant—and another on this end of the island; and they dare the commander to interfere, while they are getting ready to fight sixty men. In this weak little fort, I suppose, President Buchanan and Secretary Floyd intend the Southern Confederation to be cemented with the blood of this brave little garrison. Their names shall be handed down to the end of time. When the last man is shot down, I presume they will think of sending troops. The soldiers here deserve great credit. Though they know not but an unequal number is coming to massacre them, yet they are in good spirits, and will fight desperately. Our commander says, he never saw such a brave little band. I feel desperately myself. Our only hope is in God."

[1] See *Memoir of Lieutenant-General Scott, LL. D., written by Himself*, ii. 622.

[2] *Memoir of Scott*, ii. 614.   [3] The same, ii. 614.

[4] "The plan invented by General Scott to stop secession," said the Richmond *Examiner*, in a eulogy of Floyd, "like all campaigns devised by him, was very able in its details, and nearly certain of general success. The Southern States are full of arsenals and forts, commanding their rivers and strategic points. General Scott desired to transfer the Army of the United States to these forts as speedily and quietly as possible. The Southern States could not cut off communication between the Government and the fortresses without a great fleet, which they cannot build for years,—or take them by land without one hundred thousand men, many

The appeals of Major Anderson and the urgent recommendations of General Scott produced much feeling in the Cabinet at Washington. General Cass, the Secretary of State, warmly urged the President to order re-enforcements to be sent at once, not only to Charleston, but elsewhere. Most of the other members of the Cabinet, being conspirators yet hidden from public view, opposed the measure. This opposition, and the threats of the South Carolina delegation in Congress, as we have observed,[1] caused the President to refuse such order.[2] It was on account of that refusal that Cass withdrew,[a] after which the Cabinet was almost a unit in sentiment for [a December 14, 1860.] about a fortnight, when, as we shall observe presently, there was a grand disruption of the ministry. For this patriotic act, the *Charleston Mercury*, ungrateful for the steady support which Mr. Cass had given to the policy of the Southern leaders during Buchanan's administration, denounced him[b] as a " hoary-headed trickster and humbug," who [b December 19.] had retired from the Cabinet "because war was not made on South Carolina."[3]

Anderson found it necessary for him to assume grave responsibilities, for he was evidently abandoned to his fate by his Government. He sent engineers and workmen to repair Castle Pinckney, and, as vigorously as possible, he pushed on the labor of strengthening Fort Moultrie.

When the Ordinance of Secession was passed, still more menacing became the actions of the South Carolinians. Anderson knew that commissioners had been appointed to repair to Washington, to demand the surrender of the forts in Charleston harbor; and he was conscious that preparations for seizing them, the very moment when the expected refusal to surrender should be made known, were in active progress. He knew, too, that if he should remain in Moultrie, their efforts would be successful; and two days after the passage of that ordinance, he wrote to the Department,[c] [c December 22.] saying :—" I have heard from several sources that, last night and the night before, a steamer was stationed between this island and Fort

---

hundred millions of dollars, several campaigns, and many a bloody siege. Had Scott been able to have got these forts in the condition he desired them to be, the Southern Confederacy would not now exist."

[1] See page 102.

[2] The President offered as a reason for his refusal to give orders for the re-enforcement of Major Anderson the fear of giving offense to the South Carolinians, and bringing on a collision. Apparently unsuspicious that the politicians of other States were equally determined to commence a rebellion at a favorable moment, he professed to believe that if the Government did not begin actual hostilities, South Carolinians would keep the peace, for fear of provoking the other Cotton-producing States. If, on the contrary, the Government should provoke the South Carolinians to strike, those of the other States would join them. Mr. Buchanan also offered as a reason, that there were not sufficient troops at command, at any time, to garrison the forts. His mistake is apparent when we consider the ease with which Forts Sumter, Pickens, Taylor, and Jefferson held out with very small garrisons against all the forces that the insurgents could bring. Anderson could have held out in Sumter for a long time with less than one hundred men, if he had possessed food and water for them.

[3] A public banquet was given to Secretary Floyd at Richmond, on the 11th of January, 1861, and, in an after-dinner speech, he stated some interesting matters concerning the proceedings of the Cabinet in relation to the forts in Charleston harbor. He said the President was at first anxious to send re-enforcements. "I would rather be at the bottom of the Potomac," he said, "than that these forts should be in the hands of those who intend to take them. It will destroy me—it will cover your [Floyd's] name with infamy, for you will never be able to show that you had not some complicity in it." Floyd called in to his aid Jefferson Davis, James M. Mason, and R. M. T. Hunter, "with other patriots, Northern and Southern." The President yielded, and said, "I am content with your policy—we will send no more troops to the harbor of Charleston." But General Cass was firm. "These forts," he said, "must be strengthened. I demand it." The President replied, "I am sorry to differ with the Secretary of State, but the interests of the country do not demand a re-enforcement of the forts at Charleston. I cannot do it. I take the responsibility." This was on the 13th of December—General Cass resigned the next day.—*Report of Floyd's Speech in the Richmond Enquirer*, January 12, 1861.

Sumter. I am certain that the authorities of South Carolina are determined to prevent, if possible, any troops from being placed in that fort; and that they will seize upon that most important work as soon as they think there is any reasonable ground for a doubt whether it will be turned over to the State. I think that I could, however, were I to receive instructions to do so, throw my garrison into that work; but I should have to sacrifice the greater part of my stores, as it is now too late to attempt their removal. Once in that work with my garrison, I could keep the entrance of this harbor open until they constructed works outside of me, which might, I presume, prevent vessels from coming into the outer harbor. . . . No one can tell what will be done. They may defer action until their commissioners return from Washington; or, if assured by the nature of the debates in Congress

FORT SUMTER IN 1860.

that their demand will not probably be acceded to, they may act without waiting for them. I do not think we can rely upon any assurances, and wish to God I only had men enough here to man fully our guns. Our men are perfectly conscious of the dangerous position they are placed in, but are in as fine spirits as if they were certain of victory."[1]

To this letter no response came. Hour after hour the danger seemed to Anderson more threatening. Watch-boats were out continually, spying his movements, and ready to report the approach of a relief vessel of any kind. Four days had passed, and no word came from his Government. He had resolved to save the forts if possible, and he would wait no longer for instructions. He was commander of *all* the forts in the harbor, and might occupy

---

[1] Anderson's MS. Letter-book.

whichever he pleased.[1] He resolved to assume the responsibility, for the public good, of abandoning the weaker and occupying the stronger.

Great caution and circumspection were essential to success. There were vigilant eyes upon Anderson on every side. There was wide-spread disaffection everywhere among Southern-born men. Whom can I trust? was a question wrung almost hourly from loyal men in public station. Anderson had lately been promoted to his present command, and had been so little with his officers and men, that his acquaintance with them was extremely limited. He revealed his secret intentions only to Captain (afterward Major-General) John G. Foster, his second in command, and two or three other officers.

Anderson's first care was to remove the women and children, with a supply of provisions, to Fort Sumter. To do so directly and openly would invite an immediate attack. He resolved on strategy. He would give out that they were going to Fort Johnson, on James Island. Wherefore? would be asked by the watchful Charlestonians. His reply might properly be : Because I know you are about to attack me. I cannot hold out long. I wish to have the helpless ones, with food, in safety.

This was substantially the course of events. On Wednesday, the 26th of December, the women and children in Fort Moultrie, and ample provisions, were placed in vessels and sent to Fort Johnson. The commandant there had been instructed to detain them on board until evening, under a pretext of a difficulty in finding quarters for them. The firing of three guns at Moultrie was to be the signal for them all to be conveyed immediately to Fort Sumter, and landed. The expected question was asked, and the plausible answer was given. The people of Charleston, as Anderson desired, talked about his movement as a natural and prudent measure. They now felt sure of their speedy possession of the forts. All suspicion was allayed. The stratagem was successful.

Just at the close of the evening twilight, when the almost full-orbed moon was shining brightly in the Southern sky, the greater portion of the little garrison at Fort Moultrie embarked for Fort Sumter. The three signal-guns were fired soon afterward, and the women and children were taken from before Fort Johnson to the same fortress. Captain Foster, Surgeon Crawford, and two or three other officers were left at Fort Moultrie, with a few men, with orders to spike the great guns, destroy their carriages, and cut down the flag-staff, that no " banner with a strange device" should be flung out from the peak from which the Stars and Stripes had so long fluttered. That accomplished, they were to follow the garrison to Sumter.

The movement was successful. The garrison departed. The voyage was short, but a momentous one. A guard-boat had been sent out from Charleston just as the last vessel left Sullivan's Island. At the same time a steam-tug was seen towing a vessel in from sea. She might have revealed the secret. Providentially, the moon shone full in the faces of her people when looking in the direction of the flotilla, and they could not see them. Sumter

---

[1] In the instructions communicated to Anderson by Buell, on the 11th of December, he was authorized, as the smallness of his force would not permit him to occupy more than one of the three forts, to put his command in either of them, in case he should be attacked, or if there should be attempts made to take possession of either one of them.

was gained. The soldiers and their families, and many weeks' provisions, were safe within its walls, and at eight o'clock the same evening,[a]
[a] December 26, 1860. Major Anderson wrote to the Adjutant-General from his snug quarters, nearly over the sally-port :—"I have the honor to report that I have just completed, by the blessing of God, the removal to this fort, of all my garrison except the surgeon, four North Carolina officers, and seven men."

Electricity, speedier than steam, conveyed intelligence of the movement to the War Department from the Charleston conspirators, long before Anderson's message reached the National Capital. It fell among the disunionists [b] December 27. in that capital like an unlooked-for thunderbolt, and the wires flashed back from the dismayed Floyd these angry words:— "Intelligence has reached here this morning[b] that you have abandoned Fort Moultrie, spiked your guns, burnt the carriages, and gone to Fort Sumter. It is not believed, because there is no order for any such movement. Explain the meaning of this report."[1]

Anderson calmly replied by telegraph:—"The telegram is correct. I abandoned Fort Moultrie because I was certain ·that if attacked my men must have been sacrificed, and the command of the harbor lost. I spiked the guns and destroyed the carriages to keep the guns from being turned against us. If attacked, the garrison would never have surrendered without a fight."[2]

When this last dispatch was written, the flag of the Union had been floating over Sumter for four hours. It had been flung to the breeze at meridian, after impressive religious services. The commander, a devout man, took that opportunity to impress upon the garrison, then entering upon a

COLUMBIAD ON THE PARADE IN FORT SUMTER.[3]

season of great trial, the important truth, that to God alone they must look for strength to bear it. His companions were anxious to hoist the National ensign before the dawn of the 27th, but the Major would not consent to the act before the return of the chaplain. He came at noon; and around the flag-staff, not far from the great columbiad, mounted on the parade of the fort, all the inmates of Sumter were congregated. The commander, with the halliards in hand, knelt at the foot of it. The chaplain prayed earnestly for encouragement, support, and mercy; and when his supplications ceased, an impressive "Amen!" fell from the lips of many

---

[1] Anderson's MS. Letter-book.   [2] The same.
[3] This 10-inch columbiad was designed to throw shells into Charleston, if necessary. See Chapter XII.

and stirred the hearts of all. Anderson then hoisted the flag to the head of the staff. It was greeted with cheer after cheer, while the band saluted it with the air of " Hail Columbia."

While this impressive scene was occurring in the fort, a boat was approaching from Charleston. It contained a messenger from the Governor of South Carolina, conveying a demand, in courteous but peremptory phrase, for Major Anderson's immediate withdrawal from Sumter, and return to Moultrie. The Governor said that when he came into office, he found that " there was an understanding between his predecessor and the President, that no re-enforcements were to be sent to any of the forts," and especially to Sumter ; and that Anderson had violated that agreement by thus re-enforcing it. The demand was refused ; and the Major was denounced in the Secession Convention, in the South Carolina Legislature, in public and private assemblies, and in the streets of Charleston, as a " traitor to the South " (he having been born in a Slave-labor State), and an enemy of its people. The South Carolinians felt the affront most keenly, for on the very day when he went from Moultrie to Sumter, a resolution, offered by Mr. Spain, was considered in secret session in the disunion Convention, which requested the Governor to communicate to that body any information he might possess concerning the condition of the forts in the harbor—what work was going on within them, how many men were employed, the number and weight of guns, number of soldiers, and whether assurances had been given that they would not be re-enforced ; also, what steps had been taken for the defense of Charleston and the State. It was afterward known that these conspirators intended to seize Castle Pinckney and Fort Sumter within twenty-four hours from that time, but their plans were frustrated by the timely movement of Anderson.

The conspirators in Charleston and Washington were filled with rage. At the very hour when the old flag was flung out defiantly to the breeze over Sumter, in the face of South Carolina traitors, Floyd, the Secretary of War, was declaring vehemently in the Cabinet that " the solemn pledges of the Government had been violated " by Major Anderson, and demanding of the President permission to withdraw the garrison from Charleston harbor. The President refused. A disruption of the Cabinet ensued ; and the next communication that Major Anderson received from the War Department, after the angry electrograph of Floyd, was from Joseph Holt, a loyal Kentuckian like himself, whom the President had called to the head of that bureau.[a] He assured Major Anderson of the approval [a] December 31, 1860. of his Government; and that his movement in transferring the garrison from Moultrie to Sumter " was in every way admirable, alike for its humanity and patriotism as for its soldiership.'"

Earlier than this, words of approval had reached Anderson from the loyal North; and five days after the old flag was raised over Sumter, the Legislature of Nebraska, two thousand miles away toward the setting sun, greeted him, by telegraph, with " A Happy New Year!" Other greetings from the outside world came speedily, for every patriotic heart in the land made lips evoke benedictions on the head of the brave and loyal soldier. In many

---

[1] Secretary Holt to Major Anderson, January 10, 1861. Anderson's MS. Letter-book.

places guns were fired in honor of the event; and never did a public servant receive such spontaneous praise from a grateful people, for his deed seemed like a promise of safety to the Republic. Pen and pencil celebrated his praises; and a poet, in a parody of a couple of stanzas of a dear old Scotch song, made "Miss Columbia," addressing Anderson, thus express the sentiments of the people :—

> "Bob Anderson, my beau, Bob, when we were first acquent,
> You were in Mex-i-co, Bob, because by order sent;
> But now you are in Sumter, Bob, because you chose to go,
> And blessings on you anyhow, Bob Anderson, my beau.

> "Bob Anderson, my beau, Bob, I really don't know whether
> I ought to like you so, Bob, considering that feather.
> I don't like standing armies, Bob, as very well you know,
> But I love a man that dares to act, Bob Anderson, my beau."[1]

From the hour when Anderson and his little band[2] entered Sumter, their position was an extremely perilous one. His friends knew this, and were very uneasy. His devoted wife, a daughter of the gallant soldier, General Clinch, of Georgia, with her children and nurse, were in New York City. She knew, better than all others, the perils to which her husband might be exposed from ferocious foes without, and possible traitors within. With an intensity of anxiety not easily imagined, she resolved in her mind a hundred projects for his relief. All were futile. At length, while passing a sleepless night, she thought of a faithful sergeant who had been with her husband in Mexico, and who had married their equally faithful cook. If he could be placed by the side of Major Anderson in Sumter, that officer would have a tried and trusty friend, on whom he could rely in any emergency. Where was he? For seven long years they had not seen his face. Seven years before, they heard that he was in New York. She resolved to seek him. At dawn she sent for a city directory. The Sergeant's name was Peter Hart. She made a memorandum of the residence of every Hart in the city; and, in a carriage, she sought, for a day and a half, for the man she desired to find. Then she obtained a clew. He might be in the Police establishment—there was a man of that name who had been a soldier. She called on the Superintendent of the Police, and was satisfied. She left a request for Peter Hart to call on her.

Mrs. Anderson had resolved to go with Peter to Fort Sumter, if he would accompany her. She was an invalid. Her physician and friend, to whom alone she had intrusted the secret of her resolve, protested vehemently against the project. He believed its execution would imperil her life. She had resolved to go, and would listen to no protests or entreaties. Seeing her determination, he gave her every assistance in his power.

Peter Hart came, bringing with him his wife, the faithful Margaret. They were delighted to see their former mistress and friend. Hart stood erect before her, with his heels together, soldier-like, as if to receive orders.

---

[1] *Harper's Weekly*, January 26, 1861.
[2] The garrison was composed of ten officers, fifteen musicians, and fifty-five artillerists—eighty in all.

"I have sent for you, Hart," Mrs. Anderson said, "to ask you to do me a favor." "Any thing Mrs. Anderson wishes, I will do," was his prompt reply. "But," she said, "it may be more than you imagine." "Any thing Mrs. Anderson wishes," he again replied. "I want you to go with me to Fort Sumter," she said. Hart looked toward Margaret for a moment, and then promptly responded, "I will go, Madam." "But, Hart," continued the earnest woman, "I want you to *stay* with the Major. You will leave your family and give up a good situation." Hart again glanced inquiringly at Margaret and then quickly replied, "I will go, Madam." "But, Margaret," Mrs. Anderson said, turning to Hart's wife, "What do *you* say?" "Indade, Ma'am, and it's Margaret's sorry she can't do as much for you

PETER HART.

as Pater can," was the warm-hearted woman's reply. "When will you go, Hart?" asked Mrs. Anderson. "To-night, Madam, if you wish," replied her true and abiding friend. "Be here to-morrow night at six o'clock," said Mrs. Anderson, "and I will be ready. Good-by, Margaret."

All things were speedily arranged. The two travelers were to take only a satchel each for the journey. Hart was to play the part of a servant to Mrs. Anderson, and to be ready, at all times, to second her every word and act. What difficulties and trials awaited them, no one knew. The brave, patriotic, loving woman did not care. It was enough for her to know that her husband and country were in peril, and she was seeking to serve them.

The travelers left New York on Thursday evening, the 3d of January.[a] None but her good physician—not even the nurse of her ^{a 1861.} children—knew their destination. She was completely absorbed with the subject of her errand. They traveled without intermission until their arrival in Charleston, late on Saturday night. She neither ate, drank, nor slept during that time. From the Cape Fear to Charleston, she was the only woman in the railway train, which was filled with rough men hurrying to Charleston to join in an attack on Fort Sumter. They were mostly shaggy-haired, brutal, and profane, who became drunken and noisy, and filled the cars with tobacco-smoke. "Can't you prevent their smoking here?" she gently asked the conductor. His only reply was, "Wal, I reckon they'll have to smoke." Her appeal to two rough men in front of her was more successful. With sweet voice, that touched the chords of their better nature, she said, "Will you please to throw away your cigars? they make me *so* sick." One of them glanced at the speaker, and said to his companion, "Let's do it; she's a lady." During the remainder of the journey these rude men were very respectful. In that train of cars, Mrs. Anderson was compelled to hear her husband cursed with the most horrid oaths, and threatened with savage violence should he fall into the hands of the exasperated mob. But she endured all heroically.

It was late in the evening when they reached Charleston. When the drunken soldiers were carried out, she asked an agent at the station for a carriage. "Where are you from?" he asked. "New York," she replied. "Where are you going?" "To Charleston." "Where else?" "Don't know; get me a carriage to go to the Mills House." "There are none." "I know better." "I can't get one." "Then give me a piece of paper that I may write a note to Governor Pickens; he will send me one." The man yielded at the mention of the Governor's name. He supposed she must be some one of importance; and a few minutes afterward, she and Hart were in a carriage, on their way to the Mills House. There the parlor into which she was ushered was filled with excited people of both sexes, who were exasperated because of her husband's movements. His destruction of the old flagstaff at Moultrie was considered an insult to the South Carolinians that might not be forgiven. Their language was extremely violent.

Mrs. Anderson met her brother at the Mills House. On the following morning he procured from Governor Pickens a permit for her to go to Fort Sumter. She sought one for Hart. The Governor could not allow a man to be added to the Sumter garrison, he said; he would be held responsible to the Commonwealth of South Carolina for any mischief that might ensue in consequence! Mrs. Anderson did not conceal the scorn which the suggestion and excuse elicited. The State of South Carolina—now claiming to be a sovereign power among the nations of the earth—endangered by the addition of one man to a garrison of seventy or eighty, while thousands of armed hands were ready and willing to strike them! Pickens was her father's old friend. "Tell him," she said, "that I shall take Hart to the fort, with or without a pass." Her words of scorn and her demand were repeated to the Governor. He saw the absurdity of his conduct, and gave a pass for Hart, but coupled the permission with a requirement that her messenger should obtain from Major Anderson a pledge that he should not be enrolled as a soldier! The pledge was exacted, given, and faithfully kept. Peter Hart served his country there better than if he had been a mere combatant.

At ten o'clock on Sunday morning, the 6th of January, Mrs. Anderson,

with Hart and a few personal friends then in Charleston, started in a small boat for Sumter, carrying with her a mail-bag for the garrison, which had lately been often kept back. It was a most charming morning. The air was balmy and the bosom of the bay was unrippled. Nature invited to delicious enjoyment; but the brave woman, absorbed in the work of her holy mission of love and patriotism, heeded not the invitation. Everywhere were seen strange banners. Among them all was not a solitary Union flag. She felt like an exile from her native land. Presently, as the boat shot around a point of land, some one exclaimed, "There's Sumter!" She turned, and

MRS. ANDERSON.

saw the national ensign floating gently over it. It seemed, as it waved languidly in the almost still air, like a signal of distress over a vessel in the midst of terrible breakers. "The dear old flag!" she exclaimed, and burst into tears. For the first time since she left New York, Emotion had conquered the Will.

Sentinel-boats were now passed, and proper passwords were given. They approached Sumter, when a watchman on its walls trumpeted the inquiry, "Who comes there?" A gentleman in the boat replied through a trumpet, "Mrs. Major Anderson." She was formally ordered to advance. As her friends conveyed her up the rocks to the wharf, her husband came running out of the sally-port. He caught her in his arms, and exclaimed in a vehement whisper, for her ear only, "My glorious wife!" and carried her into the fort. "I have brought you Peter Hart," she said. "The children are well. I return to-night." Then, turning to the accompanying friends, she said, "Tell me when the tide serves; I shall go back with the boat." She then retired with her husband to his quarters nearly over the sally-port, and took some refreshments; the first since leaving New York.

ANDERSON'S QUARTERS IN FORT SUMTER.

The tide served in the course of two hours. When Mrs. Anderson was placed in the boat by her husband, she experienced almost an irresistible desire to draw him after her—to take him away from the great peril. With the plashing of the oars, when the boat was shoved off, came a terrible impression as if she had buried her husband and was returning from his funeral. But she leaned lovingly, by faith, on the strong arm of the All-Father, and received strength. Invalid and a woman as she was, she had performed a great service to her husband and country. She had given them a faithful and useful friend in Peter Hart—how faithful and useful, the subsequent history of Fort Sumter until it passed into the hands of armed insurgents, three months later, only feebly reveals.

Unheeding the entreaties of friends, who tried to persuade her to remain, and offered to bring her family to her; and the assurance of a deputation of Charlestonians, who waited upon her, that she might reside in their city, dwell in Sumter, or wherever she pleased, Mrs. Anderson started for the National Capital that evening,[a] accompanied by Major Anderson's brother. Charleston was no place for her while her husband was under the old flag; and she would not add to his cares by remaining with him in the fort. A bed was placed in the cars, and on that she journeyed comfortably to Washington. She was insensible when she arrived at Willard's Hotel, into which she was conveyed by a dear friend from New York, a powerful man, whose face was the first that she recognized on the return of her consciousness. After suffering for forty-eight hours from utter exhaustion, she proceeded to New York, and was for a long time threatened with brain fever.

Thus ended the mission of this brave woman. She alone had done what the Government would not, or dared not do. She had not sent, but taken, a valuable re-enforcement to Fort Sumter. When we look back to the beginning of the great civil war, the eye of just appreciation perceives no heroism more genuine and useful than that displayed by this noble woman; and history and romance will ever delight to celebrate her deed.

We have observed that the occupation of Sumter created great exasperation among the conspirators. They had been outgeneraled, and were mortified beyond measure. They did not expect so daring an assumption of responsibility by the gentle, placid Major, who, only the day before, had accepted their proffered hospitality, and eaten a Christmas dinner in Charleston with some of the magnates of the city and State. Little did they suspect, when seeing him quietly participating in the festivities of the occasion, that, within thirty hours, he would extinguish, for a season, the most sanguine hopes of the South Carolina conspirators. It was even so; and they had no alternative but to consider his movement as an "act of war." They did so, and proceeded upon that assumption. The *Charleston Courier* declared that "Major Robert Anderson, of the United States Army, has achieved the unenviable distinction of opening civil war between American citizens, by an act of gross breach of faith. He has, under counsels of panic,

THE CITADEL (MILITARY) ACADEMY AT CHARLESTON.

deserted his post at Fort Moultrie, and, under false pretexts, has transferred his garrison, and military stores and supplies, to Fort Sumter."

Such was the sentiment of the deceived, offended, astonished, and bewildered Charlestonians, who, at dawn, on the morning of the 27th,[a] had seen clouds of heavy smoke rolling up from Fort Moultrie. They had crowded the Battery, the wharves, and the roofs of their houses, and gazed seaward for two hours before they comprehended the meaning of the startling apparition. The conflagration was a mystery, and wild conjecture alarmed the timid, and filled every mind with anxiety. There was in it an aspect of war, and many breakfasts in Charleston were left untasted on that eventful morning. At length, some workmen came from the vicinity of Fort Moultrie, and revealed the truth. Exasperation succeeded wonder. The more excitable portion of the population asked to be led immediately in an attack upon Fort Sumter. They declared that they could pull it down with their unarmed hands, they felt so invincible. Martial music and the tramp of military columns were soon heard in the streets. The Secession Convention at once requested Gov-

[a] December, 1860.

ernor Pickens to take military possession of Forts Moultrie and Johnson, and Castle Pinckney. The order for such occupation was speedily given. The hall of the Citadel Academy, the great military school of the State, that opens on the largest of the public squares of the city, was made the place of rendezvous for the military officers, and the grounds near it were covered by an excited populace. The Government Arsenal, into which Secretary Floyd had crowded a vast amount of arms and ammunition, taken from those of Massachusetts and New York,[1] was seized in the name of the State. It had, for some time, been held by only a sufficient number of men to insure its safety in a time of profound peace. For a while a guard of State militia had been there, under the pretext of defending it from injury by an excited population; and these, by order of the State authorities, took full possession of it on Sunday, the 30th of December. Seventy thousand stand of arms, and a vast amount of military stores, valued at half a million of dollars, were thus placed in the hands of the conspirators. These were used at once. Men in Charleston were armed and equipped from this National treasure-house; and within three hours after the ensign of the Republic had been raised over Sumter,[a] two armed steamers (*General Clinch* and   [a] December 27, 1860. *Nina*), which had been watching Anderson's movements, left the city, with about four hundred armed men, under General R. G. M. Dunovant (who had been a captain in a South Carolina regiment in the war with Mexico, and was now Adjutant-General of the State), for the purpose of seizing Castle Pinckney and Fort Moultrie. One-half of these troops, led by Colonel J. J. Pettigrew, landed at Pinckney. The commandant of the garrison, Lieutenant R. K. Mead (a Virginian, who soon afterward deserted his flag and hastened to Richmond), made no resistance, but fled to Sumter. His men so strongly barricaded the door of the Castle that the assailants were compelled to enter it by escalade. They found the cannon spiked, the carriages ruined, the ammunition removed, and the flag-staff prostrated. Borrowing a Palmetto flag from the captain of one of the steamers, Petti- grew unfurled it over the Castle. It was greeted by the cheers of thousands. on the shore. It was the first flag raised by the insurgents over a National fortification.

The remainder of the troops, consisting of the Washington Artillery, the German Artillery, the Lafayette Artillery, and the Marion Artillery, in num- ber about two hundred and twenty-five, under Colonel Wilmot G. De Saus- sure, proceeded in the steamers to Fort Moultrie. The people in Charleston looked on with the greatest anxiety, for they thought the guns of Sumter might open fire upon their friends when they should land on the beach of Sullivan's Island. They did not know how tightly Major Anderson's hands. were tied by instructions from his Government. While the insurgents left Fort Sumter unassailed, he was compelled to keep its ports closed.

The insurgent troops were landed without opposition, and Fort Moultrie was surrendered by the sentinel, in accordance with orders, to Colonel Al- ston, one of Governor Pickens's aids, and Captain Humphreys of the arsenal. They found the fort much more extensive than it was a few months before,.

[1] See page 121, and note 1, page 121.

for Anderson's men had worked faithfully, under skillful direction, in preparing it to resist an attack. Old works had been repaired, and new ones constructed. But the affair was comparatively a shell now, for its interior was a scene of utter desolation. The guns were spiked; the carriages were destroyed; nearly all the ammunition and every piece of small-arms had been carried away; the flag-staff lay prone across the parade, and partly burned; and no munitions of war or military stores, of much account, were left, excepting some heavy cannon-balls and about six weeks' provisions for Anderson's garrison. The guns of Sumter looked directly into the dismantled fort, and a few shots from them would have driven De Saussure and his men out among the sand-hills. But Anderson was compelled to keep them silent; and the South Carolinians quietly took possession of the abandoned

December 27, fortress, and flung out over its desolated area the Palmetto flag.[a]
   1860.

It was then too dark for the citizens of Charleston to see it, but their hearts were soon cheered by the ascent of three rockets from Fort Moultrie, which gave them assurance that the insurgents were safely within its walls, while the garrison at Sumter seemed asleep or paralyzed.

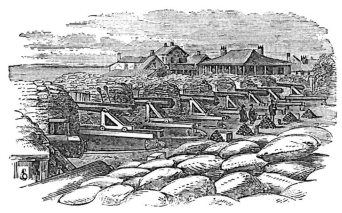

SAND-BAG BATTERY AT FORT MOULTRIE.

Under the direction of Major Ripley, late of the National Army, Fort Moultrie was enlarged and strengthened. The ramparts were covered with huge heaps of sand-bags, and new breastworks, composed of these and palmetto logs, were erected, and heavy guns were mounted on them.

On the same day when Fort Moultrie was seized, the revenue cutter *William Aikin*, lying in Charleston harbor, under the command of Captain N. L. Coste, of the revenue service, was surrendered by that faithless officer into the custody of the insurgents. With his own hands he hauled down the National flag which he had sworn to defend, ran up the Palmetto banner—the emblem of revolt—and gave himself and his vessel to the service of the conspirators. His subordinate officers, honorable and loyal, at once reported themselves for duty at Washington. This was the beginning of the defection of naval officers who were born in Slave-labor States. The first army officer who resigned his commission to take up arms against his Government was Captain R. G. M. Dunovant, mentioned on the preceding page.

Official notes now began to pass between Sumter and surrounding points. On the afternoon of the 27th, as we have observed, Governor Pickens sent a message to Anderson, requiring him to leave Sumter and return to Moultrie. That commander refused. On the following morning, Anderson sent his post-adjutant to Fort Moultrie, to inquire of the commander there by what authority he and armed men were in that fortification of the United States. He replied, " By the authority of the Sovereign State of South Carolina, and by command of her government."

Anderson's refusal caused Pickens to treat him as a public enemy within the domain of South Carolina ; and the *Charleston Mercury*, with the peculiar logic characteristic of the class it represented, declared that the " holding of Fort Sumter by United States troops was an invasion of South Carolina." In a letter written to Adjutant-General Cooper, on the 28th, Anderson said :—" I shall regret very deeply the persistence of the Governor in the course he has taken. He knows how entirely the city of Charleston is in my power. I can cut his communication off from the sea, and thereby prevent the reception of supplies, and close the harbor, even at night, by destroying the light-houses. These things, of course, I would never do, unless compelled to do so in self-defense." On the same day, the authorities of South Carolina seized and appropriated to the uses of the State the Custom House, and the Post-office kept within its walls. That building, fronting on Broad Street, was venerated as the theater of many events connected with the old war for Independence.[1]

From that time until the close of President Buchanan's administration, and even longer, Major Anderson was compelled, by Government policy, to see the insurgents gather by thousands in and around Charleston, erect fortifications within reach of his guns, and make every needful preparation

OLD CUSTOM HOUSE IN CHARLESTON.

for the destruction of Fort Sumter and its little garrison, without being allowed to fire a shot. Looking back from our present stand-point, we perceive in this forbearance either the consummate wisdom of man or the direct interposition of God.

[1] In the basement of the Custom House, Colonel Moultrie and other patriots concealed from the eyes of British officials, in 1775, nearly one hundred thousand pounds of " provincial powder." Its vaults were military prisons, and there hundreds of patriots suffered long and hopelessly, and scores perished of wounds and privations, while the British held possession of the city, from May, 1780, until the close of the war. From that building Isaac Hayne, the martyr, was taken out to execution, having been brought up from a damp vault for the purpose. This building originally fronted the sea ; but, in the course of time, stately warehouses arose between it and the water.

CHAPTER VI.

AFFAIRS AT THE NATIONAL CAPITAL.—WAR COMMENCED IN CHARLESTON HARBOR.

HEN intelligence of Anderson's occupation of Fort Sumter went abroad, it created intense excitement. In the Free-labor States, as we have observed, it produced joyful emotions. In the Slave-labor States it kindled anger, and intensified the hurricane of passion then sweeping over them. From these, proffers of sympathy and military aid were sent to the South Carolinians, and they were amazingly strengthened by the evidences of hearty co-operation in their revolutionary designs, which came not only from the Cotton-producing States, but from Virginia, Kentucky, Tennessee, Missouri, and even from Maryland.

The National Capital, in the mean time, became the theater of important and startling events, calculated to add to the feverish excitement throughout the country. Congress had not adjourned during the holidays, as usual. On the day when the South Carolina Ordinance of Secession was passed,[a] the House of Representatives was discussing the Pacific Railway Bill. Half an hour after that ordinance was adopted, the telegraph told the news to the representatives of that State in Congress, and all but two of them immediately left the hall. A little later it was publicly announced by Representative M. R. H. Garnett, of Virginia, who, contending in the discussion that his State would not be responsible for any bonds which the Government might issue for the construction of the Pacific Road, said :—" Why, Sir, even while your bill is under debate, one of the Sovereign States of this Confederacy has, by the glorious act of her people, withdrawn, in vindication of her rights, from the Union, as the telegraph announced to us at half-past one o'clock. . . . It is my solemn belief that the people of Virginia, when my State takes that course which thronging events will lead her to take, will not hold themselves responsible for the first cent of these bonds and appropriations."[1] These words were followed by applause from some of the Southern members; and Messrs. Boyce and Ashmore, the two remaining representatives of South Carolina, arose from their seats, shook hands with some of their friends, and left the hall. Four days afterward, a letter signed by the entire South Carolina delegation, then in Washington, was sent in to the Speaker, announcing, in the peculiar phraseology of the devotees of State Supremacy, that the action of their State had dissolved their connection with those whom they had " been associated with

[a] December 20, 1860.

---

[1] Report of the Proceedings of Congress, in the *Washington Globe*, December 20, 1860.

in a common agency" (meaning the National Congress), and that they should vacate their seats.[1] After drawing their pay from the public treasury up to the hour of their desertion, they departed for their homes. The South Carolina Senators, as we have observed, had already resigned.[2]

The announcement of the treasonable movements at Charleston was heard with a calm dignity quite remarkable by the representatives of the Free-labor States, who had begun to look with contempt on the dramatic performances of some of the Hotspurs of the cotton-growing region, and thought it time to rebuke them. On the same evening the New York delegation, excepting those from the city of New York, held a consultation, and passed a resolution, by unanimous vote, saying for the people of their State, that they believed that the appropriate remedy for every existing grievance might be applied under the Constitution, and that they should insist upon "a prompt and energetic enforcement of all the laws of the General Government." This resolution, which was applauded by representatives from other States, was sent to the Governor of New York (Morgan), with a suggestion, that in his forthcoming message he should give such expression that the enemies of the Government should know that "New York, at least, will never submit to the doctrine of secession;" also, suggesting the propriety of recommending the Legislature to adopt measures for forming "volunteer companies, to sustain, if need be, the Union—to protect the Federal property, and aid in enforcing the Federal laws."[3] It was felt that the time for public meetings, for political speeches, and for moral suasion, had passed, and that the people should rise in their majesty, and say, with the vehemence of conscious power, to the traitors everywhere—Touch the Ark of our Covenant with parricidal hands at your peril!

While there was calmness in Congress on the annunciation of the action of South Carolinians, there was great excitement throughout the Capital. The writer was in Washington at the time, and was in conversation with General Cass, at his house, on the great topic of the hour, when a relative brought to him a bulletin concerning the act of secession. The venerable statesman read the few words that announced the startling fact, and then throwing up his hands, while tears started from his eyes, he exclaimed, with uncommon emotion:—"Can it be! Can it be! Oh," he said, "I had hoped to retire from the public service, and go home to die with the happy thought, that I should leave to my children, as an inheritance from patriotic men, a united and prosperous republic. But it is all over! This is but the beginning of the end. The people in the South are mad; the people in the North are asleep. The President is pale with fear, for his official household is full of traitors, and conspirators control the Government. God only knows what is to be the fate of my poor country! To Him alone must we look in this hour of thick darkness."

The writer left the venerable ex-Minister of State, and went over to the War and Navy Departments. The offices were closed for the day, but the

[1] This letter was signed by John McQueen, Milledge L. Bonham, W. W. Boyce, and J. D. Ashmore. Lawrence M. Keitt and William Porcher Miles were then in the Secession Convention at Charleston.
[2] See page 51.
[3] Letter of John B. Haskin, member of Congress, to Governor Morgan, December 20, 1860.

halls and lobbies were resonant with the voices of excited men. There were treasonable utterances there, shocking to the ears of loyal citizens. I went to the hotels on Pennsylvania Avenue—"Willard's," the "Kirkwood," "Brown's," and "The National," and found them swarming with guests, for it was then the late dinner-hour. There was wild excitement among them; secession cockades were plentiful, and treason and sedition walked as boldly and defiantly in these hotels, and in the streets of the National Capital, as in the "Mills House," and the streets of Charleston. I took up the newspapers, and found no word of comfort therein for the lovers of the country. "The long-threatened result of Black Republican [1] outrage and autocracy," said one, "has taken place in South Carolina; secession is a fixed fact."[2] Another, the Government gazette, praised the dignity of the South Carolina Convention. "If the telegraphic abstract may be relied upon," it said, "it is not easy to conceive of any thing more calm, more thoughtful, more dignified, than the utterances which followed the taking of the decisive step. . . . Almost Spartan simplicity animates the oratory. . . . A few days will bring the issue to the chambers of the Capitol. South Carolina, through her representatives, will reappear in Washington, in a character that will test the virtue of the Federal system, and the good sense of Congress. Let us hope that the solemnity of Charleston will not be left to stand in contrast to frivolity or passion in this the metropolis of the Union."[3] I went home with a friend living near Bladensburg. His family physician—a small, fiery man, named Garnett, and son-in-law of ex-Governor Wise, of Virginia—came to see a sick child. He was full of passion. "Noble South Carolina," he said, "has done her duty bravely. Now Virginia and Maryland must immediately raise an armed force sufficient to control the district, and never allow Abe Lincoln to set his foot on its soil." The little enthusiast was only the echo of the Virginia conspirators. A few days before, the *Richmond Enquirer*, edited by Wise's son, who perished while in arms against his country, thus insolently concluded an article on the subject of sending commissioners from that State to others: —"Let the first convention, then, be held between Maryland and Virginia, and, these two States agreeing, let them provide sufficient force to seize the city of Washington, and if coercion is to be attempted, let it begin with subjugating the States of Maryland and Virginia. Thus practical and efficient fighting in the Union will prevent the powers of the Union from falling into the hands of our enemies. We hope Virginia will depute her commissioners to Maryland first, and, providing for the seizure of Washington and Old Point, Harper's Ferry and Gosport Navy Yard, present these two States in the attitude of rebels inviting coercion. This was the way Patrick Henry brought about the Revolution, and this is the best use that Virginia can make of commissioners of any kind."

Governor Wise had already publicly announced that, in the event of an attempt at "coercion" on the part of the National Government, Fortress Monroe, the Navy Yard at Gosport, and the armory and arsenal at Harper's

---

[1] The prefix "Black" was given to the Republican party because, being favorable to the abolition of Slavery, its members were ranked as friends of the negro. This name was applied by the Oligarchy in the South, and was freely used by their partisans in the North.

[2] Washington *States*.

[3] Washington *Constitution*, the organ of the Administration.

Ferry would be seized, and held for the purpose of opposing the Government. Already Judge A. H. Handy, a commissioner from Mississippi, had visited Maryland for the purpose of engaging that State in the Virginia scheme of seizing the National Capital, and preventing the inauguration of Mr. Lincoln. The conspirators were so confident of the success of their schemes, that one of the leading Southern Senators, then in Congress, said:—"Mr. Lincoln will not dare to come to Washington after the expiration of the term of Mr. Buchanan. This city will be seized and occupied as the capital of the Southern Confederacy, and Mr. Lincoln will be compelled to take his oath of office in Philadelphia or in New York."[1] And the veteran editor, Duff Green, the friend and confidential co-worker with Calhoun when the latter quarreled with President Jackson, and who naturally espoused the cause of the secessionists, told Joseph C. Lewis, of Washington, while under the half-finished dome of the Capitol, early in 1861:—" We intend to take possession of the Army and Navy, and of the archives of the Government; not allow the electoral votes to be counted; proclaim Buchanan provisional President, if he will do as we wish, and if not, choose another; seize the Harper's Ferry Arsenal and the Norfolk Navy Yard simultaneously, and sending armed men down from the former, and armed vessels up from the latter, take possession of Washington, and establish a new government."

There is ample evidence that the seizure of Washington City, the Government buildings, and the archives of the nation, was an original and capital feature in the plan of the conspirators; and their assertions, after they were foiled in this, that they sought only for "independence," and that all they asked was "to be let alone," was the most transparent hypocrisy. They aimed at *revolution* at first, and *disunion* afterwards. They had assurances, they believed, that the President would not interfere with their measures. Should Congress pass a Force Bill, he was pledged by the declarations of his annual Message to withhold his signature from it; and most of them were satisfied that they might, during the next seventy days, establish their "Southern Confederacy," and secure to it the possession of the Capital, without governmental interposition. Yet *all* were not satisfied. Some vigilant South Carolina spies in Washington would not trust the President. One of them, signing only the name of "Charles," in a letter to Rhett, the editor of the *Charleston Mercury*, said: "I know *all* that has been done here, but *depend upon nothing that Mr. Buchanan promises. He will cheat us*

---

[1] Correspondence (Occasional) of the Philadelphia *Press*, December 21, 1860. In the same letter, which was a trumpet-call to the country to arouse it to a sense of its danger and to act, the writer (J. W. Forney) said:—"The Administration of the Government is in the hands of the enemies of the country. The President of the United States has ceased to be the Chief Magistrate of a free people, and may be called the chief of those who are seeking to enslave a free people. He is quoted by the secessionists, if not as their active, at least as their quiescent ally! He refuses to exercise his functions, and to enforce the laws! He refuses to protect the public property, and to re-enforce the gallant Anderson at Fort Moultrie! He sends the Secretary of the Interior to North Carolina, with the intention of forcing that loyal and conservative State into the ranks of the disunionists! While sending General Harney to Kansas with a large military force to suppress a petty border insurgent, he folds his arms when General Scott and his brave subordinates in the South appeal to him for succor. His Attorney-General argues with all his ingenuity against the power of the Federal Government to enforce the laws of the country. His confidants are disunionists. His leaders in the Senate and in the House are disunionists! and while he drives into exile the oldest Statesman in America, simply and only because he dares to raise his voice in favor of the country, he consults daily with men who publicly avow, in their seats in Congress, that the Union is dissolved, and that the laws are standing still! Is it not time, then, for the American people to take the country into their own hands, and to administer the Government in their own way?"

unless we are too quick for him."[1] He then urged the seizure of the forts, Sumter particularly, without a moment's delay. Neither would the conspirators fully trust each other. William H. Trescot, already mentioned, a South Carolinian, and then Assistant Secretary of State and who for years had been conspiring against the Government, was thought to be tricky. The writer just quoted said :—"Further, let me warn you of the *danger of Governor Pickens making Trescot his channel of communication with the President*, for the latter will be informed of every thing that transpires, and that to our injury. Tell Governor Pickens this at once, before matters go further."[2] And the elder Rhett commenced a letter to his son, of the *Charleston Mercury*, by saying :—" Jefferson Davis is not only a dishonest man, but a liar !"[3] These politicians seem to have had a correct appreciation of each other's true character.

While the excitement in Washington because of the doings at Charleston was at its hight, it was intensified by a new development of infamy, in the discovery of the theft of an enormous amount of the Indian Trust-Fund, which was in the custody of the conspirator, Jacob Thompson, the Secretary of the Interior. The principal criminal in the affair was undoubtedly Floyd, the Secretary of War. He had been chiefly instrumental in getting up a military expedition into the Utah Territory, in which about six millions of dollars of the public treasure were squandered, to the hurt of the national credit, at a critical time. The troops were stationed there at a point called Camp Floyd ; and the Secretary had contracted with the firm of Russell, Major, & Waddell for the transportation of supplies thither from Fort Leavenworth, and other points on the Missouri River. For this service they were to receive about one million of dollars a year. Floyd accepted from them drafts on his Department, in anticipation of service to be performed, to the amount of over two millions of dollars.[4] These acceptances were so manifestly illegal, that they could with difficulty be negotiated. The contractors became embarrassed by the difficulty, and hit upon a scheme for raising money more rapidly.

Russell had become acquainted with Goddard Bailey, a South Carolinian and kinsman of Floyd, who was the clerk in the Interior Department in whose special custody were the State bonds composing the Indian Trust-Fund. He induced Bailey to exchange these bonds [a] for Floyd's illegal acceptances. These were hypothecated in New York, and money raised on them. When, as we have observed, the financial affairs of the country became clouded, late in 1860,[b] these bonds depreciated, and the holders called on Russell for additional security. Bailey supplied him with more bonds,[b] until the whole amount was the sum of eight hundred and seventy thousand dollars. When the time approached for him to be called upon by the Indian Bureau for the coupons payable on the 1st of January, on the abstracted bonds, Bailey found himself in such a position that he was driven to a confession. Thompson, his employer, was then in North Carolina, on the business of conspiracy, as Commissioner of the " Sovereign State of Missis-

a July, 1860.

b December 18.

---

[1] Autograph letter, dated Washington, December 22, 1860.   [2] The same.   [3] Autograph letter.
[4] Report of the Committee of Investigation of the House of Representatives, February 12, 1861.
[5] See page 115.

sippi." Bailey wrote a letter to him, antedated the 1st of December, disclosing the material facts of the case, and pleading, for himself, that his motive had been only to save the honor of Floyd, which was compromised by illegal advances.

Thompson returned to Washington on the 22d, when the letter was placed in his hands. After consultation, it is said, with Floyd, he revealed the matter to the President, who was astounded. The farce of discovering the thief was then performed, Thompson being chief manager. The Attorney-General, and Robert Ould the District Attorney (who afterward became one of the most active servants of the confederated conspirators at Richmond), were called to take a part. Neither the robber, nor the key of the safe in which the bonds were kept, could be found. Mayor Berret was required to detail a special police force to guard every avenue leading to the Interior Department, so that no clerks might leave. These clerks were all examined touching their knowledge of the matter. Nothing was elicited. Then the safe was broken open, and the exact amount of the theft was speedily made known. At length Bailey was discovered, and made a full confession.

The wildest stories as to the amount of funds stolen immediately went abroad. It was magnified to millions.[1] It was already known that Cobb had impoverished the Treasury ; it was now believed that plunder was the business of the Cabinet, for the public held Floyd and Thompson responsible for the crime which Bailey had confessed. The blow given to the public credit was a staggering one. The Grand Jury of Washington soon acted on the matter, and Floyd was indicted on three counts, namely, malversation in office, complicity in the abstraction of the Indian Trust Fund, and conspiracy

JOHN B. FLOYD.

against the Government. The House of Representatives appointed a Committee to make a thorough investigation of the affair, and they concluded their report [a] with the expression of an opinion, mildly drawn. that Floyd's conduct in the matter "could not be reconciled with purity of private motives and faithfulness to public trusts."[2] When the indictment of the Grand Jury and the report of the Committee were made, Floyd was far beyond the reach of marshals and courts. He had fled in disgrace from the National Capital, and was an honored guest of the public authorities at Richmond,[3] who boldly defied the national power.

[a] February 12, 1861.

The excitement on account of the robbery in the Interior Department was followed by intelligence of the proceedings at Pittsburg, already mentioned,[4] where an immense meeting of the citizens was held in the street, in front of the Court House, in the evening of the 27th,[b] and they resolved that it was the duty of the President "to purge his

[b] December, 1860.

---

[1] The Government lost over six hundred thousand dollars.
[2] Report of the Investigating Committee, February 12, 1861.   [3] See note 3, page 127.   [4] See page 123.

Cabinet of every man known to give aid and comfort to, or in any way countenancing, the revolt of any State against the authority of the Constitution and the laws of the Union." On the morning of the same day,[a] the news of the occupation of Fort Sumter by the garrison of Fort Moultrie reached Washington, and produced the greatest consternation among the conspirators. The Cabinet assembled at midday. They had a stormy session. Floyd urgently demanded an order for Anderson's return to Fort Moultrie, alleging that the President, by withholding it, was violating the "solemn pledges of the Government." The latter, remembering his implied, if not actual pledges, was inclined to give the order;[1] but the warning voices of law, duty, and public opinion made him hesitate. They spoke to his conscience and his prudence about faithfulness, impeachment, and a trial for treason; and to his patriotism concerning the goodness and the greatness of his native land, and its claims upon his gratitude. He paused, and the Cabinet adjourned without definite action.

[a] December 27, 1860.

The position of the aged President, during the eventful week we are here considering, was a most painful one. He was evidently involved in perilous toils into which he had fallen in less troublous times, when he believed that he had called into his counsels true men, as the world of politicians goes. He found himself, if not deceived, unexpectedly subjected to the control of bad men; and for two or three days after this Cabinet meeting, as the writer was informed by an intimate acquaintance of the President, he was in continual fear of assassination.

On the morning after the stormy cabinet meeting just mentioned, news came that Fort Moultrie and Castle Pinckney had been seized by South Carolina troops. The President breathed more freely. He felt himself relieved from much embarrassment, for the insurgents had committed the first act of war. He now peremptorily refused to order the withdrawal of the garrison from Sumter, and on the following day[b] the disappointed Floyd resigned the seals of his office, fled to Richmond, and afterward took up arms against his country. In his letter of resignation, this man, covered, as with a garment, with some of the darkest crimes known in history, spoke of "patriotism" and "honor." He said:—"I deeply regret that I feel myself under the necessity of tendering to you my resignation as Secretary of War, because I can no longer hold it under my convictions of patriotism, nor with honor, subjected as I am to a violation of solemn pledges and plighted faith."[2] His resignation was immediately accepted, and his place filled by the patriotic Kentuckian, Joseph Holt. Then a load of anxiety was lifted from the burdened hearts of the loyal people of the Republic. The purification of Buchanan's Cabinet went on, and there was a general change in the ministry by the middle of January. When Attorney-General Black succeeded General Cass as Secretary of State, his office was filled by Edwin M. Stanton, afterward Secretary of War under President Lincoln; Philip F. Thomas, of Maryland, had succeeded Cobb as Secretary of the Treasury.

[b] December 29.

---

[1] See Letter of President Buchanan to the "Commissioners of South Carolina," December 30, 1860.

[2] In reply to a statement made by General Scott, concerning the apparent remissness of duty on the part of the Administration at that crisis, published in the *National Intelligencer* on the 21st of October, 1862, Mr. Buchanan says that it was at his request that Floyd resigned. This allegation of the President, which is undoubtedly true, makes Floyd's high-sounding words about wounded patriotism and honor, in connection with his infamous official career, appear extremely ridiculous.

Unwilling to assist the Government in enforcing the laws, Thomas resigned,[1] and was succeeded by John A. Dix, a staunch patriot of New York. Thompson left the Interior Department on the 8th,[a] and, like Floyd, hastened to his own State to assist in the work of rebellion. *January, 1861.*

There was still another cause for excitement in Washington and throughout the country, during the eventful week we are considering. It was the arrival and action of Messrs. Barnwell, Adams, and Orr, the "Commissioners" for South Carolina. They evidently expected to stay a long time, as embassadors of their "Sovereign State" near the Government of the United States. Their fellow-conspirator, W. H. Trescot, who had just left the State Department, in which he could be no longer useful to the enemies of his country, had hired the fine dwelling-house of the widow of Captain Joseph Smoot, of the United States Navy, No. 352 (Franklin Row) K Street, as their ministerial residence.

JOSEPH HOLT.

There they took up their abode on their arrival, on the 26th, with servants and other necessaries for carrying on a domestic establishment, and Trescot was duly installed their Secretary. They were greeted with distinguished consideration by their fellow-conspirators, and the multitude of sympathizers in the National Capital; and they doubtless had roseate dreams of official and social fellowship with Lord Lyons, M. Mercier, Baron

RESIDENCE OF THE "COMMISSIONERS."[2]

Von Gerolt, and other foreign ministers then in Washington. That dream, however, assumed the character of a nightmare, when, on the following day, they heard of Anderson and his gallant little band being in Fort Sumter.

On the 28th,[b] the "Commissioners" addressed a formal diplomatic letter to the President, drawn up, it is said, *December, 1860.*
by Orr, who was once Speaker of the National House of Representatives, and who had been denounced in his own State as "the prince of demagogues."[3] That letter informed the President

---

[1] See his Letter of Resignation, January 11, 1861.

[2] The house next to the open space in the picture.

[3] Orr's views seem to have undergone a change. In a letter to the editor of the *Charleston Mercury,* dated January 24, 1858, Andrew Calhoun said:—" I found, on my return to this State, that Orr, that prince of demagogues, had, by all kinds of appliances, so nationalized public opinion about here, that sentiments are habitually uttered suited to the meridian of Connecticut, but destructive to the soil and ancient faith of the State." This Calhoun and other conspirators found it necessary to work upon the people continually, to keep them prepared for treasonable work at the proper moment. Whenever they found a man of influence true to the Union, they denounced and persecuted him, and men in more humble spheres were cowed into meek submission by the truculent Oligarchy.

that they were authorized and empowered to treat with the Government of the United States for the delivery of the forts, magazines, light-houses, and other real estate, with their appurtenances, in the limits of South Carolina; and also for an apportionment of the public debt, and for a division of all other property held by the Government of the United States as agent of the Confederated States, of which South Carolina was recently a member; and generally to negotiate as to all other measures and arrangements proper to be made and adopted in the existing relation of the parties, and for the continuance of peace and amity between the Commonwealth and the Government at Washington.   They also furnished him with a copy of the

JAMES L. ORR.

Ordinance of Secession. They said it would have been their duty, under their instructions, to have informed him that they were ready to negotiate, " but (referring to Anderson's movements) the events of the last twenty-four hours " had altered the condition of affairs under which they came. They reminded him that the authorities of South Carolina could, at any time within the past sixty days, have taken possession of the forts in Charleston harbor, but they were restrained by pledges given in a manner that they could not doubt.[1] They assured him that until the circumstances of Anderson's movements were explained in a manner to relieve them of all doubt as to the spirit in which the negotiations should be conducted, they would be compelled to suspend all discussion. In conclusion, they urged the President to immediately withdraw all the National troops from Charleston harbor, because, under the circumstances, they were a "standing menace," which rendered negotiations impossible, and threatened to "bring to a bloody issue questions which ought to be settled with temperance and judgment."[2]

The arrogance and insolence visible in this letter, considering the criminal position of the men who signed it, and the circumstances to which it related, offended the President, who would have been applauded by every loyal man in the country if he had arrested them on a charge of treason.[3] Yet he treated the " Commissioners " and their letter with marked

[a] December, 1860.

courtesy in a reply written on the 30th.[a] He referred them to his Annual Message for a definition of his intended course concerning the property of the United States and the collection of the revenue. He could only meet them as private gentlemen of the highest character, and

---

[1] See page 102.

[2] Letter of the "Commissioners" to the President, dated Washington, December 28, 1861.

[3] Three weeks later, Francis C. Treadwell, of New York, a counselor of the Supreme Court, offered to Chief-Justice Taney an affirmation, in due form, that certain persons (naming most of the public men known to have been engaged in the great conspiracy) were guilty of conspiring against the Constitution and Government of the United States, and had committed the crime of treason, or misprision of treason, and praying for their arrest. This paper was returned to Mr. Treadwell by the Clerk of the Supreme Court, Benjamin C. Howard, with the remark, that the Chief Justice deemed it "an improper paper to be offered to the Court."

was willing to lay before Congress any proposition they might make. To recognize their State as a foreign power would be usurpation on his part; he should refer the whole matter of negotiation to Congress. He denied ever having made any agreement with the Congressional delegates from South Carolina concerning the withholding of re-enforcements from the Charleston forts, or any pledge to do so;[1] but declared that it had been his intention, all along, not to re-enforce them, and thus bring on a collision, until they should be attacked, or until there was evidence that they were about to be attacked. "This," he said, "is the whole foundation of the alleged pledge." He then referred them to the instructions to Major Anderson, already noticed,[2] in which that officer was authorized to occupy any one of the forts with his small force in case of an attack, and to take similar steps when he should "have tangible evidence of a design to proceed to a hostile act." He also referred to the fact that the South Carolinians had already committed an act of war by seizing two forts belonging to the National Government in Charleston harbor, and had flung out the Palmetto flag over them, in place of the old standard of the Union. "It is under all these circumstances," he said, with evident indignation, "that I am urged immediately to withdraw the troops from the harbor of Charleston, and am informed that without this negotiation is impossible. This I cannot do; *this I will not do.* Such an idea was never thought of by me in any possible contingency." He informed them that he had just heard of the capture of the Arsenal at Charleston and half a million of dollars' worth of property by the insurgents, and said,—"Comment is needless;" and then gave them to understand that he considered it his duty to defend Fort Sumter, as a portion of the public property of the United States. He concluded with expressing "great personal regard" for the "Commissioners."

Two days later,[a] the "Commissioners" replied to this note in a long and extremely insolent and insulting letter. As representatives of a "sovereign power," they said, they "had felt no special solicitude" as to the character in which the President might receive them, and they had no reason to thank him for permitting them to have their propositions laid before Congress. They then referred to the declarations in his Message, that he had no right, and would not attempt, "to coerce a seceding State," and pointed to his subsequent acts, as virtual pledges that such were his honest convictions of duty. "Some weeks ago," they said, "the State of South Carolina declared her intention, in the existing condition

[a] January 1, 1861.

---

[1] See page 102. When Jacob Thompson, the Secretary of the Interior, reached Oxford, Mississippi, after leaving office, he was honored by a public reception. In the course of a speech on that occasion, he said, speaking of affairs in Charleston harbor:—"The President agreed with certain gentlemen, undertaking to represent South Carolina, that no change should be made in the military status of the forts; and when Major Anderson, adopting an extreme measure of war, only justified in the presence of an overpowering enemy, spiked his guns and burned his gun-carriages, and moved, with his garrison, from Fort Moultrie to Fort Sumter, and thus committed an act of hostility, the President heard of the movement with chagrin and mortification."

It is the deliberate conviction of Joseph Holt, the loyal Secretary of War during the last seventy days of Mr. Buchanan's administration, that no such pledge was ever given. See his reply to allegations in a speech of ex-Postmaster-General Blair, at Clarkesville, Maryland, in August, 1865. It is fair to conclude that men like the "Commissioners" from South Carolina, and Jacob Thompson, all engaged in the commission of the highest crime known, namely, treason to their Government, would not be slow in the use of the more venal and common sin of making false accusations, especially when such accusations might furnish some excuse for their iniquity. No proof has ever been given that the President violated his oath by making such pledg-

[2] See page 125, and note 1, page 129.

of public affairs, to secede from the United States. She called a convention of her people to put her declaration in force. The Convention met, and passed the Ordinance of Secession. All this you anticipated." They then taunted him with dereliction of duty. "You did not re-enforce the garrison in the harbor of Charleston. You removed a distinguished and veteran officer from the command of Fort Moultrie because he attempted to increase his supply of ammunition.[1] You refused to send additional troops to the same garrison when applied for by the officer appointed to succeed him. You accepted the resignation of the oldest and most eminent member of your Cabinet, rather than allow the garrison to be strengthened. You compelled an officer, stationed at Fort Sumter, to return immediately to the Arsenal forty muskets which he had taken to arm his men. You expressed, not to one, but to many, of the most distinguished of our public characters, your anxiety for a peaceful termination of this controversy, and your willingness not to disturb the military status of the forts, if Commissioners should be sent to the Government, whose communications you promised to submit to Congress. You received, and acted on, assurances from the highest official authorities of South Carolina, that no attempt would be made to disturb your

SIGNATURES OF THE SOUTH CAROLINA "COMMISSIONERS."

possession of the forts and property of the United States, if you would not disturb their existing condition until the Commissioners had been sent, and the attempt to negotiate had failed. You took from the members of the House of Representatives a written memorandum that no such attempt should be made, 'provided that no re-enforcements should be sent into those forts, and their relative military status shall remain as at present.'[2] . . . You sent orders to your officers, commanding them strictly to follow a line of conduct in conformity with such an understanding." They then mentioned the circumstances of their arrival and personal interview :—"On Friday," they said, " we saw you, and we called upon you then to redeem your pledge. You could not deny it." Because of the resignation of Floyd, expressly in consequence of the alleged violation of the pledged faith of the Government, they said, " denial was impossible. You did not deny it. You do not deny it now, but seek to escape from its obligations on the ground that we terminated all negotiations by demanding, as a preliminary measure, the withdrawal of the United States troops from Charleston, and the hostile action of the

---

[1] See page 118.   [2] See page 102.

authorities of South Carolina."[1] They told him that they had felt kindly, and, by forbearance, had acted kindly toward him, because of the delicacy of his position, but he had deceived them. "You have decided," they said. "You have resolved to hold by force what you have obtained by misplaced confidence; and by refusing to disavow the act of Major Anderson, have converted his violation of orders into a legitimate act of your executive authority. Be the issue what it may, of this we are assured, that if Fort Moultrie has been recorded in history as a memorial of Carolina gallantry, Fort Sumter will live upon the succeeding page as an imperishable testimony of Carolina faith. By your course you have probably rendered civil war inevitable. Be it so. If you choose to force this issue upon us, the State of South Carolina will accept it, and, relying upon Him who is the God of Justice, as well as God of Hosts, will endeavor to perform the great duty which lies before her, bravely and thoroughly."

The President made no reply to this letter, but returned it to the " Commissioners," indorsed with these words:—"This paper, just presented to the President, is of such a character that he declines to receive it." This occurred on New Year's Day. The usual calls on the President were very few and formal. The "East Room," which is the great hall of "The White House," as the official residence of the President is called, and which is usually very much crowded on such

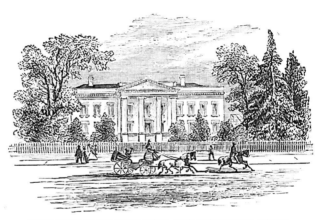

NORTH FRONT OF THE WHITE HOUSE, FROM PENNSYLVANIA AVENUE.

occasions, was almost deserted. Only a few Army and Navy officers made their appearance. Many Unionists and secessionists, it is said, declined to

---

[1] Much has been said concerning the visit to Charleston, at about this time, of Caleb Cushing, the distinguished citizen of Massachusetts who presided over the Democratic Convention in that city, seven months before. One of the most careful chroniclers of the events immediately preceding, and at the outbreak of the civil war, says, that he was sent there by President Buchanan as his confidential agent, to assure the insurgents that he would not "re-enforce Major Anderson, nor initiate any hostilities against the Secessionists, provided they would evince a like pacific spirit, by respecting the Federal authority down to the close of his Administration." He says the time of this mission was at "the middle of December," and that General Cushing, having been informed that his being a "representative of the Federal authority had cast a sudden mildew on his popularity in that stronghold of secession," remained there but five hours, when he returned to Washington, and his report was "the theme of a stormy and protracted Cabinet meeting." See *The American Conflict:* by Horace Greeley, i., 409. I have the authority of a letter from General Cushing himself, dated 26th March, 1865, for saying, that the single and sole object of his visit (which was on the 20th of December) was to endeavor to "counteract the mad scheme of secession." The visit was suggested or promoted by gentlemen at Washington of the very highest authority, North and South, including the President. At the very moment when General Cushing entered Charleston, the bells were beginning to ring, and salutes to be fired, in honor of the passage of the Ordinance of Secession. Of course there was nothing for him to do at Charleston, and he left for Washington the next morning. His agency went no further. He had no authority to say any thing on the subject of the forts or of hostilities, and, of course, he did not.

shake hands with the President. He appeared, according to the newspaper correspondents, " pale, haggard, care-worn, and weary." The city, at the same time, was heaving with excitement. Union and secession cockades were worn by men and women in the streets. Full fifty Union flags were displayed; and that night a police force was detailed to guard the house where the " Commissioners" dwelt.

Thus terminated the diplomatic correspondence between the President of the Republic and the Embassadors of a treasonable Oligarchy in one of the weaker States of the Union. Having occupied the ministerial residence on K Street ten days, they left it,[a] and returned home, to engage in the work of conspiracy with all their might. Trescot had started for Charleston on New Year's Day.

[a] January 5, 1861.

With the opening of the new year, the faith of the people in the Administration was somewhat revived by evidences of its determination to enforce the laws. The President, under better counselors, seemed disposed to do his duty boldly. It was evident that plans for the seizure of Washington City and the Government were fast ripening. Lieutenant-General Scott was called into cabinet meetings for consultation; and measures were taken for the military defense of the Capital, by the organization of the militia of the District of Columbia, and the concentration at Washington of a few companies of artillery, under the charge of Captain Charles P. Stone, of the Ordnance Department. It was also resolved to strengthen the garrisons of the forts on the coasts of the Slave-labor States, particularly in Charleston harbor. For the latter purpose, the naval force at hand was totally inadequate. The steam-frigate *Brooklyn*, which had lately arrived at Norfolk, after a three years' cruise, was the only armed vessel of any importance on the Atlantic coast, the conspirators having managed to procure the dispersion of the Navy in distant seas.

In view of the threatening aspect of affairs, the crew of the *Brooklyn* was not discharged on her arrival, but was kept in readiness for duty. At the Cabinet meeting whose proceedings compelled Secretary Cass to resign,[b] it was proposed to send her with troops to Charleston. The Secretary of the Navy (Toucey), it is alleged, refused to give the order for the purpose,[1] and the President yielded; now, under the advice of General Scott and Secretary Holt, orders were given for her to be made ready to start at a moment's notice. This order was revealed to the conspirators. Virginians were ready to seize any vessels that might attempt to leave Norfolk with troops; and the lights of the shore-beacons in Charleston harbor were extinguished, and the buoys that marked the channels were removed. Informed of this betrayal of his secret, the President countermanded the order; and when Thompson, the Secretary of the Interior, who was doubtless the criminal in the matter, threatened the President with his resignation because of such order, the latter promised that none like it should be issued, " without the question being first considered and decided in the Cabinet."[2]

[b] December 14, 1860.

---

[1] "I should have told you that Toucey has refused to have the *Brooklyn* sent from Monroe."—*Autograph Letter of " Charles " to the Editor of the Charleston Mercury*, December 22, 1860, already cited on page 143.

[2] Speech of ex-Secretary Thompson at Oxford, Mississippi.

Pledges to men had to yield to the public interest. It was evident that there were those in the Cabinet who could not be trusted. Dangers were thickening. Fortunately, the President listened to his new counselors, Secretary Holt and General Scott; and it was resolved to send troops and supplies to Fort Sumter by a more secret method than had yet been devised. Instead of employing a vessel-of-war for the purpose, the stanch merchant-steamer *Star of the West*, built to run between New York and Aspinwall, on the California route, was chartered by the Government and quickly laden with supplies. She was cleared for New Orleans and Savannah, in order to mislead spies. She left her wharf at New York at sunset on the 5th of January, and far down the bay she received, under the cover of thick darkness, four officers and two hundred and fifty artillerists and marines, with their arms and ammunition. She crossed the bar at Sandy Hook at nine o'clock the same evening, and proceeded to sea under her commander, Captain John McGowan.

In consequence of the reception of a letter from Major Anderson, stating that he regarded himself secure in his position, and intelligence that the

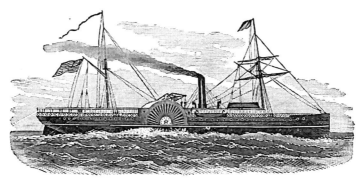

THE STAR OF THE WEST.

insurgents had erected strong batteries at the mouth of Charleston harbor that could destroy an unarmed vessel, the Government, with the concurrence of General Scott, countermanded the order for the sailing of the *Star of the West*.[1] The countermand was sent by the General-in-chief to Colonel H. L. Scott, of his staff, then in New York, by telegraph, but it reached that city after the vessel had left. It is a pity that it was too late. The American people will ever recur to the page of their history on which the record of that expedition is written with regret and humiliation, because it tells the fact that their powerful Government was so weakly administered, that it seemed necessary to resort to clandestine acts in the maintenance of its rightful authority.

The South Carolinians, meanwhile, were making preparations to attack Fort Sumter and strengthen their position. They affected to regard the refusal of the President to hold further intercourse with their arrogant representatives as an insult to their "Sovereign State." Every man in

---

[1] Letter of Secretary Holt to ex-Secretary Thompson, March 5, 1861.

Charleston and vicinity, liable to do military duty, was immediately called to arms. Measures were taken to increase the strength and armament of Fort Moultrie. A garrison composed of the Charleston Rifles, under Captain J. Johnson, was sent to occupy Fort Johnson. The erection of batteries that would command the ship-channel of the harbor, and bear heavily upon Fort Sumter, was commenced on Morris and Sullivan's Islands, and a thousand negro slaves were employed in the work. The commander of Castle Pinckney ordered that no boat should approach its wharf-head except by permission. The city of Charleston was placed under the protection of a military patrol. Look-out boats scouted the outer harbor at night. The telegraph was placed under the most rigid censorship, and Major Anderson was denied all communication with his Government. The United States Sub-treasurer at Charleston (Pressley) was forbidden by the author. ities to cash any more drafts from Washington.[1] The National Collector of the Port (Colcock), participating in the treasonable work, announced that all vessels from and for ports outside of South Carolina must enter and clear at Charleston. The Convention, assuming supreme authority, passed an ordinance on the 1st of January, defining treason against the State; and with a barbarous intent unknown in a long obsolete British law, and with a singular misunderstanding of its terms, they declared the punishment to be " death, without benefit of *the*

• January 1, 1861. clergy."[2] On that morning• they had received intelligence from the " Commissioners" at Washington that their mission would be fruitless; and the Rev. Mr. Du Pré, in the prayer at the opening of the Convention, evidently believing that war was inevitable, supplicated the Almighty, saying:—" Wilt thou bring confusion and discomfiture upon our enemies, and wilt thou strengthen the hearts, nerves, and arms of our sons to meet this great fire." Then a bust of John C. Calhoun, cut from pure white marble, was placed on the table before the President, bearing a curious inscription on a piece of paper.[3]

Frantic appeals were now made to the politicians of other Southern coast States to seize the forts and arsenals of the Republic within their borders. The organs of the South Carolina conspirators begged that Fort Pickens, and the Navy Yard and fortifications on the shores of Pensacola Bay, and Forts Jefferson and Taylor, at the extremity of the Florida Peninsula, might be seized at once—also Fort Morgan, near Mobile; for a grand scheme of piracy, which was inaugurated a hundred days later, was then in embryo.

---

[1] This dishonest order plagued Governor Pickens in a way that provoked much merriment. With amazing assurance, that officer, then in open insurrection against his Government, wrote to the Secretary of the Treasury for three thousand dollars, due him on his salary as Minister to Russia. The Secretary sent him a draft on the Sub-treasurer at Charleston, who, pursuant to his instructions, refused to honor it. See Harper's *History of the Great Rebellion*, page 36.

[2] The term in the old criminal law was, " without benefit of clergy," not of *the* clergy; for it had no reference to the attendance of a clergyman upon a criminal, of which favor the South Carolinians intended to deprive him. It was a law in Roman Catholic countries, or where that form of Christianity, as a system, prevailed. That church claimed the right to try its own clergy at its own tribunals. When a man was condemned, and was about to be sentenced, he might, if he had the right, claim that he was a clergyman, and he was relieved from the power of the civil law and remanded to the ecclesiastical tribunal, under the privilege called "benefit of clergy." In certain cases of heinous offenses, this "benefit of clergy " was denied.

[3] Associated Press Dispatch from Charleston, January 1, 1861. The following is the inscription:—" Truth, Justice, and Fraternity, you have written your name in the Book of Life, fill up the page with deliberation— that which is written, execute quickly—the day is far spent, the night is at hand. Our names and honor summon all citizens to appear on the parade-ground for inspection."

Speaking for those who, true to the instructions of their ancestral traditions, were anxious to revive that species of maritime enterprise which made Charleston so famous and so rich in far back colonial times, the *Mercury* shouted, Seize those forts, and then "the commerce of the North in the Gulf will fall an easy prey to our bold privateers; and California gold will pay all such little expenses on our part." There was a wild cry for *somebody*, in the interest of the conspirators, to capture the California treasure-ships; and the Louisianians were invoked to seize the mint at New Orleans, and to put into the coffers of their State its precious metals. This piracy— this plunder—this violation of every principle of honor—were counseled by the South Carolina conspirators before the politicians in any other State had even held a convention to determine on secession! It was the spirit of an outlaw, whose life is forfeit to offended justice, armed to the teeth, and with the frenzy of desperation, defying all power, denying all right, and, desiring to drag every one down to his own base level.

Cut off by the insurgents from communication with his Government, Major Anderson could not know whether his appeals for re-enforcements and supplies had been heard or heeded. Anxiously all eyes in Sumter were hourly turned ocean-ward, with a desire to see some vessel bearing the National flag that might promise relief. With that apparition they were greeted on the morning of the 9th of January,* when *1861.
the *Star of the West* was seen coming over the bar, and making her way toward the fort. She had arrived at the bar at half-past one o'clock, and finding all the lights put out, extinguished her own, and lay there until morning. At dawn she was discovered by the scouting steamer, *General Clinch*, which at once burned colored lights as signals, passed the bar into the ship-channel, and ran for the inner harbor. The *Star of the West* followed her, after putting all the soldiers below, and giving her the appearance of a mere merchant vessel, with only crew enough to manage her. The deception was fruitless. Her name, her character, and the object of her voyage, had already been made known to the authorities of South Carolina, by a telegraphic dispatch to the *Charleston Mercury*,[1] and by Thompson, one of the conspirators in Buchanan's Cabinet, who was afterward an accomplice in deeds exceeding in depravity of conception the darkest in the annals of crime. Some spy had revealed the secret to this man, and he, while yet in the pay of the Government, betrayed it to its enemies. "As I was writing my resignation," he said, "I sent a dispatch to Judge Longstreet that the *Star of the West* was coming with re-enforcements."[2] He also gave a messenger another dispatch to be sent, in which he said, as if by authority, "Blow the *Star of the West* out of the water." The messenger patriotically withheld the dispatch.

[1] On the 24th of January, 1861, the following card appeared in the New York *Tribune*:—
"I have to state that I am no spy, as charged in your paper of this morning. I utterly detest the name, and am incapable of acting the part of one.
"I have been for some time employed as a special telegraph news reporter for a few Southern newspapers, including one in Charleston. My business has been to send them, when occasion required it, important commercial intelligence and general news items of interest. *Hence,* in the discharge of my duty as a telegraph reporter, *I did send an account of the sailing of the Star of the West.* If that was treason, all I have to say in conclusion is, make the most of it.   "ALEXANDER JONES.
"HERALD OFFICE, NEW YORK, *January 23, 1861.*"
[2] Speech at Oxford, Mississippi.

The insurgents at Charleston were thus enabled to prepare for her reception. They did so; and when she had arrived within two miles of Forts Moultrie and Sumter, unsuspicious of danger, a shot came *ricocheting* across her bow from a masked battery on Morris Island, three-fourths of a mile distant, the only indication of its presence being a red Palmetto flag. The battery was under the command of Major Stevens, Principal of the State Military School, kept in the Citadel Academy, and his gunners, called the Citadel Cadets, were his pupils. He was supported by about two hundred and sixty-five soldiers under Lieutenant-Colonel J. L. Branch.

The National flag was flying over the *Star of the West* at the time, and, as soon as possible, Captain McGowan displayed a large American ensign at the fore. Of course the assailants had no respect for these emblems of the Union, and for ten minutes, while the vessel went forward, a continuous fire was kept up from the battery, and one or two shots were hurled at her from Fort Moultrie, without producing serious damage. The heavy balls flew over her deck and through her rigging, " and one," said the Captain, " came within an ace of carrying away our rudder." Fort Moultrie, well armed and garrisoned, was then just ahead, and from it two steam-tugs were seen to put out, with an armed schooner, to intercept the *Star of the West*. Hemmed in, and exposed to a cannonade without power to offer resistance (for his vessel was unarmed), Captain McGowan perceived that his ship and all on board of her were in imminent peril of capture or destruction; so he turned her bow ocean-ward, after seventeen shots had been fired at her, put to sea, and returned to New York on the 12th.[1] Major Stevens, a tall, black-eyed, black-bearded young man of thirty-five years, was exceedingly boastful of his feat of humbling the flag of his country. The friends of Colonel Branch claimed the infamy for him.

The garrison in Sumter had been in a state of intense excitement during the brief time when the *Star of the West* was exposed to danger. Major Anderson was ignorant of her character and object, and of the salutary official changes at Washington, or he would have instantly resented the insult to the old flag. Had he known that the Executive and the new members of his Cabinet approved his course, and were trying [a January 7, 1861.] to aid him—had he known that, only two days before,[a] a resolution of such approval had passed the National House of Representatives by a large majority[2]—the *Star of the West* and her precious freight of men and stores would not have been driven to sea by a band of less than three hundred insurgents. He was ignorant of all this. She appeared as only a merchant vessel on a commercial errand to Charleston. When the first shot was fired upon her, he suspected her of being a relief-ship. When she ran up the old ensign at the fore, he could no longer doubt. His guns bearing on Moultrie, Morris Island, and the channel, were shotted and

[1] Report of Captain McGowan, January 12, 1861.
[2] The resolution, offered by Mr. Adrain of New Jersey, was as follows:—"*Resolved*, That we fully approve o f the bold and patriotic act of Major Anderson in withdrawing from Fort Moultrie to Fort Sumter, and of the determination of the President to maintain that fearless officer in his present position; and that we will support the President in all constitutional measures to enforce the laws and preserve the Union." This resolution was adopted by a vote of one hundred and twenty-four against fifty-six. For the yeas and nays, see *Congressional Globe's* report of the proceedings of the Thirty-sixth Congress, page 281.

run out, and his officers earnestly desired leave to fire. His peremptory instructions restrained him. He had not been "attacked." Yet he was on the point of assuming the responsibility of giving the word to fire, because

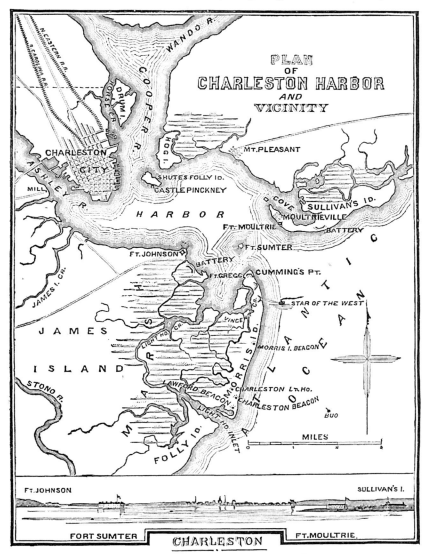

MAP OF CHARLESTON HARBOR IN JANUARY, 1861.

the sovereignty of the nation was insulted by this dishonoring of its flag, when the vessel that bore it turned about and went to sea.

This assault upon the *Star of the West* was an open act of war. The conspirators of South Carolina had struck the first blow that was to inaugurate a destructive civil war—how specially destructive to themselves, and to the hundreds of thousands of the innocent people in the Slave-labor States whom they deceived, betrayed, and ruined, let the history of that war declare. They gloried in the infamy. The Legislature resolved unanimously, "That this General Assembly learns with pride and pleasure of the successful resistance this day by the troops of this State, acting under orders of the Governor, to an attempt to re-enforce Fort Sumter." The organ of the conspirators, speaking in their name, said, exultingly:—"Yesterday, the 9th of January, will be remembered in history. Powder has been burnt over the decree of our State, timber has been crashed, perhaps blood spilled. The expulsion of the *Star of the West* from Charleston harbor yesterday morning, was the opening of the ball of revolution. We are proud that our harbor has been so honored. We are more proud that the State of South Carolina, so long, so bitterly, so contemptuously reviled and scoffed at, above all others, should thus proudly have thrown back the scoff of her enemies. Intrenched upon her soil, she has spoken from the mouth of her cannon, and not from the mouths of scurrilous demagogues, fanatics, and scribblers. Contemned, the sanctity of her waters violated with hostile purpose of re-enforcing enemies in our harbor, she has not hesitated to *strike the first blow*, full in the face of her insulter. Let the United States Government bear, or return at its good-will, the blow still tingling about its ears—the fruit of its own bandit temerity. We would not exchange or recall that blow for millions! It has wiped out half a century of scorn and outrage. Again South Carolina may be proud of her historic fame and ancestry, without a blush upon her cheek for her own present honor. The haughty echo of her cannon has ere this reverberated from Maine to Texas, through every hamlet of the North, and down along the great waters of the Southwest. The decree has gone forth. Upon each acre of the peaceful soil of the South, armed men will spring up as the sound breaks upon their ears; and it will be found that every word of our insolent foe has been, indeed, a dragon's tooth sown for their destruction. And though grisly and traitorous ruffians may cry on the dogs of war, and treacherous politicians may lend their aid in deceptions, South Carolina will stand under her own Palmetto-tree, unterrified by the snarling growls or assaults of the one, undeceived or deterred by the wily machinations of the other. And if that red seal of blood be still lacking to the parchment of our liberties, and blood they want—blood they shall have—and blood enough to stamp it all in red. For, by the God of our fathers, the soil of South Carolina *shall be free!*"[1]

Four years after the war was so boastfully begun by these South Carolina conspirators, it had made Charleston a ghastly ruin, in which not one of these men remained; laid Columbia, the capital of the State, in ashes; liberated every slave within the borders of the Commonwealth; wholly disorganized society; filled the land with the mourning of the deceived and bereaved people, and caused a large number of those who signed the Ordinance of Secession, and brought the curse of War's desolation upon the innocent inhabitants of most of the Slave-labor States, to become fugitives from their homes, utterly ruined.[2] The retribution was terrible!

[1] *Charleston Mercury*, January 10, 1861.
[2] A letter written in Charleston just after the National troops took possession of it, in February, 1865, contained the following paragraph:—
"The wharves looked as if they had been deserted for half a century—broken down, dilapidated, grass and

Major Anderson accepted the insult to his country's flag as an act of war, and promptly sent a letter to Governor Pickens *under a flag of truce,* borne by Lieutenant Hall, as he would to a belligerent enemy, stating the fact of the firing upon an unarmed vessel bearing the flag of the Republic, and asking him whether the outrage had been committed in obedience to his orders. It was a humiliating but unavoidable confession of the weakness of the Government, when a commander of one of its powerful forts was compelled, with a supplicating flag of truce, to seek communication with the Governor of one of the most unimportant members of the Republic—the proconsul of a province. Anderson felt the humiliation keenly; but acted prudently. His demand for an explanation was made with courtesy, but with firmness. He notified the Governor, that if the outrage was not disavowed by him he should regard it as an act of war, and should not, after a reasonable time allowed for the return of his messenger, permit any vessel to pass within range of his guns. "In order to save, as far as it is in my power," he said, "the shedding of blood, I beg you will take due notification of my decision, for the good of all concerned."

Governor Pickens replied promptly. He assumed the act as that of the State of South Carolina; and assured Anderson that any attempt to re-enforce Sumter would be resisted. He left him to decide for himself, whether he would carry out his threat concerning the interception of vessels passing the channel, which the Governor would regard as an attempt to "impose on the State the conditions of a conquered province." The affair assumed an aspect of too much gravity for Anderson to act further upon his sole responsibility, and he resolved to refer the whole subject to his Government. He wrote to Pickens to that effect, expressing a hope that he would not prevent the bearer of his letter, Lieutenant Talbot, proceeding at once to Washington. No objections were interposed, and Talbot carried to the North the first full tidings, from

FRANCIS W. PICKENS.

Sumter, of the outrage upon the old flag, and the failure of the expedition of the *Star of the West.* It created an intense excitement in the Free-labor

moss peeping up between the pavements, where once the busy feet of commerce trode incessantly. The warehouses near the river; the streets as we enter them; the houses and the stores and the public buildings—we look at them and hold our breaths in utter amazement. Every step we take increases our astonishment. No pen, no pencil, no tongue can do justice to the scene. No imagination can conceive of the utter wreck, the universal ruin, the stupendous desolation. Ruin—ruin—ruin—above and below; on the right hand and the left; ruin, ruin, ruin, everywhere and always—staring at us from every paneless window; looking out at us from every shell-torn wall; glaring at us from every battered door and pillar and veranda; crouching beneath our feet on every sidewalk. Not Pompeii, nor Herculaneum, nor Thebes, nor the Nile, have ruins so complete, so saddening, so plaintively eloquent, for they speak to us of an age not ours, and long ago dead, with whose people and life and ideas we have no sympathy whatever. But here, on these shattered wrecks of houses—built in our own style, many of them doing credit to the architecture of our epoch—we read names familiar to us all; telling us of trades and professions and commercial institutions which every modern city reckons up by the hundred: yet dead, dead, dead; as silent as the grave of the Pharaohs, as deserted as the bazars of the merchant princes of Old Tyre."

States, composed of disgust and indignation—disgust, because the Government had attempted to do secretly and deceptively what it should have done openly and honorably, with a strong arm ; and indignation, because traitors in arms had dishonored the old flag, and boasted of their crime.   How that indignation, as a sentiment, speedily ripened into positive action, we shall observe hereafter.

Two days after the attack on the *Star of the West*, Governor Pickens sent his Secretary of State, Magrath, and Secretary of War, Jamison, as commissioners, to make a formal demand on Major Anderson for the immediate surrender of Fort Sumter to the authorities of South Carolina. They tried every art to persuade and alarm him, but in vain.   He assured them that, sooner than suffer such humiliation, he would fire the magazine, and blow fort and garrison in the air.   They returned fully impressed with the conviction that only by starvation or assault could the fortress be secured for South Carolina ; and, to prevent re-enforcements or supplies coming into the harbor, four old hulks filled with stones were towed into the ship-channel that afternoon and sunk.   From that time, the insurgents worked diligently in preparations to attack the fort, and the garrison worked as diligently in preparations for its defense.

Here, besieged in Fort Sumter, we will leave Major Anderson and his little band, while we observe the progress of revolutionary movements in the six Gulf States.

CHAPTER VII.

SECESSION CONVENTIONS IN SIX STATES.

URING the first thirty days of the year 1861, the disloyal politicians in six States of the Union, following the example of those of South Carolina, passed ordinances of secession and appointed delegates to a General Convention for the purpose of forming a Southern Confederacy. These ordinances were passed in the following chronological order:—In Mississippi, on the 9th of January; in Florida, on the 10th; in Alabama, on the 11th; in Georgia, on the 19th; in Louisiana, on the 26th; and in Texas, on the 1st of February. At the same time, large numbers of "Minute-men" in Virginia, under the control of ex-Governor Henry A. Wise, and others in Maryland, under leaders unknown to the public, were organized and drilled for the special purpose of seizing the City of Washington, and the Government buildings and archives there.

At the same time the conspirators, in several places, acting upon the counsel of those of South Carolina, began to plunder the National Government, by seizing its property in the name of certain States in which such property happened to be. Even in the loyal State of North Carolina, where there was no pretense of secession until four months later,[a] the Governor, John W. Ellis, seized the forts within its borders,[b] and the Arsenal at Fayetteville (into which Floyd had lately thrown seventeen thousand small arms, with accouterments and ammunition), under the pretext of securing them from occupation by mobs. He then wrote a letter to the President, telling him that if he (the Governor) could receive assurances that no troops would be sent to that State prior to the 4th of March (the day fixed upon by many as the one on which the first blow at the life of the Republic should be struck), then all would be "peace and quiet" there. "If, however," he said, "I am unable to get such assurances, I will not undertake to answer for the consequences. The forts in this State have long been unoccupied, and these being garrisoned at this time will unquestionably be looked upon as a hostile demonstration, and will, in my opinion, certainly be resisted."[1] The State troops were soon afterward withdrawn from the forts and the Arsenal.

The politicians of Mississippi were the first to follow the example of those of South Carolina. We have already observed initial movements there, by the Legislature authorizing a State Convention, and the appointment of Commissioners to visit other Slave-labor States.[2] Immediately

a May, 1861.

b January 8.

---

[1] Letter of Governor Ellis to the President, January 12, 1861.   [2] See page 59.

afterward the whole State was excited by preparations for the election of delegates to the Convention, ninety-nine in number. The 20th day of December was the time appointed for the election, and the 7th of January[a] was the day selected for the Convention to assemble. Public meetings were held in all parts of the State, at which the most distinguished men in the Commonwealth were speakers.[1] '

[a] 1861.

There was a diversity of sentiment among the politicians in Mississippi, mainly on the question whether there should be immediate, separate, and independent State action, or whether they should wait for the co-operation of other States. Two parties were formed, one called the " Secessionists " proper, the other " Co-operationists." Each was zealous in a bad cause, for all had determined on secession in some form. "These are but household quarrels," said one of the " Co-operationists;" "as against Northern combination and aggression, we are united. We are all for resistance. We differ as to the mode; but the fell spirit of Abolitionism has no deadlier, and, we believe, no more practical foes than the ' Co-operationists' of the South. We are willing to give the North a chance to say whether it will accept or

---

[1] There were also speakers who were not distinguished beyond their own immediate neighborhoods. These were more numerous and influential than the others. Their persons, manner, and language commended them to the great mass of the people who attended these gatherings. Their harangues were forcible and inflammatory. One of these is here given as a specimen of a fair average of the speeches made to the people all over the Slave-labor States at this time, at their primary gatherings. It is quoted from *The Iron Furnace; or, Slavery and Secession:* by the Rev. John H. Aughey, a Presbyterian clergyman of Mississippi:—

"LADIES AND GENTLEMEN:—I am a secessionist out and out; voted for Jeff. Davis for Governor in 1850, *when the same issue was before the people.*" After announcing, in vile language, the election of Mr. Lincoln, he said:—" Shall he be permitted to take his seat on Southern soil? No, never! I will volunteer as one of thirty thousand to butcher the villain if he ever sets foot on slave territory. Secession or submission! What patriot would hesitate for a moment which to choose? No true son of Mississippi would brook the idea of submission to the rule of the baboon, Abe Lincoln—a fifth-rate lawyer, a broken down hack of a politician, a fanatic, an abolitionist. I, for one, would prefer an hour of virtuous liberty to a whole eternity of bondage under Northern, Yankee, wooden nutmeg rule. The halter is the only argument that should be used against the submissionists [that is to say, loyal men in the State], and I predict that it will soon, very soon, be in force.

" We have glorious news from Tallahatchie. *Seven Tory submissionists* [Union men] *were hanged there in one day,* and the so-called Union candidates, having the wholesome dread of hemp before their eyes, are not canvassing the county; therefore the heretical dogma of submission, under any circumstances, disgraces not their county. Compromise! Let us have no such word in our vocabulary. . . . No concession of the scared Yankees will now prevent secession.

" We are now threatened with internecine war. The Yankees are an inferior race; they are cowardly in the extreme. They are descended from the Puritan stock, who never bore rule in any nation. We, the descendants of the Cavaliers, are the Patricians; they the Plebeians. The Cavaliers have always been the rulers, the Puritans the ruled." Then mounting the Delphic stool on which the elder Rhett (see page 96) had prophesied, this disciple attempted to imitate his master. "The dastardly Yankees," he said, "will never fight us; but if they, in their presumption and audacity, venture to attack us, let the war come—I repeat it, let it come ! The conflagration of their burning cities, the desolation of their country, and the slaughter of their inhabitants, will strike the nations of the earth dumb with astonishment, and serve as a warning to future ages, that the Slaveholding Cavaliers of the sunny South are terrible in their vengeance. . . . We will drive back to their inhospitable clime every Yankee who dares to pollute our shores with his cloven foot. Go he must, and, if necessary, with the blood-hounds on his track. The scum of Europe and the mudsills of Yankeedom shall never be permitted to advance a step south of 36° 30′, the old *Missouri Compromise line.* South of that latitude is ours—westward to the Pacific. With my heart of hearts I hate a Yankee; and I will make my children swear eternal hatred to the whole Yankee race.

"In battle, one Southron is equivalent to ten Northern hirelings; but I regard it a waste of time to speak of Yankees—they deserve not our attention. . . . We have a genial clime, and a soil of uncommon fertility. We have free institutions—freedom for the white man, bondage for the black man, as Nature and Nature's God designed. We have fair women and brave men. The lines have truly fallen to us in pleasant places. We have indeed a goodly heritage. The only evil we complain of is our bondage to the Yankees, through the Federal Union. Let us burst these shackles from our limbs, and we will be free indeed."

Four years later, the State of Mississippi was marked in every direction by the dark lines of War's desolating paths, and in almost every district were heard the anathemas of a deceived, betrayed, and suffering people, against those Oligarchs whose folly and wickedness had laid the Commonwealth and its thousands of happy homes in ruins.

reject the terms that a united South will agree upon. If accepted, well and good; if rejected, a united South can win all its rights, in or out of the Union." The Co-operationists, swayed by reason rather than by passion, counseled waiting for an overt act of wrong on the part of the incoming Administration, before raising the resisting arm. This counsel the Hotspurs denounced as cowardly in thought and disastrous in practice; and one of their poets, with bitter irony, put submissive words into their mouths, calculated to stir up the passions of the people. He said:—

> "We are waiting till Abe Lincoln grasps the *purse* and grasps the *sword*,
> And is sending down upon us all his Abolition horde;
> Waiting till our friends are murdered, and our towns and cities sacked
> And 'poor Sambo' gets his freedom—waiting for the 'overt act.'
> Waiting till our fields of cotton, cane, and rice, and waving grain,
> All are desolate and lonely, 'neath *King Cuffee's* stupid reign;
> Till our sisters, wives, and daughters are compelled to his embrace;
> Yes, we're waiting, only waiting, for this horrible disgrace."

The Convention met on the 7th of January, at Jackson, the State capital, a town of about two thousand five hundred inhabitants. It was found that only about one-third of the members were "Co-operationists." This gave the "Secessionists" entire confidence, and made them exceedingly arrogant in speech and manner. Efforts were made by the "Co-operationists" to postpone action, but these were put down by decided majority votes. This unanimity made the progress of business easy.

Delegates from South Carolina and Alabama, who were present, were invited to seats in the Convention, and were received with great applause. A committee appointed to draft an Ordinance of Secession, having their work all prepared for them by the leaders, were not long at their labor. An ordinance was reported on the 8th, and many of the "Co-operationists" were so intimidated by threats, that on the final vote on the measure only fifteen had the courage to say No. It was adopted on the 9th, by a vote of eighty-four ayes and fifteen noes, and was afterward declared unanimous. It was brief, and arranged in four sections. The first was a simple declaration, in set terms, that all connection with the old Union was forever broken, and that Mississippi was a "free, sovereign, and independent State." The second decreed that the clause in the State Constitution, which required all officers to take an oath to support the National Constitution, was thereby "abrogated and annulled." The third declared that all rights acquired and vested under the National Constitution, or any act of Congress, and not incompatible with the Ordinance, should remain in full force and effect. The fourth, speaking for the people of the State, said, that they would "consent to form a Federal Union with such of the States as have seceded or may secede from the Union of the United States of America," upon the basis of the National Constitution, with a qualification.

The next step was to assert the sovereignty of Mississippi by acts. That sovereignty was formally acknowledged by Judge Samuel J. Gholson, of the United States District Court, who resigned his office because his State, in the exercise of sovereignty, had cut the bond that held it to the old Union. South Carolina was formally acknowledged as a Sovereign State by the younger but not less ardent sister, who, like herself, had a population of slaves greater in number than her population of freemen.—a distinction then not vouchsafed to any other States in the Union.[1]

Steps were taken, through committees, to sever effectually every connection with the National Government, excepting the convenient one of the postal system. They also assumed the right to dictate the terms upon which the Mississippi River should be navigated, in the portion that washed the borders of their commonwealth. By order of Governor

January 12, 1861. Pettus,* the "Quitman Battery," as a company of frantic artillerists called themselves, hastened from Jackson to Vicksburg, and planted cannon on the bluff there, with orders to hail and examine every vessel that should attempt to pass. On Tuesday, the

January, 18th,[b] the river steamer *A. O. Tyler* was brought to by a shot athwart her bows, and others were soon served in the same way. This battery was a representative of sovereignty, which the arrogant Oligarchs in power in Mississippi set up, in the very wantonness of pride, to command the obeisance of others. The act was sanctioned by the confederated conspirators assembled at Montgomery a month later, who followed up this attempt to blockade the great aqueous highway, by establishing a custom-house at Neine's Landing, near the boundary between Mississippi and Tennessee, and the erection of other batteries, whose guns for more than two years obstructed the river-trade. That first steamer (*A. O. Tyler*) arrested at Vicksburg, was afterward converted into a national gunboat, and did good service in putting down the rebellion. The blockade at Vicksburg created intense exasperation among the navigators of the river, and threats of vengeance came down from Cincinnati and St. Louis.[2]

Measures were taken by the Convention, and by the Legislature, which had reassembled, in order to give force to the Ordinance of Secession, to increase the military power of the State. The Governor, on hearing that the Chief Magistrate of Louisiana had seized the National Arsenal at Baton Rouge, with its fifty thousand small arms, heavy cannon, and munitions of war, sent Colonel C. G. Armistead, to ask him to share his plunder with his brother of Mississippi, "on such terms as he might deem just." Pettus asked for ten thousand stand of arms. He got eight thousand muskets, one thousand rifles, six 24-pound cannon and equipage, and a considerable amount of ammunition. Private munificence was exhibited to some degree. "Patriotic citizens," said the Governor, "in various portions of the State, have extended to me pecuniary aid in arming the State. Hon. A. G. Brown sent me a bill on New York for five hundred dollars. Colonel Jeff. Davis and Hon. Jacob Thompson have guaranteed the payment, in May or June, of twenty-five thousand dollars, for the purchase of arms."[3]

[1] The population of South Carolina, in 1860, was 703,812, of whom 402,541 were slaves, or 101,270 more slaves than free persons. The population of Mississippi, at the same time, was 791,396, of whom 436,696 were slaves, or 82,000 more slaves than free persons.

[2] "Cincinnati steamboat men have been thrown into a fever, from the Governor of Mississippi ordering cannon and a military company to Vicksburg, to hail all steamboats passing. The Abolition journals of Cincinnati howl over it, and are greatly incensed. We would like to see them help themselves."—*Memphis Evening Argus,* January 17, 1861.

[3] Message of Governor Pettus to the Legislature of Mississippi, January 15, 1861. Brown and Davis were members of the Senate of the United States, and left their seats because of the alleged secession of their State. Thompson had been a member of Buchanan's Cabinet until the day before the Mississippi Ordinance of Secession was passed.

The Legislature of Mississippi levied an additional tax of fifty per cent. upon the amount of the existing State tax, and authorized the Governor to borrow two millions of dollars at ten per cent. interest, payable in one, two, and three years, out of the resources of the State, raised chiefly by taxation. These measures alarmed the capitalists and large property-holders, who desired no change; but many of them had already been threatened with personal violence and confiscation of their estates, and all were compelled to acquiesce in any measures which the leaders of secession saw fit to employ. Already a system of terrorism, sharp and implacable, had begun to make the expressed voice of the people of Mississippi a "unit in favor of secession." By these means the conspirators silenced all opposition. The hopes of the late General Quitman (a former Governor of the State), a native of the State of New York, one of the most persistent and dangerous enemies of American nationality, and on whom fell the mantle of Calhoun, as the chief leader of secessionists, were soon realized. The State was placed in an attitude of open revolt in the maintenance of the doctrine of State Supremacy.

When the Mississippi Convention had finished the business for which it had assembled, it adjourned until the 25th of March, for an object which will be hereafter considered.

Florida, purchased of Spain less than half a century ago,ᵃ and the most unimportant State in the Union in population[1] and   ᵃ 1820. developed resources, was early made the theater of seditious speech and treasonable action. Its politicians at home, and its representatives in Congress, were more haughty and pretentious, if possible, than those of South Carolina, in the assumption of supreme sovereignty for their dependent commonwealth, as we have already observed.[2] They were anxious to establish an independent empire on the borders of the Gulf; and early in January, 1861, they met in Convention to take the first step in the necessary revolution, by declaring Florida no longer a member of the Union. The Convention assembled at Tallahassee, the capital of the State, a city of less than two thousand inhabitants, on the 3d, when Colonel Petit was chosen temporary Chairman, and Bishop Rutledge invoked the blessing of God upon the wicked acts it was about to perform. The number of its members was sixty-nine; and it was found that not more than one-third of them were "Co-operationists." The Legislature, fully prepared to work in harmony with the Convention, assembled at the same place on the 5th.

On the 10th of January an Ordinance of Secession was adopted by the Florida Convention, by a vote of sixty-two ayes to seven noes. Its preamble set forth, that "all hopes of preserving the Union upon terms consistent with the safety and honor of the Slaveholding States" had been "fully dissipated;" and it was declared that the State, acting in its "sovereign capacity," was, by this ordinance, withdrawn from the Union, and Florida had become "a sovereign and independent nation." On the following day the ordinance was signed, amidst the firing of cannon and the

---

[1] The population of the State, in 1860, was one hundred and forty thousand nine hundred and thirty-nine, of whom only a little more than half were white.   [2] See page 60.

---

ringing of bells; and the glad tidings were sent swiftly over the Gulf States and other portions of the Union by the telegraph. The representatives of Florida in the National Congress, and especially Senators Mallory and Yulee, received the announcement with great satisfaction, but, unlike the South Carolina Senators, they remained in their seats, that they might be more mischievous to the Government than they could be out of them. On the 14th,[a] Yulee wrote to the Chairman of the Convention, from his desk in the Senate Chamber, to ·that effect, saying:—"It seemed to be the opinion [at a conference of conspirators in Washington] that if we left here, force, loan, and volunteer bills might be passed, which would put Mr. Lincoln in immediate condition for hostilities; whereas, by remaining in our places until the 4th of March, it is thought we can keep the hands of Mr. Buchanan tied, and disable the Republicans from effecting any legislation which will strengthen the hands of the incoming Administration."[1] Other Senators, as we shall observe hereafter, wrote similar letters to their constituents. These infamous epistles were sent free in the national mail, under the official frank of their more infamous authors.

[a] January, 1861.

DAVID L. YULEE.

The Convention at Tallahassee was addressed by L. W. Spratt, of South Carolina, the great advocate of the African Slave-trade. Delegates were appointed to a general convention, to assemble at Montgomery, Alabama; and other measures were adopted to secure the "sovereignty" of Florida. The Legislature authorized the emission of the sum of five hundred thousand dollars in treasury notes; and they defined the crime of treason against the State to be, in one form, the holding of office under the National Government, in the event of actual collision between the State and Government troops, to be punished with death.

Before the Ordinance of Secession was passed, the Governor of Florida (Perry) made secret preparations, in conjunction with the Governor of Alabama, to seize the national property within the limits of the State. This consisted of Fort Jefferson, at the Garden Key, Tortugas; Fort Taylor, at Key West; Forts Pickens, McRee, and Barrancas, near the entrance to Pensacola Bay (a fine expanse of water at the mouth of the Escambia River), and the Navy Yard, at the little village of Warrington, five miles from the entrance to the Bay. He ascertained that the defenders and defenses of Forts Jefferson and Taylor were too strong for any force Florida might send against them, so he prudently confined his efforts to the harbor of Pensacola. He issued orders, immediately after the passage of the

[1] The original letter, now before me, was found at Fernandina, Florida, when the national troops took possession of that place, on the 3d of March, 1862. It was directed to "Joseph Finegan, Esq. (Sovereignty Convention), Tallahassee, Florida."

Ordinance of Secession, for the seizure of these forts and the Navy Yard, and disloyal men were in them ready to assist in the work. Fortunately, the command of the forts was in the hands of Lieutenant A. J. Slemmer, a young, brave, and patriotic officer from Pennsylvania, who, like Anderson, could not be moved by the threats or persuasions of the enemies of his country. Governor Perry had already been to New York and Philadelphia, and purchased one thousand Maynard rifles and five thousand Minié muskets for the use of the State.

ADAM J. SLEMMER.

Fort Pickens is on Santa Rosa Island, and commands the entrance to the harbor. Nearly opposite, but a little farther seaward, on a low sand-spit, is Fort McRee. Across from Fort Pickens, on the main, is Fort Barrancas, built by the Spaniards, taken from them by General Jackson, and repaired by the National Government. Nearly a mile eastward of the Barrancas, was the Navy Yard (since destroyed), then in charge of Commodore Armstrong, a veteran captain in the Navy.

Rumors reached Slemmer early in January, that the works in his charge would be seized by the Governor of Florida, when a Secession Ordinance should be passed. He believed the report when word came to him that the forts near Mobile had been surrendered to Alabama troops, and he resolved to take immediate measures to save those at Pensacola, if possible. On the 7th of January, accompanied by Lieutenant Gilman, he called on Commodore Armstrong, and asked his co-operation. Armstrong declined it, because he had no special orders to do so. Slemmer resolved to do what he might without his co-operation, and he at once took measures to secure the powder in Fort Barrancas, which he had been occupying. He caused the batteries to be put in working order, strengthened the guard, and, at sunset,* raised the draw-bridge. That evening about   * January 8, twenty armed men approached the fort, with the evident inten-   1861. tion of seizing it. They were discovered by a sentinel, and an alarm was given. Perceiving this, and finding the draw-bridge up, the insurgents fled.

On the following day, Slemmer received instructions from his Government to use all diligence and power for the protection of the forts. At the same time, Armstrong received instructions to co-operate with Slemmer. These commanders held a consultation. It was agreed that the small garrison could hold only one fort, and it was resolved that that one should be Pickens, the stronger, less liable to be attacked, and the one that might most easily be re-enforced. It was arranged for Armstrong to send the steamship *Wyandot*, Captain Berryman, to take the little garrison from the Barrancas to Fort Pickens, increase the force by as many men as could be spared from the Navy Yard, and order the *Wyandot* and the store-ship *Supply*, Captain Walke, to anchor under the guns of the fort.

Slemmer was soon ready for the movement, but Armstrong failed to perform an essential part of his business in the matter.   He could only send the garrison over in the *Wyandot*, and furnish some provisions from the Navy Yard.   Slemmer went immediately to the Commodore for an explanation.   He charged Armstrong with deception, and inquired, indignantly, how he supposed the fort, calculated for twelve hundred men, could be defended with only forty-six, the actual number of the garrison then fit for duty?   Slemmer did not know that the Commandant was surrounded by traitors just ready to desert their flag and betray their country.   He did not know that when, at that interview, he sent for Commander E. Farrand and Lieutenant F. B. Renshaw, and ordered them to see that the plans agreed upon by himself and Slemmer were carried out, these very men were then foremost at that post in disloyal designs.   It was even so.

FORTS PICKENS AND M'REE.[1]

On the morning of the 10th,[a] the *Wyandot* carried over Slemmer's command.   All night long, and all the day before, the men, the officers and their wives, and even children, worked without ceasing in preparations for removal.   For twenty-four hours no one slept, or even rested.   Among those workers were the heroic wives of Lieutenants Slemmer and Gilman, who bore a conspicuous part in the history of Fort Pickens at that time, because of their labor and fortitude.

[a] January, 1861.

The families at the Barrancas were embarked on the *Supply*, while the war-ship bore the garrison.   The latter landed at Pickens at ten o'clock, and was re-enforced by only about thirty ordinary seamen from the Navy Yard, who were without arms or equipments of any kind.   Nearly all the powder and fixed ammunition at the Barrancas were also carried over to the strong fort on the same day; and all the guns of the abandoned post,

----

[1] Fort McRee, on the main, is seen in the distance, on the extreme right of the picture.

fifteen in number, bearing upon the bay, were, by Slemmer's orders, spiked in position, for he had neither time nor means to dismount them.

The arrangement for the *Wyandot* and *Supply* to anchor near Fort Pickens was not carried out; and, to the astonishment of Slemmer, he was informed that Commodore Armstrong had ordered both vessels away, the former to the south side of Cuba, and the latter to her final destination off Vera Cruz, with coals and stores for the Home Squadron there. He remonstrated, but in vain. That night Captain Berryman sent him some muskets which he had procured, with difficulty, from the Navy Yard, to arm his seamen; and Captain Walke assured him that he would afford him all the aid in his power, in defense of the fort.

On the morning of the 10th, about five hundred troops of Florida and Alabama, and a few from Mississippi, commanded by Colonel Lomax, of Florida, appeared at the Navy Yard, and demanded its immediate surrender to the authorities of the State. Armstrong was powerless. Of the sixty officers and men under his command, he afterward said, more than three-fourths of them were disloyal, and some were active traitors. Commander Farrand was actually among the insurgents who demanded the surrender

NAVY YARD AT PENSACOLA.

of the post. These disloyal men would have revolted, had the Commodore made the least resistance, and he was compelled to yield. Lieutenant Renshaw, the Flag-officer, and one of the leading traitors there, immediately ordered the National standard to be pulled down. When at a little less than half-mast it was allowed to fall suddenly to the ground, when a greater portion of the men present, led by Lieutenant J. R. Eggleston, of the *Wyandot*, greeted the dishonored banner with derisive shouts. The command of the Navy Yard was then given to Captain V. M. Randolph, another naval officer who had abandoned his flag; and the post, with ordnance stores valued at one hundred and fifty-six thousand dollars, passed into the hands of the authorities of Florida.[1] At the same time Colonel Lomax and some men took possession of Fort Barrancas, and restored the disabled guns; and another party was soon afterward thrown into Fort McRee. Farrand, Renshaw, Randolph, and Eggleston had already sent their resignations to

[1] When Colonel Lomax demanded the surrender of the Navy Yard, Commodore Armstrong said, that he had served his country faithfully all his life; that he loved the old flag, and had protected it in sunshine and in storm; that his heart was bleeding because of the distractions of his country; that he was a native of Kentucky, which had no navy, and, therefore, he knew not where he should go to make a livelihood in his declining years; that he had no adequate force to make resistance, and if he had, he would rather lose his own life than to destroy the lives of his countrymen. He then said that he "relinquished his authority to the representatives of the Sovereignty of Florida."—*Pensacola Observer*, January 15, 1861.

Washington, and they were accepted before the Government was aware of their treachery. At the same time, the insolent leaders of the insurrection in Florida sent word to the President, through Senators Yulee and Mallory, that the seizure of the public property within the limits of the State of Florida was in consequence of the transfer of troops to Fort Pickens, and proposed a restoration when that strong fortress should be evacuated !

Already, even before the Ordinance of Secession was passed, Florida

January 6, 1861. troops had seized the Chattahoochee Arsenal,[a] with five hundred thousand rounds of musket cartridges, three hundred thousand rifle cartridges, and fifty thousand pounds of gunpowder.[1] They had

January 7. also taken possession of Fort Marion,[b] at St. Augustine, formerly the Castle of St. Mark, which was built by the Spaniards more than a hundred years before. It contained an arsenal, the contents of which fell into the hands of the insurgents. On the 15th they seized the Coast-survey schooner *F. W. Dana*, and appropriated it to their use.

A CASEMATE IN FORT PICKENS.[2]

Slemmer heard of the movement at the Navy Yard through Commander Walke, who had received instructions from Armstrong to put to sea immediately with the *Supply*, if the post should be attacked. Slemmer sent a note at once to the Commodore, saying:—"I am informed that the Navy Yard is besieged. In case you determine to capitulate, please send the marines to strengthen my command." To this he received no reply. A few hours afterward, he saw the old flag go down at the Navy Yard, and heard, with mingled surprise and indignation, that the Commodore had ordered the *Wyandot* to co-operate with Fort Pickens under strange restrictions. Captain Berryman was ordered not to fire a shot unless his vessel should be attacked. In case Pickens should be assailed,

---

[1] The Arsenal was in the keeping of Sergeant Powell and three men. Powell had been in the employment of the Government for twenty years. He made the following speech on this occasion:—

"OFFICERS AND SOLDIERS:—Five minutes ago I was the commander of this Arsenal; but, in consequence of the weakness of my command, I am obliged to surrender—an act which I have hitherto never had to do during my whole military career. If I had a force equal to, or half the strength of yours, I'll be d—d if you would have ever entered that gate until you walked over my dead body. You see that I have but *three* men. These are laborers, and cannot contend against you. I now consider myself a prisoner of war. Take my sword, Captain Jones."

Jones returned it, saying, "Take your sword; you are too brave a man to disarm." The troops then gave three cheers for Powell.—*Correspondence of the Jacksonville Southern Confederacy.*

[2] To those not familiar with military names, it may be proper to observe, that a *casemate* is a vaulted chamber in a fort, with an opening outward for the use of cannon, and spacious enough, in large regular works, to be used as quarters and hospital to a garrison during war. They are made bomb-proof, so that these terrible missiles cannot enter them. Our little picture is a good delineation of a casemate, seen from the interior of the fort. Sometimes they are made only large enough for a gun and the gunners.

the *Wyandot* must be a passive spectator! She might as well have been on the south side of Cuba, if these instructions had been obeyed.

Slemmer was now left to his own resources. He was in one of the strongest forts on the Gulf coast, but his garrison consisted of only eighty one souls, officers and men. There were fifty-four guns in position and fit for service, and five months' provisions. The casemate guns, of which there were fourteen in order, were 32-pounders. Beside these there were seven 12-pounders; one 8-inch sea-coast howitzer; one 10-inch columbiad; six field-pieces; and twenty-five 24-pound howitzers for flank defense. The garrison labored unceasingly in putting every thing in working order, doing guard duty, &c., for an attack was hourly expected.

On the 12th,[a] Captain Randolph, Major Marks, and Lieutenant Rutledge, all in military dress, presented themselves at the gate of Fort Pickens, and demanded admittance as citizens of Florida and Alabama. They were not permitted to enter, but were allowed an interview at the gate with Lieutenant Slemmer. "We have been sent," they said, "to demand a peaceable surrender of this fort, by the Governors of Florida and Alabama." Slemmer immediately replied:— "I am here under the orders of the President of the United States, and by direction of the General-in-chief of the Army; and I recognize no right of any governor to demand a surrender of United States property. My orders are distinct and explicit." The intruders immediately withdrew, and Slemmer prepared for an attack that night, which was dark and stormy. All night long sentinels were posted beyond the glacis,[1] and the men stood at their guns.

On the 15th,[b] Colonel William H. Chase, of Massachusetts, formerly of the United States Army, but now in command of all of the insurgent troops in Florida, accompanied by Farrand, of the Navy, who had just abandoned his flag, asked for an interview with Slemmer. It was granted. Chase informed him that he had full power from the Chief Magistrate of Florida to take possession of the fort, and he desired to do so without bloodshed. "You can contribute toward this desirable result," he said, "and, in my judgment, without the sacrifice of the honor of yourself or your gallant officers and men." He said he came to demand a surrender of the fort, which was to be held subject to any agreement that might be entered into between the Commissioners of the State (Senators Mallory and Yulee, then in their official seats at Washington) and the National Government. "I would not counsel you to do aught that was dishonorable," said the tempter. "On the contrary, to do that which will secure for you the commendation of all Christian gentlemen." He entreated him not to be guilty of allowing fraternal blood to flow. "Listen to me then," he continued, "I beg of you, and act with me in preventing the shedding of the blood of your brethren." He promised Slemmer and his garrison comfortable quarters at Barrancas, if he would only prove unfaithful to his trust; and, in conclusion, he said:—"Consider this well, and take care that you will so act as to have no fearful recollections of a tragedy

[a] January, 1861.

[b] January.

---

[1] The glacis is the superior slope of the parapet of the covered way, extended in a gentle declivity to the surrounding country.

that you might have avoided, but rather to make the present moment one of the most glorious, because Christian-like, of your life." The Serpent could not charm the Patriot. Slemmer did so act as to make it the most glorious moment of his life, by first consulting with the Commanders of the *Wyandot* and *Supply*, and then positively refusing to give up the fort.[1]

The insurgents on shore now commenced preparations for assailing Fort Pickens, and on the 18th,[a] Chase again demanded its surrender, saying he was re-enforced, and more troops were expected. Slemmer remained firm. Then commenced the siege of Fort Pickens, which will be considered hereafter.

[a] January, 1861.

While these events were transpiring near Pensacola,[2] the Convention at Tallahassee were working in harmony with the Legislature. They appointed Senators Mallory and Yulee, then in the Senate at Washington, commissioners to treat with the National Government concerning its property within the limits of Florida, and also appointed delegates to a general convention at Montgomery.

On the day after the Florida Ordinance of Secession was passed, the politicians of Alabama assembled at Montgomery, the capital of the State, committed a similar act of folly and crime. We have already observed the preliminary movements to this end, in that State, with Governor Moore as an active leader.[3] The election of members of the Convention was held on the 24th of December,[b] and, as in other States, the politicians were divided into two classes, namely, "immediate Secessionists" and "Co-operationists." The latter were also divided; one party wishing the co-operation of all the Slave-labor States, and the other caring only for the co-operation of the Cotton-producing States. The vote, as reported, for all but ten counties was, for secession, twenty-four thousand four hundred and forty-five; and for co-operation, thirty-three thousand six hundred and eighty-five. Of the ten counties, some were for secession and others for co-operation.

[b] 1860.

The Convention assembled at Montgomery on the 7th of January.[c] Every county in the State was represented, and the number of delegates was one hundred. William Brooks was chosen President. On the same day, the representatives of Alabama[4] in the Congress at Washington, on consultation, resolved to telegraph to the Convention their advice to pass an ordinance of secession immediately.

[c] 1861.

The Convention was marked by a powerful infusion of Union sentiment, which found expression in attempts to postpone secession under the plea of the desirableness of co-operation. Resolutions of this tenor were offered on the 9th; while another proposed that the powers of the State should be pledged to "resist any attempt on the part of the Federal Government to

---

[1] The foregoing brief narrative of the movements in Pensacola Bay, immediately after the passage of the Ordinance of Secession by the Convention of Florida politicians, is compiled chiefly from the manuscript report of Lieutenant Slemmer, now before me, made to Adjutant-General Thomas, on the 26th of January, 1861.

[2] The city of Pensacola is eight miles northeastward from the Navy Yard, and about ten miles from the entrance to the bay. It contained about two thousand inhabitants at the time we are considering.

[3] See page 60.

[4] Benjamin Fitzpatrick and Clement C. Clay, *Senators;* James L. Pugh, David Clopton, Sydenham Moore, George S. Houston, W. R. W. Cobb, J. A. Stallworth, J. L. M. Curry, *Representatives.*

coerce any seceding State." After discussing various resolutions, it was finally resolved, by unanimous vote, that the people of Alabama would not submit to a Republican administration.

On the 10th an ordinance of secession was reported by the majority of a Committee of Thirteen, appointed to draft it, of whom seven were "Secessionists" and six "Co-operationists." It was longer than any of its predecessors, but similar to them in tenor. With that groundless sophistry and reckless disregard of the plainest historic truths which characterized the speeches and writings of the men of the State Supremacy school, they assumed that their commonwealth, which was created by the National Government, first a Territory[a] and then a State,[b] had "delegated sovereign powers" to that Government, which were now "resumed and vested in the people of the State of Alabama." This was an act as sensible as if Man should say to his Maker, "I will resume the life I have delegated to you, vest it in myself, and henceforth there shall be no union between us!" The ordinance favored the formation of a confederacy of Slave-labor States, and formally invited the others to send delegates to meet those of Alabama in convention, on the 4th of February, in the city of Montgomery, for consultation on the subject.

[a] 1817.
[b] 1819.

The Alabama Convention was not harmonious. Some seriously discordant notes were heard. The Union element was not inclined to yield every thing without a struggle. There was a minority report on secession; and many men were favorable to postponing action altogether, until the 4th of March, with the hope of preserving the Union. So doubtful was the final result, that, so late as the 17th,[c] a dispatch was sent by telegraph to the Alabama delegation in Congress, to retain their seats until further advised. This opposition exasperated the ultra-secessionists, and they became very violent. When, in the debate that followed the presentation of the two reports, Nicholas Davis, of Huntsville, in northern Alabama, declared his belief that the people of that section would not submit to any disunion schemes of the Convention, William L. Yancey, whose business for many months had been to "fire the Southern heart and precipitate the Cotton States into revolution," sprang to his feet, denounced the people of northern Alabama as "Tories, traitors, and rebels," and said they ought to be coerced into submission. This high criminal, who had talked so defiantly about the sin of "coercion" on the part of the National Government, when its authority was resisted, was now ready to use brute force to coerce Union-loving and loyal men into submission to the treasonable schemes of a few politicians assembled in convention! Mr. Davis was not intimidated by Yancey's bluster, but calmly assured the conspirators that the people of his section would be ready to meet their enemies on the line, and decide the issue at the point of the bayonet.

[c] January, 1861.

The final vote on the Ordinance of Secession was taken at about two o'clock on the 11th,[d] and resulted in sixty-one ayes to thirty-nine noes. This result created great joy. An immense mass meeting was held in front of the State House in Montgomery, during the afternoon; and weak-kneed "Co-operationists," carried away by the popular enthusiasm, pledged their constituents to a support of the ordinance. A secession flag, which the women of Montgomery had pre-

[d] January.

sented to the Convention, was raised over the Capitol, amidst the firing of cannon, the ringing of bells, and the shouts of the multitude. There was no less excitement in Mobile, whither the news went with lightning speed. It continued until late at night, and was intensified by intelligence of the so-called secession of Florida. Government Street was filled with jubilant people of both sexes. They gathered in a dense crowd around a "secession pole" that had been erected at the foot of the street, from the top of which a "Southern banner" was displayed. A hundred and one guns were fired in honor of Alabama, and fifteen in praise of Florida. The bells rang out merrily, and all business ceased. The crowd formed in procession, and followed a band of music, that played the "Southern Marseillaise," to the Custom House, over which waved a Lone-star flag. On all sides was seen the fluttering of women's handkerchiefs, and the voices of men speaking to surging crowds were heard, while the military thronged the public square and there fired salvos of artillery. At night the city blazed with fireworks of every description; and the most popular pieces of all were the "Southern Cross" and the "Lone Star."

When the excitement of the hour was over, the Convention resumed its sittings. From beginning to end, these were in secret, and the public were indulged with only a crumb of intelligence that fell occasionally from the table of the conclave. It leaked out, however, that the Union feeling in the Convention was potently mischievous toward the ultra-secessionists, and that several delegates absolutely refused to sign the Ordinance, unless its action should be postponed until the 4th of March.

The Convention adjourned on the 30th of January until the 4th of March, after having resolved against the opening of the African Slave-trade, and making provision for the due execution of the Ordinance of Secession. At the close of the session, the President (Brooks) said:—"The people of Alabama are now independent; sink or swim, live or die, they will continue free, sovereign, and independent. Dismiss the idea of a reconstruction of the old Union, now and forever." Soon afterward, Thomas J. Judge was appointed a commissioner to negotiate with the National Government for the surrender of forts and other property to the authorities of Alabama.

A week before the Ordinance of Secession was passed at Montgomery, volunteer troops, in accordance with an arrangement made with the Governors of Louisiana and Georgia, and by order of the Governor of Alabama, had seized the Arsenal at Mount Vernon, about thirty miles above Mobile, and Fort Morgan, at the entrance to the harbor of Mobile, about thirty miles below the city. The expedition to seize the Mount Vernon Arsenal was commanded by Captain Danville Leadbetter, of the United States Engineer Corps, and a native of the State of Maine.[1] For this purpose the Governor made him his special aid, with the rank of colonel. He left Mobile on the steamer *Selma*, at near midnight of the 3d of January,ª with four companies of volunteers, and at dawn surprised Captain Reno, who was in command of the Arsenal. By

ª 1861.

---

[1] This man appears to have been one of the most fiendish of the persecutors of Union men in Alabama and East Tennessee, at the beginning of the civil war. His atrocious conduct in East Tennessee is darkly portrayed by Governor Brownlow, in his *Sketches of the Rise, Progress, and Decline of Secession*, page 311.

this seizure, the Alabama insurgents came into possession of fifteen thousand stand of arms, one hundred and fifty thousand pounds of powder, some cannon, and a·large quantity of munitions of war.

At about the same hour on the night of the 3d, when Leadbetter started for Mount Vernon, Colonel John B. Todd, acting under the orders of Governor Moore, embarked, at Mobile, in the steamer *Kate Dale*,[1] with four companies of volunteers, for Fort Morgan. They reached it at about three o'clock in the morning, and at five o'clock they were in possession of the post. The garrison not only made no resistance out an eye-witness declared, that when the State flag of Alabama r. .is unfurled, in place of the National flag that had been pulled down, they cheered it. It was a bloodless conquest. One of the insurgents, writing at the fort that morning, said:—"We found here about five thousand shot and shell; and we are ready to receive any distinguished strangers the Government may see fit to send on a visit to us." Fort Gaines, on Dauphin Island, opposite Fort Morgan, was taken possession of by the insurgents at the same time; and, on the same morning, the revenue cutter *Lewis Cass* was surrendered to T. Sandford, the Collector of the Port of Mobile, by Commander Morrison. On the 9th, five companies of volunteers left Montgomery for Pensacola, at the request of the Governor of Florida, to assist the insurgents of that State in the seizure of the forts and Navy Yard. These formed a part of the force to whom Armstrong surrendered his post.

When the Ordinance of Secession was passed, the Mayor of Mobile called for a thousand laborers, to prepare defenses for the city. These, and an ample amount of money, were at once supplied. The Common Council, in a frenzy of passion and folly, passed an ordinance, changing the names of several streets of the city which bore those of Free-labor States to those of places in the Slave-labor States. The name of *Maine* Street was changed to Palmetto Street; of *Massachusetts* Street, to Charleston Street; of *New Hampshire* Street, to Augusta Street; *Rhode Island* Street, to Savannah Street, &c. And now, at the close of January, the authorities of the State of Alabama, and of its commercial metropolis, were fully committed to the great work of treason, which brought terrible suffering upon large numbers of the peaceful citizens of that Commonwealth.

A week after the so-called secession of Alabama, the politicians of Georgia, assembled in convention at Milledgeville, the State capital, announced to the world that that Commonwealth was no longer a part of the great American Republic. We have already observed the preliminary secession movements in that State,[2] under the manipulations of Toombs, Cobb, Iverson, and some less notable conspirators, and the reluctance of the greater portion of the more intelligent citizens to follow the lead of these selfish and ambitious men. Their exalted positions (one a Cabinet Minister, and the other two named, National Senators) enabled them to work powerfully, through subservient politicians, in deceiving, misleading, exciting, and coercing the people. Toombs, in particular, whose thirst for power and

---

[1] This vessel was destroyed by a terrible powder explosion, at Mobile, on the afternoon of the 25th of May, 1865.
[2] Pages 51 to 58, inclusive.

personal aggrandizement, and contempt for "common folks," made him impatient of the popular will, and consequently inimical to republican institutions, was unceasing in his efforts to destroy the confidence of the people in their free Government. He employed falsehood, menaces, and the low arts of the mere demagogue in his unholy work; and he seems to have been the chief manager, while at home and in Washington, of a system of subtle terrorism, by which a majority of the members of the Convention, called to consider secession, were chosen from among the politicians of his disloyal school. In Georgia, as in Virginia, and most of the other Slave-labor States, there were "Minute-men," "Vigilance Committees," "Defense Committees," "Brotherhoods," "Knights of the Golden Circle," "Southern Rights," and other associations, all working in the interest of the conspirators. These were used before the election, and at the ballot-box, with great effect. "It is a notable fact," said a leading Georgia journal,[1] "that wherever the 'Minute-men,' as they are called, have had an organization, those counties have voted, by large majorities, for immediate secession. Those that they could not control by persuasion and coaxing, they dragooned and bullied by threats, jeers, and sneers. By this means, thousands of good citizens were induced to vote the immediate secession ticket through timidity. Besides, the towns and cities have been flooded with sensation dispatches and inflammatory rumors, manufactured in Washington City for the especial occasion. To be candid, there has never been as much lying and bullying practiced, in the same length of time, since the destruction of Sodom and Gomorrah, as has in the recent campaign. The fault has been at Washington City; from that cesspool have emanated all the abominations that ever cursed a free people."

The Georgia journalist told the truth at that time, for Washington City was, indeed, the place where the voltaic pile of active treason was to be found, in the persons of the congregated conspirators in Congress.

• 1860.

So early as the 13th of December,[a] about twenty of them assembled at night, at the rooms of Reuben Davis, a Representative from Mississippi (one of the Committee of Thirty-three[2]), and there signed the following letter to their constituents:—"The argument is exhausted. All hope of relief in the Union, through the agency of Committees, Congressional legislation, or Constitutional amendments, is extinguished, and we trust the South will not be deceived by appearances or the pretense of new guaranties. The Republicans are resolute in the purpose to grant nothing that will or ought to satisfy the South. We are satisfied the honor, safety, and independence of the Southern people are to be found only in a Southern Confederacy—a result to be obtained only by separate State secession—and that the sole and primary aim of each Slaveholding State ought to be its speedy and absolute separation from an unnatural and hostile Union."

This declaration, signed by a large number of Senators and Representatives, was scattered broadcast over the Slave-labor States, first by the telegraph and then in print.[3] It was one of the many "sensation dis-

---

[1] The *Southern Confederacy*, published at Atlanta, Georgia.   [2] See page 87.
[3] The document was sent out by Reuben Davis, with the following statement:—"Signed by J. L. Pugh, David

patches" spoken of by the Georgia journalist. It was also presented by Mr. Davis to the Committee of Thirty-three, with the expectation, no doubt, that it would frighten the Northern men into acquiescence with the demands of those of the South. It failed to do so; and on the 22d,[a] Toombs, who had lately arrived in Washington, telegraphed an address to the people of Georgia, half true and half untrue, in which he said:—"I came here to secure your constitutional rights, or to demonstrate to you that you can get no guaranties for these rights from your Northern confederates." He then informed them that the Republicans in the Senate Committee of Thirteen were, to a man, against making any concessions to the South. "That Committee is controlled," he said, "by Black Republicans—your enemies—who only seek to amuse you with delusive hopes until your election, in order that you may defeat the friends of secession. . . . I now tell you, upon the faith of a true man, that all further looking to the North, for security for your constitutional rights in the Union, ought to be instantly abandoned. It is fraught with nothing but ruin to yourselves and your posterity. Secession by the 4th of March next, should be thundered from the ballot-box by the unanimous voice of Georgia on the 2d day of January next. Such a voice will be your best guaranty for LIBERTY, SECURITY, TRANQUILLITY, and GLORY."

[a December, 1860.]

This dispatch produced, as it was intended to, a profound sensation in Georgia. "It has unsettled conservatives here," telegraphed[b] a number of citizens of Atlanta,' to Messrs. Douglas and Crittenden. "Is there any hope for Southern rights in the Union?" they inquired. "We are for the Union of our fathers," they said, "if Southern rights can be preserved in it. If not, we are for secession. Can we yet hope the Union will be preserved on this principle? You are looked to in this emergency. Give us your views by dispatch."

[b December 26.]

"We have hopes," said Douglas and Crittenden, in reply,[c] "that the rights of the South, and of every State and section, may be protected within the Union. Don't give up the ship. Don't despair of the Union."

[c December 29.]

To counteract this assurance, Toombs and others sent numerous "sensation dispatches" to Georgia. On the first of January,[d] the day before the election was to be held, Toombs telegraphed to an Augusta journal,[2] saying:—"The Cabinet is broken up; Mr. Floyd, Secretary of War, and Mr. Thompson, Secretary of the Interior, having resigned.[3] A coercive policy has been adopted by the Administration. Mr. Holt, of Kentucky, our bitter foe, has been made Secretary of War. *Fort Pulaski*

[d 1861.]

Clopton, Sydenham Moore, J. L. M. Curry, and J. A. Stallworth, of Alabama; Alfred Iverson, J. W. H. Underwood, L. J. Gartrell, James Jackson (Senator Toombs is not here, but would sign), John J. Jones, and Martin J. Crawford, of Georgia; George S. Hawkins, of Florida. It is understood Mr. Yulee will sign it. T. C. Hindman, of Arkansas. Both Senators will also sign it. A. G. Brown, William Barksdale, O. R. Singleton, and Reuben Davis, of Mississippi; Burton Cragie and Thomas Ruffin, of North Carolina; J. P. Benjamin and John M. Landrum, of Louisiana. Mr. Slidell will also sign it. Senators Wigfall and Hemphill, of Texas, will sign it." Davis added, that he had presented it to the Committee of Thirty-three, when a resolution was passed "avowedly intended to counteract the effect of the above dispatch, and, as I believe, to mislead the people of the South."

[1] William Ezzard, Robert W. Sims, James P. Hambleton, Thomas S. Powell, S. G. Howell, J. A. Hayden, G. W. Adair, and R. C. Honlester.

[2] *True Democrat.*

[3] This was eight days before Thompson resigned.

is in danger. The Abolitionists are defiant." On the same day, Jamison, President of the South Carolina Convention, telegraphed to the Mayor of Macon, saying:—"Holt has been appointed Secretary of War. He is for *coercion,* and war is inevitable. We believe re-enforcements are on the way. We shall prevent their entrance into the harbor at every hazard."

These dispatches, it is said, decided the wavering vote of Georgia for secession, at the election on the 2d of January, and yet the ballot-box showed twenty-five or thirty-thousand fewer votes than usual, and of these there was a decided majority against immediate secession. "With all the appliances brought to bear, with all the fierce, rushing, maddening events of the hour, the Co-operationists had a majority, notwithstanding that falling off of nearly thirty thousand, and an absolute majority of elected delegates of twenty-nine. But, upon assembling, by coaxing, bullying, and all other arts, the majority was changed.'"

The Convention assembled on the 16th of January. The number of members was two hundred and ninety-five. They chose Mr. Crawford to preside over them, and invited Commissioners Orr, of South Carolina, and Shorter, of Alabama, to seats in the Convention. On the 18th, a resolution was passed, by a vote of one hundred and sixty-five ayes to one hundred and thirty noes, declaring it to be the right and the duty of the State to withdraw from the Union. On the same day, they appointed a committee to draft an Ordinance of Secession. It was reported almost immediately, and was shorter than any of its predecessors. It was in a single paragraph, and simply declared the repeal and abrogation of all laws which bound the commonwealth to the Union, and that the State of Georgia was in "full possession and exercise of all those rights of sovereignty which belong and appertain to a free and independent State." The debate on the ordinance elicited many warm expressions of Union sentiments; and it was on this occasion that Alexander H. Stephens, made the speech already cited.[2] Toombs was in the Convention, and the chief manager of the secession machinery. He worked it with energy, and many changes among the Co-operationists were apparent. A. H. Stephens, his brother Linton, Herschel V. Johnson (the candidate of the Douglas Democrats for Vice-President), B. H. Hill, and others who afterward took an active part in rebellion, tried to prevent immediate secession, but in vain. Toombs and his party were strong enough to give to the ordinance, when it came up for a final vote, two hundred and eight ballots against eighty-nine. The vote was taken at two o'clock in the afternoon. That evening the event was celebrated in the Georgia capital, by a grand display of fireworks, a torchlight procession, music, speeches, and the firing of cannon. Similar demonstrations of joy were made at Savannah and Augusta.

An effort to postpone the operation of the Ordinance of Secession until the 3d of March failed. A resolution was then adopted, requiring every member of the Convention to sign the ordinance. Another, proposing to submit the ordinance to a final consideration by the people through the ballot-box, was rejected by a large majority. A copy of a resolution by

---

[1] *The American Annual Cyclopedia, and Register of Important Events of the year* 1861, page 338.
[2] See page 56.

the Legislature of the State of New York was received[a] from the Governor of Georgia at this point in the proceedings, and produced much excitement. It tendered to the President of the United States all ^{a January 20, 1861.} the available power of the State to enable him to enforce the laws, and uphold the authority of the National Government; and declared that, in defense of the Union, which had conferred prosperity and happiness upon the American people, renewing the pledge given and redeemed by their fathers, they were ready to devote their fortunes, "their lives, and their sacred honor." As soon as this resolution was read, Toombs offered the following, which was adopted by unanimous vote :—"*Resolved*, As a response to the resolutions of New York, that this Convention highly approves of the energetic and patriotic conduct of the Governor of Georgia, in taking possession of Fort Pulaski by Georgia troops, and requests him to hold possession until the relations of Georgia with the Federal Government be determined by this Convention; and that a copy of this resolution be ordered to be transmitted to the Governor of New York."

The allusion above to the seizure of forts brings us to the consideration of the fact that Governor Brown, following the advice of the South Carolina conspirators, and the recommendations of Toombs and others, at

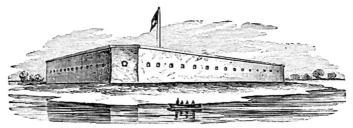

FORT PULASKI.

Washington, ordered the seizure of the coast defenses more than a fortnight before the Secession Convention met. Fort Pulaski, on Cockspur Island, at the mouth of the Savannah River, and Fort Jackson, nearer the city of Savannah, were seized on the 3d of January. The National Arsenal at the same city was taken possession of by insurgents on that day. On the 24th, the Arsenal at Augusta was seized by seven hundred State troops, in the presence of the Governor, and by his orders. The National troops in charge were allowed to salute their flag when they left, and were soon sent to New York. In the Arsenal were twenty-two thousand muskets and rifles, some cannon, and a large amount of powder and other munitions of war. The forts were without garrisons, and each was in charge of only two or three men. Fort Pulaski was intended for one hundred and twenty-eight guns, and a garrison of six hundred and fifty men. The walls were more than six feet in thickness, very solid, and well built of hard gray brick. It contained three furnaces for heating shot. It effectually guarded the main entrance to the Savannah River, and its possession was a great advantage to the insurgents during the earlier part of the war that ensued.

The Convention at Milledgeville adopted measures in accordance with the new order of things which they had decreed, and made preparations for maintaining, by force of arms, the independence of Georgia.   They appointed delegates to the proposed General Convention at Montgomery, and adjourned to an early day in March.

Just one week after the so-called secession of Georgia, the politicians of Louisiana declared the withdrawal of that State from the Union.   It was one of the most suicidal acts that madmen ever committed.   The prosperity of its great commercial capital (New Orleans, containing one hundred and eighty thousand inhabitants) was a blessing almost wholly derived from the Union.   Indeed, no State of the Republic was more dependent on the Union for its permanent growth in population and wealth than Louisiana. The device upon the Great Seal of the Commonwealth was a perpetual acknowledgment of the fact—a Pelican brooding over and feeding her young, emblematic of the fostering care of the National Government for its children, the States created by its will.

We have already observed the early movements of the politicians of Louisiana, led by Slidell, Benjamin, Moore, Walker of the *Delta*, and others, in drawing the people into the vortex of revolution.[1]   In the Legislature, which assembled at Baton Rouge in special session on the 10th of December, the Union sentiment was powerful, yet not sufficiently so to avert mischief to the Commonwealth.   An effort was made to submit the question of "Convention or No Convention" to the people.   It failed; and an election of delegates to a convention was ordered to be held on the 8th of January, the anniversary of the battle of New Orleans, in 1815.   No efforts, fair or unfair, were spared to excite the people against the Government, and elect secessionists.

The activity of the politicians in New Orleans was wonderful.   They expected the example of the city would be followed in the rural districts, and they sought to make that example boldly revolutionary by frequent public displays of their disunion feelings.   On the 21st of December, they publicly celebrated the so-called secession of South Carolina, with demonstrations of great enthusiasm. They fired cannon a hundred times; paraded the streets with bands of mu-

CUSTOM HOUSE AT NEW ORLEANS.[2]

sicians playing the Marseillaise Hymn and polkas, but no National air; flung out the Pelican flag of the State from the Custom House and other public buildings; and their orators addressed the excited multitude in favor of immediate secession.   Four days afterward, there was a public ratification of the nomination of secession or "Southern Rights" candidates, with the accompaniments of cannon, and flags, and speeches.   Yet, with all these manifestations of disaffection in the city, the great mass of the people of the State remained loyal—passively if not actively so. "In our section," a gentleman from the lower part of the State wrote, "the excitement is confined to the politicians; the people generally being borne along with the current, and feeling the natural disposition of sustaining their section. I think that ninety-nine out of every hundred of the people sincerely hope that some plan will yet be devised to heal up the dissensions, and to settle our difficulties to the satisfaction of both the North and the South."[1]

The popular vote at the election on the 8th of January was small. It was of such a complexion, however, that it made the secessionists confident of success—so confident that on the following day,[a] prompted by advice from Slidell, Benjamin, and other representatives of the State at Washington, the Governor sent military expeditions from New Orleans to seize Forts Jackson and St. Philip on the Mississippi, below the city, then in command of Major Beauregard; also Fort Pike on Lake Pontchartrain, and the Arsenal at Baton Rouge, then in charge of Major Haskin.   [a January 9, 1861.]

The expedition against the forts down the Mississippi consisted of a part of General Palfrey's Division. They left the city in the steamer *Yankee*, at near midnight, cheered by a multitude on the levee and vessels. They reached Fort St. Philip at eight o'clock the next evening.[b] It was in charge of a man named Dart, who had a few negroes at work there. Dart gladly gave the fort into the custody of the Louisiana Foot Rifles, who garrisoned it in the name of the State. Fort Jackson was taken possession of on the same evening, at nine o'clock. Sergeant Smith, of the National Army, gave the keys to the insurgents, under protest, and a company of the Washington Artillery took possession of the fort. At the same time, Fort Livingston, on Grand Terre Island, Barataria Bay, was seized by State troops; and on the 20th of the month, the unfinished fort on Ship Island, off the coast of Mississippi, was seized, and held by the insurgents. Another unfinished fort (Clinch) on Amelia Island, off the coast of Georgia, was taken possession of by insurgents of that State.   [b January 10.]

The troops detailed for the capture of the Government Arsenal and Barracks at Baton Rouge left New Orleans on the evening of the 9th, on the steamer *National*, and arrived at their destination the next evening. Baton Rouge insurgents had already prepared to attack and seize the Arsenal, but at the critical moment their courage had failed them, notwithstanding there were only eight men under arms, with Major Haskin, to defend it.

The New Orleans troops, three hundred in number, were commanded by Colonel Walton, of the Washington Artillery. They were paraded at dawn, on the morning of the 11th, and proceeded immediately to surround the property to be seized. Major Haskin had no adequate means for defense, and was compelled to surrender without offering resistance. By this success, the insurgents procured fifty thousand small arms, four howitzers, twenty heavy pieces of ordnance, two field batteries (one of 6 and the other of 12 pounders), three hundred barrels of gunpowder, and a

---

large quantity of other munitions of war. Governor Moore, as we have seen, turned over to Governor Pettus, of Mississippi, a part of this plunder.[1]

On the 11th, the barracks below New Orleans, which had been for some time occupied as a Marine hospital by the National Government, were seized by Captain Bradford, of the State infantry, in the name of Louisiana, by order of the Governor. The Collector at New Orleans was required to remove the two hundred and sixteen patients immediately, as the State wanted the buildings for the use of the gathering insurgents. General Dix was then at the head of the Treasury Department. As soon as he was fully informed of the matter, he wrote to the Collector (Hatch) that he could not "believe that a proceeding so discordant with the character of the people of the United States, and so revolting to the civilization of the age, had been sanctioned by the Governor of the State of Louisiana." He directed him to remonstrate with the Governor. Humanity or shame prevailed, and the invalids were permitted to remain.

The Legislature of Louisiana convened at Baton Rouge on the 21st of January, when a flag with fifteen stars (the number of the Slave-labor States) was raised over the Capitol. The Convention met at the same place on the 23d. The number of delegates present was one hundred and thirty. Ex-Governor Alexander Mouton, an intimate friend and willing instrument of Slidell,[2] was chosen President, and J. Thomas Wheat, Secretary. J. L. Manning, of South Carolina, and J. A. Winston, of Alabama, Commissioners from their respective States, were invited to seats in the Convention, and made vehement speeches in favor of secession. The Governor was formally

---

[1] See page 164.

[2] The politicians more directly under the influence of Slidell seem to have had the management of the Convention. It had been all arranged beforehand, apparently, that Mouton should be made President of that body. He was elected on the first ballot. As early as the 14th of the month (January), nine days before the Convention assembled, a letter written by Slidell, and signed by himself and Judah P. Benjamin, and Representatives J. M. Landrum and J. G. Davidson, of Lonisiana, was addressed, from the Capitol at Washington, "To the Convention of the State of Louisiana," directed to "Hon. Alexander Mouton, *President* of the Convention," &c. This letter (the original is before me) occupies six pages of large foolscap paper, and contains an expression of the views of the arch-conspirator and his colleagues on the great topic of the hour. It urges the necessity of immediate and energetic action; and after referring to the fact, that many of the people of the State were unwilling to accept secession as a remedy for grievances, because it seemed like revolution, it avers the right of a people to resist oppression, and says:—"You may well treat the difference between secession and revolution as one more of words than of substance—of ideas rather than of things." It denounces Holt as "the unconstitutional head of the War Department—an open and virulent enemy of the South"—who had submitted a plan to the Government "of a campaign on a gigantic scale for the subjugation of the seceding States." They confess that they united in a recommendation to the Governor, on the accession of Holt, to "take possession at once of the forts and arsenals of the United States within the jurisdiction of Louisiana." They recommend "immediate and unqualified secession," and express a belief that every Slaveholding State, except Maryland and Delaware, will join in the revolutionary movement. "Without slavery, we perish!" they exclaim. They then express an earnest desire that the Convention should fully recognize the right of navigating the Mississippi freely by all citizens on its borders, and the lands watered by its tributaries, with "a wish and hope," they say, "to reconstruct our Confederacy with such materials as are not irreconcilably hostile." It was the delusive dream of some of the conspirators, and the hope of the politicians of Louisiana, that the people of

FAC-SIMILE OF A PART OF SLIDELL'S LETTER.

the Western and Northwestern States, governed by self-interest alone, would become partners in their revolutionary schemes.*

"It had been a subject of earnest deliberation," they say, "among the delegations of the States wherein Conventions had been held, whether, even after their States had seceded, they might not possibly render better service to their constituents by remaining here, and opposing the passage of any measures tending to strengthen the incoming Administration in a policy of coercion." It says that they came to the conclusion that no certainty existed of their being able to do so. See extract of Yulee's letter, on page 166. A *fac-simile* of the above paragraph (the whole letter is in Slidell's handwriting) is given on this page. I am indebted to the Hon. Mark D. Wilbur, afterward in the National military service at Baton Rouge, for the original.

---

* A year earlier than this, a Cincinnati paper noticed the fact, that "agents of the politicians of the Gulf States had been in that city, consulting with leading politicians of the Buchanan party, and endeavoring to create a sentiment among business men favorable to the establishment of a Confederacy, leaving out Pennsylvania, New Jersey, New York, and all New England. Free trade was to be the basis of union. These agents, it asserted, were in all of the Northwestern States, and their aim was to spring the issue soon among the citizens of those States."—*McPherson's Political History of the Great Rebellion*, page 42.

thanked by the Convention for seizing the forts. A Committee of Fifteen was appointed to draft an Ordinance of Secession. It reported on the 24th, by their Chairman, John Perkins, Jr., and its ordinance was adopted, two days afterward, by a vote of one hundred and thirteen ayes to seventeen noes. Like Mississippi, Florida, and Alabama, Louisiana, the creature of the National Government, speaking in this ordinance through disloyal politicians, declared that it resumed the rights and powers "heretofore delegated to the Government of the United States of America," its creator.

The galleries of the hall were densely crowded with spectators at this time, who observed the casting of the ballots in profound silence. When the result was known, there was an outburst of the most enthusiastic applause. It ceased, and then President Mouton arose, with great solemnity of manner, and said :—"In virtue of the vote just announced, I now declare the connection between the State of Louisiana and the Federal Union dissolved, and that she is a free, sovereign, and independent power."

Then Governor Moore entered the hall with a military officer (Captain Allen), bearing a Pelican flag.[1] This was placed in the hands of the President, while the mass of spectators and delegates were swayed with excitement, and cheered vehemently.

THE PELICAN FLAG.

When all became quiet, a solemn prayer was offered, and the flag was "blessed according to the rites and forms of the Roman Catholic Church, by Father Hubert."[2] Then a hundred heavy guns were fired, and to each member was presented a gold pen wherewith to sign the Ordinance. After their signatures were affixed, to the number of one hundred and twenty-one, the Convention adjourned,[a]

[a] January 26, 1861.

to meet in the City Hall, at New Orleans, on the 29th, at which time the session was opened with prayer by the Rev. Dr. Palmer, whose Thanksgiving sermon, a few weeks before, we have already considered.[3]

Before the adjournment, the Convention, sensible of the folly of the Mississippi insurgents in planting a blockading battery at Vicksburg, and in accordance with the recommendation of Slidell and his Congressional colleagues,[4] resolved unanimously, that they recognized the right of a "free navigation of the Mississippi River and its tributaries by all friendly States bordering thereon ;" also "the right of egress and ingress of the mouths of the Mississippi by all friendly States and Powers." A motion to submit the Secession Ordinance to the people, for ratification or rejection, was lost.

[b] January 29.

On the day when the Convention reassembled at New Orleans,[b] an event occurred there which produced a profound sensation throughout the Union. Secretary Dix had sent William Hemphill

---

[1] The Committee of the Convention appointed to prepare a new flag and seal for the State, discovering that the device of a Pelican feeding her young had the idea of Union in it, were glad to find, also, that the pelican was not a fit emblem of Louisiana, because its form was unsightly, its habits filthy, and its nature cowardly, and so they had a good excuse for dispensing with the time-honored device on the flag and seal of Louisiana. The flag adopted by the Convention was composed of fifteen stripes, alternate red, white, and blue, with a red square in one corner, on which was a single yellow star. It was the National flag deprived of its beauty and significance.

[2] Journal of the Convention, page 18.   [3] See note 3, page 38.   [4] See note 2, page 182.

Jones as special agent of the Treasury Department, to secure from seizure the revenue cutters *Lewis Cass* at Mobile, and *Robert McClelland* at New Orleans. He found the *Cass*, as we have observed, in possession of the authorities of Alabama.[1] He hastened to New Orleans, and in a note to Captain J. G. Breshwood, of the *McClelland*, inclosing one from Secretary Dix,[2] he directed that officer to proceed immediately with his vessel to New York. Breshwood instantly replied:—"Your letter, with one of the 19th of January from the Honorable Secretary of the Treasury, I have duly received, and, in reply, refuse to obey the order." Jones immediately communicated the fact of this refusal to the Secretary, by telegraph, and informed him that Collector Hatch sustained the action of the rebel. Dix instantly telegraphed back, saying:—"Tell Lieutenant Caldwell to arrest Captain Breshwood, assume command of the cutter, and obey the order through you. If Captain Breshwood, after arrest, undertakes to interfere with the command of the cutter, tell Lieutenant Caldwell to consider him as a mutineer, and treat him accordingly. *If any one attempts to haul down the American flag, shoot him on the spot.*"

The conspirators, who held control of the telegraph in New Orleans, did not allow this dispatch to pass. Collector Hatch was in complicity with them, and the *McClelland* fell into the hands of the insurgents. Two days afterward, the National Mint and the Custom House, with all the precious metals that they contained, in coin and bullion, were seized as legitimate plunder by the authorities of Louisiana.[3] By an ordinance of the State Convention, a greater part of the coin and bullion then seized, to the amount of five hundred and thirty-six thousand dollars, was placed in the coffers of the State.

General Dix's order soon went over the land by telegraph and newspapers; and its

JOHN A. DIX.

last sentence thrilled every loyal heart with a hope that the hour of hesitation and temporizing, on the part of the Administration, had forever passed by. It had the ring of true loyalty and patriotism; and the words, "If any one attempts to haul down the American flag, shoot him on the spot," went from lip to lip like electric fire, and became a proverb in every true American's thoughts. It was heard with dismay by the more timid insurgents, while its promises gave joy to the lover of his country.[4] A small medal was

---

[1] See page 175.

[2] The original is before me. It reads thus: "This letter will be presented to you by Wm. Hemphill Jones, a special agent of this Department. You are required to obey such directions as may be given you, either verbally or in writing, by Mr. Jones, with regard to the vessel under your command."

[3] The value of gold and silver then in the Mint was $118,311, and in the Sub-treasury, in the Custom House, $483,984. Soon after this seizure a draft for $300,000 was received from the Treasury Department. The Sub-treasurer refused to pay it, saying, "The money in my custody is no longer the property of the United States, but of the Republic of Louisiana." Provision was made by the Convention for the payment of certain drafts; and the funds in the Post-office, amounting to $31,164, remained untouched by the insurgents.

[4] When Farragut's fleet approached New Orleans, in April, 1862, and the *McClelland* was set on fire and abandoned by the traitors in charge of her, David Ritchie, a bold sailor, boarded her, and saved from the flames the flag to which Secretary Dix alluded; also the "Confederate" flag which had been raised in its place. These

struck by private hands, commemorative of the event, of the exact size given in the engraving below. The words are not quite correctly quoted.

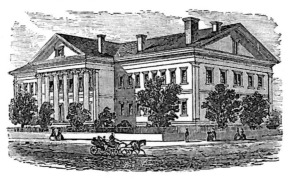

THE MINT AT NEW ORLEANS.

The disloyal politicians of Texas, a province purchased by the people of the United States at the cost of a war with Mexico (in which two hundred millions of dollars of treasure, and thousands of precious lives, were squandered), and by an after payment of ten millions of dollars more, followed the example of the conspirators of South Carolina, and their coadjutors in crime in other Cotton-growing States. That province had been a State of the Union only little more than fifteen years, when these bold bad men set up the banner of revolt. Its Governor, the venerable Samuel Houston, the hero of its war for independence, in 1836, and the real founder of the State as a sovereign commonwealth, adhered to the Union. He had been elected by almost ten thousand majority,[1] but the Legislature was filled with disloyal men. By these and others, immediately after the election of Mr. Lincoln, he was urged to either call the Legislature to a special session, or else a State Convention. He knew how mischievous the action of the Legislature and of such a convention would be at that very critical time, and he

THE DIX MEDAL.

steadily refused. The great mass of the people of the State were with him in sentiment; and as late as at the middle of December, there was an enthusiastic Union demonstration at Austin, the capital of the Commonwealth. Several young men drove through the streets, with the "Star-spangled Banner" floating over each carriage. They were greeted with loud cheers from the citizens; and on the 23d, an immense Union meeting was held there, when a pole, ninety feet in hight, was erected, and the National flag was thrown to the breeze from its top. The crowd was composed of men, women, and children, many of whom had come from afar to greet the old flag, and to hear the airs of "Hail Columbia" and "Yankee Doodle" played by the band of musicians and sung by patriotic young women. It was a bright and joyous day in Texas, and the hearts of the lovers of the Union were made glad.

flags were sent to General Dix by General Butler, who wrote, saying:—"When I read your instructions to shoot on the spot any one who should attempt to haul down the American flag, my heart bounded for joy. It was the first bold stroke in favor of the Union, under the past Administration."—*General Butler in New Orleans:* by James Parton, page 67.

[1] In 1859, the politicians of Texas nominated a State ticket pledged to favor the reopening of the African Slave-trade, one of the prime objects of the conspirators in the Gulf States, in plotting against the Union. It was headed by Hardin R. Runnels, a Mississippian. The people were alarmed by the movement, and when Sam. Houston took the field as an independent Union candidate for Governor, they rallied around him, and he was elected by an overwhelming majority.

That 23d of December, 1860, was almost the last bright day vouchsafed for Texas during years of civil war that ensued. At that moment there was a deadly enemy to free institutions and the most sacred rights of man working secretly in the vitals of the Commonwealth, and sapping the citadel of its life. This was an organization known as *Knights of the Golden Circle*, formed primarily, it is asserted, for the destruction of the nationality of the Republic, the seizure of the richest provinces of Mexico and the island of Cuba, and the establishment of an empire with slavery for its corner-stone. That empire was to be included in a golden circle, as its projectors termed it, having its center at Havana, in Cuba, with a radius of sixteen degrees of latitude and longitude, and reaching northward to the Pennsylvania line, and southward to the Isthmus of Darien. It would include the West India Islands and those of the Caribbean Sea, with a greater part of Mexico and Central America. The organization composed of the Knights of the Golden Circle was the soul of all the "fillibustering" movements from 1850 to 1857; and when these failed, its energies were concentrated to the accomplishment of one of its prime objects—the destruction of the Union. At the time we are considering, two adventurers (George W. Bickley and his nephew) were busily engaged in the establishment of "castles" or lodges all over Texas, creating a powerful band of secret plotters against the Government, and receiving, as rich compensation for their work, all the initiation-fees paid by members.[1] These "castles" included many members of the Legislature and active politicians in all parts of the State. Sixty of these irresponsible men, early in January, 1861, called a State Convention, to meet at Austin on the 28th of that month; and a single member of the Legislature issued a call for the assembling of that body at the same time and place. Already a system of terrorism had been inaugurated, and there was general alarm.[2]

Under the management of the Knights of the Golden Circle, or "K. G. C.," as they styled themselves by initials, and the disloyal judges of the State, an election of delegates to the Convention was held. The whole movement seemed so ridiculous,—so illegally and harmlessly revolutionary, —that the great body of the people regarded it as a farce, and not one-half of the voters of the State appeared at the polls. Alas! it proved to be the beginning of a bloody tragedy.

Governor Houston now felt it his duty to take measures to counteract these revolutionary movements. He summoned the Legislature to meet in extraordinary session on the 22d of January, for the purpose, primarily, of considering the "Federal relations" of the State, and, secondarily, to provide against Indian hostilities and the wants of an exhausted treasury.

The Legislature and the revolutionary Convention met at the appointed times. The former betrayed the liberties and rights of the people by the adoption of a joint resolution declaring the election of delegates to the latter as proper, and recognizing the Convention as a legally constituted body.

---

[1] *Secession Times in Texas:* by J. P. Newcomb, editor of the *Alamo Express*, page 6. Concerning this Order, we shall have much more to observe hereafter. It is authoritatively asserted that it was founded by John C. Calhoun and other South Carolina conspirators, in the year 1835.

[2] As early as the beginning of December, it had been asserted in the National Senate that men were *hanging from the trees in Texas because of their Union* sentiments! See quotation from Clingman's speech, on page 79.

Governor Houston protested against the assumption of any powers by the Convention beyond the reference of the question of secession to the people.

The Revolutionary Convention assembled in the Hall of the House of Representatives, at Austin, on the 28th of January. One of the chief managers was John H. Reagan, a judge, who afterward became the "Post-master-general" of the so-called "Confederate States of America." McQueen, a commissioner from South Carolina, was there to assist in working the machinery. It was easily managed, for it was so well constructed that there was but little friction. Of the one hundred and twenty-two counties in the State, not one-half were represented. The whole affair was a stupendous fraud upon the people. But what cared the representatives of the Oligarchy for the rights and privileges of the *people?* Their whole movement in the Slave-labor States, since the Presidential election, had been in contravention of those rights.

On the 1st of February the Convention, by an almost unanimous vote, passed an Ordinance of Secession. There were one hundred and sixty-six voices for it, and only seven against it. It declared that the National Government had failed "to accomplish the purpose of the compact of Union between the States," falsely charging that it had not furnished the inhabitants of Texas with protection against Indian depredations on its frontiers, when a large portion of the Army had been, and then was, actually employed in that very work. They charged that the National Government would no longer uphold the slave system. This was their chief grievance, and therefore they abrogated, in the name of the people of Texas, the Ordinance of Annexation adopted on the 4th of July, 1845. They talked of a "resumption of sovereign powers" with some propriety, for Texas is the only State of the Union that ever really possessed them, as an absolutely independent Commonwealth. They also did what the politicians in the other "Seceding States" refused to do, namely, decreed that the ordinance should be submitted to a vote of the people. But the merit of this seeming concession to the popular will was counterbalanced by the most outrageous usurpation and practical denial of the rights of the people. They appointed a day for the delivery of the popular verdict so early (February 23) that there could be no opportunity for a public discussion of the Ordinance. This, however, was a slight affront compared to two others, namely, the appointment of a "Committee of Safety," and of delegates to the Montgomery Convention.

The "Committee of Safety" was simply a powerful revolutionary machine for the purpose of carrying on effectually a system of terrorism already begun. That Committee at once appointed two of its number (Devine and Maverick) commissioners to treat with General Twiggs, then in command of the National troops in Texas, for the surrender of his army and the public property under his control. The Committee also managed the voting on the Ordinance of Secession, on the 23d of February, so adroitly, by means of misrepresentations and the arguments of the rope and fire-brand, that the voice of a really loyal people appeared in favor of secession by an alleged majority of over twenty-three thousand.

Having completed the preliminary work of treason, the Convention adjourned to meet again on the 2d day of March. In the mean time General Twiggs, as we shall observe presently, had fully performed his allotted part in the conspiracy, and given the State over to the absolute rule of the Secessionists; and when the Convention again assembled, its work was easy. The votes of the people on secession were counted on the 5th, and when the result was announced by the President there was great cheering, and he proceeded to declare Texas to be an independent State. On the following day the Convention instructed its delegates at Montgomery to ask for the admission of their State into the "Southern Confederacy," and appointed a committee to inform Governor Houston of the new political relations of the Commonwealth. To these communications the Governor replied, in substance, that the Convention had transcended its powers and that its acts were usurpations. He promised to lay the whole matter before the Legislature, which was to assemble on the 18th, until which time he should consider it his duty to perform the functions of his office regardless of all alleged changes.

SAMUEL HOUSTON.

The reply of the Governor produced great excitement in the Convention, and it was believed that he had issued orders for assembling the militia of the State to resist the action of that body. By an ordinance passed on the 8th, it defied his authority, and then he appealed to the people in a stirring address, which strengthened the hearts of the Union men of the State. He recounted his services and his difficulties, and complained bitterly of the usurpations of the Convention, which had "transferred the people, like sheep, from the shambles," from the Union to an unlawful league. He loved Texas too well, he said, to do aught that should kindle civil war on its soil, and he should not attempt, under the circumstances, to exercise his authority as Governor, nor would he take the oath of allegiance to the "Southern Confederacy."[1]

[1] "My worst anticipations," said the Governor, "as to the assumption of power by this Convention, have been realized. To enumerate all its usurpations would be impossible, as a great portion of its proceedings have been in secret. This much has been revealed:—

"It has elected delegates to the provisional council of the Confederate States, at Montgomery, before Texas had withdrawn from the Union, and who, on the 2d day of March, annexed Texas to the Confederate States, and constituted themselves members of Congress, when it was not officially known by the Convention until the 4th of March that a majority of the people had voted in favor of secession. While a portion of these delegates were representing Texas in the Congress of the Confederate States, two of them, still claiming to be United States Senators, have continued to represent Texas in the United States Senate, under the administration of Mr. Lincoln, an administration that the people of Texas have declared odious and not to be borne. Yet Texas has been exposed to obloquy, and forced to occupy the ridiculous attitude, before the world, of attempting to maintain her position as one of the United States, and at the same time claim to be one of the Confederate States.

"It has created a Committee of Safety, a portion of whom have assumed the executive powers of the Government, and to supplant the executive authority, have entered into negotiations with Federal officers. This committee, and commissioners acting under it, have caused the Federal troops to be removed from posts in the country exposed to Indian depredations, and had them located with their arms and field-batteries on the coast, where, if their desire is to maintain a position in the country, they can not only do so successfully, but destroy the commerce of the State. They have usurped the power to draw these troops from the frontier; but though in possession of ample stores, munitions of war, and transportation, have failed to supply troops in the place of those removed. As a consequence, the wail of women and children is heard upon the border. Devastation and ruin has thus come upon the people; and though the Convention, with all the means in its power, has been in session two weeks, no succor has been sent to a devastated frontier.

"The Committee of Safety has brought danger instead of safety. It has involved the State in an enormous

On the 20th, the Convention proceeded to depose Governor Houston and other State officers who refused to take the new oath. The disloyal Legislature sanctioned the measure, and on the 21st, the seals and the archives of the Commonwealth were resigned into the hands of Lieutenant-Governor Clarke, who assumed the functions of Provisional Governor, and who speedily issued a proclamation, forbidding all intercourse with the people of the Northern States.

Texas was now under the absolute control of the secessionists, and they managed public affairs with a high hand. They persecuted every proclaimer of Union sentiments; and Houston himself actually renounced his allegiance to his Government, and, descending from the proud patriotic position which he at first assumed, became a maligner of the President, and used the vocabulary of treasonable speech with great fluency. He declared that he was loyal so long as there was any loyalty left in Texas. So early as the 18th of May, in a speech at Independence, he recognized the validity of the "Southern Confederacy," and recommended obedience to its government. In September following, he found it necessary to explain his position, which he did in a long letter, in which he declared that " Union " and " reconstruction " were obsolete terms. "If there is any Union sentiment in Texas," he said, " I am not aware of it." He charged Mr. Lincoln and his Cabinet with the crime of usurping the .powers of Congress and waging war against "Sovereign States," thereby absolving their allegiance to the National Government. He also charged that they had, "with more than Vandalic malignity and Gothic hate, sought to incite a servile insurrection in Missouri." He denounced the President as an invader of Virginia, and declared that the South could never unite with the North, and that the latter could never subjugate the. South. The course of Governor Houston was a painful assurance to the people of Texas that the heel of a vile despotism was too firmly planted upon their necks to give them any hope of relief while the war continued, and they sat down to wait with faith and patience for the hour when Right should triumph and they should be redeemed.

We have now noted the principal events connected with the so-called secession of seven Cotton-growing States, namely, South Carolina, Florida,

---

expense for an army, where no army was needed, and left unprotected those who needed protection. It has exposed the State to ridicule, and wounded the chivalry and historic pride of the people, by sending an army of over a thousand men to attack a single post upon the Rio Grande, which has been permitted to defy them, until such time as its commander saw fit to withdraw. It has assumed to appoint agents to foreign States, and created offices, military and civil, unknown to the laws, at its will, keeping secret its proceedings.

"This Convention has deprived the people of a right to know its doings, by holding its sessions in secret.

"It has appointed military officers and agents under its assumed authority.

"It has declared by ordinance that the people of Texas ratify the constitution of the provisional government of the Confederate States, and has changed the State Constitution and established a test oath of allegiance to the Confederate States, requiring all persons now in office to take the same, or suffer the penalty of removal from office; and, actuated by a spirit of petty tyranny, has required the executive, and a portion of the other officers at the seat of government, to appear at its bar at a certain hour and take the same.

"It has assumed to create organic laws, and to put the same in execution. It has overthrown the theory of free government, by combining in itself all the departments of government, and exercising the powers belonging to each. Our fathers have taught us that freedom requires that these powers shall not be all lodged in, and exercised by, one body. Whenever it is so, the people suffer under a despotism.

"Fellow-citizens, I have refused to recognize this Convention. I believe it has derived none of the powers which it has assumed, either from the people or the Legislature. I believe it guilty of an usurpation, which the people cannot suffer tamely, and preserve their liberties. I am ready to lay down my life to maintain the rights and liberties of the people of Texas. I am ready to lay down office rather than yield to usurpation and degradation."

Alabama, Mississippi, Louisiana, Georgia, and Texas, and their preparations for a convention of delegates, to be held, by common consent, at the city of Montgomery, Alabama, on the 4th of February, 1861, for the purpose of forming a confederacy of Slave-labor States. We have seen how, in these States, the serpent of Treason was hatched from the egg of Secession. We have seen how absolutely the secession movement was the work of ambitious politicians, evidently in opposition to the feelings of the great majority of the people, and how carefully they excluded the people from any participation in the matter, after they had used them in putting the revolutionary machinery in motion. Only in Texas did they ask them to sanction their acts, and the concession in that case, as we have observed, was a most transparent fraud, to cheat the world into a belief that secession was accomplished by the legally expressed will of the people. Each convention unwarrantably stretched the powers given it, by choosing from among its own class of partisans, without the consent of the people, delegates to a General Convention to form a confederacy independent of the old Union; and in order to carry out the bold design of the conspirators, of having that confederacy consist of the fifteen Slave-labor States, four of the conventions appointed commissioners to go to these several States as seductive missionaries in the bad cause.[1] We have had glimpses of these Commissioners at several conventions.

Let us now observe relative events in the other States of the Union.

---

[1] The names and destination of these Commissioners were as follows:—
South Carolina.—To Alabama, A. P. Calhoun; to Georgia. James L. Orr; to Florida, L. W. Spratt; to Mississippi, M. L. Bonham; to Louisiana, J. L. Manning; to Arkansas, A. C. Spain; to Texas, J. B. Kershaw.
Alabama.—To North Carolina, Isham W Garrett; to Mississippi, E. W. Pettus; to South Carolina, J. A. Elmore; to Maryland, A. F. Hopkins; to Virginia. Frank Gilmer; to Tennessee, L. Pope Walker; to Kentucky, Stephen F. Hale to Arkansas, John A. Winston.
Georgia.—To Missouri, Luther J. Glenn; to Virginia, Henry L. Benning.
Mississippi.—To South Carolina, C. E. Hooker; to Alabama, Joseph W. Matthews; to Georgia, William L. Harris; to Louisiana, Wirt Adams; to Texas, H. H. Miller; to Arkansas, Geo. R. Fall; to Florida, E. M. Yerger; to Tennessee, T. J. Wharton; to Kentucky, W. S. Featherstone; to North Carolina, Jacob Thompson; to Virginia, Fulton Anderson; to Maryland, A. H. Handy; to Delaware, Henry Dickinson; to Missouri, ——— Russell.—*McPherson's Political History of the Great Rebellion*, page 11.

CHAPTER VIII.

ATTITUDE OF THE BORDER SLAVE-LABOR STATES, AND OF THE FREE-LABOR STATES.

HILST the politicians of the Gulf States were perfecting their scheme for forming a confederacy, there was universal agitation on the subject all over the Union, and especially in the Border Slave-labor States, where there were bonds of interest, and association, and consanguinity with both sections. Emissaries of the conspirators, resident and itinerant, were in those States, working assiduously for the corruption of public sentiment concerning nationality, and for the seduction of leading and influential men into ways of treasonable transgression. They were specially active in Maryland and Virginia, because the co-operation of the people of those States would be vitally important, in efforts to seize and hold Washington City in the interest of the conspirators. That city lay in the District of Columbia, contiguous to and between Maryland and Virginia, and was completely surrounded and filled with a Slave-holding population.

In Virginia, where disunion sentiments had been uttered and fostered, and from which they had been widely disseminated ever since the birth of the nation, the conspirators and politicians were anxious, at first, not so much for secession by States, or the formation of a new confederacy, as for a combined effort to seize the Capital and national archives, and establish an

aristocratic government, with Slavery for its corner-stone, on the ruins of the Republic. In the day-dreams of the politicians, Washington City appeared as a deserted capital (for the seat of government was to be nearer the Gulf), and its magnificent buildings were to be "consecrated to the genius of Southern Institutions." At the same time, the great majority of the people in those States were loyal to the Constitution, and willing to be obedient to the laws; and those of the western section of Virginia—the mountain region—as we shall observe hereafter, remained so, and

JOHN LETCHER.

were spared much of the misery inflicted by civil war.

John Letcher, formerly a member of Congress, and a willing instrument of the conspirators, was then Governor of Virginia. He and his associates watched the course of public events with great interest, for it was difficult for them to choose the most expedient course of action. While the authorities were cautious, the press was loud in its demands for revolutionary action.

Thoughtful men clearly discerned portents of a desolating storm, and, on the solicitation of many citizens, Governor Letcher called the Legislature to meet in extraordinary session on the 7th of January.ᵃ In his message, he renewed a proposition previously made by himself, ᵃ 1861. for a convention of all the States; and, with a seeming desire to save the Republic, he proposed that all constitutional remedies should be exhausted before withdrawing from the Union, saying :—" Is it not monstrous to see a Government like ours destroyed, merely because men cannot agree about a domestic institution which existed at the formation of the Government, and which is now recognized by fifteen out of the thirty-three States comprising the Union ?" At the same time, he instituted inquiries concerning the strength and garrison of Fortress Monroe, within the limits of his State, and the probability of success, should available Virginia troops attempt to seize it. He was advised, by a competent judge, that the attempt would fail, and he abandoned the contemplated scheme.

Letcher, no doubt, knew the plans of the conspirators of his section, and counseled inaction for the moment, until the revolutionary movements in the Gulf region should be more fully developed. " A disruption is inevitable," he said, " and if new confederations are formed, we must have the best guaranties before we can attach Virginia to either." His counsel was denounced by the more Southern leaders, as selfish and unpatriotic. Yet they applauded his declaration, that he should regard any attempt of the National troops to pass through Virginia, " for the purpose of coercing any Southern State, as an act of invasion, which would be repelled." In support of this assertion, the Legislature passed resolutions,ᵇ declaring that " any attempt to coerce a State " would be resisted by ᵇ January 8. Virginia.

Governor Letcher was at first opposed to a State Convention, but the Legislature authorized the assembling of one on the 15th of February, and appointed the 4th of that month as the day on which the delegates should be elected. It also decreed that, at the same election, the question whether the acts of the Convention on the subject of secession should be submitted to the people for ratification or rejection, should be decided by the popular vote. The secessionists denounced this decree as an emasculation of the Convention Bill, and subjecting to imminent peril " all that the people of Virginia hold most sacred and dear, both as to the Federal Constitution and the honor of the State"¹—in other words, imperiling the scheme of the conspirators to drag the people of Virginia into revolution. The decree delighted the loyal people of the State, and numerous Union meetings were held in Western Virginia.

While the Legislature seemed to be thoroughly inoculated with the revolutionary virus, it felt the restraints of the popular sentiment too forcibly to allow it to disregard the popular will, and several measures looking to a

---

¹ *Richmond Enquirer.*

settlement of existing difficulties were proposed in that body. Finally, on the 19th of January, a series of resolutions were adopted, recommending a National Convention to be held in the City of Washington on the 4th day of February, for the alleged purpose of effecting a general and permanent pacification; commending the "Crittenden Compromise,"[1] as a just basis of settlement; and appointing two commissioners, one to go to the President of the United States, and the other to the Governors of the "Seceding States," to ask them to abstain from all hostile action, pending the proceedings of the proposed Convention.[2] Copies of these resolutions were sent by telegraph to the President and to the Governors of all the States, North and South.

The proposition for a Peace Convention was received with great favor. President Buchanan laid the matter before Congress, with a commendatory Message, in which he said:—"If the seceding States abstain from any and all acts calculated to produce a collision of arms, then the danger so much deprecated will no longer exist. Defense, and not aggression, has been the policy of the Administration from the beginning."

The Virginians accompanied their propositions for securing peace with a menace. On the same day they resolved, "That if all efforts to reconcile the unhappy differences between the sections of our country shall prove abortive, then every consideration of honor and interest demands that Virginia shall unite her destinies with her sister Slaveholding States." Virginia was made to say to the North, substantially in the words of an epigrammatist of the time:—

> "FIRST.—Move not a finger; 'tis coercion,
>   The signal for our prompt dispersion.
>
> "SECOND.—Wait, till *I* speak my full decision,
>   Be it for Union or division.
>
> "THIRD.—If *I* declare my ultimatum,
>   Accept my terms as I shall state 'em.
>
> "FOURTH.—Then I'll remain, while I'm inclined to;
>   Seceding when I have a mind to."[3]

The Virginia Legislature appropriated one million of dollars for the defense of the State,[a] and made other hostile preparations; and the conspirators were so alarmed by the Peace Congress proposition, and by the waning hope of seizing Washington, that they took measures to precipitate the people of that Commonwealth into revolution. In order to stir up the smoldering fires of enmity against the people of the

* January 23.

---

[1] See page 89.

[2] Already a joint resolution had been introduced, to appoint a commission to represent to the President that, "in the judgment of the General Assembly of Virginia, any additional display of military power in the North will jeopardize the tranquillity of the Republic; and that the evacuation of Fort Sumter is the first step that should be taken to restore harmony and peace."

For the purpose of procuring abstinence from hostile action, pending the proceedings of the proposed Peace Congress, ex-President John Tyler was sent to President Buchanan, and Judge John Robertson to Governor Pickens, and the Governors of "other seceding States." The President informed Mr. Tyler that he had no power to make such agreement; and the Legislature of South Carolina said haughtily, by resolution, "The separation of this State from the Federal Union is final, and we have no further interest in the Constitution of the United States. The only appropriate negotiations between South Carolina and the Federal Government are as to their mutual relations as foreign States."

[3] New York *Commercial Advertiser*, March 1, 1861.

North, created by John Brown's raid, representatives of Virginia in Congress issued a manifesto, nine days before the election of delegates to the State Convention.[a] After mentioning proceedings in Con- ^a *January 26, 1861.* gress looking toward " guaranties for the South," they said :—" It is our duty to warn you that it is in vain to hope for any measure of concili- ation or adjustment which you could accept. We are also satisfied that the Republican party designs, by civil war alone, to coerce the Southern States, under the pretext of enforcing the laws, unless it shall become speedily apparent that the seceding States are so numerous, determined, and united, as to make such an attempt hopeless. . . . There is nothing to be hoped from Congress. The remedy is with you alone, when you assemble in sovereign convention. . . . We conclude by expressing our solemn convic- tion that prompt and decided action, by the people of Virginia, in convention, will afford the surest means, under the providence of God, of averting an impending civil war, and preserving the hope of reconstructing a Union already dissolved." This manifesto was signed by R. M. T. Hunter and nine others.[1] Hunter was the ablest man among them, and one of the most dangerous of the chief conspirators against the Government.

R. M. T. HUNTER.

The election was held on the appointed day,[b] and of the one ^b *February 4, 1861.* hundred and fifty-two delegates chosen, a large majority were opposed to secession. Concealing this fact, and using the other fact, that the unconditional Unionists were few, the newspapers in the interest of the conspirators declared that " not twenty submissionist Union men" had been chosen. " Virginia," said the leading organ of the secessionists in that State, " will, before the 4th of March, declare her- self absolved from all further obligation to the Federal Government. It is eminently proper that the State which was the leader in the Revolution, and the first to proclaim the great doctrine of State Rights in 1799, should lead the column of the Border States."[2]

We will consider the proceedings of the Virginia Convention hereafter.

The conspirators felt great anxiety and doubt concerning the position of MARYLAND. To the disloyalists of that State, with those of Virginia, they had looked for the most efficient aid in the work of seizing the National Capital. Maryland lay between the Free-labor States and that capital, and might be a barrier against Northern troops sent to protect it. Emissaries and commissioners from the Cotton-growing States were early within its borders plying their seductive arts, and they found so many sympathizers among the slaveholders, and a large class in Baltimore, connected by blood, affection, and commerce with the South, that they entertained, for a while,

---

[1] The following are the names attached to the document:—James M. Mason, R. M. T. Hunter, D. C. De Jarnette, M. R. H. Garnett, Shelton F. Leake, E. S. Martin, H. A. Edmonston, Roger A. Pryor, Thomas S. Bocock, A. G. Jenkins.
[2] *Richmond Enquirer*, February 5, 1861.

bright hopes of the co-operation of the people of that State. It is said that on the 1st of January, 1861, no less than twelve thousand men were organized in that State, bound by the most solemn oaths to do the bidding of their leaders, whose purpose was to seize Washington City.[1]

Independent of the innate loyalty of the greater portion of the people of Maryland to the flag of the Union, there were considerations of material interests calculated to make them weigh well the arguments for and against revolution that were presented to them. The value of the "slave property" of the State was then estimated to be at least fifty millions of dollars. This would be imperiled, for, if war should be kindled, that "property," possessing manhood and its instincts, would fly toward the free air of the North, so near and so inviting. A blight would fall suddenly upon Maryland, for the withdrawal, by such an exodus, of seven hundred thousand laborers from the fields would leave the soil untilled. And yet the madmen of the State—conspirators and demagogues and their dupes—blinded by passion, were ready and anxious to risk every thing, by clinging to the destinies, whatever they might be, of the Slave-labor States.

Fortunately for Maryland and the Republic, the Governor of the State, Thomas H. Hicks, his age on the borders of threescore and ten, was a prudent, loyal man. When Judge Handy, the Commissioner from Mississippi,
a 1860. visited him officially, at the middle of December,[a] and set forth the object of his mission, and the causes which justified secession, and desired him to call a special session of the Legislature, that they might authorize a State Convention, Hicks assured him, that while the people of his State were in sympathy with the institutions, habits, and feelings of the Slave-labor States, they were conservative, and ardently attached to the Union. He was disposed to consult the opinions of the people of the Border Slave-labor States before acting in the matter, and gave assurance that Maryland would undoubtedly act with those States. Handy was well convinced that his treasonable schemes found no favor in the mind and heart of Governor Hicks, and he departed. From that time the Governor was vehemently importuned by the politicians to convene the Legislature. Twelve of the twenty-two State Senators jointly addressed him, urging the necessity of an extraordinary session; and disloyal politicians took steps for calling an informal convention of prominent citizens, in order to get an expression of opinion in favor of such session. At the same time, the friends of the Union as strenuously urged him to refuse the call.

Governor Hicks was firm. He well knew the political complexion of the Legislature, and foresaw the mischief it might accomplish; so he steadily
b January 6, 1861. refused to call the members together. To this refusal he added an appeal to the people,[b] in the form of a protest against the attempt of demagogues to make Maryland subservient to South Carolina. "We are told," he said, "by the leading spirits of the South Carolina Convention, that neither the election of Mr. Lincoln, nor the non-execution of the Fugitive Slave Law, nor both combined, constitute their grievances. They declare that the real cause of their discontent dates as far

---

[1] Baltimore Correspondent of the New York *World.*

back as 1833. Maryland, and every other State in the Union, with a united voice, then declared the cause insufficient to justify the course of South Carolina. Can it be that this people, who then unanimously supported the course of General Jackson, will now yield their opinions at the bidding of modern secessionists? . . . The people of Maryland, if left to themselves, would decide, with scarcely an exception, that there is nothing in the present causes of complaint to justify immediate secession; and yet, against our judgments and solemn convictions of duty, we are to be precipitated into this revolution, because South Carolina thinks differently. Are we not equals? Or shall her opinions control our actions? After we have solemnly declared for ourselves, as every man must do, are we to be forced to yield our opinions to those of another State, and thus, in effect, obey her mandates? She refuses to wait for our counsels. Are we bound to obey her commands? The men who have embarked in this scheme to convene the Legislature will spare no pains to carry their point. The whole plan of operations, in the event of the assembling of the Legislature, is, as I have been informed, already marked out; the list of embassadors who are to visit the other States is agreed on; and the resolutions which they hope will be passed by the Legislature, fully committing the State to secession, are said to be

THOMAS H. HICKS.

already prepared. In the course of nature, I cannot have long to live, and I fervently trust to be allowed to end my days a citizen of this glorious Union. But should I be compelled to witness the downfall of that Government inherited from our fathers, established as it were by the special favor of God, I will at least have the consolation, at my dying hour, that I, neither by word nor deed, assisted in hastening its disruption."[1] Already Henry Winter Davis, a Representative of a Baltimore district in the National Congress, had published a powerful appeal[a] against the calling of the Legislature, or the assembling of a Border State Convention, as some had proposed. Nothing, he said, but a convention of *all* the States could be useful.　　　　　　　　　　　　　　　[a] January 2, 1861.

The address of Governor Hicks was read with delight and profound gratitude by the loyal people of Maryland, while the secessionists at home and abroad denounced him as a "traitor to the Southern cause." He steadily maintained the position of an antagonist to their treasonable designs. They tried hard, but in vain, to counteract his influence. At the middle of February, they held an irregular convention in Baltimore, and issued an address and resolutions. Their operations were abortive. The best men of the State, of all parties, frowned upon their work. A Union party was organized, composed of vital elements, and grew in strength and stature every day. Maryland, and especially Baltimore, became a great battle-field of opinions between the champions of Right and Wrong. The former triumphed gloriously; and

---

[1] Governor Hicks died suddenly at Washington City, on the morning of the 13th of February, 1865, where he was engaged in his duties as a member of the National Senate.

in less than four years from that time, slavery became utterly extinct in Maryland, by the constitutional act of its own authorities.

DELAWARE, lying still farther than Maryland within the embrace of the Free-labor States, had but little to say on the subject of secession, and that little, officially spoken, was in the direction of loyalty. Its Governor, several of its Senators, its Representatives in the National Senate, and many leading politicians, sympathized with the secessionists, but the people were conservative and loyal. The Legislature convened at Dover, the capital, on the 2d of January, when the Governor (William Burton) declared that the cause of all the trouble was "the persistent war of the Abolitionists upon more than two billions of property; a war waged from pulpits, rostrums, and schools, by press and people—all teaching that slavery is a crime and a sin, until it had become the opinion of one section of the country. The only remedy," he said, "for the evils now threatening, is a radical change of public sentiment in regard to the whole question. The North should retire from its untenable position immediately." On the following day, Henry Dickinson, Commissioner from Mississippi, addressed them. He declared, with supporting arguments, that a State had a right to secede, and invited Delaware to join the "Southern Confederacy" about to be formed. He was applauded by some, and listened to courteously by all. Then the House, by unanimous vote, adopted a resolution (concurred in by a majority of the Senate), saying, that they deemed it proper and·due to themselves, and the people of Delaware, to express their unqualified disapproval of the remedy for existing evils proposed by Mr. Dickinson, in behalf of Mississippi. This ended his mission. Delaware maintained that position during the war that ensued; and it is a notable fact, that it was the only Slave-labor State whose soil was not moistened with the blood of the slain in battle. No insurgent soldier ever appeared within the limits of that State, except as a prisoner of war.

Great efforts were made to force NORTH CAROLINA into revolution. The South Carolinians taunted them with cowardice; the Virginians treated them with coldness; and the Alabamians and Mississippians coaxed them by the lips of commissioners. These efforts were vain. Thompson, of Buchanan's Cabinet, went back to Washington,[1] convinced that the radical secessionists of that State were but a handful. The Legislature did, indeed, authorize a convention; but directed that the people, when they elected delegates for it, should vote on the question of Convention or No Convention. The delegates were elected,[a] one hundred and twenty in number, eighty-two of whom were Unionists; at the same time, the people decided not to have a convention. The Legislature also appointed delegates to the Peace Congress at Washington; also, commissioners to represent the State in the proposed General Convention at Montgomery, but with instructions to act only as "mediators to endeavor to bring about a reconciliation." They also declared, by resolution,[b] that if peace negotiations should fail, North Carolina would go with the Slave-labor States. They provided for the arming of ten thousand volunteers, and the reorganization of the militia of the State. Further than this the legislative branch of the State Government refused to go at that

[a] January 28, 1861.

[b] February 4.

---

[1] See pages 45 and 144; note 1, page 143, and note 3, page 91.

time, and the people, determined to avoid war if possible, kept steadily on in their usual pursuits. They heard the howling of the tempest without, but heeded not its turmoil for a time; and they were but little startled by the thunderbolt cast in their midst to alarm them, by Senator Cling-man, when, at the middle of February,[a] he telegraphed from Washington:—"There is no chance for Crittenden's proposition. North Carolina must secede, or aid Lincoln in making war on the South."[1] Finally, by pressure from without, and especially by the machinations of traitors nestled in her own bosom, the State was placed in an attitude of open rebellion.

a February 18, 1861.

The people of TENNESSEE, the daughter of North Carolina, like those of the parent State, loved the Union supremely; but their Governor, Isham G. Harris, was an active traitor, and had been for months in confidential correspondence with the conspirators in the Gulf States and in South Carolina and Virginia. He labored unceas-ingly, with all of his official power, to place his State in alliance with the enemies of the Union. For that pur-pose he called a special session of the Legislature, to assemble at Nashville on the 7th of January. In his message, he recited a long list of so-called grievances which the people of the State had suffered under the National Govern-ment; appealed to their passions and prejudices, and recommended several amendments to the Constitution, which would give to the support of Slavery all that its advocates desired, as a remedy for those grievances.

ISHAM G. HARRIS.

The Legislature provided for a State Conven-tion, but decreed that when the people should elect the delegates, they should vote on the question of Convention or No Convention; also, that any ordinance adopted by the Convention, concerning "Federal Relations," should not be valid until submitted to the people for ratification or rejection.

The election, held on the 9th of February,[b] was very gratify-ing to the loyal people of the State. The Union candidates were chosen by an aggregate majority of about sixty-five thousand; and, by a majority of nearly twelve thousand, they decided not to have a convention. The result produced great rejoicings, for it was believed that the secession movements in the State would cease. It was a delusive hope, as we shall observe hereafter.

b 1861.

KENTUCKY, a Border State of great importance, having a population, in 1860, of one million one hundred and fifty-five thousand seven hundred and thirteen, of whom two hundred and twenty-five thousand were slaves, was, like Maryland, strongly attached by triple bonds to both sections of the Union. Its action at this crisis, whatever it might be, would have great

---

[1] McPherson's *Political History of the United States during the Rebellion*, page 41.

influence, and that action was awaited with anxiety. The sympathies of the
Governor of the State, Beriah Magoffin, were with the Southern people and
their slave-system of labor; yet in his public acts, at this time, he opposed
secession. The people of his State were decidedly hostile to the revolutionary movements in the Gulf region; yet, whenever the question was raised
concerning the right and the duty of the National Government to enforce
the laws by its constitutional power, that enforcement was. called, in the language of the disloyal sophists, " coercing a Sovereign State," and therefore,
they said, it must not be tolerated.

      At a convention of Union and Douglas men of the State, held
^a 1861.   on the 8th of January,^a it was resolved that the rights of Ken-
tucky should be maintained *in the Union.* They were in favor
of a convention of the Slave and Free-labor Border States, to decide upon

some just compromise, and declared their
willingness to support the National Government, unless the incoming President
should attempt to "coerce a State or
States." The Legislature, which assembled
at about the same time, was asked by the
Governor to declare, by resolution, the
" unconditional disapprobation " of the
people of that State of the employment
of force against " seceding States." Accordingly, on the 22d of January, the
Legislature resolved that the Kentuckians, uniting with their brethren of the
South, would resist any invasion of the
soil of that section, at all hazards and to

BERIAH MAGOFFIN.

the last extremity. This action was taken by the authorities of Kentucky,
because the Legislatures of several of the Free-labor States had offered
troops for the use of the Government, in enforcing the laws in " seceding
States." The Legislature also decided against calling a convention, and
appointed delegates to the Peace Congress to meet at Washington City.
Such was the attitude of Kentucky at the beginning. A little later,
its public authorities and other leading men endeavored to give to it a
position of absolute neutrality.

    Missouri, lying west of the Mississippi River, was another Border State
of great importance. Its population in 1860 was one million one hundred
and eighty-two thousand three hundred and seventeen, of whom one hundred
and fifteen thousand were slaves. Its inhabitants had been agitated more or
less by the troubles in Kansas, a State stretching along almost the whole of
its western border, where the friends and enemies of the Slave system of
labor had quarreled and fought for several years previous to the year 1858.
In that school of experience, the Missourians had been pretty well instructed
concerning the questions at issue in the now impending conflict; and when
they were called upon to act, they did so intelligently. They knew the value
of the Union; and the great body of the people reprobated the teachings of
the disloyal politicians, and determined to stand by the Union so long as it
seemed to them a blessing.

The 4th of January, 1861, was an unfortunate day for Missouri. On that day Claiborne F. Jackson, an unscrupulous politician, and a conspirator against the Republic, was inaugurated Governor of the State. In his message to the Legislature, he insisted that Missouri should stand by its sister Slave-labor States in whatever course they might pursue at that crisis. He recommended the calling of a State Convention to consider "Federal Relations;" and on the 16th,[a] the Legislature re- *January, 1861.* sponded by authorizing one, decreeing, however, that its action on the subject of secession should be submitted to the vote of the people. The election resulted in the choice of a large majority of Union delegates by a heavy majority of the popular vote. They

CLAIBORNE F. JACKSON.

assembled at Jefferson City on the 28th of February. Their proceedings will be considered hereafter.

Adjoining Missouri on the south, and lying between it and Louisiana, is ARKANSAS, a rapidly growing Cotton-producing State. The people were mostly of the planting class, and were generally attached to the Union; and it was only by a rigorous system of terrorism that they were finally placed in an attitude of rebellion.

An emissary of treason, named Hubbard, was sent into Arkansas at the middle of December, by the Alabama conspirators. He was permitted to address the State Legislature[b] assembled at Little *December 20, 1860.* Rock, when he assured them that Alabama would soon secede, whether other States did or did not, and advised Arkansas to do the same. Ten days afterward there was an immense assemblage of the people at Van Buren, on the Arkansas River, in the extreme western part of the State. They resolved, on that occasion, that separate State action would be unwise, and that co-operation was desirable. It was evident, from many tests, that nine-tenths of the people were averse to the application of secession as a remedy for alleged evils.

On the 16th, the Legislature of Arkansas provided for the submission of the question of a State Convention to the people, and if they should decide to have one, the Governor was directed to appoint a day for the election of delegates. A majority of twelve thousand voted in favor of a convention. An election was held, when, out of about forty thousand votes, there was a popular majority of about six thousand for Union delegates. How that Convention was managed by the conspirators, and the people were cheated, will be considered hereafter.

We have now observed the revolutionary movements in the Slave-labor States down to the so-called secession of seven of them;[c] their preparations for a General Convention, at the beginning of Feb- *February 1, 1861.* ruary, to form a confederacy; and the construction of machinery, in the form of State conventions, for sweeping most of the other Slave-labor States into the vortex of revolution. Let us see what, in the mean time, was done in the matter in the Free-labor States, beginning with New England.

MAINE, lying on the extreme eastern border of the Republic, and adjoining the British possessions, had, in 1860, a population of over six hundred thousand. Its people watched the rising tide of revolution with interest, and were among the first to offer barriers against its destructive overflow. The idea of nationality, so universally a sentiment among intelligent men all over the Free-labor States, made such action instinctive; and everywhere assurances of aid were given to the Chief Magistrate of the Republic.

Israel Washburne, Jr., was then Governor of Maine. In his message to the Legislature, on the day of its assembling at Augusta, he ably reviewed the history of the Slavery question, and recommended the repeal of any laws that were unconstitutional. "Allow no stain," he said, "on the faith and

devotion of the State to the Constitution and the rights of the States." He declared that the concessions demanded by the politicians of the Slave-labor States were wholly inadmissible, and incompatible with the safety of the Constitution, as the exponent and defender of republican institutions. He stigmatized secession as a crime without the shadow of a right. "There is no such right in the Constitution," he said. "Congress cannot grant it; the States cannot concede it, and only by the people of the States, through a change in the Constitution, can it be conferred. The laws, then, must be

ISRAEL WASHBURNE, JR.

executed, or this, the best, because the freest and most beneficent Government that the world has ever seen, is destroyed." He pledged the State to a support of the Union, and he was sustained in this by the Legislature, who, on the 16th, declared by a large majority the attachment of the people of that State to the Union, and loyalty to the Government, and requested the Governor to assure the President of that attachment and loyalty, and "that the entire resources of the State, in men and money," were "pledged to the Administration in defense and support of the Constitution and Union." Willing to make concessions for the

a March 11, 1861.

sake of peace, the State Senate afterward passed a bill[a] repealing the Personal Liberty Act.

MASSACHUSETTS was an early and conspicuous actor in the great drama we are considering. In many aspects, in nature and society, it was totally unlike South Carolina, the cradle of the rebellion. Its people were the most energetic, positive, and ever-active of any State in the Union, and its wealth for each person was greater than any other. It was regarded by the people of the Slave-labor States as the central generator of the Abolition force that threatened the destruction of Slavery; and South Carolina orators and journalists made Massachusetts the synonym of Puritanism, which they affected to despise, as vulgar in theory and in practice. It must be confessed that much that was done in religion, in politics, and in social life in Massachusetts, did not harmonize with the opinions, habits, and feelings of the people of South Carolina. The representatives of Massachusetts in the National Senate (Henry Wilson and Charles Sumner) were known in every part of the Union as the most able and uncompromising opponents of the Slave system; and its Governor at that time (John A. Andrew) was an earnest co-worker with them in the cause of the final emancipation of the slaves within the borders of the Republic. Its Personal Liberty Act was most offensive to the slaveholders; and the ill-timed and irritating perform-ances of a few zealous men in Boston, on the 3d of December, 1860, as we have observed, in celebrating the anniversary of the execution of John Brown,[1] added intensity to the flame of passion—of hatred and disgust of New Englanders—in all the region below the Potomac and the Ohio, and far away to the Rio Grande.

It was evident at the beginning of January, 1861, that the contagion of secession was spreading too rapidly, and was too malignant in its character, to be arrested either by moral suasion or by compromises and concessions. The time had arrived for courageous, conscientious, and manly action. Nathaniel P. Banks, the retiring Governor of Massachusetts, in his valedictory address to the Legislature,[a] took open and un-equivocal ground against secession, declaring that the North would *a January 3, 1861.* never submit to the revolutionary acts of the Southern conspirators. His successor, Governor Andrew, was equally energetic and outspoken. His words constantly grew into action. He saw approaching danger, and dispatched agents to other New England States, to propose a military com-bination in support of the Government, first in defending Washington City from seizure by the insurgents, within and around it, and afterward in enforcing the laws. At the same time, all of the volunteer companies of the State, with an aggregate membership of about five thousand, commenced drilling nightly in their armories. Governor Andrew also sent one of his staff (Lieutenant-Colonel Ritchie) to Washington, to consult with General Scott and other officers, civil and military, concern-ing the dispatch of Massachusetts troops to the Capital, in the event of insurrectionary movements against it. A satisfactory arrange-ment was made, and troops were held in readiness to start at a moment's notice. How

JOHN A. ANDREW.

well they played an important part in the drama, at the beginning of the war, will be related hereafter. It was the blood of Massachusetts soldiers that was first poured out in the terrible war for the life of the Republic, that soon commenced.

RHODE ISLAND, the smallest of the States, was full of patriotic zeal. Her large manufacturing interests were intimately connected with the States in which insurrections had commenced, yet no considerations of self-interest could allure her people from their love of the Union and allegiance to the National Government. Her youthful Governor (William Sprague), anxious for peace and union, recommended, in his message to the Legislature of

---

Rhode Island, the repeal of the Personal Liberty Act on its statute-book, "not from fear or cowardice," he said, "but from a brave determination, in the face of threats and sneers, to live up to the Constitution and all its guaranties, the better to testify our love for the Union, and the more firmly to exact allegiance to it from all others." The act was repealed at the close of January;[a] and this measure was regarded as the forerunner of other concessions that might bring about reconciliation.

[a] 1861.

The spirit of the conspirators was unknown and unsuspected. They had resolved to accept no compromises or concessions, and they sneered at generous acts like this as the "pusillanimity of cowardly Yankees." It was the first and the last olive-branch offered to the traitors by Rhode Island. When they struck the blow, with deadly intent, at the life of the Republic, ten weeks later, she sent against them a sword in the hands of her Governor and others, that performed brave deeds in the cause of our nationality.

In the remaining New England States, namely, New Hampshire, Vermont, and Connecticut, nothing specially noteworthy was done in relation to the secession movement, before the insurgents commenced actual war, in April; but in the great State of NEW YORK, whose population was then nearly three millions nine hundred thousand, and whose chief city was the commercial metropolis of the Republic, much was done to attract public attention.

WILLIAM SPRAGUE.

The Legislature assembled at the beginning of January, and the Governor, Edwin D. Morgan, in a conciliatory message, proposed to cast oil on the turbulent political waters, by offering concessions to the complaining politicians of the South. The members of the Legislature were not so yielding; and on the first day of the session[b] patriotic resolutions were introduced by Mr. Spinola, of the lower house.

[b] January 3, 1861.

They were referred to a Select Committee of Five, who reported a series of resolutions and a spirited preamble, that were adopted on the 11th. They seemed to comprehend the true character of the conspirators and the duty of all loyal men. The preamble spoke of the "insurgent State of South Carolina;" its seizure of the public property; its act of war, in firing on the *Star of the West;*[c] the seizure of forts and arsenals elsewhere; and the treasonable words of the representatives of Southern States in the National Congress. The first resolution then declared that the people of New York were firmly attached to the Union, and that, impressed with the value of that Union, they tendered to the President, through their Chief Magistrate, whatever aid in men and money might be required to enable him to enforce the laws. They directed the Governor to send a copy of these resolutions to the President, and to the Governors of all the States. These produced much irritation in the Slave-labor States, and at the same time profoundly impressed the people therein with a distrust of the assu-

[c] January 9.

rance of their politicians that secession would be peaceful, and that there would be no war.[1]

At that time a notorious character named Fernando Wood was Mayor of the City of New York. He was a special favorite of the worst elements of society in that cosmopolitan city, and sympathized with the conspirators against the Republic, during the civil war that ensued. Four days before[a] the Legislature of the State passed its patriotic reso- [a] January 7, 1861. lutions, this disloyal man sent a message to the Common Council of the city, in which he mentioned the advantages which the people might secure by following the example of those of South Carolina in revolutionary measures.

"Why should not New York City," he said, "instead of supporting by her contributions in revenue two-thirds the expenses of the United States, become also equally independent? As a free city, with but a nominal duty on imports, her local government could be supported without taxation upon her people. Thus we could live free from taxes, and have cheap goods, nearly duty free. In this she would have the whole and united support of the Southern States, as well as of all other States, to whose interests and rights, under the Constitution, she has always been true. If the

EDWIN D. MORGAN.

Confederacy is broken up," he continued, "the Government is dissolved; and it behooves every distinct community, as well as every individual, to take care of themselves. When disunion has become a fixed and certain fact, why may not New York disrupt the bands which bind her to a venal and corrupt master—to a people and a party that have plundered her revenues, attempted to ruin her commerce, taken away the power of self-government, and destroyed the confederacy of which she was the proud Empire City? Amid the gloom which the present and prospective condition of things must cast over the country, New York, as a *free city*, may shed the only light and hope for a future reconstruction of our blessed confederacy."[2] His own treasonable words seemed to have startled him,

---

[1] See Toombs's counter-resolution in the Georgia Convention. The Legislature of Virginia, on the 17th of January, ordered the resolutions to be returned to Governor Morgan.

[2] One of the favorite writers for *De Bow's Review* (already mentioned as the most stately and pretentious of the periodical publications in the Slave-labor States), and who was a leader of the peculiar "Virginia aristocracy" based on the ownership of slaves, pronounced this proposition, "the most brilliant that these eventful times have given birth to," and then proceeded in the following style, characteristic of the writers and speakers of his class at that time, to give his views on the subject:—

"Should New York fail to erect herself into a free port and separate republic; should she remain under the dominion of the corrupt, venal wire-workers of Albany, and of the immoral, infidel, agrarian, free-love Democracy of western New York; should she put herself under the rule of Puritans, the vilest, most selfish, and unprincipled of the human race; should she join a northern confederacy; should she make New England, western New York, northern Ohio, northern Indiana, or northern Illinois her masters; should she make enemies of her Southern friends, and deliver herself up to the tender mercies of her Northern enemies, she will sink to rise no more. Better, a thousand times better, to come under the dominion of free negroes, of gipsies, than of Yankees, or low Germans, or Canadians. Gipsies and free negroes have many amiable, noble, and generous traits; Yankees, sour-krout Germans, and Canadians none. Senator Wade says, and Seward too, that the North will absorb Canada. They are half true; the vile, sensual, animal, brutal, infidel, superstitious democracy of

and given him visions of a felon's cell, for he immediately added, meekly:—
"Yet I am not prepared to recommend the violence implied in these views."[1]

The seditious suggestions of this Mayor, and the opposing and defiant tone of the Legislature, alarmed the commercial classes and large capitalists, and these hastened to seek some method for pacifying the Southern insurgents. War seemed inevitable. Its besom would sweep thousands of the debtors of New York merchants and manufacturers in the Slave-labor States into the mill of absolute ruin, and millions of dollars' worth of bills receivable in the hands of their creditors must be made as worthless as so much soiled white paper. This material consideration, and an almost universal desire for peace and quiet, developed a quick willingness to make every concession to the demands of the discontented Southerners consistent with honor. As an expression of this feeling, and with the hope of practical results, a memorial for compromise measures, largely signed by merchants, manufacturers, and capitalists, was forwarded to Congress on the 12th of January. The memorialists prayed that body to legislate so as to give assurances "with any required guaranties," to the slaveholders, that their right to regulate Slavery within the borders of their respective States should be secured; that the Fugitive Slave Law should be faithfully executed; that Personal Liberty Acts in "possible conflict" with that law should be "readjusted;" and that they should have half the Territories, whereof to organize Slave-labor States. They were assured, the memorialists said, that such measures would "restore peace to their agitated country."

This memorial was followed by another, adopted on the 18th of January, at a meeting of merchants in the rooms of the Chamber of Commerce, similar in tone to the other, and substantially recommending the "Crittenden Compromise" as a basis for pacification. They appointed a committee to take charge of the memorial, to procure signatures to it, and forward it to Congress. It was taken to Washington early in February, with forty thousand names attached to it.

On the 28th of January, an immense meeting of citizens was held at the Cooper Institute, in New York, when it was resolved to send three Commissioners to six of the "seceded States," instructed to confer with the "delegates of the people," in convention assembled, in regard to "the best measures calculated to restore the peace and integrity of the Union." James T. Brady, Cornelius K. Garrison, and Appleton Oaksmith were appointed such Commissioners. At about the same time, the "Democratic State Central Committee" called for the appointment of four delegates from each

---

Canada and the Yankee States will coalesce; and Senator Johnson of Tennessee will join them. But when Canada, and western New York, and New England, and the whole beastly, puritanic, 'sour-krout,' free negro, infidel, superstitious, licentious, democratic population of the North become the masters of New York—what then? Outside of the city, the State of New York is Yankee and puritanical; composed of as base, unprincipled, superstitious, licentious, and agrarian and anarchical population as any on earth. Nay, we do not hesitate to say, it is the vilest population on earth. If the city does not secede, and erect a separate republic, this population, aided by the ignorant, base, brutal, sensual German infidels of the northwest, the stupid democracy of Canada (for Canada will, in some way, coalesce with the North), and the arrogant and tyrannical people of New England will become masters of the destinies of New York. They hate her for her sympathies with the South, and will so legislate as to divert all her western trade to outlets through Chicago, the St. Lawrence, Portland, and Boston. She will then be cut off from her trade North and South. In fine, she must set up for herself or be ruined."—George Fitzhugh in *De Bow's Review* for February, 1861.

[1] The Board of Aldermen ordered three thousand copies of this message to be "printed in document form."

Assembly district in the State, to meet as representatives of the party in convention at Albany on the 31st of January. They assembled on that day, and the delegates were addressed by the venerable ex-Chancellor Walworth, ex-Governor Seymour, and men of less note, and a series of resolutions were adopted, expressive of the sense of the party on the great topic of the day. They declared, substantially, that a conflict of sectional passions had produced present convulsions; that the most ineffective argument to be presented to the "seceding States" was war, which would not restore the Union, but would "defeat forever its reconstruction;" that the restoration of the Union could only be obtained by the exercise of a spirit of conciliation and concession; that there was nothing in the nature of the impending difficulties that made an adjustment by compromise improper; and that the Union could only be preserved by the adoption of a Border-State policy, embodied in the Crittenden Compromise. They appointed a committee to prepare, in behalf of the Convention, "a suitable memorial to the Legislature, urging them to submit the Crittenden Compromise to a vote of the electors of the State, at the earliest practicable day."

At about this time there seemed to be concerted action all over the State to discountenance anti-slavery movements, and to silence those men whose agency, it was alleged, had caused the "public sentiment of the North to have the appearance of a hostility to the South, incompatible with its continuance in the Union." Anti-slavery meetings were broken up by violence; and early in March[a] an association was formed in New York City, called *The American Society for the Promotion of National Union,* of which Professor Samuel F. B. Morse, the inventor of the perfected electro-magnetic telegraph, was chosen President.[1] Its professed object was "to promote the union and welfare of our common country, by addresses, publications, and all other suitable means adapted to elucidate and inculcate, in accordance with the Word of God, the duties of American citizens, especially in relation to Slavery." Reiterating the idea put forth a few weeks before by the Rev. Dr. Smythe, of Charleston, in denunciation of the doctrines of the Declaration of Independence,[2] this society, in its "Programme," said.—"The popular declaration that all men are created equal, and entitled to liberty, intended to embody the sentiments of our ancestors respecting the doctrine of the Divine right of kings and nobles, and perhaps, also, the more doubtful sentiment of the French school, may be understood to indicate both a sublime truth and a pernicious error." Again:—"Our attention will not be confined to Slavery, but this will be, at present, our main topic. Four millions of immortal beings, incapable of self-care, and indisposed to industry and foresight, are providentially committed to the hands of our Southern friends. This stupendous trust they cannot put from them if they would. Emancipation, were it possible, would be

[a] March 6, 1861.

---

[1] The officers of the society were:—*President,* Samuel F. B. Morse. *Executive Committee,* John W. Mitchell, Sidney E. Morse, Benjamin Douglass, Lucius Hopkins, J. T. Moore, J. H. Brower, Thomas Tileston, A. G. Jennings, Francis Hopkins, H. J Baker, Edwin Crosswell, William H. Price, Cornelius Du Bois, J. B. Waterbury, J. Holmes Agnew. *Ex-officio,* S. F. B. Morse, James T. Soutter, Hubbard Winslow, Seth Bliss. *Treasurer,* James T. Soutter. *Secretaries,* Hubbard Winslow, Seth Bliss. The New York *Journal of Commerce,* speaking of the society, expressed its regret that something like it had not been formed thirty years before, in the "infancy of the Abolition heresy," and employing a small "army of talented lecturers to follow in the wake, or precede Abolition lecturers."

[2] See note 3, page 88.

rebellion against Providence, and destruction to the colored race in our land." These sentences indicate the scope of this society's operations. It was the germ of that powerful "Peace Party" which played a conspicuous part, as we shall observe, during the last three years of the civil war that ensued.

While the Legislature of New York was firmly resolved to support the National Government with arms, if necessary, it was ever willing to try first the power of peaceful measures. It responded to Virginia's proposition for a Peace Congress, by appointing five delegates thereto, who were instructed not to take any part in the proceedings, unless a majority of the Free-labor States were represented. From that time forth, the people of New York watched the course of events with intense interest; and when the National flag was dishonored at Fort Sumter, their patriotism was most conspicuous, as we shall observe hereafter.

NEW JERSEY, intimately connected with New York, was the theater of early movements in relation to secession. So early as the 11th of December, 1860, a convention of "all national men in favor of constitutional Union measures" was held at Trenton, the capital. They adopted a series of resolutions declaring that there was danger of a dissolution of the Union; that the interference of "Northern agitators with the rights and property of fifteen States of the Union" was the cause of "the portentous crisis;" that they saw no remedy excepting in the "avowal of the North, in the most prompt and explicit manner," of its determination to remove all political agitation for the abolition of Slavery; repeal all Personal Liberty Acts; execute the Fugitive Slave Law; allow the slaveholder to have the attendance of his slaves during his temporary sojourn in any of the Free-labor States, "on business or pleasure;" accord to the South all the rights of property in man, and accept the decrees of the Supreme Court of the United States, on the Slavery question, as their rule of action. They appointed five commissioners to confer with sister States on the great topic of the time.

The Legislature of New Jersey met at Trenton, the capital, on the 8th of January. The Governor, Charles S. Olden, in his message, expressed a hope that the compromise measures in Congress might be adopted; if not, he recommended a convention of all the States, to agree upon some plan of pacification. On the 15th, a majority of the Committee on National Affairs reported a series of resolutions as the sense of the people of New Jersey, the vital point of which was the indorsement of the Crittenden Compromise. They were adopted on the 31st of January, the Democrats voting in the affirmative. The Republican members adopted a series of resolutions, totally dissenting from the declaration of the majority, that their indorsement of the Crittenden Compromise was "the sentiment of the people of the State." They declared the willingness of the people to aid in the execution of all the laws of Congress; affirmed their adhesion to the doctrine of Popular Sovereignty, with a qualification; asserted the nationality of the Government, in opposition to the doctrine of State Supremacy; declared it to be the duty of the National Government to maintain its authority everywhere within the limits of the Republic, and pledged the faith and power of New Jersey in aid of that Government, to any required extent. This pledge the people of that State nobly redeemed.

The great State of PENNSYLVANIA, with its three millions of inhabitants, and its immense and varied interests, was profoundly moved by the events in the Gulf region. Even before there had been any Secession Conventions, and the muttering thunders of treason in that section were only echoed from the halls of Congress, there was an immense assemblage of citizens in Independence Square, in the city of Philadelphia, to counsel together on the state of public affairs. It was called by the Mayor, Alexander Henry, and was held on the 13th of December, 1860. Disunion—the separation of the States—seemed inevitable, the Mayor said in his proclamation, "unless the loyal people, casting off the spirit of party, should, in a special manner,

VIEW IN INDEPENDENCE SQUARE.[1]

avow their unfailing fidelity to the Union, and their abiding faith in the Constitution and laws." The meeting was opened with prayer by the thoroughly loyal Bishop of the Protestant Episcopal Church of that diocese, Right Rev. Alonzo Potter, and was addressed by men of all parties. The tone of every speech was deprecatory of war; and nearly every one expressed a willingness to make every possible concession to the demands of the Oligarchy necessary for the preservation of Union and peace. The troubled aspect of the nation was generally attributed to the interference of the "North" with Slavery, such as "the misplaced teachings of the pulpit, the unwise rhapsodies of the lecture-room, and the exciting appeals of the press,"[2] on the subject. It was urged that these "must be frowned

---

[1] In this view, at the end of the avenue of trees is seen the Walnut Street front of the venerable State House, in whose great hall the Declaration of Independence was discussed, adopted, and signed.
[2] Speech of Mayor Henry at the opening of the meeting.

down by a just and law-abiding people."[1]   There were some who demurred, and counseled a manly and energetic assertion of the sovereign authority of the National Government; but the prevailing sentiment was highly conservative, and even submissive. The resolutions adopted by the meeting proposed the repeal of the Personal Liberty Act of Pennsylvania, and the recognition of the obligations of the people to assist in the full execution of the Fugitive Slave Law; pointed, with " pride and satisfaction, to the recent conviction and punishment, in Philadelphia," of those who had attempted to rescue an alleged fugitive from bondage; recommended the passage of a law providing for the payment of full remuneration to the owner of a slave who might lose him by such rescue; declared that they recognized slaves as property, in accordance with the decision of the Supreme Court of the United States; and also, " that all denunciations of Slavery, as existing in the United States, and of our fellow-citizens who maintain that institution, and who hold slaves under it, are inconsistent with the spirit of brotherhood and kindness which ought to animate all who live under and profess to support the Constitution of the American Union."

The newly elected Governor of Pennsylvania, Andrew G. Curtin, was inaugurated on the 15th of January, 1861, and his address on that occasion resounded with the ring of the true metal of loyalty and positiveness of character, which he displayed throughout the war that ensued.   He coun- seled forbearance, and kindness, and a conciliatory spirit; proposed the

repeal of the Personal Liberty Act of that State, if it was in contravention of any law of Congress; and denounced the wicked doings of the conspirators and their servants.   Two days afterward, the Legislature, by resolutions, approved of the conduct of Major Anderson in Charleston harbor, and of Governor Hicks, in Maryland.   In another series of resolutions, passed on the 24th, it severely rebuked the conduct of the South Carolinians; declared that the Constitution gave the Government full power to maintain its authority, and pledged the " faith and power of Penn- sylvania " to the support of all such

ANDREW G. CURTIN.

measures as might be required to put down insurrection, saying :—" All plots, conspiracies, and warlike preparations against the United States, in any section of the country, are treasonable in their character," and that all the powers of Government should be used, if necessary, to suppress them, " without hesitation or delay."   How fully these pledges of Pennsyl-

---

[1] Speech of Mayor Henry. Such was the alleged irritated state of public feeling in Philadelphia at that time (strenuously denied by many), that only three days before this meeting, the Mayor, in a note to the Chairman of a committee of the " People's Literary Institute " of that city, deprecated, as " extremely unwise," the appear- ance before them, as a lecturer on " The Policy of Honesty," of George William Curtis, known to be an earnest lover of his country, and as earnest a foe to the Slave system. " If I possessed the lawful power," said the Mayor, "I would not permit his presence on that occasion." The proprietor of the hall in which Curtis was to lecture was officially informed that a riot might be expected if that gentleman should appear, and he refused its use.

vania were redeemed, and its patriotism, fidelity, and prowess were attested, let the records of the generous gifts of men and money to the cause, and the sufferings of the people of that State, testify.

Next west of Pennsylvania lay OHIO, with two millions three hundred thousand inhabitants. It was first settled chiefly by New Englanders, and was a part of the great Northwestern Territory, which was solemnly consecrated to free-labor by the Congress of the old Confederation, in 1787.[1] It was a vast agricultural State, filled with industrious and energetic inhabitants, who loved freedom, and revered the National Government as a great blessing in the world. Their chief magistrate, at the beginning of the troubles, was William Dennison, Jr., who was an opponent of the Slave system, and loyal to the Government and the Constitution.

The Legislature of Ohio met on the 7th of January, 1861. In his message, the Governor explained his refusal to surrender alleged fugitive slaves on the requisition of the authorities of Kentucky and Tennessee; denied the right of secession; affirmed the loyalty of his State; suggested the repeal of the obnoxious features of the Fugitive Slave Law, as the most effective method for procuring the repeal of Personal Liberty Acts; and called for a repeal of the laws of Southern States which interfered with the constitutional rights of the citizens of the Free-labor States.

WILLIAM DENNISON, JR.

"Determined to do no wrong," he said, "we will not contentedly submit to wrong."

Five days afterward,[a] the Legislature passed a series of resolutions in which they denounced the secession movements, and promised, for the people of Ohio, their firm support of the National Government, in its efforts to maintain its just authority. Two days later,[b] they reaffirmed this resolution, and pledged "the entire power and resources of the State for a strict maintenance of the Constitution and laws by the General Government, by whomsoever administered." This position the people of Ohio held throughout the war with marvelous steadfastness, in spite of the wicked machinations of traitors among themselves, who were friends of the conspirators and their cause.

[a January 12, 1861.]

[b January 14.]

Adjoining Ohio, on the west, lay INDIANA, another great and growing State carved out of the Northwestern Territory, with over one million three hundred and fifty thousand inhabitants, and real and personal estate valued at about five hundred and thirty millions of dollars. There was burning in the hearts of the people of that State the most intense loyalty to the Union, but there was no occasion for its special revealment until the attack on Fort Sumter, in April, 1861, when it blazed out terribly for the enemies of the Republic. The sons of its soil were found on every battle-

---

[1] See *The Journal of Congress*, July 13, 1787, Folwell's edition, xii. 58.

field during the first year and a half of the war, and the people were grandly faithful to the end, as our record will show.

North of Ohio and Indiana, on a vast peninsula, whose shores are washed by magnificent inland seas, lies MICHIGAN, with a population of almost eight hundred thousand. Its Legislature met at the beginning of January,[a] when the retiring Governor, Moses Wisner, in a message to that body, denounced the President of the United States as a

a January 2. 1861.

AUSTIN BLAIR.

partisan, and the Democratic party as the cause of the discontent, alarm, and hatred in the South, because of its misrepresentations of the principles and intentions of the Republican party. He declared the Personal Liberty Act of that State, and other measures inimical to the Fugitive Slave Law, to be right, and the exponents of the sentiments of the people. "Let them stand," he said; "this is no time for timid and vacillating counsels, while the cry of treason is ringing in our ears." The new Governor, Austin Blair, who was inaugurated the next day,[b] took

b January 3.

substantially the same ground; argued that secession was disintegration, and that the Republic was a compact Nation, and not a League of States. He recommended the Legislature to make the loyalty and patriotism of the people of Michigan apparent to the country; whereupon, that body passed some resolutions,[c] pledging to the National Government all the military power and mate-

c February 2.

RICHARD YATES.

rial resources of the State. They expressed an unwillingness to offer compromises and concessions to traitors, and refused to send delegates to the Peace Congress, or to repeal the Personal Liberty Act. The best blood of Michigan flowed freely in the war, and the people nobly sustained the Government in the struggle for the life of the Republic.

ILLINOIS, the home of the President elect, and more populous than its neighbor, Indiana, the number of its inhabitants being over one million seven hundred thousand, had a loyal Governor at the beginning of 1861, in the person of Richard Yates. The Legislature of the State assembled at Springfield, on the 7th of January. The Governor's message was temperate and patriotic; and he summed up what he believed to be the sentiment of the people of his State, in the words of General Jackson's toast,[1] thirty years

---

[1] John C. Calhoun, and other conspirators against the Republic, inaugurated the first act in the great drama of treason, in the spring of 1830, in the form of the assertion that a "Sovereign State may nullify or disobey an Act of the National Congress." As Thomas Jefferson was the author of the Kentucky and Virginia Resolutions

before:—" Our Federal Union : it must be preserved." Little was done at that time, excepting the appointment of delegates to the Peace Congress; but throughout the war, Governor Yates and the people of Illinois performed a glorious part.

Northward of Illinois, WISCONSIN was spread out, between Lakes Michigan and Superior and the Mississippi River, with a population of nearly eight hundred thousand. Its voters were Republicans by full twenty thousand majority. Its Governor, Alexander W. Randall, was thoroughly loyal. In his message to the Legislature, which convened at Madison on the 10th of January,[a] he spoke of the doctrine of State Supremacy as a fallacy, and said :—" The signs of the times indicate, in my opinion, that there may arise a contingency in the condition of the Government, under which it may become neces-

ALEXANDER W. RANDALL.

[a] 1861.

sary to respond to the call of the National Government for men and means to sustain the integrity of the Union, and thwart the designs of men engaged in an organized treason." The Legislature was ready to respond to these words by acts, but no occasion seemed to call for them at that time, and nothing·was done until after the attack on Fort Sumter. Then the people of Wisconsin gave men and money freely to the great cause of American Nationality.

Westward of the Mississippi River, and stretching away northward along its course from the borders of Missouri, were the young and vigorous States of Iowa and Minnesota ; and across the continent, on the shores of the Pacific Ocean, was California. The hearts of the people of these States beat responsive to Union sentiments whenever uttered. Iowa had nearly seven hundred thousand inhabitants. Its Governor, Samuel J. Kirkwood, was thoroughly loyal, and spared no exertions in raising troops for the defense of the State against lawless insurgents that might come up from Missouri, and in aid of the National Government, when the President called for

SAMUEL J. KIRKWOOD.

them. " In this emergency," the Governor said, " Iowa must not, and does not, occupy a doubtful position. For the Union, as our fathers formed it, and for the Government they framed so wisely and so well, the

<hr>

of 1798, which seemed to favor the doctrine of nullification, they resolved to plant their standard of incipient revolt under the auspices of his great name. A dinner was prepared at Washington City, on the birthday of Jefferson. professedly to honor his memory. It was the work of Calhoun and others. President Jackson and

people of Iowa are ready to pledge every fighting man in the State, and every dollar of her money and credit." That pledge was nobly redeemed. One-tenth of the entire population of the State, or seventy thousand men, went to the field !

The people of Minnesota were equally faithful to the old flag. Alexander

Ramsay was Governor. The Legislature that assembled on the 26th of January passed a series of loyal resolutions, declaring the Constitution as it was to be sufficient for the whole Union ; denouncing secession as revolution ; condemning in severest terms the treasonable acts at Charleston, saying, that when one or more States appear in military array against the Government, it could discover no other honorable or patriotic resource than to test, by land and sea, "the full strength of the Federal authority under our National flag." It gave assurance of an earnest desire for peace with and good-will

ALEXANDER RAMSAY.

toward the people of the South; thanked General Scott for his patriotic efforts, and declared that the people of Minnesota would never consent to the obstruction of the free navigation of the Mississippi River, "from its source to its mouth, by any power hostile to the Federal Government."

By a careful observation of the aspect of public sentiment in the various States of the Union at the period when a new Administration was about to assume the conduct of national affairs, as delineated in brief outline in this chapter, the reader will perceive that the great majority of the people were thoroughly loyal to the National Government, and desired peace upon any honorable terms. At the same time, it cannot be denied that there was a large class of politicians who, misrepresenting the greater portion of their partisans, seemed incapable of rising above the selfish considerations of party domination. With amazing sycophancy, they hastened to assure the Slave power of their sympathy and subserviency. At home, in speeches, through the public press, and sometimes through the pulpit, they clamored loudly for concessions to its most extravagant demands, and begged the sturdy patriots of the Free-labor States, who loved freedom more than power, to bend the knee of abject submission to the arrogant Oligarchy rather than raise a resisting hand to save the Republic from destruction. They talked oracularly of that phantom, the "coercion of a sovereign State," and denounced every

his Cabinet were invited to attend. There was a numerous company. The doctrine of Nullification had lately been put forth as an orthodox dogma of the Democratic creed, and the movements of Calhoun and his political friends were looked upon with suspicion. At this dinner, it was soon apparent that the object was, next to honor Jefferson's memory, but to commence treasonable work with the sanction of his name and deeds. Jackson perceived this plainly, and offered as a toast, "Our Federal Union: it must be preserved." Calhoun immediately arose and offered the following:—"The Union: next to Liberty, the most dear; may we all remember that it can only be preserved by respecting the rights of the States, and distributing equally the benefits and burdens of the Union." "The proceedings of that day," said Mr. Benton, who was present, "revealed to the public mind the fact of an actual design tending to dissolve the Union." See Benton's *Thirty Years' View,* i. 148.

public expression of a determination to uphold the National authority by force of arms, if necessary, as puerile, unmeaning, and mischievous. Hundreds of letters, some of them written by men who had been honored by high social and official positions, were borne by the mails southward, in which it was asserted, again and again, that the people of the Free-labor States would never allow the Government to make war upon a "seceding State;" and when the conspirators struck the first deadly blow at the life of the nation, they did so with the assurance that their political friends in the North would keep the sword of the Republic immovably in its scabbard, until the black crime should be consummated.[1]   They were mistaken.

---

[1] An ex-President of the United States wrote to the man who afterward became chief leader of the conspirators, saying:—" Without discussing the question of right—of abstract power to secede—I have never believed that actual disruption of the Union can occur without blood; and if, through the madness of Northern Abolitionists, that dire calamity must come, the fighting will not be along Mason and Dixon's line, merely.   It will be within our own borders, in our own streets, between the two classes of citizens to whom I have referred. Those who defy law and scout constitutional obligations will, if we ever reach the arbitrament of arms, find occupation enough at home."—*Extract of a Letter from Franklin Pierce to Jefferson Davis*, January 6, 1860.

After the South Carolina Ordinance of Secession was adopted, an ex-Governor of Illinois wrote to the same man, saying:—" I am, in heart and soul, for the South, as they are right in the principles and possess the Constitution.   If the public mind will bear it, the seat of Government, the Government itself, and the Army and Navy, ought to remain with the South and the Constitution.   I have been promulgating the above sentiment, although it is rather revolutionary.   *A Provisional Government should be established at Washington to receive the power of the outgoing President, and for the President elect to take the oath of office out of Slave Territory.* . . . If the Slave States would unite and form a convention, they might have the power to coerce the North into terms to amend the Constitution so as to protect Slavery more effectually."—*Extract of a Letter from John Reynolds, of Belleville, Illinois, to Jefferson Davis and ex-Governor William Smith, of Virginia,* dated December 28, 1860.

Many influential public journals in the Free-labor States advocated the right of secession and the wrong of "coercion."   One of these, more widely read and more frequently quoted in the South than any other, as the exponent of public opinion in the North, said :—" For far less than this [the election of Mr. Lincoln] our fathers seceded from Great Britain ; and they left revolution organized in every State, to act whenever it is demanded by public opinion.   The confederation is held together only by public opinion.   Each State is organized as a complete government, holding the purse and wielding the sword, possessing the right to break the tie of the confederation as a nation might break a treaty, and to repel coercion as a nation might repel invasion."—*New York Herald,* November 9, 1860.

At a large political meeting in Philadelphia, on the 16th of January, 1861, one of the resolutions declared :— " We are utterly opposed to any such compulsion as is demanded by a portion of the Republican party; and the Democratic party of the North will, by all constitutional means, and with its moral and political influence, oppose any such extreme policy, or a fratricidal war thus to be inaugurated."   On the 22d of February, a political State Convention was held at Harrisburg, the capital of Pennsylvania, when the members said, in a resolution:—" We will, by all proper and legitimate means, oppose, discountenance, and prevent any attempt on the part of the Republicans in power to make any armed aggressions upon the Southern States, especially so long as laws contravening their rights shall remain unrepealed on the Statute-books of Northern States, and so long as the just demands of the South shall continue to be unrecognized by the Republican majorities in these States, and unsecured by proper amendatory explanations of the Constitution."   Such utterances in the great State of Pennsylvania, and similar ones elsewhere, by the chosen representatives of a powerful party in convention assembled, encouraged the conspirators in a belief that there would be no war made upon them, and for that reason they were defiant everywhere and on all occasions.

CHAPTER IX.

PROCEEDINGS IN CONGRESS.—DEPARTURE OF CONSPIRATORS.

HILST the country at large, solemnly impressed by the thick gathering portents of a fearful storm, was violently agitated, and all eyes and hearts were turned anxiously toward the National Congress and the Executive of the Government for assurances of safety, the halls of that Congress presented some strange spectacles for the patriot, the philosopher, and the historian. The line of demarkation between the patriots and the conspirators in that body had been early and distinctly drawn by the latter, as we have observed, with amazing boldness; and while the former, sincerely wishing to be just, were ardently seeking for some honorable way for conciliating the malcontents, the traitors were implacable and defiant. At all times they plainly revealed their determination not to agree to any terms for conciliation, even if such terms should offer more than they demanded; and they looked upon the yielding spirit of the true men in Congress as an exhibition of that subserviency, born often of an intense love for the Union, which had forever been making concessions to the Slave interest, to the mortal hurt of the nation.

There was perfect unity of action between the conspirators in Congress and the conspirators and politicians working in the Slave-labor States. They wrought harmoniously; those at the seat of Government directing important movements, and those who controlled political affairs in the several States executing them with energy, secrecy, and success, for the corrupt State Legislatures were auxiliaries in the business of the enslavement of the people by the Oligarchy. This evident harmony of action we have observed while considering the secession movements in the seven Cotton-growing States.

^a 1860. The public suspected it after the rebellious acts of the South Carolina politicians, late in December;[a] and early in January it was authoritatively proclaimed, in an anonymous communication published in the *National Intelligencer* at the seat of Government, and signed EATON. It was written by a "distinguished citizen of the South, who formerly represented his State in the popular branch of Congress," and was then tem-
^b January 5, 1861. porarily sojourning in Washington.[1] He charged that a caucus was held on the preceding Saturday night[b] in that city, by the Senators from seven of the Cotton-producing States (naming them[2]), who,

---

[1] *National Intelligencer*, January 9, 1861.

[2] These were, Benjamin Fitzpatrick and Clement C. Clay, Jr., of Alabama; R. W. Johnson and William K. Sebastian, of Arkansas; Robert Toombs and Alfred Iverson, of Georgia; Judah P. Benjamin and John Slidell,

at that time, resolved, in effect, to assume to themselves the political power of the South, and to control all political and military operations for the time ; that they telegraphed directions to complete the seizure of forts, arsenals, custom houses, and other public property, as already recorded in preceding pages, and advised conventions then in session, or soon to assemble, to pass ordinances for immediate secession. They agreed that it would be proper for the representatives of the "seceded States" to remain in Congress, in order to prevent the adoption of measures by the National Government for its own security.

"They also," said this writer, "advised, ordered, or directed the assembling of a convention of delegates from the seceding States, at Montgomery, on the 15th of February. This can, of course, only be done by the revolutionary conventions usurping the powers of the people, and sending delegates over whom they will lose all control in the establishment of a provisional government, which is the plan of the dictators." They resolved, he said, to use every means in their power to force the Legislatures of Tennessee, Kentucky, Missouri, Arkansas, Texas, Virginia, and Maryland, into the adoption of revolutionary measures. They had already possessed themselves of all the avenues of information in the South—the telegraph, the press, and the wide control of the postmasters; and they relied upon a general defection of all the Southern-born members of the Army and Navy. "The spectacle here presented," he said, "is startling to contemplate. Senators, intrusted with the representative sovereignty of States, and sworn to support the Constitution of the United States, while yet acting as the privy counselors of the President, and anxiously looked to by their constituents to effect some practical plan of adjustment, deliberately conceive a conspiracy for the overthrow of the Government through the military organizations, the dangerous secret order of the Knights of the Golden Circle, Committees of Safety, Southern Leagues, and other agencies at their command. They have instituted as thorough a military and civil despotism as ever cursed a maddened country."

These charges were sustained by an electrograph, which appeared in the *Charleston Mercury* on the 7th,[a] dated at Washington City on the 6th. "The Senators," it said, "from those of the Southern States which have called conventions of the people, met in caucus last night, and adopted the following resolutions:— [a] January, 1861.

"*Resolved*, That we recommend to our respective States immediate secession.

"*Resolved*, That we recommend the holding of a General Convention of the said States, to be holden in the city of Montgomery, Alabama, at some period not later than the 15th day of February, 1861."

These resolutions, and others which the correspondent did not feel at liberty to divulge, were telegraphed to the conventions of Alabama, Mississippi, and Florida. He said there was much discussion concerning the propriety of the members of Congress from seceding States retaining their seats, in order to embarrass legislation, and added, "It is believed that the opinion that they should remain, prevailed." The truth of these statements

---

of Louisiana; Jefferson Davis and Albert G. Brown, of Mississippi; John Hemphill and Lewis T. Wigfall, of Texas; and David L. Yulee and Stephen R. Mallory, of Florida.

was confirmed by the letter written by Senator Yulee (already referred to[1]), on the 14th of January, in which he inclosed a copy of the resolutions passed at that meeting, in one of which they resolved to ask for instructions, whether the delegations from "seceding States" were to remain in Congress until the 4th of March, "for the purpose of defeating hostile legislation." The other, and last, resolved "That a committee be, and are hereby, appointed, consisting of Messrs. Davis, Slidell, and Mallory, to carry out the objects of the meeting." It was also stated, in a dispatch from Washington to the Baltimore press, dated the day after "Eaton's" revelations appeared, that "the leaders of the Southern movement are consulting as to the best mode of consolidating their interests in a confederacy under a provisional government. The plan is to make Senator Hunter, of Virginia, Provisional President, and Jefferson Davis Commander-in-chief of the Army of Defense. Mr. Hunter possesses, in a more eminent degree, the philosophical character of Jefferson than any other statesman now living."

These revelations; the defiant attitude of the traitors in Congress, in speech and action; the revolutionary movements at Charleston; the startling picture of the perilous condition of the country, given in a Special Message of the President on the 8th,[a] and the roar of the tornado of secession, then sweeping fearfully over the Gulf States, pro-duced the most intense and painful excitement in the public mind. That Message of the 8th, under the circumstances, seemed like a cry of despair or a plea for mercy from the President, who seemed painfully conscious, after the departure of the South Carolina Commissioners and the disruption of his Cabinet, that faith in the promises of the conspirators, which had lured him all along into a fatal conciliatory policy, could no longer be entertained or acted upon without imminent peril to the nation and his own reputation. He perceived that the golden moment, when vigorous action on his part might have crushed the serpent of secession, had passed, and that the reptile had become a fearful dragon; and now he earnestly entreated Congress to appease the voracious appetite of the monster, and still the turbulence that alarmed the Executive, by concessions equivalent to the Crittenden Compro-mise. He assured that body that he considered secession a crime, and that he should attempt to collect the public revenue everywhere, so far as practicable under existing laws; at the same time he declared that his execu-tive powers were exhausted, or were wholly inadequate to meet existing difficulties. To Congress alone, he said, "belongs the power to declare war, or to authorize the power to employ military force, in all cases contemplated by the Constitution," and on it "alone rests the responsibility." And yet he did not ask that body to delegate powers to him for the purpose of protect-ing the life of the nation. "It cannot be denied," he said, "that we are in the midst of a great revolution;" but instead of imploring Congress, and his political friends in it, with the spirit of a vigilant and determined patriot, to give him the means to stay its progress, he contented himself with offering insufficient reasons why he had not already done so, by re-enforcing and provisioning the garrison in Fort Sumter before it was too late, and also by urging Congress to submit to the demands of the revolutionists.

a January,
1861.

---

[1] See page 166. See also a notice of Slidell's Letter in note 2, page 182.

In this the President acted consistently. He well knew that the political constitution of the two Houses at that time was such, that no Force-bill could be passed. Besides, Attorney-General Black had expressed his doubts whether Congress had the ability "to find constitutional powers to furnish the President with authority to use military force"[1] in the execution of the laws; and in view of the position which he had assumed in his Annual Message on the subject of "coercion" and "subjugation of a State,"[2] he would feel in conscience bound to veto any Force-bill looking to such action. He did not ask Congress for any more power, nor did he give a word of encouragement to the loyal people that he would heed the warning voice of the veteran General Wool, and others, who implored the Government not to yield Fort Sumter to the insurgents, and thereby cause the kindling of a civil war. "So long as the United States keep possession of that fort," said Wool, "the independence of South Carolina will only be in name, and not in fact." Then, with prophetic words, whose predictions were fulfilled a few weeks later, he said:—"If, however, it should be surrendered to South Carolina, the smothered indignation of the Free States would be roused beyond control. It would not be in the power of any one to restrain it. *In twenty days two hundred thousand men would be in readiness to take vengeance on all who would betray the Union into the hands of its enemies.* Be assured that I do not exaggerate the feelings of the people."[3] The soldier, with a statesman's sagacity, correctly interpreted the will of that people.

As the plot thickened, and the designs of the conspirators became more manifest, the loyal men in Congress were more firmly rooted in a determination to withstand the further aggressions of the Slave interest and the malice of the public enemies. This determination was specially apparent when the Crittenden Compromise, and other measures looking toward conciliation, were considered in the Senate and House of Representatives. Appalled by visions of civil war, distracted by discordant oracles and counselors, and anxious to have reconciliation, and union, and peace at almost any sacrifice, the people, no doubt, would have acquiesced in Mr. Crittenden's propositions.[4] But their true representatives, better instructed by experience and observation concerning the perfidy of the traitors before them, who might accept those measures as a concession, but not as a settlement, and would be ready to make a more insolent demand another year, could not be induced to wrong posterity by a desertion of the high and holy principles of the Declaration of Independence for the sake of temporary ease. They could not consent to have the National Constitution so amended, that it should be forever subservient to the truculent Slave interest and its desolating influence. They plainly saw that such would be the effect of the most vital of the amendments of it proposed by Mr. Crittenden. They did not doubt *his* patriotism, yet they deemed it wise and prudent to act upon the suggestions of the first President of the Republic, when, warning his countrymen against attempts to destroy the Union, he said:—"One method of assault may be to effect, in the forms of the Constitution, alterations which impair the energy of the system, and

---

[1] See page 70.
[2] See page 72.
[3] Letter to General Cass, dated Troy, December 31, 1860.
[4] See the substance of these propositions recorded on pages 89 and 90.

thus to undermine what cannot be directly overthrown."[1]—"I most cheer-fully accord to the Senator from Kentucky purity of motive and patriotic intentions and purposes," said Henry Wilson, one of the most active and vigilant men in the Senate. "While I believe every pulsation of his heart throbs for the unity and perpetuity of this Republic; while I cherish for him sentiments of sincere respect and regard, I am constrained to say here, and now, that his policy has been most fatal to the repose of the country, if not to the integrity of the Union and the authority of the Government. Whether his task be self-imposed, or whether it be imposed upon him by others, he has stood forth, day by day, not to sustain the Constitution, the Union, and the enforcement of the laws; not to rebuke seditious words and treasonable acts; but to demand the incorporating into the organic law of the nation of irrepealable, degrading, and humiliating concessions to the dark spirit of slavery."[2]

It was plainly perceived that Jefferson Davis, one of the most cold, crafty, malignant, and thoroughly unscrupulous of the conspirators, had embodied the spirit of Crittenden's most vital propositions in a more compact and perspicuous form, in a resolution offered in the Senate on the 24th of December,[a] saying, "That it shall be declared, by amend-ment of the Constitution, that property in slaves, recognized as such by the local law of any of the States of the Union, shall stand on the same footing, in all constitutional and Federal relations, as any other species of property so recognized; and, like other property, shall not be subject to be divested or impaired by the local law of any other State, either in escape thereto or by the transit or sojourn of the owner therein. And in no case whatever shall such property be subject to be divested or impaired by any legislative act of the United States, or any of the territories thereof."[3] In other words, the Constitution was to be made to recognize property in man, and slavery as a national institution. Speaking for the Oligarchy, Senator Wigfall, in a speech on the Crittenden Compromise, exclaimed:—"We say that man has a right to property in man. We say that our slaves are our *property*. We say that it is the duty of every government to protect its property everywhere. . . . If you wish to settle this matter, declare that slaves *are* property, and, like all other property, entitled to be protected in every quarter of the globe, on land and on sea. Say that to us, and then the difficulty is settled." Because the majority of the people of the United States would not consent to abase their Constitution, and make it subservient to the cause of injustice and inhumanity, the Oligarchy rebelled and kindled a horrible civil war!

We have observed that a Committee of Thirteen was chosen by the Senate, and another of Thirty-three by the House of Representatives, to receive, consider, and report upon plans for pacification.[4] These committees labored sedulously, but at every step they were met by evidence that the conspirators would not be satisfied with any thing that might be offered. These men were holding their seats in Congress, and committing perjury every hour, for no other purpose than to further their plans for the destruc-tion of the Republic; and when they could be no longer useful there, they

[1] Washington's Farewell Address to his Countrymen.
[2] Speech in the National Senate, February 21, 1861.
[3] *Congressional Globe*, December 24, 1860.
[4] See pages 86 and 89.

cast off all disguise, insolently flaunted the banner of treason in the faces of true men, and fled to the fields of open and defiant revolt, there to work the infernal engines of rebellion with fearful power. Yet all the while, earnest, loyal men patiently labored, in committees and out of them, in the halls of Congress and out of them, to produce reconciliation, preserve the Union, and secure the stability and prosperity of the Republic. No less than seventeen Representatives offered amendments to the Constitution, all making concessions to the Slave interest; and petitions and letters came in from all parts of the Free-labor States, praying Congress to adopt the Crittenden Compromise as the great pacificator.

Finally, it became so evident that the labors of the committees were only wasted, that Daniel Clark, of New Hampshire, offered in the Senate [a] two resolutions as an amendment to Mr. Crittenden's propositions. The first declared that the provisions of the Constitution were ample for the preservation of the Union and the protection of all the material interests of the country; that it needed to be obeyed rather than amended; and that an extrication from the present dangers was to be looked for in strenuous efforts to preserve the peace, protect the public property, and enforce the laws, rather than in new guaranties for particular interests, compromises for particular difficulties, or concessions to unreasonable demands. The second declared that "all attempts to dissolve the Union, or overthrow or abandon the National Constitution, with the hope or expectation of constructing a new one, were dangerous, illusory, and destructive; that, in the opinion of the Senate of the United States, no such reconstruction is practicable, and therefore to the maintenance of the existing Union and Constitution should be directed all the energies of the Government and the efforts of all good citizens."[1]

[a] January 9, 1861.

This amendment, so thoroughly wise and patriotic, and so eminently necessary at that critical moment in averting the most appalling national danger, was adopted by a vote of twenty-five against twenty-three.[2] The leading conspirators in the Senate, who might have defeated the amendment and carried the Crittenden Compromise, did not vote. This reticence was preconcerted. They had resolved not to accept any terms of adjustment. They were bent on disunion, and acted consistently.[3]

In the Senate Committee of Thirteen, which was composed of five Republicans and eight opposed to them, Mr. Crittenden's proposition to restore the line of the Missouri Compromise (36° 30') was, after full discussion, voted down. The majority of the Committee were favorable to the remainder of his propositions, but, under the rule made by the Committee at the beginning, that no resolution should be considered adopted unless it received a majority both of the Republicans and anti-Republicans, they were not passed. Finally, Mr. Seward proposed that no amendment should be made to the Constitution which would authorize or give to Congress any

---

[1] *Congressional Globe*, January 9, 1861.
[2] The vote was as follows:—YEAS, Messrs. Anthony, Baker, Bingham, Cameron, Chandler, Clark, Collamer, Dixon, Doolittle, Durkee, Fessenden, Foote, Foster, Grimes, Hale, Harlan, King, Seward, Simmons, Sumner, Ten Eyck, Trumbull, Wade, Wilkinson, and Wilson. NAYS, Messrs. Bayard, Bigler, Bragg, Bright, Clingman, Crittenden, Fitch, Green, Gwin, Hunter, Johnson of Tennessee, Kennedy, Lane of Oregon, Mason, Nicholson, Pearce, Polk, Powell, Pugh, Rice, Saulsbury, and Sebastian.
[3] See notice of "The 1860 Association," on page 95.

power to abolish or interfere, in any State, with the domestic institutions thereof, including that of persons held to service or labor by the laws of such State. Only Jefferson Davis and Robert Toombs voted against it. He then proposed that the Fugitive Slave Law of 1850 should be so amended as to secure to the alleged fugitive a trial by jury. Stephen A. Douglas amended it so as to have the alleged fugitive sent for trial to the State from which he had escaped. This was voted down, the Republicans and Mr. Crittenden alone voting for it. Mr. Seward further proposed that Congress should pass an efficient law for the punishment of persons engaged in the armed invasion of any State from another State, and all persons in complicity with them. This, too, was rejected; and so was every thing short of full compliance with the demands of the Slave interest.

In the House Committee of Thirty-three were seen like failures to please the Oligarchy, notwithstanding great concessions were offered. These concessions were embodied in an elaborate report submitted by Mr. Corwin,[a] the Chairman of the Committee. It condemned legislative interference with the Fugitive Slave Law. It recommended the repeal of Personal Liberty Acts, in so far as they conflicted with that law. It recognized Slavery as existing in fifteen States of the Union, and denied the existence of any power, outside of a State, competent to interfere with it. It urged the propriety of a faithful execution of the Fugitive Slave Law. It recognized no conflicting elements in the National Constitution and laws that might afford sufficient cause for a dissolution of the Union, and enjoined upon Congress the duty of measuring out exact justice to all the States. It declared it to be essential for the peace of the country for the several States faithfully to observe their constitutional obligations to each other; and that it was the duty of the National Government to maintain its authority and protect its property everywhere. It proposed that each State should be requested to revise its statutes, or to so amend the same, that citizens of other States therein might enjoy protection against popular violence, or illegal summary punishment for implied crimes without trial in due form of law; also, that the States should be requested to provide by law against the setting in motion, within their respective borders, any lawless invasion of another State. The President was requested to send a copy of this report to the Governors of the States, asking them to lay it before their respective Legislatures.

In addition to this report, Mr. Corwin submitted a joint resolution proposing an amendment to the Constitution, whereby any further amendment, giving Congress power over Slavery in the States, was forbidden. By a portion of the Committee the report was considered too yielding, and two minority reports were submitted. One by Messrs. Washburne and Tappan declared that, in view of the rebellion then in progress, no concessions should be made; and then they submitted, as a distinct proposition, Senator Clark's substitute for Crittenden's plan. Another, by Messrs. Burch and Stout, proposed a convention of the States to amend the Constitution. A proposition was also made to substitute the Crittenden Compromise for Corwin's report. Albert Rust, of Arkansas, offered in the Senate a proposition, substantially the same as Crittenden's, as "the ultimatum of the South;" and Henry Winter Davis, of Maryland, proposed a resolution to

[a] January 14, 1861.

request the several States to revise their statutes, to ascertain whether any of them were in conflict with the Fugitive Slave Act, and, if so, to repeal them forthwith.

The consideration of reports and propositions concerning pacification occupied a large portion of the session, and nearly every debater in both Houses of Congress was engaged in the discussion. It was fairly opened in the Senate on the 7th of January,[a] when Mr. Crittenden called up a resolution which he had offered on the 2d, to provide by law for submitting his proposed amendments to the Constitution to a vote of the people. He saw no chance for any agreement on the subject in Congress, and he perceived no other course for him to pursue than to make an appeal to the people. He earnestly desired to save the Union and prevent civil war. He felt that the danger to which the Republic was exposed was imminent, and he pleaded earnestly for the people to take care of the Constitution and the Union, saying:—"The Constitution will take care of you; the Union will be sure to protect and preserve you." He proposed, he said, to take the Slavery question from Congress forever. He did not think he was asking any one to make concessions, but only to grant equal rights. He was opposed to secession, as a violation of the law and the Constitution. "If a State wishes to secede," he said, "let them proclaim revolution boldly, and not attempt to hide themselves under little subtleties of law, and claim the *right* of secession. A constitutional right to break the Constitution was a new doctrine."

[a] 1861.

Senator Toombs followed Senator Crittenden. His speech was characteristic of the man—coarse, treasonable, and defiant. "The Abolitionists," he said, "have for long years been sowing dragons' teeth, and they have finally got a crop of armed men. The Union, Sir, is dissolved. That is a fixed fact lying in the way of this discussion, and men may as well hear it. One of your confederates [South Carolina] has already wisely, bravely, boldly, met the public danger and confronted it. She is only ahead and beyond any of her sisters because of her greater facility of action. The great majority of those sister States, under like circumstances, consider her cause as their cause." He then declared that "the patriotic men of the country," having appealed to the Constitution, to justice, and to fraternity in vain, were "prepared for the arbitrament of the sword. Now, Sir," he said, "you may see the glitter of the bayonet and hear the tramp of armed men from your Capital to the Rio Grande."

Toombs then proceeded, with great insolence of speech and manner, to define his own position and demands. "They are what you," he said, "who talk of constitutional right, call treason. I believe that is the term. I believe for all the acts which the Republican party call treason and rebellion, there stands before them as good a traitor and as good a rebel as ever descended from revolutionary loins. What does this rebel demand?" The right, he said, of going into all the Territories with slaves, as property, and that property to be protected there by the National Government. "Shall I not do it?" he asked. "You say No. You and the Senate say No; the House says No; and throughout the length and breadth of your whole conspiracy against the Constitution, there is one shout of No! It is the price of my allegiance. Withhold it, and you can't get my obedience. There is the philosophy of the armed men that have sprung up in this country, and I had rather see the population of my own, my native land beneath the sod, than that they should support for one hour such a Government."

Toombs further demanded that offenders against Slave codes in one State, fleeing into another, should be delivered up for punishment; that the Fugitive Slave Law should be rigidly enforced, and that no State should pass Personal Liberty Acts. He denounced the National Constitution as having been made by the fathers for the purpose of getting "at the pockets of the people." With a wicked perversion of history, he declared that a "large portion of the best men of the Revolution voted against it," and that it was "carried in some of the States by treachery." He sneered at the venerable Senator from Kentucky (who had fought for his country when this traitor was yet an infant, and had entered Congress as a member when this conspirator was a schoolboy), because of his attachment to that Constitution, and his denial of the constitutional right of a State to secede. "Perhaps he will find out after a while," said Toombs, "that it is a fact accomplished. You have got it in the South pretty much in both ways. South Carolina has given it to you regularly, according to the approved plan. You are getting it just below there [in Georgia], I believe, irregularly, outside of law, without regular action. You can take it either way. You will find armed men to defend both. . . . We are willing to defend our rights with the halter around our necks, and to meet these Black Republicans, their myrmidons and allies, whenever they choose to come on." The career of this Senator during the war that ensued was a biting commentary upon these high words before there was any personal danger to the speaker, and illustrated the truth of Spenser's lines in the *Fairy Queen:*—

> " For highest looks have not the highest mind,
> Nor haughty words most full of highest thought;
> But are like bladders blown up with the wind,
> That being pricked evanish out of sight."

Toombs concluded his harangue by a summing up of charges not unfavorable to the Government against which he was rebelling, but against the political party that had outvoted his own party at the late election, and was about to assume the conduct of that Government. "Am I a freeman?" he asked. "Is my State a free State, to lie down and submit, because political fossils [referring to the venerable Crittenden] raise the cry of 'the glorious Union?' Too long, already, have we listened to this delusive song. We are freemen. We have rights; I have stated them. We have wrongs; I have recounted them. I have demonstrated that the party now coming into power has declared us outlaws, and has determined to exclude four thousand millions of our property [slaves] from the common Territories." He then said:—"They have refused to protect us from invasion and insurrection by the Federal power, and," he added truly, "the Constitution denies to us in the Union the right either to raise fleets or armies for our own defense. All these charges I have proven by the record." He then said, with gross perversion of the truth, that they had appealed in vain for the exercise of their constitutional rights. Restore them and there would be peace. "Refuse them," he said, "and what then? We shall then ask you, 'Let us depart in peace.' Refuse that, and you present us war. We accept it; and, inscribing upon our banners the glorious words, 'iberty and Equality,' we will trust to the blood of the brave and the d of battles for security and tranquillity." With these words ringing in ears of Senators, and these declarations of premeditated treason hurled the face of the President, this conspirator left the Senate amber and the National Capital forever,[a] and hastened to   [a] January 7, orgia, to cheat the people of their rights and precipitate them   1861. to the seething caldron of civil war.

The Georgia Senator was followed, a few days later,[b] by two of the ablest embers of that House, namely, Hunter of Virginia, and Seward New York. Their speeches were marked by great dignity of   [b] January 11 anner and language, but irreconcilable opposition of sentiment.   and 12.

unter's foreshadowed the aims and determination of the conspirators, while eward's as clearly foreshadowed the aims and determination of the loyal people of the country and of the incoming Administration, of which he was to be the Prime Minister.

Mr. Hunter was one of the most polished, subtle, and dangerous of the conspirators. Like Calhoun, his logic was always masterly, and powerfully persuasive. He led the judgments of men with great ease. For years, as the champion of State Supremacy— the intimate friend and disciple of Calhoun —he had been laboring to sap the life of the National Government. He now boldly proposed radical changes in the Constitution and the Government, and advocated the right and duty of secession. He declared that "the South" must obtain by

WILLIAM H. SEWARD.

such changes guaranties of *power*, so as not to be governed by the majorities of "the North."[1] His whole speech favored the widening of the line of separation between the Free-labor and Slave-labor States. and consequently practical disunion.[2]

Mr. Seward was regarded as the oracle of the Republican party, now about to assume the administration of National affairs, and his words were listened to with eager attention. It was felt that he was to pronounce for

---

[1] He proposed Calhoun's favorite plan of a dual executive, modified, as he thought, to adapt it to the circumstances of the hour. He proposed that "each section," as he called the Free-labor and Slave-labor States, should elect a President, to be called the First and Second President, the first to serve for four years, and the President next succeeding him to serve for four other years, and afterward be re-eligible. During the term of the President, the second should be President of the Senate, having a casting vote in the event of a tie. No treaty or law should be valid without the signatures of both Presidents; nor should any appointments to office be valid without the sanction of both Presidents or of a majority of the Senators. He also proposed a sectional division of the Supreme Court, which should consist of ten members, five from the Free-labor States and five from the Slave-labor States, the Chief-Justice to be one of the five. These judges were to be appointed by the President of each section.

[2] It is a significant fact, that the closing formula of legal documents which usually have the words: "Done in the —— year of American Independence," had been for many years made subservient in Virginia and other Slave-labor States to the heresy of State Supremacy, by the form of "Done in the —— year of Virginia" or "North Carolina Independence."

peace or war. He spoke guardedly, and yet not enigmatically. He skillfully analyzed the treasonable movements of the Oligarchy, exposed the falsehood of their pretenses, the real springs of their ambition and their crime, and pleaded with powerful argumentation for affiliation and union. He declared his adherence to the Union in its integrity and with all its parts, with his friends, with his party, with his State, with his country, or without either, as they might determine; in every event, whether of peace or war, with every consequence of honor or of dishonor, of life or of death. He concluded by saying :—" I shall cheerfully lend to the Government my best support in whatever prudent, yet energetic efforts it shall make to preserve the public peace, and to maintain and preserve the Union, advising only that it practice, as far as possible, the utmost moderation, forbearance, and conciliation."

The speeches of Toombs, Hunter, and Seward were key-notes to all that succeeded on the great topic of the hour. There were others of eminent ability, and worthy of careful preservation in the annals of the great Civil

War, as exponents of the conflicting views entertained concerning the Government, its character, and its power.[1] Several of these were from representatives of Slave-labor States, and were extremely loyal. Foremost among them was that of Andrew Johnson, Senator from Tennessee, now [a]

[a] 1865.

President of the Republic—a man who had come up from among the common people, planted himself firmly on the foundation of human rights and popular prerogatives, and performed valorous service against the pretensions and claims of the imperious Oligarchy.

ANDREW JOHNSON.

" I will not give up this Government,"
he said, " that is now called an experiment, which some are prepared to abandon for a constitutional monarchy. No! I intend to stand by it, and I entreat every man throughout the nation who is a patriot, and who has seen

---

[1] Charles Sumner, Henry Wilson, Benjamin F. Wade, and others in the Senate; and John Sherman, Charles Francis Adams, Thomas Corwin, and others in the House of Representatives, made powerful speeches against Mr. Crittenden's propositions, and in favor of universal freedom. One of the most remarkable passages in the great debate was the speech of Sherrard Clemens, of Western Virginia, who took such decided ground against the pretensions of the Oligarchy, that its representatives in Congress called him a traitor. With the most biting scorn, he thus referred to the conspirators in Congress:—" Patriotism has become a starveling birdling, clinging with unfledged wings around the nest of twigs where it was born. A statesman *now* must not only

——————— ' Narrow his mind,
And to party give up what was meant for mankind,'

but he must become as submissive as a blind horse in a bark-mill to every perverted opinion which sits, whip in hand, on the revolving shaft at the end of which he is harnessed, and meekly travels. To be considered a diamond of the first water, he must stand in the Senate House of his country [like Toombs and his fellow-traitors], and, in the face of a forbearing people, glory in being a traitor and a rebel. He must solemnly proclaim the death of the nation to which he had sworn allegiance, and, with the grave stolidity of an undertaker, invite its citizens to their own funeral. He must dwarf and provincialize his patriotism to the State on whose local passions he thrives, to the county where he practices court, or to the city where he flaunts in all the meretricious dignity of the Doge of Venice. He can take an oath to support the Constitution of the United States, but he

and is compelled to admit the success of this great experiment, to come forward, not in heat, not in fanaticism, not in haste, not in precipitancy, but in deliberation, in full view of all that is before us, in the spirit of brotherly love and fraternal affection, and rally round the altar of our common country, and lay the Constitution upon it as our last libation, and swear by our God, by all that is sacred and holy, that the Constitution shall be saved and the Union preserved." From this lofty attitude of patriotism he never stooped a line during the fierce struggle that ensued.

Senator Baker, of Oregon, who attested his devotion to his country by giving his life in its defense on the battle-field a few months later,[a] made a most eloquent appeal for the preservation of the Union.[b] He and others had been powerfully moved by the treasonable speech of Toombs. He drew a graphic picture of the terrible effects that might be expected from secession—nationality destroyed, and on its ruins several weak republics established, without power to carry on any of the magnificent schemes in hand for the development of the resources of the continent. He spoke of the continual incentives to war between the separated States, and the contempt into which all would fall in the estimation of the world. "With standing armies consuming the substance of our people on the land," he said, "and our Navy and our postal steamers withdrawn from the ocean, who will protect, or respect, or who will even know by name our petty confederacies? The American man-of-war is a noble spectacle. I have seen it enter an ancient port in the Mediterranean. All the world wondered at it and talked about it. Salvos of artillery, from forts and shipping in the harbor, saluted its flag. Princes and princesses and merchants paid it homage, and all the people blessed it, as a harbinger of hope for their own ultimate freedom. I imagine now the same noble vessel again entering the same haven. The flag of thirty-three stars and thirteen stripes has been hauled down, and in its place a signal is run up which flaunts the device of a lone star or a palmetto-tree. Men ask, 'Who is the stranger that thus steals into our waters?' The answer, contemptuously given, is, 'She comes from one of the obscure republics of North America—let her pass on.'"

The plan of this work does not contemplate the recording of Congressional debates in detail; so we will proceed to notice, in few words, the result of the great discussion on pacification. It was continued from time to

[a] October 21, 1861.

[b] January 12.

can enter with honor into a conspiracy to overthrow it. He is ready to laugh in your face when you tell him, that before he was 'muling and puking in his nurse's arms,' there lived an obscure person by the name of George Washington, and who, before he died, became eminent, by perpetuating the immortal joke of advising the people of the United States that 'it is of infinite moment that we should properly estimate the immense value of our National Union, that we should cherish a cordial, habitual, and immovable attachment to it; that we should watch for its preservation with jealous anxiety, discountenancing whatever may suggest even a suspicion that it can, in any event, be abandoned; and indignantly frowning upon the first dawning of every attempt to alienate any portion of our country from the rest, or to enfeeble the sacred ties which now link together the various parts.'"

With greater bitterness Mr. Clemens denounced the Abolitionists, and quoted from the writings and speeches of William Lloyd Garrison and Wendell Phillips, in which they advocated a dissolution of the Union. "All hail disunion!" cried Phillips, in one of these. "Sacrifice every thing for the Union? God forbid! Sacrifice every thing to keep South Carolina in it? Rather build a bridge of gold and pay her toll over it. Let her march off with banners and trumpets, and we will speed the parting guest. Let her not stand upon the order of her going, but go at once. Give her the forts and arsenals and sub-treasuries, and lend her jewels of silver and gold, and Egypt will rejoice that she has departed."—*Congressional Globe*, 1860, '61. Appendix, pages 103, 104.

time until the last days of the session, when many of the conspirators had left Congress and gone home.

On the 2d of March, two days before the close of the session, Mason of Virginia called up the Crittenden resolutions in the Senate, when Clarke's substitute[1] was reconsidered and rejected, for the purpose of obtaining a direct vote on the original proposition.   After a long debate, continuing until late in the "small hours" of Sunday morning,[a] the Crittenden Compromise was finally rejected by a vote of twenty against nineteen.[2]   It might have been carried had the conspirators retained their seats.   The question was then taken in the Senate on a resolution of the House of Representatives, to amend the Constitution so as to prohibit forever any amendment of that instrument interfering with slavery in any State.   This resolution was adopted.

[a] March 3, 1861.

In the atmosphere of to-day, made clear by the tempest of war, we perceive that this result was most auspicious.   We may now see clearly the peril to which the nation would have been subjected had that Compromise, or kindred propositions for perpetuating and nationalizing slavery, been adopted.   Had the Constitution been amended in accordance with the propositions of the patriotic but short-sighted Crittenden, the Republic would have been bound in the fetters of one of the most relentless and degrading despotisms that ever disgraced the annals of mankind.

On the 12th of January, the conspirators commenced withdrawing from Congress.   On that day the Representatives of the State of Mississippi sent in a communication to the Speaker, saying they had been informed of the secession of their State, and that, while they regretted the occasion for that action, they approved the measure.   Two days afterward,[b] Albert G. Brown, one of the Senators from Mississippi, withdrew from active participation in the business of the Senate. His colleague, Jefferson Davis, did not take his leave, on account of sickness, until the 21st, when he made a parting speech.   He declared his devotion to the doctrine of State Supremacy to be so zealous, that if he believed his State had no just cause for leaving the Union, he should feel bound by its action to follow its destiny.   He thought it had just cause for withdrawing, and declared that he had counseled the people (in other words, the *politicians*) of that State to do as they had done.   He drew a distinction between nullification and secession, and asserted, in the face of history and common sense, that Calhoun advocated nullification in order to save the Union!   With the most transparent sophistry he then argued in favor of the right of secession, and against the prevailing idea, that when the preamble of the Declaration of Independence asserts that " *all* men are created equal," it means all without distinction of race or country.   Then, with a wicked perversion of the plainest teachings of history, he said:—" When you deny to us the right to withdraw from a

[b] January 14.

---

[1] See page 221.

[2] The vote was as follows:—

AYES.—Messrs. Bayard, Bright, Bigler, Crittenden, Douglas, Gwin, Hunter, Johnson of Tennessee, Kennedy, Lane, Latham, Mason, Nicholson, Polk, Pugh, Rice, Sebastian, Thompson, Wigfall—19.

NOES.—Messrs. Anthony, Bingham, Chandler, Clarke, Dixon, Doolittle, Durkie, Fessenden, Foote, Foster, Grimes, Harlan, King. Morrill, Sumner, Ten Eyck, Trumbull. Wade, Wilkinson, Wilson—20.

government which threatens to be destructive of our rights, we but tread in the path of our fathers when we proclaim our independence, and take the hazard." In direct conflict with truth, and with the most shameless hypocrisy, which his subsequent conduct revealed, he declared that the step was taken by himself and his State not for any selfish purpose, but "from the high and solemn motive of defending and protecting the rights we have inherited, and which it is our sacred duty to transmit unshorn to our children." He concluded with an expression of a hope that peaceful relations between the two sections might be maintained, and declared that he left the Senate without any animosity toward a single member personally. "I carry with me," he said, "no hostile remembrance. Whatever offense I have given which has not been redressed, or for which satisfaction has not been demanded, I have, Senators, at this hour of our parting, to offer you my apology for any pain which, in the heat of discussion, I have inflicted. . . . Having made this announcement, which the occasion seemed to me to require, it only remains for me to bid you a final adieu." Davis then left the Senate Chamber, and immediately entered more openly upon his treasonable work, in which he had been engaged for many years.

On the same day when Davis left the Senate, the representatives of Alabama and Florida in that House formally withdrew. Yulee and Mallory, the Florida Senators, spoke in temperate language; but Clement C. Clay, Jr., of Alabama, one of the most malignant foes of the Republic, and who was a secret plotter in Canada, during the war, of high crimes against the people of the United States, signalized his withdrawal by a harangue marked by the intensest venom. He commenced his speech by the utterance of what he knew to be untrue, by saying:— "I rise to announce, for my colleague and myself, that the people of Alabama have adopted an Ordinance of Separation, and that they are *all* in favor of withdrawing from the Union. I wish it to be understood that this is the act of the *people* of Ala-

CLEMENT C. CLAY, JR.

bama."[1] He then uttered a tirade of abuse against the people of the Free-labor States, and closed by saying: "As a true and loyal citizen of Alabama, approving of her action, acknowledging entire allegiance, and feeling that I am absolved by her act from all my obligations to support the Constitution of the United States, I withdraw from this body, intending to return to the bosom of my mother, and share her fate and maintain her fortunes." His white-haired colleague, Fitzpatrick, indorsed his sentiments, and both withdrew.

A week later,[a] Senator Iverson, of Georgia, having received a copy of the Ordinance of Secession from the Convention of the politicians of his State, formally withdrew, when he took the occasion to say, in contemplation of war:—"You may possibly overrun

[a] January 28, 1861.

---

[1] See an account of the opposition of the people to secession, on page 173.

us, desolate our fields, burn our dwellings, lay our cities in ruins, murder our people, and reduce us to beggary, but you cannot subdue or subjugate us to your Government or your will. Your conquest, if you gain one, will cost you a hundred thousand lives, and more than a hundred million dollars. Nay, more, it will take a standing army of a hundred thousand men and millions of money, annually, to keep us in subjection. You may whip us, but we will not stay whipped. We will rise again and again to vindicate our right to liberty, and to throw off your oppressive and cursed yoke, and never cease the mortal strife until our whole white race is extinguished, and our fair land given over to desolation. You may have ships of war, and we may have none. You may blockade our ports and lock up our commerce. We can live, if need be, without commerce. But when you shut out our cotton from the looms of Europe, we shall see whether other nations will not have something to say and something to do on that subject. *Cotton is King!* and it will find means to raise your blockade and disperse your ships."

Iverson prudently kept himself away from all personal danger during the war that ensued ; and in less than a year he saw his overrated monarch dethroned, and heard the cry of the great distress of his own people. His truculent colleague, Toombs, had already, as we have seen, gone home to work the machinery by which the people of Georgia were unwillingly placed in an attitude of rebellion. Toombs had also been bringing one of his Northern admirers in subserviency to his feet, in this wise :—Early in January, it became known to the Superintendent of the Metropolitan Police of New York, who were not under the control of the Mayor, that large quantities of arms, purchased of Northern manufacturers and merchants, were going southward. It was resolved to put a stop to traffic that would evidently prove injurious to the Government, and late in the month[a] nearly forty boxes of arms, consigned to parties in Georgia and Alabama, and placed on board the steamer *Monticello*, bound for Savannah, were seized by the New York police. The fact was immediately telegraphed to Governor Brown, at Milledgeville.

a January 22, 1861.

Toombs was there, and took the matter into his own hands. He telegraphed[b] as follows to the Mayor of New York :—"Is it true that arms, intended for, and consigned to the State of Georgia, have been seized by public authorities in New York ? Your answer is important to us and New York. Answer at once."

b January 24.

This insolent demand of a private citizen—one who had lately boasted, in his place in the National Senate, that he was a rebel and a traitor (and who, no one doubted, wanted these very arms for treasonable purposes), was obsequiously complied with. The Mayor (Fernando Wood) expressed his regret, but disclaimed for the city of New York any "responsibility for the outrage," as he called it. "As Mayor," he said, "I have no authority over the police. If I had the power, I should summarily punish the authors of this illegal and unjustifiable seizure of private property."

Toombs determined to retaliate. The Governor, who seems to have been a plastic servant of this conspirator, had asked the Legislature for power to retaliate, should there be an occasion, but his request had not been granted. Toombs advised him to act without law, and he did so. By his order, ships of several Northern owners were seized at Savannah and held as hostages. This act produced great excitement throughout the country. The more cautious leaders of the insurgents advised the release of the vessels. In the mean time a larger portion of the arms seized at New York had been given up, and the little tempest of passion was soon allayed. Investigations caused by this transaction revealed the fact that the insurgents were largely armed, through the cupidity of Northern merchants and manufacturers, who had made very extensive sales to the agents of the conspirators during the months of December, 1860, and January, February, and March, 1861.

On the 4th of February, John Slidell[1] and Judah P. Benjamin, of Louisiana, withdrew from the National Senate they were so dishonoring. Slidell made a speech which was marked by a cool insolence of manner, an insulting exhibition of contempt for the people of the Free-labor States, and a consciousness of power to do all that, in smooth rhetoric, he threatened. He spoke as if there would be a peaceable separation, and sketched a line of policy which the new "Confederacy" would pursue. But, he said, in the event of an attempt of the Government to enforce its laws in so-called seceded States, "you will find us ready to meet you with the outstretched hand of fellowship or in the mailed panoply of war, as you may will it. Elect between these alternatives." He then sneeringly referred to the utter failure which the Government would experience in any attempt to assert its authority over the "seceders." "You

JOHN SLIDELL.

may," he said, "under color of enforcing your laws or collecting your revenue, blockade our ports. This will be war, and we shall meet it with different but equally efficient weapons. We will not permit the introduction or consumption of any of your manufactures. Every sea will swarm with our volunteer militia of the ocean, with the striped bunting floating over their heads, for we do not mean to give up that flag without a bloody struggle—it is ours as much as yours[2]; and although for a time more stars may shine on your banner, our children, if not we, will rally under a constellation more numerous and more resplendent than yours. You may smile at this as an impotent boast, at least for the present, if not for the future; but," he said, with well-pointed irony, "if we need ships and men for privateering, we shall be amply supplied from the same sources as now, almost exclusively, furnish the means for carrying on with unexampled vigor the African Slave-trade—New York and New England. Your mercantile marine," he added, "must either sail under foreign flags or rot at your wharves."

With the blind spirit of false prophecy which had taken possession of the

---

[1] See page 61.

[2] The Louisiana conspirators, as we have observed, adopted as a device for their flag thirteen stripes, alternate red, white, and blue, and a single yellow star on a red ground in one corner. The blue stripe soiled the purity of appearance of the old flag. It was, indeed, dishonored.

conspirators, Slidell pointed to the inevitable hostility, as he conceived, of the European naval powers, when commerce and the supply of cotton should be interfered with by "mere paper blockades," and asked : " What will you be when, not only emasculated by the withdrawal of fifteen States, but warred upon by them with active and inveterate hostility ?" This significant question was answered four years afterward, when the naval powers of Europe had been so offended without committing acts of resentment, and the threatened civil war had raged inveterately, by the fact that the Republic was stronger, wealthier, and more thoroughly respected by foreign powers than ever. The crowning infamy of this farewell speech of Slidell was the utterance of the libel upon the *people* of Louisiana, in his declaration that the secession movement was theirs, and not of political leaders !

Benjamin followed Slidell in a temperate and argumentative speech on the right of secession. He bade the Senators from the Slave-labor States farewell, with the expectation of a speedy reunion ; and he eulogized those

Representatives from the Free-labor States who sympathized with himself and fellow-traitors in their rebellious movements, predicting that they would be honored above all others. " When in after days the story of the present shall be written," he said, " and when your children shall hear repeated the familiar tale, it will be with glowing cheek and kindling eye; their very souls will stand a-tiptoe as their sires are named, and they will glory in their lineage from men of spirit as generous, and of patriotism as high-hearted, as ever illustrated or adorned the American Senate."

JUDAH P. BENJAMIN.

This peroration was quite different in language and in its reception from that of his speech delivered on the same spot a month before,[a] when, with insinuations which only his own malignant nature could conceive, concerning the intentions of the supporters of the Government, and with the usual bravado of his class, he said :—"The fortunes of war may be adverse to our arms ; you may carry desolation into our peaceful land ; and with torch and fire you may set our cities in flames ;[1] you may even emulate the atrocities of those who, in the war of the Revolution, hounded on the bloodthirsty savage to attacks upon the defenseless frontier; you may, under the protection of your advancing armies, give shelter to the furious fanatics who desire, and profess to desire, nothing more than to add all the horrors of a servile insurrection to the calamities of civil war ; you may do all this—and more too, if more there be—but you never can subjugate us ; you never can convert the free sons of the soil into vassals,

[a] December 31, 1860.

___

[1] Benjamin was afterward convicted by testimony in open court, at the trial of the assassins of President Lincoln, of having been one of the chief plotters at Richmond, while he was the so-called "Secretary of State" of Jefferson Davis, of schemes for burning the cities, steamboats, hospitals, &c., and poisoning the public fountains of water in the Free-labor States.

paying tribute to your power; and you never, never can degrade them to the level of an inferior and servile race—never, *never*, NEVER !"[1]   The galleries of the Senate Chamber were crowded with Benjamin's sympathizers, who then filled the public offices and society at large in Washington. They greeted the closing sentences of this speech with the wildest shouts and other vehement demonstrations, which Breckinridge, the presiding officer, did not restrain. The tumult was so disgraceful that even Senator Mason, of Virginia, was ashamed of it, and he proposed, by a motion, to clear the galleries.

The House of Representatives were spared the infliction of farewell speeches overflowing with treasonable sentiments. The members from the "seceding States," with a single exception, sent up to the Speaker brief notices of their withdrawal. These were laid silently upon the table when read, and were no further noticed. Almost imperceptibly those traitors disappeared from the Legislative Hall. The exception referred to was Miles Taylor, of Louisiana, who took the occasion to warn the men of the Free-labor States of the peril of offending the cotton interest. He assured them that France and England would break any blockade that might be instituted, and that all the Border Slave-labor States would join those farther South in making war upon the National Government, if any attempt was made to "coerce a State," as the enforcement of law was falsely termed.   His remarks became so offensive to loyal ears, that Representative Spinner, from the interior of New York, interrupted him, saying, "I think it is high time to put a stop to this countenancing treason in the halls of legislation."   He made it a point of order whether it was competent for a member of Congress, sworn to support the Constitution and laws, to openly advocate treason against the Republic, and justify the seizure of forts and arsenals belonging to it by armed insurgents.   The Speaker allowed Taylor to proceed; and he finished his harangue by a formal   [a] February 5, 1861. withdrawal from his seat in the House.[a]

Thus ended the open utterances of treason in the Halls of Congress. The National Legislature was purged of its more disloyal elements, and thenceforth, during the remaining month of the session, its legitimate business was attended to.   There were turbulent and disloyal spirits left in that body, but they were less demonstrative, and were shorn of their power to do serious mischief. The Union men were now in the majority in the Lower House, and they controlled the Senate. Before the session closed, acts were passed for the organization of three new Territories, namely, Colorado, Nevada, and Dakotah. Not a word was said about Slavery in those Territories. The subject was left for decision to the people, when they should make a State Constitution. This silence was expressive of the honest determination of the party just rising into power, not to meddle with Slavery by means of the National Government, but leave it, as it always had been left, a subject for municipal law alone. In this behavior "the South" might have seen, if they had not been blinded by passion and misled by false teachers, an exhibition of justice full of promise for the future. They had been repeatedly assured of this during the progress of the session. So early as

---

[1] *Congressional Globe*, December 31, 1860.

the 27th of December, Charles Francis Adams, a distinguished citizen of Massachusetts, whose people were the chief offenders of the Oligarchy, offered in the House Committee of Thirty-three a resolution, "That it is expedient to propose an amendment to the Constitution, to the effect that no future amendments of it in regard to Slavery shall be made unless proposed by a Slave State, and ratified by all the States." It was passed with only three dissenting voices in the Committee.[1] It offered a broad and sufficient basis for a perfect reconciliation of feeling concerning the Slavery question, and would have been accepted as such, had not that Slavery question been the mere pretext of the conspirators, who had resolved that no terms of pacification should be agreed upon. They were bent on revolution, and utterly discarded the counsels of Honor, Justice, and even Prudence. The legend on their shield in political warfare was "Rule or Ruin."[2]

---

[1] This resolution was adopted by the House of Representatives by a vote of one hundred and thirty-three against sixty-five, or more than two-thirds in its favor. The Senate passed it by a vote of twenty-four against twelve.

[2] In an able speech in the Senate on the 21st of February, Henry Wilson said:—" What a saddening, humiliating, and appalling spectacle does America now present to the gaze of mankind! Conspiracies in the Cabinet and in the halls of legislation; conspiracies in the Capital and in the States; conspiracies in the Army and in the Navy; conspiracies everywhere to break the unity of the Republic; to destroy the grandest fabric of free government the human understanding ever conceived, or the hand of man ever reared. States are rushing madly from their spheres in the constellation of the Union, raising the banners of revolt, defying the Federal authority, arming men, planting frowning batteries, arming fortresses, dishonoring the National flag, clutching the public property, arms, and moneys, and inaugurating the reign of disloyal factions. . . . This conspiracy against the unity of the Republic, which, in its development, startles and amazes the world by its extent and power, is not the work of a day; it is the labor of a generation. . . . This wicked plot for the dismemberment of the Confederacy, which has now assumed such fearful proportions, was known to some of our elder statesmen. Thomas H. Benton ever raised his warning voice against the conspirators. I can never forget the terrible energy of his denunciations of the policy and acts of the nullifiers and secessionists. During the great Lecompton struggle, in the winter of 1858, his house was the place of resort of several members of Congress, who sought his counsels, and delighted to listen to his opinions. In the last conversation I had with him, but a few days before he was prostrated by mortal disease, he declared that 'the disunionists had prostituted the Democratic party'—that they 'had complete control of the Administration;' that 'these conspirators would have broken up the Union, if Colonel Frémont had been elected;' that 'the reason he opposed Frémont's election [he was his son-in-law] was, that he knew these men intended to destroy the Government, and he did not wish it to go in pieces in the hands of a member of his family.' I expressed some doubt of the extent and power of such a conspiracy to dismember the Union or to seize the Government; to which he replied, that 'he knew their purposes to be a Southern Confederacy, for efforts were early made to enlist him in the wicked scheme;' that 'so long as the people of the North should be content to attend to commerce and manufactures, and accept the policy and rule of the disunionists, they would condescend to remain in the Union; but should the Northern people attempt to exercise their just influence in the nation, they would attempt to seize the Government, or disrupt the Union; but,' said he, with terrible emphasis, ' *God and their own crimes will put them in the hands of the people!*'" How solemnly that prophecy of the great leader of the Democratic party in its days of genuine strength has been fulfilled!

CHAPTER X.

PEACE MOVEMENTS.—CONVENTION OF CONSPIRATORS AT MONTGOMERY.

N Monday, the 4th of February, 1861, the day on which Slidell and Benjamin left the Senate, a Convention known as the Peace Congress, or Conference, assembled in Willard's Hall, in Washington City, a large room in a building originally erected as a church edifice on F Street, and then attached to Willard's Hotel.

This Convention, as we have observed,[1] was proposed by resolutions of the Virginia Legislature, passed on the 19th of January,[a] and highly approved by the President of the Republic. The proposition met with favorable consideration $^{a\,1861.}$ throughout the country. Omens of impending war were becoming more numerous every day; and at the time this proposition was made, it was evident that no plan for the adjustment of existing difficulties could be agreed upon by the National Legislature. It was thought that a convention of conservative men, fresh from the people, might devise some salutary measures that should go before Congress with such weight of popular authority as to induce acquiescence, and lead to action that would secure pacification, the great object sought.

The Legislatures of most of the States were in session when the proposition went forth, and the response was so general and so prompt, that delegates from twenty-one States—fourteen of them Free-labor and seven of them Slave-labor States—appeared in the Convention.[2] When they were not

---

[1] See page 194.

[2] Some of the delegates were then members of Congress, both of the Senate and the House of Representatives. The following are the names of the delegates:—

Maine.—William P. Fessenden, Lott M. Morrill, Daniel E. Somes, John J. Perry, Ezra B. French, Freeman H. Morse, Stephen Coburn, Stephen C. Foster.

New Hampshire.—Amos Tuck, Levi Chamberlain, Asa Fowler.

Vermont.—Hiland Hall, Lucius E. Chittenden, Levi Underwood, H. Henry Baxter, B. D. Harris.

Massachusetts.—John Z. Goodrich, Charles Allen, George S. Boutwell, Theophilus P. Chandler, Francis B. Crowninshield, John M. Forbes, Richard P. Waters.

Rhode Island.—Samuel Ames, Alexander Duncan, William W. Hoppin, George H. Browne, Samuel G. Arnold.

Connecticut.—Roger S. Baldwin, Chauncey F. Cleveland, Charles J. McCurdy, James T. Pratt, Robins Battell, Amos S. Treat.

New York.—David Dudley Field, William Curtis Noyes, James S. Wadsworth, James C. Smith, Amaziah B. James, Erastus Corning, Francis Granger, Greene C. Bronson, William E. Dodge, John A. King, John E. Wool.

New Jersey.—Charles S. Olden, Peter D. Vroom, Robert F. Stockton, Benjamin Williamson, Joseph F. Randolph, Frederick T. Frelinghuysen, Rodman M. Price, William C. Alexander, Thomas J. Stryker.

Pennsylvania.—James Pollock, William H. Meredith, David Wilmot, A. W. Loomis, Thomas E. Franklin, William McKennan, Thomas White.

Delaware.—George B. Rodney, Daniel M. Bates, Henry Ridgely, John W. Houston, William Cannon.

Maryland.—John F. Dent, Reverdy Johnson, John W. Crisfield, Augustus W. Bradford, William T. Goldsborough, J. Dixon Roman, Benjamin C. Howard.

appointed by Legislatures, they were chosen by the Governors. Many of these delegates were instructed, either by formal resolutions of the appointing power or by informal expressions of opinion. Much caution was exercised, because there were well-grounded suspicions that the Virginia politicians, who had proposed the Convention, were adroitly playing into the hands of the conspirators. One of the resolutions that accompanied their invitation to a conference declared that the Crittenden Compromise, so modified as to apply to all the territory of the Republic south of latitude 36° 30', and to provide that "Slavery of the African race" should be "effectually protected as property therein during the existence of the Territorial government;" also, to secure to the holders of slaves the right of transit with this property, "between and through the non-slaveholding States and Territories," constituted a basis of adjustment that would be acceptable to Virginia. This avowal of their demands at the outset was candid, if not modest and conciliatory.

Massachusetts instructed its delegates to confer with the General Government, or with the separate States, or with any association of delegates from such States, and to report to the Legislature. Rhode Island said:—

WILLARD'S HALL.

"Agree, if practicable, upon some amicable adjustment of present difficulties, upon the basis and spirit of the National Constitution."

New York wished it not to be understood that, in acceding to the request of Virginia, it approved of Virginia's desires, as expressed in the resolutions of its Legislature. It was willing to do all in its power to bring about an honorable settlement of the national difficulties. New Jersey earnestly

---

Virginia.—John Tyler, Wm. C. Rives, John W. Brockenbrough, George W. Summers, James A. Seddon.

North Carolina.—George Davis, Thomas Ruffin, David S. Reid, D. M. Barringer, J. M. Morehead.

Tennessee.—Samuel Milligan, Josiah M. Anderson, Robert L. Caruthers, Thomas Martin, Isaac R. Hawkins, A. W. O. Totten, R. J. McKinney, Alvin Cullum, William P. Hickerson, George W. Jones, F. R. Zollicoffer, William H. Stephens.

Kentucky.—William O. Butler, James B. Clay, Joshua F. Bell, Charles S. Morehead, James Guthrie, Charles A. Wickliffe.

Missouri.—John D. Coalter, Alexander W. Doniphan, Waldo P. Johnson, Aylett H. Buckner, Harrison Hough.

Ohio.—Salmon P. Chase, John C. Wright, William S. Groesbeck, Franklin T. Backus, Reuben Hitchcock, Thomas Ewing, V. B. Horton, C. P. Wolcott.

Indiana.—Caleb B. Smith, Pleasant A. Hackleman, Godlove S. Orth, E. W. H. Ellis, Thomas C. Slaughter

Illinois.—John Wood, Stephen T. Logan, John M. Palmer, Burton C. Cook, Thomas J. Turner.

Iowa.—James Harlan, James W. Grimes, Samuel H. Curtis, William Vandever.

Kansas.—Thomas Ewing, Jr., J. C. Stone, H. J. Adams, M. F. Conway.

urged the adoption of the Crittenden Compromise.   Pennsylvania declared its willingness to make any honorable concession for the sake of peace, but did not desire any amendment or alteration of the Constitution.   It was ready to fulfill every duty prescribed to it by that Constitution, even to the full execution of the Fugitive Slave Act.   Delaware simply declared its devotion to the Union, and instructed its delegates to do all in their power for its preservation.   Ohio was willing to meet its fellow States in convention, but felt satisfied with the Constitution as it was; while Indiana instructed its delegates not to commit that State to any action until nineteen of the States should be represented, and until they had communicated with the General Assembly of their State, and received permission to commit it to proposed measures.   Illinois wished it to be understood that its willingness to confer was not a committal of the State to any proposed policy.   It was anxious for conciliation, but saw no reason for amending the Constitution for the purpose.   Kentucky would be satisfied with the Crittenden Compromise, according to the Virginia model.   Tennessee was willing to adjust all difficulties by the same process, but with enlarged franchises for the slaveholders; while Missouri instructed its delegates to endeavor to agree upon some plan for the preservation or reconstruction of the Union.   Its delegates were always to be subordinate to the General Assembly or the State Convention of Missouri.

The Convention was permanently organized by the appointment of John Tyler, of Virginia (once President of the Republic),[a]   [a 1841–1845.] as the presiding officer, and Crafts J. Wright, of Ohio, son of one of the delegates from that State, as secretary.   Mr. Tyler delivered a short address on taking the chair, in which he said:—

JOHN TYLER.

"The eyes of the whole country are turned to this assembly, in expectation and hope.   I trust that you may prove yourselves worthy of the great occasion.   Our ancestors probably committed a blunder in not having fixed upon every fifth decade for a call of a general convention to amend and reform the Constitution.   On the contrary, they have made the difficulties next to insurmountable to accomplish amendments to an instrument which was perfect for five millions of people, but not wholly so for thirty millions.   Your patriotism will surmount the difficulties, however great, if you will but accomplish one triumph in advance, and that is a triumph over *party*.   And what is party, when compared to the work of rescuing one's country from danger?   Do this, and one long, loud shout of joy and gladness will resound throughout the land."   At the conclusion of this address, Mr. Wickliffe, of Kentucky, offered a resolution that the Convention should be opened with prayer.   It was agreed to, and the Rev. Dr. P. D. Gurley officiated.

The regular business of the Convention was opened by Mr. Guthrie, of

Kentucky, who offered a resolution that a committee of one from each State be appointed by the delegates thereof, to be nominated to the President of the Convention, and to be appointed by him, to whom should be referred the resolutions of the State of Virginia, and the other States represented, and all propositions for the adjustment of existing difficulties between the States; the committee to have authority to report what it might deem right, necessary, and proper, to restore harmony and preserve the Union. The resolution was adopted; the committee was appointed,[1] and the subjects laid before it were duly discussed, sometimes with warmth, but always with courtesy. On the 15th, Mr. Guthrie, Chairman of the Committee, made a report, in which several amendments to the Constitution were offered. It was proposed—

First, To re-establish the parallel of 36° 30' north latitude as a line, in the territory north of which Slavery should be prohibited; but in all territory south of it Slavery might live, without interference from any power, while a territorial government existed. It also proposed that when any Territory north or south of that line should contain the requisite number of inhabitants to form a State, it should,[2] if its form of government should be republican, be admitted into the Union on an equal footing with the original States, either with or without Slavery, as the constitution of the new State might determine.

Second, That territory should not be acquired by the United States, unless by treaty; nor, except for naval and commercial stations, unless such treaty should be ratified by four-fifths of all the members of the Senate.

Third, That the Constitution nor any amendment thereof should be construed to give Congress power to interfere with Slavery in any of the States of the Union, nor in the District of Columbia, without the consent of Maryland and the slaveholders concerned; and, in case of the abolition of Slavery, making compensation to those who refused to consent; nor to prohibit representatives and others from taking their slaves to and from Washington; nor to interfere with Slavery in places under the exclusive jurisdiction of the United States, such as arsenals and navy-yards, in States where it was recognized; nor to interfere with the transportation of slaves from one Slave-labor State to another; nor to authorize any higher rate of taxation on slaves than on land.

Fourth, That the clause in the Constitution relating to the rendition of fugitive slaves should not be construed to prevent any of the States, by appropriate legislation, and through the action of their judicial and ministerial officers, from enforcing the delivery of fugitives from labor to the person to whom such service or labor should be due.

---

[1] The following are the names of the delegates who composed the Committee:—Maine, Lott M. Morrill; New Hampshire, Asa Fowler; Vermont, Hiland Hall; Massachusetts, Francis B. Crowninshield; Rhode Island, Samuel Ames; Connecticut, Roger S. Baldwin; New York, David Dudley Field; New Jersey, Peter D. Vroom; Pennsylvania, Thomas White; Ohio, Thomas Ewing; Indiana, Caleb B. Smith; Illinois, Stephen F. Logan; Iowa, James Harlan; Delaware, Daniel M. Bates; North Carolina, Thomas Ruffin; Virginia, James A. Seddon; Kentucky, James Guthrie; Maryland, Reverdy Johnson; Tennessee, F. R. Zollicoffer; Missouri, A. W. Doniphan.

[2] The National Constitution says:—"New States *may* be admitted by the Congress into this Union." The proposed amendment said, any new State "*shall*, if its form of government be republican, be admitted into the Union." The importance of this difference in phraseology, as well as its intent, is obvious.

Fifth, That the foreign Slave-trade should be forever prohibited.

Sixth, That the first, second, third, and fifth of the foregoing propositions, when in the form of ratified amendments to the Constitution, and the clause relating to the rendition of fugitive slaves, should not be amended or abolished without the consent of all the States.

Seventh, That Congress should provide by law that the United States should pay to the owner the full value of his fugitive from labor, in all cases where the law-officer, whose duty it was to arrest such fugitive, should be prevented from doing so by violence or intimidation, or when such fugitive should be rescued after arrest, and the claimant thereby should lose his property.

Two members of the Committee (Baldwin, of Connecticut, and Seddon, of Virginia) each presented a minority report. Baldwin proposed a general Convention of all the States,[1] to consider amendments to the Constitution; and Seddon, afterward the so-called "Secretary of War" of the confederated traitors, affirming that the majority report would not be acceptable to Virginia, because it conceded less than the Crittenden Compromise, whereas Virginia wanted all that and *more*, proposed, in addition to an absolute guaranty of Slavery south of 36° 30', an amendment that should not only give the slaveholder a right to take his slaves through Free-labor States, but allow him protection for his slaves, as property, while on the sea on such journey. He also proposed an amendment that should forever exclude from the ballot-box and public office, "persons who are in whole or in part of the African race." He also proposed another that should recognize the right of peaceable secession. He offered his propositions as a substitute for the majority report, well knowing that they would not be adopted by the Convention.

In the open Convention, Charles A. Wickliffe, of Kentucky, proposed that that body should request the several States which had passed obnoxious Personal Liberty Acts to repeal them, and to allow slaves to cross their territory when being taken from one Slave-labor State to another. On the 18th, Amos Tuck, of New Hampshire, submitted an address and resolutions. In the former, the distractions of the country were deplored and the right of secession denied; in the latter, it was proposed that the Convention should recognize the fact that the National Constitution gives no power to Congress, nor any other branch of the General Government, to interfere with Slavery in any of the States, and that neither of the great political organizations of the country contemplated a violation of the spirit of the Constitution; that the Constitution was established for the good of the whole people, and that when the rights of any portion of them are disregarded, redress can and ought to be provided; and that a convention of all the States to propose amendments to the Constitution be recommended. Salmon P. Chase, of Ohio, proposed that the Convention should adjourn to the 4th of April, to enable all of the States to be represented in it.

These various propositions and others were earnestly discussed for several

---

[1] The Legislature of Kentucky had made application to Congress to call a convention of all the States to consider amendments to the Constitution, and Mr. Baldwin proposed that the several States should join Kentucky in this request.

days, and votes were taken upon several proposed amendments to the Constitution. These votes were by States, each State having one vote.[1]

^{• February 26, 1861.} Finally, on the twenty-second day of the session,[•] David Dudley Field, of New York, moved to amend the majority report by striking out the seventh section and inserting the words: "No State shall withdraw from the Union without the consent of all the States convened, in pursuance of an act passed by two-thirds of each House of Congress." This proposition was rejected by eleven States against ten.[2]

On the same day, Mr. Guthrie's majority report was taken up for final action, when Mr. Baldwin offered his proposition as a substitute, and it was rejected by a vote of thirteen States against eight.[3] Mr. Seddon then offered his substitute. It was rejected by a vote of sixteen States against four.[4] James B. Clay then offered as a substitute Mr. Crittenden's Compromise plan, "pure and undefiled, without the crossing of a 't' or the dotting of an 'i.'" It was rejected by a vote of fourteen States against five.[5] Mr. Tuck then offered his resolutions as a substitute, and they were rejected by a vote of eleven States against nine.[6]

When these substitutes were thus disposed of, Mr. Guthrie's report was taken up, considered by sections, and, after some modifications, was adopted. Then T. E. Franklin of Pennsylvania, moved, as the sense of the Convention, that the highest political duty of every citizen of the United States is his allegiance to the Federal Government, created ly the Constitution of the United States, and that no State of this Union has any constitutional right to secede therefrom, or to absolve the citizens of such State from their allegiance to the Government of the United States. This was indefinitely postponed by a vote of ten States against seven. Mr. Seddon proposed as an amendment to the Constitution that the assent of the majority of the Senators from the Slaveholding States, and a like majority of Senators from non-slaveholding States, should be required to give validity to any act of the Senate; as also recognizing and legalizing State secession from the Union. This was laid on the table. Mr. Guthrie then offered a preamble to the propositions agreed to, which was adopted;[7] and President Tyler was requested to present that plan of adjustment and pacification to the Con-

---

[1] The eighteenth rule for the action of the conference prescribed this, and added:—"The yeas and nays of the members shall not be given or published—only the decision by States."

[2] *Ayes*—Connecticut, Illinois, Indiana, Iowa, Maine, Massachusetts, New York, New Hampshire, Vermont, Kansas—10. *Noes*—Delaware, Kentucky, Maryland, Missouri, New Jersey, North Carolina, Ohio, Pennsylvania, Rhode Island, Virginia—11.

[3] *Ayes*—Connecticut, Illinois, Iowa, Maine, Massachusetts, New York, New Hampshire, Vermont—8. *Noes*—Delaware, Indiana, Kentucky, Maryland, Missouri, New Jersey, North Carolina, Ohio, Pennsylvania, Rhode Island, Tennessee, Virginia, Kansas—13.

[4] The four States that voted for Seddon's resolution were Kentucky, Missouri, North Carolina, and Virginia.

[5] The five that voted for it were Kentucky, Missouri, North Carolina, Tennessee, and Virginia.

[6] *Ayes*—Connecticut, Illinois, Indiana, Iowa, Maine, Massachusetts, New York, New Hampshire, and Vermont—9. *Noes*—Delaware, Kentucky, Maryland, Missouri, New Jersey, North Carolina, Ohio, Pennsylvania, Rhode Island, Tennessee, Virginia—11.

[7] The following is Mr. Guthrie's plan, as adopted, with the preamble:—

"*To the Congress of the United States :*—The Convention assembled upon the invitation of the State of Virginia, to adjust the unhappy differences which now disturb the peace of the Union and threaten its continuance, make known to the Congress of the United States, that their body convened in the city of Washington on the 4th instant, and continued in session until the 27th.

"There were in the body, when action was taken upon that which is here submitted, one hundred and thirty-three commissioners, representing the following States :—Maine, New Hampshire, Vermont, Massachusetts, Rhode Island, Connecticut, New York, New Jersey, Pennsylvania, Delaware, Maryland, Virginia, North

gress, forthwith. Thus ended the business of the Convention, when Reverdy Johnson, of Maryland, one of the leading members of that body, asked and obtained leave to place on record and have printed in the proceedings of the Convention a resolution in which the action of the politicians in the seven Cotton-growing States, who had declared their withdrawal from the Union, was deplored; and that the Convention, while "abstaining from any judgment on their conduct," and expressing a hope that they might soon see cause to "resume their honored places in this confederacy of States," did so with the conviction that the Union was formed by the assent of the people of the respective States, and that the "republican institutions guarantied to each cannot and ought not to be maintained by force;" therefore the Convention deprecated "any effort of the Federal Government to coerce, in any form, the said States to reunion or submission, as tending to irreparable breach, and leading

REVERDY JOHNSON.

Carolina, Tennessee, Kentucky, Missouri, Ohio, Indiana, Illinois, Iowa, Kansas. They have approved what is herewith submitted, and respectfully request that your honorable body will submit it to conventions in the States, as an article of amendment to the Constitution of the United States."

PROPOSED ARTICLE OF AMENDMENT.

§ 1. In all the present territory of the United States north of the parallel of 36° 30' of north latitude, involuntary servitude, except in punishment of crime, is prohibited. In all the present territory south of that line, the status of persons held to involuntary service or labor, as it now exists, shall not be changed; nor shall any law be passed by Congress or the Territorial Legislature, to hinder or prevent the taking of such persons from any of the States of this Union to said territory, nor to impair the rights arising from said relation; but the same shall be subject to judicial cognizance in the Federal courts, according to the course of the common law. When any territory north or south of said line, within such boundary as Congress shall prescribe, shall contain a population equal to that required for a member of Congress, it shall, if its form of government be republican, be admitted into the Union on an equal footing with the original States, with or without involuntary servitude, as the Constitution of such State may provide.—[Adopted by a vote of nine States against eight.]

§ 2. No territory shall be acquired by the United States, except by discovery, and for naval and commercial stations, depôts, and transit routes, without the concurrence of a majority of all the Senators from States which allow involuntary servitude, and a majority of all the Senators from States which prohibit that relation; nor shall territory be acquired by treaty, unless the votes of a majority of the Senators from each class of States, hereinbefore mentioned, be cast as a part of the two-thirds majority necessary to the ratification of such treaty.—[Adopted by a vote of eleven States against eight.]

§ 3. Neither the Constitution, nor any amendment thereof, shall be construed to give Congress power to regulate, abolish, or control, within any State, the relation established or recognized by the laws thereof, touching persons held to labor or involuntary service therein; nor to interfere with or abolish involuntary service in the District of Columbia, without the consent of Maryland, and without the consent of the owners, or making the owners who do not consent just compensation; nor the power to interfere with or prohibit Representatives and others from bringing with them to the District of Columbia, retaining, and taking away, persons so held to labor or service, nor the power to interfere with or abolish involuntary service in places under the exclusive jurisdiction of the United States, within those States and Territories where the same is established and recognized; nor the power to prohibit the removal or transportation of persons held to labor or involuntary service in any State or Territory of the United States, to any other State or Territory thereof where it is established or recognized by law or usage, and the right, during transportation by sea or river, of touching at ports or shores, and landings, and of landing in case of distress, exists; but not the right of transit in or through any State or Territory, or of sale or traffic, against the laws thereof. Nor shall Congress have power to authorize any higher rate of taxation on persons held to labor or service than on land. The bringing into the District of Columbia of persons held to labor or service, for sale, or placing them in depôts to be afterward transferred to other places for sale, as merchandise, is prohibited.—[Adopted by a vote of twelve States against seven.]

§ 4. The third paragraph of the second section of the fourth Article of the Constitution shall not be conto incalculable ills;" and for this reason it earnestly invoked "abstinence from all counsels and measures of compulsion toward them."[1]

After voting thanks to the proprietors of the Hall, who made no charge for its use; to the municipal authorities of Washington City, who agreed to pay all of the expenses of the Convention incurred for printing and stationery; and to the president, "for the dignified and impartial manner" in which he had presided over their deliberations, the delegates listened to a brief farewell address from Mr. Tyler, and then adjourned.[2] On the following day, one hundred guns were fired in Washington in honor of the "Convention Compromise."

The President of the Convention immediately sent a copy of the proposed amendments to the Constitution, adopted by that body, to Vice-President Breckinridge, who laid the matter before the Senate.[a] It was referred to a Committee of Five, consisting of Senators Crittenden, Bigler, Thomson, Seward, and Trumbull, with instructions to report the next day. Mr. Crittenden reported the propositions of the Convention, when Mr. Seward, for himself and Mr. Trumbull, presented as a substitute a joint resolution, that whereas the Legislatures of the States of Kentucky, New Jersey, and Illinois had applied to Congress to call a convention of the States, for the purpose of proposing amendments to the Constitution, the Legislatures of the other States should be invited to consider and express their will on the subject, in pursuance of the fifth Article of the Constitution. A long debate ensued; and, finally, on motion of Senator Douglas, it was decided, by a vote of twenty-five to eleven, to postpone the consideration of the "Guthrie plan" in favor of a proposition of amendment adopted by the House of Representatives, which provided that "no amendment shall be made to the Constitution which will authorize or give to Congress the power to interfere within any State with the domestic institutions thereof." In this the Senate concurred, when the Crittenden Compromise, as we have observed,[3] was called up and rejected.

Thus ended the vain attempts to conciliate the Slave interest by Congres-

a March 2, 1861.

---

strued to prevent any of the States, by appropriate legislation, and through the action of their judicial and ministerial officers, from enforcing the delivery of fugitives from labor to the persons to whom such service or labor is due.—[Adopted by a vote of fifteen States against four.]

§ 5. The foreign Slave-trade is hereby forever prohibited: and it shall be the duty of Congress to pass laws to prevent the importation of slaves, coolies, or persons held to service or labor, into the United States and the Territories, from places from beyond the limits thereof.—[Adopted by a vote of sixteen States against five.]

§ 6. The first, third, and fifth sections, together with this section of these amendments, and the third paragraph of the second section of the first Article of the Constitution, and the third paragraph of the second section of the fourth Article thereof, shall not be amended or abolished, without the consent of all the States.—[Adopted by a vote of eleven States against nine.]

§ 7. Congress shall provide by law that the United States shall pay to the owner the full value of his fugitive from labor, in all cases where the marshal or other officer, whose duty it was to arrest such fugitive, was prevented from so doing by violence or intimidation from mobs or riotous assemblages, or when, after arrest, such fugitive was rescued by like violence or intimidation, and the owner thereby deprived of the same; and the acceptance of such payment shall preclude the owner from further claim to such fugitive. Congress shall provide by law for securing to the citizens of each State the privileges and immunities of citizens in the several States.—[Adopted by a vote of twelve States against ten.]

[1] See *Report of the Debates and Proceedings of the Secret Sessions of the Conference Convention for proposing Amendments to the Constitution of the United States,* by Lucius E. Chittenden, one of the delegates, for a full account of all the proceedings of this remarkable Congress.

[2] During the session, a delegate from Ohio, the venerable John C. Wright, then seventy-seven years of age, and nearly blind, died quite suddenly. His death occurred on the 13th, when his son, who had been appointed Secretary to the Convention, returned to Ohio with the remains of his father, and J. H. Puleston served the Convention as Secretary during the remainder of the session.

[3] See page 228.

sional action. They had demanded changes in the Constitution so as to nationalize Slavery, and would not recede a line from the position they had assumed, while the true men of the nation, determined not only to defend and preserve the Union, but to defend and preserve the Constitution from abasement, were willing to meet them more than half way in efforts to compromise and pacify. The Virginians, in particular, were supercilious, dictatorial, and exacting, as usual. They assumed an air of injured innocence when they saw the precautions taken by the Secretary of War and General Scott to preserve the peace and secure the safety of the National Capital by increasing the military force there; and Tyler seems to have gone so far as to have given President Buchanan to understand that the appearance of National troops as participators in the celebration of Washington's Birthday,[a] would be offensive to the Virginians, and unfavorable to the harmony of the Peace Convention. They [a February 22, 1861.] did participate in the festivities of the occasion, for which offense the President, not unaccustomed to a kindly yielding to the wishes of the Slave interest, wrote an apologetic letter to Tyler.[1]

The failure of the Peace Conference caused much disappointment throughout the country among a large class, who earnestly desired reconciliation, and who had hoped much from its labors; while to many of those who went into the Convention as delegates, and others who had watched the movements of the Oligarchy with care, the result was not unexpected. The demands made in the Virginia resolutions foreshadowed the spirit that was to be met; while the lofty and confident tone of the conspirators in Congress, and the energy with which their friends were at work in the Slave-labor States, promised nothing but failure. It was believed by many then (and events have confirmed the suspicion) that the proposition for the Conference was made in insincerity, and that it was a scheme to give the conspirators more time, while deluding the country with pretended desires for reconciliation, to perfect their plans for securing success in the impending conflict. Henry A. Wise, a chief actor among the Virginia politicians at that time, had declared, as we have seen, two months before:—"Our minds are made up. The South will not wait until the 4th of March. *We will be well under arms before then.*"[2] John Tyler, one of the chief promoters of this Peace move-

---

[1] When, in 1862, the National troops went up the Virginia Peninsula, they took possession of "Sherwood Forest," the residence of Tyler, near Charles City Court House, which the owner, one of the leaders among the enemies of his country, had abandoned. There Assistant Adjutant-General W. H. Long found the letter alluded to. The following is a copy:—

"WASHINGTON, February 22, 1861.

"My Dear Sir:—I found it impossible to prevent two or three companies of the Federal troops from joining in the procession to-day with the volunteers of the District, without giving serious offense to the tens of thousands of people who have assembled to witness the parade.

"The day is the anniversary of Washington's birth—a festive occasion throughout the land—and it has been particularly marked by the House of Representatives.

"The troops everywhere else join such processions in honor of the birthday of the Father of our Country, and it would be hard to assign a good reason why they should be excluded from the privilege in the Capital founded by himself. They are here simply as a *posse comitatus*, to aid the civil authorities, in case of need. Besides, the programme was published in the *National Intelligencer* of this morning without my personal knowledge—the War Department having considered the celebration of the National Anniversary by the military arm of the Government as a matter of course.

"From your friend, very respectfully, JAMES BUCHANAN.

"President TYLER."
[2] See page 48.

ment in Virginia, and President of the Convention, was an advocate of the treason of the South Carolina politicians in 1832–'33, and is fully on record as a co-worker with Wise and others against the life of the Republic so early as 1856.[1]   On the adjournment of the Peace Convention he hastened to Richmond, where he and Seddon (afterward the so-called Secretary of War of Jefferson Davis) were serenaded, and both made speeches.   In his address at the close of the Convention he had just left, Tyler said :—" I cannot but hope and believe that the blessing of God will follow and rest upon the result of your labors, and that such result will bring to our country that quiet and peace which every patriotic heart so earnestly desires. . . .   It is probable that the result to which you have arrived is the best that, under all the circumstances, could be expected.   *So far as in me lies, therefore, I shall recommend its adoption.*"   Thirty-six hours afterward he was in Richmond, and in the speech alluded to he cast off the mask, denounced the Peace Convention as a worthless affair, declared that "the South" had nothing to hope from the Republican party;[2] and then, with all his might, he

WINFIELD SCOTT IN 1865.

labored to precipitate Virginia into the vortex of revolution, in which its people suffered terribly.

There were many persons of influence extremely anxious for peace, and preferring a dissolution of the Union (which they hoped would be temporary) to war, who were ready to consent to the secession of the fifteen Slave-labor States in order to secure this great desire of their hearts. Influential Republican journals expressed this willingness;[3] and Lieutenant-General Scott, who knew what were the horrors of war, seems to have contemplated this alternative without dread. In a letter addressed to Governor Seward, on the day preceding Mr. Lincoln's inauguration,[a] he suggested a limitation of the President's field of action in the premises to four measures, namely :—1st, to adopt the Crittenden Compromise ; 2d, to collect duties *outside* of the ports of "seceding States," or blockade them ; 3d, to conquer those

[a] March 3, 1861.

[1] This fact was established by letters found when our army moved up the Virginia Peninsula, in 1862.

[2] Telegraphic dispatch from Richmond, dated the evening of "Thursday, February 28, 1861," quoted by Victor, in his *History of the Southern Rebellion*, page 490.

[3] " Whenever a considerable section of our Union shall deliberately resolve to go out, we shall resist all coercive measures designed to keep it in. We hope never to live in a Republic whereof one section is pinned to the residue by bayonets."—*New York Tribune*, November 7, 1860. When, in June, 1865, Alexander H. Stephens applied to President Johnson for pardon, he alleged that, among other reasons for espousing the cause of the rebellion, was the fact that the utterances of the *Tribune*, one of the most influential of the supporters of the Republican party, made him believe that the separation and independence of the Slave-labor States would be granted, and that there could be no war.

On the 22d of January, 1861, Wendell Phillips, the great leader of the radical wing of the Anti-slavery party, in an address in Boston, on the "Political Lessons of the Hour," declared himself to be "a disunion man," and was glad to see South Carolina and other Slave-labor States had practically initiated a disunion movement. He hoped that all the Slave-labor States would leave the Union, and not "stand upon the order of their going, but go at once." He denounced the compromise spirit manifested by Mr. Seward and Charles Francis Adams, with much severity of language.—*Springfield* (Mass.) *Republican*, January 23, 1861.

States at the end of a long, expensive, and desolating war, and to no good purpose; and, 4th, to "say to the seceded States, 'Wayward sisters, go in peace!'"[1]

Another earnest pleader against "coercion," which would evidently lead to war, was Professor Samuel F. B. Morse, who gave intellectual power to the electro-magnetic telegraph. He was a conspicuous opponent of the war measures of the Government during the entire conflict. He was made President, as we have seen, of "The American Society for the Promotion of National Union," immediately after the adjournment of the Peace Convention;[2] and he worked zealously for the promotion of measures that might satisfy the demands of the slaveholders. "Before that most lamentable and pregnant error of the attack on Fort Sumter had been committed," says Professor Morse, in a letter to the author of these pages,[a] "which, indeed, inaugurated actual *physical* hostilities, and while war was confined to threatening and irritating words between the two sections of the country, there seemed to me to be two methods by which our sectional difficulties might be adjusted without bloodshed, which methods I thus stated in a paper drawn up at the time, when the project of a *Flag* for the Southern section was under discussion in the journals of the South:—

[a] May 2, 1864.

"The first and most proper mode of adjusting those difficulties is to call a National Convention, in conformity with the provisions of the Constitution; a Convention of the States, to which body should be referred the whole subject of our differences; and then, if but a moiety of the lofty, unselfish,

---

[1] This letter, written by the General-in-chief of the Armies of the Republic, on whose advice and skill the incoming President must rely for the support of the integrity of the nation and the vindication of the laws, at all hazards, is so remarkable, under the circumstances, that its suggestions are given here in full, as follows:—

"To meet the extraordinary exigencies of the times, it seems to me that I am guilty of no arrogance in limiting the President's field of selection to one of the four plans of procedure subjoined:—

"I. Throw off the *old* and assume a *new* designation—the *Union Party*; adopt the conciliatory measures proposed by Mr. Crittenden, or the Peace Convention, and, my life upon it, we shall have no new case of secession; but, on the contrary, an early return of many, if not all the States which have already broken off from the Union. Without some equally benign measure, the remaining Slaveholding States will probably join the Montgomery Confederacy in less than sixty days—when this city [Washington], being included in a foreign country, would require a permanent garrison of at least thirty-five thousand troops to protect the Government within it.

"II. Collect the duties on foreign goods *outside* the ports of which this Government has lost the command, or close such ports by act of Congress, and blockade them.

"III. Conquer the seceded States by invading armies. No doubt this might be done in two or three years, by a young and able general—a Wolfe, a Desaix, or a Hoche—with three hundred thousand disciplined men (kept up to that number), estimating a third for garrisons, and the loss of a yet greater number by skirmishes, sieges, battles, and Southern fevers. The destruction of life and property on the other side would be frightful, however perfect the moral discipline of the invaders. The conquest completed, at that enormous waste of human life to the North and Northwest, with at least two hundred and fifty millions of dollars added thereto, and *cui bono?* Fifteen desolated Provinces! not to be brought into harmony with their conquerors, to be held for generations by heavy garrisons, at an expense quadruple the net duties or taxes which it would be possible to extort from them, followed by a Protector or Emperor.

"IV. Say to the seceded States—*Wayward sisters, depart in peace!*"—*Scott's Autobiography*, ii. 625.

On the solicitation of John Van Buren, of New York, General Scott gave him the original draft of this letter, as an autographic keepsake of a strictly private nature, supposing that he was simply gratifying the wishes of an honorable man. His confidence was betrayed, and this private letter to Mr. Seward was read to a large public meeting of the friends of Horatio Seymour, during the canvass of that leader for the office of Governor of New York. The letter was used as an implied censure of the policy of the Administration of Mr. Lincoln. General Scott, in vindication of himself, then published a Report on the public defenses, which he had submitted to Mr. Buchanan before he left office, which occasioned a spicy newspaper correspondence between these venerable men. See *National Intelligencer*, October, 1862.

[2] See page 207.

enlarged, and kind disposition manifested in that noble Convention of 1787, which framed our Constitution, be the controlling disposition of the new convention, we may hope for some amicable adjustment. If for any reason this mode cannot be carried out, then the second method is one which circumstances may unhappily force upon us; but even this mode, so lamentable in itself considered, and so extreme—so repulsive to an American heart, if judiciously used, may eventuate in a modified and even stronger Union. This is the temporary yielding to the desire of the South for a separate confederacy; in other words, an assent to negotiations for a temporary *dissolution of the present Union.* My object in this mode is to secure, in the end, a more permanent perpetual Union. I well know that this is a startling proposition, and may seem to involve a paradox; but look at it calmly and carefully, and understand what is involved in such an assent. It involves, as a paramount consideration, a total cessation on our part of the irritating process which for thirty years has been in operation against the South. If this system of vituperation cannot be quelled because we have 'freedom of speech;' if we cannot refrain from the use of exasperating and opprobious language toward our brethren, and from offensive intermeddling with their domestic affairs, then, of course, the plan fails, and so will all others for a true union. If we cannot tame our tongues, neither union nor peace with neighbors, nor domestic tranquillity in our homes, can be expected."

This earnest apostle of Peace then proceeds to notice some of the formidable difficulties in the way, such as fixing the boundary-line between the "two confederacies," and the weighty necessity of maintaining, in peaceful relations, a standing military army and an army of custom house officials. These considerations, he believed (assuming that both parties should never lose their temper), would cause a perception of the necessity for compromise, "which embodies a sentiment vital to the existence of any society." There then would be the difficulty of an equitable distribution of the public property, as well as an agreement upon the terms of a treaty "offensive and defensive between the confederacies. Coercion," he said, "of one State by another, or of one Federated Union by another Federated Union," was not to be thought of. "The idea is so fruitful of crime and disaster that no man, in his right mind, can entertain it for a moment."

Supposing all these matters to be definitely settled to the perfect satisfaction of all parties, the question naturally arose in the mind of the writer, "What is to become of the *Flag* of the Union?" He answered, "The Southern section is now agitating the question of a device for their distinctive flag. Cannot this question of flags be so settled as to aid in a future Union? I think it can. If the country can be divided, why not the flag? The Stars and Stripes is the flag in which we all have a deep and the self-same interest. It is hallowed by the common victories of our several wars. We all have sacred associations clustering around it in common, and, therefore, if we must be two nations, neither nation can lay exclusive claim to it without manifest injustice and offense to the other. Neither will consent to throw it aside altogether for a new and strange device, with no associations of the past to hallow it.

"The most obvious solution of the difficulties which spring up in this respect is to *divide* the old flag, giving half to each. It may be done, and

In a manner to have a salutary *moral* effect upon both parties. Let the blue union be diagonally divided, from left to right or right to left, and the thirteen stripes longitudinally, so as to make six and a half stripes in the upper, and six and a half stripes in the lower portion. Referring to it, as on a map, the upper portion being North, and the lower portion being South, we have the upper diagonal division of the blue field in each flag to contain the stars to the number of States embraced in each confederacy. The reasons for such division are obvious. It prevents all dispute on a claim for the old flag by either confederacy. It is *distinctive;* for the two cannot be mistaken for each other, either at sea or at a distance on land. Each flag, being a moiety of the old flag, will retain something, at least, of the sacred memories of the past for the sober reflection of each confederacy. And then if a war with some foreign nation, or combination of nations, should unhappily occur (all wars being unhappy), under our treaty of offense and defense, the two separate flags, by natural affinity, would clasp fittingly together, and the glorious old flag of the Union, in its entirety, would again be hoisted, once more embracing all the sister States.[1]

"NORTHERN" FLAG.

field and the upper six and a half stripes for the *Northern Flag,* and the lower diagonal division of the blue field and the lower six and a half stripes for the *Southern Flag.* The portion of the blue

"SOUTHERN" FLAG.

Would not this division of the old flag thus have a salutary moral effect inclining to union? Will there not also be felt a sense of shame when either flag is seen by citizens of either confederacy? Will the old time-honored banner, bequeathed to us by our honored ancestors of every State, shall be flung to the breeze in its original integrity, as the rallying-point for a common defense, will not a shout of welcome, going up from the Rio Grande to Maine, and from the Atlantic to the Pacific, rekindle in patriotic hearts in both confederacies a fraternal yearning for the old Union?"

REUNITED FLAG.

it not speak to them of the divisions which have separated members of the same household, and will not the *why* be forced from their lips, Why is the old flag divided? And when once

Such was the notable plan for reconciliation put forth by the most distinguished of the leaders of the Peace party, that played an important part during the civil war. This novel proposition—this disjunctive conjunctive plan of conciliation, like the experiment of making a delicate China vase stronger and more beautiful by first breaking it into fragments, and cementing it by foreign agency, shared the fate of others in Congress and in the Peace Convention. It was rejected as insufficient. The *conspirators* had resolved on absolute, wide, and eternal separation, while the vast majority of the *people* of the Republic had as firmly resolved that there should be no division of the flag, of the territory, or of the "sacred associations of the Past;" for out of that Past came the voice of the Father of his Country,

---

[1] The sketches of the divided Flag are from drawings made for me by Professor Morse.

saying: "It is of infinite moment that you should properly estimate the immense value of your National Union to your collective and individual happiness; that you should cherish a cordial, habitual, and immovable attachment to it; accustoming yourselves to think and speak of it as of the palladium of your political safety and prosperity; watching for its preservation with jealous anxiety; discountenancing whatever may suggest even a suspicion that it can, in any event, be abandoned; and indignantly frowning upon the first dawning of every attempt to alienate any portion of our country from the rest, or to enfeeble the sacred ties which now link together the various parts."[1]

On the same day when the Peace Convention assembled at Washington to deliberate upon plans for preserving the Union, a band of usurpers, chosen by the secession conventions of six States without the consent or sanction of the people, met in the State House at Montgomery, in Alabama (a city of

STATE HOUSE AT MONTGOMERY.

sixteen thousand inhabitants, on the Alabama River, and over three hundred miles by water from the Gulf of Mexico), for the purpose of perfecting schemes for the destruction of the Union. They were forty-two in number, and represented the disloyal politicians of South Carolina, Georgia, Alabama, Mississippi, Louisiana, and Florida.[2] For days heavy rains had been flooding the whole region between the Savannah and Tombigbee Rivers, damaging railways, and making traveling perilous. The train that conveyed Stephens, and Toombs, and T. R. Cobb, of Georgia, and Chesnut, and Withers, and Rhett, of South Carolina, was thrown from the track between West Point and Montgomery, and badly broken up. Everybody was frightened, but nobody was hurt; and at a late hour, on the 4th, these leaders in conspiracy entered Montgomery. Not long afterward the Convention assembled in the Legislative Hall, around which were hung, in unseemly intermingling, the portraits

---

[1] Washington's Farewell Address to his countrymen.
[2] The following are the names of the delegates:—
South Carolina.—R. B. Rhett, James Chesnut, Jr., W. P. Miles, T. J. Withers, R. W. Barnwell, C. G. Memminger, L. M. Keitt, W. W. Boyce. *Georgia.*—Robert Toombs, Howell Cobb, Benjamin H. Hill, Alexander H. Stephens, Francis Barbour, Martin J. Crawford, E. A. Nisbett, Augustus B. Wright, Thomas R. R. Cobb, Augustus Keenan. *Alabama.*—Richard W. Walker, Robert H. Smith, Colin J. McRae, John Gill Shorter, S. F. Hale, David P. Lewis, Thomas Fearn, J. L. M. Curry, W. P. Chilton. *Mississippi.*—Willie P. Harris, Walker Brooke, A. M. Clayton, W. S. Barry, J. T. Harrison, J. A. P. Campbell, W. S. Wilson. *Louisiana.*—John Perkins, Jr., Duncan F. Kenna, C. M. Conrad, E. Spencer, Henry Marshall. *Florida.*—Jackson Morton, James Powers, W. B. Ochiltree.

of George Washington and John C. Calhoun; of Andrew Jackson and William L. Yancey; of General Marion, Henry Clay, and the historian of Alabama, A. J. Pickett.   Robert W. Barnwell, of South Carolina, was chosen temporary chairman; and the blessing of a just God was invoked upon the premeditated labors of these wrong-doers by the Rev. Basil Manly.

. That assembly of conspirators was permanently organized by the appropriate choice of Howell Cobb, of Georgia, as presiding officer.   Johnson F. Hooper, of Montgomery, was chosen clerk.[1]   On taking the chair, Cobb made a short speech, in which he said, truly, that their assemblage was of no ordinary character.   They met, he said, as representatives of sovereign and independent States, who had dissolved the political associations which connected them with the United States.   He declared that the separation was a "fixed and irrevocable fact"—that it was "perfect, complete, and perpetual." The duty imposed upon them was to make provision for the Government of the "seceded States."   It was desirable to maintain the most friendly relations with their "late sister States, as with the world," and especially with the Slave-labor States.   He doubted not that he, and the men before him, would prove equal to the task assigned them.   He counseled them to assume all responsibility necessary to the accomplishment of the work they had entered upon.   "With a consciousness of the justice of our cause," he said, "and with confidence in the guidance and blessings of a kind Providence, we will this day inaugurate for the South a new era of peace, security, and prosperity."

As the delegates assumed to be representatives of "Sovereign States," it was agreed that all votes should be taken by States.   Having adopted rules for the guidance of the Convention, they at once proceeded to business with great diligence.   It was soon discovered that perfect harmony was not to be expected.   There were too many ambitious men in that little assemblage to allow the prevalence of sweet concord, or serenity of thought and manner. They were nearly all aspirants to high positions in the inchoate empire. Each felt himself, like Bottom the Weaver, capable of performing any part in the drama about opening, either as "Lion," "Pyramus," "Wall," or "Moonshine."   The South Carolinians were specially ambitious for distinction.   They longed for the most lofty honors and the most prodigal emoluments.   Had they not been leaders in the revolutionary movements?   Had they not struck the first blow for the destruction of the Republic, on whose ruins they were about to build the majestic fabric of "free government," founded on Slavery?[2]   Had they not, therefore, a pre-emptive right to the best domain in the new commonwealth?   Judge Magrath, who with ludicrous solemnity laid aside his judicial robes at Charleston,[3] sent word that he would like to put them on again at Montgomery as attorney-general.[4] Robert Barnwell Rhett, the most belligerent of the demagogues of the

---

[1] Hooper was at one time editor of the *Montgomery Mail*, a violent secession sheet.   He had for assistant clerks Robert S. Dixon and A. R. Lamar.   Hooper died in great poverty in Richmond, some time in the year 1862.

[2] See picture of banner, page 106.   [3] See page 48.

[4] "Memminger mentioned to the delegates that he was requested by Judge McGrath to say to them, that he would be glad to be appointed attorney-general by the President of the Confederacy.   There will be solicitations enough from South Carolina for offices.   But keep this to yourself."—*Autograph Letter of R. B. Rhett to his Son*, February 11, 1861.

"Palmetto State"—the perfect representative of the disloyal politicians of South Carolina—thought himself peculiarly fitted for a secretary of war, and evinced special sensitiveness because his claims to distinction were overlooked. Of this he wrote complaining letters to his son, the editor of the *Charleston Mercury*. Some of these are before me, and are rich revelations of disappointed ambition.[1] Memminger aspired to be secretary of the treasury, and James Chesnut, Jr., who had "patriotically" made a sacrifice of his seat in the National Senate,[2] was spoken of as a fitting head of the new nation.

The policy advocated by Rhett and his class,. and the *Mercury*, their organ, had been that of violence from the beginning. From the hour when Anderson entered Sumter,[3] they had counseled its seizure. In the Convention at Montgomery, Rhett urged that policy with vehemence, and tried to infuse his own spirit of violence into that assembly. He was met by calm and steady opposition, under which he chafed; and privately he denounced his associates there as cowards and imbeciles.[4] Men like Stephens, and Hill, and Brooke, and Perkins, controlled the fiery spirits in that Convention, and it soon assumed a dignity suited to the gravity of the occasion.

The sessions of the Montgomery Convention were generally held in secret.[5] That body might properly be called a conclave—a conclave of conspirators. On the second day of the session, Mr. Memminger, of South Carolina, offered a series of three resolutions, declaring that it was expedient forthwith to form a confederacy of "seceded States," and that a committee be appointed to report a plan for a provisional government, on the basis of the Constitution of the United States; that the committee consist of thirteen members; and that all propositions in reference to a provisional government be referred to that committee. Alexander H. Stephens then moved that the word "Congress" be used instead of "Convention," when applied to the body then in session, which was agreed to.

On the following day,[a] commissioners from North Carolina appeared, and were invited to seats in the Convention.[6] They came only as commissioners from a State yet "a part of the Federal Union," and had no right to appear as delegates. Their object was, according to instructions,[7] to effect an "honorable and amicable adjustment of all the

<a>a February 6, 1861.</a>

---

[1] "That they have not put me forward for office," said Rhett, "is true. I have two enemies in the [South Carolina] delegation. *One* friend, who, I believe, wants no office himself, and will probably act on the same principle for his friend—and the rest, personally, are indifferent to *me*, whilst some of them are not indifferent to *themselves*. There is no little jealousy of me, by a part of them, and they never will agree to recommend me to any position whatever under the Confederacy. I expect nothing, therefore, from the delegation lifting me to position. . . . Good-by, my dear son. I have never been wise in pushing myself forward to office or power, and, I suppose, never will be. I cannot change. Prepare for disappointment."—*Autograph Letter*, February 11, 1861.

[2] See page 51.   [3] See page 199.

[4] "If the people of Charleston," he said, "should burn the whole crew in effigy, I should not be surprised. No reasoning on earth can satisfy the people of the South, that within two months a whole State could not take a fort defended by but seventy men. The thing is absurd. We must be disgraced."—*Autograph Letter*, February 11, 1861.

The Alabamians seem to have been special objects of Rhett's dislike. "Alabama," he said, "has the meanest delegation in this body. There is not a statesman amongst them; and they are always ready for all the hasty projects of fear. *Our* policy has but little chance in this body."—*Autograph Letter*, February 13, 1861.

[5] On one or two occasions, propositions were made to employ two stenographers to take down the debates. These propositions were voted down, and no reporters were allowed. They had open as well as secret sessions. Their open sessions they called the "Congress," and their secret sessions they called the "Convention."

[6] The Commissioners were David L. Swain, M. W. Ransom, and John L. Bridges.   [7] See page 198.

difficulties that distract the country, upon the basis of the Crittenden Resolutions, as modified by the Virginia Legislature." They soon perceived that their mission would be fruitless, and they returned to their homes.

On the 7th a resolution was received by the Convention, from the Alabama Legislature, placing at the disposal of the "Provisional Government of the Confederacy of the Seceding States" the sum of five hundred thousand dollars as a loan, for the purpose of setting the machinery of the new government in motion. It was accepted with thanks. The preliminary measures for the formation of that provisional government had been taken. Mr. Memminger, Chairman of the Committee to report a plan, had submitted one.[1] It was discussed that day and a part of the next, in secret session, when the Constitution of the United States, with some important modifications, was adopted as a form of government for the new "Confederacy," which was afterward known by the false title of "CONFEDERATE STATES OF AMERICA." It was a false title, because no States, as *States*, were parties to the unholy league. The "government," so called, was composed only of a band of confederated traitors, who had usurped the powers and trampled upon the rights of the people, who constitute the State, and were about to make war upon the Republic to the hurt of that people.

The Provisional Constitution declared that the Convention at Montgomery was a "Congress," vested with all the legislative powers of that of the United States. It provided that the Provisional President should hold his office for one year, unless superseded by the establishment of a permanent government; that each State should be a judicial district, and that the several district judges should compose the supreme court of the Confederacy; that the word "Confederacy" should be substituted for "Union," as used in the National Constitution; that the President might veto a separate appropriation without affecting a whole bill; that the African Slave-trade should be prohibited; that the Congress should be empowered to prohibit the introduction of slaves from any State not a member of the Confederacy;[2] that all appropriations should be made upon demands of the President or heads of departments; and that members of the Congress might hold offices of honor and emolument under the Provisional Government. No mention was made of taxes, excepting those in the form of a tariff for revenue; nor the keeping of troops and ships of war by the States; nor for any ratification of the Constitution, it being only provisional. The word "slave" was used where, in the National Constitution, it is avoided. The Provisional Government was required to take immediate steps for a settlement of all matters concerning property, between the United States and the "Confederacy." All legislative powers were vested in the "Congress" then assembled, until otherwise ordained. Only in the above-named features did the Provisional Constitution adopted by the Convention differ essentially from the National Constitution.

Notwithstanding the Provisional Constitution received the unanimous vote of the Convention, it did not satisfy all the members. The violent

---

[1] The original draft of the Provisional Constitution is in the handwriting of Mr. Memminger. It is among the archives of the "Confederate Government," at Washington City.

[2] This would bear most injuriously upon Virginia, whose annual income from the sale of slaves to the cotton planters now included in the "Confederacy," was counted by millions of dollars. This prohibition was calculated to make Virginia hasten to join the Southern league against the Republic. See page 94.

Rhett fulminated anathemas against it through the *Charleston Mercury*, especially on account of its tariff clause, the prohibition of the African Slave-trade, and the adoption of the three-fifths rule of representation for slaves, in the National Constitution.[1] "Let your people," he said, "prepare their minds for a failure in the future permanent Southern Constitution, for South Carolina is about to be saddled with almost every grievance, except Abolition, for which she long struggled, and has just withdrawn from the United States Government. Surely McDuffie lived in vain, and Calhoun taught for naught, if we are again to be plundered, and our commerce crippled, destroyed by tariffs—even discriminating tariffs. Yet this is the inevitable prospect. The fruit of the labors of thirty odd long years, in strife and bitterness, is about to slip through our fingers." Of the three-fifths rule, he said:—"It most unfairly dwarfs the power of some of the States in any Federal representation." He called that rule, which was really a compromise in favor of the slaveholders, "one of the many Yankee swindles put upon us, in the formation of the old Constitution." As the slave population of South Carolina was the majority, he complained that two-fifths or more of the people were unrepresented. "South Carolina," he said, "is small enough without again flinging away what legitimate power she possesses. *That power is in her slaves—socially, politically, economically.*" He complained of the prohibition of the Slave-trade. "A stigma," he said, "is thus broadly stamped upon the whole institution, before the whole world, and sealed by ourselves. It is an infamous slur upon the whole

JEFFERSON DAVIS.

institution—the lives and the property of every slaveholder in the land." Rhett and his fellows were restive in view of the restraints to which the "sovereignty" of South Carolina would be subjected as a member of a Confederacy, and seemed inclined, at one time, to reject all leagues, and have their "gallant State" stand alone as an independent nation.[2]

On the sixth day of the [a] February 9, 1861. session,[a] the President of the Convention and all of the members took the oath of allegiance to the Provisional Constitution, and at noon the doors of the hall were thrown open to the public, and the Convention proceeded to the election of a President and Vice-President of the "Confederacy." Jefferson Davis, of Mississippi, received six votes (the whole number) for President, and Alexander H. Stephens, of Georgia, the same number, for Vice-President. The announcement of the result was received with the most vehement applause

---

[1] See third clause, second section of the first Article of the Constitution.

[2] The arrogance of the South Carolina politicians was sometimes gently rebuked by their friends. The *Mobile Mercury*, at this time, said:—"They will have to learn to be a little more conforming to the opinions of others, before they can expect to associate comfortably with even the Cotton States, under a federative Government."

by the vast multitude that thronged the building, inside and out; and a salute of one hundred guns, in honor of the event, was immediately given. That evening, Stephens was serenaded. He made a brief speech to the crowd, in which he spoke of the new government as one which, while it surrendered none of their ancient rights and liberties, would secure them more perfectly. He predicted for the "Confederacy" a glorious career, if it should be supported by "the virtue, intelligence, and patriotism of the people." With institutions, he said, so far as regarded their organic and social policy, "in strict conformity to nature and the laws of the Creator, whether read in the Book of Inspiration or the great Book of Manifestations around us, we have all the natural elements essential to attainment in the highest degree of power and glory. These institutions have been much assailed, and it is our mission to vindicate the great truth on which they rest, and with them exhibit the highest type of civilization which it is possible for human society to reach." He was followed by Keitt, and Chesnut, and Conrad, who all made predictions of the future grandeur of the nation they were then attempting to create.

On the following day, Stephens formally accepted the office to which he had been chosen, and made a speech to the Convention, acknowledging with gratitude the expression of their confidence in calling him to that high station. He was in an embarrassing position. His Union speeches in November and January[1] were yet ringing in the ears of the people, and his present attitude needed explanation. He thought it prudent not to attempt any explanation, and simply remarked : " It is sufficient for me to say, that it may be deemed questionable if any good citizen can refuse to discharge any duty which may be assigned him by his country in her hour of need." At Milledge-ville, in November,[2] Mr. Stephens's vision of his "country" embraced the whole Republic, from the Atlantic to the Pacific ocean, and from the region of ice to the region of perpetual bloom, with a population of more than thirty millions. At Montgomery, in February—ninety days later—he saw his "country" dwarfed to the insignificant area of six Cotton-producing States on the coast, with a population of four millions five hundred thousand, nearly one-half of whom were bond-slaves, and a seventh (Texas) just march-ing up to join the sad assemblage of recusants.

After the election of Davis and Stephens, the Convention directed its chairman to appoint Committees on Foreign Relations, Postal Affairs, Finance, Commerce, Military and Naval Affairs, Judiciary, Patents and Copy-rights,[3] and Printing.[4] All the laws of the United States, not incompatible with

---

[1] See pages 54 to 57, inclusive. [2] See page 54.

[3] The first application to the "Confederate Government" for a patent was made on the 16th of February, when J. M. Waldron, of Georgia, asked leave to file a caveat and drawings, setting forth an improvement he had made in railroad switches.

[4] The most important committees were constructed as follows :—

Foreign Affairs.—Messrs. Rhett, Nisbett, Perkins, Walker, and Keitt.

Finance.—Messrs. Toombs, Barnwell, Kenner, Barry, and McRae.

Commercial Affairs.—Messrs. Memminger, Crawford, Martin, Curry, and De Clouet.

Judiciary.—Messrs. Clayton, Withers, Hale, T. R. Cobb, and Harris.

Naval Affairs.—Messrs. Conrad, Chesnut, Smith, Wright, and Owens.

Military Affairs.—Messrs. Bartow, Miles, Sparrow, Keenan, and Anderson.

Postal Affairs.—Chilton, Hill, Boyce, Harrison, and Curry.

Mr. Brooke, of Mississippi, was made Chairman of the Committee on Patents and Copyrights—an almost useless office.

the new order of things, were continued in force, temporarily. The Finance Committee, in the face of the solemn promises of the conspirators to the people and to foreign governments to the contrary, were instructed to report a tariff bill; and a committee was appointed to report a Constitution of Permanent Government for the "Confederacy." The committee consisted of twelve, or two from each State; and nothing was now wanting but the presence of the President elect to make perfect that powerful legislative and executive engine, of which Davis became chief manager, that waged a desolating war for four years against the Government of the Republic.

While the Committee had the matter of a permanent government under consideration, the Convention discussed the important subject of a national flag, during which much warmth of feeling was exhibited. Several models had been offered. Two of these were presented by Mr. Memminger. One of them was from some young women of Charleston, and was composed of a blue cross on a red field, with seven stars; the other was from a gentleman of the same city. It was a cross with fifteen stars. On presenting them, Mr. Memminger said:—

"Now, Mr. President, the idea of Union, no doubt, was suggested to the imagination of the young ladies by the beauteous constellation of the Southern cross, which the Great Creator has placed in the Southern heavens, by way of compensation for the glorious constellation at the north pole. The imagination of the young ladies was, no doubt, inspired by the genius of Dante and the scientific skill of Humboldt. But, Sir, I have no doubt that there was another idea associated with it in the minds of the young ladies—a religious one—and although we have not seen in the heavens the '*In hoc Signo vinces*,' written upon the Labarum· of Constantine, yet the same sign has been manifested to us upon the tablets of the earth; for we all know that it has been by the aid of revealed religion we have achieved over fanaticism the victory which we this day witness; and it is becoming, on this occasion, that the debt of the South to the Cross should be thus recognized. I have also, Mr. President, another commission from a gentleman of taste and skill in the city of Charleston, who offers another model, which embraces the same idea of a cross, but upon a different ground. The gentleman who offers this model appears to be more hopeful than the young ladies. They offer one with seven stars—six for the States already represented in this Congress, and the seventh for Texas, whose deputies we hope will soon be on their way to join us. He offers a flag which embraces the whole fifteen States. God grant that his hope may be realized, and that we may soon welcome their stars to the glorious constellation of our Southern Confederacy."

These remarks were highly applauded, and a committee, consisting of one delegate from each State, was appointed to report upon a device for a national flag and seal.[1] Mr. Brooke, of Mississippi, offered a resolution to instruct the Committee to report a design for a flag as similar as possible to that of the United States, making only such changes as should give them distinction. In his speech he talked with the fervor of a patriot of the associations which clustered around the old ensign — associations which

---

[1] The Committee consisted of Messrs. Shorter, Morton, Bartow, Sparrow, Harris, and Miles.

could never be effaced. "Sir," he said, "let us preserve it as far as we can. Let us continue to hallow it in our memory, and still pray that—

> " 'Long may it wave,
> O'er the land of the free and the home of the brave.' "

His eulogy of the old flag, which the leading traitors now affected to despise, was so full of Union sentiment that it was regarded as almost treasonable, and Brooke was severely rebuked. William Porcher Miles, of South Carolina, the Chairman of the Committee, protested against the resolution and the utterances of the mover. He gloried more a thousand times in the Palmetto flag of his State. He had regarded, "from his youth, the Stars and Stripes as the emblem of oppression and tyranny." This bold conspirator was so warmly applauded, that menaced Brooke, " at the suggestion of a friend," withdrew his motion.

W. W. Boyce, of South Carolina, who had been a member of the National Congress for seven years, presented a model for a flag, which he had received, with a letter, from a woman of his State (Mrs. C. Ladd, of Winnsboro'), who described it as "tri-colored, with a red union, seven stars, and the crescent moon." She offered her three boys to her "country;" and suggested "Washington Republic" as the name of the new nation.[1] In presenting the flag and letter, Boyce indulged in the usual turgid oratory of his class, saying:—"I will take the liberty of reading her letter to the Congress. It is full of authentic fire. It is worthy of Rome in her best days, and might well have been read in the Roman Senate on that disastrous day when the victorious banner of the great Carthaginian was visible from Mont Aventine. And I may add, Sir, that as long as our women are impelled by these sublime sentiments, and our mountains yield the metals out of which weapons are forged, the lustrous stars of our unyielding Confederacy will never pale their glorious fires, though baffled oppression may threaten with its impotent sword, or, more dangerous still, seek to beguile with the siren song of conciliation."

Chilton, Toombs, Stephens, and others, also presented devices for flags.[2] They were sent in almost daily from various parts of the Cotton-growing States, a great many of them showing attachment to the old banner, yet accompanied by the most fervid expressions of sympathy with the "Southern cause."[3] The Committee finally made an elaborate report on the subject, in which they confessed that they did not share in the sentiment of attachment to the "Stars and Stripes" too often repeated in communications.

---

[1] Many members liked the suggestion, but the more radical men, like Rhett and Toombs, opposed it, probably because it might have such strong associations with the old Government as to cause a desire for "reconstruction." So powerful became the feeling in the Convention in favor of the name of "Washington Republic," that it was voted down by only one majority.

[2] Two young women, Rebecca C. Ferguson and Mollie A. D. Sinclair, in the Art Department of the "Tuscogee Female College," sent in seven designs. In their accompanying letter they said, that "amidst all their efforts at originality, there ever danced before them visions of the star-gemmed flag, with its parti-colored stripes, that floated so proudly over the late United States. . . . Let us snatch from the eagle of the cliff our idea of independence, and cull from the earth diamonds, and gems from the heavens, to deck the flag of the Southern Confederacy. With Cotton for King, there are seven States bound by a chain of sisterly love that will strengthen by time, as onward, right onward, they move up the glorious path of Southern independence." In the seven devices offered, the principal members were an eagle, stars, and a cotton-bale. These devices were presented with highly commendatory words by Mr. Chilton, of Alabama.

[3] These drawings are among the archives of the "Confederate Government," at Washington City.

They thought there was no propriety in retaining the emblems of a Government which had become so oppressive and injurious to their interests as to require a separation from it. Yet they did pay deference to that sentiment in others, by recommending a flag that had a certain resemblance to the one they were deserting. It was to consist of "a red field with a white space extending horizontally through the center, and equal in width to one-third

the width of the flag"—in other words, three stripes, two of them red, and one white: the union, blue, extending down through the white space, and stopping at the lower red space. In the center of the union a circle of white stars, corresponding in number with the States of the "Confederacy." This was the flag under which the maddened hosts of that "Confederacy" rushed to

THE CONSPIRATORS' FLAG.

battle, at the beginning of the war that ensued. It was first displayed in public on the 4th of March, when it was unfurled over the State House at Montgomery.

The first assumption of sovereignty on the part of the Convention was on the 12th,[a] when it was resolved that the new Government should take under its charge all questions and difficulties then existing "between the Sovereign States of this Confederacy and the Government of the United States," relating to the occupation of forts, arsenals, navy yards, and other public establishments. The President of the Convention was requested to communicate this resolution to the Governors of the several States. This was extremely offensive to the South Carolinians. They saw in it dark visions of the passing away of the "sovereignty" of their State. That Commonwealth, so lately proclaimed a "nation," was thereby shorn of its greatness, and placed on a common level with "sister States." The *Mercury*, speaking for the Hotspurs of the coast region, at once preached rebellion against the usurpers at Montgomery. It declared[b] that Fort Sumter belonged to South Carolina alone. It was the pet victim of the Palmettoese, and no other wolf should seize it. "After two efforts," said the *Mercury*, "to obtain peaceable possession of Fort Sumter, and a submission, for two months, to the insolent military domination in our bay of a handful of men, the honor of the State requires that *no further intervention, from any quarter, should be tolerated,* and that this fort should be taken, and taken *by South Carolina alone.* By any other course, it appears to us, unless all the positions of the Governor are false, *the State must be disgraced.*" The South Carolinians were pacified by promises, and, as we shall observe, were gratified in their belligerent desires.

On the 13th, John Gregg, one of the delegates from Texas, appeared[1] and took a seat in the Convention, although the Ordinance of Secession adopted in that State had not been ratified by the people, according to legal requirement. The rest of the delegation were on their way. In this act, as in all others, the conspirators utterly disregarded the will of the people. On the same day, the Convention commenced preparations for war, by instructing

[a] February, 1861.

[b] February 14.

[1] The delegation was composed of Louis T. Wigfall, J. H. Reagan, J. Hemphill, T. N. Waul, John Gregg, W. S. Oldham, and W. B. Ochiltree.

the Military and Naval Committees to report plans for the organization of an army and navy, and to make provision for the officers in each service who had deserted their flag and were seeking employment from the Confederates at Montgomery.

Preparations were now[a] made for the reception and inauguration of Davis. He was at his home near Vicksburg when apprised of his election, and he hastened to Montgomery on the circuitous railway route by the way of Jackson, Grand Junction, Chattanooga, and West Point. His journey was a continuous ovation. He made twenty-five speeches on the way, all breathing treason to the Government by whose bounty he had been educated and fed, and whose laws he had frequently sworn to uphold. A committee of the Convention and the public authorities of Montgomery met him eight miles from the city.[b] At Opelika, two companies from Columbus, Georgia, joined the escort. He reached his destination at ten o'clock at night, where he was received with unbounded enthusiasm. Cannon thundered a welcome, and the shouts of a vast multitude filled his ears. At the railway station he was formally received, and made a speech, in which he briefly reviewed the then position of the South, and said the time for compromises had passed. "We are now determined," he said, "to maintain our position, and make *all who oppose us smell Southern powder and feel Southern steel*." He had no doubts of the result, if coercion should be persisted in. "We will maintain our rights and our government," he said, "at all hazards. We ask nothing; we want nothing; and will have no complications. If the other States join our Confederacy, they can freely come in on our terms. Our separation from the old Union is complete, and no compromise, no reconstruction can now be entertained."

[a] February 15, 1861.

[b] February 15.

Davis was conducted from the station to the Exchange Hotel, where a large crowd, many of them women, awaited his arrival. He made a speech from the balcony or gallery to the assembled populace, while on each side of him stood a negro, with a candle, that the people might see his face. He addressed them as "Brethren of the Confederated States of America." He expressed undoubting confidence in the success of the revolution they had just inaugurated. They had nothing to fear at home, for they were united as one people; and they had nothing to fear from abroad, for if war should come, their valor would be sufficient for any occasion.

The inaugural ceremonies took place at noon on the 18th,[c] upon a platform erected in front of the portico of the State House. Davis and Stephens, with the Rev. Dr. Manly, riding in an open barouche, and followed by a large concourse of State officials and citizens, moved from the Exchange Hotel to the Capitol, while cannon were thundering. The eminence on which the Capitol stands was crowded at an early hour. It is said that so grand a spectacle had not been seen in the Slave-labor States since the ovation given in New Orleans to the victorious General Jackson, in January, 1815.

[c] February.

At one o'clock in the afternoon, after a prayer by Dr. Manly, Davis commenced pronouncing his Inaugural Address. He defended the right of secession; and he declared that, "moved by no interest or passion to invade the rights of others, and anxious to cultivate peace and commerce with the nations," if they could not hope to avoid war, they might at least expect that posterity would acquit them of having needlessly engaged in it. "Doubly justified," he said, "by the absence of wrong on their part, and by wanton aggression on the part of others," there could be no doubt of success. The world must have their "agricultural productions" (meaning cotton), and mutual interest would invite good-will and kind offices, especially from the manufacturing and navigating States of the Union. "If, however," he said, "passion or lust of dominion should cloud the judgment or inflame the ambition of those States, we must prepare to meet the emergency, and maintain, by the final arbitrament of the sword, that position which we have assumed among the nations of the earth." He declared that they had separated from the old Union from necessity, and not from choice. Having done so, they must prepare to stand alone; and he recommended the immediate organization of an army and navy. He suggested privateering or piracy as an arm of strength for them. "Besides the ordinary remedies," he said, "the well-known resources for retaliation upon the commerce of an enemy will remain to us." He closed by invoking the protection of the Almighty, while they should be performing the work of destroying the noble fabric of free institutions erected by the fathers. At the close of the address, the oath of office was administered to Davis by Howell Cobb, the President of the Convention.

In the evening, after the inauguration, Davis, in imitation of the custom at the National Capital, held a levee at Estelle Hall; and Montgomery was brilliantly lighted up by bonfires and illuminations. A spacious mansion was soon afterward provided for Davis and his family, and it became distinguished as the "White House of the Southern Confederacy."[1]

THE "WHITE HOUSE" AT MONTGOMERY.

Davis chose, from among the most active of his fellow-conspirators, fitting agents to assist him in his nefarious work, and ostentatiously titled them in imitation of the National Government. He called Robert Toombs to act as "Secretary of State;" Charles G. Memminger, as "Secretary of the Treasury;" Le Roy Pope Walker, as "Secretary of War;" Stephen R. Mallory, as "Secretary of the Navy," and John H. Reagan, as "Postmaster-General." Afterward, Judah P. Benjamin was appointed to be "Attorney-General." William M. Browne, late editor of the *Washington Constitution*,

---

[1] The official residence of the President of the United States, at Washington City, being white, has always been better known by the title of "The White House" than by any other.

President Buchanan's official organ, was appointed "Assistant Secretary of State," and Philip Clayton, of Georgia, "Assistant Secretary of the Treasury." He offered John Slidell a seat in his "cabinet," but that conspirator preferred a safer sphere of action, as minister to some foreign court. He was gratified; and Davis's leading associates in crime were all soon supplied with places of honor and profit.

JOHN H. REAGAN.

Jefferson Davis was about fifty-four years of age at the time we are considering. His person was sinewy and light, a little above the middle hight, and erect in posture. His features were regular and well-defined; his face was thin and much wrinkled; one eye was sightless, and the other was dark and piercing. He was born in Kentucky, and was taken to reside in Mississippi in early boyhood. He was educated at the Military Academy at West Point, on the Hudson River; served under his father-in-law, General Taylor, in the war with Mexico; occupied a seat in the National Senate, and was a member of President Pierce's Cabinet, as Secretary of War. He was a man of much ability, and considerable refinement of manner when in good society. As a politician, he was utterly unscrupulous. In public life, he was untruthful and treacherous. He was not a statesman, nor a high-toned partisan. He was calm, audacious, reticent, polished, cold, sagacious, rich in experience of State affairs, possessed of great concentration of purpose, an imperious will, abounding pride, and remarkable executive ability. He was a relentless foe, and was well fitted to be the leader in the commission of a crime greater in magnitude than any recorded in the annals of mankind.

Alexander H. Stephens, the lieutenant of the chief of the conspirators, was a few years the junior of Davis, having been born in Georgia in 1812. He had climbed to distinction from obscurity by the force of his own genius. Sickness had kept his frame weak from boyhood, and he never weighed a hundred pounds avoirdupois. His voice was effeminate, yet, when it was used in glowing oratory, of which he was often a charming master, it became, at times, quite sonorous. He was for several years an able representative of his State in the National Congress. More conservative and honest, and less courageous than Davis, he performed a comparatively passive part in the great drama of crime in which he was an actor. Three of the members of Davis's privy council, namely, Toombs, Mallory, and Benjamin, had lately left their seats in the National Senate. Their previous career we shall hereafter consider. Memminger was a man of fine culture, and eminent as a lawyer. So also was Walker, whose social and professional position in northern Alabama was inferior to but few. Reagan was a lawyer of ability, and was a judge in Texas when he rebelled against his Government.

The Confederates, having assumed for their league a national character, at once presented their claims to recognition as such by the powers of the earth. They sent commissioners to Europe to secure formal recognition by, and make commercial arrangements with, the leading governments there. These Commissioners were William L. Yancey, of Alabama; P. A. Rost, of Louisiana; A. Dudley Mann, of Virginia; and T. Butler King, of Georgia. Yancey was to operate in England, Rost in France, and Mann in Holland and Belgium. King seems to have had a sort of roving commission. Yancey had more real ability and force of character than either of the others. He was not a statesman, but a demagogue, and lacked almost every requisite for a diplomatist. He could fill with wild passion an excitable populace at home, but he utterly failed to impress the more sober English mind with a sense of his wisdom or the justice of his cause. Rost was a Frenchman, who emigrated to Louisiana in early life, married a woman of fortune, and finally reached a seat on the bench of the Supreme Court of that State. Mann was a dull statistician of very moderate ability; and King was an extensive farmer and slaveholder. These men so fitly represented their bad cause in Europe, that confidence in the justice or the ultimate success of that cause was speedily so impaired, that they went wandering about, seeking in vain for willing listeners among men of character in diplomatic circles; and, finally, they abandoned their missions in disgust, to the relief of statesmen who were wearied with their importunities and offended by their duplicity.

Mr. Stephens assumed the office of expounder of the principles upon which the new government was founded and was to be established. He made the occasion of a speech to the citizens of Savannah, Georgia,[a] the opportunity for giving that exposition to the world.

a March 21, 1861.

He declared that the immediate cause of the rebellion was African Slavery existing in the United States; and said that Jefferson, in his forecast, had anticipated this as the " rock on which the Union would split." He doubted whether Jefferson understood the truth on which that rock stood. He, and "most of the leaders at the time of the formation of the old Constitution," entertained the erroneous idea that " the enslavement of the African was in violation of the laws of nature; that it was wrong in principle, socially, morally, and politically." They erroneously believed "that in the order of Providence the institution would be evanescent and pass away." That, he said, was " the prevailing idea of the fathers," who rested upon the false assumption put forth in the Declaration of Independence, that " all men are created equal." [1]

" Our new government," said the Expounder, " is founded upon exactly the opposite idea; its foundations are laid, its corner-stone rests upon the great truth, that *the negro is not equal to the white man ;* that Slavery—subordination to the superior race—is his natural and normal condition. This, our new government, is the first, in the history of the world, based upon this great physical and moral truth. This truth has been slow in the process of its development, like all other truths in the various departments of science. It has been so, even among us. Many who hear me, perhaps, can recollect well that this truth was not generally admitted even within their day. The errors of the past generation still clung to many as late as twenty

---

[1] This was in flat contradiction of the extra-judicial opinion of the late Chief-Justice Taney, who said that the "prevailing opinion of the time " was, that the negroes were " so far inferior that they had *no rights which the white man was bound to respect.*" See his decision in the Dred Scott case.

years ago.[1] . . . In the conflict, thus far, success has been, on our side, complete throughout the length and breadth of the Confederate States. *It is upon this, as I have stated, our actual fabric is firmly planted ;* and I cannot permit myself to doubt the ultimate success of a full recognition of this principle throughout the civilized and enlightened world." After reiterating the assurance that SLAVERY was the special, strong, and commendable foundation of the new " government," he blasphemously used the substance of the words which the Apostle applied to Christ, saying :—" This stone, which was rejected by the first builders, 'is become the chief stone of the corner' in our new edifice."

By these frank avowals of one of the chief men in the Confederacy, that SLAVERY was the corner-stone of their government, so called—that it was founded upon the principle that a superior race has a divine right to enslave an inferior race—that its ethics were those of the savage, who insists that " Might makes Right ;" and the explicit avowal of the chief leader, that " all who oppose us shall smell Southern powder and feel Southern steel,"[2] mankind were plainly notified that an outlaw against the principles of Christianity, of Civilization, and of the Age was abroad, heavily mailed in political and social prejudices, brandishing a gleaming dagger, poison-tipped, and defying the authority of God and Man. How that outlaw was sheltered, and fed, and caressed, and strengthened, until more than half a million of precious lives had been sacrificed by his " steel," we shall observe hereafter.

---

[1] See note on page 38.
[2] Jefferson Davis's speech at Montgomery. See page 257.

CHAPTER XI.

HE arrogance and folly of the conspirators, especially of the madmen of South Carolina, often took the most ludicrous forms and expression. They were so intent upon obliterating every trace of connection with the "Yankees," as they derisively called the people of the Free-labor States, and upon showing to the world that South Carolina was an "independent nation," that so early as the first of January," when that "nation" was just nine days old—a "nine days' wonder"—it was proposed to adopt for it a new system of civil time.[1] Whether it was to be that of Julius Cæsar, in whose calendar the year began in March; or of the French Jacobins, whose year began in September, and had five sacred days called *Sansculottides;* or of the Eastern satrap

a 1861.

> " Who counted his years from the hour when he smote
> His best friend to the earth, and usurped his control;
> And measured his days and his weeks by false oaths,
> And his months by the scars of black crimes on his soul,"

is not recorded. Three days after the Montgomery Convention had formed a so-called government, by the adoption of a Provisional Constitution, and the election of Jefferson Davis to be the chief standard-bearer in the revolt, one of the organs of the conspirators said, in view of the dreamed-of power and grandeur of the new Empire :—" The South *might,* under the new Confederacy, treat the disorganized and demoralized Northern States as *insurgents*, and deny them recognition. But if peaceful division ensues, the South, *after taking the Federal Capital and archives*, and being recognized by all foreign powers as the Government *de facto*, can, if they see proper, recognize the Northern Confederacy or Confederacies, and enter into treaty stipulations with them. Were this not done, it would be difficult for the Northern States to take a place among nations, and their flag would not be respected or recognized."[2]

---

[1] Charleston Correspondence of the Associated Press, January 1, 1861.

[2] *Charleston Courier*, February 12, 1861. Only a week earlier than this (February 5th), the late Senator Hammond, one of the South Carolina conspirators, in a letter to a kinswoman in Schenectady, New York, after recommending her to read the sermon of a Presbyterian clergyman in Brooklyn, named Van Dyke, preached on the 9th of December, 1860, for proofs that the buying and selling of men, women, and children was no sin, said: "We dissolve the Union—and it is forever dissolved, be assured—to get clear of Yankee meddlesomeness and Puritanical bigotry. I say this, being half a Yankee and half a Puritan." His father was a New England

Notwithstanding this arrogance and childish folly of the politicians—notwithstanding the tone of feeling among the leading insurgents at Montgomery was equally proud and defiant, they were compelled to yield to the inexorable laws of necessity, and make a compromise with expediency. It would not do to give mortal offense to Kentucky, Tennessee, and Missouri, by obstructing the navigation of the Mississippi River;[1] so, on the 22d of February, the Convention declared the absolute freedom of the navigation of that stream. Money was necessary to carry on the machinery of government, and equip and feed an army; so, abandoning the delightful dreams of free-trade, which was to bring the luxuries of the world to their doors, they proposed tariff laws; and even went so far as to propose an export duty on the great staple of the Gulf States, relying upon the potential arm of "King Cotton" for support in the measure. "I apprehend," said Howell Cobb, who proposed it, "that we are conscious of the power we hold in our hands, by reason of our producing that staple so necessary to the world. I doubt not that power will exert an influence mightier than armies or navies. We know that by an embargo we could soon place not only the United States, but many of the European powers, under the necessity of electing between such a recognition of our independence as we require, or domestic convulsions at home." Such were the shallow conclusions of one of the leading "Southern statesmen," of whose superior wisdom the newspapers in the interest of the Oligarchy were always boasting.

The Convention authorized Davis to accept one hundred thousand volunteers for twelve months, and to borrow fifteen millions of dollars, at the rate of eight per cent. interest a year. Provision was also made for the establishment of a small naval force for coast defense. Laws were passed for carrying on postal operations.—

CONFEDERATE STATES

FIVE CENTS

"CONFEDERATE"
POSTAGE STAMP.

The franking privilege was disallowed, excepting for the Post-office Department. The rates of postage were fixed, and stamps for two, five, and ten cents were soon issued, bearing the portrait of Jefferson Davis. A variety of laws, necessary for the operations of a legitimate government, were made; and on the 11th of March, a permanent Constitution was adopted. Its preamble fully recognized the doctrine of State Supremacy, and was in the following words:—"We, the people of the Confederate States, each State acting in its sovereign and independent character, in order to form a permanent Federal Government, establish justice, insure domestic tranquillity, and insure the blessings

school-teacher. "*We absolve you by this,*" he continued, "*from all the sins of Slavery, and take upon ourselves all its supposed sin and evil, openly before the world, and in the sight of God.*" With a similar spirit, the revilers of the great Preacher of Righteousness cried: "Crucify him! Crucify him! *His blood be on us, and on our children!*" In the judgments which speedily fell upon the presumptuous Jew and the Slaveholder, do we not see a remarkable "historical parallel?"

The conspirator continued:—"Let us alone. Let me tell you, my dear cousin, that if there is any attempt at war on the part of the North, we can soundly thrash them on any field of battle; and not only that, we can give them over to Jean Jaques, and leave them to manage that. We know our strength. Why, we export over two hundred millions of produce, which the world eagerly seeks and cannot do without. A six months' failure of our exports to Europe would revolutionize every existing government there, as well as at the North. *All know it.* The North exports some sixty millions, *in competition* with the European producers. Why drive them over to Jean Jaques, and leave them to manage that. We know our strength. Why, we export more nor less, the poorest portion of the civilized world. To that it has come on an *infidel* and abstract idea."—*Letter of Jas. H. Hammond to Mrs. F. H. Pratt, published in the Albany Statesman.*

[1] See page 164.

of liberty to ourselves and to our posterity—invoking the favor and guidance of Almighty God[1]—do order and ordain this Constitution for the Confederate States of America."

This Constitution was that of the United States, with the alterations and omissions seen in the Provisional Constitution,[2] and others made by the Committee. It prohibited the giving of bounties from the Treasury, or the laying of duties for the purpose of protecting any branch of industry. It made the Post-office Department rely wholly upon its own revenue to pay its expenses; it attempted to prevent fraudulent legislation by prohibiting the introduction of more than one subject in any act; it fixed the term of service of the "President and Vice-President" at six years, and made the former ineligible to re-election; it provided for the government of new Territories, and prohibited the enactment of any law "denying or impairing the right of property in negro slaves." There were several provisions for securing an economical expenditure of money. The delegates from South Carolina and Florida voted against the clause prohibiting the African Slave-trade.

Davis had already been authorized by the Convention[a] to assume control of "all military operations between the Confederate States," or any of them, and powers foreign to them; and he was also authorized to receive from them the arms and munitions of war "acquired from the United States." At the middle of March, it recommended the several States to cede to the "Confederate States" the forts, arsenals, dock-yards, and other public establishments within their respective limits. These recommendations were cheerfully responded to by all except the South Carolinians, who were tardy in relinquishing the means for maintaining their "sovereignty." Already P. G. T. Beauregard, a Louisiana Creole, who had abandoned the flag of his country, and sought employment among its enemies, had been appointed brigadier-general,[b] and ordered from New Orleans to Charleston, to take charge of all the insurgent

[a] March 28, 1861.

[b] March 3.

JOHN FORSYTH.

forces there. Already John Forsyth, Martin J. Crawford, and A. B. Roman had been appointed Commissioners to proceed to Washington, and make a settlement of all questions at issue between the United States and the conspirators; and Memminger had made preparations for establishing Custom Houses along the frontier "between the two confederacies." After

---

[1] This expression called forth much debate. Some opposed the introduction of the sentiment in *any* form. Chilton wished it stronger, by adding, " who is the God of the Bible and the rightful source of all government." As the word " Bible" would include the New Testament, this suffix was opposed because it might offend Mr. Benjamin, who was a Jew, and did not admit the divinity of Jesus. It was voted down. One of the Cobbs proposed to introduce in the Constitution a clause recognizing the Christian Sabbath, in the following form :— "No man shall be compelled to do civil duty on Sunday." This was voted down, partly out of deference to Mr. Benjamin, the Jew, and partly because Perkins, of Louisiana, declared that the people of that State would not accept of such a provision. Delegates from Texas made the same declaration concerning the people of their State.

[2] See page 251

agreeing, by resolution, to share in the crime of plundering the National Government by accepting a portion of the money which the Louisiana politicians had stolen from the Mint and Custom House at New Orleans,[1] the Convention adjourned.[2] At that time vigorous preparations for war were seen on every hand. Volunteers, even from Tennessee, offered their services. In many places in the Gulf States enlistments went rapidly on; and by the first of April, probably twenty thousand names were on the rolls of the growing insurgent army.

The conspirators of Texas, we have observed, were represented in the Convention at Montgomery. The people of that State had lately suffered the most flagrant wrongs at the hands of disloyal men; and that Common-wealth had been the theater of an act of treachery of the vilest and most injurious nature, performed by the vet-eran soldier, General David E. Twiggs, of Georgia, who was next in rank to Lieutenant-General Scott, in the Army of the Republic.

DAVID E. TWIGGS.

We have observed that the conspir-ators and disloyal politicians of Texas had placed the people of that State, who, by an overwhelming majority, were for the Union, in an attitude of rebellion before the close of February, and that the Revolutionary Committee[3] had appointed Messrs. Devine and Maverick, Commissioners to treat with General Twiggs, the Commander of the Department, for the surrender into their hands of all the property of the National Government under his control. Twiggs was a favorite of the Administration, and his conduct denotes that he was in complicity with the conspirators at Washington.

---

[1] See page 185.

[2] The proceedings of this Convention, and of the "Provisional Government of the Confederate States," have never been printed. The original manuscripts were discovered by some of General Wilson's command at Athens, in Georgia, after the downfall of the rebellion. They were in three boxes, in one of the recitation-rooms of the University of Georgia. A correspondent of the *New York Herald*, writing from Athens, on the 19th of June, 1865, gives the following interesting history of these papers, which consist of journals, correspondence, *et cætera*:—

"As the Provisional Congress was about to expire, a proposition was made that the journals should be published. This was objected to, on the ground of furnishing much valuable information, and a law was passed authorizing and requiring the President of the Congress, Howell Cobb, to have three copies made of all the journals. He was at that time in the Army, commanding the Sixteenth Georgia Regiment, and down on the Peninsula, below Richmond. He at once engaged J. D. Hooper, former clerk, to undertake the job. Whatever were his hinderances it is not known; but he did very little, and after having them on hand for a long time, died. They were then shipped to a gentleman in Georgia, with a request to complete the work. Papers were missing, requiring months to find; materials hard to get, and the work, therefore, never was completed. They were at one time held in Atlanta, but the Unionists coming too near, were hurried off to West Point, Georgia. There a strong rumor of a raid springing up, they were carried to Tallapoosa County, Alabama, on a plantation. In marching from Dadeville to Loachapoka, General Rousseau passed within four miles of the house where they were; and when his men were destroying the railroad at Notasulga, and were having the little fight near Chehaw, the boxes were hid out in the woods, two miles off, and were watched by two negro men. They were then removed to Augusta, Georgia, and thence, when Sherman came, tearing down through Georgia like a wild horse, they were pushed along into the upper part of South Carolina. Thence in the spring they were brought over to this place." These journals are among the archives of the "Confederate Government," at Washington City.   [3] See page 188.

He was placed in command of the Department of Texas only a few weeks before he committed the treasonable act we are about to record. For forty years he had served his Government acceptably, and was honored with its confidence; but the virus that poisoned so many noble characters, destroyed the life of his patriotism. Not content with deserting his flag himself, he tried to seduce his officers from their allegiance. He began by talking gloomily of the future, and expressing doubts of the ability of the Government to maintain its authority. He soon spoke disparagingly of that Government; and finally he said to his officers :—" The Union will be at an end in less than sixty days, and if you have any pay due you, you had better get it at once, for it is the last you will ever get."

Intimations of Twiggs's disloyalty had reached the Secretary of War, Holt, and on the 18th of January, in a general order, the veteran was relieved from the command of the Department of Texas, and it was turned over to Colonel Carlos A. Waite, of the First Regiment of Infantry. But the anticipated mischief was accomplished before the order could perform its intended work. When the Commissioners were informed of its arrival at Twiggs's head-quarters, at the Alamo, in the city of San Antonio, they took

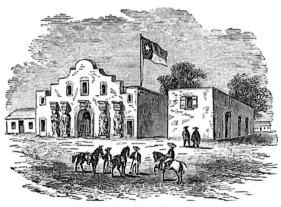

THE ALAMO.[1]

measures to prevent its reaching Colonel Waite, whose regimental head-quarters was at the least sixty miles distant, on the Verde Creek, a branch of the Guadaloupe River. But the vigilance and activity of the patriotic Colonel Nichols, Twiggs's Assistant Adjutant-General, who watched his chief with the keen eye of full suspicion, foiled them. He duplicated the orders, and sent two couriers by different routes. One of them was captured and taken back to San Antonio, and the other reached Waite, with the order, on the 17th of February.

Twiggs was cautious and had adroitly avoided committing himself to treason in writing. He always said to the impatient Commissioners :—" I will give up every thing." But the time had now arrived when temporizing must end. He was ready to act; but he must have a decent excuse for his surrendering the force under his immediate command, which consisted of only two skeleton companies under Captains King and Smith. Other troops had been ordered away from San Antonio by Twiggs when the danger of revolution became pressing, and they might be called to put down insurrection.

---

[1] This is a very old building. It was a church, erected by the Spaniards, and was afterward converted into a fortress. There, during the war for the independence of Texas, many Americans, who had joined the Texans in the struggle, were massacred by the Mexicans. Among those who fell were Colonel David Crockett, and Colonel Bowie, the inventor of the famous bowie-knife, so much used by desperadoes in the Southwest.

The excuse for Twiggs was readily found.   Ben. McCulloch, the famous Texan Ranger, was stationed at Seguin, not far off.   The Commissioners employed him to prepare and lead a sufficient military force to capture the National troops in San Antonio.   He received directions to that effect on the 9th,[a] and he at   [a] February, 1861. once pushed forward toward the city with almost a thousand men. He was joined, near the town, by two hundred Knights of the Golden Circle, who went out well armed and equipped, each having forty rounds of ammunition.

BEN. M'CULLOCH.

At two o'clock on Sunday morning, the 16th, two hundred mounted men, led by McCulloch, rushed into the city, breaking the slumbers of the inhabitants with unearthly yells.   These were soon followed by about five hundred more.   They took possession of the Main Plaza, a large vacant square in the center of the city, and placed guards over the Arsenal, the park of artillery, and the Government buildings.   A traitor in the Quartermaster's Department, named Edgar, had, at the first dash into the city, taken possession of the Alamo.[1]

General Twiggs and Colonel Nichols met McCulloch in the Main Plaza, where terms of surrender were soon agreed to; and there, at noon,[b] was fully consummated the treasonable act which Twiggs   [b] February 16, 1861. had commenced by negotiation so early as the 7th.[2]   He surrendered all the National forces in Texas, numbering about two thousand five hundred, and composed of thirty-seven companies.   Fifteen companies of infantry and five of artillery were on the line of the Rio Grande, and the other seventeen were in the interior.   With the troops Twiggs surrendered public stores and munitions of war, valued, at their cost, at one million two hundred thousand dollars.[3]   Beside these, he surrendered all the forts, arsenals, and other military posts within the limits of his command, including Fort Davis, in the great cañon of the Lympia Mountains, on the San Antonio and San Diego mail-route, five hundred miles from the former city.   It was then the head-quarters of the Eighth Regiment of Infantry, and, because of its situation in the midst of the country of the plundering Mescalaro Apaches, and in the path of the marauding Comanches into Mexico, it was a post of great importance.

---

[1] *Galveston News*, February 22, 1861.   *Sketch of Secession Times in Texas:* by J. P. Newcomb, editor of the *Alamo Express,* page 11.   *Texas, and its Late Military Occupation and Evacuation:* by an Officer of the Army.

[2] On that day, Twiggs issued an order to his troops, informing them that the "Secession Act had passed the Convention" of the State, to take effect on the 2d day of March; but that he could not say what disposition would be made of the troops.   He promised to remain with them until something was done, and make them as comfortable as possible.   He seems to have made up his mind, as soon as the Secession Ordinance was passed, to betray his troops and the public property into the hands of the public enemy.

[3] "Their value in Texas is much greater, and worth to the State at least a million and a half of dollars."— *San Antonio Herald*, February 26.

By this act Twiggs deprived his Government of the most effective portion of its Regular Army, in strict accordance with the plans of his employers, Davis and Floyd. When the Government was informed of his *a March 1, 1861.* actual treason, an order was issued,[a] directing him to be " dismissed from the Army of the United States, for treachery to the flag of his country." [1] Earlier than this, " Charity Lodge " of the " Knights of Malta," in New Orleans, who had heard of his infamy, expelled *b February 25.* him from their order[b] by unanimous vote. On the 4th of March the Secession Convention of Louisiana, that had assembled that day, resolved to unite with the citizens of New Orleans in honoring Twiggs with a public reception. That honor was conferred eight days after he was dismissed from the service of his country for a high crime.

On the 18th,[c] Twiggs issued a general order, in which he announced the fact of the surrender of his forces, and directed the garrisons *c February.* of all the posts, after they should be handed over to agents of the insurgents, to make their way to the sea-coast as speedily as possible, where,

FORT DAVIS.

according to the terms made with the Commissioners, they would be allowed to leave the State, taking with them their arms, clothing, and necessary stores. With this order went out a circular from the Commissioners, in the name of the State of Texas, whose authority they had usurped, in which they solemnly agreed that the troops should have every assistance, in the way of transportation and otherwise, for leaving the State, for, they said, " they are our friends, who have hitherto afforded us all the protection in their power; and it is our duty to see that no insult or indignity is offered them." It is apparent that at that very time the conspirators had determined to cast every obstacle in the way of the betrayed men on their way to the coast, and their departure from it, with the hope of persuading a portion of them to join the insurgents. In this they were mistaken. In all the vicissitudes to which

---

[1] The *Charleston Courier*, on the 18th of May, 1861, published a letter written by General Twiggs to President Buchanan, threatening to visit Lancaster, and call him to a personal account for branding him as a traitor. " This was personal," he said, " and I shall treat it as such—not through the papers—but *in person*."

they were afterward exposed, the private soldiers and most of the officers remained true to the old flag. The writer saw some of them at midsummer in Fort Hamilton, at the entrance to New York Bay; and never was a curse by "bell, book, and candle," more sincerely uttered, than were those that fell from the compressed lips of these betrayed soldiers. These troops were the first who left Texas. They came from posts on the line of the Rio

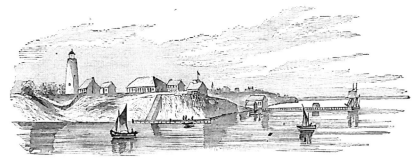

POINT ISABEL, TEXAS, IN 1861.

Grande, and embarked in the *Daniel Webster* at Point Isabel, a place of much note in the history of the war with Mexico.[a] They arrived at Fort Hamilton on the 30th of March, 1861.

[a] 1846-1848.

At five o'clock on the evening of the 16th,[b] the little band of National troops in San Antonio marched sullenly out of the city, to the tune of "The Red, White, and Blue," and encamped at San Pedro Springs, two miles from the Plaza, there to remain until the arrival of Colonel Waite. They were followed by a crowd of sorrowing citizens. The tears of strong men were mingled with those of delicate women, when they saw the old flag disappear; and sullen gloom hung over the town that night, and for many days.[1] San Antonio was full of loyal men, and so was the State. There was wide-spread sorrow when the calamity of Twiggs's treason became known. It was a calamity for the nation, and it was a special calamity for the Texans, for these troops, now about to leave them, had been their protectors against the incursions of the savage Indian tribes, that were hanging, like a portentous cloud, along their frontier. The surrendered forts were to be garrisoned by Texas militia, but in these the people had little confidence.

[b] February, 1861.

Colonel Waite, who started for San Antonio, with an escort of fifteen cavalry, immediately after receiving his order from the War Department, arrived there early in the afternoon of the 18th. McCulloch had stationed troops on the regular route to intercept him. By taking by-paths he eluded them. But he was a few hours too late. Twiggs had consummated his treason, and Texan soldiers occupied the post. Waite was compelled to recognize the capitulation. Sadly he rode out to San Pedro Springs, joined the little handful of National troops there, and, on the following day,[c] assumed the command of the department. Already Twiggs's order for the evacuation of the posts in Texas had been sent, but

[c] February 19.

[1] *Secession Times in Texas*, page 11

some of these were so distant and isolated, and the traveling so difficult at that season of the year, that it was several weeks before the order reached them.   One of these is Fort Arbuckle, in Franklin County, situated west

FORT ARBUCKLE.

from Arkansas, on the False Wachita River.   It protects the northern frontiers of the State from the forays of the wild Comanches.   At the time we are considering, it was garrisoned by detachments from the First Cavalry and one company of the First Infantry Regiment.   Another was Fort

FORT WACHITA.

Wachita, sixty miles southeasterly from Fort Arbuckle, and, like it, on the Indian Reserve.   It was garrisoned by two companies of the First Cavalry Regiment.   Near this post, in the autumn of 1858, Major Earle Van Dorn, a gallant officer of the National Army, who appears for the first time, in

FORT LANCASTER.

connection with Twiggs's treason, as an enemy of his country, had a successful battle with a band of warlike Comanches.   Another important post was Fort Lancaster, on the mail-route between San Antonio to San Diego,

In the midst of the remarkable table-lands near the junction of Live Oak Creek and the Pecos River. It is a place of much importance, for it protects the great ford of the Pecos, where nearly all the trains from Texas cross it, on their way to California. These are really mere military posts rather than forts, quite sufficient in strength, however, for the uses of the service in that region. The military power under Twiggs's control was ample, with the co-operation of the Union citizens, to hold the State firmly in a position of loyalty to the National Government, and to defy the Arch-Conspirator at Montgomery, who, before Texas had become a member of the "Confederacy," wrote, through his so-called Secretary of War, to the Texas Convention, that if, after a reasonable time, the United States Government should refuse to withdraw the troops, "all the powers of the Southern Confederacy should be used to expel them."[1]

Colonel Waite found himself at once entangled in most serious embarrassments. In violation of the terms of Twiggs's treaty for surrender, adequate means of transportation for the troops in the interior were withheld; and officers born in Slave-labor States, such as Lieutenant Thornton Washington, Major Larkin Smith, and others, in whom he confided, betrayed their trusts in a most shameful manner, and joined the insurgents.

Captain Hill, who commanded Fort Brown, on the Rio Grande, opposite

FORT BROWN.

Matamoras, refused to obey the order of Twiggs to evacuate it, and prepared to defend it. He soon found that he could not hold it with the small force under his command, and he was compelled to yield. The troops along the line of the Rio Grande soon left the country, but those in the interior, who made their way slowly toward the coast, became involved in great difficulties.

Toward the middle of April, Major Earle Van Dorn, who was a favorite in the army of that department, appeared in Texas with the commission of a colonel, from Jefferson Davis. He was a native of Mississippi. He had abandoned his flag, and was now in the employment of its enemies. He was there to secure for the use of the insurgent army, by persuasion and glowing promises of great good to themselves, the remnant of the betrayed forces of the Republic, or to make them useless to their Government. Simultaneously with his appearance, the newspapers in the interest of the conspirators teemed with arguments to show that the National soldiers were absolved from their allegiance, because the "Union was dissolved;" and Van Dorn held out brilliant temptations to win them to his standard. His labor was vain.

They were too patriotic to be seduced, or even to listen patiently to his wicked overtures.

At about the time when Van Dorn appeared, seven companies of National troops, under Major Sibley, were at Indianola, on Matagorda Bay, preparing to embark on the *Star of the West*, which had been ruthlessly expelled from Charleston harbor in January. This vessel had been sent, with twenty thousand rations and other supplies, under convoy of the gunboat *Mohawk*, to bear away the troops. Supposing the vessel to be at the mouth of the harbor, Sibley embarked the troops on two small steam lighters, and proceeded down the bay. He had suspected treasonable designs concerning his command. His suspicions were confirmed by the absence of the *Star of the West* and its convoy, and he resolved to go on in the lighters to Tampico, in Mexico. A lack of provisions and coal compelled him to turn back. His troops were disembarked, and, on the following day, Lieutenant Whipple gave him proof of hostile designs against his troops, by reporting the existence of a small battery at Saluria, some distance down the bay. Whipple was ordered to capture it, but when he and his little party approached the place, the cannon were not there.

As speedily as possible, Major Sibley re-embarked his troops on two schooners, and these, towed by the steam lighters, proceeded toward the Gulf. Heavy easterly winds were sweeping the sea, and no pilots were to be seen. Darkness came on before they reached the entrance to the bay, and they anchored within it. There they lay a greater part of two days and two nights, anxiously awaiting the arrival of the *Star of the West* and *Mohawk*. At ten o'clock, when the darkness was profound, and the storm heavy, thick volumes of smoke were discerned above the schooners. At daylight three steamers lay near, with side-barricades of cotton-bales; and, a little later, a larger steamship than either of these, armed with. heavy cannon, came over the bar and anchored near the schooners. The four vessels bore about fifteen hundred well-armed Texans, under Van Dorn. He sent commissioners to demand the surrender of the troops on the schooners. Sibley called a council of war. It was unanimously agreed that resistance to such a heavy and active force would be madness, and Sibley surrendered.[a] The spoils, besides the seven companies made prisoners of war, four hundred and fifty in number, were over three hundred fine rifles and the camp equipage of the whole party of captured troops. Many of these men wept because they had not an opportunity to fight, and threw their arms overboard. At about the same time, a party of volunteers from Galveston boarded the *Star of the West* off Indianola, and captured her, with all her stores.[b]

[a] April 24, 1861.

[b] April 17.

On the day preceding this surrender near Saluria, Colonel Waite, with his staff and all of the officers on duty at San Antonio, were made prisoners,[c] under most aggravating circumstances. When Colonel Waite pointed to the plighted faith of the self-constituted Texan authorities with whom Twiggs had treated, and argued that the present act was in violation of a solemn covenant, he was given to understand that no arguments would be heard—that he and his officers were prisoners, and, if they were not quiet, physical force would be used to compel them to keep silence. One of the most insolent of these representatives of "authority"

[c] April 23.

was a Major Maclin, of Arkansas, who until a short time before had held the office of paymaster in the Regular Army.

At this time, seven companies of the Eighth Regiment, three hundred and thirty-six strong, under Colonel Reese, were making their way from the interior, slowly and wearily, toward the coast, along El Paso Road. On reaching Middle Texas, Colonel Reese found all the supplies necessary for the subsistence of his troops in the hands of the insurgents; and at the ranche of Mr. Adams, near San Lucas Springs, twenty miles west from San Antonio, on the Castroville Road, he was confronted by Van Dorn, who had full fifteen hundred men and two splendid batteries of 12-pounders, one of them under Captain Edgar, the traitor who seized the Alamo.[1] Van Dorn sent Captains Wilcox and Major to demand an unconditional surrender. Reese refused, until he should be convinced that Van Dorn had a sufficient force to sustain his demand. Van Dorn allowed him to send an officer (Lieutenant Bliss) to observe the insurgent strength. The report convinced Reese that his force was greatly outnumbered, and he surrendered unconditionally,[a] giving his word of honor that he would report ^a^ May 9, 1861. at Van Dorn's camp, on the Leon, at six o'clock that evening.

The little column of Colonel Reese comprised all of the National troops remaining in Texas, and these were held close prisoners at San Antonio, whilst Colonel Waite and his fellow-captives, and Major Sibley's command, were paroled. The men were compelled to take an oath that they would not bear arms against the insurgents. Embarking soon afterward, they reached New York in safety, after a voyage of thirty days. Texas was now completely prostrated beneath the heel of that grinding and infernal despotism whose central force was at Montgomery; and that commonwealth, as we have already observed, soon became an important member of the revolutionary league called THE CONFEDERATE STATES OF AMERICA.[2]

After the adoption of the permanent Constitution at Montgomery, and the establishment of the so-called "Confederation," or plan of "permanent Federal Government," that Constitution was submitted to the revolutionary conventions of the several States named in the league, for ratification or rejection. The Convention of Alabamians, who reassembled on the 4th of March, ratified it on the 13th, by a vote of eighty-seven against five. That of Georgians reassembled on the 7th of March, and on the 16th ratified it by unanimous vote, saying that the State of Georgia acted "in its sovereign and independent character." That of Louisianians, which reassembled on the 4th of March, ratified the Constitution on the 21st of the same month, by a vote of one hundred and seven against seven. The South Carolina politicians reassembled their Convention on the 26th of March, and on the 3d day of April that assembly relinquished the boasted sovereignty of the State, by giving a vote of one hundred and forty against twenty-nine for the Constitution of the new "Confederacy."[3] The Convention of Mississippians

---

[1] See page 267.
[2] See the closing pages of Chapter VII.
[3] R. Barnwell Rhett made strenuous opposition to the Constitution. On the 27th of March, he submitted an ordinance for consideration, which provided for the calling a Convention in South Carolina, in the event of a Free-labor State being admitted into the new Confederacy. And on the 2d of April, he offered a resolution that the Convention should expressly declare "that in ratifying and adopting the above Constitution, they suppose that it establishes a Confederacy of Slaveholding States; and this State does not consider herself bound

reassembled on the 25th of March.   There were able men among them, who
contended that the *people* and not that Convention should decide whether or
not the new Constitution should be the supreme law of their land.   These
democratic ideas were scouted as heterodox, and the Convention proceeded
 to act as the embodied sovereignty of the State, by adopting the
* March 26, new plan of government by a vote of seventy-eight against seven.*
   1861.
          Such was the method by which a few arrogant politicians in
seven of the States of the Union, usurping the rights and powers of the
people, formed a league against the rightful and beneficent Government of
that people, and in their name plunged their peaceful and highly prosperous
country into a civil war unparalleled in the history of mankind in its extent,
energy, and waste of life and treasure.   The confiding, misled, and betrayed
people had given them leave to meet in conventions, only to consider alleged
grievances, and to deliberate upon the subject of their relations to the
Union.   From that time, the politicians acted as if there were no people to
consult or to serve—as if they, and they alone, constituted the State.   Their
constituents were never allowed to express their opinions by vote concerning
the Ordinances of Secession, excepting in Texas, and the proceedings there
were fraudulent and outrageous.   And when seven of the revolutionary
conventions, transcending the powers delegated to them by the people,
appointed from among themselves commissioners to meet in General Convention at Montgomery, and that Convention assumed the right to found a
new empire, the people were not only not consulted, and not allowed to
express their views, by ballot, on a subject of such infinite gravity to themselves and their posterity, but, under the reign of a terrible military despotism, unequaled in rigor, lawlessness, and barbarity, they were not allowed
to utter a dissenting word ever so privately, without danger of being
relentlessly persecuted.   Davis, the head of that despotism, had said (and
his words applied equally to the people of the South, the North, and the
world):—"Whoever opposes us, shall smell Southern powder and feel
Southern steel."
   While Jefferson Davis was on his way from his home in Mississippi to
the city of Montgomery, near the Southern extremity of the Republic, there
to be inaugurated leader of a band of conspirators and the chief minister of
a despotism, Abraham Lincoln was journeying from his home in Springfield,
Illinois, hundreds of miles farther north, on his way toward the National
Capital, there to be installed in office as Chief Magistrate of a nation.   The
contrast in the characters and political relations of the two men was most
remarkable.   One was a usurper, prepared to uphold Wrong by violence
and the exercise of the gravest crimes; the other was a modest servant of
the people, appointed by them to execute their will, and anxious to uphold
Right by the majesty and power of law and the exercise of virtue and
justice.
   Mr. Lincoln was an eminent representative American, and in his own
career illustrated in a most conspicuous and distinguished manner the

to enter or continue in confederation with any State not tolerating the institution within its limits by fundamental law." Rhett and his friends seemed fully determined on revolutionary measures, if the new Confederacy
did not act in accordance with their views. See *Journal of the Conventions of the People of South Carolina*, pages 199 and 229.

beneficent and elevating operations of republican government and republican institutions. He was born in comparative obscurity, in the State of Kentucky, early in the year 1809; and when he was inaugurated President, he had just passed his fifty-second birthday. His earlier years had been spent in hard labor with his hands on the farm, in the forest, and on the waters of the Mississippi. His later years had been equally laborious in the profession of the law, a knowledge of which he had acquired by painful study, in the midst of many difficulties. In that profession he had advanced rapidly to distinction, in the State of Illinois, wherein he had settled with his father in the year 1830. His fellow-citizens discovered in him the tokens of statesmanship, and they chose him to represent them in the National Congress. He served them and his country therein with great diligence and ability, and, as we have observed, his countrymen, in the autumn of 1860, chose him to fill the most exalted station in their gift.[1] How he filled that station during the four terrible years of our history, while the Republic was ravaged by the dragon of civil war, will be recorded on succeeding pages.

On the 11th of February, Mr. Lincoln left his home in Springfield for the seat of the National Government, accompanied by a few friends.[2] At the railway station, a large concourse of his fellow-townsmen had gathered to bid him adieu. He was deeply affected by this exhibition of kindness on the part of his friends and neighbors, and with a sense of the great responsibilities he was about to assume. "My friends," he said, when he was about to leave, "no one not in my position can appreciate the sadness I feel at this parting. To this people I owe all that I am. Here I have lived more than a quarter of a century; here my children were born, and here one of them lies buried. A duty devolves upon me which is, perhaps, greater than that which has devolved

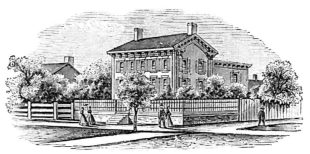

MR. LINCOLN'S RESIDENCE AT SPRINGFIELD.

upon any other man since the days of Washington. He never would have succeeded, except for the aid of Divine Providence, upon which he at all times relied. I feel that I cannot succeed without the same Divine aid which sustained him, and on the same Almighty Being I place my reliance for support; and I hope you, my friends, will all pray that I may receive that Divine assistance without which I cannot succeed, but with which success is certain. Again I bid you farewell."[3]

[1] See page 34.
[2] The following persons accompanied Mr. Lincoln:—J. G. Nicolay, private secretary of the President elect; John Hay; Robert L. Lincoln, Major Hunter, United States Army; Colonel Sumner, United States Army; Colonel E. E. Ellsworth, Hon. John K. Dubys, State Auditor; Colonel W. H. Lamon, Aid to Governor Yates; Judge David Davis, Hon. O. H. Browning, E. L. Baker, editor of the Springfield *Journal;* Robert Irwin, N. B. Judd, and George Lotham.
[3] Before Mr. Lincoln left home, J. Young Scammon, member of the Legislature of Illinois, presented to

We will not follow the President elect through the details of his long travel of hundreds of miles through Illinois, Indiana, Ohio, New York, New Jersey, Pennsylvania, Delaware, and Maryland. During all that journey, which occupied several days, he was everywhere greeted with demonstrations of the most profound respect; and at a few places he addressed the crowds who came out to see. him in plain words, full of kindness and forbearance and tenderness and cheerfulness. "Let us believe," he said, at Tolono, "that behind the cloud the sun is shining." Common prudence counseled him to say but little on the grave affairs of State, the administration of which he was about to assume; yet here and there, on the way, a few words responsive to friendly greetings would sometimes well up to his lips from a full heart, and give such utterances to his thoughts as to foreshadow dimly their general scope. He often alluded to the condition of the country. "It is my intention," he said, "to give this subject all the consideration I possibly can before specially deciding in regard to it, so that when I do speak, it may be as nearly right as possible. I hope I may say nothing in opposition to the spirit of the Constitution, contrary to the integrity of the Union, or which will prove inimical to the liberties of the people or to the peace of the whole country."—"When the time does come for me to speak, I shall then take the ground that I think is right—right for the North, for the South, for the East, for the West, for the whole country."[2]

It was evident that the President elect had no conception of the depth, strength, and malignity of the conspiracy against the life of the Republic which he was so soon afterward called upon to confront. He had been too long accustomed to the foolish threats of the Oligarchy, whenever their imperious will was opposed, to believe them more in earnest now than they ever had been, or that their angry and boastful menaces, and the treasonable conduct of their representatives in Congress, would ripen into more serious action; and as he went along from city to city, talking familiarly to magistrates, and legislators, and crowds of citizens, he tried to soothe their troubled spirits and allay their apprehensions by honestly given assurances that there was "no crisis but an artificial one—none excepting such a one as may be gotten up at any time by turbulent men, aided by designing politicians. Keep cool," he said. "If the great American people on both sides of the line will only keep their temper, the troubles will come to an end, just as surely as all other difficulties of a like character which have originated in this Government have been adjusted."[3]

On the 20th of February Mr. Lincoln was received by the municipal authorities of New York, in the City Hall, when the Mayor, who, as we have observed, had recently, in an official communication, set forth the peculiar advantages which that metropolis would secure by seceding from the State

Mr. Lincoln a fine picture of the flag of the Union, with an inscription upon the folds of the same, in Hebrew, being the fourth, fifth, sixth, seventh, eighth, and ninth verses of the first chapter of Joshua. The verses are those in which Joshua is commanded to reign over the whole land. The last one is as follows:—"9th. 'Have not I commanded thee? Be strong and of a good courage; be not afraid, neither be thou dismayed: for the Lord thy God is with thee whithersoever thou goest.'" The picture was surrounded by a gilt frame, and accompanied by a letter to Mr. Scammon from the donor, Abr. Kohn, City Clerk of Chicago.

1 Speech at Pittsburg, Pennsylvania, February 15, 1861.
2 Speech at the Astor House, New York, on the evening of the 19th of February.
3 Speech at Pittsburg, Pennsylvania, February 15.

and the Union, and establishing an independent government as a free city,[1] admonished him, " because New York was deeply interested in the matter," that his great duty was to so conduct public affairs as to preserve the Union. " New York," said the Seceder, " is the child of the American Union. She has grown up under its maternal care, and been fostered by its maternal bounty, and we fear that if the Union dies, the present supremacy of New York will perish with it." The President elect assured him that he should endeavor to do his duty. On the following day,[a] he passed on through New Jersey to Philadelphia, declaring at Trenton, on the way, to the assembled legislators of that State, that he was " exceedingly anxious that the Union, the Constitution, and the liberties of the people " should be perpetuated. " I shall be most happy," he said, " if I shall be an humble instrument in the hands of the Almighty and of this, his most chosen people, as the chosen instrument—also in the hands of the Almighty—for perpetuating the object of the great struggle" in which Washington and his compatriots were engaged.

[a] February 21, 1861.

Mr. Lincoln was in Philadelphia on Washington's birthday,[b] and with his own hands, in the presence of an immense assemblage of the citizens, he raised the American flag high above the old State House, in which the Declaration of Independence was debated and signed almost eighty-five years before. The place and its hallowed associations suggested the theme of a brief speech, which he made a short time before raising the flag over the Hall wherein the great deed was done. " I have never had a feeling," he said " politically, that did not spring from the sentiments embodied in the Declaration of Independence. I have often pondered over the dangers which were incurred by the men who assembled here and framed and adopted that Declaration of Independence. I have pondered over the toils that were endured by the officers and soldiers of the army who achieved that independence. I have often inquired of myself what great principle or idea it was that kept the Confederacy so long together. It was not the mere matter of the separation of the Colonies from the mother land, but that sentiment in the Declaration of Independence which gave liberty, not alone to the people of this country, but, I hope, to the world, for all future time.[2] It was that which gave promise that, in due time, the weight would be lifted from the shoulders of men. This is the sentiment embodied in the Declaration of Independence. Now, my friends, can this country be saved upon that basis ? If it can, I will consider myself one of the happiest men in the world if I can help to save it. If it cannot be saved upon that principle, it will be truly awful. But if this country cannot be saved without giving up this principle, I was about to say, *I would rather be assassinated on this spot than surrender it.* . . . My friends, I have said nothing but what I am willing to live by, and, if it be the pleasure of Almighty God, die by." Then, in beautiful contrast with the truculent speech of Davis at Montgomery a week earlier, in which that bold leader said that those who opposed himself and his fellow-conspirators, must expect " to smell

[b] February 22.

---

[1] See page 205.

[2] " We hold these truths to be self-evident: that all men are created equal; that they are endowed by their Creator with certain inalienable rights; that among these are life, liberty, and the pursuit of happiness."— *Declaration of Independence*, adopted July 4, 1776.

Southern powder and feel Southern steel,"[1] Mr. Lincoln added:—"Now, in my view of the present aspect of affairs, there need be no bloodshed or war. There is no necessity for it. I am not in favor of such a course; and I may say in advance, that there will be no bloodshed unless it be forced upon the Government, and then it will be compelled to act in self-defense." He had said the day before, at Trenton, "I shall do all that may be in my power to promote a peaceful settlement of all our difficulties. The man does not live who is more devoted to peace than I am—no one who would do more to preserve it; *but it may be necessary to put the foot down firmly.*"

The declaration of Mr. Lincoln, that he was about to say that he would

THE TAYLOR BUILDING.[2]

rather be assassinated than to give up the great principles of the rights of man embodied in the Declaration of Independence, came back to the ears of the American people like a terrible echo, a little more than four years afterward, when he *was* assassinated because he firmly upheld those principles; and in the very hall wherein they were first enunciated in the clear voice of Charles Thomson, reading from the manuscript of Thomas Jefferson, his lifeless body lay in state all through one Sabbath day,* that his face might be looked upon for the last time by a sorrowing people.

* April 23, 1865.

Perhaps the thought of assassination was in Mr. Lincoln's mind at that time, because he had been warned the night before that a band of men in Baltimore in the interest of the conspirators, and who held secret meetings in a room over a billiard and drinking saloon on Fayette Street, near Calvert, known as "The Taylor Building," had made preparations to take his life. Before he left home, threats had found their way to the public ear that he would never reach Washington alive. On the first day of his journey an attempt was made to throw the railway train in which he was conveyed from the track; and just as he was about leaving Cincinnati, a hand-grenade was found secreted in the car in which he was to travel. These and other suspicious circumstances had led to a thorough investigation, under the direction of a sagacious police detective. It resulted in the discovery of the conspiracy at Baltimore, and the revelation of the fact, that a small number of assassins, led, it was said, by an Italian who assumed the name of Orsini,[3] the would-

---

[1] See page 257.

[2] This is from a sketch made in December, 1864. The front is of brown freestone. It is No. 66 Fayette Street. In this building, as we shall observe hereafter. the meetings of the Baltimore conspirators were held, to arrange for the attack on the Massachusetts troops, on the 19th of April, 1861.

[3] *History of the Administration of President Lincoln*, by H. J. Raymond, page 109. A Baltimore correspondent of the New York *Evening Post* said that a notorious gambler of Baltimore, named Byrne, who went to Richmond soon after the events in question, was arrested there on a charge of keeping a gambling-

be murderer of Louis Napoleon, were to kill Mr. Lincoln whilst passing through the streets in a carriage. General Scott and Mr. Seward were so well satisfied that such a plot was arranged, that they sent a special messenger to meet the President elect, and warn him of his danger. He heeded the warning, passed through Baltimore twelve hours earlier than he was expected there; and, to the astonishment of the people, the delight of his friends, and the chagrin and dismay of the conspirators, he appeared in Washington City early on the morning of the 23d of February.

This movement gave life and currency to many absurd stories. It was asserted that Mr. Lincoln had assumed all sorts of disguises to prevent recognition—that he was muffled in a long military cloak and wore a Scotch cap—that he was wrapped in the shaggy dress of a hunter, et cætera ; and for a while his political opponents made merry at his expense, and the pencils of the caricaturists supplied fun for the public. Thoughtful men were made sad. They felt humiliated by the fact that there was a spot in our fair land where the constitutionally chosen Chief Magistrate of the nation might be in danger of personal injury at the hands of his fellow-citizens; and especially mortifying was the allegation that he had been compelled to go in full disguise, by stealth, like a fugitive from justice, to the National Capital. It was properly felt to be a national disgrace.

The occurrence was not so humiliating as represented by the politicians, the satirists, and caricaturists. The President did not travel in disguise ; and the hired assassins or their employers were doubtless too timid or too prudent to attempt the execution of their murderous plan at the critical moment. While in Washington City, early in December, 1864, the writer called on the President, with Isaac N. Arnold, Member of Congress from Chicago, one of Mr. Lincoln's most trusted personal friends. We found him alone in the room wherein the Cabinet meetings are held (in the White House), whose windows overlook the Potomac and the Washington Monument.[1] At the request of the writer, the President related the circumstances of his clandestine journey between Philadelphia and Washington. The narrative is here given substantially in his own words, as follows:—

"I arrived at Philadelphia on the 21st. I agreed to stop over night, and on the following morning hoist the flag over Independence Hall. In the evening there was a great crowd where I received my friends, at the Continental Hotel. Mr. Judd, a warm personal friend from Chicago, sent for me to come to his room. I went, and found there Mr. Pinkerton, a skillful police detective, also from Chicago, who had been employed for some days in Baltimore, watching or searching for suspicious persons there. Pinkerton informed me that a plan had been laid for my assassination, the exact time when I expected to go through Baltimore being publicly known. He was well informed as to the plan, but did not know that the conspirators would have pluck enough to execute it. He urged me to go right through with him to Washington that night. I didn't like that. I had made engagements to visit Harrisburg, and go from there to Baltimore, and I resolved to do so.

---

house, and of disloyalty to the "Southern Confederacy." His loyalty was made apparent by the notorious Senator Wigfall, who testified that he "was captain of the gang who were to kill Mr. Lincoln." This evidence of his complicity in the premeditated crime was sufficient to cover every other sin of which he was guilty, and he was discharged from custody.

[1] See the Frontispiece to this volume.

I could not believe that there was a plot to murder me. I made arrangements, however, with Mr. Judd for my return to Philadelphia the next night, if I should be convinced that there was danger in going through Baltimore. I told him that if I should meet at Harrisburg, as I had at other places, a delegation to go with me to the next place (then Baltimore), I should feel safe, and go on.

" When I was making my way back to my room, through crowds of people, I met Frederick Seward. We went together to my room, when he told me that he had been sent, at the instance of his father and General Scott, to inform me that their detectives in Baltimore had discovered a plot there to assassinate me. They knew nothing of Pinkerton's movements. I now believed such a plot to be in existence.

" The next morning I raised the flag over Independence Hall, and then went on to Harrisburg with Mr. Sumner, Major (now General) Hunter, Mr. Judd, Mr. Lamon, and others. There I met the Legislature and people, dined, and waited until the time appointed for me to leave.[1] In the mean time, Mr. Judd had so secured the telegraph that no communication could pass to Baltimore and give the conspirators knowledge of a change in my plans.

" In New York some friend had given me a new beaver hat in a box, and in it had placed a soft wool hat. I had never worn one of the latter in my life. I had this box in my room. Having informed a very few friends of the secret of my new movements, and the cause, I put on an old overcoat that I had with me, and putting the soft hat in my pocket, I walked out of the house at a back door, bareheaded, without exciting any special curiosity. Then I put on the soft hat and joined my friends without being recognized by strangers, for I was not the same man. Sumner and Hunter wished to accompany me. I said no; you are known, and your presence might betray me. I will only take Lamon (now Marshal of this District), whom nobody knew, and Mr. Judd. Sumner and Hunter felt hurt.

" We went back to Philadelphia and found a message there from Pinkerton (who had returned to Baltimore), that the conspirators had held their final meeting that evening, and it was doubtful whether they had the nerve to attempt the execution of their purpose. I went on, however, as the arrangement had been made, in a special train. We were a long time in the station at Baltimore. I heard people talking around, but no one particularly observed me. At an early hour on Saturday morning,[a] at about the time I was expected to leave Harrisburg, I arrived in Washington."[2]

^{a February 23, 1861.}

Mr. Lincoln was received at the railway station in Washington by Mr. Washburne, member of Congress from Illinois, who was expecting him. He was taken in a carriage to Willard's Hotel, where Senator Seward was in waiting to receive him. Mrs. Lincoln had joined him at Philadelphia, on

---

[1] Six o'clock in the evening.

[2] According to a statement in the *Albany Evening Journal*, a confidential agent was sent by Mr. S. M. Felton with Mr. Lincoln who was called "George," and whose authority was recognized by engineer, conductor, fireman, and brakeman. He bore a large package marked *Dispatches*, and this was the pretext for sending the special train at near midnight. The telegraph wires leading toward Washington had been cut. They were reunited after sufficient time had elapsed for the train to reach its destination, when " George," on its arrival, sent back the following electrograph :—" The Dispatches have arrived, and are safely delivered."

the 22d, and she, Mr. Sumner, and others left Harrisburg at the time appointed, and passed on to the National Capital without interference.

There has never been a public legal investigation concerning the alleged plot to assassinate the President elect at that time. Sufficient facts have been made known through the testimony of detectives to justify the historian in assuming that such a plot was formed, and that it failed only because of the change in Mr. Lincoln's movements. It was alleged that "statesmen, bankers, merchants, and others" were engaged in the conspiracy,[1] and that these were meeting secretly then, and did meet secretly a long time thereafter, in a private room in Taylor's Building. The plan, as revealed, seems to have been to create a mob of the most excitable elements of society in Baltimore, ostensibly against the Republican Committee in that city, while they and the nobly loyal citizens were honoring Mr. Lincoln by a public reception at the railway station. In the confusion created by the mob, the hired assassins were to rush forward, shoot or stab the President elect while in his carriage, and fly back to the shelter of the rioters.

The policemen of Baltimore at that time were under the direction of George P. Kane, as Chief Marshal. He was a violent secessionist, and seems to have been the plastic instrument of conspirators in Baltimore, who were chiefly of the moneyed Oligarchy, connected by blood or marriage with the great land and slave holders in the more Southern States. Kane afterward fled beyond the Potomac, took up arms against his country, and received a commission in the insurgent army. It is asserted that an arrangement had been made for him to so control the police on that occasion, as not to allow a suppression of the mob until the terrible deed should be accomplished. His complicity in the movements which resulted in the murder of Massachusetts troops while passing through Baltimore, a few weeks later, makes it easy to believe that he was concerned in the plot to assassinate the President elect.

GEORGE P. KANE.

The disloyal press of Baltimore seemed to work in complicity with the conspirators on this occasion. A leading editorial in the *Republican*, on the 22d, was calculated to incite tumult and violence; and on the following morning, the day on which Mr. Lincoln was expected to arrive in Baltimore, the *Exchange*, in a significant article, said to its readers :—" The President elect of the United States will arrive in this city, with his suite, this afternoon, by special train from Harrisburg, and will proceed, we learn, directly to Washington. It is to be hoped that no opportunity will be afforded him—or that, if it be afforded, he will not embrace it—to repeat in our ears the sentiments which he is reported to have expressed yesterday in Philadelphia."[2]

Intelligence of Mr. Lincoln's arrival at Washington soon spread over the

---

[1] Baltimore Correspondence of the *New York Times*, February 23, 1861.

[2] For these sentiments, see page 277.

town, and at an early hour Willard's Hotel was crowded with his friends, personal and political, who came to give him a cordial welcome. Loyal men of all parties rejoiced at his safe arrival ; and, because of it, there was gladness throughout the land. That gladness was mingled with indignation because of the circumstances attending that arrival, and the journey preceding it. .Had the danger at Baltimore been made known, and protectors called for, two hundred thousand loyal citizens of the Free-labor States would have escorted the President elect to the Capital.

At an early hour, accompanied by Mr. Seward, Mr. Lincoln called on President Buchanan. The latter could scarcely believe the testimony of his own eyes. He gave his appointed successor a cordial greeting. The Cabinet was then in session. By invitation, the President elect passed into their chamber. He was received with demonstrations of delight. He then called to see General Scott, at his head-quarters. The veteran was absent. Mr. Lincoln returned to Willard's, and there received his friends unceremoniously during the remainder of the day. In the evening he was formally waited upon by the Peace Convention,[1] in a body, and afterward by loyal women of Washington City. Only the secessionists (and they were a host) kept aloof. Foiled malice, disappointment, and chagrin made them sullen. A capital plan in their scheme had been frustrated ; and General Scott, whose defection had been hoped and prayed for, and expected *because he was born in Virginia*, was standing firm as a rock in the midst of the surges of secession, and had filled the National Capital with so many troops that its security against the machinations of the conspirators, secret or open, was considered complete.

On Wednesday, the 27th, the Mayor and Common Council waited upon Mr. Lincoln, and gave him a welcome. On the same day, he and Mrs. Lincoln were entertained at a dinner-party given by Mr. Spaulding, Member of Congress from Buffalo, New York ; and on that evening, they were visited at Willard's by several Senators, and Governor Hicks of Maryland, and were serenaded by the members of the Republican Association at Washington, to whom he made a short speech—the last one previous to his inauguration.[2]

Having followed the President elect from his home to the Capital, and left him there on the eve of his assuming the responsibilities of Chief Magistrate of the Republic, let us turn a moment and hold brief retrospective intercourse with the actual President, who seemed to be as anxious as were the people for the close of his official career. We have seen him, from the opening of the session of Congress until the disruption of his Cabinet, at the close of December, working or idling, voluntarily or involuntarily, in seeming harmony with the wishes of the conspirators. We have seen him after that surrounded by less malign influences, and prevented, by loyal men in his Cabinet, from allowing his fears or his inclinations to do the Republic serious

a January 4, 1861. harm. And when the National Fast-day which he had recommended had been observed,[a] he spoke some brave words in a

b January 8. message sent in to Congress,[b] saying, it was his right and his duty to " use military force defensively against those who resist the Federal

---

[1] See page 237.
[2] *History of the Administration of President Lincoln :* by Henry J. Raymond, page 110. Vice-President Hamlin and Thomas Corwin also made speeches.

officers in the execution of their legal functions, and against those who assail the property of the Federal Government;" yet he refused to support these brave words by corresponding dutiful action, and cast the whole responsibility of meeting the great peril upon Congress, at the same time suggesting to it the propriety of yielding to the demands of the disloyal Oligarchy, by adopting, substantially, the Crittenden Compromise.

Mr. Buchanan seemed determined to get through with the remainder of his term of office as quietly as possible, and as innocent of all offense toward the conspirators as "a decent respect for the opinions of mankind" would allow.[1] In his efforts to please his "Southern friends," he sometimes omitted to be just. While the country was ringing with plaudits for Major Anderson, because of his gallant and useful conduct at Fort Sumter, and Lieutenant-General Scott asked the President to show his regard for the faithful soldier, and act as "the interpreter of the wish of millions" by nominating Anderson for the rank of lieutenant-colonel by brevet, for his "wise and heroic transfer of the garrison of Fort Moultrie to Fort Sumter;" also by nominating him for the rank of colonel by brevet, "for his gallant maintenance of the latter fort, under severe hardships, with but a handful of men, against the threats and summons of a formidable army,"[2] the President, who might, in that act, have won back much of the lost respect of his countrymen, refused, saying in substance:—"I leave that for my successor to do." And with a seeming desire to maintain his inoffensive position toward the conspirators, he pursued a timorous and vacillating policy, which greatly embarrassed his loyal counselors, and paralyzed their efforts to strengthen the ship of State, so as to meet safely the shock of the impending tempest.

Notwithstanding his efforts to please his "Southern friends," they would not allow the current of the President's official life to flow smoothly on, after Holt and Dix, loyal Democrats, became his counselors. They would not trust him with such advisers at his ear. It has been said that he "preached like a patriot, but practised like a traitor." His preaching offended and alarmed them, especially the South Carolina politicians, for its burden was against the dignity of their "Sovereign nation." While Sumter was in possession of National troops, they felt that South Carolina was insulted and her sovereignty and independence were denied. So, on the 11th of January, two days after the attack on the *Star of the West*, Governor Pickens, as we have observed,[3] sent A. G. Magrath and D. F. Jamison, of his Executive Council, to demand its surrender to the authorities of the State. Major Anderson refused to give it up, and referred the matter to the President; whereupon Pickens sent Isaac W. Hayne, the Attorney-General of the State, in company with Lieutenant Hall, of Anderson's command, to Washington City, to present the same demand to the National Executive. Hayne bore a letter from the Governor to the President, in which the former declared, that the demand for surrender was suggested because of his "earnest desire to avoid the bloodshed which a persistence in the attempt to retain posses-

---

[1] In his Message on the 8th of January he said:—"At the beginning of these unhappy troubles, I determined that no act of mine should increase the excitement in either section of the country. If the political conflict were to end in civil war, it was my determined purpose not to commence it, nor even to furnish an excuse for it in any act of this Government."

[2] Letter of Lieutenant-General Scott to President Buchanan, February 26, 1861.

[3] See page 160.

sion of that fort would cause, and which would be unavailing to secure that possession." Commissioner Hayne was authorized to "give the pledge of the State" that the valuation of the public property within Fort Sumter should be "accounted for by the State, upon the adjustment of its relations with the United States, of which it was a part."[1]

Mr. Hayne arrived in Washington City on the 13th of January, when ten of the disloyal Senators, still holding seats in Congress,[2] advised him, in

ISAAC W. HAYNE.

writing, not to present the letter of Pickens to the President until after the Southern Confederacy should be formed, a month later. They proposed to ask the President to agree not to re-enforce Fort Sumter, in the mean time. "I am not clothed with power to make the arrangement you suggest," Mr. Hayne replied, in writing; "but, provided you can get assurances, with which you are entirely satisfied, that no re-enforcements will be sent to Fort Sumter in the interval, and that the public peace will not be disturbed by any act of hostility toward South Carolina, I will refer your communication to the authorities of South Carolina, and, withholding the communication with which I am at the present charged, will await further instructions."

This correspondence was laid before the President[a] by Senators Slidell, Fitzpatrick, and Mallory, and the President was asked to consider [a] January 16, 1861. the matter.[3] He replied, through Mr. Holt, the Secretary of War, that he could not give such pledge, for the simple reason that he had no authority to do so, being bound as an Executive officer to enforce the laws as far as practicable. He informed them that it was not deemed necessary to re-enforce Major Anderson at that time; but told them, explicitly, that should the safety of that officer at any time require it, the effort to give him re-enforcements and supplies would be made. He reminded them that Congress alone had the power to make war, and that it would be an act of

---

[1] Letter of Francis W. Pickens to President Buchanan, January 11, 1861.

[2] These were Wigfall, Hemphill, Yulee, Mallory, Jefferson Davis, C. C. Clay, Jr., Fitzpatrick, Iverson, Slidell, and Benjamin.

[3] The boldness and impunity of the conspirators in Congress, at this time, is illustrated by this correspondence which they laid before the President, and asked that he would "take into consideration the subject of said correspondence." In their letter to Hayne, signed by the ten Senators, they assure him that they "represent States which have already seceded from the United States, or will have done so before the 1st of February next," and which would meet South Carolinians "in convention on or before the 15th of that month." "Our people," said these conspirators to Mr. Hayne, "feel that they have a common destiny with your people, *and expect to form with them, in that convention, a new confederation and provisional government.* We must and will share your fortunes, suffering with you the evils of war, if it cannot be avoided, and enjoying with you the blessings of peace if it can be preserved."

This letter was written on the 15th of January, the day after several of these Senators had written to the conventions of their several States, intimating that it might be well for them to retain their seats in Congress, in order to more effectually carry on their treasonable work. These men were not only not arrested, but their request was responded to by the Secretary of War, under the direction of the President, as courteously and considerately as if they were true and loyal to their Government.

usurpation on the part of the Executive to give any assurance that Congress would not exercise that power.

When this correspondence reached Charleston, Governor Pickens ordered Hayne to present the demand for the surrender of Sumter forthwith. He did so,* in a letter of considerable length, to which [*] ^{January 31, 1861.} Secretary Holt gave a final answer on the 6th of February, in which, as in his reply to Senators Fitzpatrick, Mallory, and Slidell, he claimed for the Government the right to send forward re-enforcements when, in the judgment of the President, the safety of the garrison required them—a right resting on the same foundation as the right to occupy the fort. He denied the right of South Carolina to the possession of the fort, and said :—" If the announcement, so repeatedly made, of the President's pacific purpose in continuing the occupation of Fort Sumter until the question shall be settled by competent authority, has failed to impress the government of South Carolina, the forbearing conduct of the Administration for the last few months should be received as conclusive evidence of his sincerity. And if this forbearance, in view of the circumstances which have so severely tried it, be not accepted as a satisfactory pledge of the peaceful policy of this Administration towards South Carolina, then it may be safely affirmed that neither language nor conduct can possibly furnish one. If, with all the multiplied proofs which exist of the President's anxiety for peace, and of the earnestness with which he has pursued it, the authorities of that State shall assault Fort Sumter, and peril the lives of the handful of brave and loyal men shut up within its walls, and thus plunge our common country into the horrors of civil war, then upon them and those they represent must rest the responsibility."

Here ended the attempt of the conspirators of South Carolina to have the sovereignty of that State acknowledged by diplomatic intercourse. It had utterly failed. The President refused to receive Governor Pickens's agent, excepting as " a distinguished citizen of South Carolina," and also refused any compliance with the demands of the authorities of that State. He had been strongly inclined to yield to these demands; but recent manifestations of public opinion convinced him that he could not do so without exciting the hot indignation of the loyal portion of the people. Coincident with these manifestations were the strong convictions of Holt, Dix, and Attorney-General Stanton of his Cabinet.[1]

---

[1] The secret history of these public demonstrations of a desire to hold Fort Sumter has been given by General Daniel E. Sickles, in a brief eulogy of Mr. Stanton, the Secretary of War during a greater portion of Mr. Lincoln's Administration. "Toward evening, on one of the gloomy days in the winter of 1861," says Sickles, " the Attorney-General [Stanton] sent for one of the representatives in Congress from New York, and informed him that unless the public opinion of the North was instantly manifested, the President would yield to the demand of South Carolina, and order Major Anderson back from Sumter to Moultrie. It was decided at once that an envoy should go to the principal Northern cities and announce that the President had decided to maintain Anderson in Sumter at all hazards. ' Fire some powder,' said Stanton; ' all we can do yet is to fire blank cartridges; a thousand bullets or a bale of hemp would save us from a bloody rebellion. The President will not strike a blow, but he will resist if he sees the temper of the people demands resistance. Go and fire some cannon, and let the echoes come to the White House.' The next day salutes were fired in New York, Philadelphia, Albany, and other cities, in honor of President Buchanan's determination to sustain the gallant Anderson. Congratulating telegrams were sent from prominent men in all these cities to the President ; the corporate authorities of New York passed earnest resolutions of support; several journals, in leading articles of remarkable power, indorsed and commended the decision of the President. The next day the decision was made. The demand of South Carolina for the evacuation of Fort Sumter was refused; it remained only for the South to secede, or make war."—*Address at the Opening of the American Institute Fair, in New York, on the 12th of September*, 1865.

Before " Commissioner" Hayne was dismissed, " Commissioner" Thomas J. Judge appeared on the stage at Washington, as the representative of Alabama, duly authorized " to negotiate with the Government of the United States in reference to the forts, arsenals, and custom houses in that State, and the debt of the United States." He approached the President [a] through Senator C. C. Clay, Jr., who expressed his desire that when Judge might have an audience, he should. " present his credentials and enter upon the proposed negotiations."[1] The President placed Mr. Judge on the same footing with Mr. Hayne, as only a " distinguished" private gentleman, and not as an embassador; whereupon Senator Clay wrote an angry letter to the President,[b] too foolish in matter and manner to deserve a place in history. The " Sovereign State of Alabama" then withdrew, in the person of Mr. Judge, who argued that the course of the President implied either an abandonment of all claims to the National property within the limits of his State, or a desire that it should be retaken by the sword.[2]

[a] February 1, 1861.

[b] February 1.

No further attempts to open diplomatic intercourse between the United States and the banded conspirators in " seceded States" were made during the remainder of Mr. Buchanan's Administration; and he quietly left the chair of State for private life, a deeply sorrowing man. " Governor," said the President to Senator Fitzpatrick, a few weeks before,[c] when the latter was about to depart for Alabama, " the current of events warns me that we shall never meet again on this side the grave. I have tried to do my duty to both sections, and have displeased both. I feel isolated in the world."[3]

[c] January 24.

---

[1] Letter of Senator Clay to the President, February 1, 1861.

[2] Letter of Senator Clay to " Commissioner" Judge, February 4, 1861.

[3] *Harper's Weekly*, February 2, 1861.

CHAPTER XII.

THE INAUGURATION OF PRESIDENT LINCOLN, AND THE IDEAS AND POLICY OF THE GOVERNMENT.

 ONDAY, the 4th of March, 1861, will ever be a memorable day in the annals of the Republic. On that day a Chief Magistrate was installed who represented the loyal and free spirit of the nation, which had found potential expression in a popular election. That election proclaimed, in the soft whispers of the ballot, an unchangeable decree, that slave labor should cultivate no more of the free land of the Republic. Professedly on account of that decree, the advocates of such labor commenced a revolt; and it was in the midst of the turmoil caused by the mad cry of insurgents, that Abraham Lincoln went up to the National Capital, and was inaugurated the Sixteenth President of the United States of America.

The inaugural ceremonies were performed quietly and orderly, at the usual place, over the broad staircase at the eastern front of the Capitol, whose magnificent dome was only half finished. In order to insure quiet and safety, and the performance of the ceremony in the usual peaceful form, General Scott had collected about six hundred regular troops in the city, but they were so scattered that their presence was scarcely perceptible. They had been making their way to the capital in small numbers from different points for several weeks, and the conspirators were so impressed with the belief that the total force was enormous in strength—that a vast number of troops were hidden all about the city—that they abandoned the scheme of seizing Washington, preventing the inauguration of Mr. Lincoln, and placing one of their number in the Executive Chair.[1] They were undeceived, four days before the inauguration, by a Message of the President,[a] in response to an inquiry by Congress concerning the number of troops in the city.[2] It was then too late for them to organize

[a] March 1, 1861.

---

[1] See page 143.

[2] Mr. Burnett, of Kentucky, offered a resolution in the House of Representatives on the 11th of February, which was adopted, asking the President for his reasons for assembling a large number of troops in Washington; why they were kept there; and whether he had any information of a conspiracy to seize the Capital, and prevent the inauguration of the President elect. On the 5th of the same month, Wigfall had offered a resolution in the Senate, asking the President why, since the commencement of the session of Congress, troops had been gathering in Washington; munitions of war collected there; from what points they had been called, &c., and under the authority of what law they were held for service in the National Capital. The President did not answer these inquiries until the 1st of March, when he declared that there were only six hundred and fifty-three private soldiers in the city, besides the usual number of marines at the Navy Yard, and that they were ordered to Washington to "act as a *posse comitatus*, in strict subordination to the civil authority, for the purpose of preserving peace and order," should that be necessary, before or at the period of the inauguration of the President elect. In the mean time a Committee of the House had investigated the subject of a conspiracy; and the members of that body were so well convinced of its existence, that a resolution, expressing the opinion that "the regular troops now in this city ought to be forthwith removed therefrom," was laid on

the "Minute-men" of Maryland and Virginia. This condition, and the natural belief that many of the thousands of the loyal people who were pouring into the Capital to participate in the ceremonies were well armed, kept the enemies of the Republic in perfect restraint.

SCENE OF THE INAUGURATION.

The dawn of the 4th of March was pleasant, and the day was a bright one. Washington City was crowded by more than twenty-five thousand strangers, a large portion of them the political friends of the President elect. The streets around Willard's Hotel were densely packed, at an early hour, with eager watchers for the appearance of Mr. Lincoln. The forenoon wore away, and he was yet invisible to the public eye. He was waiting for Mr. Buchanan, who was engaged almost up to twelve o'clock, the appointed hour for the inaugural ceremonies, in signing bills at his room in the Capitol. Then he was conveyed rapidly to the White House, where he entered a barouche, waited upon by servants in livery, and hastened to Willard's. The President elect, with the late Senators Pearce and Baker, there entered the carriage, and at a little before one o'clock the procession, under the direction of Chief Marshal Major French, moved along Pennsylvania Avenue toward the Capitol.[1] Mounted troops, under the direction of General Scott, moved on the flanks on parallel streets,

the table by a very large majority. The alarm for the safety of the Government archives, which prevailed throughout the country, had instantly subsided when it was known that troops were called to Washington.

[1] Marshal French was assisted by thirteen aids and twenty-nine assistant marshals, representing loyal States and Territories. Besides these were eighty-three assistants. The marshal's aids wore blue scarfs and white rosettes. Their saddle-cloths were blue, trimmed with gilt. The assistant marshals wore blue scarfs and white rosettes. Their saddle-cloths were white, trimmed with blue. Each carried a *baton* two feet in length, of blue color, with ends gilt two inches deep. The procession was composed as follows:—

Aids.   Marshal-in-Chief.   Aids.
A National Flag, with appropriate emblems.
The President of the United States, with the President Elect and Suite, with Marshals on their left, and the Marshal of the United States for the District of Columbia (Colonel William Selden) and his Deputies on their right.
The Committee of Arrangements of the Senate.
Ex-Presidents of the United States.
The Republican Association.
The Judiciary.
The Clergy.
Foreign Ministers.
The Corps Diplomatique.
Members elect, Members, and ex-Members of Congress, and ex-Members of the Cabinet.
The Peace Congress.
Heads of Bureaus.
Governors and ex-Governors of States and Territories, and Members of the Legislatures of the same.
Officers of the Army, Navy, Marine Corps, and Militia, in full uniform.
Officers and Soldiers of the Revolution, of the War of 1812, and subsequent periods.
The Corporate Authorities of Washington and Georgetown.
Other Political and Military Associations from the District, and other parts of the United States.
All organized Civil Societies.
Professors, Schoolmasters, and Students within the District of Columbia.
Citizens of the District, and of States and Territories.

There was a military escort under Colonels Harris and Thomas, and Captain Taylor. The carriage in

ready for action at a concerted signal.[1] They were not needed. The procession passed on without interruption, excepting by the enormous crowd.

At half-past one the two Presidents left the carriage, went into the
Capitol, and, preceded by Major French, entered the Senate Chamber arm
in arm. Mr. Buchanan was pale and nervous; Mr. Lincoln's face was
slightly flushed with emotion, but he was a model of self-possession. They
sat waiting a few minutes before the desk of the President of the Senate.
"Mr. Buchanan," an eye-witness said, "sighed audibly and frequently.
Mr. Lincoln was grave and impassive as an Indian martyr." The party
soon proceeded to the platform over the ascent to the eastern portico, where
the Supreme Court, the Senate and House of Representatives, Foreign Ministers, and other privileged persons were assembled, while an immense congregation of citizens filled the space below.

Mr. Lincoln was introduced to the people by Senator Baker, of Oregon;
and as he stepped forward, his head towering above most of those around
him (for his hight was six feet and four inches),[2] he was greeted with
vehement applause. Then, with a clear, strong voice, he read his
Inaugural Address, during which service Senator Douglas, lately his competitor for the honors and duties he was now assuming, held the hat of the
new President.[3] At the close of the reading, the late Chief-Justice Taney

which the two Presidents rode was surrounded by military, so as to prevent any violence, if it should be
attempted.

[1] "I caused to be organized," says General Scott, "the *élite* of the Washington Volunteers, and called
from a distance two batteries of horse artillery, with small detachments of cavalry and infantry, all regulars."—
Autobiography of General Scott. iii. 611. The General says, that during the two months preceding the
inauguration, he received more than fifty letters from various points, some earnestly dissuading him from being
present at the ceremony, and others threatening him with assassination if he dared to protect the ceremony by
a military force.

[2] The best description of the personal appearance of Mr. Lincoln, according to the author's own vivid
recollection of him in January, 1865, is the following:—

"Conceive a tall and gaunt figure, more than six feet in hight, not only unencumbered with superfluous
flesh, but reduced to the minimum working standard of cord, and sinew, and muscle, strong and indurated by
exposure and toil, with legs and arms long and attenuated, but not disproportionately so to the long and
attenuated trunk. In posture and carriage not ungraceful, but with the grace of unstudied and careless ease,
rather than of cultivated airs and high-bred pretensions. His dress is universally of black throughout, and
would attract but little attention in a well-dressed circle, if it hung less loosely upon him, and the ample white
shirt collar was not turned over his cravat in the Western style. The face that surmounts this figure is half
Roman and half Indian, bronzed by climate, furrowed by life-struggles, seamed with humor; the head is
massive, and covered with dark, thick, and unmanageable hair; the brow is wide and well developed; the nose
large and fleshy; the lips full; cheeks thin, and drawn down in strong corded lines, which, but for the wiry
whiskers, would disclose the machinery which moves the broad jaw. The eyes are dark gray, sunk in deep
sockets, but bright, soft, and beautiful in expression, and sometimes lost and half abstracted, as if their glance
was reversed and turned inward, or as if the soul which lighted them was far away. The teeth are white and
regular, and it is only when a smile, radiant, captivating, and winning, as was ever given to mortal, transfigures
the plain countenance, that you begin to realize that it is not impossible for artists to admire and woman to
love it."—*Eulogy on Abraham Lincoln:* by Henry Champe Deming, before the General Assembly of Connecticut, at Hartford, June 8, 1865.

[3] On that day the veteran journalist, Thurlow Weed, wrote as follows for the editorial column of his paper,
the *Albany Evening Journal:*—

"The throng in front of the Capitol was immense, and yet the President's voice was so strong and clear
that he was heard distinctly. The cheers went up loud and long.

"After he commenced delivering his Inaugural I withdrew, and passing north on Capitol Hill, saw Generals
Scott and Wool, in full uniform, standing by their battery—the battery memorable for its prowess in Mexico.
I could not resist the impulse to present myself to those distinguished veterans, the heroes of so many battles
and so many victories. They received me cordially, General Scott inquiring how the inauguration was going
on. I replied, 'It is a success.' Upon which the old hero raised his arms and exclaimed, 'God be praised!
God in His goodness be praised!'

"In leaving these scarred and seamed veterans, my mind went back to the long interval and striking events
which have occurred since 1812, when I *first* saw them—General Scott a major of artillery, and General Wool
a captain in the Thirteenth Infantry, both alert, active, buoyant young men—General Scott tall and erect, but
remarkably slender in form, with flowing flaxen hair. Nearly half a century has passed. They have fought

administered the oath of office to him, when the President and ex-President re-entered the Capitol, and the former proceeded immediately to the White House. Mr. Buchanan drove to the house of District-Attorney Ould,[1] and on the following day left for his beautiful seat of "Wheatland," near Lancaster, in Pennsylvania, which he reached on the 6th.[2] There he was received by a large concourse of his fellow-citizens, with a fine display of military, and civic societies. He was welcomed home by an address; and, in response, he congratulated himself on his retirement from public life, and announced his intention to pass the remainder of his existence as a "good citizen, a faithful friend, an adviser of those who needed advice, and a benefactor of the widows and the fatherless." He alluded to public affairs only to express a hope that the Constitution and the Union might be preserved. .

President Lincoln's Inaugural Address was waited for with intense interest and anxiety throughout the Republic. At no period in its wonderful career had the nation been in so great peril as at that time. Already a rebellion had been allowed to acquire formidable moral and physical proportions, and republican institutions and a republican form of government, against which its deadly blows were to be aimed, were now put upon their trial before the bar of the great powers of the earth. Mr. Lincoln was their chosen counsel and defender; and he now entered upon the momentous task of vindicating their might and invincible vitality, with no precedents to guide him, and no statutes for support other than the opinions and theories of the fathers, sometimes only dimly shadowed, and the plain letter of the National Constitution. With these helps, the exercise of sound judgment, abounding common sense, an honest purpose, patriotism without alloy, and with the illumination that comes down to the earnest seeker for Divine light and assistance, Mr. Lincoln stood up bravely before that bar with his brief, and entered upon the cause.

"Apprehensions," said Mr. Lincoln in his Inaugural, "seem to exist among the people of the Southern States, that by the accession of a Republican Administration, their property and their peace and personal security are to be endangered. There has never been any reasonable cause for such apprehension. Indeed, the most ample evidence to the contrary has all the while existed and been open to their inspection. It is found in nearly all the published speeches of him who now addresses you. I do but quote from one of these speeches, when I declare that ' I have no purpose directly or indirectly to interfere with the institution of Slavery in the States where it exists. I believe I have no lawful right to do so, and I have no inclination to do so.' Those who nominated and elected me, did so with full knowledge that I had made this and similar declarations, and had never recanted them. And, more than this, they placed in the platform for my acceptance, and as a law to themselves and to me, the clear and emphatic resolution which I now read :—

" ' Resolved, That the maintenance inviolate of the rights of the States, and especially the right of each State to order and control its own domestic

---

through all the wars of their country, terminating them all gloriously. They are spared for a severer trial of courage and patriotism, unless Heaven, in its wisdom and mercy, averts the threatened dangers."

[1] Robert Ould. See page 145.

[2] Mr. Buchanan was escorted to the railway station at Washington by a committee of gentlemen from Lancaster, and two companies of mounted infantry. He was well received at Baltimore by the citizens; and from that city he was escorted to his home by the Baltimore City Guards.

institutions according to its own judgment exclusively, is essential to the balance of power on which the perfection and endurance of our political fabric depend;[1] and we denounce the lawless invasion by armed force of the soil of any State or Territory, no matter under what pretext, as among the gravest of crimes.'

"I now reiterate these sentiments; and, in doing so, I only press upon the public attention the most conclusive evidence of which the case is susceptible, that the property, peace, and security of no section are to be in any wise endangered by the now incoming Administration. I add, too, that all the protection which, consistently with the Constitution and the laws, can be given, will be cheerfully given to all the States, when lawfully demanded, for whatever cause—as cheerfully to one section as to another."

The President referred to the Fugitive Slave Act as constitutional, but suggested that it should have provisions that would throw around it "all the safeguards of liberty known in civilized and humane jurisprudence," so that "a free man be not in any case surrendered as a slave." He also suggested that it might be well to provide by law "for the enforcement of that clause in the Constitution which guaranties that 'the citizens of each State shall be entitled to all privileges and immunities of citizens in the several States.'" These "privileges and immunities" had not been fully enjoyed by citizens of the Free-labor States while in the Slave-labor States, for many years.

The President then spoke of the political construction and character of the Republic. "I hold," he said, "that in contemplation of universal law and of the Constitution, *the Union of these States is perpetual.* Perpetuity is implied, if not expressed, in the fundamental law of all national governments. It is safe to assert that no government proper ever had a provision in its organic law for its own termination. Continue to execute all the express provisions of our National Constitution, and the Union will endure forever—it being impossible to destroy it, except by some action not provided for in the instrument itself. If the United States be not a government proper, but an association of States in the nature of a contract merely, can it, as a contract, be peaceably unmade by less than all the parties who made it? One party to a contract may violate it—break it, so to speak; but does it not require all to lawfully rescind it?

"Descending from these general principles, we find the proposition that, in legal contemplation, the Union is perpetual, confirmed by the history of the Union itself. The Union is much older than the Constitution. It was formed, in fact, by the Articles of Association, in 1774. It was matured and continued by the Declaration of Independence, in 1776. It was further matured, and the faith of all the then thirteen States expressly plighted and engaged that it should be perpetual, by the Articles of Confederation, in 1778. And finally, in 1787, one of the declared objects for ordaining and establishing the Constitution was, 'to form a more perfect Union.' But if the destruction of the Union, by one or by a part only of the States, be lawfully possible, the Union is less perfect than before, the Constitution having lost the vital element of perpetuity."[2]

[1] See page 82.
[2] For a quarter of a century, conspirators against the nationality of the Republic had been teaching the opposite doctrine, until, at the beginning of the war, it was proclaimed as a fundamental dogma of the political

"It follows, from these views, that no State, upon its own mere motion, can lawfully get out of the Union ; that resolves and ordinances to that effect are legally void; and that acts of violence within any State or States, against the authority of the United States, are insurrectionary or revolutionary, according to circumstances. I, therefore, consider that, in view of the Constitution and the laws, the Union is unbroken, and, to the extent of my ability, I shall take care, as the Constitution itself expressly enjoins upon me, that the laws of the Union be faithfully executed in all the States. Doing this I deem to be only a simple duty on my part, and I shall perform it, so far as practicable, unless my rightful masters, the American people, shall withhold the requisite means, or in some authoritative manner direct the contrary. I trust this will not be regarded as a menace, but only as the declared purpose of the Union, that it will constitutionally defend and maintain itself.

"In doing this, there need be no bloodshed or violence; and there shall be none, unless it be forced upon the National authority. The power confided to me will be used to hold, occupy, and possess the property and places belonging to the Government, and to collect the duties and imposts ; but beyond what may be but necessary for these objects, there will be no invasion, no using of force against or among the people anywhere. Where hostility to the United States in any interior locality shall be so great and universal as to prevent competent resident citizens from holding the Federal offices, there will be no attempt to force obnoxious strangers among the people for that object. While the strict legal right may exist in the Government to enforce the exercise of these offices, the attempt to do so would be so irritating, and so nearly impracticable withal, I deem it better to forego for the time the uses of such offices."

The President then declared that he should endeavor, by justice, to reconcile all discontents, with a hope of bringing about a "peaceful solution of the National troubles." If there were any who sought to destroy the Union in any event, to those he need "address no word." To those who really loved the Union, he spoke in terms of zealous and earnest pleading, asking them to consider well so "grave a matter as the destruction of our national fabric, with all its benefits, its memories, and its hopes," before undertaking it. He asked the malcontents to point to a single instance where "any right, plainly written in the Constitution," had been denied. He declared that if, "by the mere force of numbers, a majority should deprive a minority of any clearly written constitutional right, it might, in a moral point of view, justify revolution—certainly would if such right were a vital one. But such is not our case," he said. "All the vital rights of minorities and of individuals are so plainly assured to them, by affirmations and negations, guaranties and prohibitions in the Constitution, that controversies never arise concerning them."

---

creed of the conspirators and the Oligarchy, that the Union was a temporary compact, and the National Government no government at all, but only the "agent of the Sovereign States." Edward A. Pollard editor of the *Richmond Examiner,* who wrote a history of the war, opens his first volume with these remarkable words as the key-note to his whole performance :—"The American people of the present generation were born in the belief that the Union of the States was destined to be perpetual. A few minds rose superior to this natal delusion," *et cætera.*

The President then spoke of the necessity of acquiescence of 'either minorities or majorities in the decisions of questions. Without such acquiescence, the Government could not exist. "If a minority in such case," he said, " will secede rather than acquiesce, they make a precedent which, in turn, will divide and ruin them; for a minority of their own will secede from them whenever a majority refuses to be controlled by such minority. For instance, why may not any portion of a new Confederacy, a year or two hence, arbitrarily secede again, precisely as portions of the present Union now claim to secede from it? . . . Plainly, the central idea of secession is anarchy. A majority, held in restraint by constitutional checks and limitations, and always changing easily with deliberate changes of popular opinions and sentiments, is the only true sovereign of a free people. Whoever rejects it, does of necessity fly to anarchy or to despotism."

The President referred to the binding character of the decisions of the Supreme Court in all special cases; but he said, evidently with the action of Chief-Justice Taney in the Dred Scott case in his mind,[1] "The candid citizen must confess, that if the policy of the Government upon vital questions affecting the whole people is to be irrevocably fixed by decisions of the Supreme Court, the instant they are made in ordinary litigation between parties in personal actions, the people will have ceased to be their own rulers, having to that extent practically resigned their government into the hands of that eminent tribunal." He referred to the impossibility of a dissolution of the Union, physically speaking. The people of the respective sections, who differed widely in opinions, might, like a divorced husband and wife, separate absolutely, by going out of the reach of each other, but the territory of the respective sections must remain "face to face," and intercourse, either amicable or hostile, must continue between them. The question then arises, whether that intercourse would be more agreeable after separation. "Can aliens," asked the President, "make treaties easier than friends can make laws? Can treaties be more faithfully enforced among aliens than laws can among friends? Suppose you go to war, you cannot fight always; and when, after much loss on both sides and no gain on either, you cease fighting, the identical old questions as to terms of intercourse are again upon you."

The President recognized the right of the people to change their existing form of government when they should become weary of it, either by amending the Constitution or by revolution; and, in view of present difficulties, he expressed his concurrence in the proposition for a Convention of Representatives of all the States, to deliberate on constitutional amendments; and he went so far as to say, that he had no objections to any amendment which should, by an express and irrevocable decree, provide that the National Government should never interfere with Slavery in the States where it existed. The Chief Magistrate, he said, had no power to fix any terms for a separation of States. That was for the people to do. His business was only to execute the laws. He believed in the ultimate wisdom and justice of the American people. "Why not have a patient confidence in that justice?" he asked. "Is there any better or equal hope in the world? In our present differences, is either party without faith of being in the right?

If the Almighty Ruler of Nations, with His eternal truth and justice, be on your side of the North, or on yours of the South, that truth and that justice will surely prevail, by the judgment of this great tribunal of the American people." He concluded by an earnest exhortation to his countrymen to think calmly and well upon the whole subject. He begged them to take time for serious deliberation. "Such of you," he said, "as are now dissatisfied, still have the old Constitution unimpaired, and, on the sensitive point, the laws of your own framing under it; while the new Administration will have no immediate power, if it would, to change either. . . . In your hands, my dissatisfied fellow-countrymen, and not in mine, is the momentous issue of civil war. The Government will not assail you. You can have no conflict without being yourselves the aggressors. You have no oath registered in heaven to destroy the Government; whilst I shall have the most solemn one to 'preserve, protect, and defend it.' I am loth to close. We are not enemies, but friends. We must not be enemies. Though passion may have strained, it must not break our bonds of affection. The mystic chords of memory, stretching from every battle-field and patriot grave to every living heart and hearthstone all over this broad land, will yet swell the chorus of the Union, when again touched, as surely they will be, by the better angels of our nature."

Long before sunset on that beautiful 4th of March, the brilliant pageant of the inauguration of a President had dissolved, and thousands of citizens, breathing more freely now that the first and important chapter in the history of the new Administration was closed without a tragic scene, were hastening homeward. But Washington City was to be the theater of another brilliant display the same evening, in the character of an Inauguration Ball. Notwithstanding a pall of gloom and dark forebodings overspread the land, and the demon of Discord, with his torch and blade, was visibly on the wing, expediency seemed to declare that none of the usual concomitants of the inauguration ceremonies should be omitted on this occasion, but that every thing should move on after the old fashion, as if the Government were perfectly undisturbed by the stormy passions of the time.

The preparations for the ball had been made in the usual manner. A large temporary building had been erected for the purpose near the City Hall, whose council-chamber and committee-rooms were used as dressing-rooms for the guests. The hall, a parallelogram in shape, was decorated with red and white muslin, and many shields bearing National and State arms. Several foreign ministers and their families, and heads of departments and their families, were present. The dancing commenced at eleven o'clock. Ten minutes later the music and the motion ceased, for it was announced that Mr. and Mrs. Lincoln, in whose honor the ball was given, were about to enter the room. The President appeared first, accompanied by Mayor Berret, of Washington, and Senator Anthony, of Rhode Island. Immediately behind him came Mrs. Lincoln, wearing a rich watered silk dress, an elegant point-lace shawl, deeply bordered, with camelias in her hair and pearl ornaments. She was leaning on the arm of Senator Douglas, the President's late political rival. The incident was accepted as a proclamation of peace and friendship between the champions. Mr. Hamlin, the Vice-President, was already there; and the room was crowded with many distinguished men and beautiful and elegantly dressed women. The utmost gayety and hilarity prevailed; and every face but one was continually radiant with the unmixed joy of the hour. That face was Abraham Lincoln's. The perennial good-humor of his nature could not, at all times, banish from his countenance

COSTUMES WORN AT THE INAUGURATION BALL. [1]

that almost painfully sad thoughtfulness of expression, more frequently seen afterward, when the cares of State had marred his brow with deeper furrows. Of all that company, he was the most honored and the most burdened; and with the pageantry of that Inauguration Day and that Inauguration Ball, ended, for him, the poetry of his Administration. Thereafter his life was spent in the sober prose of dutiful endeavor to save and redeem the nation.

On the day after Mr. Lincoln's inauguration, the Senate, in extraordinary session, confirmed his appointments of Cabinet ministers. He had chosen for Secretary of State, William H. Seward, of New York; for Secretary of the Treasury, Salmon P. Chase, of Ohio; for Secretary of War, Simon Cameron, of Pennsylvania; for Secretary of the Navy, Gideon Welles, of Connecticut; for Secretary of the Interior, Caleb Smith, of Indiana; for Postmaster-General, Montgomery Blair, of Maryland; and for Attorney-General, Edward Bates, of Missouri.[2] Mr. Seward had been a prominent candidate for a nomination for the Presidency, at Chicago. On that account,

---

[1] The dress of one of the ladies was thus described by an eye-witness:—"The robe was of white illusion, décolleté, puffed sleeves, with six flounces, embroidered with cherry silk; an overskirt of cherry satin, looped up with clusters of white roses; a pointed waist of same, edged with a quilling of white satin; head-dress, a chaplet of ivy; ornaments, diamonds and opals."

[2] See the Frontispiece to this volume. The picture represents the President and his Cabinet, with General Scott, in consultation concerning military affairs. I have endeavored to give this picture an historic value, by presenting not only a correct portraiture of the men, but also of the room in which the meetings of the Cabinet were held, in the White House. The drawing of the room was made for me, with great accuracy, by Mr. C. K. Stellwagen, of the Ordnance Department, in October, 1864, and the grouping of the figures by Mr. Schuselle, an accomplished artist of Philadelphia. This council chamber of the Executive is on the southern side of the White House, overlooking the public grounds, the Smithsonian Institute, the unfinished Washington Monument, and the Potomac River. The Washington Monument is seen, in the picture, through one of the windows.

and because of his known eminent ability, and unswerving fidelity to his country and the principles of justice and right, his appointment was acceptable to all loyal people, and especially to his political friends. How well he performed the very important and delicate duties of prime minister during the four succeeding years, let the recorded diplomacy of the Republic for that time answer.

The ship of State was now fairly launched upon the tide under the guidance of the new pilot. It was evident that terribly stormy seas were before it. Premonitions of tempests were darkening the air, alarming the timid, and filling the hearts of the brave with anxiety. There was peril on every side.

The President's Inaugural Address, calm, dignified, conciliatory even to pathos in tone, clear in its enunciation of the great truths concerning the political construction and character of the nation, and as clear in its annunciation of the duties and determination of the Chief Magistrate, satisfied the loyal people of the country everywhere. It promised peace, security, and justice to every law-abiding citizen and community. It was a pledge that the integrity of the territory of the Republic should be maintained, and its laws executed. It denied the existence of State *supremacy*, but not of State *rights*. It denied the right of secession, and plainly told the advocates of such pretended right that to attempt it would be an essay at criminal revolution, that would be resisted with all the powers of the Government. It was denounced by the conspirators and their partisans, South and North, as belligerent—as threatening war, because it contemplated the " coercion " of law-breakers into submission.[1] It was mutilated and interpolated while passing through the newspapers in the interest of the conspirators; and the

---

[1] That conspicuous counterfeit of a statesman, Senator Wigfall, whose mendacity and cowardice at Fort Sumter, a month later, were as prominent as his vulgarity and bluster in Congress, kept his seat in the Senate, in defiance of all decency; and on the last days of its session uttered his treasonable words more insolently than ever. He took it upon himself to treat the Inaugural with scorn. " It is easy to talk about enforcing the laws, and holding, occupying, and possessing the forts," he said. " When you come to do this, bayonets, and not words, must settle the question. And he would here say, that Fort Pickens and the Administration will soon be forced to construe the Inaugural. Forts Moultrie, and Johnston, and Castle Pinckney are in possession of the Confederate States; but the confederated States will not leave Fort Sumter in possession of the Federal Government. . . . Seven Southern States have formed a confederation, and to tell them, as the President has done, that the acts of secession are no more than blank paper, is an insult." He repeated: "There is no Union left; the seceded States will never surely come back under any circumstances. They will not live under this Administration. Withdraw your troops. Make no attempt to collect tribute, and enter into a treaty with those States. Do this, and you will have peace. Send your flag of thirty-four stars thither, and it will be fired into, and war will ensue. Divide the public property; make a fair assessment of the public debt; or will you sit stupidly and idly till there shall be a conflict of arms, because you cannot compromise with traitors? Let the remaining States reform their government, and if it is acceptable, the Confederacy will enter into a treaty of commerce and amity with them. If you want peace, you shall have it. If war, you shall have it. The time for platforms and demagogism has passed. Treat with the Confederate States as independent, and you will have peace. Treat with them as States of this Union, and you will have war. Mr. Lincoln has to remove the troops from Forts Pickens and Sumter, or they will be removed for him. He has to collect the revenue at Charleston, Savannah, and New Orleans, or it will be collected for him. If he attempts to do so, resistance will be made. It is useless to blind your eyes. No compromise or amendment to the Constitution, no arrangement you may enter into, will satisfy the South, unless you recognize slaves as property, and protect it as any other species of property."

Senator Douglas reminded Wigfall that, according to his own doctrine, he was " a foreigner," and yet he retained his seat in the Senate of the United States. The insolent conspirator replied:—" It was because he had no official information that Texas has abolished the office of United States Senator. When he should be so notified, he would file a notice of his withdrawal at the desk; and if, after being so informed, his name should continue to be called, he should answer to it, if it suited his convenience; and if called upon to vote, he would probably give his reasons for voting, and regard this as a very respectable public meeting."

misled and excited people were made to believe that a war for subjugation was about to be waged against them. "It is our wisest policy," said the satanic *Charleston Mercury*, "to accept it as a declaration of war;" and urged its readers not to waste time in thinking, but to raise the arm of resistance immediately. The conspirators were most afraid of deliberation. They would not allow the people to reflect, but hurried them on, willing or unwilling, into open armed rebellion. "To carry out his threats," they said, "not only on the forts now in possession of the Federal Government to be held, but fortresses along the coast, and owned [by virtue of unlawful seizure] by the Confederate States Government, are to be 'possessed' and 'held' by the United States Government. This warns us that our course now must be entirely one of policy and war strategy."[1] A member (Mr. Harvie, of Amelia) of the politicians' convention in Virginia, then in session in Richmond, introduced a resolution declaring that it was Mr. Lincoln's purpose to plunge the country into civil war by "coercive policy," and asked the Legislature to take measures for resistance; and some were so indiscreet as to rejoice because the Inaugural seemed to give a pretext for rebellion. Every thing that unholy ambition and malice could devise was used to distort the plain meaning of the address, and inflame the passions of the people against those of the Free-labor States.[2] It was falsely asserted that it breathed hostility to the *people* of the Slave-labor States, when it was only hostile to the conspirators and their friends. For that reason they sought to blind and mislead the people; and they illustrated the truth, that

"No rogue e'er felt the halter draw
With good opinion of the law."

The first business of the President and his Cabinet was to inform themselves about the condition of public affairs, the resources of the Government, and the powers at its command. They first turned to the Treasury Department, and there found, under the skillful management of Secretary Dix, cheerful promises, because of evidences of renewed public confidence. The national debt was something more than sixty millions of dollars, and was slowly increasing, because of the necessity for loans. After the Presidential election, in November, 1860, as we have seen, the public inquietude and the dishonest operations of Secretary Cobb caused much distrust among capitalists, and they were loth to buy Government stocks. Of a loan of twenty millions of dollars, authorized by Congress in June,[a] one-half of it was asked for in October. It was readily subscribed for, but only a little more than seven millions of dollars were paid in. A few days after Cobb left the Treasury, Congress authorized the issue of treasury notes[b] to the amount of ten millions of dollars, payable in one year, at the lowest rates of interest offered. Of these, five millions of dollars were offered on the 28th of December.

[a] 1860.

[b] December 14.

[1] *Charleston Mercury*, March 6, 1861.
[2] The Richmond newspapers were specially incendiary. "No action of our Convention can now maintain the peace, and Virginia must fight," said the *Enquirer*. "Every Border State ought to go out within twenty-four hours," said the *Despatch*. "The positions taken are a declaration of war, laying down doctrines which would reduce the Southern section to the unquestioned dominion of the North, as a section," said the *Sentinel*. Even the conservative *Whig* blazed with indignation. "The policy indicated toward the seceding States will meet with stern, unyielding resistance by the united South," said this professedly Union paper.

The buoyancy of feeling in financial circles, after the retirement of Cobb, had now given way to temporary despondency because of a want of confidence in Thomas, his immediate successor, and the robbery of the Indian Trust-Fund.[1] There were bids for only five hundred thousand dollars. The semi-annual interest on the national debt would be due on the first of January, and the Government would be greatly embarrassed. Loyal bankers stepped forward, and took a sufficient quantity of the treasury notes to relieve the pressing wants of the Government. Nothing was now needed to inspire capitalists with confidence but the appointment of General Dix to the head of the Treasury, which was made soon afterward.[a] When he offered the remaining five millions of dollars of the author-
[a] January 11, 1861. ized loan, it was readily taken, but at the high average rate of interest of ten and five-eighths per centum.

Congress perceived the necessity for making provision for strengthening the Government financially. By far the larger proportion of all the expenses of the Government, from its foundation, had been paid from customs' revenue. To this source of supply the National Legislature now directed their attention, and the tariff was revised so that it would produce a much larger revenue. An act passed Congress on the 2d of March, to go into effect on the 1st of April, which restored the highest protective character to the tariff. A bill was also passed on the 8th of February, authorizing a loan of twenty-five millions of dollars, to bear six per cent. interest, to run not less than ten, nor more than twenty years, the stock to be sold to the highest bidder. The Secretary offered eight millions of dollars of this stock on the 27th of February, when there were bids to the amount of fourteen millions three hundred and fifty-five thousand dollars, ranging from seventy-five to ninety-six. All bids below ninety were refused. The new tariff bill, and the faith in the Government shown by the eagerness to lend money on its securities, were the cheerful promises found in the Treasury Department.

The President and his Cabinet turned to the Army and Navy, and saw little in that direction to encourage them. The total regular force was sixteen thousand men, and these were principally in the Western States and Territories, guarding the frontier settlers against the Indians. The forts and arsenals on the seaboard, especially those within the Slave-labor States, were so weakly manned, or really not manned at all, that they became an easy prey to the insurgents. The consequence was, that they were seized; and when the new Administration came into power, of all the fortifications within the Slave-labor States, only Fortress Monroe, and Forts Jefferson, Taylor, and Pickens, remained in possession of the Government. The seized forts were sixteen in number.[2] They had cost the Government about seven millions of dollars, and bore an aggregate of one thousand two hundred and twenty-six guns. All the arsenals in the Cotton-growing States had been seized. That at Little Rock, the capital of the State of

---

[1] See page 144.

[2] The following are the names and locations of the seized forts:—*Pulaski* and *Jackson*, at Savannah; *Morgan* and *Gaines*, at Mobile; *Macon*, at Beaufort, North Carolina; *Caswell*, at Oak Island, North Carolina; *Moultrie* and *Castle Pinckney*, at Charleston; *St. Philip*, *Jackson*, *Pike*, *Macomb*, and *Livingston*, in Louisiana; and *McRee*, *Barrancas*, and a *redoubt* in Florida.

Arkansas, was taken possession of by the militia of that State, under the direction of the disloyal Governor Rector, on the 5th of February. They came from Helena, and readily obtained the Governor's sanction to the movement.   Far-off Fort Kearney, on Grand Island, in the Platte River,

ARSENAL AT LITTLE ROCK.

was also seized on the 19th of February, and a Palmetto flag was raised over it.   It was soon retaken by the Union men.

The little Navy of the United States, like the Army, had been placed far beyond the reach of the Government for immediate use.   The total number of vessels of all classes belonging to the Navy was ninety, carrying or designed to carry two thousand four hundred and fifteen guns.   Of this number, only forty-two were in commission.   Twenty-eight ships, bearing in the aggregate eight hundred and seventy-four guns, were lying in ports, dismantled, and none of them could be made ready for sea in less than several weeks' time; some of them would require at least six months.   The most of those in commission had been sent to distant seas; and the entire available force for the defense of the whole Atlantic coast of the Republic was the *Brooklyn*, of twenty-five guns, and the store-ship *Relief*, of two guns.   The *Brooklyn* drew too much water to enter Charleston harbor, where war had been commenced, with safety; and the *Relief* had been ordered to the coast of Africa with stores for the squadron there.   Many of the officers of the Navy were born in Slave-labor States, and a large number of them abandoned their flag at this critical moment.   No less than sixty of them, including eleven at the Naval Academy at Annapolis, had resigned their commissions.

Such was the utterly powerless condition of the Navy to assist in the preservation of the life of the Republic, when Isaac Toucey, of Connecticut, for four years at the head of the Navy Department, handed the seals of his office to his successor, Gideon Welles, of the same State.   The amazing fact stands upon official record, that Mr. Buchanan's Secretaries of War and of the Navy had so disposed the available military forces of the Republic that it could not command their services at the critical moment when the assassin was preparing to strike it a deadly blow.

The public offices were found to be swarming with disloyal men.   It was difficult to decide as to who were or were not trustworthy.   It was necessary for the President to have proper instruments to work with; and for a month after his inauguration, he was busily engaged in relieving the Government of unfaithful servants, and supplying their places with true men. So intent was he upon the thorough performance of this work before he should put forth the arm of power to maintain the laws and keep down

rising rebellion, that many of his best friends were filled with apprehensions. They thought they discovered signs of that weakness which had characterized the late Administration, and began to seriously doubt the ability of the Republic to preserve its own life. They did not know the man. Like a prudent warrior of old, he was unwilling to go out to battle before he should prove his armor. He would be sure of the temper of his blade before he unsheathed it. Mr. Lincoln wisely strengthened the Executive arm, by calling to its aid loyal men, before he ventured to speak out with authority.

ISAAC TOUCEY.

The rebellion could not be put down by proclamations, unless the insurgents saw behind them the invincible power of the State, ready to be wielded by the President with trusty instrumentalities.

The firmness of the new Administration was soon put upon its trial. We have already observed that three Commissioners were appointed by the confederated conspirators at Montgomery to proceed to Washington, for the alleged purpose of treating with the National Government upon various

topics of mutual interest, that there might be a "settlement of all questions of disagreement between the Government of the United States and that of the Confederate States, upon principles of right, justice, equity, and good faith."[1] Two of these Commissioners (John Forsyth, of Alabama, who had been a Minister of the United States in Mexico a few years before, and Martin J. Crawford, of Georgia, a member of Congress from that State) arrived in Washington on the 5th of March. On the 11th they made a formal application, through "a distinguished Senator," for an unofficial interview with the Secretary of State. It

MARTIN J. CRAWFORD.

was declined, and on the 13th they sent to the Secretary a sealed communication, in which they set forth the object of their mission, and asked the appointment of an early day on which to present their credentials to the President.[2]

---

[1] See page 264.
[2] See Secretary Seward's Memorandum for Messrs. Forsyth and Crawford, dated March 15, 1861.

This first attempt of the conspirators adroitly to win for the so-called government of the Confederated States the solid advantage of a recognition of inherent sovereignty, was met by Mr. Seward with his accustomed suavity of manner and unanswerable logic. He told them, not in a letter, for he would hold no such communication with them, but in a Memorandum, in pleasant phrases and explanatory sentences, that he was not at liberty to know them in any other character than that of citizens of the Republic. The Commissioners had said : "Seven States of the late Federal Union having, in the exercise of the inherent right of every free people to change or reform their political institutions, and through conventions of their people, withdrawn from the United States, and resumed the attributes of sovereign power delegated to it, have formed a government of their own. The Confederate States constitute an independent nation *de facto* and *de jure*, and possess a government perfect in all its parts, and endowed with all the means of self-support."

"The Secretary of State," Mr. Seward replied in his Memorandum,[a] "frankly confesses that he understands the events which have recently occurred, and the condition of public affairs which ⁣[a] March 15, 1861. actually exists in the part of the Union to which his attention has thus been directed, very differently from the aspect in which they are presented by Messrs. Forsyth and Crawford. He sees in them, not a rightful and accomplished revolution, and an independent nation, with an established government, but rather a perversion of a temporary and partisan excitement to the inconsiderate purposes of an unjustifiable and unconstitutional aggression upon the rights and authority vested in the Federal Government, and hitherto benignly exercised, as from their very nature they always must be so exercised, for the maintenance of the Union, the preservation of Liberty, and the security, peace, welfare, happiness, and aggrandizement of the American people. The Secretary of State, therefore, avows to Messrs. Forsyth and Crawford that he looks patiently, but confidently, to the cure of evils which have resulted from proceedings so unnecessary, so unwise, so unusual, and so unnatural—not to irregular negotiations, having in view new and untried relations with agencies unknown to, and acting in derogation of, the Constitution and laws, but to regular and considerate action of the people of those States, in co-operation with their brethren in the other States, through the Congress of the United States; and such extraordinary conventions, if there shall be need thereof, as the Federal Constitution contemplates and authorizes to be assembled." Mr. Seward then referred them to the President's Inaugural Message, saying that, "guided by the principles therein announced," he could not admit that any States had withdrawn from the Union, or that they could do so, excepting with the consent of the people of the United States, given through a National Convention. Therefore, the so-called "Confederate States" were not a foreign power, "with whom diplomatic relations ought to be established," and that he could not "recognize them as diplomatic agents, or hold correspondence or other communication with them."

Thus, at the outset, both in the Inaugural Address, and in the Memorandum of the Secretary of State for the representatives of the conspirators, the Government took the broad national ground that secession was an impossibility; that no State, as a State, had seceded or could secede; that the National Government is a unit, and that it knows no States in the exercise of its executive authority, but deals only with the individuals of the people; therefore the "coercing of a State" was an impossibility, the contemplation of it an absurdity, and the assertion of its possibility a positive misrepresentation. And during the entire war that ensued, the Government acted upon the plain fact, declared by the very nature of the construction of the nation, that no State, as a State, was at any time in insurrection or rebellion, but only certain persons in certain States were acting in open defiance of the Law and of the Constitution. Individual citizens, not *States*, any more than counties or towns, were held amenable to the outraged Constitution and laws.[1]

Mr. Seward's Memorandum remained uncalled for and undelivered for twenty-three days, when, on the 8th of April, J. F. Pickett, Secretary of the Commissioners, applied for it.[2] The Commissioners explained the delay in seeking a reply to their note, by asserting that they had been assured by "a person occupying a high official station in the Government," and who, they believed, was speaking by authority, that Fort Sumter would soon be evacuated, and that there would be no change in the relations of Fort Pickens to the "Confederacy," prejudicial to the "new government." They were also informed, they said, on the 1st of April, that an attempt might be made to send provisions to Fort Sumter, but nothing was said about re-enforcing the garrison. Governor Pickens, they understood, was to be informed before any attempt to send supplies should be made. With the belief that no hostile act would be undertaken unheralded, they had consented to wait, that they might secure the great object of their mission, namely, "a peaceful solution of existing complications."

The "person occupying a high official station" was John A. Campbell, a judge of the Supreme Court of the United States, who soon afterward resigned his seat on the bench, and joined the conspirators in their unholy work. He had received from Secretary Seward such assurances of peaceful intentions on the part of the Government, that on the day when the Secretary wrote his Memorandum for the Commissioners, Judge Campbell advised them not to press the matter of their mission. "I feel an entire confidence," he said, "that an immediate demand for an answer to your communication will be productive of evil and not of good." They acted upon his advice, and waited. It was from Judge Campbell that they received from Mr. Seward, on the 1st of April, the assurance that he was "satisfied that the Government would not undertake to supply Fort Sumter without giving notice to Governor Pickens." When, on the 8th, they were informed that

---

[1] At Indianapolis, while on his way to Washington, Mr. Lincoln asked, significantly:—"In what consists the special sacredness of a State? I speak of that assumed primary right of a State to rule all which is *less* than itself, and ruin all which is greater than itself. If a State and a county, in a given case, should be equal in extent of territory and equal in number of inhabitants, in what, as a matter of principle, is the State better than the county? Would an exchange of *names* be an exchange of *rights*, upon principle? On what rightful principle may a State, being not more than one-fiftieth part of the Nation in soil and population, break up the Nation, and then coerce a proportionably larger subdivision of itself, in the most arbitrary way? What mysterious right to play tyrant is conferred on a district of country, with its people, by merely calling it a State?"

[2] The original Memorandum is in the office of the Secretary of State. On it is an indorsement, setting forth that its delivery was delayed by the consent of the "Commissioners," and that, when called for, a verified copy was delivered to their Secretary.

Governor Pickens had been so notified, they sent for the Secretary's reply, and received the Memorandum alluded to; and on the 9th they returned a response characteristic of the cause which they represented. It was disingenuous, boastful, and menacing. They spoke of their government—the band of usurpers at Montgomery—as one seeking the good of the *people*, who (they falsely alleged) "had intrusted them with power, in the spirit of humanity, of the Christian civilization of the age," *et cætera;* and who, among its first acts, had sent to the Government of the United States, which they were attempting to revolutionize, the olive-branch of peace.

The Commissioners proceeded to give the Secretary a lecture, composed of a curious compound of truth, untruth, prophecy, and sophistry. "Persistently wedded," they said, "to those fatal theories of construction of the Federal Constitution always rejected by the statesmen of the South, and adhered to by those of the Administration school, until they have produced their natural and often-predicted result of the destruction of the Union, under which we might have continued to live happily and gloriously together, had the spirit of the ancestry who framed the common Constitution animated the hearts of all their sons, you now, with a persistence untaught and uncured by the ruin which has been wrought, refuse to recognize the great fact presented to you of a complete and successful revolution; you close your eyes to the existence of the government founded upon it, and ignore the high duties of moderation and humanity which attach to you in dealing with this great fact. Had you met these issues with the frankness and manliness with which the undersigned were instructed to present them to you and treat them, the undersigned had not now the melancholy duty to return home and tell their government and their countrymen that their earnest and ceaseless efforts in behalf of peace had been futile, and that the Government of the United States meant to subjugate them by force of arms. Whatever may be the result, impartial history will record the innocence of the Government of the Confederate States, and place the responsibility of the blood and mourning that may ensue upon those who have denied the great fundamental doctrine of American liberty, that 'governments derive their just powers from the consent of the governed;' and who have set naval and land armaments in motion to subject the people of one portion of the land to the will of another portion. That it can never be done while a freeman survives in the Confederate States to wield a weapon, the undersigned appeal to past history to prove. *   *   *   *   *   *   *   *

"It is proper, however, to advise you, that it were well to dismiss the hopes you seem to entertain that, by any of the modes indicated, the people of the Confederate States will ever be brought to submit to the authority of the Government of the United States. You are dealing with delusions, too, when you seek to separate our people from our government, and to characterize the deliberate sovereign act of the people as a 'perversion of a temporary and partisan excitement.' If you cherish these dreams you will be awakened from them, and find them as unreal and unsubstantial as others in which you have recently indulged. The undersigned would omit the performance of an obvious duty, were they to fail to make known to the Government of the United States, that the people of the Confederate States have declared their independence with a full knowledge of all the responsibilities of that act, and with as firm a determination to maintain it by all the means with which Nature has endowed them, as that which sustained their fathers when they threw off the authority of the British crown.[1] . . . The undersigned, in behalf of their government and people, accept the gage of battle thus thrown down to them; and, appealing to God and the judgment of mankind for the righteousness of their cause, the people of the Confederate States will defend their liberties to the last against this flagrant and open attempt at their subjugation to sectional power.'' In conclusion, these bold conspirators offended truth and insulted the Chief Magistrate by saying, it was clear "that Mr. Lincoln had determined to appeal to the sword, to reduce the people of the Confederate States to the will of the section or party whose President he was."

In a memorandum of a few lines, on the 10th of April the Secretary of State acknowledged the receipt of this communication, and declined to make a reply. So ended the first attempt of the so-called Government of the "Confederate States of America" to hold diplomatic intercourse with the National Government, whose forbearance they had reason to admire. The Commissioners left Washington on the morning of the 11th.

In their communication, Messrs. Forsyth and Crawford recited the assurances concerning Fort Sumter which they had received from the Secretary of State through Judge Campbell, and charged the Administration with bad faith, because, early in April, it attempted to send supplies to the Fort. Judge Campbell, finding himself suspected of treachery, or at best of duplicity, by his friends at Montgomery, hastened, on the day after the attack on Fort Sumter, to exculpate himself by a letter to the Secretary of State, intended for publication. "On the 7th of April," he said, "I addressed you a letter on the subject of the alarm that the preparations by the Government had created, and asked you if the assurances I had given were well or ill founded in respect to Sumter. Your reply was:—'Faith, as to Sumter, fully kept—wait and see.' In the morning's paper I read:—'An authorized messenger from President Lincoln informed Governor Pickens and General Beauregard that provisions will be sent to Fort Sumter—peaceably, or otherwise by force.' This was on the 8th, at Charleston, the day following your last assurance, and is the evidence of the faith I was invited to *wait* for and *see*. In the same paper, I read that intercepted dispatches disclosed the fact that Mr. Fox, who had been allowed to visit Major Anderson, on the pledge that his purpose was pacific, employed his opportunity to devise a plan for supplying the fort by force, and that this plan had been adopted by the Washington Government, and was in process of execution. My recollection of the date of Mr. Fox's visit carries it to a day in March. I learn he is a near connection of a member of the Cabinet. My connection with the Commissioners and yourself was superinduced by a conversation with Justice Nelson. He informed me of your strong disposition in favor of peace, and that you were pressed with a demand of the Commissioners of the Confederate States for a reply to their first letter, and that you desired to avoid it at that time."

---

[1] How cruelly the *people* were kept silent on the subject of the formation of an independent government, the careful reader of these pages may easily comprehend.

Judge Campbell then mentioned his interview with the Secretary, and the pledge given for the evacuation of Sumter, as the ground of his advice to the Commissioners to wait, and added :—"The Commissioners who received those communications conclude they have been abused and overreached. The Montgomery Government holds the same opinion. . . . I think no candid man, who will read over what I have written, and consider for a moment what is going on at Sumter, but will agree that the equivocating conduct of the Administration, as measured and interpreted in connection with these promises, is the proximate cause of the great calamity. I have a profound conviction that the telegrams of the 8th of April, of General Beauregard, and of the 10th of April, of General Walker, the Secretary of War, can be referred to nothing else than their belief that there has been systematic duplicity practiced on them, through me.[1] It is under an oppressive sense of the weight of this responsibility that I submit to you these things for your explanation." The Secretary did not reply to this letter, nor to another note, again asking for explanations, written on the 20th of April.

The correspondence of the Commissioners, and the letter of Judge Campbell to Secretary Seward, were soon published to the world, and made an unfavorable impression concerning the dignity and good faith of the Government. The Commissioners disingenuously affected to be ignorant of the reason why an answer was not immediately given by the Secretary to their letter, when, as we have seen, they had made arrangements themselves with Campbell, their friend and adviser, to delay asking for it. Campbell's letter to the Secretary was also unnoticed ; and the charges, actual and implied, of bad faith on the part of the Government, went out uncontradicted. The friends of the conspirators everywhere denounced the Administration as faithless. It was held up to scorn by the organs of the ruling classes in England and on the Continent; and its friends, in the absence of explanations, were unable to defend it with success. State policy, which allowed the President to give a partial explanation three months later,[2] commanded silence at that time. The pledges concerning Sumter, and the charge that they had been violated by the Government, were obscured in mystery, and month after month the Opposition pointed significantly to the seeming bad faith of the Secretary of State. The following facts, communicated to the author of this work, semi-officially, in September, 1864, may, in connection with Mr. Lincoln's Message, just referred to, make it plain that he and his advisers acted in good faith, and that Mr. Seward's assurances were honestly given :—

On the 4th of March, the day when Mr. Lincoln was inaugurated, a

---

[1] The following are the telegraphic dispatches alluded to :—

"CHARLESTON, April 8, 1861.

"To L. P. WALKER, *Secretary of War* :—

"An authorized message from President Lincoln just informed Governor Pickens and myself that provisions will be sent to Fort Sumter peaceably, or otherwise by force. G. T. BEAUREGARD."

"MONTGOMERY, April 10, 1861.

"General G. T. BEAUREGARD:—

"If you have no doubt as to the authorized character of the agent who communicated to you the instructions of the Washington Government to supply Fort Sumter by force, you will at once demand its evacuation ; and if this is refused, proceed, in such manner as you may determine, to reduce it. "L. P. WALKER."

[2] See the President's Message to Congress, July 4, 1861, sixth and seventh paragraphs.

letter was received at the War Department from Major Anderson, dated the 28th of February,[a] in which that officer expressed an opinion that re-enforcements " could not be thrown into Fort Sumter within the time for his relief, rendered necessary by the limited supply of provisions, and with a view of holding possession of the same, with a force of less than twenty thousand good and well-disciplined men."[1] This letter was laid before the President and his Cabinet on the 5th, and the first question of importance which that council was called upon to decide was, whether Fort Sumter should be surrendered to the demands of the South Carolina authorities. General Scott was called into the council,[2] and he concurred in opinion with Major Anderson. No sufficient force was then at the control of the Government, nor could they be raised and taken to the ground before Anderson's supplies would be exhausted. In a military point of view, the Administration was reduced to the simple duty of getting the garrison safely out of the fort.

[a] 1861.

Mr. Lincoln, governed by the advice of General Scott, who had been earnest some weeks earlier, while there was yet time, for re-enforcing the fort, was in favor of abandoning any further attempts to hold it. Every member of his Cabinet but two—anxious for peace, and believing further efforts to hold Sumter would be useless, and perhaps mischievous—coincided with the views of the President and of General Scott. Those members were Messrs. Chase and Blair. Finding himself alone in support of the idea that the fort must be held at all hazards, Mr. Blair sent[b] for his kinsman by marriage, Gustavus V. Fox, who had resigned his commission of lieutenant in the Navy several years before.

[b] March 12.

Mr. Fox had already, through Secretary Holt, presented[c] to Mr. Buchanan a plan for provisioning and re-enforcing the garrison of Sumter, which was highly approved by General Scott. This plan, which Mr. Blair now wished to lay before President Lincoln, proposed the preparation of necessary supplies in packages of portable form; to appear off Charleston bar with them and the troops in a large ocean steamer; to have three or four men-of-war as a protecting force; to have the steamer accompanied by three fast New York tug-boats, and, during the night, to send in the supplies and troops in these tugs, or in launches, as should seem best, after arrival and examination. The channel between Cummings's Point and Fort Moultrie is one mile and one-third in width; and this plan was based on the feasibility of passing the line of fire, from batteries that commanded this channel, with impunity. Experience has taught us that it was so. Farragut's successes during the late war were achieved by action based upon the same plan; and the impunity with which vessels passed up and down the Potomac, after the insurgents had established batteries upon its banks, shows that the plan was feasible.

[c] January 7.

The President was strongly urged to give up Fort Sumter for the sake of peace; but the Postmaster-General argued against it, in opposition to the opinions of the General-in-Chief and other military men, with great pertinacity. Aided by the practical suggestions of Mr. Fox, he succeeded in

---

[1] Anderson's MS. Letter-book. President Lincoln's Message, July 4, 1861.
[2] See the Frontispiece of this volume.

convincing the President of the feasibility of the plan, and that sound policy required that the attempt should be made, whether it should succeed or not. " It was believed," as the President said in his Message, already referred to,[a] " that to abandon that position, under the circum- stances, would be utterly ruinous; that the *necessity* under which [a] July 4, 1861. it was done would not be fully understood; that by many it would be con- strued as a part of a *voluntary* policy ; that at home it would discourage the friends of the Union, embolden its adversaries, and go far to insure to the latter a recognition abroad; that, in fact, it would be our national destruction commenced."

Although satisfied of the feasibility and the necessity of strengthening Major Anderson, by sending him provisions and men, the President, extremely anxious for peace and reconciliation, hesitated to make any movement that might lead to collision with the insurgents. He favored Mr. Fox's propo- sitions, and that gentleman, with the approval of the Secretary of War and General Scott, visited Charleston harbor. In company with Captain Hartstene, of the Navy, who had joined the insurgents, he visited Fort Sumter on the 21st of March, by permission of Governor Pickens,[1] and ascer- tained that Major Anderson had provisions sufficient for his command until the 15th of April;[2] and it was understood between them that he must sur- render or evacuate the fort at noon on that day. Mr. Fox gave him no assurances, such as Judge Campbell mentioned, of relief, nor any information of a plan for that purpose.

On his return to Washington, Mr. Fox reported to the President that any attempt to succor Major Anderson must be made before the middle of April. The President was perplexed. He yearned for peace, if it could be had without dishonor. The Virginia Convention was then in session, and he sent for one of the prominent members of that body, known to be a professed Union man, and assured him that if the Convention would adjourn instead of staying in session, menacing the Government, he would immediately direct Major Anderson to evacuate Sumter. Had the Virginia politicians desired peace, this reasonable request would have been complied with. On the con- trary, this professed Virginia Unionist replied: " The United States must instantly evacuate Fort Sumter and Fort Pickens, and give assurances that no attempts shall be made to collect revenue in Southern ports." This was a demand, in effect, for the President to recognize the band of conspirators at Montgomery as a government possessed of sovereign powers.

Mr. Lincoln was now satisfied that a temporizing policy would not do. He had said in a little speech to the New Jersey Legislature,[b] [b] February 1. when on his way to Washington, as we have observed, " it may be necessary to put the foot down firmly." That necessity now pre- sented itself, and the President did " put the foot down firmly." Over- ruling the persistent objections of the General-in-Chief, and other military

---

[1] On that occasion, Mr. Fox carried a letter to Governor Pickens from General Scott, in compliance with orders from the President. Pickens sent the following note to Major Anderson:—
 " I have permitted Mr. Fox and Captain Hartstene to go to you under peculiar circumstances, and I deeply regret General Scott could not have been more formal to me, as you well know I have been in a peculiar position for months here, and I do this now because I confide in you as a gentleman of honor."
[2] Lieutenant Norman J. Hall, one of Anderson's trusty men, furnished Mr. Fox with a memorandum of supplies in Fort Sumter.

authorities, and regarding the affair more as a naval than as a military operation, he at once sent for Mr. Fox, and verbally authorized him[a]
[a] March 29. to fit out an expedition for the relief of Sumter, according to that
gentleman's plan.   The written order for that service was not given until the
afternoon of the 4th of April, when the President informed Fox that, in order
that "faith as to Sumter" might be kept, he should send a messenger at once
to Charleston, to inform Governor Pickens that he was about to forward provisions, only, to the garrison, and that if these supplies should be allowed to
enter, no more troops would be sent there.   This was done.   Colonel Lamon
(afterward marshal of the District of Columbia) was sent as a special messenger to Governor Pickens, who was also informed that supplies must go
into Sumter peaceably, if possible, if not, by force, as the Governor might
choose.

Mr. Fox arrived in the city of New York the second time, on his important
errand, on the evening of the 5th of April, and delivered to Colonel H. L.
Scott, of the staff of the General-in-Chief, a copy of his instructions.   That
officer ridiculed the idea of relieving Sumter, and stood as an obstacle in the
way as far as possible.   The plan was highly approved by Commodores
Stewart and Stringham; and, as Mr. Fox's orders were imperative, he
performed his duty in spite of all official detentions, and with that profes-

sional skill, untiring industry, and in-
domitable energy which, as Assistant
Secretary of the Navy, he displayed
throughout the entire war that ensued,
he fitted out the expedition (having
made some previous preparations)
within the space of forty-eight hours.
He sailed on the morning of the 9th,
with two hundred recruits, in the
steamer *Baltic*, Captain Fletcher.—
The entire relief squadron consisted of
that vessel, the United States ships
Powhatan, *Pawnee*, *Pocahontas*, and
Harriet Lane, and the tugs *Yankee*,
Uncle Ben, and *Freeborn;* and all of
them were ordered to rendezvous off

GUSTAVUS VASA FOX.

Charleston.[1]   The frigate *Powhatan*
bore the senior naval officer of the expedition, and men sufficient to man
the boats for the relief party.

Soon after leaving New York, the expedition encountered a heavy storm.
One of the tugs (the *Freeborn*) was driven back; a second (*Uncle Ben*) put
into Wilmington, North Carolina, and was captured by the insurgents there;
and the third, losing her smoke-stack, was not able to reach Charleston bar
until it was too late.   The *Powhatan*[2] was also lost to the expedition.

---

[1] The frigate *Powhatan*, Captain Mercer, left New York on the 6th of April.   The *Pawnee*, Commodore
Rowan, left Norfolk on the 9th, and the *Pocahontas*, Captain Gillis, on the 10th.   The revenue cutter *Harriet
Lane*, Captain Faunce, left the harbor of New York on the 8th, in company with the tug *Yankee*.   The *Free-
born* and *Uncle Ben* left on the previous day.   The *Yankee* was fitted to throw hot water.

[2] The energy displayed in getting the *Powhatan* ready for sea was wonderful.   She had been put out of

While passing down New York Bay, Captain Meigs, who was Quartermaster-General during the war, and Lieutenant (afterward Rear-Admiral) Porter went on board of her, with an order from the President to take any man-of-war they might select and proceed immediately with her crew to Pensacola. Under this order they took possession of and sailed away in the flag-ship of the relief expedition.[1]

The *Baltic* reached Charleston bar on the morning of the 12th, just as the insurgents opened fire on Fort Sumter. The *Pawnee* and the *Harriet Lane* were already there, with orders to report to the *Powhatan*, but she had gone to Fort Pickens, then, like Fort Sumter, threatened by armed insurgents. All day long the ocean and Charleston harbor were swept by a storm. A heavy sea was rolling inward, and there were no signs of abatement until the morning of the 13th. It was then determined to seize a schooner lying at anchor near, load her with provisions, and take her to Fort Sumter the following night. She was accordingly prepared, but before the time for her departure, Fort Sumter was in the hands of the insurgents. How that happened will be related in the next chapter.

It was fortunate for the Republic that the effort to relieve Major Anderson was made at that time. It gave practical assurances to the country that the new Administration would employ all its energies in support of the Constitution and the laws; and it also gave to the Government one whose services can only be appreciated by those who know their amount and value. The judgment and energy displayed by Mr. Fox caused him to be appointed Assistant Secretary of the Navy. He was then in the prime of life, and endowed with great physical endurance. As the lieutenant of Secretary Welles, invested with wide discretionary powers, he was to the Navy what the General-in-Chief is to the Army.

---

commission, and was "lying up," and her crew were on the receiving-ship *North Carolina*. She was put into commission at the Brooklyn Navy Yard, and sent to sea in the space of three days.

[1] The order (issued by the President) changing the destination of the *Powhatan* did not pass through the Navy Department, or it would have been arrested there. It was calculated to prevent the success of Fox's expedition, because the *Powhatan* carried the sailors and launches provided for the landing of supplies and re-enforcements. The President was not aware of this when he signed the order. In the whole matter there was nothing more serious than a blunder, which was caused by the secrecy with which two expeditions were simultaneously fitted out, namely, one for the relief of Fort Sumter, and the other for the relief of Fort Pickens. Mr. Fox was not aware of the change in the destination of the *Powhatan* until he arrived off Charleston bar.

CHAPTER XIII.

THE SIEGE AND EVACUATION OF FORT SUMTER.

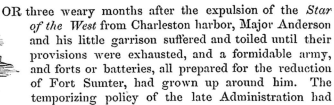

OR three weary months after the expulsion of the *Star of the West* from Charleston harbor, Major Anderson and his little garrison suffered and toiled until their provisions were exhausted, and a formidable army, and forts or batteries, all prepared for the reduction of Fort Sumter, had grown up around him. The temporizing policy of the late Administration had compelled him to keep his guns muzzled while the treasonable operations were going on, and the new Administration continued the same policy until it was prepared to act with some vigor.

From the hour when the South Carolina politicians declared that State to be an independent sovereignty, they had striven with all their might to sustain that declaration. The garrison in Sumter was a standing refutation of it, and every effort was used to wipe that disgrace from the newly made escutcheon of the Palmetto Empire. The *Charleston Mercury* almost daily published articles calculated to inflame the public mind, and, in spite of the prudent restraints of the band of conspirators at Montgomery, cause Sumter to be attacked. Its appeals were frantic, and assumed every phase of entreaty, remonstrance, and menace. Styling Fort Sumter "The Bastion of the Federal Union," it said :—"No longer hoping for concessions, let us be ready for war; and when we have driven every foreign soldier from our shores, then let us take our place in the glorious republic our future promises us. Border Southern States will not join us until we have indicated our power to free ourselves—until we have proven that a garrison of seventy men cannot hold the portal of our commerce. The fate of the Southern Confederacy hangs by the ensign halliards of Fort Sumter."[1]

The Convention and the Legislature of South Carolina worked in unison for the great end of securing the independence of the State. The latter appropriated eight hundred and fifty thousand dollars for general purposes; nine hundred and eighty thousand dollars for military and cognate expenses; and fifty thousand dollars for the postal service, when the National mail-routes should be closed. They also made preparations to organize a force of ten thousand men; and Milledge L. Bonham, a late member of Congress, was appointed major-general of the forces of that State. Volunteers from every part of the "Confederacy" flocked into Charleston; and at the close of March, not less than seven thousand armed men and one hundred and twenty

---

[1] *Charleston Mercury*, January 24, 1861. The "Southern Confederacy" was not yet formed.

cannon were menacing Anderson and his little garrison. These were under the command of Major Peter Gustavus Toutant Beauregard, a Louisiana Creole, who had deserted his flag, resigned his commission,[a] and received from the Montgomery conspirators the appointment of brigadier general. He arrived at Charleston on the 4th of March.

[a] February, 1861.

MILLEDGE L. BONHAM.

Fort Sumter was built for defense against external and not against internal foes. Its stronger sides were toward the sea; its weakest side was toward Morris Island, three-fourths of a mile distant, and the nearest land. On that side were its sally-port and docks. The builders never suspected that a hostile gun would be pointed toward that face; now Morris Island was selected as the position for one of the most formidable of the batteries of the insurgents, which was built of heavy yellow pine logs, with a slanting roof toward the fort of the same material, over which was laid a shield of railway iron, strongly clasped, and forming a perfect foil to bomb-shells. The embrasures were closed with iron-clad doors; and within were three 64-pounder columbiads. This was known as the Stevens Battery, so named in honor of its inventor and constructor, Major P. F. Stevens, who was conspicuous in the attack on the *Star of the West*. There were two other batteries on Cummings's Point of Morris Island, the principal one being known as the Cummings's Point Battery, which was armed with two 42-pounder columbiads, three 10-inch mortars, and a 12-pounder Blakely gun from England. All of the troops on Morris Island were under the command of Brigadier-General James Simons, who had been Speaker of the South Carolina House of Representatives, and the artillery battalion was in charge of Lieutenant-Colonel De Saussure. The iron-clad battery was served under the immediate direction of Captain George B. Cuthbert. The batteries at Cummings's Point were manned by the Palmetto Guards.

The spiked guns of Fort Moultrie, on Sullivan's Island, had been restored to good order, and others added to them. Traverses had been constructed, the ramparts strengthened by sand-bags, and eleven heavy siege-guns and

IRON-CLAD BATTERY ON MORRIS ISLAND.

several mortars had been placed in position. Beside Fort Moultrie and some small channel batteries, there were six formidable ones on Sullivan's Island bearing on Fort Sumter, some of which will be mentioned hereafter. All the forces on that island were commanded by Brigadier-General Dunnovant, and the artillery battalion was in charge of Lieutenant-Colonel R. S. Ripley, late of the National Army. On Mount Pleasant was a battery of two 10-inch mortars; and on James Island, nearer Charleston, was Fort Johnston, which had been strengthened, and was flanked by two batteries, known as the Upper and Lower. The latter was a mortar battery. Assistant Adjutant-General N. G. Evans was in command of that post. The sandy shores of Morris, Sullivan, and James Islands were literally dotted with fortifications, about twenty in number, of varied strength, armed with heavy guns, and well manned. Several of them were commanded by officers of the National Army who had abandoned their flag.

JAMES SIMONS.

In addition to the land-works was a curious monster in the character of a floating battery, which had been constructed at Charleston, under the direction of Lieutenant J. R. Hamilton, a deserter from the National Navy.[1] It was made of heavy pine timber, filled in with Palmetto logs, and covered with a double layer of railway iron. It appeared on the water like an immense shed, about twenty-five feet in width, and, with its appendages, about a hundred feet in length. Its front, in which were four enormous siege cannon, sloped inward from the top; and the iron-clad roof, intended to be shell-proof, sloped to its outer edge. Just back of the cannon was an open space with water to extinguish the fuze of any shell that might fall into it. The powder-maga-

FLOATING BATTERY AT CHARLESTON.

zine was in the rear, below the water-line, and protected by bags filled with sand. Farther back was a platform extending the whole width of the battery. This was loaded with sand-bags, which served to balance the heavy guns, and to protect the floating hospital attached to the rear. The hospital was fitted up with every necessary article, and was placed in charge of Dr. De Veza, of Charleston. The monster was to be towed to a position so as to have its guns brought to bear upon the weakest part of Sumter.

During those three weary months, Major Anderson had suffered extremely from anxiety and annoyances of every kind. It was evident that his letters were regularly opened at Charleston, and the contents noted. His valor and his prudence sustained the dignity of his Government under the most trying circumstances, and his bearing toward the civil and military authorities at Charleston won for him their most cordial esteem. He communicated with his Government almost daily, sometimes by a messenger, but generally by

---

[1] See note 3, page 97.

mail. The faithful Peter Hart was his judicious mail-carrier between Sumter and the main, and his trusted caterer for the garrison in fresh provisions in the Charleston markets, so long as they were open to them. Lieutenant George W. Snyder[1] was his chief messenger in bearing written and oral dispatches to and from Governor Pickens; and Lieutenant Theodore Talbot was his personal messenger to the President.[2] These young officers, since dead, were gallant and true on all occasions. His other officers were brave, and also loyal, with the exception of Lieutenant Meade, a Virginian,[3] and several of them have since held distinguished positions in the Army. His little garrison, with one or two exceptions, were true to the old flag when tempted. Yet, with all these advantages, Anderson was sorely tried by the practical weakness of his Government, and the malice of its enemies.

At the beginning of February, one source of much anxiety for the garrison was removed. On Sunday, the 3d of that month, the wives and children (about twenty in number) of the officers and soldiers in Sumter were borne away in the steamer *Marion* for New York. The parting scenes of fortitude and tenderness were touching.[4] They had left the fort on the

---

[1] Lieutenant George W. Snyder was one of Major Anderson's most energetic and trusted young officers. He had been the highest of the three higher graduates of his class at West Point, who were entitled to enter the Engineer Corps. He carried a number of messages from Major Anderson to Governor Pickens. On one occasion the Governor told him that the rebellion would have been delayed if the Republican majorities in 1860 had not been so large. They had resolved on rebellion when their political power, "sustained by the Democratic party in the North," should pass from them. They saw no chance for that party to recover its power, and there was no reason for the conspirators to wait any longer. The exigency mentioned by Calhoun in 1812 (see note 2, page 41) had occurred.

A colonel's commission, as commander of a volunteer regiment, was offered to Lieutenant Snyder, but he preferred his position in the regular Army. He died while assisting in the construction of the defenses of Washington City. His remains are under a neat monument in his family burial-ground, near Schoharie Court House, New York, forty miles west of Albany. On the monument are the following inscriptions:—

WEST SIDE.—Lieutenant GEO. W. SNYDER, born at Cobleskill, July 30, 1833. Died at Washington City, D. C., November 17, 1861.

NORTH SIDE.—A graduate of Union College; also of the Military Academy at West Point, with the highest honors of his class.

EAST SIDE.—One of the gallant defenders of Fort Sumter.

SOUTH SIDE.—Aide-de-Camp to General Heintzelman at the battle of Bull's Run.

On the west side of the monument, in relief, is a military hat and sword. I am indebted to Mr. Daniel Knower for the drawing of the monument.

SNYDER'S MONUMENT.

[2] On one occasion, when Lieutenant Talbot went to President Buchanan, the latter met the young officer with much agitation, and laying both his hands on his shoulders, said: "Lieutenant, what shall we do?" Talbot, when he related this fact to Lieutenant Snyder, said: "I never felt so in my life. The President seemed like an old man in his dotage. It seemed so strange to me that I should have lived to see the day when a President of the United States should put his hands imploringly on the shoulders of a poor lieutenant, and ask what he should do to save his country! A meeting of the Cabinet was immediately called (January 1, 1861), when none of the Ministers had any resolution, excepting Mr. Holt, the new Secretary of War, who said that the Union must be saved at whatever cost of blood and treasure."—*Letter of Daniel Knower to the Author.*

[3] Soon after leaving Fort Sumter, Meade abandoned his flag and joined the insurgents. He was active in the construction of the defenses of Petersburg, in the second and third years of the war.

[4] "Many a woman and child departed that day who, to the utmost of their ability, would have done and dared as much as their husbands and fathers. 'We have been seven years married,' said one, 'and I never

25th,[a] and embarked at Charleston. When the *Marion* neared Sumter, the whole garrison was seen on the top of the ramparts. While the ship was passing, they fired a gun and gave three hearty cheers, as a parting farewell to the beloved ones on board. The response was waving of handkerchiefs, and tears and sobs, and earnest prayers, both silent and audible.

[a January, 1861.]

Late in March, rumors reached Governor Pickens that the garrison in Sumter would soon be transferred to some other post. It doubtless came from the Commissioners at Washington, who were waiting in expectation of that event. Accordingly, Beauregard wrote to Major Anderson,[b] apprising him of the rumor, and saying that when he should be prepared to leave the fort, he and the authorities at Charleston would be happy to give him every facility. "All that will be required of you," he said, " will be your word of honor, as an officer and a gentleman, that the fort, all public property therein, its armaments, &c., shall remain in their present condition, without any arrangements or preparations for their destruction or injury after you shall have left the fort. On our part, no objection will be raised to your retiring with your side and company arms, and to your saluting your flag on lowering it."[1] To this the indignant commander replied :—" I feel deeply hurt at the intimation in your letter about the conditions which will be exacted of me, and I must state most distinctly, that if I can *only* be permitted to leave on the pledge you mention, I shall never, so help me God, leave this fort alive."[2] Beauregard apologized, and there the matter rested.

[b March 26.]

Rumors concerning the evacuation of Fort Sumter now came from the North as thickly as falling leaves. Major Anderson was sorely perplexed. He received no instructions from his Government, and his discretionary powers were made very limited by unrepealed restrictions. On the 1st of April he wrote to Lieutenant-General Scott, saying, after referring to the fact that he had been at times cut off from all communication with Washington: "I think the Government has left me too much to myself. It has given me no instructions, even when I have asked for them, and I think that responsibilities of a higher and more delicate character have devolved upon me than was proper." He wrote to Adjutant-General Thomas (the successor of Cooper, the traitor), on the 5th, because of rumors from the North, and the non-reception of replies to earnest letters for advice, saying: "I am sure that I shall not be left without instructions, even though they may be confidential. After thirty odd years of service, I do not wish it to be said that I have treasonably abandoned a post, and turned over to unauthorized persons public property intrusted to my charge. I am entitled to this act of justice at the hands of my Government, and I feel confident that I shall not be disappointed. What to do with the public property, and where to take my

---

had reason to find fault with you; now, whatever may happen, I *know* I shall never have cause to blush for you.' Another, whose swollen eyes belied her words, said: ' I don't want you to think of *us*, Ben; the children and myself will get along, and you'll have enough to think of *here*.' And another, holding a large warm hand between her own, and leaning her head against the brawny shoulder, whispered, with quivering lips, 'May God bless an' take care o' you, Thomas: I'll never cease to pray for you; but do your juty, do your juty, darlint. God forbid that my love should interfere with that.'. Her husband, Thomas Carroll, did his 'juty' well when the hour for duty came, and carried a wounded face away from Fort Sumter."—*Within Fort Sumter :* by one of the Company. page 25.

[1] Anderson's MS. Letter-book.   [2] Anderson's MS. Letter-book.

command, are questions to which answers will, I hope, be at once returned. Unless we receive supplies, I shall be compelled to stay here without food or to abandon this fort very early next week."[1] Again, on the 6th, he wrote, " The truth is, that the sooner we are out of this harbor, the better.   Our flag runs an hourly risk of being insulted, and my hands are tied by my orders; and even if that were not the case, I have not the power to protect it.   God grant that neither I nor any other officer of our Army may be again placed in a position of such humiliation and mortification."

Whilst Anderson was thus chafing in Fort Sumter, the Government at Washington, as we have observed, was very much perplexed, for it was evident that a crisis was at hand.

Lieutenant Talbot was on his way to the seat of government, with an earnest plea from Anderson for instructions, when a note from Beauregard informed the Major that orders had been received from Montgomery, that " on account of delays and apparent vacillation of the United States Government, in relation to the evacuation of Fort Sumter," no further communication between that fort and Charleston, for mails or for the

P. G. T. BEAUREGARD.

purpose of procuring supplies, would be permitted.   Once before there had been a like restriction, and when a removal of it was offered, in the form of a courtesy, and he was proffered[a] " fresh meat and vegetables, under the direction of an officer of the State of South Carolina," Major Anderson declined receiving any supplies by " permission." He had not, he said, represented that he was in need of supplies.   " If the permission is founded on courtesy and civility, I am compelled respectfully to decline accepting it."[2]   No objections were made for a time thereafter to his free use of the Charleston markets for fresh meat and vegetables.

[a] January 19, 1861.

The crisis came.   The message of President Lincoln to Governor Pickens, concerning the sending of supplies to Fort Sumter, was made known on the morning of the 8th.[b]   It produced the most intense excitement.   Beauregard immediately sent the electrograph to Montgomery, already noticed, and the reply came back on the 10th, conditionally authorizing him to demand the surrender of Fort Sumter.[3]   " The demand will be made to-morrow at twelve o'clock," replied Beauregard.   The news of this determination spread instantly over the city, and to the various camps and batteries of the insurgents.   The Floating Battery, finished, armed, and manned, was taken out and anchored near the west end of Sullivan's Island; and fire-ships—vessels filled with wood and rosin, to be set on fire and run among the relief squadron, to burn it, if it should enter the harbor—were towed out at the same time.

[b] April.

---

[1] Anderson's MS. Letter-book.   [2] Anderson's MS. Letter-book.

[3] See note 1, page 305.

Charleston was full of demagogues at that time, busily engaged in infla‑
ming the populace and the soldiers; and that city became, in miniature, what
Paris was just before the attack on the Bastile.

Among the demagogues in Charleston was Roger A. Pryor, lately a
member of the National House of Representatives; and also Edmund
Ruffin,[1] both from Virginia. Their State Convention was then in session at
Richmond. The Union sentiment in that body seemed likely to defeat the
secessionists. Something was needed to neutralize its power, by elevating
passion into the throne of judgment. It was believed by many that this
could be done only by shedding blood. Pryor and Ruffin were self-consti‑
tuted preachers of the sanguinary doctrine. They were earnest missionaries;
and on the evening of the 10th, while the city was rocked with excitement,
a rare opportunity was offered to Pryor for the utterance of his incendiary
sentiments. He was serenaded, and made a fiery speech to the populace, in
response to the compliment. " Gentlemen," he said, " I thank you, especially,
that you have at last annihilated this cursed Union, reeking with corruption,
and insolent with excess of tyranny. Thank God! it is at last blasted and
riven by the lightning wrath of an outraged and indignant people. Not
only is it gone, but gone forever. In the expressive language of Scripture, it
is water spilt upon the ground, and cannot be gathered up. Like Lucifer,
son of the morning, it has fallen, never to rise again. For my part, gentle‑
men, if Abraham Lincoln and Hannibal Hamlin, to-morrow, were to abdicate
their office, and were to give me a blank sheet of paper to write the condi‑
tions of reannexation to the defunct Union, I would scornfully spurn the
overture. . . . I invoke you, and I make it in some sort a personal appeal—
personal so far as it tends to our assistance in Virginia—I do invoke you, in
your demonstrations of popular opinion, in your exhibitions of official inter‑
est, to give no countenance to the idea of reconstruction. In Virginia, they
all say, if reduced to the dread dilemma of this alternative, they will espouse
the cause of the South as against the interests of the Northern Confederacy;
but they whisper of reconstruction, and they say Virginia must abide in the
Union, with the idea of reconstructing the Union which you have anni‑
hilated. I pray you, gentlemen, rob them of that idea. Proclaim to the
world that upon no condition and under no circumstance will South Carolina
ever again enter into political association with the Abolitionists of New
England. Do not distrust Virginia. As sure as to-morrow's sun will rise
upon us, just so sure will Virginia be a member of the Southern Confedera‑
tion. And I will tell you, gentlemen," said the speaker, with great vehe‑
mence, " what will put her in the Southern Confederacy in less than an hour
by Shrewsbury clock—STRIKE A BLOW! The very moment that blood is
shed, old Virginia will make common cause with her sisters of the South.
It is impossible she should do otherwise."[2]

This speech was vehemently applauded. It was in consonance with the
diabolical spirit of the more zealous conspirators and insurgents everywhere
The cry of Pryor for blood was sent to Montgomery by telegraph the next
morning, and Mr. Gilchrist, a member of the Alabama Legislature, said to
Davis and a portion of his " Cabinet" (Walker, Benjamin, and Memminger):—

---

[1] See page 48.   [2] *Charleston Mercury*, April 11, 1861.

" Gentlemen, unless you sprinkle blood in the face of the people of Alabama, they will be back in the old Union in less than ten days."[1] The " sober second thought " of the people was dreaded. The conspirators knew that there was solemn truth in the assertion, that " the big heart of the people is still in the Union. It is now subjugated temporarily to the will of the politicians. *Less than a hundred thousand politicians are endeavoring to destroy the liberties and usurp the rights of more than thirty millions of people.*"[2]

At two o'clock in the afternoon of Thursday, the 11th of April, Beauregard sent Colonel James Chesnut, Jr., Colonel Chisholm, and Captain Stephen D. Lee, of his staff, with a letter to Major Anderson, in which he conveyed a demand for the evacuation of Fort Sumter.[3] This reached the fort at four o'clock. Major Anderson, who was in expectation of such demand, at once replied, that his sense of honor and obligations to his Government would not allow him to comply. At the same time he informed Beauregard's aids, orally, that the condition of his supplies was such that he would be compelled, by menaces of starvation, to leave the fort in a few days. They returned to Beauregard under a red flag, thereby indicating to the commanders of the forts and batteries that no peaceful arrangement had yet been made. That officer instantly communicated Anderson's remark to Walker, the " Confederate Secretary of War," at Montgomery, giving as his words:—" I will await the first shot, and if you do not batter us to pieces, we will be starved out in a few days." Walker telegraphed back, that if Major Anderson would state the time when he would evacuate, and agree that, meanwhile, he would not use his guns against them, unless theirs should be employed against Fort Sumter, Beauregard was authorized thus to avoid

---

[1] Speech of Jeremiah Clemens, formerly United States Senator from Alabama, at Huntsville, in that State, on the 13th of March, 1864.

[2] *Raleigh* (North Carolina) *Banner.*

[3] The original of Beauregard's letter is before me while I write. It is as follows:—

" HEAD-QUARTERS PROVISIONAL ARMY, C. S. A., }
" CHARLESTON, S. C., April 11, 1861.   }

" SIR:—The Government of the Confederate States has hitherto forborne any hostile demonstrations against Fort Sumter, in the hope that the Government of the United States, with a view to the amicable adjustment of all questions between the two governments, and to avoid the calamity of war, would voluntarily evacuate it. There was reason at one time to believe that such would be the course pursued by the Government of the United States, and, under that impression, my government has refrained from making any demand for the surrender of the fort. But the Confederate States can no longer delay assuming actual possession of a fortification commanding the entrance of one of their harbors, and necessary to it.

" I am ordered by the Government of the Confederate States to demand the evacuation of Fort Sumter. My aids, Colonel Chesnut and Captain Lee, are authorized to make such demand of you. All proper facilities will be afforded for the removal of yourself and command, together with company arms and property, and all private property, to any post in the United States which you may elect. The flag which you have upheld so long, and with so much fortitude, under the most trying circumstances, may be saluted by you on taking it down.

" Colonel Chesnut and Captain Lee will, for a reasonable time, await your answer.

" I am, Sir, your obedient servant,
" G. T. BEAUREGARD,
" *Brigadier-General Commanding.*

" Major ROBERT ANDERSON,
" *Commanding at Fort Sumter, S. C.*"

It is a noteworthy fact, that the paper on which was written this demand from the conspirators for a recognition of their right and power to destroy the Union, bore, in its water-mark, the emblem of Union, namely, the Union shield, with its full complement of stars on and around it, and in the segment of a circle over it the words, E PLURIBUS UNUM. In a corner, surrounded in an ellipse formed by the words *Evans and Cogswell, Charleston,* was a picture of the National Capitol at Washington.

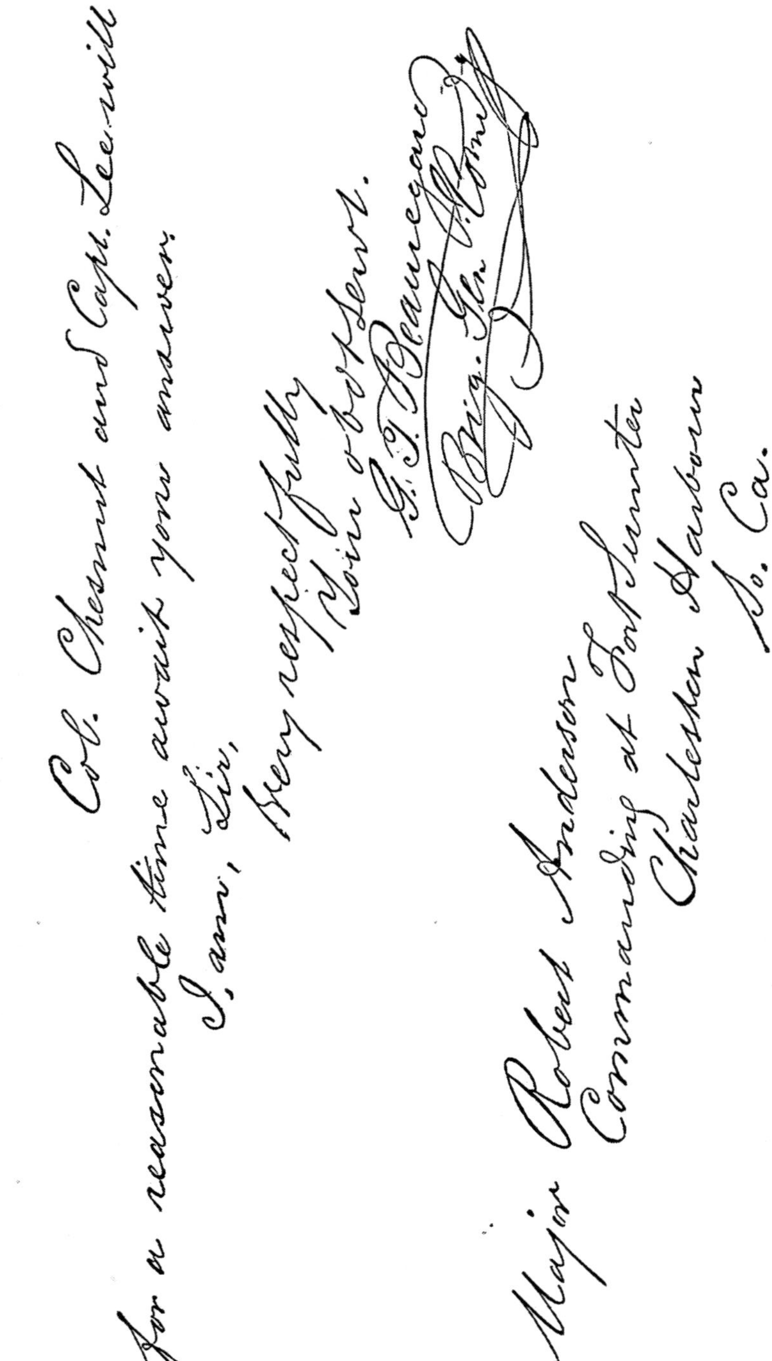

Col. Chesnut and Capt. Lee will

for a reasonable time await your answer.

I am, Sir,

Very respectfully

Your obt servt.

G. T. Beauregard

Brig. Gen. Army

Major Robert Anderson

Commanding at Fort Sumter

Charleston Harbor

So. Ca.

FAC-SIMILE OF A PART OF BEAUREGARD'S LETTER TO ANDERSON.

the effusion of blood." "If this or its equivalent be refused," he said, "reduce the fort, as your judgment decides to be the most practicable."

At eleven o'clock the same night, Beauregard sent Colonels Chesnut, Chisholm, Pryor (Roger A.), and Captain Lee, with the proposition of Walker, to Major Anderson, when the latter replied that he cordially united with them in a desire to prevent bloodshed, and would therefore agree, in accordance with the proposed stipulations, to leave the fort by noon on the 15th, should he not, previous to that time, "receive controlling instructions" from his Government, or additional supplies. The messenger had arrived at one o'clock on the morning of the 12th, and the answer was written at half-past two. At the request of Chesnut and his companions, it was handed to them unsealed.

LE ROY POPE WALKER.

Anderson was ignorant of what his Government had been doing for his relief during the last few days. He had notice of its intentions, but his special messenger, Lieutenant Talbot, who had been sent to Washington after the notice was given, had not been allowed by the authorities at Charleston to return to the fort.[1] These authorities had better information than Anderson. Scouts had discovered, during the previous evening, the *Pawnee* and the *Harriet Lane* outside the bar, and had reported the fact to Beauregard. That there might be no delay, that officer had directed his aids, sent to Anderson, to receive an open reply from him, and if it should not be satisfactory, to exercise discretionary powers given them. They consulted a few minutes in the room of the officer of the guard, and, deciding that it was not satisfactory, at twenty minutes past three o'clock in the morning,[*] they addressed a note to Anderson, saying:—   * April 12, 1861. "By authority of Brigadier-General Beauregard, commanding the provisional forces of the Confederate States, we have the honor to notify you that he will open the fire of his batteries on Fort Sumter in one hour from this time." They immediately left the fort, when the flag was raised, the postern was closed, the sentinels were withdrawn from the parapet, and orders were given by the commander, that the men should not leave the bomb-proofs without special orders.

The night of the 11th of April, 1861, will be long remembered by the then dwellers in Charleston. It became known early in the evening that a demand for the surrender of Fort Sumter would be made. Orders had been issued for all the military in the city, and surgeons, to hasten to their respective posts. The telegraph called four full regiments of a thousand men each from the country. Conveyances for wounded men were prepared, and every

---

[1] Governor Pickens professed to give his permission with great cheerfulness for Talbot to go to Washington. A perfidious trick was practiced. At Florence, the car in which Talbot was seated was detached, by order, it is said, of the authorities at Charleston, and the train went on, thus detaining Anderson's messenger while they were preparing to attack Fort Sumter.

thing necessary to meet the demands of suffering caused by battle was made
ready.   At midnight, seven discharges from heavy cannon aroused all sleepers.
They were signals for the assembling of all the reserves immediately.   The
people rushed to the streets in alarm.   The roll of the drum, the tramp of
horses, and the rumbling of wagons were heard in every direction, while
from the southwestern horizon a heavy thunder-storm was approaching.   The
streets were soon crowded with people, who hurried to East Bay Battery
and other places, and watched eagerly for an attack on Fort Sumter.

> " In the town—through every street,
>   Tramp, tramp, went the feet,
>   For they said the Federal fleet
>   Hove in sight;
>   And down the wharves they ran,
> ' Every woman, child, and man,
>   To the fight."

Hours passed on, and all was quiet.   The disappointed inhabitants made
their way slowly back toward their homes, and very soon the gathering
thunder-storm burst over the city.

Patiently, firmly, almost silently, the little band in Fort Sumter awaited
the passage of that pregnant hour.   Each man could hear his own heart beat
as the expiring moments brought him nearer to inevitable but unknown perils.
Suddenly the dull booming of a gun at a signal-battery on James Island,
near Fort Johnson, was heard,[1] and a fiery shell, sent from its broad throat,
went flying through the black night and exploded immediately over Fort
Sumter.   It was a malignant "shooting star," coursing through the heavens
like those, in appearance, which in the olden time affrighted the nations.   It
was one of fearful portent, and was the "forerunner" of terrible calamities.
Then, no man was wise enough to interpret its full augury.

The sound of that mortar on James Island was the signal for battle.   It
awakened the slumberers in Charleston.   The streets of the city were again
thronged with an excited populace.   After a brief pause, the heavy cannon
on Cummings's Point, comprising Battery Stevens (so named in honor of the
inventor), opened fire upon Fort Sumter.   To the late Edmund Ruffin,[2] of
Virginia, belongs the infamy of firing its first shot, and the first hurled against
that fort, the mute representative of the nationality under whose benign
overshadowing he had reposed in peace and security for more than seventy
years.   He had hastened to Morris Island when hostilities seemed near, and
when asked there to what company he belonged, he replied, " To that in
which there is a vacancy."[3]   He was assigned to duty in the Palmetto
Guard, and implored the privilege of firing the first gun on Fort Sumter.   It
was granted, and he at once acquired Ephesian fame.   That wretched old
man appears in history only as a traitor and a suicide[4]—a victim to the
wicked teachings of stronger and wiser men.

That first shot from Cummings's Point was followed quickly by others
from the Floating Battery, which lay beached on Sullivan's Island, under the

---

[1] That signal-gun was fired by Lieutenant H. S. Farley.   [2] See page 48.
[3] *Charleston Mercury*, April 13, 1861.   [4] See note 1, page 48.

command of Lieutenants Yates and Harleston; from Fort Moultrie, commanded by Colonel Ripley; from a powerful masked battery on Sullivan's Island, hidden by sand-hills and bushes, called the Dahlgren Battery,[1] under Lieutenant J. R. Hamilton; and from nearly all the rest of the semicircle of military works arrayed around Fort Sumter for its reduction. Full thirty heavy guns and mortars opened at once. Their fire was given with remarkable vigor, yet the assailed fort made no reply. The tempest of lightning, wind, and rain that had just been skurrying through the heavens, leaving behind it heavy clouds and a drizzling mist, and the angry storm of shot and shell, seemed to make no impression on that "Bastion of the Federal Union." For two hours and more, Fort Sumter seemed to the outside world as silent as the grave, bravely bearing the brunt of assault with wonderful fortitude or the stolidity of paralysis. This silence mortified the insurgents, for they longed for the glory of victory after resistance. A contemporary poet sang :—

> "The morn was cloudy, and dark, and gray,
> When the first columbiad blazed away,
> Showing that there was the devil to pay
> With the braves on Morris Island;
> They fired their cannon again and again,
> Hoping that Major Anderson's men
> Would answer back, but 'twas all in vain,
> At first, on Morris Island."[2]

It had been plainly seen by Anderson and his officers that the *barbette* and area guns could not be used, if all the batteries of the insurgents should open upon the fort at the same time.[3] This was a fatal misfortune, for the *barbette* guns could have hurled heavy crushing shot upon the Floating Battery and the armored work on Cummings's Point. On the parade, in the fort, were five heavy columbiads, arranged for throwing shells. These, too, would have been effective, but they could not be manned with safety. For this reason, Anderson gave his orders for the men to remain in the bomb-proofs. He had men sufficient to work only nine guns well, and it was necessary to guard against casualties as effectually as possible.

At half-past six o'clock, the garrison were summoned to breakfast in the usual manner, and they ate as hearty a meal as their scanty supplies would allow, little disturbed by the terrible uproar around them. It was now broad daylight. The officers and men in Fort Sumter were arranged in three reliefs. The first was commanded by Captain Doubleday, the second by Surgeon Crawford, and the third by Lieutenant Snyder. Thus prepared they went to work, under the most trying disadvantages. They had plenty

---

[1] This battery was composed of two heavy Dahlgren guns, which had been sent from the Tredegar Works at Richmond, and arrived at Charleston on the 28th of March. Five 10-inch mortars were put into the same battery with the Dahlgrens. On the same day, fifty thousand pounds of powder, sent from Pensacola, reached Charleston, and twenty thousand pounds from Wilmington, North Carolina. At that time neither Virginia nor North Carolina had passed ordinances of secession. See *Charleston Mercury*, April 13, 1861.

[2] From *The Battle of Morris Island :* a "Cheerful Tragedy," in *Vanity Fair*, April 27, 1861.

[3] Fort Sumter was armed at this time with fifty-three effective guns. Of these, twenty-seven were mounted *en barbette*, twenty-one were in the lower tier of casemates, and five were on the parade. The embrasures of the second tier of casemates had been filled with masonry. One of the guns on the parade was a 10-inch columbiad, arranged to throw shells into Charleston. (See page 130.) The others were 4-inch columbiads, to throw shells upon the Cummings's Point Battery. There were only seven hundred cartridges when the action commenced.—*Engineer's Journal of the Bombardment of Fort Sumter :* by Captain J. G. Foster.

of powder, but few cartridges made up. They had no scales for weighing powder, and only six needles for sewing cartridge-bags. They had no instruments for sighting the guns; and other deficiencies was numerous. The wood-work of the barracks and officers' quarters was exposed to ignition by the bursting bomb-shells, every moment. The garrison was composed of only about eighty men; the insurgents numbered several thousands. The odds were fearful, but, leaning trustfully on the arm of the Almighty, the commander determined to resist. At seven o'clock in the morning, he ordered a reply to the attack. The first gun was fired from the battery at the right gorge angle, at the Stevens Battery on Morris Island, by Captain (afterward Major-General) Abner Doubleday. A fire from the fort upon all of the principal attacking batteries immediately followed; and for four hours the contest was kept up so steadily and vigorously on the part of Fort Sumter, that the insurgents suspected that it had been stealthily re-enforced during the night.

The first solid shot from Fort Sumter, hurled at Fort Moultrie, was fired by Surgeon (afterward Major-General) S. W. Crawford. It lodged in the sand-bags, and was carried by a special reporter of the *Charleston Mercury* to the office of that journal. It was a 32-pound shot, and was soon afterward forwarded by Beauregard, it is said, to Marshal Kane, of Baltimore, who appears as a worthy recipient of the gift from such hands. The writer saw that shot at the police head-quarters in the old City Hall on Holliday Street, in Baltimore, when he visited that building in December, 1864, where it was carefully preserved, with the original presentation label upon it, namely, " *To George P. Kane, Marshal of Police, Baltimore, from Fort Sumter.*"

ROUND SHOT FROM FORT SUMTER.

Anderson's order for the men to remain in the bomb-proofs could not restrain them when the firing commenced. The whole garrison, officers and men, were filled with the highest excitement and enthusiasm by the events of the morning, and the first relief had been at work but a few minutes when the other two joined in the task. Hence it was that the fort was enabled to assail all of the principal insurgent batteries at the same time. The surgeon (Crawford), musicians, engineers, and workmen, inspired by example, fell in and toiled vigorously with the soldiers. There were no idle hands. Yet after four hours of hard and skillful labor, it was evident that Fort Sumter could not seriously injure the works opposed to it. One of Fort Moultrie's guns had been silenced for a while; its embrasures were injured, its barracks were riddled, and three holes were torn in its flag. A shot had penetrated the Floating Battery; but the iron-plated battery (Stevens) on Cummings's Point was absolutely invulnerable. It was uninjured at the end of the engagement, though frequently hit by heavy shot.

In the mean time, the firing of the assailants was becoming more accurate and effective. At first, many of their shot actually missed Fort Sumter, and those that struck it were so scattering that there seemed no chance for breaching the walls. But the firing became more and more concentrated, and began to tell fearfully upon the walls and the parapets. Some of the barbette guns were dismounted or otherwise disabled,[1] and at length the fearful cry of *Fire!* was raised.   The barracks were burning.

From the hour when the garrison had been made to expect relief, their eyes had been turned much and anxiously toward the sea.   And now, when the tempest of war was beating furiously upon them, and not three days' supply of food was left, they looked out from the oceanward port-holes more anxiously than ever.   At noon on that fearful day, Surgeon Crawford, who had volunteered to ascend to the parapet, amid the storm of missiles, to make

EFFECT OF CANNON SHOT ON FORT SUMTER.[2]

observations, reported, to the infinite delight of the garrison, that through the vail of the misty air he saw vessels bearing the dear old flag.   They were a part of Fox's relief squadron, namely, the *Pawnee*, ten guns; the *Harriet Lane*, five guns, and the transport *Baltic*.   They signaled greetings by dipping their flags.   Sumter could not respond, for its ensign was entangled in the halliards, which had been cut by the enemy's shot, but it was still waving defiantly at about half-mast.   The vessels could not cross the bar.   The sinuous and shifting channels were always difficult, in fine weather;

---

[1] Alluding to the firing from Fort Moultrie upon Fort Sumter, the *Charleston Mercury* of the 13th said:— "Many of its shells dropped into that fort, and Lieutenant John Mitchell, the worthy son of that patriot sire who has so nobly vindicated the cause of the South, has the honor of dismounting two of its parapet guns by a single shot from one of the columbiads, which, at the time, he had the office of directing." The "patriot sire" here spoken of was John Mitchell, an Irish revolutionist, who was sent to Australia as a traitor to the British Government, was paroled, violated his parole, and escaped to the United States, the asylum for the oppressed. Here he pursued his vocation of newspaper editor, first in New York and then in the Slave-labor States, where he upheld Slavery as a righteous system, advocated the reopening of the horrible African Slave-trade, joined the conspirators, and, through the newspaper press of Richmond, Virginia, became one of the most malignant of the revilers of the Government whose protection he had sought and received. Lieutenant Mitchell afterward perished in Fort Sumter. A London correspondent of the *New York Tribune*, in a graphic account of this young man, says that he met him in Charleston in 1860, "when he boasted of having assisted to murder an Abolitionist, by lynching."

[2] This little picture is from a photograph taken by an operator in Charleston immediately after the evacuation of the fort. It shows the appearance, at that time, of the portion of the gorge of Fort Sumter nearest Cummings's Point, and the effect of the cannonade and bombardment from the iron-clad battery there.

now the buoys had been removed, ships laden with stones had been sunken therein, and a blinding storm was prevailing.

The battery on Cummings's Point became very formidable in the afternoon. The guns were rifled. A Blakely cannon, already mentioned, was specially mischievous, and heavy shot, aimed accurately at the embrasures, were extremely destructive and annoying. The gunners in Sumter on that side were frequently stunned, or otherwise injured, by splinters of the masonry. In every part of the fort in which they were engaged they worked without intermission, and received food and drink at their guns. As the hours wore away, they became very weary. The supply of cartridges began to fail, and before sunset all the guns were abandoned but six. These were worked continually, but not rapidly, until dark, when the port-holes were closed, and the little garrison was arranged for alternate repose, and work, and watching. Several men had been wounded, but not one was mortally hurt. So closed the first day of actual war between the servants of the OLIGARCHY and those of the PEOPLE.

BLAKELY GUN.[1]

The night of the 12th was dark and stormy, with high wind and tide. The telegraph was not yet silenced, and it had carried tidings of the fight all over the land before sunset. Thousands of anxious heads, hundreds of miles away from Sumter, were laid upon their pillows that night, and thousands of prayers went up to the Almighty for the salvation of the Republic. In Charleston and in its harbor there was but little sleep. All night long the mortars of the insurgents kept up a slow bombardment of the fort, sufficient to deprive the wearied garrison of all but intermittent slumbers. Anderson continually expected an attack from armed men in boats, and was prepared for their reception. He hoped to welcome other boats filled with friends and stores. He was disappointed in all his expectations. The naval commanders outside did, as we have observed, take measures to send in relief, but the storm kept them from performing their errand of mercy until it was too late.[2]

The storm ceased before the dawn.[a] Only a few vanishing clouds flecked the morning sky. The sun rose in splendor. Already the cannonade and bombardment had been renewed with increased vigor and additional terrors. Red-hot shot were hurled into the fort. One passed along the course of a water-pipe through the wall that masked the magazine for fixed ammunition. Fortunately, it did not penetrate the inner wall. By that shield the fiery demon was foiled. Four times

[a] April 12, 1861.

---

[1] This is a view of the English rifled cannon that produced the chief destructive effects on Fort Sumter during the siege. Its projectiles are seen in front of its carriage.
[2] See page 309.

on Friday the buildings in the fort had been set on fire, and each time the flames were extinguished. Now the barracks and officers' quarters were again and again ignited. They could not be saved, and no attempt to do so was made, for precious lives would have been imperiled by the act. Means for that purpose had been diminished. On the previous day, three of the iron cisterns over the hall-ways had been destroyed by the shots of the insurgents, by which the quarters below had been deluged and the flames checked, Now there was no resource of the kind. The garrison must be starved out within three days, and shelter would be no longer needed, so the buildings were abandoned to the flames. The safety of the magazine, and the salvation of sufficient powder to last until the 15th, became the absorbing care of the commander. Blankets and flannel shirts were used for making cartridges; and every hand within the fort was fully employed. On that morning the

INTERNAL APPEARANCE OF FORT SUMTER AFTER THE BOMBARDMENT.[1]

last parcel of rice had been cooked, and nothing was left for the garrison to eat but salt pork.

The flames spread, and the situation of the garrison became extremely distressing. The heat was almost intolerable. The fire approached the magazine, when its doors were closed and locked. In fearful eddies the glowing embers were scattered about the fort. The main gate took fire, and very soon the blackened sally-port was open to the besiegers. The powder brought out into the service magazine was so exposed to the flames, that ninety barrels of it were thrown into the sea by Lieutenant Snyder and Surgeon Crawford.

Out of Sumter immense volumes of smoke rose sluggishly on the still air.

[1] This is from a photograph taken immediately after the evacuation of Fort Sumter. It is a view of that portion of the officers' quarters to the left of the gateway, and of that of the men's quarters nearest the powder-magazine, the entrance to which was at the junction of these two buildings. In front of this entrance are seen the ruins of a traverse. The gateway or sally-port is also seen, the doors of which were burned. In the foreground is seen the great lantern that was taken down from the top of the fort, where it was used as a beacon.

The assailants knew that the fort was on fire, and that its inmates were dwellers in a heated furnace, yet they inhumanly intensified the fury of the attack from all points.[1] The heat and vapor became stifling, and the garrison were compelled, frequently, to lie upon the ground, with wet cloths on their faces, to prevent suffocation by smoke.[2] Yet they would not surrender. They bravely kept the old flag flying. Eight times its staff had been hit without serious injury; now, at twenty minutes before one o'clock, it was shot away near the peak, and the flag, with a portion of the staff, fell down through the thick smoke among the gleaming embers. Through the blinding, scorching tempest, Lieutenant Hall rushed and snatched up the precious ensign, before it could take fire. It was immediately carried by Lieutenant Snyder to the ramparts, and, under his direction, Sergeant Hart, who for weeks had been Major Anderson's faithful servant and friend, but was a non-combatant by agreement,[3] sprang upon the sand-bags, and with the assistance of Lyman, a mason from Baltimore, fastened the fragment of the staff there, and left the soiled banner flying defiantly,[4] while shot and shell were filling the air like hail. Almost eighty-five years before, another brave and patriotic Sergeant (William Jasper) had performed a similar feat, in Charleston harbor, near the spot where Fort Moultrie now stands.[5] One was assisting in the *establishment* of American nationality, the other in *maintaining* it.

At half-past one o'clock, the notorious Senator Wigfall (who, as soon as he had received his salary from the National Treasury, had hastened to Charleston, and there became a volunteer aid on the staff of General Beauregard) arrived at Sumter in a boat from Cummings's Point, accompanied by one white man and two negroes. Leaving the boat at the wharf, Wigfall passed around the fort until he came to the first embrasure, or port-hole, through which he saw private John Thompson, of the fort. The Texan was carrying a white handkerchief on the point of his sword, as a flag of truce. He asked permission to enter the embrasure, but was denied. "I am General Wigfall," he said, "and wish to see Major Anderson." The soldier told him to stay there until he could see his commander. "For God's sake let me in!" cried the conspirator, "I can't stand it out here in the firing." The privilege was denied him for the moment. He then hurried around to the sally-port, at which place he had asked an interview with Anderson. Finding the passage strewn with the burning timbers of the gate, the poor fellow, in utter despair, ran around the fort, waving his white handkerchief imploringly toward his fellow-insurgents, to prevent them from firing. It was useless. The missiles fell thick and fast, and he was permitted to crawl into an embra-

[1] Captain Foster, in his report, says:—"As soon as the flames and smoke burst from the roof of the quarters, the enemy's batteries redoubled the rapidity of their fire, firing red-hot shot from most of their guns."

[2] Afterward, on the occasion of his being presented with a sword by the citizens of Taunton, Massachusetts, Major Anderson, alluding to the inhumanity of his assailants, said:—"It is one of the most painful recollections of that event, that when our barracks were on fire, and the men were compelled to cover their faces with wet handkerchiefs, and lie with their faces upon the ground, to avoid suffocation, instead of sending a white flag, with assistance to extinguish the flames, then threatening us with destruction, they rapidly increased their fire upon us from every battery, in total disregard of every feeling of humanity."

[3] See page 134.

[4] See the device on the Sumter Medal, near the close of this chapter, in which Hart is represented in the act of planting the flag-staff.

[5] For a full account of this, and attending circumstances, see *Lossing's Pictorial Field-book of the Revolution*, ii. 550.

sure, after he had given up his sword to a private soldier there. He was almost exhausted by fatigue and affright.

At his place of entrance, Wigfall met Captain J. G. Foster, Lieutenant J. C. Davis, and Surgeon S. W. Crawford, all of whom were afterward general officers in the Army; also Lieutenant R. K. Meade. Trembling with excitement, he said :—"I am General Wigfall; I come from General Beauregard, who wants to stop this bloodshed. You are on fire, and your flag is down; let us stop this firing." One of the officers replied: "Our flag is not down, Sir. It is yet flying from the ramparts." Wigfall saw it where Peter Hart and his comrade had nailed it, and said: "Well, well, I want to stop this." Holding out his sword and handkerchief, he said to one of the officers:— "Will you hoist this?" "No, Sir," replied the officer; "it is for you, General Wigfall, to stop them." "Will any of you hold this out of the embrasure?" he asked. No one offering, he said: "May I hold it, then?" "If you wish to," was the cool reply. Wigfall sprang into the embrasure, or port-hole, and waved the white flag several times. A shot striking near frightened him away, when he cried out excitedly: "Will you let some one show this flag?" Corporal Charles Bringhurst, by permission, took the handkerchief and waved it out of the port-hole, but he soon abandoned the perilous duty, exclaiming: "I won't hold that flag, for they don't respect it. They are firing at it." Wigfall replied, impatiently: "They fired at me two or three times, and I stood it; I should think you might stand it once." Turning to Lieutenant Davis, he said: "If you will show a white flag from your ramparts, they will cease firing."—"It shall be done," said Davis, "if you request it for the purpose, and that alone, of holding a conference with Major Anderson."

The commander, in the mean time, with Lieutenant Snyder and Surgeon Crawford, had passed out of the sally-port to meet Wigfall. He was not there, and they returned, and just as Davis had agreed to display a white flag, they came up. Wigfall said to Major Anderson: "I come from General Beauregard, who wishes to stop this, Sir."—"Well, Sir!" said Anderson, rising upon his toes and settling firmly upon his heels, as he looked the traitor in the face, with sharp inquiry. "You have defended your flag nobly, Sir," continued Wigfall; "you have done all that can be done, Sir. Your fort is on fire. Let us stop this. Upon what terms will you evacuate the fort, Sir?" Anderson replied: "General Beauregard already knows the terms upon which I will evacuate this fort, Sir. Instead of noon on the 15th, I will go now."—"I understand you to say," said Wigfall, eagerly, "that you will evacuate this fort now, Sir, upon the same terms proposed to you by General Beauregard?" Anderson answered: "Yes, Sir; upon those terms only, Sir."—"Then," said Wigfall, inquiringly, "the fort is to be ours?"— "Yes, Sir; upon those conditions," answered Anderson. "Then I will return to General Beauregard," said Wigfall, and immediately left.[1] Believing what had been said to him to be true, Major Anderson allowed a white flag to be raised over the fort.

---

[1] This account of Wigfall's adventure I derived from the written statements of Captain (afterward General) Seymour, Surgeon (afterward General) Crawford, and private John Thompson, and from the verbal statements of Major (afterward Major-General) Anderson.

At a little before two o'clock, Colonels Chesnut, Pryor, Miles (W. P., who was a volunteer aid on Beauregard's staff), and Captain Lee, went over to Sumter directly from the presence of their commanding general, who was at Fort Moultrie, to inquire the meaning of the white flag. When informed of the visit of Wigfall, they exchanged significant glances and smiles, and Colonel Chesnut frankly informed Major Anderson that the Texan conspirator had not seen Beauregard during the last two days. Wishing to secure for himself alone the honor of procuring the surrender of Fort Sumter, Wigfall had, by misrepresentations, obtained leave from the commander on Morris Island to go to the beleaguered fort. He went there with a white flag in his hand and a black falsehood on his lips, and played a most ludicrous part. He was an acknowledged and cherished leader of the rebellion, and was an admirable representative of the cause in which he was engaged, for it was the offspring of falsehood and fraud.

Assured of Wigfall's mendacity, the deceived and indignant commander said to the new deputation:—" That white flag shall come down immediately." They begged him to leave matters as they were until they could see Beauregard. He did so, and the firing ceased.

* April 13, 1861. The bombardment on Saturday* was seen by thousands of spectators. About three thousand insurgent troops were engaged in the work, while almost double that number were held in reserve—mere spectators. Beside these observers were the inhabitants of Charleston, who covered the roofs of houses, the Battery, the wharves, and every place where a view might be obtained. It was like a holiday in that city. The Battery was crowded with women, gayly dressed; and to most of the inhabitants it had only the significance of a sublime spectacle.

During the afternoon and early evening, several deputations from Beauregard visited Major Anderson, for the purpose of obtaining from him better terms than he had proposed. He was firm. They offered him assistance in extinguishing the flames in Sumter. He declined it, regarding the offer as an adroit method of asking him to surrender, which he had resolved never to do. Finally, between seven and eight o'clock in the evening, Major D. R. Jones, accompanied by Colonels Miles and Pryor, and Captain Hartstene,[1] arrived at the fort with a communication from Beauregard, which contained an agreement for the evacuation of the fort according to Anderson's terms,. namely, the departure of the garrison, with company arms and property, and all private property, and the privilege of saluting and retaining his flag.[2] Anderson accepted the agreement, and detailed Lieutenant Snyder to accom-

---

[1] Captain Hartstene had been an excellent officer in the National Navy, and had some fame as an explorer of the Arctic seas, in search of Sir John Franklin. He had resigned his commission, abandoned his flag, and entered the service of its enemies. He was now a volunteer aid to Beauregard. His kindness to the garrison was conspicuous.

[2] A ludicrous incident occurred at this interview. Colonel Pryor, armed with sword, pistols, and bowie-knife, and assuming the air of a man who possessed the fort and all within it, seeing a tumbler on a table, and what he supposed to be a whisky-bottle near it, poured out of the latter a sufficient quantity of liquid to half fill the former, and drank it, supposing it to be "old Bourbon." The taste not agreeing with its appearance, he inquired if it was water, when Surgeon Crawford informed him that he had swallowed a strong solution of the iodide of potassium, a dangerous poison. Pryor, with face pale with terror, begged the surgeon to give him relief at once. His weapons were laid aside, a powerful emetic was administered, and in the course of an hour or so, that infamous Virginian went on his way rejoicing in his deliverance. Surgeon Crawford, wearing the stars of a major-general, met the traitor, just at the close of the war, in a really sadder condition than when he administered the friendly emetic.

pany Captain Hartstene to the little relief-squadron outside, to make arrangements for the departure of the garrison. A part of that night, the brave defenders of Fort Sumter[1] enjoyed undisturbed repose. Not one of their number had been killed or very seriously hurt during the appalling bombardment of thirty-six hours, when over three thousand shot and shell were hurled at the fort.[2] The same extraordinary statement was made concerning the insurgents. It was too extraordinary for ready belief, and for a long time there was doubt about the matter, at home and abroad, and grave journalists and sparkling satirists had food for many a telling paragraph.[3] Testimony seems to show that it was true.[4]

Governor Pickens watched the bombardment on Saturday morning with a telescope, and that evening he made a most extraordinary speech to the excited populace from the balcony of the Charleston Hotel. "Thank God!"

---

[1] The following are the names of the defenders of Fort Sumter:—

OFFICERS.—Major Robert Anderson; Captains, J. G. Foster and Abner Doubleday; First Lieutenants, Jefferson C. Davis, George W. Snyder, Truman Seymour (then brevet captain), Theodore Talbot (then assistant adjutant-general), and Norman J. Hall; Second Lieutenant, Richard K. Mead; and Assistant Surgeon Samuel W. Crawford.

NON-COMMISSIONED OFFICERS.—Quartermaster-Sergeant, William H. Hamner; Sergeants, James E. Gallway, John Renshaw, John Carmody, John McMahon, John Otto, Eugene Sheibner, James Chester, William A. Harn, and Thomas Kiernan; Ordnance-Sergeant, James Kearney; Corporals, Christopher Costolow, Charles Bringhurst, Henry Ellerbrook, Owen McGuire, and Francis J. Oakes; Musicians, Robert Foster and Charles Hall; Artificers, Henry Straudt, John E. Noack, and Philip Andermann; Confidential Mail and Market Man, Peter Hart.

PRIVATES.—Patrick Murphy, Tedeschi Onoratto, Peter Rice, Henry Schmidt, John Urquhart, Andrew Wickstrom, Edward Brady, Barney Cain, John Doran, Dennis Johnson, John Kehoe, John Klein, John Lanagan, John Laroche,* Frederick Lintner, John Magill, Frederick Meier, James Moore, William Morter, Patrick Neilan, John Nixon, Michael O'Donald, Robert Roe, William Walker, Joseph Wall, Edmund Walsh, Henry R. Walter, Herman Will, Thomas Wishnowski, Casper Wutterpel, Cornelius Baker, Thomas Carroll, Patrick Clancy, John Davis, James Digdam, George Fielding, Edward Gallway, James Gibbons, James Hays, Daniel Hough, John Irwin, James McDonald, Samuel Miller, John Newport, George Pinchard, Frank Rivers, Lewis Schroeder, Carl A. Sellman, John Thompson, Charles H. Tozer, William Witzmann.

All of the officers but three were highly promoted during the war. Major Anderson was commissioned a brevet Major-General; Captains Foster and Doubleday were raised to full Major-Generals; Lieutenants Davis, Seymour, and Hall, were commissioned Brigadiers; and Surgeon Crawford received the same appointment. Lieutenant Snyder died in November following, and Lieutenant Talbot died in April, 1862. Lieutenant Meade resigned his commission and joined the insurgents. Major Anderson performed gallant service in the war with Mexico. Captain Seymour had been an extensive traveler. His ascent of Popocatapetl, in Mexico, the highest mountain in North America, has been frequently mentioned. Captain Foster was severely wounded at Molino del Rey, in Mexico; Lieutenant Davis was in the battle of Buena Vista; and Lieutenant Talbot had crossed the Rocky Mountains with Frémont's first expedition.

[2] Captain Foster, in his report, said that of the 10-inch shells, thrown from seventeen mortars, one-half went within or exploded over the parapet of the fort, and only about ten buried themselves in the soft earth of the parade without exploding. This statement shows how impossible it was to man the barbette and area guns.

[3] The London *Times*, alluding to the bombardment, the conflagration, *et cetera*, without causing serious personal injury, said:—"Many a 'difficulty' at a bar has cost more bloodshed. Was this a preconcerted feat of conjury? Were the rival Presidents saluting one another in harmless fireworks to amuse the groundlings? The whole affair is utterly inexplicable. . . . The result is utterly different from all we are accustomed to hear of the Americans. There, 'a word and a blow' has been the rule. In this case, the blow, when it does at last come, falls like snow, and lights as gently as thistle-down."

Vanity Fair, a humorous weekly sheet then published in New York, contained the following stanzas, in a poem called *The Battle of Morris Island*, already quoted from in the text:—

> "Then came the comforting piece of fun,
> Of counting the noses, one by one,
> To see if any thing had been done
>   On glorious Morris Island.
> 'Nobody hurt!' the cry arose;
> There was not missing a single nose,
> And this was the sadly ludicrous close
>   Of the Battle on Morris Island."

[4] "It is said that the only living creature killed in the conflict was a fine horse belonging to General Dunnovant, which had been hitched behind Fort Moultrie."—*Duyckinck's War for the Union*, i. 115. .

* Deserted on the 22d of April, 1861.

he exclaimed, "the war is open, and we will conquer or perish. . . . We have humbled the flag of the United States. I can here say to you, it is the first time in the history of this country that the Stars and Stripes have been humbled. That proud flag was never lowered before to any nation on the earth. We have lowered it in humility before the Palmetto and Confederate flags; and we have compelled them to raise by their side the white flag, and ask for an honorable surrender. The flag of the United States has triumphed for seventy years; but to-day, the 13th of April, it has been humbled, and humbled before the glorious little State of South Carolina." The populace were wild with delight, and while brave soldiers were sleeping in Fort Sumter, the insurgents were indulging in a saturnalia of excitement in the rebellious city.

On the following day—the holy Sabbath—the fall of Fort Sumter was commemorated in the churches of Charleston. The venerable "Bishop of the Diocese, wholly blind and physically feeble," said a local chronicler,[1] "was led by the Rector to the sacred desk," in old St. Philip's Church, when he addressed the people with a few stirring words. Speaking of the battle, he said :—"Your boys were there, and mine were there, *and it was right that they should be there.*" He declared it to be his belief that the contest had been begun by the South Carolinians "in the deepest conviction of duty to God, and after laying their cause before God—and God had most signally blessed their dependence on Him." Bishop Lynch, of the Roman Catholic Church, spoke exultingly of the result of the conflict; and a *Te Deum* was chanted, in commemoration of the event, in the Cathedral of St. John and St. Finbar, where he was officiating.

On Sunday morning,[a] long before the dawn, Major Anderson and his command began preparations for leaving the fort. These were completed at an early hour. Lieutenant Snyder and Captain Hartstene soon returned, accompanied by Captain Gillis, commander of the *Pocahontas;* and at about the same time the Charleston steamer *Isabel,* provided by the military authorities at that city for carrying the garrison out to the *Baltic,* where Mr. Fox was waiting to receive them, approached the fort. When every thing was in readiness, the battle-torn flag which had been unfurled over Fort Sumter almost four months before, with prayers for the protection of those beneath it, was raised above the ramparts, and cannon commenced saluting it. It was Anderson's intention to fire one hundred guns, but only fifty were discharged, because of a sad accident attending the firing. Some fixed ammunition near the guns was ignited, and an explosion instantly killed private Daniel Hough, mortally wounded private Edward Gallway, and injured some others. The Palmetto Guard,[2] which had been sent over from Morris Island, with the venerable

[a] April 14, 1860.

---

[1] *The Battle of Fort Sumter and First Victory of the Southern Troops:* a pamphlet published in Charleston soon after the evacuation of Fort Sumter. The Bishop of the Protestant Episcopal Church alluded to was Thomas Frederick Davis, D. D., then and now (1865) residing at Camden, South Carolina.

[2] The Palmetto Guard received honors as the chief instrument in the reduction of Fort Sumter. "The mothers, wives, sisters, and sweethearts of the Guard," said the *Charleston Mercury* of the 1st of May, "contributed the sum of two hundred dollars for the purpose of presenting a gold medal to that corps." It was completed at that date, the devices on it having been made with a graver instead of a die. On one side was a Palmetto-tree, with a rattle-snake in coil and rattles sprung. Over the tree the name of the company, and around the border the words : "From their mothers, sisters, wives, and daughters." On the other side was a

Edmund Ruffin as color-bearer, entered the fort when the salute was ended and the garrison had departed, and buried the dead soldier with military honors.   Two private soldiers of the company erected a board at the head of his grave.[1]

When the flag was lowered, at the close of the salute, the garrison, in full dress, left the fort, and embarked on the *Isabel*, the band playing "Yankee Doodle."   When Major Anderson and his officers left the sally-port, it struck up "Hail to the Chief."   The last one who retired was Surgeon Crawford, who attended poor Gallway until the latest moment possible. Soon afterward a party from Charleston, composed of Governor Pickens and suite, the Executive Council, General Beauregard and his aids, and several distinguished citizens, went to Fort Sumter in a steamer, took formal posses-

RUINS OF FORT SUMTER IN 1864.

sion of the abandoned stronghold, and raised the Confederate and Palmetto flags over it.[2]   It had been *evacuated*, not *surrendered*.   The sovereignty of the Republic, symbolized in the flag, had not been yielded to the insurgents. That flag had been lowered, but not given up—dishonored, but not captured. It was borne away by the gallant commander, with a resolution to raise it

---

picture of the Stevens Battery in the foreground, with the State flag, gun No. 1 just fired ; Fort Sumter, over which the National flag was just falling, and a squadron in the distance. Above was the motto: "None but the Brave deserve the Fair." Below: "April 12th and 13th, 1861." A richly engraved border surrounded the whole. The engraving was by a German named Bornemann.

    [1] *Charleston Mercury*, May 2, 1861."

    [2] The editor of the *Charleston Mercury*, who was one of the party who first entered Sumter after the evacuation, described the appearance of the interior. "Every point and every object," he said, "to which the eye was turned, except the outer walls and casemates, which are still strong, bore the impress of ruin. Brooded over by the desolation of ages, it could scarcely have been developed to a more full maturity of ruin. It were as if the Genius of Destruction had tasked its energies to make the thing complete. The walls of the internal structures, roofless, bare, blackened, and perforated by shot and shell, hung in fragments, and seemed in instant readiness to totter down. Near the center of the parade-ground was the hurried grave of one who had fallen from the recent casualty. To the left of the entrance was a man who seemed to be at the verge of death. In the ruins to the right there was another. The shattered flag-staff, pierced by four balls, lay sprawling on the ground. The parade-ground was strewn with fragments of shell and dilapidated buildings. At least four guns were dismounted on the ramparts ; and at every step the way was impeded by portions of the broken structure." See sketch of the interior of Fort Sumter on page 325.

again over the battered fortress, or be wrapped in it as his winding-sheet at the last. Precisely four years from that day,[a]—after four years

a April 14, 1865.

of terrible civil war—Major Anderson, bearing the title of Major-General in the Armies of the United States, again raised that tattered flag over all that remained of Fort Sumter—a heap of ruins.[1]

The *Isabel* lay under the battered walls of the fort, waiting for a favoring tide, until Monday morning,[b] when she conveyed the garrison

b April 15, 1861.

to the *Baltic*, then commanded by Captain Fletcher. The insurgent soldiers had been so impressed with the gallantry of the defense of the fort, that, as the vessel passed, they stood on the beach with uncovered heads, in token of profound respect.[2] After the surrender, every courtesy was extended to Major Anderson and his men by the military authorities at Charleston.

When all the garrison were on board the *Baltic*, the precious flag, for which they had fought so gallantly, was raised to the mast-head and saluted with cheers, and by the guns of the other vessels of the little relief-squadron. It was again raised when the *Baltic* entered the harbor of New York, on the morning of the 18th, and was greeted by salutes from the forts there, and the plaudits of thousands of welcoming spectators. Off Sandy Hook, Major Anderson had written a brief dispatch to the Secretary of War, saying:—"Having defended Fort Sumter for thirty-four hours, until the quarters were

GOLD BOX PRESENTED TO ANDERSON.

entirely burned, the main gates destroyed by fire, the gorge wall seriously injured, the magazine surrounded by flames, and its doors closed from the effects of heat, four barrels and four cartridges of powder only being available, and no provisions but pork remaining, I accepted terms of evacuation offered by General Beauregard, being the same offered by him on the 11th inst., prior to the commencement of hostilities, and marched out of the fort Sunday afternoon, the 14th instant, with colors flying and drums beating, bringing away company and private property, and saluting my flag with fifty guns."[3] This was immediately forwarded to the War Department.

The praises of Major Anderson, his officers and men, were unbounded. The gratitude of the American people was overflowing; and honors were showered upon the commander without stint. Already the citizens of

[1] See picture of the ruins on the preceding page.   [2] *Charleston Mercury.*
[3] Major Anderson to Simon Cameron, Secretary of War, April 18, 1861. I am indebted for the facts concerning the occupation and evacuation of Fort Sumter, to statements made to me by Major Anderson during several interviews, and to his official correspondence, in manuscript, which he kindly lent me, by permission of the War Department. Also, to the very interesting Manuscript Diary of Surgeon (afterward Major-General) S. W. Crawford, and the official report of Lieutenant (afterward Major-General) J. G. Foster.

Taunton, Massachusetts, impressed with a sense of his patriotism and prowess, had voted him an elegant sword, the handle of which is of carved ivory, surmounted by a figure of Liberty. The scabbard was of beautiful design and workmanship, wrought of the richest gold plate, and ornamented with a view of Fort Sumter, and with military emblems.[1] The authorities of New York presented him with the freedom of the city in an elegant Gold Box, in the form of a casket, oblong octagonal in shape.[2] The citizens of New York presented to him a beautiful gold medal, appropriately inscribed;[3] and those of Philadelphia gave him a very elegant sword, the handle and upper part of the scabbard of which are delineated in the engraving.[4] From other sources, such as societies and legislative bodies, he received pleasing testimonials of the good-will of his countrymen. Finally, the *Chamber of Commerce of the State of New York* ordered[a] the execution of a series of medals, of an appropriate character, to be presented to Major Anderson, and to each officer, non-commissioned officer, and soldier engaged in the defense of Fort Sumter. These were of four classes. The first, for presentation to Major Anderson, was six inches in diameter, bearing, on one side, a medallion portrait of the commander, and on the other the Genius or Guardian Spirit of America rising from Fort Sumter, with the American flag in the left hand, and the flaming torch of war in the right. The idea symbolized was the loyal spirit of the country, calling upon all patriots to arouse and resent the insult to the

ANDERSON'S SWORD.

a June 6, 1861.

---

[1] On the scabbard was the following inscription:—"*Deo duci, ferro comitante.*" Upon the handle, on a solid gold shield, was the following inscription:—"*Et decus et pretium recte. The citizens of Taunton, Massachusetts, to Major Robert Anderson, U. S. A. A tribute to his courage and fidelity. Acquirit qui tactus.*" This sword was presented to Major Anderson at the Brevoort House, New York, by W. C. Lovering, on the 22d of April.

[2] This box, represented on the preceding page, was five and a half inches in length, two inches in width, and not quite three inches in depth. Its whole surface, excepting the place of the inscription, was elaborately wrought in arabesque figures, giving it a very rich appearance. On the top of the clasp was an American eagle about to soar. On the top of the lid were two figures. One represented Major Anderson, kneeling on one knee in the attitude of the recipient of knighthood. In one hand he clasps a flag-staff, over which droops the American ensign. In the other hand he holds a sword. Near him stands a figure of *Liberty*, with her right hand pointing toward heaven, and with the left hand placing a laurel crown on the head of the kneeling hero. On the front of the box was the following inscription:—"The freedom of the city of New York conferred upon Major ROBERT ANDERSON by its corporate authorities, in recognition of his gallant conduct in defending Fort Sumter against the attack of the rebels of South Carolina, April 12, 1861."

[3] The gold medal was two and a half inches in diameter. On one side was a representation of the bombardment of a fort on fire; on the other a wreath of laurel, just within the outer rim, clasped by the American shield. Inside of this wreath the words, "*Prudens fidelis et audax invictæ fidelitatis præmium.*" Then there was a little circle of thirty-four stars, within and across the face of which were the words:—"To Major ROBERT ANDERSON, U. S. A., from the citizens of New York City, as a slight tribute to his patriotism."

[4] The handle and guard of this sword were set with stones. The guard was open basket-work at the broad part, in which was a shield of blue enamel bearing the cipher, in script, of Major Anderson, neatly wrought in gold and set in brilliants. On the handle were three lozenge-shaped amethysts bordered with brilliants. The scabbard is heavy gilt. At the first belt-ring are seen the arms of Pennsylvania on an escutcheon, and between them the words:—"The city of Philadelphia to ROBERT ANDERSON, U. S. A., April 22, 1861. A loyal city to a loyal soldier, the hero of Fort Sumter." At the next belt-ring the arms of Pennsylvania on another escutcheon.

flag and the sovereignty of the Republic, by the attack on the fort.[1] The second class, for presentation to the officers, was of the same design, but only four inches in diameter.[2] The third class, three and a half inches in

diameter, bore on one side the medallion portrait of Major Anderson, and on the other, Peter Hart raising the Stars and Stripes on the burning fort.[3] This is represented in the engraving below. The fourth class, for the common soldiers, was two inches in diameter, and the same as the third in design and inscription. These medals were all of bronze.

The President of the United States gave Major Anderson a more substantial evidence of appreciation, by honoring him with the rank and pay of a brigadier-general,[a] precisely one month after

OBVERSE OF THE FIRST AND SECOND CLASS MEDALS.

[a] May 14, 1861.

his evacuation of Fort Sumter. At the earnest solicitation of Garrett Davis (Congressman) and other leading Kentuckians, he was then appointed to command in that State; but his terrible experience in Fort Sumter had prostrated his nervous system, and he was compelled to abandon active

FORT SUMTER MEDAL.—THIRD AND FOURTH CLASS.

service. He was placed upon the retired list in the autumn of 1863, and the following year he was breveted a major-general. We shall hereafter meet his gallant officers in high rank, and in the performance of noble deeds, during the great war that ensued.

---

[1] On the portrait side were the words:—"ROBERT ANDERSON, 1861." On the other side were the words:— "The Chamber of Commerce, New York, honors the Defender of Fort Sumter—the patriot, the hero, and the man."

[2] The same words around the portrait. On the other side the words:—"The Chamber of Commerce, New York, honors the Defenders of Fort Sumter—first to withstand treason." This was for the officers.

[3] See page 326. The inscription on this was precisely the same as on the second class. These were for the non-commissioned officers. These medals were designed and executed by Charles Müller, sculptor, of New York City. They occupied the artist and several assistants during the period of five months.

CHAPTER XIV.

THE GREAT UPRISING OF THE PEOPLE.

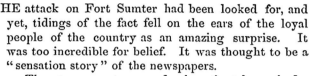HE attack on Fort Sumter had been looked for, and yet, tidings of the fact fell on the ears of the loyal people of the country as an amazing surprise. It was too incredible for belief. It was thought to be a "sensation story" of the newspapers.

The story was true; and when the telegraph declared that the old flag had been dishonored, and that "a banner, with a strange device," was floating over that fortress, which everybody thought was impregnable, and the story was believed, the latent patriotism of the nation was instantly and powerfully aroused. It seemed as if a mighty thunderbolt had been launched from the hand of the Omnipotent, and sent crashing, with fearful destructiveness, through every party platform—every partition wall between political and religious sects—every bastile of prejudice in which free thoughts and free speech had been restrained, demolishing them utterly, and opening a way instantly for the unity of all hearts in the bond of patriotism, and of all hands mailed for great and holy deeds. Heart throbbed to heart; lip spoke to lip, with a oneness of feeling that seemed like a Divine inspiration; and the burden of thought was,

> "Stand by the Flag! all doubt and treason scorning,
> Believe, with courage firm and faith sublime,
> That it will float until the eternal morning
> Pales, in its glories, all the lights of Time!"

The Sabbath day on which Anderson and his men went out of Fort Sumter was a day of wild excitement throughout the Union. Loyalists and disloyalists were equally stirred by the event—the former by indignation, the latter by exultation. The streets of cities and villages, every place of public resort, and even the churches, were filled with crowds of people, anxious to obtain an answer to the question in every mind—What next? That question was not long unanswered. Within twenty-four hours from the time when the Stripes and Stars were lowered in Charleston harbor, the President of the United States had filled every loyal heart in the land with joy and patriotic fervor, by a call for troops to put down the rising rebellion. That call answered the question.

In a proclamation issued on the 15th,[a] the President declared that the laws of the Republic had been for some time, and were then, opposed in the States of South Carolina, Georgia, Alabama, Florida, Mississippi, Louisiana, and Texas, "by combinations too powerful to be suppressed by the ordinary course of judicial proceedings, or by the powers vested in the marshals by law ;" and he therefore, by virtue of the power in him vested by the Constitution and the laws, called forth the militia of the several States of the Union, to the aggregate number of seventy-five thousand, in order to suppress those combinations and to cause the laws to be duly executed. The President appealed to all loyal citizens to "favor, facilitate, and aid this effort to maintain the honor, the integrity, and existence of our National Union, and the perpetuity of popular government, and to redress wrongs already long enough endured." He deemed it proper to say, that the first service assigned to the forces thereby called forth would probably be "to repossess the forts, places, and property which had been seized from the Union ;" and he assured the people that in every event the utmost care would be observed, consistently with the objects stated, to

a April, 1861.

SIMON CAMERON.

"avoid any devastation, any destruction of, or interference with property, or any disturbance of peaceful citizens of any part of the country." He commanded the persons composing the combinations mentioned to disperse, and retire peaceably to their respective abodes, within twenty days from the date of his proclamation.[1]

Impressed with the conviction that the then condition of public affairs demanded an extraordinary session of the Congress, he, in the same proclamation, summoned the Senators and Representatives to assemble at their respective chambers in Washington City, at noon on Thursday, the 4th day of July next ensuing, then and there to consider and determine such measures as, in their wisdom, the public safety might seem to demand.

Simultaneously with the President's Proclamation, the Secretary of War, under the authority of an Act of Congress, approved in February, 1795,[2] issued a telegraphic dispatch to the Governors of all the States of the Union, excepting those mentioned in the proclamation, requesting each of them to cause to be immediately detailed from the militia of his State the quota designated in a table, which he appended, to serve as infantry or riflemen for a period of three months (the extent allowed by law[3]), unless sooner

---

[1] Proclamation of President LINCOLN, April 15, 1861.
[2] See *The Military Laws of the United States:* by John F. Callan, page 108. G. W. Childs, Philadelphia. 1863. The President's authority for the proclamation may be found in the second and third sections of the Act approved February 28, 1795.
[3] The law declared that the militia should not be "compelled to serve more than three months after arrival

discharged. He requested each to inform him of the time when his quota might be expected at its rendezvous, as it would be there met, as soon as practicable, by an officer or officers, to muster it into the service and pay of the United States.[1] He directed that the oath of fidelity to the United States should be administered to every officer and man; and none were to be received under the rank of a commissioned officer who was apparently under eighteen, or over forty-five years of age, and not in physical health and vigor. He ordered that each regiment should consist, on an aggregate of officers and men, of seven hundred and eighty, which would make a total, under the call, of seventy-three thousand three hundred and ninety-one. The remainder of the seventy-five thousand called for was to be composed of troops in the District of Columbia.[2]

The President's Proclamation, and the requisition of the Secretary of War, were received with unbounded favor and enthusiasm in the Free-labor States; while in six of the eight Slave-labor States included in the call, they were treated by the authorities with words of scorn and defiance. The exceptions were Maryland and Delaware. In the other States disloyal Governors held the reins of power. "I have only to say," replied Governor Letcher, of Virginia, "that the militia of this State will not be furnished to the powers at Washington for any such use or purpose as they have in view. Your object is to subjugate the Southern States, and a requisition made upon me for such an object—an object, in my judgment, not within the province of the Constitution or the Act of 1795—will not be complied with. You have chosen to inaugurate civil war, and, having done so, we will meet it in a spirit as determined as the Administration has exhibited toward the South." Governor Ellis, of North Carolina, answered:—"Your dispatch is received, and if genuine, which its extraordinary character leads me to doubt, I have to say in reply, that I regard the levy of troops, made by the Administration for the purpose of subjugating the States of the South, as in violation of the Constitution, and a usurpation of power. I can be no party to this wicked violation of the laws of the country, and to this war upon the liberties of a free people. You can get no troops from North Carolina." Governor Magoffin, of Kentucky, replied:—"Your dispatch is received. I say emphatically that Kentucky will furnish no troops for the wicked purpose of subduing her sister Southern States." Governor Harris, of Tennessee, said:—"Tennessee will not furnish a single man for coercion, but fifty thousand, if necessary, for the defense of our rights, or those of our Southern brethren." Governor Rector, of Arkansas, replied:—"In answer

---

at the place of rendezvous, in any one year." It was hoped that three months would be sufficient time to put down the insurrection.

[1] The quota for each State was as follows. The figures denote the number of regiments.

State	No.	State	No.	State	No.
Maine	1	Pennsylvania	16	Missouri	4
New Hampshire	1	Delaware	1	Ohio	13
Vermont	1	Tennessee	2	Indiana	6
Massachusetts	2	Maryland	4	Illinois	6
Rhode Island	1	Virginia	3	Michigan	1
Connecticut	1	North Carolina	2	Iowa	1
New York	17	Kentucky	4	Minnesota	1
New Jersey	6	Arkansas	1	Wisconsin	1

[2] Letter of Simon Cameron, Secretary of War, to the Governors of States, April 15, 1861.

to your requisition for troops from Arkansas to subjugate the Southern States, I have to say that none will be furnished. The demand is only adding insult to injury. The people of this Commonwealth are freemen, not slaves, and will defend, to the last extremity, their honor, their lives, and property, against Northern mendacity and usurpation." Governor Jackson, of Missouri, responded:—"There can be, I apprehend, no doubt that these men are intended to make war upon the seceded States. Your requisition, in my judgment, is illegal, unconstitutional, and revolutionary in its objects, inhuman and diabolical, and cannot be complied with. Not one man will the State of Missouri furnish to carry on such an unholy crusade."

There is such a coincidence of sentiment and language in the responses of the disloyal governors, that the conviction is pressed upon the reader that the conclave of conspirators at Montgomery was the common source of their inspiration.

Governor Hicks, of Maryland, appalled by the presence of great dangers, and sorely pressed by the secessionists on every side, hastened, in a proclamation, to assure the people of his State that no troops would be sent from Maryland unless it might be for the defense of the National Capital, and that they (the people) would, in a short time, " have the opportunity afforded them, in a special election for members of the Congress of the United States, to express their devotion to the Union, or their desire to see it broken up." Governor Burton, of Delaware, made no response until the 26th, when he informed the President that he had no authority to comply with his requisition. At the same time he recommended the formation of volunteer companies for the protection of the citizens and property of Delaware, and not for the preservation of the Union. The Governor would thereby control a large militia force. How he would have employed it, had occasion required, was manifested by his steady refusal, while in office, to assist the National Government in its struggle with its enemies.

In the seven excepted Slave-labor States in which insurrection prevailed, the proclamation and the requisition produced hot indignation, and were assailed with the bitterest scorn. Not in these States alone, but in the border Slave-labor States, and even in the Free-labor States, there were vehement opposers of the war policy of the Government from its inception.[1] One of the most influential newspapers printed west of the Alleghanies, which had opposed secession valiantly, step by step, with the keen cimeter of wit and the solid shot of argument, and professed to be then, and throughout the war, devoted to the cause of the Union, hurled back the proclama-

---

[1] The utterances of two of the leading newspapers in the city of New York, whose principal editors were afterward elected to the National Congress, gave fair specimens of the tone of a portion of the Northern press at that time. The New York *Express* said:—"The South can never be subjugated by the North, nor can any marked successes be achieved against them. They have us at every advantage. They fight upon their own soil, in behalf of their dearest rights—for their public institutions, their homes, and their property. . . . The South in self-preservation, has been driven to the wall, and forced to proclaim its independence. A servile insurrection and wholesale slaughter of the whites will alone satisfy the murderous designs of the Abolitionists. The Administration, egged on by the halloo of the Black Republican organs of this city, has sent its mercenary forces to pick a quarrel and initiate the work of desolation and ruin. A call is made for an army of volunteers, under the pretense that an invasion is apprehended of the Federal Capital; and the next step will be to summon the slave population to revolt and massacre."

The New York *Daily News*, assuming to be the organ of the Democratic party, said:—"Let not this perfidious Administration invoke the sacred names of the Union and the Constitution, in the hope of cheating fools into the support of the war which it has begun. . . . He is no Democrat who will enter the Army, or

tion, to the great delight and encouragement of the conspirators, and the dismay of the friends of American nationality, in the following words:—

"The President's Proclamation has reached us. We are struck with mingled amazement and indignation. The policy announced in the Proclamation deserves the unqualified condemnation of every American citizen. It is unworthy not only of a statesman, but of a man. It is a policy utterly hare-brained and ruinous. If Mr. Lincoln contemplated this policy in his Inaugural Address, he is a guilty dissembler; if he has conceived it under the excitement aroused by the seizure of Fort Sumter, he is a guilty Hotspur. In either case, he is miserably unfit for the exalted position in which the enemies of the country have placed him. Let the people instantly take him and his Administration into their own hands, if they would rescue the land from bloodshed and the Union from sudden and irretrievable destruction."[1]

Thus spoke the organ of the "Conservatives" of the great and influential State of Kentucky,[2] and, indeed, of the great Valley of the Mississippi below the Ohio. Its voice was potential, because it represented the feelings of the dominant class in the Border Slave-labor States. From that hour the politicians of Kentucky, with few exceptions, endeavored to hold the people to a neutral attitude as between the National Government and the insurgents. They were successful until the rank perfidy of the conspirators and the destructive invasions of the insurgent armies taught them that their only salvation from utter ruin was to be found in taking up arms in support of the Government. The effect of that neutral policy, which, in a degree, was patriotic, because it seemed necessary to prevent the State from being properly ranked with the "seceding" States, will be observed hereafter.

There seemed to be calmness only at Montgomery, the head-quarters of the conspirators. These men were intoxicated with apparent success at Charleston. In profound ignorance of the patriotism, strength, courage, temper, and resources of the people of the Free-labor States, and in their pride and arrogance, created by their sudden possession of immense power which they had wrested from the people, they coolly defied the National Government, whose reins of control they expected soon to hold. Already the so-called Secretary of War of the confederated conspirators (L. P. Walker) had revealed that expectation, in a speech from the balcony of the Exchange Hotel in Montgomery, in response to a serenade given to Davis and himself, on the evening of the day on which Fort Sumter was attacked.[*] "No man," he said, "can tell when the war this day commenced[3] will end; but I will prophesy that the flag which

* April 12, 1861.

volunteer to aid this diabolical policy of civil war." These utterances found echoes in many places. We may notice here only one, that of a newspaper published in Bangor, Maine. After declaring that the South Carolinians were simply imitators of the Fathers of the Republic, it said:—"When the Government at Washington calls for volunteers to carry on the work of subjugation and tyranny, under the specious phrases of 'enforcing the laws,' retaking and 'protecting the public property,' and collecting the revenue, let every Democrat fold his arms and bid the minions of Tory despotism do a Tory despot's work."—Quoted by Whitney in his *History of the War for the Preservation of the Federal Union*, i. 313.

[1] *Louisville Journal*, April 16, 1861.
[2] Kentucky was largely represented, at that time, by men prominent in public life. It was the native State of President Lincoln; Jefferson Davis; the late Vice-President Breckenridge; Senator John J. Crittenden; James Guthrie, Chairman of the committee on resolutions in the Peace Convention at Washington; Major Anderson; Joseph Holt, late Secretary of War; General Harney, and several others of less note.
[3] During the war it was often asserted by the conspirators, and by the opponents of the war in the Free-

now flaunts the breeze here will float over the dome of the old Capitol at Washington before the first of May. Let them try Southern chivalry and test the extent of Southern resources, and it may float eventually over Faneuil Hall in Boston."[1] Already Hooper, the Secretary of the Montgomery Convention,[2] had replied to the question of the agent of the Associated Press in Washington, "What is the feeling there?" by saying:—

"Davis answers, rough and curt,
With mortar, Paixhan, and petard;
'Sumter is ours and nobody hurt.
We tender Old Abe our Beau-regard.'"[3]

Already General Pillow, of Tennessee, had hastened to Montgomery and offered the "Confederate Government" ten thousand volunteers from his

STREET VIEW IN MONTGOMERY IN 1861.—THE STATE HOUSE.

State; and assurances had come by scores from all parts of the "Confederacy," and of the Border Slave-labor States, that ample aid in men and money would be given to the "Southern cause." And an adroit knave named Sanders, who had been a conspicuous politician of the baser sort in the North, and who was in Montgomery as the self-constituted representative of the "Northern Democracy," "drinking with the President [Davis], shaking hands and conversing with crowds at the hotels, and having long

labor States, that the conflict was commenced by the National Government. This authoritative declaration of the War Minister of the "Confederacy"—"the war *this day commenced*"—settles the question.

[1] Robert Toombs once boasted, in the Senate of the United States, that he would yet call the roll of his slaves on Bunker's Hill.

[2] See page 249.

[3] The *Charleston Mercury* of the 16th said:—"Jefferson Davis replies to President Lincoln as follows:—

"With mortar, Paixhan, and petard,
We tender Old Abe our Beau-regard."

talks with the Cabinet,"[1] had assured Davis and his associates that his party would "stand by the South at all hazards," and that there would be such a " divided North," that war would be impossible.[2] Thus surrounded by an atmosphere of sophistry and adulation, which conveyed to their ears few accents of truth or reason ; confident of the support of kings, and queens, and emperors of the Old World, who would rejoice if a great calamity should overtake the menacing Republic of the West, and sitting complacently at the feet of " King Cotton,"

" The mightiest monarch of all,"

these men received the President's Proclamation with " derisive laughter,"[3] and for the moment treated the whole affair as a solemn farce.[4]

The press in the so-called " Confederate States," inspired by the key-note at Montgomery, in dissonance with which they dared not be heard, more vehemently than ever, and without stint ridiculed the " Yankees," as they called the people of the Free-labor States. They were spoken of as cowards, ingrates, fawning sycophants ; a race unworthy of a place in the society of " Southern gentlemen ;" infidels to God, religion, and morality ; mercenary to the last degree, and so lacking in personal and moral courage, that " one Southron could whip five of them easily, and ten of them at a pinch."[5] The

---

[1] Montgomery Correspondence of the *Charleston Mercury*, April 10, 1861.

[2] To impress his new political associates with exalted ideas of his power as a " Democratic leader " in the North, Sanders sent, by telegraph, the following pompous dispatch to his political friends in New York :—

" MONTGOMERY, April 14.

" To Mayor WOOD, DEAN RICHMOND, and AUGUSTE BELMONT :—

" A hundred thousand mercenary soldiers cannot occupy and hold Pensacola. The entire South are under arms, and the negroes strengthen the military. Peace must come quickly, or it must be conquered. Northern Democrats standing by the South will not be held responsible for Lincoln's acts, unless indorsing them. State Sovereignty must be fully recognized. Protect your social and commercial ties by resisting Republican Federal aggression. Philadelphia should repudiate the war action of the Pennsylvania Legislature. The commerce of Rhode Island and New Jersey is safe, when distinguished. Hoist your flag !

" Davis's answer is rough and curt—
'Sumter is ours, and nobody hurt;
With mortar, Paixhan, and petard,
We tender Old Abe our Beau-regard.'

" GEORGE N. SANDERS."

This man, as we shall observe hereafter, was a conspicuous actor in the most infamous work of the conspirators during the war that ensued.

[3] *First Year of the War :* by E. A. Pollard, page 59.

[4] The following advertisement is copied from the first inside business column of the *Mobile Advertiser* of April 16, now before me :—

" 75,000 COFFINS WANTED.

" Proposals will be received to supply the Confederacy with 75,000 BLACK COFFINS.

" ☞ No proposals will be entertained coming north of Mason and Dixon's Line. Direct to

" JEFF. DAVIS, Montgomery, Ala.

" Ap. 16, 1t."

This was intended as an intimation that the 75,000 men called for by President Lincoln would each need a coffin. It has been alleged, by competent authority, that Davis, in the folly of his madness, sanctioned the publication of this advertisement, to show contempt for the National Government.

[5] The *Mobile Advertiser*, one of the ablest and most respectable of the Southern newspapers, held the following language :—" The Northern ' soldiers' are men who prefer enlisting to starvation ; scurvy fellows from the back slums of cities, whom Falstaff would not have marched through Coventry with. But these are not soldiers—least of all to meet the hot-blooded, thoroughbred, impetuous men of the South. Trencher soldiers, who enlisted to war upon their rations, not on men. They are such as marched through Baltimore [the Massachusetts Sixth, admirably clothed, equipped, and disciplined, and composed of some of the best young men of New England], squalid, wretched, ragged, and half-naked, as the newspapers of that city report them. Fellows who do not know the breech of a musket from its muzzle, and had rather filch a handkerchief than fight an enemy in manly combat. White slaves, peddling wretches, small-change knaves and vagrants, the dregs and offscourings of the populace ; these are the levied ' forces' whom Lincoln suddenly arrays as candidates for the honor of being slaughtered by gentlemen—such as Mobile sends to battle. Let them come South, and we will put our negroes to the dirty work of killing them. But they will not come South. Not a wretch of them will live on this side of the border longer than it will take us to reach the ground and drive them off."

most absurd stories were told concerning starvation, riots, and anarchy in the Free-labor States, by the brawling politicians, the newspapers, and the men in public office who were under the absolute control of the conspirators;[1] and every thing calculated to inflame the prejudices and passions and inflate the pride of the people—inspire an overweening confidence in their own prowess and the resources of their so-called government—and to fill them with contempt and hatred for "the North," was used with great prodigality. A military despotism was suddenly erected. It was supreme in power and inexorable in practice; more withering to true manhood and more destructive of national prosperity than any written about by historians. It prevailed from this time until the close of the terrible war that ensued. It took the place of civil government everywhere, permitting only the skeleton of the latter to exist. Press, pulpit, courts of law, were all overshadowed by its black wing; and its fiat produced that "united South" about which the conspirators and their friends prated continually. It raised great armies, that fought great battles so valiantly, that American citizens everywhere contemplate with honest pride their courage and endurance, while loathing the usurpers who, by force and fraud, compelled the many to combat for wrong for the benefit of the few.

The foolish boastings of the newspaper press in the Slave-labor States. were imitated by many of the leading journals in the Free-labor States. "The nations of Europe," said one,[2] "may rest assured that Jeff. Davis & Co. will be swinging from the battlements at Washington at least by the 4th of July. We spit upon a later and longer deferred justice."—"Let us make quick work," said another.[3] "The 'rebellion,' as some people designate it, is an unborn tadpole. Let us not fall into the delusion, noted by Hallam, of mistaking a 'local commotion' for a revolution. A strong, active 'pull together' will do our work effectually in thirty days." Another[4] said that "no man of sense could for a moment doubt that this much-ado-about-nothing would end in a month," and declared that "the Northern people are simply invincible. The rebels—a mere band of ragamuffins—will fly like chaff before the wind on our approach." A Chicago newspaper[5] said:—"Let the East get out of the way; this is a war of the West. We can fight the battle, and successfully, within two or three months at the furthest. Illinois can whip the South by herself. We insist on the matter being turned over to us." Another[6] in the West said:—"The rebellion will be crushed out before the assemblage of Congress."

There were misapprehensions, fatal misapprehensions, in both sections. Neither believed that the other would fight. It was a sad mistake. Each

<hr/>

[1] A contributor to *De Bow's Review* for February, 1861, wrote as follows:—

"Our enemies, the stupid, sensual, ignorant masses of the North, who are foolish as they are depraved, could not read the signs of the times, did not dream of disunion, but rushed on as heedlessly as a greedy drove of hungry hogs at the call of their owners. They were promised plunder, and find a famine; promised 'bread, and were given a stone.' Our enemies are starving and disorganized. The cold, naked, hungry masses are at war with their leaders. They are mute, paralyzed, panic-stricken, and have no plan of action for the future. Winter has set in, which will aggravate their sufferings, and prevent any raid into or invasion of the South. They who deluded them must take care of them. The public lands will neither feed nor clothe them; they cannot plunder the South, and are cut off by their own wicked folly from the trade of the South, which alone could relieve and sustain them." And so the readers of this magazine were wickedly deceived.

[2] *New York Tribune.*
[3] *New York Times.*
[4] *Philadelphia Press.*
[5] *Chicago Tribune.*
[6] *Cincinnati Commercial.*

appealed to the Almighty to witness the rectitude of its intentions, and each was quick to discover coincident omens of Heaven's approval. "God and justice are with us," said the loyalists, "for we contend for union, nationality, and universal freedom."—"God is equally with us," said the insurgents, "for we contend for rightful separation, the supreme sovereignty of our respective States, and the perpetuation of the Divine institution of Slavery." And when, on the Sunday after the promulgation of the President's summons for troops to put down rising rebellion, the first Lesson in the Morning Service of the Protestant Episcopal Churches of the land was found to contain this battle-call of the Prophet:—"Proclaim ye this among the Gentiles; Prepare war, wake up the mighty men, let all the men of war draw near; let them come up: beat your plowshares into swords, and your pruning-hooks into spears: let the weak say, I am strong,"[1] the loyalists said: "See how Revelation summons us to the conflict!" and the insurgents answered, "It is equally a call for us;" adding, "See how specially we are promised victory in another Lesson of the same Church!—' I will remove far off from you the Northern army, and will drive him into a land barren and desolate, with his face toward the east sea, and his hinder part toward the utmost sea. . . . Fear not, O land! be glad and rejoice: for the Lord will do great things.'"[2] In this temper multitudes of the people of the Republic, filled with intelligent convictions of the righteousness of the cause they had respectively espoused, left their peaceful pursuits in the pleasant spring-time, and the alluring ease of abounding prosperity, and prepared for war, with a feeling that it would be short, and little more than an exciting though somewhat dangerous holiday pastime. No one seemed to think that it was the beginning of a sanguinary war that might cost the Nation a vast amount of blood and treasure.

The uprising of the people of the Free-labor States in defense of Nationality was a sublime spectacle. Nothing like it had been seen on the earth since the preaching of Peter the Hermit and of Pope Urban the Second filled all Christian Europe with religious zeal, and sent armed hosts, with the cry of "God wills it! God wills it!" to rescue the sepulcher of Jesus from the hands of the infidel. Men, women, and children felt the enthusiasm alike; and, as if by concerted arrangement, the National flag was every-where displayed, even from the spires of churches and cathedrals. In cities, in villages, and by wayside taverns all over the country, it was unfurled from lofty poles in the presence of large assemblages of the people, who were addressed frequently by some of the most eminent orators in the land. It adorned the halls of justice and the sanctuaries of religion; and the "Red, White, and Blue," the colors of the flag in combination, became a common ornament of women and a token of the loyalty of men. Every thing that might indicate attachment to the Union was employed; and in less than a fortnight after the President's Proclamation went forth, the post-offices were made gay with letter envelopes bearing every kind of device, in brilliant colors, illustrative of love of country and hatred of rebellion. The use of these became a passion. It was a phenomenon of the times. Not less than

---

[1] Joel iii. 9, 10.
[2] Joel ii. 20, 21. Letter of W. T. Walthall, of Mobile, to the editor of the *Church Journal*, May 17, 1861.

four thousand different kinds of Union envelopes were produced in the course of a few weeks. Sets of these now find a careful depository in the cabinets of the curious.

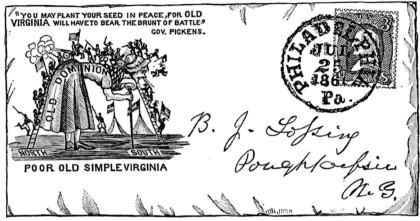

UNION ENVELOPE.[1]

The uprising in the Slave-labor States at this time, though less general and enthusiastic, was nevertheless marvelous. The heresy of State Supremacy, which Calhoun and his followers adroitly called State *rights*, because the latter is a sacred thing cherished by all, was a political tenet generally accepted as orthodox. It had been inculcated in every conceivable form and on every conceivable occasion;[2] and men who loved the Union and deprecated secession were in agreement with the conspirators on that point. Hence it was that in the tornado of passion then sweeping over the South, where reason was discarded, thousands of intelligent men, deceived by the grossest misrepresentations respecting the temper, character, and intentions of the people of the Free-labor States, flew to arms, well satisfied that they were in the right, because resisting what they believed to be usurpation, and an unconstitutional attempt at the subjugation of a free people, on the part of the National Government.

The writer was in New Orleans at the time of the attack on Fort Sumter, in quest of knowledge respecting the stirring military events that occurred in that vicinity at the close of the year 1814 and the beginning of 1815. He was accompanied by a young kinswoman. We arrived there on the 10th,[a] having traveled all night on the railway from Grand Junction, in Tennessee. At Oxford, Canton, Jackson, and other places, we heard rumors of an expected attack on the fort. These were brought to us by a physician, who had been a member of the Secession Con-

[a] April, 1861.

---

[1] This specimen of the Union envelopes has been chosen from several hundreds of different kinds in possession of the author, because it contains, in its design and words, a remarkable prophecy. The leaders of the rebellion in the more Southern States comforted their people with the assurance, when it was seen that war was inevitable, that it could not reach their homes, for in the Border Slave-labor States, and especially in Virginia, would be the battle-fields. It was indeed so, until in the last year of the war; and "Poor Old Virginia," as Governor Pickens predicted, had to bear the brunt. She was the Mother of Disunion, and the hand of retributive justice was laid heavily upon her.

[2] See note 1, page 63.

vention of Mississippi—a man of sense, moderation, and courtesy, who was our pleasant traveling companion from Decatur, in Northern Alabama, to Magnolia, in Mississippi, where we parted with him at breakfast. In the same car we met a Doctor Billings, of Vicksburg, who had been for several years a surgeon in the Mexican army, and was then returning to the city of Mexico, to carry out the preliminaries of a scheme of leading men in the Southwest for seizing some of the richest portions of Mexico. Wine or something stronger had put his caution asleep, and he communicated his plans freely. He was a Knight of the Golden Circle, and was charged with the duty of procuring from the Mexican Congress permission for American citizens to construct a railway from the Rio Grande, through Chihuahua and Sonora, to the Gulf of California. He intended to get permission to commence the work immediately, with five thousand men, armed ostensibly for defense against the Indians. Once in the country, these men would seize and hold possession of those States until sufficiently re-enforced to make the occupation permanent. This was to be the end of the railway enterprise. It was to be a movement, in co-operation with the secessionists of Texas, to open the way for the extension toward Central America of that grand empire to be established on the foundation of Slavery, whose political nucleus was at Montgomery.[1] Billings left New Orleans for Mexico a few days afterward. His scheme failed.

We found much excitement in New Orleans. The politicians were giving out ominous hints of great events near at hand. Ben. McCulloch[2] was at the St. Charles Hotel, having arrived on the 6th, and was much of the time in consultation with the leading secessionists. Howell Cobb[3] was also there. I called on some of the active politicians for local information, but found them too intently engaged in matters of immediate and pressing importance to listen or reply to many questions. On the following morning, intelligence that Fort Sumter had been attacked was brought by the telegraph. The absorbing occupation of the politicians was explained. They foreknew the event. All day long the spaces around the bulletin-boards were crowded by an excited multitude, as dispatch after dispatch came announcing the progress of the conflict.

WASHINGTON ARTILLERY.

At an early hour on Saturday, we left the city in a barouche for Jackson's battle-field below. We passed the head-quarters of the celebrated Washington Artillery,[4] who were afterward in the battle at Bull's Run. They were on parade, in the uniform in which they afterward appeared on the field. We rode down the levee as far as Villere's, where Pakenham and other British officers had their head-quarters in 1815; and returning, stopped to visit and sketch the remains of the famous old battle_

---

ground. At a little past two o'clock in the afternoon, while sitting on the base of the unfinished monument commemorative of the conflict, making a drawing of the plain of Chalmette, where it occurred, we heard seven discharges of heavy guns at the city—the number of the States in the Confederacy. "Fort Sumter is doubtless gone," I said to my companion. It was so. The news had reached the city at that hour, and under the direction of Hatch, the disloyal Collector of the port of New Orleans,[1] the guns of the *McClelland*, which the insurgents had seized, were fired in honor of the event.

On our return to the city, at five o'clock in the evening, we found it alive with excitement. The Washington Artillery were just marching by the statue of Henry Clay, on Canal Street, and members of many other corps, some of them in the brilliant and picturesque Zouave uniform, were hurrying, singly or in squads, to their respective places of rendezvous. The cry in all that region then was: "On to Fort Pickens!" The seizure of that strong-

LOUISIANA ZOUAVE.

hold was of infinite importance to the insurgents; and to that end the conspirators at Montgomery called the military power of the Confederacy to hasten to Pensacola before Fort Pickens should be re-enforced.

The next day was Sunday. The bulletin-boards were covered with the most exciting telegraphic placards early in the morning. Among others seen on that of the *Delta*, was one purporting to be a copy of a dispatch from Richmond, saying substantially that "Ben. McCulloch, with ten thousand men, was marching on Washington!" I had seen the chief editor of the *Delta* with McCulloch on the previous evening. Another declared that General Scott had resigned, and had offered his services to his native State, Virginia. Many similar misrepresentations were posted, calculated to inspire the people with hope and enthusiasm and to promote enlistments, while they justified the charge of the Union men, that those pretended dispatches, and a host of others, originated in New Orleans. Around the bulletin-boards were exultant crowds, sometimes huzzaing loudly; and at the usual hour for Divine Service, the solemn music of the church bells tolling was mingled with the lively melody of the fife and drum.[2] Many citizens were seen wearing the secession rosette and badge; and small secession flags fluttered from many a window. The banner of the so-called Southern Confederacy—the "Stars and Bars"[3]—

---

[1] See page 185.

[2] A sturdy old negro, named Jordan Noble, celebrated in New Orleans as a drummer at the battle near there in January, 1815, and who went as such to Mexico under General Taylor, was now drumming for the volunteers. He accompanied New Orleans troops to Virginia, and was at the first battle of Bull's Run.

[3] See page 256. "We protest against the word 'stripes,' as applied to the broad *bars* of the flag of our Confederacy. The word is quite appropriate as applied to the Yankee ensign or a barber's pole; but it does not correctly describe the red and white divisions of the flag of the Confederate States. The word is *bars*—we have removed from under the stripes."—*Montgomery Mail*, March, 1861.

was everywhere seen, but nowhere the flag of the Union. The latter would not be tolerated. The reign of terror had commenced in earnest. The voices of Union men were silenced; and the fact of a revolution accomplished seemed painfully apparent when we saw these strange banners, and heard, in a Protestant Episcopal Church, a prayer for "the President of the Confederate States of America."

On Monday, the President's call for seventy-five thousand men was placarded on the bulletin-boards. That proclamation was unexpected. It exhibited an unsuspected resoluteness in the Government that threatened trouble for the insurgents. The effect was marked. The groups around the placards were no longer jubilant. There was visible uneasiness in the mind of every looker-on, and all turned away thoughtful. There was a menace of war, and war would ruin the business of New Orleans. Even the marching of troops through the streets when they departed for Pensacola failed to excite much enthusiasm; and when, on the 17th, the subscription-books for the fifteen millions of dollars loan, authorized by the Convention of conspirators at Montgomery,[1] were opened, there were very few *bona-fide* bids for large amounts. But that proclamation gave heart-felt satisfaction to the Union men of New Orleans, and they were counted by thousands among the best citizens. These were silent then. The editor of the *True Delta*, a Union journal, had been compelled to fling out the secession flag, to prevent the demolition of his office by a mob. "No one dares to speak out now," said the venerable Jacob Barker, the banker, as he stealthily placed in the writer's hand a broadside, which he had had printed on his eighty-first birthday,[a] as a gift of good for his countrymen, containing a series of argumentative letters against secession, first published in a Natchez newspaper. "If," said another, one of the oldest citizens of New Orleans, "the Northern people shall respond to that call, and the United States shall 'repossess and hold' the forts and other public property—if the power of the Government shall pull down the detested secession flags now flaunting in our faces over our Mint and Custom House, and show that it has power to maintain the old banner in their places,[3] the Union men in the South will take Kentucky hemp, and hang every traitor between the Gulf and the Ohio and Potomac!"

SECESSION ROSETTE AND BADGE.[2]

[a] December 7, 1860.

---

[1] See page 263.

[2] The rosette was made of blue satin ribbon, surrounding a disk, containing two circles. On one were the words, "OUR FIRST PRESIDENT. THE RIGHT MAN IN THE RIGHT PLACE." On the other, seven stars and the words "JEFF. DAVIS." On the badge of white satin was printed, in proper colors, the "Confederate" flag. Over it were the words, "THE SOUTH FOREVER. SOUTHERN CONFEDERATION." Below it, "JEFF. DAVIS, PRESIDENT. A. H. STEPHENS, VICE-PRESIDENT."

[3] The last time the National Flag had been publicly displayed in New Orleans was on Washington's Birthday, the 22d of February. A citizen flung out one on Front Levee Street, on which were two clasped hands and the words, "United we stand; divided we fall." The enraged secessionists went to pull it down, but found armed men there to defend it, and it was kept flying until evening, when it was taken down voluntarily.

We left New Orleans for the North on the morning of Wednesday, the 17th,[a] and spent that night at the little village of Canton, in Mississippi. We went out in search of a resident of the place, whom we had met at Niagara Falls the previous summer. He was absent. A war-meeting was gathering in the Court House, on the village green, when we passed, and a bugle was there pouring forth upon the evening air the tune of the Marseillaise Hymn of the French Revolution.[1] We had observed that every National air which hitherto had stirred the blood of all Americans was discarded throughout the "Confederacy," and that the performance of any of them was presumptive evidence of treason to the traitors. We felt great desire to respond to the bugle with Yankee Doodle or Star-spangled Banner,[2] but prudence counseled silence.

[a] April, 1861.

We went on to Grand Junction the next morning, where we were detained thirty-six hours, in consequence of our luggage having been carried to Jackson, in Tennessee. All along the road, we had seen recruiting-officers gathering up men here and there from the sparse population, to swell the ranks of the insurgents assembling at Pensacola under General Bragg, who had abandoned the old flag. The negroes were quietly at work in the fields, planting cotton, little dreaming of their redemption from Slavery being so nigh.

The landlord of the "Percey House" at Grand Junction was kind and obliging, and made our involuntary sojourn there as agreeable as possible. We were impatient to go forward, for exasperation against Northern men was waxing hot. We amused ourselves nearly half a day, "assisting," as the French say, at the raising of a secession flag upon a high pole. It was our first and last experience of that kind. After almost five hours of alternate labor, rest, and consultation, during which time the pole was dug up, prostrated, and re-erected, because of defective halliards, the flag was "flung to the breeze," and was saluted by the discharge of a pocket-pistol in the hands of a small boy. This was followed by another significant amusement at which we "assisted." At Grand Junction, four railway trains, traveling respectively on the New Orleans and Jackson and the Charleston and Memphis roads, which here intersect, met twice a day, and the aggregation of passengers usually formed a considerable crowd. On one of these occasions we heard two or three huzzas, and went out to ascertain the cause. A man of

---

[1] This stirring hymn was parodied, and sung at social gatherings, at places of amusement, and in the camps throughout the "Confederacy." The following is the closing stanza of the parody:—

> "With needy, starving mobs surrounded,
>   The zealous, blind fanatics dare
> To offer, in their zeal unbounded,
>   Our happy slaves their tender care.
> The South, though deepest wrongs bewailing,
>   Long yielded all to Union's name;
> But INDEPENDENCE now we claim,
>   And all their threats are unavailing.
>   To arms! to arms! ye brave!
>   The avenging sword unsheathe!
>   March on! march on!
>   All hearts resolved
>   On Victory or Death!"

[2] A Charleston correspondent of the *Richmond Examiner* said, just before the attack on Fort Sumter, "Let us never surrender to the North the noble song, the 'Star-spangled Banner.' It is Southern in its origin; in its association with chivalrous deeds, it is ours." See Frank Moore's *Rebellion Record*, i. 20.

middling stature, with dark hair, and whiskers slightly sprinkled with white, apparently fifty years of age, was standing on a bale of cotton, haranguing the listeners:—"Every thing dear to you, fellow-citizens," he exclaimed, " is in peril, and it is your duty to arm immediately in aid of the holy Southern cause. The Northern Goths and Vandals—offscourings of the Yankee cities —two hundred thousand strong, are gathering north of the Ohio to invade your State, to liberate your slaves or incite them to insurrection, to ravish your daughters, to sack your cities and villages, to lay waste your plantations, to plunder and burn your dwellings, and to make you slaves to the vilest people on the face of the earth." He had spoken in this strain about three minutes, when the conductor's summons, "All aboard!" dispersed the audience, and the speaker entered a car going westward to Memphis. The orator was General Gideon J. Pillow, who played an inglorious part in the war that ensued. He had just come from the presence of Jefferson Davis at Montgomery. Although his State (Tennessee) had lately, by an overwhelming vote, pronounced for Union, this weak but mischievous man, the owner of hundreds of acres of cotton lands in the Gulf and Trans-Mississippi States, and scores of slaves, was working with all his might, with the traitorous Governor of the Commonwealth (Harris), to excite the people to revolt, by such false utterances as we have just noticed.[1]

GIDEON J. PILLOW.

He was ambitious of military fame, and had already, as we have observed, offered to Jefferson Davis the services of ten thousand Tennessee soldiers, without the least shadow of

[1] On the day after his harangue at Grand Junction, Pillow was in Memphis, where he assumed the character of a military chief, and issued a sort of proclamation, dated April 20, in which he said: "All organized military companies of foot, cavalry, and artillery will be needed for the defense of the Southern States against invasion by the tyrant who has established a military despotism in the city of Washington. These forces will be received in companies, battalions, or regiments, as they may themselves organize, and will be received into the service of the Confederate States (for Tennessee has no other place of shelter in this hour of peril), and the officers commissioned with the rank of command with which they are tendered for the field.

"They will not be required for the defense of the Southern coast. Kentucky and Virginia will be the fields of conflict for the future. The city of Memphis is safe against the possibility of approach from the Gulf, and will be equally so by the construction of a battery of 24 and 32-pounders at Randolph, and the point indicated to the Committee of Safety, above the city. Such batteries, with the plunging fire, could sink any sized fleets of steamboats laden with Northern troops. If such batteries are promptly constructed, Memphis will never even be threatened.

"The object of seizing Cairo by the Lincoln Government (if it should be done, as I take it for granted it will) will be to cut off supplies of subsistence from the Northwest, to prevent the approach through the Ohio of Southern troops, and to cut off Missouri from Southern support; and when she is thus isolated, to invade and crush her. The safety of Missouri requires that she should seize and hold that position at whatever cost. Without it, she will soon cease to breathe the air of freedom.

"All the forces tendered from Tennessee, to the amount of fifty thousand men, will be received as they are fitted by their state of drill for the field. Sooner, they would not be efficient, and they will not be called into the service without proper provision for subsistence and the best arms within the resources of the government. The entire South must now unite and make common cause for its safety—no matter about the political relations of the States at present—else all will be crushed by the legion of Northern Goths and Vandals with which they are threatened.

"The revolution which is on us, and invasion which is at our doors, will unite the Southern States with or without formal ordinances of separation. I speak not without authority.

"I desire to receive official reports from all organized corps of the State—giving me the strength of the rank and file of each separate organization. These reports will reach me at Nashville."

authority.[1]   Inquiring of a leading Nashville secessionist, on the evening after hearing Pillow's harangue, what authority the General had for his magnificent offer, he smiled and said, in a manner indicative of the disesteem in which the conspirator was held in his own State, " The authority of Gid. Pillow." In the course of the war that ensued, which this disloyal Tennessean strove so hard to kindle, the hand of retributive justice fell upon him, as upon all of his co-workers in iniquity, with crushing force.

Our detention at Grand Junction was fortunate for us.   We intended to travel eastward through East Tennessee and Virginia to Richmond, and homeward by way of Washington and Baltimore.   The car in which we left our place of detention was full of passengers, many of them from the North, and all of them excited by the news in the Memphis papers of that morning.

WOOD-CUT FROM A MEMPHIS NEWSPAPER.

The telegraphic dispatches from the East were alarming and distressing, and the tone of the papers containing them was exultant and defiant.   It was asserted that on the day before,[a] eight hundred Massachusetts troops had been captured, and more than one hundred killed, while trying to pass through Baltimore.   The annunciation was accompanied by a rude wood-cut, made for the occasion, representing the National flag tattered and humbled beneath the secession banner, that was waving over a cannon discharging.[2]   It was also announced that Harper's Ferry had been seized and was occupied by the insurgents ; that the New York Seventh Regiment, in a fight with

[a] April 19, 1861.

Marylanders, had been defeated with great loss ; that Norfolk and Washington would doubtless be in the hands of the insurgents in a day or two ; that General Scott had certainly resigned his commission and offered his services to Virginia ;[3] and that President Lincoln was about to follow his

[1] See page 340.

[2] At about the same time, according to an informant of the Philadelphia *North American* (May 9, 1861), the National flag was more flagrantly dishonored in Memphis.   A pit was dug by the side of the statue of General Jackson, in the public square at Memphis.   Then a procession, composed of about five hundred citizens, approached the spot slowly, headed by a band of music playing the "Dead March."   Eight men, bearing a coffin, placed it in the pit or grave, when the words, "Ashes to ashes, dust to dust," were pronounced, and the grave filled up.   The coffin contained nothing but the American flag!   It was an act significant of an eternal separation from the Union.

[3] This story was so persistently iterated and reiterated, that it was believed.   Scott was eulogized by the press in the interest of the conspirators.   "And now," said the *New Orleans Picayune*, "how·many of those gallant men who, in various positions, have for years gloried in Winfield Scott, will linger in the ranks of the army which, in losing him, has lost its ablest and most signal ornament?"   The slander was soon set at rest by the old hero himself.   Senator Crittenden, at his home in Kentucky, anxiously inquired of him whether there was any truth in the story, and instantly received the following dispatch:—

"WASHINGTON, April 20, 1861.

"Hon. J. J. CRITTENDEN:—I have not resigned.   I have not thought of resigning.   Always a Union man.

"WINFIELD SCOTT."

Commenting on this answer, a Virginia newspaper, differing from its *confrère*, the *Picayune*, in its esti

example.[1] At Decatur we were met by still more alarming rumors, underlying which there was evidently some truth, and we thought it prudent to turn our faces northward. Had we not been detained at Grand Junction, we should then have been in Virginia, possibly in Washington or Baltimore, subjected to the annoyances of that distressing week when the National Capital was cut off from all communication with the States north and east of it. We spent Sunday in Columbia, Tennessee; Monday, at Nashville; ^a and at four o'clock on Tuesday morning,^a departed for Louisville.   ^{a April 23, 1861.}

At Columbia we received the first glad tidings since we left New Orleans. There we met a bulletin from the Nashville *Union and American*, containing news of the great uprising in the Free-labor States—the rush of men to arms, and the munificent offers of money from city corporations, banking institutions, and private citizens, all over the country. Our faith in the patriotism of the people was amazingly strengthened; and when, on the following day, at Franklin and one or two other places, Pillow, who was our fellow-passenger, repeated his disreputable harangue at Grand Junction, and talked of the poverty, the perfidy, the acquisitiveness, and the cowardice of the "Northern hordes of Goths and Vandals," he seemed like a mere harlequin, with cap and bells, trying to amuse the people with cunning antics. And so the people seemed to think, for at Franklin, where there was quite a large gathering, there was not a single response to his foolish speech. Nobody seemed to be deceived by it.

Pillow was again our fellow-passenger on Tuesday morning, when we left Nashville. We had been introduced to him the day before, and he was our traveling-companion, courteous and polite, all the way to Louisville. When we crossed the magnificent railway bridge that then spanned the Green River at Mumfordsville, in Kentucky, he leaned out of the car window and viewed it with great earnestness. I spoke of the beauty and strength of the structure, when he replied: "I am looking at it with a military eye, to see how we may destroy it, to prevent Northern troops from invading Tennessee." He seemed to be persuaded that a vast host were mustering on the Ohio border. He was evidently on his way to Louisville to confer, doubtless by appointment, with leading secessionists of Kentucky, on the subject of armed rebellion. The register of the "Galt House"[b] in ^{b April 23.} that city showed that Pillow, Governor Magoffin, Simon B. Buckner, and other secessionists were at that house on that evening.[2]

We did not stop at Louisville, but immediately crossed the Ohio River to Jeffersonville, and took passage in a car for Cincinnati. The change was wonderful. For nearly three weeks we had not seen a National flag, nor heard a National air, nor scarcely felt a thrill produced by a loyal sentiment audibly uttered; now the Stars and Stripes were seen everywhere, National melodies were heard on every hand, and the air was resonant with the shouts

---

mate of Scott's character, said, after calling him "a driveling old fop," "With the red-hot pencil of infamy, he has written on his wrinkled brow the terrible, damning words, 'Traitor to his native State!'"—*Abingdon Democrat.*

  [1] These dispatches produced the greatest exultation throughout the South and Southwest. Salvos of cannon and the ringing of bells attested the general joy. The editor of the Natchez *Free Trader* said, after describing the rejoicings there, "The pen fails to make the record a just one. We are hoarse with shouting and exalted with jubilancy."

  [2] Letter of General Leslie Coombs to the author.

of loyal men. Banners were streaming from windows, floating over house-tops, and fluttering from rude poles by the waysides. Little children waved them with tiny huzzas, as our train passed by, crowded to its utmost capacity with young men hastening to enroll themselves for the great Union Army then forming.

Cincinnati was fairly iridescent with the Red, White, and Blue. From the point of the spire of white cut stone of the Roman Catholic Cathedral, two hundred and twenty-five feet in the air, the loyal Archbishop Purcell had caused to be unfurled, with " imposing ceremonies," it was said, a mag-nificent National flag, ninety feet in length;[1] and on the day of our visit, it seemed as if the whole population were on the streets, cheering the soldiers

STREET SCENE IN CINCINNATI, IN APRIL, 1861.

as they passed through the city.[2] There was no sign of doubt or lukewarm-ness. The Queen City gave ample tokens that the mighty Northwest, whose soil had been consecrated to freedom forever by a solemn act of the Congress of the old Confederation,[3] was fully aroused to a sense of the perils that threatened the Republic, and was sternly determined to defend it at all hazards. How lavishly that great Northwest poured out its blood and trea-sure for the preservation of the Union will be observed hereafter.

As we journeyed eastward through Ohio, by way of Columbus, Newark, and Steubenville, to Pittsburg, the magnitude and significance of the great

---

[1] " The 'ceremonies' attending the raising of the flag," wrote the Archbishop in a letter to the author, July 23, 1865, in reply to a question concerning it, " consisted of the hurrahs, the tears of hope and joy, the prayer for success from the blessing of God on our cause and arms by our Catholic people and our fellow-citizens of various denominations, who saluted the flag with salvos of artillery. The flag was really ninety feet long, and broad in proportion. One of less dimensions would not have satisfied the enthusiasm of our people."

[2] The scene depicted in the engraving was on Fourth Street, the fashionable and business thoroughfare of Cincinnati, in the vicinity of Pike's Opera House. The view is from a point near the Post-office.

[3] See the famous Ordinance passed on the 13th of July, 1787, by the unanimous vote of the eight States then represented in Congress, namely, Massachusetts, New York, New Jersey, Delaware, Virginia, North Caro-lina, South Carolina, and Georgia. In that ordinance, the most perfect freedom of person and property was decreed. See *Journals of Congress*, Folwell's edition, xii. 58.

uprising became hourly more and more apparent.   The whole country seemed to have responded to the call:—

> "Lay down the ax, fling by the spade;
> Leave in its track the toiling plow:
> The rifle and the bayonet-blade
> For arms like yours were fitter now;
> And let the hands that ply the pen
> Quit the light task, and learn to wield
> The horseman's crooked brand, and rein
> The charger on the battle-field."[1]

In the evening we saw groups drilling in military maneuvers in the dim moonlight, with sticks and every kind of substitute for a musket.   Men were crowding the railway cars and other vehicles, as they pressed toward designated places of rendezvous; and at every station, tearful women and children were showering kisses, and farewells, and blessings upon their loved ones, who cheered them with assurances of speedy return.   Pittsburg, with its smoke and forges, was bright with banners, and more noisy with the drum than with the tilt-hammer.   All the way over the great Alleghany range, and down through the beautiful valleys of the Juniata and Susquehanna, we observed the people moving to "the music of the Union." Philadelphia—staid and peaceful Philadelphia—the Quaker City—was gay and brilliant with the ensigns of war.   Her streets were filled with resident and passing soldiery, and her great warm heart was throbbing audibly with patriotic emotions, such as stirred her more than fourscore years before, when the Declaration of Independence went out from her venerated State House.   Her Mayor (Henry) had just said:—"By the grace of Almighty God, treason shall never rear its head or have a foothold in Philadelphia.   I call upon you as American citizens to stand by your flag, and protect it at all hazards."[2]   The people said Amen! and no city in the Union has a brighter record of patriotism and benevolence than Philadelphia.   New Jersey was also aroused.   Burlington, Trenton, Princeton, Brunswick, Rahway, Elizabethtown, Newark, and Jersey City, through which we passed, were alive with enthusiasm.   And when we had crossed the Hudson River, and entered the great city of New York,[a] with its almost a million of inhabitants, it seemed as if we were in a vast military camp.   The streets were swarming with soldiers.   Among the stately trees at the Battery, at its lower extremity, white tents were standing.   Before its iron gates sentinels were passing.   Rude barracks, filled with men, were covering portions of the City Hall Park; and heavy cannon were arranged in line near the fountain, surrounded by hundreds of soldiers, many of them in the gay costume of the Zouave.   Already thousands of volunteers had gone out from among the citizens, or had passed through the town from other parts of the State, and from New England ; and already the commercial metropolis of the Republic, whose disloyal Mayor, less than four months before, had argued officially in favor of its raising the standard of secession and

^a May 1, 1861.

---

[1] *Our Country's Call:* by William Cullen Bryant.

[2] Speech of Mayor Henry to a crowd of citizens who were about to attack the printing-office of *The Palmetto Flag*, a disloyal sheet, on the corner of Fourth and Chestnut Streets.   The Mayor exhorted the citizens to refrain from violence.   The proprietor of the obnoxious sheet displayed the American flag.   The Mayor hoisted it over the building, and the crowd dispersed.

revolt,[1] had spoken out for the Union in a monster meeting of men of all
political and religious creeds, gathered around the statue of Washington,
at Union Square,[a] where all party feeling was kept in abeyance,
and only one sentiment—THE UNION SHALL BE PRESERVED—was
the burden of all the oratory.

[a] April 20, 1861.

THE BATTERY, NEW YORK, IN MAY, 1861.

That New York
meeting, the type
of others all over the
land, had a peculiar
significance, and a
vast and salutary in-
fluence. That city
had been regarded
as eminently "con-
servative" and friend-
ly to "the South,"
on account of the
many ties of commer-
cial interest. Politi-
cally it was opposed
to the Administra-
tion by thirty thou-
sand majority. The
voice of the metropo-
lis, at such a crisis, was therefore listened for with the most anxious solicitude.
It could not keep silence. Already the insurgents had commenced their
movements for the seizure of the seat of Government. Harper's Ferry and
the Gosport Navy Yard were just passing into the hands of rebellious men.
Already the blood of Union soldiers had been spilt in Baltimore, and the cry
had come up from below the Roanoke: "*Press on toward Washington!*"
Already the politicians of Virginia had passed an Ordinance of
Secession,[b] and were inviting the troops from the Gulf States to
their soil. The secessionists of Maryland were active, and the National
Capitol, with its archives, was in imminent peril of seizure by the insurgents. It was under such a condition of public affairs that the meeting had
assembled, on the 20th of April. Places of business were closed, that all
might participate in the proceedings. It was estimated, that at least one
hundred thousand persons were in attendance during the afternoon. Four
stands were erected at points equidistant around Union Square; and the soiled
and tattered flag that Anderson had brought away from Fort Sumter, was
mounted on a fragment of its staff, and placed in the hands of the statue
of Washington. The meeting was organized by the appointment of a
President at each of the four stands, with a large number of assistants;[2]
and it was addressed by representative men of all political parties, who,

[b] April 17.

---

[1] See page 205.
[2] The four Presidents were John A. Dix, ex-Governor Hamilton Fish, ex-Mayor William F. Havemeyer,
and Moses H. Grinnell. These were assisted by numerous vice-presidents and secretaries, who were chosen
from among men holding opposing opinions.

as we have observed, were in perfect agreement on this occasion, in a determination to support the Government in maintaining its authority.[1]

John A. Dix, a life-long Democrat, and lately a member of Buchanan's Cabinet, presided at the principal stand, near the statue of Washington. The meeting was then opened by prayer by the venerable Gardiner Spring, D. D., when the President addressed a few sentences to the multitude, in which he spoke of the rebellion being without provocation on the part of the Government, and said:—"I regard the pending contest with the secessionists as a death-struggle for constitutional liberty and law—a contest which, if successful on their part, could only end in the establishment of a despotic government, and blot out, whenever they were in the ascendant, every vestige of national freedom.

UNION SQUARE, NEW YORK, ON THE 20TH OF APRIL, 1861.

. . . We stand before the statue of the Father of his Country. The flag of the Union which floats over it, hung above him when he presided over the Convention by which the Constitution was framed. The great work of his life has been rejected, and the banner by which his labors were consecrated has been trampled in the dust. If the inanimate bronze, in which the sculptor has shaped his image, could be changed for the living form which led the armies of the Revolution to victory, he would command us, in the name of the hosts of patriots and political martyrs who have gone before, to strike for the defense of the Union and the Constitution."

Daniel S. Dickinson, a venerable leader of the Democratic party, said:— "We are called upon to *act*. This is no time for hesitation or indecision— no time for haste or excitement. It is a time when the people should rise in the majesty of their might, stretch forth their strong arm, and silence the angry waves of tumult. It is a question between Union and Anarchy— between law and disorder."

Senator Baker, of Oregon, a leading member of Congress, who afterward gave his life for his country at Ball's Bluff, made an eloquent speech. "Young men of New York," he said—"Young men of the United States—

---

[1] An account of the proceedings of this meeting, containing the names of the officers, and abstracts of the several speeches, may be found in the first volume of the *Rebellion Record*, edited by Frank Moore.

you are told this is not to be a war of aggression. In one sense, that is true; in another, not. We have committed aggression upon no man. In all the broad land, in their rebel nest, in their traitor's camp, no truthful man can rise and say that he has ever been disturbed, though it be but for a single moment, in life, liberty, estate, character, or honor. The day they began this unnatural, false, wicked, rebellious warfare, their lives were more secure, their property more secure by us—not by themselves, but by us—guarded far more securely than any people ever have had their lives and property secured, from the beginning of the world. We have committed no oppression, have broken no compact, have exercised no unholy power; have been loyal, moderate, constitutional, and just. We are a majority of the Union, and we will govern our own Union, within our own Constitution, in our own way. We are all Democrats. We are all Republicans. We acknowledge the sovereignty of the people within the rule of the Constitution; and under that Constitution, and beneath that flag, let traitors beware. . . . I propose that the people of this Union dictate to these rebels the terms of peace. It may take thirty millions; it may take three hundred millions. What then? We have it. Loyally, nobly, grandly do the merchants of New York respond to the appeal of the Government. It may cost us seven thousand men; it may cost us seventy-five thousand men in battle; it may cost us even seven hundred and fifty thousand men? What then? We have them. The blood of every loyal citizen of this Government is dear to me. My sons, my kinsmen, the young men who have grown up beneath my eye and beneath my care, they are all dear to me; but if the country's destiny, glory, tradition, greatness, freedom, government—written Constitutional Government—the only hope of a free people—demand it, let them all go. I am not here now to speak timorous words of peace, but to kindle the spirit of manly, determined war. . . . I say my mission here to-day is, to kindle the heart of New York for war. The Seventh Regiment is gone. Let seventy and seven more follow. . . . Civil War, for the best of reasons upon one side, and the worst upon the other, is always dangerous to liberty—always fearful, always bloody; but, fellow-citizens, there are yet worse things than fear, than doubt and dread, and danger and blood. Dishonor is worse. Perpetual anarchy is worse. States forever commingling and forever severing is worse. Traitors and secessionists are worse. To have star after star blotted out—to have stripe after stripe obscured—to have glory after glory dimmed—to have our women weep and our men blush for shame throughout generations yet to come; that and these are infinitely worse than blood.

"The President himself," continued the eloquent speaker, "a hero without knowing it—and I speak from knowledge, having known him from boyhood—the President says, 'There are wrongs to be redressed, already long enough endured.' And we march to battle and to victory, because we do not choose to endure these wrongs any longer. They are wrongs not merely against us; not against you, Mr. President; not against me, but against our sons and against our grandsons that surround us. They are wrongs against our ensign; they are wrongs against our Union; they are wrongs against our Constitution; they are wrongs against human hope and human freedom. . . . While I speak, following in the wake of men so eloquent, so conservative, so eminent, so loyal, so well known—even while I speak, the object of your meeting is accomplished. Upon the wings of the lightning it goes out throughout the world that New York, the very heart of a great State, with her crowded thoroughfares, her merchants, her manufacturers, her artists— that New York, by one hundred thousand of her people, declares to the country and to the world, that she will sustain the Government to the last dollar in her treasury—to the last drop of your blood. The National banners leaning from ten thousand windows in your city to-day, proclaim your affection and reverence for the Union."

Robert J. Walker, of Mississippi, who was Secretary of the Treasury in the Democratic Administration of President Polk, denounced secession as a crime, and said :—"Much as I love my party, I love my country infinitely more, and must and will sustain it, at all hazards. Indeed, it is due to the great occasion here frankly to declare that, notwithstanding my earnest opposition to the election of Mr. Lincoln, and my disposition most closely to scrutinize all his acts, I see, thus far, nothing to condemn in his efforts to save the Union. . . . And now let me say, that this Union must, will, and shall be perpetuated ; that not a star shall be dimmed or a stripe erased from our banner ; that the integrity of the Government shall be preserved, and that from the Atlantic to the Pacific, from the lakes of the North to the Gulf of Mexico, never shall be surrendered a single acre of our soil or a drop of its waters."

David S. Coddington, an influential member of the Democratic party, gave a scathing review of the efforts of disunionists recorded in our history, and said :—"Shall I tell you what secession means? It means *ambition in the Southern leaders and misapprehension in the Southern people. Its policy is to imperialize Slavery, and to degrade and destroy the only free republic in the world.* . . . Nothing so disappoints secession as the provoking fidelity of New York to the Constitution. From the vaults of Wall Street, Jefferson Davis expected to pay his army, and riot in all the streets and in all the towns and cities of the North, to make their march a triumphant one. Fifty thousand men to-day tread on his fallacy."

Such was the response of some of the ablest representatives of the venerable Democratic party to the slanderers of that party, such as Sanders and his like in the South, and its trading politicians in the North.[1] It was the

---

[1] Representative men of the Democratic party in different loyal States made speeches, and took substantially the same ground. The venerable General Cass, late Secretary of State, made a stirring speech at Detroit, on the 24th of April. "He who is not for his country," he said, "is against her. There is no neutral position to be occupied. It is the duty of all zealously to support the Government in its efforts to bring this unhappy civil war to a speedy and satisfactory conclusion, by the restoration, in its integrity, of that great charter of freedom bequeathed to us by Washington and his compatriots."

The veteran General Wool, a Democrat of the Jefferson and Jackson school, and then commander of the Eastern Department, said, in response to the greetings of the citizens of Troy, who, at the close of an immense meeting, on the 16th of April, went to his house in a body:—"Will you permit that flag to be desecrated and trampled in the dust by traitors? Will you permit our noble Government to be destroyed by rebels, in order that they may advance their schemes of political ambition and extend the area of Slavery? No, indeed, it cannot be done. The spirit of the age forbids it. My friends, that flag must be lifted up from the dust into which it has been trampled, placed in its proper position, and again set floating in triumph on the breeze. I pledge you my heart, my hand, all my energies to the cause. The Union shall be maintained. I am prepared to devote my life to the work, and to lead you in the struggle!"

Caleb Cushing, who presided at the Charleston Convention (page 20) and at the Seceders' Convention at Baltimore (page 27), in 1860, made an eloquent speech at Newburyport, Massachusetts, on the same day, in which he said that he cordially participated in the patriotic manifestations around him. He would yield to no man in faithfulness to the Union, or in zeal for the maintenance of the laws and the constitutional authorities

unbiased sentiment of the great body of that organization then and throughout the war, who were truly loyal in sentiment, and formed a strong element of the powerful Union party that faithfully sustained the Government, in spite of the machinations of demagogues. That meeting relieved the citizens of the commercial metropolis of the nation from the false position of apparent selfish indifference to the fate of the Republic, in which they had been placed before Europe by an able correspondent of the London *Times*, who had been utterly misled by a few men among whom he unfortunately fell on his arrival in this country.[1] It gave assurance of that heart-felt patriotism of the great body of the citizens of New York, who attested their devotion to the country by giving about one hundred thousand soldiers to the army, and making the sacrifice, it is estimated, in actual expenditures of money, the loss of the labor of their able-bodied men, private and public contributions, taxes, *et cætera*, of not less than three hundred millions of dollars in the course of four years. That meeting dismayed and exasperated the conspirators,[2] for they saw that

of the Union; and to that end he stood prepared, if occasion should call for it, to testify his sense of public duty by entering the field again, at the command of the Commonwealth or of the Union. Mr. Cushing did offer his services in the field to the Governor of Massachusetts, but they were not accepted.

At a public reception of Senator Douglas, Mr. Lincoln's opponent for the Presidency, at Chicago, Illinois, on the 1st of May, that statesman, in a patriotic speech, said:—"There are only two sides to this question. Every man must be for the United States or against it. There can be no neutrals in this war; only *patriots* or *traitors*. . . . I express it as my conviction before God, that it is the duty of every American citizen to rally round the flag of his country."

[1] This was William Howard Russell, LL. D., whom we have mentioned in note 2, page 91. He had acquired much reputation by his graphic pictures of the war in the Crimea. He was instructed to keep the readers of the *Times* advised of the progress of events in the United States during the civil war that then seemed inevitable. Dr. Russell arrived in the city of New York at the middle of March, 1861, while the ground was covered with snow. The center of the society into which he was invited and retained during his stay in that city was an eminent banker, whom he speaks of as "an American by theory, an Englishman in instincts and tastes—educated in Europe, and sprung from British stock. His friends," he said, "all men of position in New York society, had the same dilettanti tone, and were as little anxious for the future. or excited by the present, as a party of *savans*, chronicling the movements of a 'magnetic storm.'" He mentions the names of some of the gentlemen whom he met there, among whom were some who were distinguished throughout the war as the most persistent opposers of their Government in its efforts to save the nation from ruin. The impression their conversation and arguments made on the mind of Dr. Russell was, he said, "that, according to the Constitution, the Government could not employ force to prevent secession, or to compel States which had seceded by the will of the people to acknowledge the Federal power. In fact, according to them, *the Federal Government was a mere machine put forward by a society of sovereign States*, as a common instrument for certain ministerial acts, more particularly those which affected the external relations of the Confederation. . . . There was not a man who admitted the Government had any power to coerce the people of a State, or to force a State to remain in the Union, or under the action of the Federal Government; in other words, the symbol of power at Washington is not at all analogous to that which represents an established government in other countries. Although they admitted the Southern leaders had meditated 'the treason against the Union' years ago, they could not bring themselves to allow their old opponents, the Republicans now in power, to dispose of the armed force of the Union against their brother Democrats of the Southern States."

The conclusion at which Dr. Russell arrived, in consequence of the expressed opinions of these "men of position in New York," among whom he associated while there, was, that "there was neither army nor navy available, and the ministers had no machinery of rewards, and means of intrigue, or modes of gaining adherents known to European Governments. The Democrats," he said, "behold, with silent satisfaction, the troubles into which the Republican triumph has plunged the country, and are not at all disposed to extricate them. The most notable way of impeding their efforts is to knock them down with the Constitution every time they rise to the surface, and begin to swim out. New York society, however, is easy in its mind just now, and the upper world of millionaire merchants, bankers, contractors, and great traders, are glad that the vulgar Republicans are suffering for their success."—*My Diary North and South:* by William Howard Russell, Chapters III. and IV. Harper & Brothers, 1863.

[2] Alluding to the meeting, the *Richmond Despatch* (April 25) said:—"New York will be remembered with special hatred by the South, to the end of time. Boston we have always known where to find; but this New York, which has never turned against us until this hour of trial, and is now moving heaven and earth for our destruction, shall be a marked city to the end of time." That special hatred, not of "the South," but of the conspirators, was evinced in attempts to lay the city in ashes, and, it is said, to poison the Croton water with which the city is supplied from forty miles in the interior.

This exasperation of those who had been greatly deceived was very natural. The disloyal official propo-

they had been deceived, and observed that, unlike themselves, their political brethren in the Free-labor States loved their country more than their party —were more patriotic than selfish—and would boldly confront with war, if necessary, every enemy of the Union and of American nationality. It also amazingly encouraged and strengthened the President and his Cabinet in their efforts to suppress the rising rebellion.

In that meeting the profound intellect—the science of the Free-labor States—was represented by Professor O. M. Mitchel, one of the brightest lights of the century, who also gave his services and his life in defense of the Union. No speech on that occasion thrilled the vast multitude who heard his voice more than that of Professor Mitchel. "I have been announced to you," he said, "as a citizen of Kentucky. Once I was, because I was born there. I love my native State as you love your native State. I love my adopted State of Ohio as you love your adopted State, if such you have; but, my friends, I am not a citizen now of any State. I owe allegiance to no State, and never did, and, God helping me, I never will. *I owe allegiance to the Government of the United States.*" After referring to his own education at the Military Academy at West Point, he said:—"My father and my mother were from Old Virginia, and my brothers and sisters from Old Kentucky. I love them all; I love them dearly. I have my brothers and friends down in the South now, united to me by the fondest ties of love and affection. I would take them in my arms to-day with all the love that God has put into this heart; but, if I found them in arms against my country, I would be compelled to smite them down. You have found officers of the Army who have been educated by the Government, who have drawn their support from the Government for long years, who, when called upon by their country to stand for the Constitution and for the right, have basely, ignominiously, and traitorously either resigned their commissions or deserted to traitors, and rebels, and enemies. What means all this? How can it be possible that men should act in this way? There is no question but one. If we ever had a Government and a Constitution, or if we ever lived under such, have we ever recognized the supremacy of right? I say, in God's name, why not recognize it now? Why not to-day? Why not forever? Suppose those friends of ours from Old Ireland—suppose he who made himself one of us, when a war should break out against his own country, should say, 'I cannot fight against my own countrymen,' is he a citizen of the United States? They are countrymen no longer when war breaks out. The rebels and the traitors in the South we must set aside; they are not our friends. When they come to their senses, we will receive them with open arms; but till that time, while they are trailing our glorious banner in the dust; when they scorn it,

<hr>

sition of Mayor Wood, only three or four months before; the intimate and extensive commercial relations of New York with the Slave-labor States; the known financial complicity of some of its citizens in the African Slave-trade, and the daily utterances of some of its politicians, gave assurance that in a crisis such as had arrived, it would "stand by the South." While the writer was at the St. Charles Hotel, in New Orleans, on the day when the President's call for troops reached that city, he heard a gentleman (Colonel Hiram Fuller), who had been prominently connected with the newspaper press of New York, say to a group of bystanders: "Our city will never countenance the Black Republicans in making war. I belong to a secret society [Knights of the Golden Circle?] in that city, fifty thousand strong, who will sooner fight for the South than for the Abolition North." This was less than a week before the great meeting at Union Square.

condemn it, curse it, and trample it under foot, then I must smite. In God's name I will smite, and, as long as I have strength, I will do it. Oh! listen to me! listen to me! I know these men; I know their courage; I have been among them; I have been with them; I have been reared with them; they have courage; and do not you pretend to think they have not. I tell you what it is, it is no child's play you are entering upon. They will fight; and with a determination and a power which is irresistible. Make up your mind to it. Let every man put his life in his hand, and say: 'There is the altar of my country; there I will sacrifice my life.' I, for one, will lay my life down. It is not mine any longer. Lead me to the conflict. Place me where I can do my duty. There I am ready to go. I care not where it may lead me. I am ready to fight in the ranks or out of the ranks. Having been educated in the Academy; having been in the Army seven years; having served as commander of a voluntary company for ten years, and having served as an adjutant-general, I feel I am ready for something. I only ask to be permitted to act, and, in God's name, give me something to do!"

While the speakers at the great meeting illustrated the enthusiasm of the people of the Free-labor States, the resolutions there adopted indicated the calm judgment and unalterable determination that would govern them in the trial before them. In those resolutions, they averred that the Declaration of Independence, the war of the Revolution, and the Constitution of the United States had given origin to our Government, the most equal and beneficent hitherto known among men; that under its protection the wide expansion of our territory, the vast development of our wealth, our population, and our power, had built up a nation able to maintain and defend before the world the principles of liberty and justice upon which it was founded; that by every sentiment of interest, of honor, of affection, and of duty, they were engaged to preserve unbroken for their generation, and to transmit to their posterity, the great heritage they had received from heroic ancestors; that to the maintenance of this sacred trust they would devote whatever they possessed and whatever they could do; and in support of that Government under which they were happy and proud to live, they were prepared to shed their blood and lay down their lives. In view of future reconciliation, they added:—"That when the authority of the Federal Government shall have been re-established, and peaceful obedience to the Constitution and laws prevail, we shall be ready to confer and co-operate with all loyal citizens throughout the Union, in Congress or in convention, for the consideration of all supposed grievances, the redress of all wrongs, and the protection of every right, yielding ourselves, and expecting all others to yield, to the will of the whole people, as constitutionally and lawfully expressed."

For many months after this great meeting, and others of its kind in the cities and villages of the land, the Government had few obstacles thrown in its way by political opponents; and the sword and the purse were placed at its disposal by the people, with a faith touching and sublime.

CHAPTER XV.

SIEGE OF FORT PICKENS.—DECLARATION OF WAR.—THE VIRGINIA CONSPIRATORS AND
THE PROPOSED CAPTURE OF WASHINGTON CITY.

E have observed that on the fall of Fort Sumter the conspirators were very anxious to seize Fort Pickens before it should be re-enforced. We left Lieutenant Slemmer and a small garrison there, besieged by insurgents, who were continually increasing in number.[1] We have also observed that the Governor of Florida had made secret preparations to seize Forts Jefferson and Taylor before the politicians of his State had passed an Ordinance of Secession.

Fort Jefferson[2] is at the Garden Key, one of the Tortugas Islands, off the southern extremity of the Florida peninsula, and Fort Taylor is at Key West, not far distant from the other. The walls of Fort Jefferson were finished, as to hight, and the lower tier of ports was completed, in the

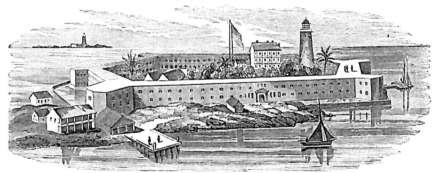

FORT JEFFERSON IN 1861.

autumn of 1860; but the upper embrasures were entirely open; temporary sally-ports, for the convenience of laborers, remained unstopped, and the works were exposed to easy capture at any time. Fort Taylor was nearer completion. Its casemate-battery was mounted, and Captain (afterward Brigadier-General) J. M. Brannan, with a company of the First Artillery, occupied barracks about half a mile distant.

The seizure of these forts by the secessionists was delayed chiefly because the laborers employed on them were mostly slaves belonging to

---

[1] See page 172.
[2] This fort covers an area of about thirteen acres, or nearly the whole of the Garden Key. It is calculated for an armament of four hundred and fifty guns when complete, and a garrison of one thousand men. It commands the inner harbor of Key West.

the friends of the conspirators, and their owners did not wish to lose the revenue derived from their labor any sooner than would be absolutely necessary. It was believed that the forts might be seized by the Floridians at any time. There was an armed band of secessionists at Key West, headed by the clerk of Fort Taylor, whose second in command was the editor of a violent secessionist newspaper there. Military officers connected with the forts were known to be secessionists, and these afterward abandoned their flag and joined its enemies; and some of the most respectable of the residents, holding office under the Government, had declared their intention to oppose Captain Brannan to the utmost, if he should attempt to take possession of and occupy Fort Taylor. The disaffected were so numerous that Brannan was compelled to act with the greatest circumspection. At one time it seemed impossible for him to be of any practical service to his country, so completely was he in the power of the secessionists, civil and military.

At that time the United States steamer *Mohawk*, Captain T. A. Craven, was cruising for slave-ships in the vicinity of the Florida Keys and the coast of Cuba; and at about the time of Mr. Lincoln's election,[a] Captain (afterward Quartermaster-General) M. C. Meigs arrived, to take charge of the works at the Tortugas. He went by land, and was satisfied from what he heard on the way that an attempt would be made by the secessionists to seize the forts at the Keys, for their possession would be an immense advantage to the conspirators in the event of war.

[a] November 6, 1860.

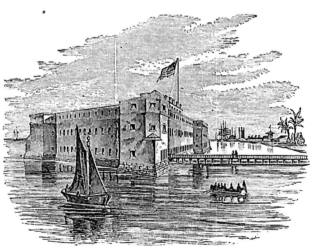

FORT TAYLOR IN 1861.[1]

It was determined to defeat their designs, and to this end Captain Meigs worked assiduously, with his accustomed energy and prudence, in conjunction with Captain Brannan and the officers of the Navy at that station, whom he supposed he could trust.

Within a week after the arrival of Captain Meigs, a crisis seemed to be approaching, and preparations were made to throw Captain Brannan's company into Fort Taylor, and strengthen both fortresses against all enemies A little

---

[1] This fort is near Key West, and, with Fort Jefferson, commands the northern entrance to the Gulf of Mexico. It is of great strength. It is calculated for an armament of one hundred and seventy-eight guns, arranged in three tiers. This picture is from a sketch made by one of the garrison, and published in *Harper's Weekly* in 1861.

stratagem was necessary; so the *Mohawk*, which had been lingering near Key West, weighed anchor and departed, professedly on a cruise in search of slave-ships. This was to lull into slumber the vigilance of the secessionists, who were uneasy and wide awake when the *Mohawk* was there. She went to Havana on the 16th,[a] where her officers boarded two of the steamers of lines connecting Key West with both New Orleans and Charleston, and requested to be reported as "after slavers." As soon as they were gone she weighed anchor, and on Sunday morning, the 18th, returned to Key West. The *Wyandotte*, Captain Stanley, was there, and had taken position so that her battery would command the bridge that connected Fort Taylor with the island.

[a] November, 1860.

While the inhabitants of Key West were in the churches, Captain Brannan quietly marched his company by a back path, crossed the bridge, and took possession of the fort. He had sent munitions and stores by water. The two forts were immediately put in a state of defense, and they and the port of Key West were irretrievably lost to the insurgents.

The Administration did not like these performances of loyal commanders, because they were "irritating" to the secessionists; and Captain Craven received peremptory orders from the Navy Department to go on a cruise. He lingered around the Keys, believing that his services would be needed near those important forts that guarded the northern entrance to the Gulf of Mexico. He was not mistaken. The presence of his vessel admonished the secessionists to be cautious. At length, on the 18th of January, the day on which the insurgents at Pensacola demanded, a second time, the surrender of Fort Pickens,[1] the steamer *Galveston*, from New Orleans, bearing a military force for the purpose of capturing the forts near Key West, appeared in sight. At the same time the United States transport *Joseph Whitney* was there; and a company of artillery, under Major Arnold, was disembarking from her at Fort Jefferson, then in command of Captain Meigs. This apparition caused the *Galveston* to put about and disappear. Forts Taylor and Jefferson were now in a condition to resist the attacks of ten thousand men. Various plans of the secessionists to capture these forts were partially executed, but no serious attack was ever attempted afterward.[2]

Let us now consider the siege of Fort Pickens.

From the 18th of January, on which day Colonel Chase, the commander of the insurgents near Pensacola, demanded the surrender of Fort Pickens, and was refused,[3] Lieutenant Slemmer and his little garrison, like Anderson and his men in Fort Sumter, worked faithfully, in the midst of hourly perils, to strengthen the fort. Like the dwellers in Fort Sumter, they were compelled to be non-resistant while seeing formidable preparations for their destruction. The country, meanwhile, was in a state of feverish anxiety, and loyal men at the seat of Government, like Judge Holt, the Secretary of War, and General Scott, strongly urged the propriety of re-enforcing and supplying that fort. The President was averse to any "initiatory" move-

---

[1] See page 171.

[2] See statement of Surgeon Delavan Bloodgood, in the *Companion to the Rebellion Record*, Document 4. Mr. Bloodgood was in service on the *Mohawk* at that time.

[3] See page 172.

ment on the part of the Government; but when, at the middle of January, it was announced that the insurgents had actually seized the Navy Yard at Warrington, and Forts Barrancas and M'Ree, and were menacing Fort Pickens, he consented to have re-enforcements sent. These, consisting of only a single company of artillery, under Captain Vogdes, ninety in number, were taken from Fortress Monroe, whose garrison was already too weak to be safe against an attack by Virginians, while at the same time General

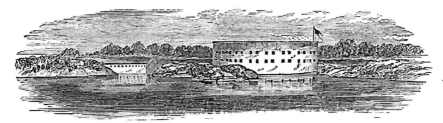

FORT M'REE AND "CONFEDERATE" BATTERY OPPOSITE FORT PICKENS.

Scott held three hundred troops in readiness for the purpose, at Fort Hamilton, in New York harbor, where they were not needed.[1]

On the 24th of January, the National war-steamer *Brooklyn* left Fortress Monroe for Fort Pickens, with Captain Vogdes and ten artillerymen, and provisions and military stores. It was also determined to employ three or four small steamers, then in the Coast-Survey service, for the same purpose, under the command of Captain J. H. Ward of the Navy,[2] who was an early martyr in the cause of his country. These movements were suspended in consequence of a telegraphic dispatch sent from Pensacola on the 28th,[a] by Senator Mallory, to Senators Slidell, Hunter, and Bigler, in which was expressed an earnest desire for peace, and an assurance that no attack would be made on Fort Pickens if the then present *status* should be preserved.[3]

[a] January, 1861.

This proposal was carefully considered, both with a view to the safety of the fort, and the effect which a collision might have upon the Peace Convention about to assemble in Washington.[4] The result was that a joint telegraphic dispatch, prepared by the Secretaries of War and the Navy, was sent, the next day, to Lieutenant Slemmer and the naval commanders off Pensacola, in which instructions were given for the *Brooklyn* not to land any troops at Fort Pickens unless it should be attacked, but to give the garrison any needed stores. The commanders of the *Brooklyn* and other vessels were charged to be vigilant, and to act promptly in the event of an attack. It was stipulated, in the sort of armistice then agreed upon, that the commander of each arm of the service should have the right of free intercourse with the Government while the arrangement should last. This proposition proved to be only a trick on the part of Mallory and his associates to gain time for the collection of a larger force near Fort Pickens, while that

[1] Statement of Lieutenant-General Scott, dated at "Washington City, March 30, 1861," and published in the *National Intelligencer*, October 21, 1862.
[2] Statement of General Scott, above cited.
[3] Reply of Ex-President Buchanan to General Scott's statement, dated "Wheatland, October 28, 1862."
[4] See page 235.

work should remain comparatively empty and absolutely weak, and so be made an easy prey through treachery or assault. Thus for more than two months re-enforcements were kept out of Fort Pickens while the rebellion was gaining head, although the armistice really ended with the closing of the Peace Convention, and its failure to effect a reconciliation.

When the new Administration came into power, on the 4th of March, a new line of policy was adopted, more consistent with the National dignity, but not less cautious. Informed that the insurgents were greatly augmented in numbers near Pensacola, and were mounting guns in Fort McRee, and constructing new batteries near, all to bear heavily on Fort Pickens, General Scott again advised the Government to send re-enforcements and supplies to the garrison of that post. The Government acted upon his advice, and by its directions on the same day[a] the General-in- Chief dispatched a note to Captain Vogdes of the *Brooklyn*, saying :—" At the first favorable moment you will land with your company, re-enforce Fort Pickens, and hold the same till further orders." It was unsafe to send such orders by mail or telegraph, for the insurgents controlled both in the Gulf States, and this was sent from New York, in duplicate, by two naval vessels. From that time unusual activity was observed in the Navy Yard at Brooklyn; also on Governor's Island and at Fort Hamilton, at the entrance to the harbor of New York. There was activity, too, in the arsenals of the North, for, while the Government wished for peace, it could scarcely indulge a hope that the wish would be gratified.

[a] March 12, 1861.

With the order for the fitting out of an expedition for the relief of Fort Sumter was issued a similar order in relation to Fort Pickens. Supplies and munitions for this purpose had been prepared in ample quantity, in a manner to excite the least attention, and between the 6th and 9th of April the chartered steamers *Atlantic* and *Illinois* and the steam frigate *Powhatan* departed from New York for the Gulf of Mexico with troops and supplies.[1] In the mean time the Government had dispatched Lieutenant John L. Worden of the Navy (the gallant commander of the first *Monitor*, which encountered the *Merrimack* in Hampton Roads), with an order to Captain Adams, of the *Sabine*, then in command of the little squadron off Fort Pickens,[2] to throw re-enforcements into that work at once. The previous order of General Scott to Captain Vogdes had not been executed, for Captain Adams believed that the armistice was yet in force. Colonel Braxton Bragg, the artillery officer in the battle of Buena Vista, in Mexico, to whom, it is said, General Taylor coolly gave the order, in the midst of the fight— "a little more grape, Captain Bragg"—was now in command of all the insurgent forces at and near Pensacola, with the commission of brigadier-general; and Captain Duncan N. Ingraham, of the United States Navy (who behaved so well in the harbor of Smyrna, a few years before, in defending the rights of American citizens, in the case of the Hungarian, Martin Kostza), had charge of the Navy Yard at Warrington. On the day of Lieutenant Worden's arrival there, Captain Adams had dined with these faithless men, and had returned to his ship.

---

[1] See page 308.

[2] This squadron consisted of the frigate *Sabine*, steam sloop-of-war *Brooklyn*, gunboats *Wyandotte* and *Crusader*, store-ship *Supply*, and the *St. Louis*.

Lieutenant Worden had acted with great energy and discretion. At eleven o'clock on the night of the 6th of April he received orders from the Secretary of the Navy to take dispatches with all possible speed to Captain Adams. He left Washington City early the next morning, arrived at Montgomery late at night on the 9th, and departed early the following

THE SABINE.[1]

morning for Pensacola, by way of Atlanta, in Georgia. He observed great excitement prevailing. Troops and munitions of war were being pushed forward toward Pensacola, and he thought it likely that he might be arrested; so, after reading his dispatches carefully, he tore them up. At dawn on the morning of the 11th, while seeking for a boat to convey him to the squadron, a "Confederate" officer interrogated him, and on ascertaining his rank and destination, directed him to report to General Bragg. An officer was sent with him to the General's head-quarters at the Naval Hospital at Warrington (whither they had been conveyed in a small steamer), where he arrived at ten o'clock in the morning. He told Bragg that he had come from Washington, under orders from the Navy Department to communicate with the commander of the squadron off that harbor. Bragg immediately wrote a "pass," and as he handed it to Worden, he remarked, "I suppose you have dispatches for Captain Adams?" Worden replied, "I have no written ones, but I have a verbal communication to make to him from the Navy Department." The Lieutenant then left Bragg and made his way to the *Wyandotte*, the flag-of-truce vessel lying inside the lower harbor. The wind was high, and the *Wyandotte* did not go outside until the next morning. At noon[a] Worden's message was delivered to Captain Adams, and Fort Pickens was re-enforced that night.[2]

a April 12, 1861.

Lieutenant Worden's arrival was timely. It frustrated a well-matured

---

[1] The *Sabine* was an old but stanch sailing vessel, and had been Commodore Shubrick's flag-ship in the Paraguay expedition, a few years before.
[2] Statement of Lieutenant Worden to the author.

plan of General Bragg's for seizing the fort, which was to have been executed on the night of the 11th, but which, on account of the rough weather, was deferred until the following night, and was not unknown to Lieutenant Slemmer. That officer had been kept acquainted with affairs in the insurgent camp at Warrington by Richard Wilcox, a loyal watchman at the Navy Yard, who addressed him over the signature of "A Friend to the Union." During the siege, Slemmer had been allowed to send a flag of truce to the yard every day. The bearer was carefully conducted from his boat to the yard and back. Wilcox was generally on hand to perform that duty, and used these opportunities to communicate with Slemmer. On the 10th of April he discovered that one of Slemmer's sergeants was holding treasonable correspondence with two secessionists on shore (Sweetman and Williams), who were employed by General Bragg. The sergeant had arranged to assist in betraying the fort into the hands of the insurgents, for which service he was to receive a large sum of money and a commission in the "Confederate" Army. He had seduced a few companions into a

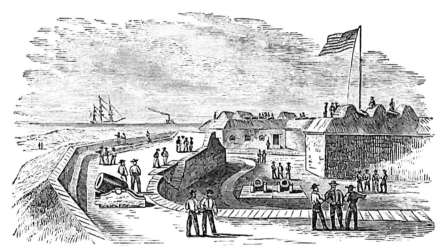

FLAG-STAFF BASTION, FORT PICKENS.

promised participation in his scheme. The act was to be performed, as we have observed, on the night of the 11th of April, when a thousand insurgents were to engage in the matter. They were to cross over in a steamboat (the same that conveyed Lieutenant Worden from Pensacola to Warrington) and escalade the fort at an hour when the sergeant and his confederates would be on guard. Wilcox informed Slemmer of the fact, and his testimony was confirmed by a Pensacola newspaper[1] that found its way into the fort. In that paper was a letter from a correspondent at Warrington, in which the intended attack on Fort Pickens was mentioned.

---

[1] *Pensacola Observer.* Its correspondent "Nemo," named Mathews, was not a traitor, but a blunderer, and was arrested and sent to Montgomery. His indiscretion was of service to the National cause, and for this the conspirators were disposed to punish him.

Slemmer prepared to frustrate the designs of the insurgents, but friends instead of enemies visited him the following night.[1]

The re-enforcement of Fort Pickens was performed as follows :—Early in the evening the marines of the *Sabine* and *St. Louis*, under Lieutenant Cash, were sent on board the *Brooklyn*, Captain Walker, when she weighed anchor and ran in as near to Fort Pickens as possible. Launches were lowered, and marines, with Captain Vogdes's artillerymen, immediately embarked. The landing was effected not far from the flag-staff bastion, at about mid-night, under the direction of Lieutenant Albert N. Smith, of Massachusetts. They had passed into the harbor, and under the guns of Forts McRee and Barrancas, unobserved. The whole expedition was in charge of Commander Charles H. Poor, assisted by Lieutenants Smith, of the *Brooklyn*, Lew and Newman, of the *Sabine*, and Belknap, of the *St. Louis*. The insurgents, in endeavoring to conceal their own movements, had assisted in obscuring those of the squadron, by extinguishing the lamp of the light-house. In the thick darkness, the expedition struck the designated landing-place with great accuracy.[2] When the important work was accomplished, heavy guns were fired on the vessels, the fort was lighted up, and the insurgents, who were on the point of making an attack on Fort Pickens, observing the ominous appearance of affairs there prudently remained on shore.[3]

Lieutenant Worden, in the mean time, had returned to Pensacola, and departed for home. He left the *Sabine* about three o'clock in the afternoon,[a] landed at Pen-

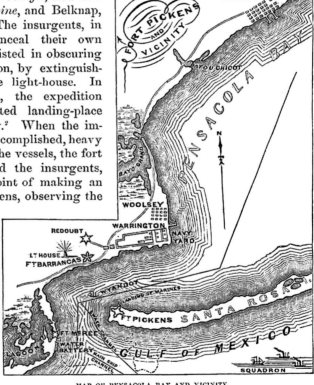

MAP OF PENSACOLA BAY AND VICINITY.

[a] April 12, 1861.

sacola, and at nine in the evening left there in a railway car for Montgomery, hoping to report at Washington on Monday night. He was disappointed. Bragg had committed a great blunder, and knew it early on the morning

---

[1] The loyal Wilcox tried to escape to the North. He reached Norfolk, where he was pressed into the "Confederate service," in which he remained, at that place, until it was taken possession of in May, 1862.

[2] Report of Commander H. A. Adams to the Secretary of the Navy, April 14, 1861.

[3] Statement of Mr. Wilcox. A correspondent of the *Charleston Mercury*, writing on the 13th, said that the firing alarmed the insurgents. An attack on Fort McRee was expected. The troops were called out, and

1 ROB'T ... HENRY M ... 4 ABSALOM BAIRD B ... 7 ABNER DOUBLEDAY, M. G. 10 WM. F. BARRY, B. G.
2 JOHN W. GEARY B ... A ... JEMMER B ... 8 WILLIAM B. HAZEN, B ... 11 P. J. OSTERHAUS, B. G.
3 AUGUST WILL... M ... D ... 9 CHARLES GRIFFIN B. G. 12 ROB'T H. MILROY, M. G.

of the 13th, when a spy informed him of the re-enforcement of Fort Pickens. That movement exasperated him, and he was deeply mortified by a sense of his own utter stupidity in allowing Lieutenant Worden to visit the squadron. To shield himself from the charge of such stupidity by his associates and superiors, he laid aside all honor as a man and a soldier, and accused the lieutenant with having practiced falsehood and deception in gaining permission to visit the *Sabine*. He telegraphed this charge to the conspirators at Montgomery, with a recommendation for his arrest. Five officers were detailed for the service, one of whom had served with Worden in the Navy. They arrested him a short distance below Montgomery, and, on their arrival at that city, placed him in the custody of Cooper, the " Adjutant-General of the Confederacy." Cooper took from him unimportant dispatches for his Government, and on Monday, the 15th, Worden was cast into the common jail. Bragg's false charge made him an object of scorn to Davis and his fellow-conspirators, and the citizens generally; and there, in that common jail, this gallant officer, whose conduct had been governed by the nicest sense of honor, suffered indignity until the 11th of November following, when he was paroled and ordered to report at Richmond, where Davis and his associates were then holding court. Cooper sent him to Norfolk, whence he was forwarded to the flag-ship of Admiral Goldsborough, in Hampton Roads,[a] when Lieutenant Sharpe, of the insurgent navy, was exchanged for him.[1] Worden was the first prisoner of war held by the insurgents.[2]

[a] November 18, 1861.

A few days after the re-enforcement of Fort Pickens, the *Atlantic* and *Illinois* arrived with several hundred troops, under the command of Colonel Harvey Brown, with an ample quantity of supplies and munitions of war. These were taken into Fort Pickens, and within ten days after the arrival of Worden, there were about nine hundred troops in that fort. Colonel Brown assumed the command, and Lieutenant Slemmer and his little band of brave men, worn down with fatigue, want of sleep, and insufficient food, were sent to Fort Hamilton, at the entrance to New York harbor, to rest. They shared the plaudits of a grateful people with those equally gallant defenders of Fort Sumter. Lieutenant Slemmer was commissioned major of the Sixteenth Regiment of Infantry; and because of brave conduct subse-

---

many of them lay on their arms all night. On the day after the re-enforcement, John Tyler, Jr., son of ex-President Tyler. who was employed under Walker, the so-called " Secretary of War," telegraphed the fact to the *Richmond Enquirer*, saying:—" Re-enforcements were thrown into Fort Pickens by the Government at Washington, in violation of the convention existing between that Government and this Confederacy." This false charge of bad faith on the part of the National Government was intended to affect the Virginia Convention, then sitting in Richmond. Tyler telegraphed " by authority of the Hon. L. P. Walker," who did not consider his order to Bragg, some time before, to attack Fort Pickens at the earliest practicable moment, as a " violation of the convention" which he pretended had existence. What was called " bad faith" on the part of the National Government, appears to have been considered highly honorable for the conspirators to practice. Such evidences of moral obliquity, on the part of the leaders in the rebellion, were continually observed throughout the war that ensued.

[1] Statement of Lieutenant Worden to the author.

[2] Lieutenant Worden's family and friends were in much distress concerning his imprisonment, for at times his life seemed to be in great jeopardy among lawless men, and was preserved, doubtless, by the Provost-Marshal of Montgomery, in whom Worden found a friend. Applications to the " Confederate Government" were for a long time treated with silent contempt. Mutual acquaintances wrote to Mrs. Davis, requesting her to use her influence in procuring his parole, for all other prisoners were allowed that privilege then. Her uniform reply was: "I shall do nothing; he is just where he ought to be." The prisoner, in the mean time, made no complaint, asked for no parole, and only once communicated with the chief conspirators. He then simply asked for the reasons why he was in prison.

quently in Tennessee, he was raised to the rank of brigadier-general. The Chamber of Commerce of New York included in their resolution to honor the defenders of Fort Sumter with a series of bronze medals,[1] those of Fort Pickens, and these were presented to Slemmer, his officers and men, at the same time. The medals were executed by the same sculptor (Charles Müller), and of the same sizes. The engraving represents the one presented to Lieutenant Slemmer, on a smaller scale than the original.[2]

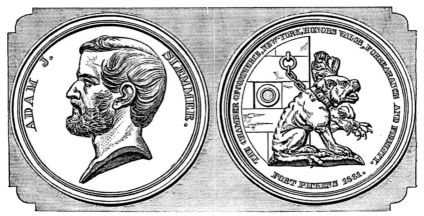

THE PICKENS MEDAL.

By the 1st of May there was a formidable force of insurgents menacing Fort Pickens, who were lying on the arc of a circle, from the water-battery beyond Fort McRee on the right, to the Navy Yard on the left. They numbered nearly seven thousand, and were arranged in three divisions. The first, on the right, was composed of Mississippians, under Colonel J. R. Chalmers; the second was composed of Alabamians and a Georgia regi-

---

[1] See pages 333 and 334.

[2] This medal, made of bronze, is six inches in diameter. On one side is a medallion portrait of Lieutenant Slemmer, and the inscription, "ADAM J. SLEMMER." On the other side is Cerberus, as the Monster of War, chained to Fort Pickens. By this design the artist intended to typify the forbearance of the Government and its servants, which was conspicuously exhibited during the defense of Fort Pickens. The initial letters U. S. on the collar of the monster indicate his owner. Amid the taunts and insults of the foe, he is kept chained to the fort. His impatience of restraint is shown by his actions. On this side of the medal is the inscription :— "THE CHAMBER OF COMMERCE, NEW YORK, HONORS VALOR, FORBEARANCE, AND FIDELITY. FORT PICKENS. 1861." Two sizes of medals bore these devices and inscriptions, and the other two, on the reverse side, a view of Fort Pickens, with the inscription:—"THE CHAMBER OF COMMERCE, NEW YORK, HONORS THE DEFENDERS OF FORT PICKENS—FAR OFF, BUT FAITHFUL."

The following are the names of the defenders of Fort Pickens:—

COMMISSIONED OFFICERS.—First Lieutenant, Adam J. Slemmer; Second Lieutenant, Jeremiah H. Gilman.

NON-COMMISSIONED OFFICERS.—First Sergeant, Alexander Jamieson; Corporals, David H. Boyd, Patrick Mangan, James P. Caldwell, and Benjamin Webster; Fifer, Thomas Smith; Drummer, William Sheppard; Artificers, Frederick Bickel and Simeon Webster; Ordnance Sergeants, Robert Granger, Elias H. Broady, and John Flynn.

PRIVATES.—John Bainfield, Michael Burns, John H. Boyer, Francis Bohnert, Joseph Clancy, John Cannon, Jacob C. Deckert, James Dolan, James Foley, Lewis Holmes, Thomas Honlahan, Edward L. Hastings, John Jackson, Thomas Jackson, Martin King, John Kerns, Owen McGair, Jackson McLeod, Thomas Manning, Thomas McGuire, James Matthews, John Mealey, Theodore Meeker, John Miller, Michael Morris, Patrick Mulligan, Michael Murphy, Michael Murray, William Nelson, Patrick Norton, James O'Brien, Frederick O'Donnell, Bartholomew O'Neil, John J. Reilly, Thomas B. Shaw, David Summers, Patrick Travers, and Francis Winters.

The whole number of officers and men who received medals was fifty-three. These were of the same regiment of Artillery (First, U. S. A.) as the defenders of Fort Sumter.

ment, under Colonel Clayton; and the third was made up of Louisianians, Georgians, and a Florida regiment, the whole commanded by Colonel Gladdin. Beside these there were about five hundred troops at Pensacola, all Louisianians, under Colonel Bradford. General Bragg was commander-in-chief. "These compose the very best class of our Southern people," wrote Judge Walker, the editor of the *New Orleans Delta*, on the 27th of April; "ardent, earnest, and resolute young men. They can never be conquered or even defeated. They may be destroyed, but not annihilated. When the Lincolnites subdue the country or the people which they have undertaken to subjugate, as long as we have such men to fight our battles, the spoils of their victory will be a blasted and desolated country, and an extinct people."

Re-enforcements continued to be sent to Fort Pickens from the North, and a considerable squadron lay outside in the Gulf. In June, Santa Rosa Island, on which Fort Pickens stands, was made lively by the encampment there of the Sixth New York Regiment of Volunteers, known as Wilson's Zouaves. They left New York on the 13th of June, on which day they were presented with a beautiful silk banner by the Ladies' Soldiers' Relief Association. The insurgents were also re-enforced; but nothing of great importance occurred in the vicinity of Fort Pickens during the ensuing summer.

WILSON'S ZOUAVES.

The attack on Fort Sumter, the re-enforcement of Fort Pickens, and the President's call for troops, aroused the entire nation to preparations for war. Although Davis and his associates at Montgomery had received the President's Proclamation with "derisive laughter," they did not long enjoy the sense of absolute security which that folly manifested. They were sagacious enough to estimate their heavy misfortune in the loss of the control of the Florida forts, and to interpret correctly the great uprising of the people in the Free-labor States, intelligence of which came flashing significantly every moment over the telegraph, with all the appalling aspect of the lightning before a summer storm.

Two days after the President's Proclamation was promulgated, Davis issued, from Montgomery,[a] an intended countervailing one.[1] In the preamble he declared that the President had "announced the intention of invading the Confederacy with an armed force for the purpose of capturing its fortresses, and thereby subverting its independence, and subjecting the free people thereof to the dominion of a foreign power." He said it had become the duty of the "government" to "repel the threatened invasion, and defend the rights and liberties of the people by all

[a] April 17, 1861.

---

[1] On the day before (16th), the Montgomery *Daily Advertiser* said, under the head of "Fine pickings for Privateers," that "the spring fleet of tea-ships from China are arriving quite freely at New York," and mentioned one of those whose cargo was valued at a million and a half of dollars.

the means which the laws of nations and usages of civilized warfare placed at its disposal." He therefore invited all persons who desired to engage in the business of legalized piracy known as *privateering*, by depredating upon the commerce of the United States, to apply to him for authority to do so, when it would be given, under certain restrictions which were set forth in the proclamation. He also enjoined all persons holding offices, civil or military, under his authority, to be vigilant and zealous in their duties; and exhorted the people of the " Confederate States," as they loved their country, as they prized the blessings of free government, as they felt the wrongs of the past, and others then threatened in an aggravated form, by those whose enmity was " more implacable, because unprovoked, to exert themselves in preserving order, in promoting concord, in maintaining the authority and efficacy of the laws, and in supporting and invigorating all the measures which may have been adopted for a common defense, and by which, under the blessing of Divine Providence," they might "hope for a speedy, just, and honorable peace."

The President at once met the proclamation of Davis, by declaring that he should immediately employ a competent force to blockade all the ports of States claimed as belonging to the Southern Confederacy; and also, that if any person, under the pretended authority of such States, or under any other pretense, should molest a vessel of the United States, or the persons or cargo on board of her, such persons should be held amenable to the laws of the United States for the prevention and punishment of piracy.[1]

Davis had already summoned[a] the so-called " Congress of the Confederate States " to meet at Montgomery on the 29th of April. That body, on the 6th of May, passed an Act with fifteen sections, " recognizing the existence of war between the United States and the Confederate States; and concerning letters of marque, prizes, and prize goods."[2] The preamble declared that the " Confederate States " had made earnest efforts to establish friendly relations between themselves and the United States; but that the Government of the latter had not only refused to hold any intercourse with the former, as a government in fact, but had prepared to make war upon them, and had avowed an intention of blockading their ports. Such being the case, they declared that war existed between the "two governments," and in accordance with a cherished design of Davis, which he hinted at in his " inaugural address " at Montgomery,[3] and had openly announced in his proclamation on the 17th, they authorized the " President of the Confederate States " to use their whole land and naval force " to meet the war thus commenced, and to issue to private armed vessels commissions or letters of marque and general reprisal, in such form as he shall think proper, under the seal of the Confederate States, against the vessels, goods, and effects of the Government of the United States, and of the citizens or inhabitants of the States and Territories thereof."[4] The tenth

[a] April 12, 1861.

---

[1] Proclamation of President Lincoln, April 19, 1861.
[2] Acts and Resolutions of the Second Session of the " Provisional Congress of the Confederate States," page 22.
[3] See page 258.
[4] The following is the form in which the letters of marque were issued:—

"JEFFERSON DAVIS, President of the Confederate States of America, to all who shall see these presents, greeting: Know ye, that by virtue of the power vested in me by law, I have commissioned, and do hereby commission, have authorized, and do hereby authorize, the schooner or vessel called the —— (more particularly

section of the Act offered a bounty of twenty dollars for each person who might be on board any armed ship or vessel belonging to the United States, at the commencement of an engagement, which should be burned, sunk, or destroyed by any vessel commissioned as a privateer, of equal or inferior force—in other words, a reward for the murder, by fire, water, or otherwise, of men, women, and children found on board of a public vessel of the United States. Happily for the credit of humanity, this Act has no parallel on the statute-books of civilized nations. They also offered a bounty of twenty-five dollars for every prisoner captured by a privateer and delivered to an agent of the "Confederation" in any of its ports. Davis did not wait for the legal sanction of his so-called "Congress," but issued letters of marque immediately after putting forth his proclamation on the 17th of April.[1]

The country controlled by the conspirators lacked the mechanical skill and many materials for the construction of a navy; therefore, while the offer of Davis to issue letters of marque created uneasiness among shipping merchants, they did not feel serious alarm, especially when it was known that the Government would institute a rigid blockade. But it was not long before privateers were on the seas. The Confederates had not the means for building vessels, but they had for purchasing them. They had already stolen six National revenue cutters,[2] which they fitted up as privateers; and

in the course of a few weeks after the "recognition of a state of war," Mr. Mallory, the so-called "Secretary of the Navy" of the conspirators, had purchased and fitted out about a dozen vessels. The owners of as many more private vessels took out letters of marque immediately after Davis's proclamation was made; and before the middle of

THE LADY DAVIS.

June, the commerce of the United States was threatened with serious mischief.

The first of the purchased vessels commissioned by Mallory was a small

described in the schedule hereunto annexed), whereof —— —— is commander, to act as a private armed vessel in the service of the Confederate States, on the high seas, against the United States of America, their ships, vessels, goods, and effects, and those of their citizens, during the pendency of the war now existing between the said Confederate States and the said United States. This commission to continue in force until revoked by the President of the Confederate States for the time being.

"Given under my hand and the seal of the Confederate States, at Montgomery, this — day of —, A. D. 1861.
"By the President:	JEFFERSON DAVIS.
R. TOOMBS, Sec'y of State."

The Act contained many regulations; and accompanying the letters of marque were explicit instructions concerning the meaning of the terms, "the high seas," the rights and treatment of neutrals, the treatment of enemies, the disposition of captured property, and as to what were considered articles contraband of war. They declared that " neutral vessels, conveying the enemy's dispatches, or military persons in the service of the enemy," were liable to capture and condemnation; but the rule was not made to apply to neutral vessels bearing dispatches from the public ministers or embassadors of the enemy, residing in neutral countries.

[1] Telegraphic communication from Montgomery to the *Charleston Mercury*, April 18, 1861.
[2] The *Lewis Cass*, *Washington*, *Pickens*, *Dodge*, *McClelland*, and *Bradford*.

steamer which Governor Pickens had bought in Richmond, for use in the defense of Charleston harbor. She was commissioned in March; and named *Lady Davis*, in honor of the wife of Jefferson Davis. She was armed with

S. R. MALLORY.

two 24-pounders, and placed under the command of Lieutenant T. B. Huger, formerly of the United States Navy. This was the beginning of the "Confederate States Navy," which never assumed formidable proportions excepting when ships, foreign built, armed, and manned, were permitted to enter the service. The number, character, and performances of the privateers commissioned by Davis and Toombs during the spring and early summer of 1861, will be considered hereafter.

With the hostile proclamations of the President and the Chief of the conspirators, the great conflict fairly began. There was no longer any tenable neutral ground for men to stand upon, and they at once, as we have observed in the case of prominent members of the Opposition in the Free-labor States, took positive positions. Two of the late candidates for the Presidency (Breckinridge and Bell) openly avowed their sympathy with the secessionists. Breckinridge, who afterward became a military leader in the rebellion, was cautious and treacherous. For a time he assumed the virtue of loyalty to the Constitution and the Union, and took his seat in the Senate of the United States, at the called session of Congress, in July. But his disguise was too thin to deceive anybody. So early as the 17th of April, he wrote to a friend at Louisville, saying:—"Kentucky should call a convention without delay, and Lincoln's extra session of Congress [in which he took a seat as a professedly loyal man] should be confronted by fifteen States. This alone can prevent a general civil war."[1] On the 20th, in a speech at Louisville, he echoed the voice of the *Journal* of that city in its denunciation of the President's call for troops.[2] He advised Kentuckians to remain neutral, but in the event of their being driven from that position, he declared it to be their duty to espouse the cause of the conspirators for the conservation of Slavery. Bell, bolder or more honest, openly linked his fortunes with those of the "Confederacy," in a speech at Nashville, on the 23d of April, in which he declared that Tennessee was virtually "out of the Union," and urged the people of his State to prepare for vigorous war upon the Government.[3] The Governor (Harris) was at the same time working with all his might in the manipulation of machinery to array Tennessee, as a State, against the National Government. In this he was aided by an address to the people by professed friends of the Union, who counseled them to "decline joining either party; for in so doing they would at once terminate her [Tennessee's] grand mission of peacemaker between the

---

[1] Telegraphic dispatch from Louisville to the *Charleston Mercury*.   [2] See page 339.
[3] *Nashville Banner.*

States of the South and the General Government. Nay, more," they said; "the almost inevitable result would be the transfer of the war within her own borders, the defeat of all hopes of reconciliation, and the deluging of the State with the blood of her own people."[1]

The Governor of Kentucky was less courageous and more cautious than his neighbor of Tennessee, but not less a practical enemy of the Union. To confirm him in disloyalty, and to commit the great State of Kentucky to the cause of the conspirators, Walker, their so-called "Secretary of War," wrote to Governor Magoffin, from Montgomery, on the 22d of April, complimenting him for his "patriotic response to the requisition of the President of the United States for troops to coerce the Confederate States,"[2] and saying that it justified the belief that his people were prepared to unite with the conspirators "in repelling the common enemy of the South. Virginia needs our aid," he continued. "I therefore request you to furnish one regiment of infantry without delay, to rendezvous at Harper's Ferry, Virginia. It must consist of ten companies, of not less than sixty-four men each. . . . They will be mustered into the service of the Confederate States at Harper's Ferry." The object of this call to Harper's Ferry will be apparent presently.

Virginia, at this time, was in a state of great agitation. Its Convention had passed through a stormy session, extending from the middle of February to the middle of April. It was held in the city of Richmond, and was organized[a] by the appointment of John Janney, of Loudon, as its President, and John L. Eubank, Clerk. In his address on taking the chair, the President favored conditional Union, saying, in a tone common to many of the public men of Virginia, that his State would insist on its own construction of its rights as a condition of its remaining in the Union. It was evident, from the beginning, that a better National sentiment than the President of the Convention evinced was largely dominant in that body, and the conspirators within it were for a long time foiled in their attempts to array Virginia on the side of the "Southern Confederacy." Even so late as the 4th of April, the Convention refused, by a vote of eighty-nine against forty-five, to pass an ordinance of secession;[3] and they resolved to send Commissioners to Washington City to ask the President to communicate to that body the policy which he intended to pursue in regard to the "Confederate States."[4] Yet the conspirators worked on, conscious of increasing strength, for one weak Unionist after another was converted by their sophistry or their threats. Pryor and Ruffin, as we have seen, went to Charleston to urge an attack upon Fort

> [a February 13, 1861.]

[1] *Address to the People of Tennessee:* by Neil S. Brown, Russell Houston, E. H. Ewing, C. Johnstone, John Bell, R. J. Meigs, S. D. Morgan, John S. Brien, Andrew Ewing, John H. Callender, and Baylie Peyton.

[2] See page 337.

[3] The resolution voted upon was introduced by Lewis E. Harvie, and was as follows:—"*Resolved*, That an ordnance of secession, reserving the powers delegated by Virginia, and providing for submitting the same to the qualified voters of the Commonwealth for adoption or rejection at the polls in the spring elections, in March next, should be adopted at this Convention."

[4] The Commissioners appointed were William Ballard Preston, A. H. H. Stuart, and George W. Randolph. It is said that Mr. Carlile, of Western Virginia, suggested the appointment of a similar committee to visit Montgomery, to ascertain what Jefferson Davis intended to do with the troops he was then raising; whereupon Henry A. Wise said, that if Mr. Carlile should be one of that committee, "that would be the last they would ever see of him." In other words, he would be murdered for his temerity in venturing to question the acts of the traitors.—*Louisville Journal,* April 23, 1863.

Sumter, believing that bloodshedding would inflame the passions of Southern men, and that, during the paroxysm of excitement that would ensue, Virginia might be arrayed against the National Government.

Suddenly, bribery or threats, or change of ownership, made the *Richmond Whig*, the only newspaper in the Virginia capital that opposed secession, become ominously silent, while the organs of the conspirators were loudly boastful of a majority in the Convention favorable to secession. The hearts of the genuine Unionists of the old State were saddened by gloomy forebodings, for they knew that their friends in that Convention were continually browbeaten by the truculent secessionists, and that the people were hourly deceived by the most astounding falsehoods put forth by the conspirators.

The Commissioners sent to Washington*a* obtained a formal audience with the President on the 13th,*b* almost at the very time when, in their State capital, the bells were ringing, "Confederate" flags were flying, and one hundred guns were thundering, in attestation of the joy of the secessionists because of the attack on Fort Sumter.

a April 4, 1861.
b April.

A telegraphic correspondent at Charleston had said the day before :— "That ball fired at Sumter by Edmund Ruffin will do more for the cause of secession in Virginia than volumes of stump speeches."[1] The assertion was correct. While the Convention was debating the question of the surrender of Fort Sumter, Governor Letcher sent in a communication from Governor Pickens, announcing the attack on that fortress, and saying :— "We will take the fort, and can sink the ships if they attempt to pass the channel. If they land elsewhere, we can whip them. We have now seven thousand of the best troops in the world, and a reserve of ten thousand on the routes to the harbor. The war has commenced, and we will triumph or perish. Please let me know what your State intends to do?" Letcher replied :— "The Convention will determine." It was this dispatch—this notice of "that ball fired on Sumter" by Ruffin—that set the bells ringing, the flags flying, the cannons thundering, and the people shouting in Richmond; and a few days afterward the Convention revealed its determination to the world.

The President replied to the Virginia Commissioners,*c* that it was his intention to pursue the policy clearly marked out in his Inaugural Address. He had discovered no reasons for changing his views. He recommended them to give that document a careful perusal, especially that portion in which he declared it to be his intention "to hold, occupy, and possess property and places belonging to the Government, and to collect the duties on imports; but beyond what is necessary for these objects, there will be no invasion, no using of force against or among the people anywhere." He informed them that if an attack had been made upon Fort Sumter, as it was at that moment rumored, he should feel himself at liberty to repossess it, if he could; for he considered it and other military posts seized by the insurgents as much the property of the United States as ever. "In any event," he said, "I shall, to the best of my ability, repel force by force." He also told them that he might feel it his duty to cause the United States mails to be withdrawn from all the States which

c April 13.

---

[1] *New York Herald*, April 13, 1861.

claimed to have seceded, "believing that this commencement of actual war against the Government justifies, and, possibly, demands it."

With this explicit declaration of the President that he should defend the life of the Republic to the best .of his ability, the Virginia Commissioners returned to their constituents.   Their report added fuel to the flames of passion then raging in the Virginia capital.   Its reading produced a scene of wild excitement in the Convention.   It was heard therein at almost the same hour when the President's call for troops to crush the rising rebellion was read.ª   Doubt, anger, joy and sorrow, and senti-   ª April 15, 1861. ments of treachery and fidelity swayed that body with varied emotions, until reason and judgment fled affrighted from the hall, and untempered feeling bore rule.   The boldest and best of the Union men bent like reeds before the storm.   In the excitement of the moment, men like Scott and Preston, warmed by the glow of innate State pride, exclaimed: " If the President means subjugation of the South, Virginia has but one course to pursue, and that is, resistance to tyranny."   The only question entertained was: Shall Virginia secede at once, or await the co-operation of the other Border Slave-labor States?   In the midst of the excitement pending that question, the Convention adjourned until morning.

On the following dayᵇ the Convention assembled in secret session.   Its aspect had changed.   For three days, threats and persuasions,   ᵇ April 16. appeals to interest, State pride and sectional patriotism, and the shafts of ridicule and scornful denunciation were brought to bear upon the faithful Union men, who were chiefly from the mountain districts of the State, or Western Virginia; and yet, at the adjournment, on the evening of the 15th, there was a clear majority of the one hundred and fifty-three members of the Convention against secession.   The conspirators became. desperate.   Richmond was in the hands of a mob ready to do their bidding, and they resolved to act with a high hand.   It was calculated that if ten Union members of the Convention should be absent, there would be a majority for secession.   Accordingly, the leading conspirators waited upon ten of them during the evening, and informed them that they were allowed the choice of doing one of three things, namely: to vote for a secession ordinance, to absent themselves, or be hanged.¹   Resistance would be useless, and the seats of the ten members were vacant on the morning of the 16th.   Other Unionists who remained in the Convention were awed by these violent proceedings, and an Ordinance of Secession was passed on Wednesday, the 17th, by a vote of eighty-eight against fifty-five.   It was similar in form and substance to that of the South Carolina politicians and those of other States, excepting that it was only to take effect when it should be ratified by "a majority of the votes of the people," to be "cast at a poll to be taken thereon, on the fourth Tuesday in May next."

The Virginia conspirators at once sent a private messenger to Montgomery to apprise Davis and his associates of their action, and to invite co-operation.   Already Governor Letcher, who had been assured by the leaders in the Convention that the Ordinance of Secession would be adopted,

---

¹ Statement of one of the members of the Convention, cited in the *Annual Cyclopedia*, 1861, page 735.

had sent* his defiant response to the President's call for troops;[1] and now,
under the direction of that Convention, which assumed supreme
authority in the State, he issued a proclamation, ordering "all
armed volunteer regiments or companies within the State forthwith to hold themselves in readiness for immediate orders."

*April 16, 1861.

When, on the following day, the passage of the Ordinance (upon which
fact a temporary injunction of secrecy had been laid) was announced, the
joy of the secessionists in Richmond was unbounded. The streets resounded
with the acclamations of great crowds. The sign, in gilt letters,— *United
States Court,*—over the north entrance to the Custom House, was taken
down and broken in pieces by the populace; and the National officers suddenly found their occupation gone. The flag of the "Southern Confederacy," with an additional star for Virginia (making eight in all), was
unfurled over the Capitol. It was also displayed from the Custom House
and other public buildings, and from hotels and private dwellings. The
Custom House was taken into the keeping of Virginia troops; and the
packets *Yorktown* and *Jamestown*, belonging to the New York and Virginia
Steamship Company, were seized and placed in charge of the same body of
armed men.

As the news from Richmond went over the land, it produced the most
profound sensation. In the cities of Slave-labor States, and especially of
the more Southern ones, there were demonstrations of great delight. At
Charleston the event caused the wildest excitement. "The news of the
secession of the mother of Presidents and Patriots," said a telegraphic dispatch to Philadelphia,[b] "was received here with great
joy. The old secession gun was fired in front of the *Courier* office, by the
venerable Edmund Ruffin. The old gentleman was surrounded by many
Virginians, who cheered lustily." The Virginians then in Montgomery,
headed by Pryor, who had gone up from Charleston,[2] fired a hundred guns
on their own account; and from the far Southwest went forth the greeting:—

April 19.

> " In the new-born arch of glory,
>   Lo! she burns, the central star;
> Never shame shall blight its grandeur,
>   Never cloud its radiance mar.
> 'Old Virginia! Old Virginia!'
>   Listen, Southrons, to the strain;
> 'Old Virginia! Old Virginia!'
>   Shout the rallying-cry again!"[3]

In the Free-labor States the action of Virginia was observed with alarm,
for it threatened immediate danger to the National Capital and the archives
of the Republic. Only the hope that the *people* of Virginia would refuse to
ratify the Ordinance, calmed the fears of the loyalists. The expectation that
they would do so, if an opportunity should be offered them, made the conspirators more active and bold. They did not wait for the people to speak
concerning the matter; but, within twenty-four hours after the passage of
the Ordinance, and while the vote was still covered by an injunction of
secrecy, they set on foot, doubtless under directions from Montgomery,

---

[1] See page 337.   [2] See page 316.   [3] *New Orleans Picayune.*

expeditions for the capture of Harper's Ferry and of the Navy Yard near Norfolk, preparatory to an attempt to seize Washington City.

A few days afterward, Alexander H. Stephens arrived in Richmond, to urge the Convention to violate its own Ordinance, and to take measures for annexing Virginia to the "Confederacy" without the consent of the people. He was clothed with full power to make a treaty to that effect. Troops were then pushing forward from the Gulf States toward her borders. The conspirators, having promised the people of the Cotton-growing States that no harm should come nigh their dwellings, and perceiving war to be inevitable, were hastening to make the Border States the theater of its operations, and, if possible, secure the great advantage of the possession of the National Capital. At various points on his journey northward, Stephens had harangued the people, and everywhere he raised the cry of "On to Washington!"[1] That cry was already resounding throughout the South. It was an echo or a paraphrase of the prophecy of the "Confederate Secretary of War."[2] "Nothing is more probable," said the *Richmond Enquirer* on the 13th of April, "than that President Davis will soon march an army through North Carolina and Virginia to Washington," and it called upon Virginians who wished to "join the Southern army," to organize at once. "The first-fruits of Virginia secession," said the *New Orleans Picayune* of the 18th, "will be the removal of Lincoln and his Cabinet, and whatever he can carry away, to the safer neighborhood of Harrisburg or Cincinnati—perhaps to Buffalo or Cleveland." The *Vicksburg* (Mississippi) *Whig* of the 20th said:—"Major Ben. McCulloch has organized a force of five thousand men to seize the Federal Capital the instant the first blood is spilled." On the evening of the same day, when news of bloodshed in Baltimore was received in Montgomery, bonfires were built in front of the Exchange Hotel, and from its balcony Roger A. Pryor said, in a speech to the multitude, that he was "in favor of an immediate march upon Washington." At the departure of the Second Regiment of South Carolina Infantry for Richmond, at about the same time, the Colonel (Kershaw), on taking the flag presented to the regiment, said, as he handed it to the Color-Sergeant (Gordon):—"To your particular charge is committed this noble gift. Plant it wherever honor calls. If opportunity offers, let it be the first to kiss the breezes of heaven from the dome of

SOUTH CAROLINA LIGHT INFANTRY.

---

[1] The New York *Commercial Advertiser* of April 25th had an account of the experience of a gentleman who had escaped from Fayetteville to avoid impressment into the insurgent army. He traveled on the same train with Stephens from Warsaw to Richmond. "At nearly every station," he says, "Stephens spoke. *The capture of Washington was the grand idea which he enforced, and exhorted the people to join in the enterprise,* to which they heartily responded. This was the only thing talked of. 'It must be done!' was his constant exclamation."

[2] See extract from Walker's speech at Montgomery on the 12th of April, page 339.

the Capitol at Washington." The *Richmond Examiner* of the 23d (the day on which Stephens arrived in Richmond), said :—"The capture of Washington City is perfectly within the power of Virginia and Maryland, if Virginia will only make the proper effort by her constituted authorities. . . . There never was half the unanimity among the people before, nor a tithe of the zeal upon any subject that is now manifested to take Washington, and drive from it every Black Republican who is a dweller there. From the mountain-tops and valleys to the shores of the sea there is one wild shout of fierce resolve to capture Washington City, at all and every human hazard." On the same day Governor Ellis, of North Carolina, ordered a regiment of State troops to march for Washington; and the *Goldsborough Tribune* of the 24th said, speaking of the grand movement of Virginia and a rumored one in Maryland :—"It makes good the words of Secretary Walker at Montgomery, in regard to the Federal metropolis. It transfers the lines of battle from the Potomac to the Pennsylvania border." The *Raleigh Standard* of the same date said :—"Our streets are alive with soldiers" (although North Carolina was a professedly loyal State of the Union), and added, "Washington City will be too hot to hold Abraham Lincoln and his Government. North Carolina has said it, and she will do all she can to make good her declaration." The *Wilmington* (N. C.) *Journal* said :—"When North Carolina regiments go to Washington, and they will go, they will stand side by side with their brethren of the South." The *Eufaula* (Alabama) *Express* said, on the 25th :[a]—"Our policy at this time should be to seize the old Federal Capital, and take old Lincoln and his Cabinet prisoners of war." The Milledgeville (Georgia) *Southern Recorder* of the 30th, inspired by men like Toombs, Cobb, Iverson, and other leaders, said :—"The Government of the Confederate States must possess the city of Washington. It is folly to think it can be used any longer as the head-quarters of the Lincoln Government, as no access can be had to it except by passing through Virginia and Maryland. The District of Columbia cannot remain under the jurisdiction of the United States Congress without humiliating Southern pride and defeating Southern rights. Both are essential to greatness of character, and both must co-operate in the destiny to be achieved." A correspondent of the *Charleston Courier*, writing from Montgomery at about the same time, said :—"The desire for taking Washington, I believe, increases every hour, and all things, to my thinking, seem tending to this consummation. We are in lively hope that, before three months roll by, the Government, Congress, departments and all, will have removed to the present Federal Capital."

We might cite utterances of this kind from the leading newspapers of the more Southern Slave-labor States, and the declarations of eminent politicians, sufficient to fill a chapter, which show that everywhere it was well understood that the seizure of Washington, the destruction of the Republic, and the erection of a confederation composed wholly of Slave-labor States, according to the plan foreshadowed in the banner of the South Carolina Secession Convention,[1] was the cherished design of Jefferson Davis and his

[a] April, 1861.

---

[1] See page 106.

confederates. Yet in the face of this testimony—in the presence of the prophecy of his so-called Secretary of War at Montgomery, and the action of Stephens, his lieutenant, while on his way to Richmond, and while there in assisting the Virginia conspirators in carrying out their scheme for seizing the Capital, the arch-traitor, with hypocrisy the most supremely impudent, declared in a speech at the opening of his so-called Congress, on the 29th of April, that his policy was peaceful and defensive, not belligerent and aggressive. Speaking more to Europe than to the "Confederacy," he said:—"We protest solemnly, in the face of mankind, that we desire peace at any sacrifice, save that of honor. . . . In independence we seek no conquest, no aggrandizement, no cession of any kind from the States with which we have lately confederated. *All we ask is to be let alone*—those who never held power over us should not now attempt our subjugation by arms. This we will, we must resist to the direst extremity." On the very next day [a] Stephens, the so-called Vice-President, said in a speech at Atlanta, in Georgia:—"A general opinion prevails that Washington City is soon to be attacked. On this subject I can only say, our object is peace. We wish no aggressions on any one's rights, and will make none. But if Maryland secedes, the District of Columbia will fall to her by reversionary right—the same as Sumter to South Carolina, Pulaski to Georgia, and Pickens to Florida. When we have the right, we will demand the surrender of Washington, just as we did in the other cases, and will enforce our demands at every hazard and at whatever cost." The burglar, using the same convenient logic, might say to the householder about to be plundered by him, after having made the intended victim's near neighbor an accomplice, and with his aid had forced his way into the dwelling: "Your plate, and your money, and your jewelry fall to my accomplice as a reversionary right, and we demand the surrender of your keys. *All we ask is to be let alone.*"[1]

[a] April 30, 1861.

---

[1] A quaint writer in the *Hartford* (Connecticut) *Courant*, at that time, made the following amusing commentary on the conspirators' untruthful assertion—"All we ask is to be let alone:"—

"As vonce I valked by a dismal swamp,
There sot an old Cove in the dark and damp,
And at everybody as passed that road
A stick or a stone this old Cove throwed;
And venever he flung his stick or his stone,
He'd set up a song of 'Let me alone.'
'Let me alone, for I loves to shy
These bits of things at the passers by;

Let me alone, for I've got your tin,
And lots of other traps snugly in;
Let me alone—I am rigging a boat
To grab votever you've got afloat;
In a veek or so I expects to come
And turn you out of your 'ouse and 'ome.
I'm a quiet Old Cove,' says he, with a groan,
'All I axes is, *Let me alone.*'"

The writer then foreshadowed the action of the Government, as follows:—

"Just then came along, on the self-same way,
Another old Cove, and began for to say:—
'Let you alone! that's comin' it strong!
You've *ben* let alone a darned sight too long!
Of all the sarce that ever I heerd!
Put down that stick! (You may well look skeered.)
Let go that stone! If you once show fight,
I'll knock you higher than any kite.
You must have a lesson to stop your tricks,
And cure you of shying them stones and sticks;
And I'll have my hardware back, and my cash,
And knock your scow into 'tarnal smash;

And if ever I catches you, round my ranch,
I'll string you up to the nearest branch.
The best you can do is to go to bed,
And keep a decent tongue in your head;
For I reckon, before you and I are done,
You'll wish you had let honest folks alone.'
The Old Cove stopped, and the t'other Old Cove,
He sot quite still in his cypress grove,
And he looked at his stick revolvin' slow,
Vether 'twere safe to shy it or no;
And he grumbled on, in an injured tone,
'All that I ax'd was, *Let me alone.*'"

CHAPTER XVI.

SECESSION OF VIRGINIA AND NORTH CAROLINA DECLARED.—SEIZURE OF HARPER'S
FERRY AND GOSPORT NAVY YARD.—THE FIRST TROOPS IN WASHINGTON FOR ITS
DEFENSE.

HE reception of Alexander H. Stephens by the Convention of Virginia politicians, the authorities of the State, and the excited populace in Richmond, gave him instant assurances of the success of his mission. He saw the "Confederate Flag" waving everywhere, and heard no complaint because of the usurpation. He perceived that in Virginia, as in the Gulf States, the heel of the usurper was firmly planted on the necks of the loyal people, and that despotism was substantially triumphant. His soul was filled with gladness, and he addressed the Virginians with the eloquence and earnestness of a man whose heart was in his work. "The fires of patriotism," he said, "I have seen blazing brightly all along my track, from Montgomery to the very gates of your city, and they are enkindling here with greater brilliancy and fervor. That constitutional liberty which we vainly sought for while in the old Union, we have found, and fully enjoy in our new one. . . . What had you, the friends of liberty, to hope for while under Lincoln? Nothing. Beginning in usurpation, where will he end? He will quit Washington as ignominiously as he entered it, and God's will will have been accomplished. Madness and folly rule at Washington,· but Providence is with us, and will bless us to the end. The people of Virginia and the States of the South are one in interest, in feeling, in institutions, and in hope; and why should they not be one in Government? Every son of the South, from the Potomac to the Rio Grande, should rally beneath the same banner. The conflict may be terrible, but the victory will be ours. It remains for you to say whether you will share our triumphs."[1]

Stephens, as we have observed, was in Richmond for the purpose of negotiating a treaty for the admission of Virginia into the "Southern Confederacy." The Convention appointed Ex-President John Tyler, William Ballard Preston, S. McD. Moore, James P. Holcombe, James C. Bruce, and Lewis E. Harvie, Commissioners to treat with him. They entered upon the business at once, and on the 24th of April agreed to and signed a "Conven-

---

[1] Speech at Richmond, April 23, 1861, cited by Whitney in his *History of the War for the Union*, i. 402. Compare what Stephens said at Milledgeville, in November, 1860, and in the Georgia Convention, in January 1861, pages 54 to 57, inclusive.

tion between the Commonwealth of Virginia and the Confederate States of America," which provided that, until the union of Virginia with the league should be perfected, "the whole military force and military operations, offensive and defensive, of said Commonwealth, in the impending conflict with the United States," should be under the chief control and direction of Jefferson Davis. So eager were the Virginia conspirators to "perfect the Union," that on the following day,* the Convention, appealing • April 25, to the Searcher of all hearts for the rectitude of their conduct, 1861. passed an ordinance ratifying the treaty, and adopting and ratifying the

SIGNATURES OF THE COMMISSIONERS.[1]

Provisional Constitution of the Montgomery League.[2] They proceeded to appoint delegates to the "Confederate Congress" that was to assemble on the 29th;[b] authorized the banks of the State to suspend specie payments; made provision for the establishment of a navy ᵇ April. for Virginia, and for enlistments for the State army, and adopted other measures preparatory for war. They also invited Jefferson Davis and his confederates to make Richmond their head-quarters. The so-called annexation of the Commonwealth to the "Confederacy" was officially proclaimed

---

[1] These were copied from the original parchment upon which the convention or treaty was engrossed and signed.

[2] John Tyler, who was a chief manager among the conspirators of the Virginia Convention, telegraphed as follows to Governor Pickens, at three o'clock that afternoon:—" We are fellow-citizens once more. By an ordinance passed this day, Virginia has adopted the Provisional Government of the Confederate States."

by Governor Letcher; and the "Mother of States," the "Mother of Presidents," and equally the Mother of Disunion, was forced into the position of an important member of the league against the Republic. Eastern and Northern Virginia soon became the theater of great battles, fought by immense armies, at various times during the war that ensued.

When the time approached for the people of Virginia to vote on the Ordinance of Secession, in accordance with its own provisions, Senator James M. Mason, one of the most malignant and unscrupulous of the conspirators, addressed a letter to them from his home near Winchester, in which, after saying that the Ordinance "withdrew the State of Virginia from the Union, with all the consequences resulting from the separation," annulling "all the Constitution and laws of the United States within its limits," and absolving "its citizens from all obligations or obedience to them," he declared that

JAMES M. MASON.

a rejection of the Ordinance by the people would reverse all this, and that Virginia would be compelled to fight under the banner of the Republic, in violation of the sacred pledge made to the "Confederate States," in the treaty or "Military League" of the 25th of April. He then said:— "If it be asked, What are those to do who, in their conscience, cannot vote to separate Virginia from the United States? the answer is simple and plain. Honor and duty alike require that they should not vote on the question; and if they retain such opinions, *they must leave the State*."[1] The answer was, indeed, "simple and plain," and in exact accordance with the true spirit of the conspirators, expressed by their chosen leader:—"All who oppose us shall smell Southern powder and feel Southern steel." Submission or banishment was the alternative offered by Mason, in the name of traitors in power, to Virginians who were true to the principles of the Father of his Country, whose remains were resting within the bosom of their State, and to the old flag under which the independence of their common country had been achieved. He well knew that his words would be received as expressions of the views of the usurpers at Richmond, and that thousands of citizens would thereby be kept from the polls, for in Virginia the votes were given openly, and not by secret ballot, as in other States.

Mason's infamous suggestion was followed by coincident action. Troops had been for some time pouring into Virginia from the more Southern a May 23, States, and the vote on the Ordinance of Secession was taken 1861. toward the close of May,a in the midst of bayonets thirsting for the blood of Union men. Terror was then reigning all over Eastern Virginia. Unionists were hunted like wild beasts, and compelled to fly from

<hr>

[1] Letter to the Editor of the *Winchester Virginian*, May 16, 1861.

their State to save their lives; and by these means the conspirators were enabled to report a vote of one hundred and twenty-five thousand nine hundred and fifty for secession, and only twenty thousand three hundred and seventy-three against it. This did not include the vote in North-western Virginia, where the people had rallied around their true representatives in the Convention, and defied the conspirators and all their power. They had already placed themselves boldly and firmly upon earnest professions of loyalty to the Union, and in Convention assembled at Wheeling, ten days before the voting, they had planted, as we shall observe hereafter, the vigorous germ of a new Free-labor Commonwealth.

The conservative State of North Carolina, lying between Virginia and the more Southern States, could not long remain neutral. Her disloyal politicians, with Governor Ellis at their head, were active and unscrupulous. We have already observed their efforts to array the State against the National Government, and the decided condemnation of their schemes by the people.[1] Now, taking advantage of the excitement caused by the attack on Fort Sumter, and the call of the President for troops, they renewed their wicked efforts, and with better success. Ellis issued a proclamation,[a] calling an extraordinary session of the   [a February 17, 1861.] Legislature on the 1st of May, in which he shamelessly declared that the President was preparing for the "subjugation of the entire South, and the conversion of a free republic, inherited from their fathers, into a military despotism, to be established by worse than foreign enemies, on the ruins of the once glorious Constitution of Equal Rights." With equal mendacity, the disloyal politicians throughout the State stirred up the people by making them believe that they were about to be deprived of their liberties by a military despotism at Washington. Excited, bewildered, and alarmed, they became, in a degree, passive instruments in the hands of men like Senator Clingman and others of his party. The Legislature acted under the same malign influences. It authorized a convention to consider the subject of the secession of the State, and ordered an election of delegates therefor, to be held on the 13th of May. It gave the Governor authority to raise ten thousand men, and appropriated five millions of dollars for the use of the State. It empowered the treasurer to issue notes to the amount of five hundred thousand dollars, in denominations as low as three cents; and by act defined treason to be the levying of war against the State, adhering to its enemies in establishing a government within the State without the consent of the Legislature, and in holding or executing any office in such government.

The Convention assembled on the 20th of May, the anniversary of the "Mecklenburg Declaration of Independence,"[2] and on the same day an Ordinance of Secession was adopted by a unanimous vote. In the mean time the Governor had issued an order for the enrollment of thirty thousand

---

[1] See pages 62 and 198.

[2] In 1775 a Convention of the representatives of the citizens of Mecklenburg County, North Carolina, held at Charlotte, passed a series of patriotic resolutions, equivalent in words and spirit to a declaration of independence of the Government of Great Britain. There is a well-founded dispute as to the day on which that declaration was adopted, one party declaring it to be the 20th of May, and another the 31st of May. For a minute account of that affair, see Lossing's *Pictorial Field-Book of the Revolution.*

minute-men, and the forces of the State had seized, for the second time, the
National forts on the sea-coast;[1] also the Mint at Charlotte,[a] and
the Government Arsenal at Fayetteville,[b] in which were thirty-
seven thousand stand of arms, three thousand kegs of gunpowder, and an immense amount of munitions of war. Within three weeks

a April 20, 1861.

b April 23.

ARSENAL AT FAYETTEVILLE, NORTH CAROLINA.

after the passage of the Ordinance of Secession, there were not less than
twenty thousand North Carolina volunteers under arms. They adopted a
flag which was composed of the colors red, white, and blue, differently
arranged from those in the National flag.[2]

NORTH CAROLINA FLAG.

The Governor of Tennessee (Harris)
and a disloyal majority of the Legislature now commenced the work of
infinite mischief to the people of their
State. Harris called the Legislature
together on the 25th of April, and delivered to that body a message, in
which he strongly urged the necessity
for the immediate secession of the
State. Remembering that
less than eighty days before[c]
the people had declared in
favor of the Union by sixty-five thousand majority, he was unwilling to
trust the question of secession to them
now. He argued, that at the opening
of a revolution so vitally important, there was no propriety in wasting the
time required to ascertain the will of the people by calling a convention,
when the Legislature had the power to submit an ordinance of secession to

c February 9, 1861.

---

[1] See page 161.
[2] The colors were arranged as follows in this flag of the "Sovereign State of North Carolina:"—The red
formed a broad bar running parallel with the staff, on which was a single star, and the dates arranged as seen in
the engraving, "May 20, 1775," which was that of the promulgation of the so-called "Mecklenburg Declaration
of Independence" (mentioned in note 2, page 385), and "May 20, 1861," on which day the politicians of North
Carolina declared the bond that bound that State to their own chosen Union was forever dissolved.

them without "encumbering them with the election of delegates." He accordingly recommended the Legislature to adopt such an ordinance at once, and call upon the people to vote upon it speedily.

A few days after the Governor's message was submitted to the Legislature, Henry W. Hilliard, a leading member of the "Methodist Church South," appeared before that body.[a] as a commissioner of Jefferson Davis and his confederates, clothed by them with authority to negotiate a treaty of alliance between the State of Tennessee and the "Confederate States of America," similar to that already completed between the Virginia politicians and the conspirators at Montgomery. He was allowed to submit his views to the Legislature. He regarded the question at issue "between the North and the South" as one "of constitutional liberty, involving the right of the people to govern themselves." He believed there was not a true-hearted man in the South who would not rather die than submit to "the Abolition North." The idea of reconstruction must be utterly abandoned. They would never think of "going back to their enemies." He considered the system of government founded on Slavery, which had been established at Montgomery, as the only permanent form of government that could be maintained in America. His views were warmly supported by some prominent Tennesseans. Ex-Governor Neil S. Brown, in a letter published at about that time, expressed his belief that it was "the settled policy of the Administration" and of "the whole North, to wage a war of extermination against the South," and urged the people to arm themselves, as the Border States, he believed, would be the battleground. Ex-Congressman Felix R. Zollicoffer declared that Tennessee was "already involved in war," and said, "We cannot stand neutral and see our Southern brothers butchered."

[a] April 30, 1861.

On the 1st of May the Legislature authorized the Governor to enter into a military league with the "Confederate States," by which the whole military rule of the Commonwealth should be subjected to the will of Davis. He appointed Gustavus A. Henry, Archibald O. W. Totten, and Washington Barrow as commissioners for the purpose. They and Mr. Hilliard negotiated a treaty, and on the 7th[b] the Governor announced to the Legislature the conclusion of the business, and submitted to it a copy of the "Convention." By it Davis and his confederates were authorized to exercise absolute military control in Tennessee until that Commonwealth should become a member of the "Confederacy" by ratifying its permanent constitution. The vote on the treaty in the Senate was fourteen ayes to six noes, and in the lower House, forty-two ayes to fifteen noes. Eighteen of the members, chiefly from East Tennessee, were absent or did not vote.[1]

[b] May.

---

[1] It was stipulated by the convention, in addition to the absolute surrender of all the military affairs of the State to Jefferson Davis, that the State of Tennessee should, "on becoming a member of said Confederacy, under the permanent Constitution of said Confederate States, if the same shall occur, turn over to said Confederate States all the public property, naval stores, and munitions of war, of which she may then be in possession, acquired from the United States, on the same terms and in the same manner as the other States of said Confederacy have done in like cases." Governor Harris had already (on the 29th of April) ordered the seizure of Tennessee bonds to the amount of sixty-six thousand dollars, and five thousand dollars in cash, belonging to the United States, which were in possession of the Collector of the Port of Nashville. The pretext for the seizure was, that the amount might be held in trust, as a sort of hostage, until the Government should return to the State and its citizens property contraband of war which had been taken from the steamer *Hillman*, at Cairo.

The Legislature, in the mean time, had passed an act, to submit to a vote of the people a "Declaration of Independence, and an Ordinance dissolving the Federal Relations between the State of Tennessee and the United States of America;" and also an Ordinance for the adoption of the Constitution of the "Provisional Government of the Confederate States."[1] The Governor was empowered to raise fifty-five thousand volunteers "for the defense of the State," and, if it should become necessary, to call out the whole available military strength of the Commonwealth, to be under the absolute control of the Governor. He was also authorized to issue the bonds of the State to the amount of five millions of dollars, to run ten years and bear an annual interest of eight per cent. Thus the purse and the sword of the violated Commonwealth were placed in the hands of its bitterest enemy, and before the day had arrived on which the vote was to be taken on the question of Separation or No Separation,[a] Harris

[a] June 8, 1861.

had organized twenty-five thousand volunteers and equipped them with munitions of war; a greater portion of which had been stolen from National arsenals, and brought to Nashville by the disloyal Ex-Congressman Zollicoffer, who had been sent by the Governor to Montgomery on a treasonable mission, at the middle of May.[2] The people found themselves practically dispossessed of the elective franchise, one of the most sacred rights of freemen, by a usurper—the head of a military despotism, in complicity with the conspirators at Montgomery. That despotism had been of quick and powerful growth under the culture of men in authority, and was possessed of amazing energy. Its will was law. The people were slaves. Its mailed heel was upon their necks, and they perceived no way to lift it. They knew that their voice at the ballot-box might be silenced by the bayonet, yet they ventured to speak; and it is asserted by the most competent authority, that a decided majority of the votes cast were against the disunion schemes of the Governor and his friends, who at once inaugurated a system of terrorism such as the history of tyrants has seldom revealed. Fraud and violence were exercised everywhere on the part of the disloyalists, and after the operation of a concerted plan for making false election returns, and the changing of figures in the

---

[1] This action was kept secret for several days. When the intrepid Brownlow (see page 85) heard of it, he denounced it vehemently in his journal, the *Knoxville Whig*. "The deed is done, and a black deed it is," he said. "The Legislature of Tennessee, in secret session, passed an Ordinance of Secession, voting the State out of the Federal Union, and changing the Federal relations of the State, thereby affecting, to the great injury of the people, their most important earthly interests." He denounced the Governor and legislators as usurpers, and called upon the people to vote against the Ordinance. "Let every man," he said, "old and young, halt and blind, contrive to be at the polls on that day. If we lose then, our liberties are gone, and we are swallowed up by a military despotism more odious than any now existing in any of the monarchies of Europe."

[2] In a letter to the Governor, after his return, Zollicoffer gave an account of his mission, and revealed facts which throw considerable light on subsequent events. He said that "President Davis" desired and expected to furnish Tennessee with fifty thousand muskets, but there were difficulties in the way. An attempt to procure arms from Havana had failed, but they expected muskets from Belgium "in British bottoms." General Pillow, it seems, had no idea of respecting Kentucky neutrality [see Chapter XIX.], but had, so early as the middle of May, proposed to occupy Columbus, in that State, as a "Confederate" military post. Davis thought such a movement at that time was premature. He said he had once proposed the same thing to Governor Magoffin, but he would not then consent. Davis was also doubtful about the propriety of "throwing the military forces of Tennessee upon the Ohio and Missouri frontiers of Kentucky," which Governor Harris had proposed, because he doubted whether Magoffin would approve of it. "He thinks Governor Magoffin, Mr. Breckinridge, and others," said the writer, "are merely floating with the tide of Southern feeling in Kentucky, not leading it." but that "Governor Jackson, of Missouri, was in advance of his people, and leading to the utmost of his power in defense of the South." Davis also thought it would be better for the Kentuckians true to "the South" to retire, under military leaders, to Tennessee, and there "rally and organize."

aggregates, at Nashville, by the Governor and his confederates, Harris asserted, in a proclamation issued on the 24th of June, that the vote in the State was one hundred and four thousand nine hundred and thirteen for Separation, and forty-seven thousand two hundred and thirty-eight against it, or a majority in favor of disunion of fifty-seven thousand six hundred and seventy-eight.[1] Even this false report showed that East Tennessee—the mountain region of the State, which, like Western Virginia, was not seriously poisoned by the virus of the Slave system—was loyal to the Republic by a heavy majority. It is said that one-half of the votes cast in favor of Separation in East Tennessee were illegal, having been given by soldiers of the insurgent army, who had no right to vote anywhere.[2] All through the war that ensued East Tennessee remained loyal, but at the cost of fearful suffering, as we shall observe hereafter.

Thus Virginia, North Carolina, and Tennessee, by the treasonable action of their respective governors, their legislatures, and their conventions, were placed in an attitude of hostility to the National Government, positively and offensively, before the people were allowed to say a word on the subject officially. These usurpers raised armies and levied war before the people gave them power to enlist a soldier, to buy an ounce of ammunition, or to move a gun.

The conspirators of Virginia had not only talked boldly and resolved courageously, but had, from the moment of the attack on Fort Sumter, labored zealously and vigorously in preliminary movements for the seizure of Washington and the National Government. Within twenty-four hours after the passage of the Secession Ordinance,[a] as we have observed, they had set forces in motion for the capture of Harper's Ferry and the arms and ammunition there, and of the Navy Yard at Gosport, near Norfolk, with its vast amount of ordnance and stores.

[a] April 17, 1861.

Harper's Ferry is a small village in Jefferson County, Virginia, clustered around the base of a rugged hill at the confluence of the Potomac and Shenandoah Rivers, where the conjoined streams pass through the lofty range of the Blue Ridge, between fifty and sixty miles northwest from Washington City. It is on the line of the Baltimore and Ohio Railway, and the Chesapeake and Ohio Canal, the powerful commercial links which connect Maryland, and especially Baltimore, with the great West. There is the outer gate of the Shenandoah or great Valley of Virginia, and was, at the time we are considering and throughout the war, a point of much strategic importance as a military post. There, for many years, a National Armory and Arsenal had been situated, where ten thousand muskets were made every year, and from eighty to ninety thousand stand of arms were generally stored.

---

[1] The items of the vote, as given in the proclamation, were as follows:—

	SEPARATION.	NO SEPARATION.
East Tennessee	14,780	32,923
Middle Tennessee	58,263	8,198
West Tennessee	29,157	6,117
Military Camps	2,714	(none)
Total	104,913	47,238

[2] See *Sketches of the Rise, Progress, and Decline of Secession, et cætera :* by W. G. Brownlow, now (1865) Governor of Tennessee, page 222.

When the secession movement began, at the close of 1860, the Government took measures for the security of this post. Orders were received there on the 2d of January for the Armory Guard, Flag Guard, and Rifle Company to go on duty; and these were re-enforced a few days afterward by sixty-four unmounted United States dragoons, under the command of Lieutenant Roger Jones, who were sent there as a precautionary measure. Colonel Barbour, of Virginia, was superintendent of the post.

Profound quiet prevailed at Harper's Ferry until after the attack on Fort Sumter, when it was disturbed by rumors that the Virginians were preparing to seize the Armory and Arsenal there. The rumor was true, and was soon verified. On the morning of the 18th of April, orders were received

HARPER'S FERRY IN MAY, 1861.[1]

from Richmond, by the militia commanders at Winchester and Charlestown, for the seizure of the Armory and Arsenal that night, and a march in force into Maryland, when the Minute-men of that State were expected to join them in an immediate attack on Washington. Notice was given to about three thousand men, but, owing to some misunderstanding, only Jefferson County troops, about two hundred and fifty strong, under Colonel Allen, were at Halltown, the designated place of rendezvous, at eight o'clock in the evening. This was a little village about half way between Charlestown Court House and Harper's Ferry, and four miles from each. Other troops, in the vicinity of Winchester, were on their march toward the Ferry at that time.

---

[1] This is a view of Harper's Ferry as it appeared just after the destruction of the Armory and Arsenal buildings. The spectator is upon the hill back of the village, and looking toward the Potomac, where, with the waters of the Shenandoah, it passes through the Blue Ridge. Maryland Hights, which have become famous in history, are seen on the left of the picture.

As a surprise seemed important to secure success, the little detachment at Halltown moved forward between nine and ten o'clock. They had four miles to march in the gloom. The infantry led, and were followed by one piece of artillery and about twenty of the Fauquier Cavalry, led by Captain Ashby, who afterward became a noted leader of horsemen in the "Confederate army."

The march was silent. When within a mile of the Ferry, the troops met sentries, who challenged them. The former halted, loaded their guns, and the officers held a consultation. Suddenly there was seen a flash of light, followed by an explosion, in the direction of the Ferry. This was quickly repeated, and in a few minutes the mountain hights in the neighborhood were lighted by an immense and increasing flame. Captain Ashby dashed forward to the town, and soon returned with the report that the Arsenal and Armory were on fire, and that the National troops had crossed the river, and taken the mountain road in the direction of Carlisle Barracks, in Pennsylvania.

Captain Ashby was correctly informed. Lieutenant Jones had been secretly warned, twenty-four hours before, of the plan for seizing the post that night. He had indications around him of trouble being nigh. The militia of the place, who had professed to be loyal, had resolved to disband that day, and the laborers who were acting as guards manifested significant uneasiness. It was evident that the secession feeling was predominant among all classes. He was satisfied that his little force of only forty trusty men could not withstand the overwhelming number of insurgents reported to be in readiness for the attack; so he caused the arms at the post, about fifteen thousand in number, to be secretly piled in heaps in the Arsenal buildings, and surrounded with combustibles for their destruction, that they might not fall into the hands of the insurgents. Suitable materials were also placed in order for burning the Government buildings, between which trains of gunpowder were laid.

At a few minutes past ten o'clock on the evening of the 18th, a sentinel notified Lieutenant Jones that the Virginians, reported to be two thousand in number, were within twenty minutes' march of the Ferry. The commander instantly fired the trains; and three minutes afterward both of the Arsenal buildings containing the arms, together with the carpenters' shop, which was at the upper end of a large and connected series of workshops of the Armory proper, were in a blaze. Every window in the buildings had been thrown open, so as to increase the fury of the conflagration. When this work was accomplished, Jones and his little garrison of forty men crossed the Potomac over the covered bridge, followed by an excited crowd of citizens, who threatened him with direst vengeance. He wheeled his men at the bridge, and threatened to fire upon the pursuers, when they fell back. He then fled up the canal, crossed the hills, and, wading streams and swamps, reached Hagerstown at about seven o'clock in the morning. There he procured vehicles to convey his command to Chambersburg,[1] and from

---

[1] Report of Lieutenant Jones to the Secretary of War, April 20, 1861. Communication of D. H. Strother (well known by the title of "Port Crayon" to the readers of *Harper's Magazine*) in *Harper's Weekly*. Mr. Strother was an eye-witness of the scenes described, and made some graphic sketches of the conflagration.

thence they went by railway to Carlisle Barracks, their destination, where they arrived at about two o'clock in the afternoon of the 19th. The Government highly commended Lieutenant Jones for his judicious act, and his officers and men for their good conduct; and the commander was immediately promoted to the office of Assistant Quartermaster-General, with the rank of captain.[1] ·

Harper's Ferry instantly became an important post, menacing Washington City. By the 20th of May full eight thousand insurgent troops were there, composed of Virginians, Kentuckians, Alabamians, and South Carolinians. They occupied Maryland Hights and other prominent points near the Ferry, on both sides of the Potomac and Shenandoah Rivers, and threw up fortifications there.

Preparations for seizing the Navy Yard near Norfolk were commenced a little earlier than the march upon Harper's Ferry. So early as the night of the 16th of April (the day before the passage of the Ordinance of Secession in the Virginia Convention), two light-boats of eighty tons each were sunk in the channel of the Elizabeth River, below Norfolk, to prevent the egress of the several ships-of-war lying near the Navy Yard. "Thus," said a dispatch sent to Richmond by the exultant insurgents, "we have secured three of the best ships of the Navy." These ships were much coveted prizes. These, with the immense number of cannon and other munitions of war at that post, the Virginia conspirators intended to seize for the use of the "Confederacy."

The Navy Yard here spoken of was at Gosport, a suburb of Portsmouth, on the side of the Elizabeth River opposite Norfolk. It was a sheltered spot on the margin of a deep and narrow body of tide-water, whose head was at the Great Dismal Swamp of North Carolina. The station was one of the oldest and most extensive of its kind in the United States. The establishment covered an area of three-fourths of a mile in length and one-fourth of a mile in width. The largest vessels of war could float there. Ship-houses, machine-shops, officers' quarters, and an immense Dry-dock built of granite, with materials for building and fitting out war-vessels, were seen there in the greatest perfection. The quantity of arms and munitions laid up there was enormous. There were at least two thousand pieces of heavy cannon fit for service, three hundred of which were new Dahlgren guns. It was estimated that the various property of the yard, of all kinds, was worth between nine and ten millions of dollars. Besides this property on land, several war-vessels were afloat there, among which was the immense three-decker *Pennsylvania*, of one hundred and twenty guns, which was constructed in 1837, but had never ventured upon a long ocean voyage. The others were the ships-of-the-line *Columbus*, eighty; *Delaware*, eighty-four, and *New York*, eighty-four, on the stocks: the frigates *United States*, fifty; *Columbia*, fifty; and *Raritan*, fifty: the sloops-of-war *Plymouth*, twenty-two, and *Germantown*, twenty-two: the brig *Dolphin*, four; and the steam-frigate *Merrimack*, afterward made famous by its attack on the National squadron in Hampton Roads and a contest with the *Monitor*. Of these vessels, one was on the stocks, others were out of order, and only the

---

[1] Letter of Simon Cameron, Secretary of War, to Lieutenant Jones, April 22, 1861.

Merrimack and *Germantown* were in a condition to be speedily put to use. The *Merrimack* needed repairs, but the *Germantown* was nearly ready for sea.

Notwithstanding the importance of the Gosport Navy Yard as a military post, and the immense value of the property there, not only to the Government but to the insurgents, the late Administration, in its endeavors to avoid irritating the secessionists of Virginia, had left the whole exposed to seizure or destruction by them. The post was circumvallated by a low structure, incompetent to offer resistance to cannon. There was neither fort nor garrison to cover it in case of an assault. In fact, it was invitingly weak, and offered strong temptations for even a few bold men to attempt its seizure. The new Administration seemed to be equally remiss in duty prescribed by common prudence until it was too late. Finally, after the lapse of more than a month from its inauguration, and when it was resolved to give aid to Forts Pickens and Sumter, Commodore Charles S. McCauley, who was in command of the Gosport station, was admonished to exercise "extreme caution and circumspection." On the 10th of April, he was instructed to "put the shipping and public property in condition to be moved and placed beyond danger, should it become necessary;" at the same time, he was warned to "take no steps that could give needless alarm."[1]

Informed that with the workmen then employed on the engine of the steam-frigate *Merrimack*, it would take thirty days to repair it, and anxious for the safety of the vessel, the Government sent Engineer-in-chief B. F. Isherwood, who discredited the report, to put the machinery in order as quickly as possible. At the same time McCauley was directed to expedite the work, and Captain Alden was ordered to take charge of the vessel, and, when ready for sea, to go with it to Philadelphia. Isherwood arrived at the yard on Sunday morning, the 14th,[a] and by applying labor night and day, he reported to McCauley on the 17th that the engine was ready for use.   [a] April, 1861.

In the mean time, Captain, now (1865) Rear-Admiral Paulding had arrived from Washington with instructions from the Secretary of the Navy for McCauley to lose no time in arming the *Merrimack*; "to get the *Plymouth* and *Dolphin* beyond danger; to have the *Germantown* in a condition to be towed out, and to put the more valuable property, ordnance stores, *et cætera*, on shipboard, so that they could, at any moment, be moved beyond danger." · The Secretary also instructed him to defend the vessels and other property committed to his charge "at any hazard, repelling by force, if necessary, any and all attempts to seize them, whether by mob violence, organized effort, or any assumed authority." On the same day, in accordance with advice offered by Paulding, the frigate *Cumberland*, which had been anchored below, with a full crew and armament on board, was moved up to a position so as to command the entire harbor, the Navy Yard, the cities of Norfolk and Portsmouth, and the channel through which they were approached. After seeing these precautionary arrangements completed, Paulding returned to Washington.

The *Merrimack* being ready for sea on the 17th, Mr. Isherwood proposed to have her fires lighted at once, that she might depart before other channel

[1] Secretary Welles to Commodore McCauley, April 10, 1861.

obstructions should be laid by the insurgents. "To-morrow morning will be in time," said the Commodore, and the lighting was deferred. At an early hour the next day, the fires were glowing, and soon every thing was in readiness for departure. Again the Commodore proposed delay. "But the orders are peremptory," said Isherwood; and he suggested that, after another day's delay, it might be difficult to pass the obstructions which the secessionists were planting between Sewell's Point and Craney Island. But the vessel was kept back, and, to the astonishment of the Engineer-in-chief and other officers, the Commodore finally gave directions not to send the *Merrimack* away at all, and ordered the fires to be extinguished.[1] McCauley afterward asserted that he was influenced in his action at that time by the advice of several of his junior officers, born in Slave-labor States, believing that they were true to their flag. "How could I expect treachery on their part?" he said. "The fact of their being Southern men was not surely a sufficient reason for suspecting their fidelity. Those Southern officers who have remained faithful to their allegiance are among the best in the service. No; I could not believe it possible that a set of men, whose reputations were so high in the Navy, could ever desert their posts, and throw off their allegiance to the country they had sworn to defend and protect. I had frequently received professions of their loyalty; for instance, on the occasion of the surrender of the Pensacola Navy Yard they expressed to me their indignation, and observed: 'You have no Pensacola officers here, Commodore; we will never desert you; we will stand by you to the last, even to the death.'"[2] Yet these men, false to every principle of honor, after having disgracefully deceived their commander, and accomplished the treasonable work of keeping the *Merrimack* and other vessels at the Navy Yard until it was too late for them to escape, offered their resignations on the 18th (the day after the Virginia Ordinance of Secession was passed), abandoned their flag, and joined the insurgents.[3]

General Taliaferro, the commander of all the forces in southeastern Virginia, arrived at Norfolk with his staff on the evening of the 18th, and at once took measures for the seizure of the Navy Yard and the ships of war. The naval officers who had abandoned their flag joined him, and the secessionists of Norfolk were eager for the drama to open. On the following day, the workmen in the yard, who had been corrupted by the disloyal

*April 18, 1861.

[1] Report of the Secretary of the Navy, July 4, 1861. "The cause of this refusal to remove the *Merrimack*," said the Secretary of the Navy, "has no explanation other than that of misplaced confidence in his junior officers, who opposed it."

[2] Letter of Commodore McCauley in the *National Intelligencer*, May 5, 1862, in reply to the Committee on the Conduct of the War, cited by Duyckinck in his *History of the War for the Union*, i. 157.

[3] Among the naval officers who resigned at about this time was Lieutenant M. F. Maury, a Virginian, who for several years was the trusted superintendent of the National Observatory at Washington. The records of that office, it is said, disclosed the fact that he had impressed upon the minds of the scientific bodies in Europe that the dissolution of the Union and the destruction of the Republic were inevitable. So said the New York *World*. The career of Maury, after he abandoned his flag and joined its enemies, was peculiarly dishonorable. Before he resigned, and while he was yet trusted and honored by his countrymen, he was perfidiously working to overthrow the Government. He went to Europe, and there used every means in his power, by the grossest misrepresentations, to injure the character of his Government. Finally, on the 25th of May, 1865, when the rebellion was crushed, he wrote a note "at sea," to Rear-Admiral S. W. Godon, then at Havana, saying:—"In peace, as in war, I follow the fortunes of my native State, Virginia:" and expressed his willingness to accept a parol on the terms granted to General Lee. He went to Mexico; and, in the autumn of 1865, Maximilian appointed him "Imperial Commissioner of Colonization," to promote immigration from the Southern States of our Republic.

officers, were absent from roll-call, yet the day passed without any hostile demonstrations. But on Saturday, the 20th, Norfolk was fearfully excited by conflicting rumors. One was that the yard was to be attacked, when the *Cumberland* would doubtless fire on the town; another, that she was about to leave, with valuable property belonging to the Government, and that the other vessels were to be scuttled; and still another, that the yard was to be destroyed. The military companies of Norfolk and Portsmouth were called out and paraded under arms. Four companies of riflemen and infantry had arrived from Petersburg, numbering in all four hundred men, and on that day were joined by two hundred more. The Richmond Grays had also arrived that morning, bringing with them fourteen pieces of heavy rifled cannon, and an ample stock of ammunition. With these re-enforcements, Taliaferro felt certain of success. McCauley felt equally certain that he could not withstand an assault from the insurgent force, so large and so well armed, and at noon he sent Taliaferro word that not one of the vessels should be moved, nor a shot fired, excepting in self-defense. This quieted the people.

Not doubting that an immediate attack would be made upon the vessels, McCauley gave orders, on the return of his flag from Norfolk, for the scuttling of all of them, to prevent their falling into the hands of the insurgents. This was done at four o'clock in the afternoon. The *Cumberland* only was spared. This work had been just accomplished when Captain Paulding again appeared. As soon as the Secretary of the Navy heard of the detention of the *Merrimack*—that "fatal error," as he called it—he dispatched Paulding in the *Pawnee* with orders to relieve McCauley, and, with "such officers and marines as could be obtained, take command of all the vessels afloat on that station, repel force by force, and prevent the ships and public property, at all hazards, from passing into the hands of the insurrectionists." Paulding added to his crew, at Washington, one hundred marines; and at Fortress Monroe he took on board three hundred and fifty Massachusetts volunteers, under Colonel David W. Wardrop, the first regiment detailed for service from that

HIRAM PAULDING.

State, who had arrived that day. He reached Norfolk just as the scuttling of the vessels was completed. But for that act every vessel afloat might have been saved.

Paulding saw at a glance the fatal error, if error it was, of McCauley, and also that much more than scuttling must be done to render the ships useless to the insurgents. He also perceived that with only the *Pawnee* and *Cumberland*, and the very small land force at his command, he could not defend the Navy Yard; so, using the discretionary power with which he was clothed, he at once prepared to burn the slowly sinking ships, destroy the cannon, and commit to the flames all the buildings and public property in the Navy Yard, leaving the insurgents nothing worth contending for.　One hundred men were sent, under Lieutenant J. H. Russell, with sledge-hammers, to knock off the trunnions of the cannon; Captain Charles Wilkes was intrusted with the destruction of the Dry-dock; Commanders Allen and Sands were charged with the firing of the ship-houses, barracks, and other buildings; and Lieutenant Henry A. Wise was directed to lay trains upon the ships and to fire them at a given signal.　The trunnions of the Dahlgren guns resisted the hammers, but those of a large number of the old pattern guns were destroyed.　Many of the remainder were spiked, but so indifferently that they were soon repaired.　Commander Rogers and Captain Wright, of the Engineers, volunteered to blow up and destroy the Dry-dock.

At about two o'clock in the morning,[a] every thing was in readiness. The troops, marines, sailors, and others at the yard, were taken on board the *Pawnee* and *Cumberland*, leaving on shore only as many as were required to start the conflagration.　At three o'clock, the *Yankee*, Captain Germain, took the *Cumberland* in tow; and twenty minutes later Paulding sent up a rocket from the *Pawnee*, which was the signal for the incendiaries to apply the match.　In a few minutes a grand and awful spectacle burst upon the vision of the inhabitants of Norfolk and Portsmouth, and of the country for leagues around.　The conflagration, starting simultaneously at different points, became instantly terrific.　Its

[a] April 21, 1861.

BURNING OF THE VESSELS AT THE GOSPORT NAVY YARD.[1]

roar could be heard for miles, and its light was seen far at sea, far up the James and York Rivers, and Chesapeake Bay, and far beyond the Dismal Swamp.　The ships and the ship-houses, and other large buildings in the Navy Yard, were involved in one grand ruin.　To add to the sublimity of the fiery tempest, frequent discharges were heard from the monster ship-of-the-line *Pennsylvania*, as the flames reached her loaded heavy guns.

When the conflagration was fairly under way, the *Pawnee* and the *Cumberland*, towed by the *Yankee*, went down the river, and all who were

---

[1] This view shows the position of some of the vessels on Sunday morning, the 21st of April. The large vessel on the right is the *Pennsylvania*. On the extreme left is seen the bow of the *United States*. In the center is seen the *Pawnee* steam-frigate, and the *Cumberland* with the *Yankee* at her side. This is from a picture in *Harper's Weekly*, May 11, 1861.

left on shore, excepting two, reaching their boats in safety, followed by the light of the great fire, and overtook the *Pawnee* off Craney Island, where the two vessels broke through the obstructions and proceeded to Hampton Roads. The two officers left behind were Commander Rogers and Captain Wright, who failed to reach the boats. They were arrested after day-dawn and were taken to Norfolk as prisoners of war.

The great object of the conflagration was not fully accomplished. The attempt was, in fact, a failure. The Dry-dock was very little injured. The mechanics' shops and sheds, timber-sheds, ordnance building, foundries, saw-

VIEW OF THE NAVY YARD AFTER THE FIRE.[1]

mill, provisions, officers' quarters, and all other buildings in the yard, were saved, excepting the immense ship-houses, the marine barracks, and riggers, sail, and ordnance lofts. The insurgents immediately took possession of all the spared buildings and machinery, the Dry-dock, and the vast number of uninjured cannon, and proceeded at once to make use of them in the work of rebellion. Several of the heavy Dahlgren guns were mounted in battery

TEMPORARY THREE-GUN BATTERY.[2]

along the river-bank, at the Navy Yard, and other places near; and soon afterward the fortifications in the Slave-labor States were supplied with heavy guns from this post. The gain to the insurgents and loss to the National Government, by this abandonment of the Gosport Navy Yard at that time, was incalculable.[3] The mere money value of the property

---

[1] This picture is from a large sketch made by a young artist, Mr. James E. Taylor, a member of a New York regiment, and kindly placed at my disposal by him.

[2] This picture is also from a sketch by Mr. Taylor. It is a view of a three-gun battery, placed so as to command the approach to the Navy Yard by the Suffolk road.

[3] William H. Peter, appointed by the Governor of Virginia a commissioner to make an inventory of the property taken from the National Government at this time, said, that he deemed "it unnecessary to speak of the vast importance to Virginia, and to the entire South, of the timely acquisition of this extensive naval dépôt, since the presence at almost every exposed point on the entire Southern coast, and at numerous inland intrenched

destroyed, estimated at seven millions of dollars, was the least of the loss to the one and the gain to the other. It also swelled amazingly the balance of advantages for the insurgents, who were quick to discern and to be encouraged by it. And it was made the topic of special discourses from the pulpit, from which disloyal ministers were continually giving words of encouragement to the conspirators.[1]

Only a portion of the vessels at the Gosport station were absolutely destroyed. The *New York*, on the stocks in one of the ship-houses, was totally consumed. The *Pennsylvania*, *Dolphin*, and *Columbia* had nothing saved but the lower bottom timbers; the *Raritan* was burnt to the water's edge; the *Merrimack* was burnt to her copper-line and sunk; the *Germantown* was also burnt and sunk; while the useless old *United States*, in which Decatur won glory, was not injured; and the *Plymouth* was not burned, but scuttled and sunk. The same fate overtook the *Columbus* and *Delaware*. The *Plymouth* was afterward raised; so was the *Merrimack*, and converted into a powerful iron-clad vessel of war.[2]

The insurgents seized old Fort Norfolk, situated a short distance below the city of Norfolk, on the 21st. It had been used as a magazine, and contained about three hundred thousand pounds of gunpowder and a large quantity of loaded shells and other missiles. On the same day, General Taliaferro issued an order prohibiting the Collector of the port of Norfolk from accepting drafts from the National Government, or allowing the removal of money or any thing else from the Custom House. At the same time troops were hastening to Norfolk from lower Virginia; and on the 22d, three companies of soldiers from Georgia arrived in the express train from Weldon, a portion of whom took post at the Marine Hospital on the Portsmouth side of the river. The hull of the old ship *United States* was towed down the river, and moored and sunk in the channel, a mile below Fort Norfolk; and a battery of heavy guns was immediately erected at Sewell's Point, and another on Craney Island, to command the entrance to the Elizabeth River and the harbor of Norfolk. The insurgents had now secured a most important military position, as well as valuable materials

---

camps in the several States, of heavy pieces of ordnance, with their equipments and fixed ammunition, fully attest the fact."—*Report in the Richmond Enquirer*, February 4, 1862.

[1] On the 13th of June, 1861, a fast-day proclaimed by Jefferson Davis, Dr. Elliott, Bishop of the Protestant Episcopal Church in Georgia, preached a sermon on "God's Presence with the Confederate States," in which he gave, as instances of that manifest presence, the ease with which Twiggs, the traitor, accomplished the destruction of the National Army in Texas; the downfall of Fort Sumter; the easy manner in which the "Confederates" had been enabled to plunder the arsenals and seize the forts, mints, and custom houses of the United States, in the absence of competent force to protect them, and the advantages gained through this most dishonorable act of treachery at the Gosport Navy Yard. In all these iniquities the venerable prelate saw "God's Presence with the Confederate States," and spoke of the failure of a handful of men against multitudes, and of human wisdom against the diabolical plottings of perjured men, as the result of fear. "Fear seemed to fall upon our enemies—unaccountable fear," he said. Then, looking down from that lofty "Presence" to temporal things, the prelate said, referring to the Gosport affair, "Nowhere could this panic have occurred more seasonably for us, because it gave us just what we most needed, arms, and ammunition, and heavy ordnance in great abundance. All this is unaccountable upon any ordinary grounds." He likened the action of the Government servants, who hastily fired and abandoned the Navy Yard and vessels, to the panic of the Syrians on one occasion, when the Lord, in order to deliver Israel, made them hear a noise like that of a mighty host coming upon them:—"Wherefore they arose and fled in the twilight, and left their tents, and their horses, and their asses, even the camp as it was, and fled for their life." The preacher did not heed the wise injunction of the king of Israel (1 Kings, xx. 11):—"Let not him that girdeth on his harness boast himself as he that putteth it off."

[2] Report of the Select Committee of the United States Senate for investigating the facts in relation to the loss of the Navy Yard, *et cætera*, submitted by Senator Hale, of New Hampshire, April 18, 1862.

of war; and they held that post, to the great hurt of the National cause, until early in May the following year, when they fled at the approach of troops under Major-General John E. Wool.

By obtaining possession of Harper's Ferry and the Gosport Navy Yard, the most important preliminary movements for the seizure of Washington City were successfully accomplished within a week after the evacuation of Sumter. The practical annexation of a greater part of Virginia to the "Southern Confederacy" within eight days after these movements, and the assembling of troops upon its soil from the more Southern States, gave increased value to those acquisitions. Fire had materially lessened their immediate value, yet they were vitally important. It now only remained for the Marylanders to follow the bad example of the Virginians, to make the seizure of the National Capital an apparently easy achievement.

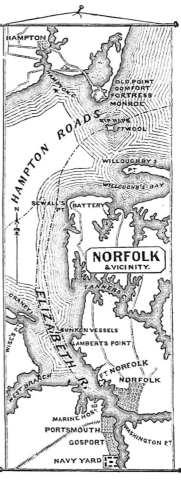

Let us consider the events at that Capital and its vicinity at this critical period in its history.

Notwithstanding the protestations of the leading conspirators everywhere, before the attack on Fort Sumter, that they had no aggressive designs against the Republic; notwithstanding the Legislature of Virginia had, on the day when the Peace Convention assembled at Washington and the Convention of conspirators began at Montgomery,[a] endeavored to lull the National Government into a sense of security most fatal to its life, by resolving that there

[a] February 4, 1861.

were "no just grounds for believing that citizens of Virginia meditate an attack on or seizure of the Federal property, or invasion of the District of Columbia, and that all preparations to resist the same are unnecessary, so far as this State is concerned," it was too well known that leading and powerful politicians in Maryland and Virginia were secretly preparing to seize the Capital, when a proper opportunity should offer, to allow the Government to relax its vigilance or its preparations for the defense of its seat, for a moment. And yet, when the crisis came—when the secession of Virginia was proclaimed, and the movements against Harper's Ferry and Gosport were begun—the foes of the Union developed such amazing proportions, vitality, and strength, that the Government was in imminent peril. The public offices were swarming with disloyal men, and the Capital held thousands of malignant secessionists of both sexes, secret and open.[1] Secession flags flaunted defiantly from many a window, and secession badges were sold openly at the doors of the Avenue hotels. It was evident to the

COSTUME OF A REBELLIOUS WOMAN.

least observant that the disloyal elements of society there were buoyant with pleasant anticipations. Information had reached the Government that the Minutemen of Virginia and Maryland, and their sympathizers in the District of Columbia, were unusually active. The leading secessionists of the city of Baltimore, comprising the "State-Rights Association," were in conference every evening; and Governor Hicks had been continually importuned to call an extraordinary session of the Legislature, that a secession convention might be authorized. Because he refused to do so, knowing how large a portion of its members were disloyal, he was abused without stint.

The Government was soon made painfully aware that the call for troops to put down the rising rebellion was not an hour too soon. There was a general impression in the Free-labor States that the Capital would be the first point of attack, and thitherward volunteers instantly began to march in large and hourly increasing numbers. Within three days after the President's call for troops went forth,[a] probably not less than one hundred thousand young men were leaving their avocations to prepare for war. The movement was simultaneous in all the Free-labor States, and the armories of volunteer companies were everywhere thronged with enthusiastic men eager to fly to the protection of the President, his Cabinet, the archives, and the Capital.

a April 15, 1861.

The Governor of Massachusetts (Andrew) had been the first of the State Executives, as we have observed,[2] to prepare for war. On the 1st of January, Brigadier-General E. W. Peirce, of the Massachusetts militia, wrote

---

[1] Taking advantage of the deference paid to their sex in this country, the women of Washington, Baltimore, and other cities within Slave-labor States yet controlled by National authority, who sympathized with the conspirators, were much more openly defiant of the Government, when the war commenced, than men. They not only worked secretly and efficiently in aid of the rebellion, and used the utmost freedom of speech, but they appeared in public places wearing conspicuously either a secession badge or the "stars and bars" of the "Southern Confederacy" in their costume. The *sacque,* then a fashionable outer garment, was sometimes made, as seen in the picture, so as to display the seven stars of the early "Confederate" flag on the bosom, and the red and white bars on the short skirt. These were flaunted in the streets: and women who wore them took every occasion to insult National soldiers, and show their hatred of the National flag. Finding at length that their conduct was more injurious to themselves than annoying to Union soldiers and Union citizens, the vulgar habit soon fell into disuetude, and sensible women who had practiced it became heartily ashamed of their folly.

[2] See page 203.

to the Governor, tendering his services to the country; and on the 5th, Andrew sent agents to the Governors of the other New England States, to press upon them the importance of placing the militia of the respective Commonwealths in condition for a prompt movement in defense of the Capital. At the same time the volunteer companies of the State, five thousand strong, began drilling nightly at their armories. Early in February, as we have observed, the Governor sent a staff officer (Ritchie) to Washington, to consult with the General-in-Chief concerning the forwarding of troops to the Capital if they should be needed; and the Massachusetts Senators (Sumner and Wilson) urged the President to call for these well-drilled companies, should the Capital be in apparent danger.

That exigency occurred when Fort Sumter was attacked; and on the day when the President called for seventy-five thousand men, Senator Wilson telegraphed to Governor Andrew to dispatch twenty companies to Washington City immediately. A few hours later, the formal requisition of the Secretary of War arrived;[1] and so promptly was the call from the Capital responded to by the Governor, that before sunset of the same day, orders were in the hands of Colonel Wardrop, of the Third Regiment, at New Bedford; of Colonel Packard, of the Fourth, at Quincy; of Colonel Jones, of the Sixth, at Lowell; and of Colonel Munroe, of the Eighth, at Lynn, to muster forthwith on Boston Common. As in 1775, so now, the first companies that appeared, in response to the call of authority for the protection of the liberties of the people, came from Marblehead. These appeared on the evening of the 15th, and early the following day the four regiments called for were on Boston Common, mustered in regular order, with banners flying and bayonets gleaming, and each company with full ranks. These companies had arrived by different railways. They had left their homes with the blessings of neighbors and friends, who assured them that their families should be taken care of during their absence, as adopted children. They were cheered on the way by the huzzas of the people in villages and at the waysides, and were welcomed in Boston with every demonstration of delight. The citizens of the New England metropolis had forgotten their usual avocations, and were intent only upon the business of saving the Republic. The old war-spirit of Faneuil Hall—the "Cradle of Liberty"—was aroused; and all over Boston there were

"Banners blooming in the air,"

in attestation of the patriotism of the people.

On the 16th, Senator Wilson again telegraphed for a "brigade of four regiments." These were then in readiness on Boston Common; and on the morning of the 17th, the Governor commissioned Benjamin F. Butler, of Lowell (then a Brigadier-General of Militia), the commander of the brigade. Butler knew the chief conspirators well. He had passed evenings with Davis, Hunter, Mason, Slidell, Benjamin, and other traitors at Washington, three months before, and had become convinced of their determination to destroy the Republic, if possible. Impelled by this conviction, he had not ceased to counsel the authorities of his State to have the militia of the Commonwealth prepared for war. He and Governor Andrew worked in unison to this end; and on the day before his appointment, he was instrumental in procuring from the Bank of Redemption, in Boston, a temporary loan to the Commonwealth, for the use of the troops, of the sum of fifty thousand dollars.

It was determined that the Sixth Regiment, Colonel Jones, which was a part of Butler's old brigade, should go forward at once to Washington, by way of New York, Philadelphia, and Baltimore. It consisted of eleven companies. To these were added the companies of Captains Sampson and Dike, making a corps of thirteen full companies. They were addressed by Governor Andrew and General Butler, in the presence of a vast multitude of citizens, and, in the afternoon,[a] departed for Washington by railway. At about the same time, Colonel Wardrop and his regiment embarked on a steamer for Fortress Monroe, in Virginia, then defended by only two companies of artillery, and in imminent peril of seizure by the insurgents of that State. These were followed by Colonel Packard and his regiment. The Eighth, under Colonel Munroe, accompanied by the General, departed for Washington on the evening train.

BENJAMIN F. BUTLER.

a April 17, 1861.

Rhode Island and Connecticut, through which these troops passed, were in a blaze of excitement. Governor Sprague, of the former State, had promptly tendered to the Government the services of a thousand infantry and a battalion of artillery, and called the Legislature together on the 17th. That body promptly provided for the State's quota, and appropriated five hundred thousand dollars for war purposes. The banks offered adequate loans to the State; and large sums were tendered by individuals. Within five days after the call for troops, the Rhode Island Marine Artillery, with eight guns and one hundred and ten horses, commanded by Colonel Tompkins, passed through New York on their way to Washington; and the First Regiment of Infantry, twelve hundred strong, under Colonel Burnside, was ready to move. It was composed of many of the wealthier citizens of the State, and was accompanied to Washington by Governor Sprague, as Commander-in-chief of the forces of Rhode Island.

RHODE ISLAND MARINE ARTILLERY.

Governor Buckingham, of Connecticut, whose labors throughout the war were unceasing and of vast importance, responded to the President's call for troops by issuing a proclamation on the same day, urging the citizens of the State to volunteer their services in aid of the Government. The banks offered all the money necessary to equip the regiment of men required by the circular letter of the Secretary of War. So enthusiastic were the people, that the Governor, in a message to the Legislature on the 1st of May, averred that forty-one volunteer companies had already been accepted. The prediction that there would be a divided North—that blood would flow in New England, in the event of an attempt of the National Government to enforce the laws against Southern insurgents,[1] was most signally falsified.

BURNSIDE'S RIFLEMEN.

New York, as we shall observe presently, responded nobly to the call; and the neighboring inhabitants of New Jersey were so full of enthusiasm, that they became impatient of the seeming lukewarmness and tardiness of Governor Olden and others in authority. The Governor was so startled by the demonstrations of patriotism around him, that he ordered Company A of the City Battalion of Trenton, the capital of the State, to watch the Arsenal, and see that the people did not run away with the arms. Two days after the President's call, he issued a formal proclamation, calling for the quota of New Jersey to assemble at the State capital. The Trenton banks tendered a loan to the State of twenty-five thousand dollars; and the authorities of the city of Newark appropriated one hundred thousand dollars for the maintenance of the families of volunteers, and five thousand dollars for the equipment of the soldiers. The Legislature met on the 30th of April, in extraordinary session, when Major-General Theodore Runyon was appointed commander of the New Jersey forces, and the movements of troops toward Washington began.

WM. A. BUCKINGHAM.

Pennsylvania, like Massachusetts, had been watchful and making preparations for the crisis. Her militia force was about three hundred and fifty thousand. The resources of the State had been pledged by the Legislature, in January, to the support of the

National Government.[1] The vigilant Governor Curtin saw the storm-clouds continually thickening, and, in a message to the Legislature on the 9th of April, he recommended the adoption of immediate measures for reorganizing the militia of the State and establishing an efficient military system.   He referred to the menacing attitude of certain States, and urged the immediate attention of the Legislature to the deplorable militia system of the Commonwealth, saying: "Pennsylvania offers no. counsel and takes no action in the nature of a menace."   An Act, in accordance with the Governor's wishes, became law on the 12th of April, and half a million of dollars were appropriated for arming and equipping the militia of the State.

When intelligence of the attack on Fort Sumter reached Philadelphia, the chief city of Pennsylvania, the excitement of the people was intense. This was hightened by the call of the President for troops, and the manifest existence of disloyal men in the city.   Great exasperation was felt against those known to be disloyal, or suspected of sympathy with the insurgents; and, at one time, full ten thousand of the populace were in the streets, engaged in putting out of the way every semblance of opposition to the Government.   The Mayor managed to control them, and when offending parties threw out the American flag the people were generally satisfied.[2]   That banner was everywhere displayed over public and private buildings, and a Union pledge was circulated throughout the city, and signed by thousands without distinction of party.   The Governor called*a an extraordinary session of the Legislature to meet at Harrisburg on the 30th; but, before that time, thousands of Pennsylvanians were enrolled in the great Union Army.   The Secretary of War (Mr. Cameron), immediately after issuing his call for troops, sent his son into Pennsylvania to expedite the work of recruiting; and within the space of three days he had the satisfaction of welcoming to Washington troops from his native State.   The Legislature authorized the organization of a reserved corps, to be armed, equipped, clothed, subsisted, and paid by the State, and drilled in camps of instruction.   It also authorized a loan of three millions of dollars for war purposes.

a April 20, 1861.

Pennsylvania has the honor of having furnished the troops that first arrived at the Capital in the hour of its greatest peril.   These composed five companies from the interior of the State, namely, the "Washington Artillery," and "National Light Infantry," of Pottsville, Schuylkill County; the "Ringgold Light Artillery," of Reading, Berks County; the "Logan Guards," of Lewistown, Mifflin County, and the "Allen Infantry," of Allentown, Lehigh County.   At the call of the President, the commanders of these companies telegraphed to Governor Curtin that they were full, and ready for service.   He immediately ordered them to assemble at Harrisburg, the State capital.   They were all there on the evening of the 17th, but

---

[2] A secession newspaper, called *The Palmetto Flag*, was hawked about the streets at that time. It was suppressed, and an American flag was displayed at its office, as we have already observed in note 2, page 353. A large number of medical students in Philadelphia were from the South, and there was much sympathy with the secessionists in that city among a certain class of politicians. Some of them, in public meetings of their party, proposed to have Pennsylvania joined to the "Southern Confederacy."

mostly without arms, expecting to receive new and improved equipments there. These were not ready. The imminence of the danger to the National Capital would admit of no delay, not even long enough for the companies to be organized as a regiment. They were ordered forward the next morning by the Northern Central Railway, to Baltimore, in company with about forty regular soldiers, who were going to re-enforce the little garrison at Fort McHenry. The battery of the Ringgold Artillery was left at Harrisburg. The muskets in the hands of the regulars, and thirty others borne by the volunteers, were the only weapons with which these prospective defenders of the Capital entered a hostile territory—Maryland being essentially such at that time. At home and on their way to Harrisburg they were cheered by the patriotic zeal and unbounded enthusiasm of the people. Men, women, and children joined in the acclamation.[1]

Baltimore, through which all troops traveling by railway from the North and East to Washington were compelled to pass, was then under the complete control of the secessionists. The wealthier classes were attached by ties of blood and marriage with the people of the South, and the system of slavery common to both was a powerful promoter of the most cordial sympathy. The dominant classes in the city were at that time disloyal, yet a large majority of the inhabitants were true to the old flag. Most of those in authority were disunionists, including the Marshal of Police (Kane[2]), and were passive, if not secretly active friends of the secession movement.

It was known that the Pennsylvania troops would go through Baltimore at a little past noon, and the Marshal, doubtless for the purpose of concealing dark designs, issued an order for his force to be vigilant, and preserve the peace, while the officers of the " State-Rights Association" hastened to publicly assure him, in the most solemn manner, that no demonstrations should be made against National troops passing through Baltimore. The Mayor (George W. Brown), whose sympathies were with the disunionists, issued a proclamation invoking all good citizens to preserve the peace and good order of the town. Notwithstanding these apparent efforts of the authorities to prevent disturbance, when the Pennsylvanians arrived, at near two o'clock in the afternoon, they were surrounded by an angry, howling mob, who only lacked the organization to which they attained twenty-four hours later, to have been the actors in a fearful tragedy on that day, instead of on the next.

News had just arrived of the passage of the Ordinance of Secession by the Virginia Convention, and it was spreading rapidly over the city. The excited multitude, of whom a large proportion were South Carolinians and

---

[1] The spirit of the women is well illustrated by the following letter from the wife of a private of the Ringgold Light Artillery, written to her husband, who was in Washington City at the time:—

"READING, April 16, 1861.

"MY DEAR HUSBAND:—The Ringgolds have been ordered to march. It is pouring down rain, and the men are flocking to the army. O, I do wish you were home to go with them. Such a time I have never seen in all my life. The people are fairly mad. I went up through all the rain to see the Captain. He said you could follow them when you came home. When he had the men all in the hall in line, he said:—'If any man is opposed to fighting for his country, he may hold up his right hand.' Only one man held up his hand, and the next minute he was kicked out of the door. Do come home as soon as you receive this letter. But you will not get it in time, as they leave this evening on the six o'clock train for Harrisburg. If you wish to join them there, telegraph, and I will send your uniform and sword by the express.

" From your true and loving wife,   SALLY G——Y."

[2] See page 281.

Georgians, then sojourning in Baltimore, followed the troops all the way from one railroad station to the other, offering the most indecent insults; shouting, "Welcome to Southern graves!" uttering the most blasphemous language, and throwing a few missiles which slightly injured some of the men. A colored man, over sixty years of age,[1] in military dress, attached as a servant to the "Washington Artillery" Company, greatly excited their ire. They raised the cry of "Nigger in uniform!" and stones and bricks were hurled at him. He received a severe wound on the face and head, from which blood flowed freely.

The Pennsylvanians left Baltimore at four o'clock and reached Washington City at about seven, where they were received by the anxious loyal inhabitants and the officers of the Government with heart-felt joy, for the rumbling volcano of revolution threatened them with an eruption every moment. For a day or two the city had been full of rumors of the movement of Virginia and Maryland secessionists for the seizure of the Capital, and many families had fled affrighted. Troops from Massachusetts, New York, and Pennsylvania had been hourly expected all that day, and when evening approached, and they did not appear, the panic increased. When the Pennsylvanians came, they were hailed as deliverers by an immense throng, who greeted them with prolonged cheers, for they were the first promise of hope and safety. The fears of the inhabitants were immediately quieted.

The Pennsylvanians were at once marched to the Capitol grounds, where they were reviewed by General McDowell, and then assigned quarters in the hall of the House of Representatives, in the south wing of the Capitol. They had been without food all day, but were soon supplied. The halls were at once lighted up and warmed, and the startling rumor spread over the city, that two thousand Northern troops, well armed with Minié rifles, were quartered in the Capitol![2] The real number was five hundred and thirty. It was the intention of the Government to arm them with muskets from Harper's Ferry, but the armory there was destroyed that very evening.[3]

It is believed by the best informed, that these troops arrived just in time to awe the conspirators and their friends, and to save the Capitol from

---

[1] This man, supposed to have been a runaway slave, was known by the name of "Nick Biddle." He had resided for a number of years in Pottsville, where he sometimes sold oysters in the winter and ice-cream in the summer. He attended the Washington Artillery company on its target and other excursions. His excursion through Baltimore was never pleasant in his memory. He was heard to say that he would go through the infernal regions with the Artillery, but would never again go through Baltimore. His was almost the first blood shed in the rebellion, that of the wounded at Fort Sumter being the first by a few days.

[2] This rumor was started by James D. Gay, a member of the Ringgold Light Artillery, who was in Washington City on business at the time of their arrival. He was already an enrolled member of a temporary home-guard in Washington, under Cassius M. Clay, which we shall consider presently, and was working with all his might for the salvation of the city. After exchanging greetings with his company at the Capitol, he hastened to Willard's Hotel to proclaim the news. In a letter to the writer, he says:—"The first man I met as I entered the doors was Lieutenant-Colonel Magruder [who afterward abandoned his flag and was a General of the "Confederate" army]. I said, 'Colonel, have you heard the good news?' 'What is it?' he asked. I told him to step to the door. He did so. Pointing to the lights at the Capitol, I said, 'Do you see that?' 'Yes,' he answered, 'but what of that?' 'Two thousand soldiers,' I said, 'have marched in there this evening, Sir, armed with Minié rifles.' 'Possible! so much!' he exclaimed, in an excited manner. Of course what I told him was not true, but I thought that, in the absence of sufficient troops, this false report might save the city." Mr. Gay's "pious fraud" had the desired effect.

[3] I am indebted to Francis B. Wallace, Esq., editor of the *Miner's Journal*, Pottsville, Pennsylvania, for the facts concerning this movement of Pennsylvania troops, and also for the muster-roll of the five companies who so patriotically hastened to the defense of the Capital. Mr. Wallace was an officer of the "Washington Artillery" Company, and was a participant in the exciting scenes of a three months' campaign.

seizure. It is believed that if they had been delayed twenty-four hours—had they not been there when, on the next day, a tragedy we are about to consider was performed in the streets of Baltimore—the President and his Cabinet, with the General-in-chief, might have been assassinated or made prisoners, the archives and buildings of the Government seized, and Jefferson Davis proclaimed Dictator from the great eastern portico of the Capitol, where Mr. Lincoln was inaugurated only forty-five days before. These citizen soldiers well deserved the thanks of the nation voted by Congress at its called session in July following,[1] and a grateful people will ever delight to do homage to their patriotism.[2]

---

[1] In the House of Representatives, July 22, 1861, on motion of Hon. James Campbell, it was "*Resolved*, That the thanks of this House are due, and are hereby tendered, to the five hundred and thirty soldiers from Pennsylvania who passed through the mob at Baltimore, and reached Washington on the 18th day of April last, for the defense of the National Capital."

[2] The Philadelphia *Press*, on the 8th of April, 1862, said:—"We understand that a gentleman of high position and good judgment, who has taken a very prominent part in public affairs ever since the inauguration of Mr. Lincoln, recently declared, that the small band of Pennsylvania troops who arrived at Washington on the 18th of April, saved the Capital from seizure by the conspirators. In his judgment, if their response to the call of the President had been less prompt, the traitors would inevitably have gained possession of the archives and public buildings of the Nation, and, probably, of the highest officers of the Government." The names of that little band are given in the following muster-rolls of the companies. It may be proper to remark, that these names are not given to mark these men as more patriotic than thousands of others who were then pressing eagerly toward Washington City, but for the obvious reason that they were the first to arrive, and give the earliest efficient check to the hands of the conspirators, uplifted to smite the Nation with a deadly blow.

The muster-rolls of the companies, on that occasion, are as follows:—

WASHINGTON ARTILLERY COMPANY, OF POTTSVILLE.

OFFICERS AND NON-COMMISSIONED OFFICERS.—Captain, James Wren; First Lieutenant, David A. Smith; Second Lieutenant, Francis B. Wallace; Second-Second Lieutenant, Philip Nagle; First Sergeant, Henry C. Russel; Second Sergeant, Joseph A. Gilmour; Third Sergeant, Cyrus Sheetz; Fourth Sergeant, William J. McQuade; Quartermaster-Sergeant, George H. Gressang; First Corporal, D. J. Ridgway; Second Corporal, Samuel R. Russel; Third Corporal, Charles Hinkle; Fourth Corporal, Reuben Snyder.

PRIVATES.—George H. Hill, Francis P. Dewees, Wm. Ramsey Potts, Thomas Johnson, Nelson T. Major, Isaac E. Severn, Edward L. Severn, Thomas Jones, George Meyer, J. C. Weaver, John Engle, Charles P. Potts, Charles P. Loeser, H. K. Downing, William H. Hardell, J. B. Brandt, Charles Slingluff, Theodore F. Patterson, Charles Evans, Charles Hause, Francis Hause, D. B. Brown, John Christian, Albert G. Whitfield, William Bates, Oliver C. Bosbyshell, Robert F. Potter, A. H. Titus, Joseph Reed, Joel H. Betz, John Curry, Robert Smith, Augustus Reese, Hugh Stevenson. H. H. Hill, Eli Williams, Benjamin Christian, Thomas Petherick, Jr., Louis T. Snyder, Edwin J. Shippen. Richard M. Hodgson, William W. Clemens, Curtis C. Pollock, William Auman, William Riley, Edward T. Leib, Daniel Moser, William Brown, Edward Nagle, Godfrey Leonard, G. W. Bratton, William Heffner, Victor Wernert, Charles A. Glenn, William Spence, Patrick Hanley, William J. Feger, William Lesher, D. C. Pott, Alba C. Thompson, Daniel Christian, Samuel Beard, Thomas Irwin, Henry Dentzer, Philip T. Dentzer, H. Bobbs, John Pass, Heber S. Thompson, B. F. Jones, John I. Hetherington, Peter Fisher, William Dagan, J. R. Hetherington, Nelson Drake, Charles A. Hesser, Samuel Shoener, Charles Maurer, James S. Sillyman, Henry Brobst, Alfred Huntzinger, Wm. Alspach, John Hoffa, J. F. Barth, William Cole, David Williams, George Rice, Joseph Kear, Charles E. Beck, F. B. Hammer, Peter H. Frailey, Thomas Corby, Charles Vanhorn, John Noble, Joseph Fyant, Alexander S. Bowen, John Jones, Francis A. Stitzer, William A. Maize, William Agin, George H. Hartman, Richard Bartolet, Lewis Douglass, Richard Price, Frederick Christ, Valentine Stichter, Francis B. Bannan, William Bartholomew, Frank P. Myer, Bernard Riley, George F. Stahlen, Edward Gaynor.

MUSICIANS.

Thomas Severn, Fifer; Albert F. Bowen, Drummer.

NATIONAL LIGHT INFANTRY, OF POTTSVILLE.

OFFICERS AND NON-COMMISSIONED OFFICERS.—Captain, E. McDonald; First Lieutenant, James Russell; Second Lieutenant, Henry L. Cake; Third Lieutenant, Lewis J. Martin; First Sergeant, La Mar S. Hay; Second Sergeant, Abraham McIntyre; Third Sergeant, W. F. Huntzinger; Fourth Sergeant, George G. Boyer; Quartermaster Sergeant, Daniel Downey; First Corporal, Ernst A. Sauerbrey; Second Corporal, Charles C. Russell; Third Corporal, Edward Moran; Fourth Corporal, Frederick W. Conrad.

PRIVATES.—J. Addison McCool, Thomas G. Bull, William Becker, John Simpson, Thomas G. Houck, Edward Thomas, Elias B. Trifoos, John Stodd, Lawrence Manayan, B. F. Barlett, Wm. Madara, Emanuel Saylor, Wm. P. Garrett, John P. Womelsdorff, George De Courcey, J. J. Dampman, John Schmidt. C. F. Hoffman, Jacob Bast, Daniel Eberle, Wm. H. Hodgson. Ernst T. Ellrich. Amos Forseman, C. F. Umberhauer, James Sammon, Wm. R. Roberts, Jonas W. Rich, Charles Weber, Terrence Smith, F. A. Schoener, William Pugh, Frank Hanley, James

Smith, Geo. W. Mennig, James Marshall, Ira Troy, Uriah Good, Wm. Irving, Patrick Curtin, John Burns, Edward McCabe, Fred. Seltzer, John Donegan, John Mullens, John Lamons, Wm. McDonald, Geo. W. Garber, F. W. Simpson, Alexander Smith, David Dilly, George Shartle, A. D. Allen, Charles F. Garrett, Geo. A. Lerch, James Carroll, John Benedict, Edmund Foley, Thomas Kelley, John Eppinger, John Rouch, David Howard, Jeremiah Deitrich, William Weller, Wm. A. Christian, Mark Walker, Ralph Corby, Henry Mehr, F. Goodyear, Wm. Carl, Anthony. Lippman, John P. Delner, Wm. A. Beidleman, Chas. J. Shoemaker, Jas. Donegan, Herman Hauser, Louis Weber, Thomas H. Parker, John Howell, Henry Yerger, Wm. Davenport, James Landefield, James R. Smith, Michael Foren, Alex. Smith, W. M. Lashorn, Levi Gloss, Samuel Heilner, Enoch Lambert, Frank Wenrich, Joseph Johnston, Henry C. Nies, Jacob Shoey, John Hartman, Wm. Buckley, Henry Quin, Thomas G. Buckley, Wm. Becker, J. P. McGinnes, Charles J. Redcay, Jr., Wm. Britton, Thomas Smith, J. M. Hughes, Thomas Martin, Henry Gehring, Dallas Dampman, John Boedefeld, M. Edgar Richards.

RINGGOLD LIGHT ARTILLERY, OF READING.

OFFICERS AND NON-COMMISSIONED OFFICERS.—Captain, James M'Knight; First Lieutenant, Henry Nagle; Second Lieutenant, Wm. Graeff; First Sergeant, G. W. Durell; Second Sergeant, D. Kreisher; Third Sergeant, H. S. Rush; First Corporal, Levi S. Homan; Second Corporal, F. W. Folkman; Third Corporal, Horatio Leader; Fourth Corporal, Jacob Womert; Bugler, John A. Hock.

PRIVATES.—James A. Fox, Samuel Evans, Amos Drenkle, Fred. Yeager, Geo. W. Silvis, Ed. Pearson, Fred. Shaeffer, Wm. C. Eben, Henry E. Eisenbeis, Daniel Maltzberger, Adam Freeze, Augustus Berger, Solomon Ash, Fred. H. Phillippi, Nathaniel B. Hill, James E. Lutz, Geo. S. Bickley, Samuel Hamilton, Amos Huyett, Andrew Helms, Wm. W. Bowers, Henry Neihart, Ferd. S. Ritter, Daniel Whitman, Jeremiah Seiders, Anthony Ammon, Henry Fleck, Henry Rush, Jacob J. Hessler, Henry G. Baus, Charles Gebhart, Henry Coleman, Chas. P. Muhlenberg, Jacob Leeds, James Gentzler, J. Hiester McKnight, B. F. Ermentrout, James Pflieger, Charles Spangler, Geo. W. Knabb, D. Dickinson, C. Levan, Albert Shirey, Adam Faust, Peter A. Lantz, Geo. D. Leaf, H. Whiteside, A. Levan, O. Frantz, Wm. Sauerbier, Jonathan Sherer, H. Geiger, Wm. Lewis, A. Seyfert, Robert Eltz, J. S. Kennedy, E. L. Smith, George Lauman, Lemuel Gries, James L. Mast, Christopher Loeser, Howard M'Ilvaine, C. B. Ansart, Wm. Haberacker, John A. M'Lenegan, George Eckert, William Herbst, Wm. Rapp, Isaiah Rambo, Daniel Levan, John Yohn, Isaac Leeds, Francis Rambo, Wm. Christ, Fred. Peck, John Freeze, Jr., William Fix, Edward Seull, Jackson Sherman, Ad. Gehry, Daniel Yohn, James D. Koch, H. Fox, F. Housum, William Smith, C. A. Bitting, Wm. P. Mack, Wm. Miller, Fred. Smeck, Milton Roy, Geo. B. Rhoads, James Anthony, David Bechtel, F. G. Ebling.

LOGAN GUARDS, OF LEWISTOWN.

OFFICERS AND NON-COMMISSIONED OFFICERS.—Captain, J. B. Selheimer; First Lieutenant, Thomas M. Hulings; Second Lieutenant, Robert W. Patton; Third Lieutenant, Francis R. Sterrett; First Sergeant, J. A. Matthews; Second Sergeant, Joseph S. Waream; Third Sergeant, H. A. Eisenbise; Fourth Sergeant, William B. Weber; Fifth Sergeant, C. M. Shull; First Corporal, E. W. Eisenbise; Second Corporal, P. P. Butts; Third Corporal, John Nolte; Fourth Corporal, Frederick Hart; Musicians, S. G. McLaughlin, William Hopper, Joseph W. Postlethwait.

PRIVATES.—William H. Irwin (subsequently elected Colonel of the Seventh Regiment Pennsylvania Volunteers), David Wasson, William T. McEwen, Jesse Alexander, James D. Burns, Robert Betts, Henry Comfort, Frank De Armint, James B. Eckebarger, Joseph A. Fiethorn, George M. Freeborn, George Hart, James W. Henry, John S. Kauffman, George I. Loff, Elias W. Link, Samuel B. Marks, William McKnew, Robert D. Morton, Thomas A. Nurce, Henry Printz, James N. Rager, Augustus E. Smith, James P. Smith, Gideon M. Tice, Gilbert Waters, David Wertz, Edwin E. Zergler, William H. Bowsun, William R. Cooper, Jeremiah Cogley, Thomas W. Dewese, Asbery W. Elberty, Abraham Files, Daniel Fessler, John Hughes, John Jones, Thomas Kinhead, John S. Langton, William G. Mitchell, John S. Miller, Robert A. Mathner, William A. Nelson, John A. Nale, John M. Postlethwait, James H. Sterrett, Theodore B. Smith, Charles W. Stahl, Thomas M. Uttley, David B. Weber, George White, William E. Benner, William Cowden, Samuel Comfort, George W. Elberty, William H. Freeborn, J. Bingham Farrer, Owen M. Fowler, John T. Hunter, James M. Jackson, Henry F. Keiser, Charles E. Laub, William R. McCay, Joseph A. Miller, John A. McKee, Robert Nelson, James Price, Bronson Rothrock, William Sherwood, Nathaniel W. Scott, George A. Snyder, Franklin H. Wentz, Henry G. Walters, Philip Winterod.

ALLEN INFANTRY, OF ALLENTOWN.

OFFICERS AND NON-COMMISSIONED OFFICERS.—Captain, Thomas B. Yeager; First Lieutenant, Joseph Wilt; Second Lieutenant, Solomon Geoble.

PRIVATES.—John G. Webster, Samuel Schneck, David Kramer, David Jacobs, Edwin Gross. Charles Deitrich, M. R. Fuller, Edwin H. Miller, Ben. Weiandt, Darius Weiss, John Romig, Isaac Gresser, Milton H. Dunlap, Wilson H. Derr, Joseph Weiss, William Kress, William Ruhe, Charles A. Schiffert, Nathaniel Hillegar, George A. Keiper, James Geidner, Gideon Frederick, Norman N. Cole, William Early, George Haxworth. Chas. A. Pfeiffer, James M. Wilson, .M. G. Frame, Joseph Hettinger, George Henry, Jonathan W. Reber, Henry Stork, John Hoke, Martin W. Leisenring, Franklin Leh, Ernest Rottman, Allen Wetherhold, George W Rhoads, Wm. H. Sigmund, William Wagner, Wm. Wolf, Lewis Seip, Edwin Hittle, William S. Davis, C. Slatterdach.

CHAPTER XVII.

EVENTS IN AND NEAR THE NATIONAL CAPITAL.

 ALTIMORE became the theater of a sad tragedy on the day after the loyal Pennsylvanians passed through it to the Capital. The conspirators and secessionists there, who were in complicity with those of Virginia, had been compelled, for some time, to be very circumspect, on account of the loyalty of the great body of the people. Public displays of sympathy with the revolutionists were quickly resented. When, in the exuberance of their joy on the "secession of Virginia," these sympathizers ventured to take a cannon to Federal Hill, raise a secession flag, and fire a salute,[a] the workmen in the iron foundries near there turned out, captured the great gun and cast it into the waters of the Patapsco, tore the banner into shreds, [a April 18, 1861.] and made the disunionists fly in consternation. At about the same time, a man seen in the streets with a secession cockade on his hat was pursued by the populace, and compelled to seek the protection of the police. These and similar events were such significant admonitions for the conspirators that they prudently worked in secret. They had met every night in their private room in the Taylor Building, on Fayette Street;[1] and there they formed their plans for resistance to the passage of Northern troops through Baltimore.

On the day when the Pennsylvanians passed through,[b] some leading Virginians came down to Baltimore from Charlestown and Winchester as representatives of many others of their class, and demanded [b April 18.] of the managers of the Baltimore and Ohio Railway not only pledges, but guaranties, that no National troops, nor any munitions of war from the Armory and Arsenal at Harper's Ferry, should be permitted to pass over their road. They accompanied their demand with a threat that, if it should be refused, the great railway bridge over the Potomac at Harper's Ferry should be destroyed. They had heard of the uprising of the loyal people of the great Northwest, and the movement of troops toward the National Capital from that teeming hive, and they came to effect the closing of the most direct railway communication for them. They had heard how Governor Dennison, with a trumpet-toned proclamation, had summoned the people of Ohio, on the very day when the President's call appeared,[c] to [c April 15.] "rise above all party names and party bias, resolute to maintain the freedom so dearly bought by our fathers, and to transmit it unimpaired

·to our posterity," and to fly to the protection of the imperiled Republic. They almost felt the tread of the tall men of the Ohio Valley,[1] as they were preparing to pass over the "Beautiful River" into the Virginia border. They had heard the war-notes of Blair, and Morton, and Yates, and Randall, and Kirkwood, and Ramsay, all loyal Governors of the populous and puissant States of that great Northwest, and were satisfied that the people would respond as promptly as had those of New England; so they hastened to bar up the nearest passage for them to the Capital over the Alleghany Mountains, until the disloyal Minute-men of Maryland and Virginia, and of the District of Columbia, should fulfill the instructions and satisfy the expectations of the conspirators at Montgomery in the seizure of the Capital. They found ready and eager sympathizers in Baltimore; and only a few hours before the coveted arms in the Harper's Ferry Arsenal were set a-blazing, and the Virginia plunderers were foiled, the "National Volunteer Association" of Baltimore (under whose auspices the secession flag had been raised on Federal Hill that day, and a salute attempted in honor of the secession of Virginia), led by its President, William Burns, held a meeting in Monument Square. T. Parkins Scott presided. He and others addressed a multitude of citizens, numbered by thousands. They harangued the people with exciting and incendiary phrases. They denounced "coercion," and called upon the people to arm and drill, for a conflict was at hand. "I do not care," said Wilson C. Carr, "how many Federal troops are sent to Washington, they will soon find themselves surrounded by such an army from Virginia and Maryland that escape to their homes will be impossible; and when the seventy-five thousand who are intended to invade the South shall have polluted that soil with their touch, the South will exterminate and sweep them from the earth."[2] These words were received with the wildest yells and huzzas, and the meeting finally broke up with three cheers for "the South," and the same for "President Davis."

With such seditious teachings; with such words of encouragement to mob violence ringing in their ears, the populace of Baltimore went to their slumbers on that night of the 18th of April, when it was known that a portion of the seventy-five thousand to be slaughtered were on their way from New England, and would probably reach the city on the morrow. While the people were slumbering, the secessionists were holding meetings in different wards, and the conspirators were planning dark deeds for that morrow, at Taylor's Building. There, it is said, the Chief of Police, Kane, and the President of the Monument Square meeting, and others, counseled resistance to any Northern or Western troops who might attempt to pass through the city.

There was much feverishness in the public mind in Baltimore on the morning of the 19th of April. Groups of excited men were seen on the corners of streets, and at the places of public resort. Well-known secessionists were hurrying to and fro with unusual agility; and in front of the

---

[1] By actual measurement of two hundred and thirty-nine native Americans in five counties in the Ohio Valley, taken indiscriminately, it appears that one-fourth of them were six feet and over in hight. As compared with European soldiers, such as the Belgians, the English, and the Scotch Highlanders, it was found that the average hight of these Ohio men was four inches over that of the Belgians, two and a half inches above that of English recruits, and one and a half inches above that of the Scotch Highlanders.

[2] Greeley's *American Conflict*, i. 462.

store of Charles M. Jackson, on Pratt Street, near Gay, where lay the only railway from Philadelphia to Washington, through Baltimore, a large quantity of the round pavement stones had been taken up during the night and piled in a heap; and near them was a cart-load of gravel, giving the impression that repairs of the street were about to be made.

Intelligence came at an early hour of the evacuation and destruction of the public property at Harper's Ferry, on the previous evening. The secessionists were exasperated and the Unionists were jubilant. Baltimore was filled with the wildest excitement. This was intensified by information that a large number of Northern troops were approaching the city from Philadelphia. These arrived at the President Street Station at twenty minutes past eleven o'clock in the forenoon, in twelve passenger and several freight cars, the latter furnished with benches. The troops, about two thousand in all, were the Sixth Regiment of Massachusetts Volunteers, Colonel Jones, and ten companies of the Washington Brigade, of Philadelphia, under General William H. Small.[1]

When the train reached the President Street Station, between which and the Camden Street or Washington Station the cars were drawn singly by horses, a mob of about five hundred men were waiting to receive them. These were soon joined by others, and the number was increased to at least two thousand before the cars were started. The mob followed with yells, groans, and horrid imprecations. Eight cars, containing a portion of the

Massachusetts Regiment, passed on without much harm. The mob threw some stones and bricks, and shouted lustily for "Jeff. Davis and the Southern Confederacy." The troops remained quietly in the cars, and reached the Camden Street Station in safety. There they were met by another crowd, who had been collecting all the morning. These hooted and yelled at the soldiers as they were transferred to the Baltimore and Ohio Railway cars, and threw some stones and bricks. One of these struck and bruised Colonel Jones, who was superintending the transfer.

The mob on Pratt Street, near the head of the Basin, became more furious every moment; and when the ninth car reached Gay Street, and there was a brief halt on account of a deranged brake, they could no longer be restrained. The

SIXTH MASSACHUSETTS REGIMENT.

heap of loose stones, that appeared so mysteriously in front of Jackson's store, were soon hurled upon the car as it passed along Pratt Street. Every window was demolished, and several soldiers were hurt. Then the cry was raised, "Tear up the track!" There were no present means for doing it, so the mob seized some anchors lying on the

wharf near Jackson's store, and, dragging them upon the railway track, effec.
tually barricaded the street. The tenth car was compelled to go back to the
President Street Station, followed by a yelling, infuriated mob, many of them
maddened by alcohol.

In the mean time the remainder of the Massachusetts troops, who were in
the cars back of the barricade, informed of the condition of affairs ahead,

SCENE OF THE PRINCIPAL FIGHTING IN PRATT STREET.[1]

alighted for the purpose of marching to the Camden Street Station. They
consisted of four companies, namely, the Lawrence Light Infantry, Captain
John Pickering; Companies C and D, of Lowell, commanded respectively by
Captains A. S. Follansbee and J. W. Hart; and the Stoneham Company,
under Captain Dike. They were speedily formed on the side-walk, and Captain Follansbee was chosen the commander of the whole for the occasion.
He wheeled them into column, and directed them to march in close order.
Before they were ready to move the mob was upon them, led by a man with
a secession flag upon a pole, who told the troops that they should never
march through the city—that "every nigger of them" would be killed before
they could reach the other station.

Captain Follansbee paid no attention to these threats, though his little
band was confronted by thousands of infuriated men. He gave the words,
"Forward, March!" in a clear voice. The order was a signal for the mob,
who commenced hurling stones and bricks, and every missile at hand, as the
troops moved steadily up President Street. At the corner of Fawn and
President Streets, a furious rush was made upon them, and the missiles filled
the air like hail. A policeman was called to lead the way, and the troops
advanced at the "double-quick." They found the planks of the Pratt Street
Bridge, over Jones's Falls, torn up, but they passed over without accident,
when they were assailed more furiously than ever. Several of the soldiers

---

[1] This is a view of the portion of Pratt Street, between Gay and South Streets, where the most severe contest occurred. The large building seen on the left is the storehouse of Charles M. Jackson, and the bow of the
vessel is seen at the place where the rioters dragged the anchors upon the railway track.

were knocked down by stones, and their muskets were taken from them; and presently some shots were fired by the populace.

Up to this time the troops had made no resistance ; now, finding the mob to be intent upon murder, Captain Follansbee ordered them to cap their pieces (which were already loaded), and defend themselves. They had reached Gay Street. The mob, full ten thousand strong, was pressing heavily upon them, hurling stones and bricks, and casting heavy pieces of iron upon them from windows. One of these crushed a man to the earth. Self-preservation called for action, and the troops turned and fired at random on the mob, who were dismayed for a moment and recoiled. The shouts of the ferocious multitude, the rattle of stones, the crack of musketry, the whistle of bullets, the shrieks of women, of whom some were among the rioters, and the carrying of wounded men into stores, made an appalling tragedy. The severest of the fight was in Pratt Street, between Gay Street and Bowley's Wharf, near Calvert Street.

The Mayor, alarmed at the fury of the whirlwind that his political friends had raised, attempted to control it, but in vain. With a large body of the police (most of whom did not share the treason of their chief, and worked earnestly in trying to quell the disturbance) he placed himself at the head of the troops, but his power was utterly inoperative, and when stones and bullets flew about like autumnal leaves in a gale, he prudently withdrew, and left the New Englanders to fight their way through to the Camden Street Station. This they did most gallantly, receiving a furious assault from a wing of the rioters at Howard Street, when about twenty shots were fired, and Captain Dike was seriously wounded in the leg. At a little past noon, the troops entered the cars for Washington. Three of their number had been killed outright, one mortally wounded, and eight were seriously and several were slightly hurt.[1] Nine citizens of Baltimore were killed, and many—how many is not known—were wounded. Among the killed was Robert T. Davis, an estimable citizen, of the firm of Paynter, Davis & Co., dry goods merchants, who was a spectator of the scene.

The cars into which the soldiers were hurried were sent off for Washington as soon as possible. The mob followed for more than a mile, and impeded the progress of the train with stones, logs, and telegraph poles, which the accompanying police removed. The train was fired into on the way from the hills, but at too long range to do much damage. That evening the Massachusetts troops, wearied and hungry, arrived at the Capitol, and found quarters in the Senate Chamber, where, on the following day, they wrote letters to their friends on the desks lately occupied by Davis and his fellow-conspirators. Their advent gave great joy to the loyal inhabitants. Already the Capitol had been fortified by General Scott. The doors and windows were barricaded with boards, and casks of cement and huge stones. The iron plates intended for the new dome of the building were used for breastworks between the marble columns; and the pictures in the rotunda and the statuary were covered with heavy planking, to shield them from harm.

While the fight between the Massachusetts Sixth[2] and the Baltimoreans

---

[1] On their arrival at Washington, eighteen of their wounded were sent to the Washington Infirmary.

[2] The following is a list of the officers of the staff and the different companies:—Colonel, Edward F. Jones,

was going on, the Pennsylvanians, under General Small, who were entirely unarmed, remained in the cars at the President Street Station. The General tried to have them drawn back out of the city, and out of reach of the mob, but failed. The rioters were upon them before an engine could be procured for that purpose. The mob had left Pratt Street when their prey had escaped, and, yet thirsting for blood, had hurried toward the armory of the Maryland Guard, on Carroll Street, to seize the weapons belonging to that corps. A small guard at the head of the stairs kept them at bay. They then rushed toward the Custom House, to seize arms said to have been deposited there, when they were diverted by information that there were more troops at the President Street Station. Thitherward they pressed, yelling like demons, and began a furious assault upon the cars with stones and other missiles. Quite a large number of the Union men of Baltimore had gathered around the Pennsylvanians. Many of the latter sprang from the cars and engaged in a hand-to-hand fight with their assailants for almost two hours, nobly assisted

THE PRATT STREET BRIDGE.[1]

by the Baltimore Unionists. The mob overpowered them, and the unarmed soldiers—some of them badly hurt—fled in all directions, seeking refuge where they might. At this juncture, and at this place, Marshal Kane appears for the first time in the history of that eventful day. He was well known to the secessionists, and his presence soon restored order, when the fugitive soldiers returned to the cars, and the Pennsylvanians were all sent

---

Lowell; Lieutenant-Colonel, Walter Shattuck, Groton; Major, Benj. F. Watson, Lawrence; Adjutant, Alpha B. Farr, Lowell; Quartermaster, James Monroe, Cambridge; Paymaster, Rufus L. Plaisted, Lowell; Surgeon, Norman Smith, Groton; Chaplain, Charles Babbidge, Pepperell. Company A, Lowell, Captain, J. A. Sawtell; Company B, Groton, Captain, E. S. Clark; Company C, Lowell, Captain, A. S. Follansbee; Company D, Lowell, Captain, J. W. Hart; Company E, Acton, Captain, David Totter; Company F, Lawrence, Captain, B. F. Chadbourne; Company H, Lowell, Captain, Jona. Ladd; Company I, Lawrence, Captain, John Pickering.

This regiment had been the recipient of the most marked attention all the way from Boston. They were greeted by crowds of cheering citizens everywhere; and when they left New York to cross the Jersey City Ferry, full fifteen thousand citizens accompanied them, while the side-walks were densely crowded. A large number of miniature American flags were presented to the soldiers, who attached them to their bayonets. The shipping in the harbor was bright with the Stars and Stripes. They crossed New Jersey in a train of fifteen cars, and were cheered by enthusiastic crowds at the stations. They arrived at Philadelphia at half-past eight o'clock on the evening of the 18th, where they were received by the authorities and a vast concourse of citizens. Huzzas were given for "Bunker Hill," "Old Massachusetts," "General Scott," and "Major Anderson," as the regiment went up Walnut and through to Chestnut Street to the "Girard House" and the "Continental Hotel." They departed for Baltimore at a little past three o'clock the next morning, accompanied by over half of the Washington Brigade, of Philadelphia. Their reception in Baltimore is recorded in the text.

[1] This is a view of the Pratt Street Bridge and its vicinity, taken in December, 1864, from the gallery of the "William Tell House." It is between President and Concord Streets. It is built of iron and heavy planks.

back to Philadelphia. After their departure, the mob proceeded to barricade the Pratt Street Bridge, and to break open the store of Henry Meyer, from which they carried off a large number of guns and pistols. At that moment General Egerton appeared in full uniform, imploring them to cease rioting. He assured them that no "foreign troops" were in the city, and that Governor Hicks had declared that no more should pass through it.[1]

The mob was quieted by four o'clock in the afternoon, when they had placed the city in the hands of the secessionists. At that hour a great meeting of the dominant party was held at Monument Square, where General George H. Stewart (who afterward joined the insurgents in Virginia[2]) had paraded the First Light Division with ball cartridges. Over the platform for the speakers floated a white flag bearing the arms of Maryland; and under this Mayor Brown, S. T. Wallis, W. P. Preston, and others, addressed the vast multitude, assuring them that no more Northern troops should pass through the city, and advising them to disperse quietly to their homes. Already Governor Hicks and Mayor Brown had sent a dispatch to President Lincoln, saying:—"A collision between the citizens and the Northern troops has taken place in Baltimore, and the excitement is fearful. Send no troops here. We will endeavor to prevent bloodshed. A public meeting of citizens has been called, and the troops of the State and city have been called out to preserve the peace. They will be enough." They had also taken measures to prevent any more troops coming over the railway from Philadelphia.

When the meeting at Monument Square was convened, a committee was appointed to invite Governor Hicks to the stand. His age was bordering on seventy years, and caution was predominant. He was appalled by the violence around him, and after listening to Mayor Brown, who declared that it was "folly and madness for one portion of the nation to attempt the subjugation of another portion—it can never be done,"—the Governor arose and said:—"I coincide in the sentiment of your worthy Mayor. After three conferences we have agreed, and I bow in submission to the people. I am a Marylander; I love my State, and I love the Union; but I will suffer my right arm to be torn from my body before I will raise it to strike a sister State."[3]

The meeting adjourned, but the populace were not quiet. They paraded the streets, uttering threats of violence to Union citizens, who were awed into silence, and driven into the obscurity of their homes. About five hundred men, headed by two drums, went to the President Street Station to seize arms supposed to be there. They found none. Disappointed, they marched to Barnum's Hotel, and called for Ex-Governor Louis E. Lowe, who made a speech to them under a Maryland flag, from a balcony, in which he

---

[1] Files of the Baltimore journals from the 20th to the 23d of April. Letter of Captain Follansbee to the *Lowell Courier.* Colonel Jones's official report to General Butler. Verbal statements to the author by citizens of Baltimore.

[2] General Stewart's abandoned mansion and beautiful grounds around it, at the head of Baltimore Street, were taken possession of by the Government, and there the *Jarvis Hospital,* one of the most perfect of its kind, was established for the use of disabled soldiers during the war. It was one of the most beautiful situations in or near Baltimore. It was on an eminence that overlooked a large portion of the city, the Patapsco, the harbor, and the land and water out to Chesapeake Bay. The mansion was built by the father of Brantz Mayer, a leading citizen of Baltimore.

[3] *Baltimore Clipper,* April 20, 1861.

assured them that they should have ample assistance from his county (Frederick), when they marched off, shouting for "Jeff. Davis and a Southern Confederacy," and saluted the Maryland flag that was waving from the head-quarters of the conspirators on Fayette Street.[1] On the same evening, Marshal Kane received an offer of troops from Bradley Johnson, of Frederick, who was afterward a brigadier in the Confederate Army. Kane telegraphed back, saying :—" Thank you for your offer. Bring your men by the first train, and we will arrange with the railroad afterward. *Streets red with Maryland blood!* Send expresses over the mountains and valleys of Maryland and Virginia for the riflemen to come without delay. Further hordes [meaning loyal volunteers] will be down upon us to-morrow. We will fight them and whip them, or die." Early the next morning Johnson posted handbills in Frederick,[2] calling upon the secessionists to rally to his standard. Many came, and with them he hastened to Baltimore,[a] and made his head-quarters in the house No. 34 Holliday Street, opposite Kane's office in the old City Hall.

a April 20, 1861.

Governor Hicks passed the night of the 19th at the house of Mayor Brown. At eleven o'clock the Mayor, with the concurrence of the Governor, sent a committee, consisting of Lenox Bond,

George W. Dobbin, and John C. Brune, to President Lincoln, with a letter, in which he assured the chief magistrate that the people of Baltimore were " exasperated to the highest degree by the passage of troops," and that the citizens were " universally decided in the opinion that no more should be ordered to come." But for the exertions of the authorities, he said, a fearful slaughter would have occurred that day ; and he conceived it to be his solemn duty, under the circumstances, to inform the President that it was " not possible for more soldiers to pass through Baltimore, unless they fight their way at every step." He concluded by requesting the President not to order or permit any more troops to pass through the city. " If they should attempt it," he said, " the responsibility for the bloodshed will not rest upon me."

JOHNSON'S HEAD-QUARTERS.

Having performed this duty, the Governor and the Mayor went to bed. Their slumbers were soon broken by Marshal Kane and Ex-Governor Lowe, who came at midnight for authority to commit further outrages upon the

---

[1] *Baltimore Clipper*, April 20, 1861. On that day Mr. Wales, the editor of the *Clipper*, spoke out boldly and ably in denunciation of the disloyal movements. Under the title of *The Madness of the Hour*, he said :— "Secession is political madness. It is an attempt to save a house by setting it on fire, and trying to tear out what can be gathered from the devouring element. The frenzy of secessionists with us is an unanswerable evidence of it."

[2] The following is a copy of Johnson's handbill :—

"MARYLANDERS, AROUSE !

" FREDERICK, Saturday, 7 A. M.

" At twelve o'clock last night I received the following dispatch from Marshal Kane, of Baltimore, by telegraph to the Junction and expressed to Frederick. [Here follows Kane's dispatch given in the text.] All men who will go with me will report themselves as soon as possible, with such arms and accouterments as they can. Double-barreled shot-guns and buck-shot are efficient. They will assemble, after reporting themselves, at half-past ten o'clock, so as to go down in the half-past eleven train."

Government and private property, which had been planned by the conspirators some days before, and "had been proclaimed in other parts of the State."[1] Kane said that he had received information by telegraph that other troops were on their way to Baltimore by the railways from Harrisburg and Philadelphia, and proposed the immediate destruction of bridges on these roads, to prevent the passage of cars. The Mayor approved the plan, but said his jurisdiction was limited to the corporate boundaries of the city. The Governor had the power to order the destruction; and to his chamber the three (with a brother of the Mayor) repaired, Mr. Hicks being too ill to rise. They soon came out of that chamber with the Governor's acquiescence in their plans, they said; but which he afterward explicitly denied in a communication to the Maryland Senate, and later[a] in an address to the people of Maryland. Their own testimony shows that his   [a] May 11, 1861.
consent was reluctantly given, if given at all, in the words:—" I suppose it must be done;" and then only, according to common rumor and common belief, after arguments such as South Carolina vigilance committees generally used had been applied.[2] With this alleged authority, Kane and Lowe, accompanied by Mayor Brown and his brother, hastened to the office of Charles Howard, the President of the Board of Police, who was waiting for them, when that officer and the Mayor issued orders for the destruction of the bridges.[3] The work was soon accomplished. A gang of lawless men hastened out to the Canton bridge, two or three miles from the city, on the

DESTRUCTION OF THE BRIDGE OVER GUNPOWDER CREEK.[4]

Philadelphia, Wilmington, and Baltimore Railway, and destroyed it. As the train from the North approached the station, it was stopped by the interference of a pistol fired at the engineer. The passengers were at once turned out of the cars, and these were filled by the mob, who compelled the engineer to run his train back to the long bridges over the Gunpowder and Bush Creeks, arms of Chesapeake Bay. These bridges were fired, and large

[1] See *Address to the People of Maryland*, May 11, 1861, by Governor Hicks.   [2] The same.
[3] *Communication from the Mayor of Baltimore with the Mayor and Board of Police of Baltimore City:* Document G, Maryland House of Delegates, May 10, 1861.
[4] This is from a sketch of the bridge made by the author in November, 1861, from the Baltimore side of Gunpowder Creek. The picture of conflagration has been added to show the relative position of the portion of the bridge that was burnt at that time.

portions of them were speedily consumed. Another party went up the North-ern Central Railway to Cockeysville, about fifteen miles north of Baltimore, and destroyed the two wooden bridges there, and other smaller structures on the road. In the mean time the telegraph wires had been cut on all the lines leading out of Baltimore, excepting the one that kept the conspirators in communication with Richmond by the way of Harper's Ferry. Thus, all communication by railway or telegraph between the seat of government and the loyal States of the Union was absolutely cut off, or in the hands of the insurgents.[1]

The Committee sent to the President by Governor Hicks and Mayor Brown had an interview with him at an early hour on the morning of the 20th. The President and General Scott had already been in consultation on the subject of the passage of troops through Baltimore, and the latter had hastily said: "Bring them *around* the city." Acting upon this hint, the President assured the Committee that no more troops should be called through Baltimore, if they could pass around it without opposition or moles-tation. This assurance was telegraphed by the Committee to the Mayor, but it did not satisfy the conspirators. They had determined that no more troops from the North should pass through Maryland, and so they would be excluded from the Capital. Military preparations went actively on in Baltimore to carry out this determination, and every hour the isolation of the Capital from the loyal men of the country was becoming more and more complete.

The excitement in Washington was fearful; and at three o'clock on the morning of the 21st (Sunday) the President sent for Governor Hicks and Mayor Brown. The former was not in the city. The latter, with Messrs. Dobbin and Brune, and S. T. Wallis, hastened to Washington, where they arrived at ten o'clock in the morning. At that interview General Scott pro-

---

[1] For a few days succeeding the riot, no person was allowed to leave Baltimore for the North without a pass from the President of the Board of Police. approved by the Mayor:* and these permissions were sparingly issued. Neither were the mails allowed to go North, for it was desirable to keep the people of the Free-labor States ignorant of affairs at Washington until the seizure of the Capital, by the insurgents, should be accomplished.

THE PRIVATE MAIL-BAG.

The first mail-bag that passed through Baltimore after the riot there. was carried by James D. Gay, a member of the Ringgold Artillery from Reading, already mentioned. He left Washington for home on the even-ing of the 19th of April, with a carpet-bag full of letters from members of his company to their friends. He was in Baltimore during the fearful night of the 19th. when the railway bridges were burned: and, after escaping many personal perils, he managed to reach Cockeysville. in a carriage with some others. on the 20th. where, north of the burnt bridges, he took the cars for home on the Northern Central Railway. He reached York that night, and Reading the next day, where the con-tents of his bag were soon distributed. These letters, some of which were addressed to editors and were published, gave the first authentic intelligence to the loyal people of the state of affairs at the Capital, and in a degree quieted the apprehensions for its safety. That private mail-bag, which. for the time, took the place of the United States mail, was afterwards placed among the curiosities of the Pennsylvania Historical Society.

---

* The following is a copy of one of the passes, now before me :—

"OFFICE OF BOARD OF POLICE, }
BALTIMORE, April 22, 1861. }

"Messrs. Edward Childe and P. H. Birkhead being about to proceed to the North upon their private business, and having Mrs. Stein-brenner under their charge, we desire that they be allowed by all persons to pass without molestation by the way of Port Deposit, or York. Pennsylvania, or otherwise, as they may see fit.

"By order of the Board :   CHARLES HOWARD, Pres't.

The Mayor of the City concurs in the above.   GEORGE HUNT BROWN.
                    "By his private Secretary,   ROBERT D. BROWN.
"Mr. F. Meredith Dryden will accompany the party.

                              "CHARLES HOWARD, *President Board of Police.*"

posed to bring troops by water to Annapolis, and march them from there, across Maryland, to the Capital, a distance of about forty miles. The Mayor and his friends were not satisfied. The soil of Maryland must not be polluted *anywhere* with the tread of Northern troops; in other words, they must be kept from the seat of government, that the traitors might more easily seize it. They urged upon the President, " in the most earnest manner, a course of policy which would give peace to the country, and especially the withdrawal of all orders contemplating the passage of troops through *any part* of Maryland."[1]

When the Mayor and his friends reached the cars to return, they were met by an electrograph from Mr. Garrett, President of the Baltimore and Ohio Railway, informing them that a large number of troops were at Cockeysville, on their way to Baltimore. They immediately returned to the President, who summoned General Scott and some of the members of the Cabinet to a conference. The President was anxious to preserve the peace, and show that he had acted in good faith in calling the Mayor to Washington ; and he expressed a strong desire that the troops at Cockeysville should be sent back to York or Harrisburg. " General Scott," said the Mayor in his report, " adopted the President's views warmly, and an order was accordingly prepared by the Lieutenant-General to that effect, and forwarded by Major Belger of the Army," who accompanied the Mayor to Baltimore.

Even this humiliation of the Government did not appease the conspirators and their friends, and they so far worked viciously upon the courage and firmness of Governor Hicks, that he was induced to send a message to the President on the 22d, advising him not to order any more troops to pass through Maryland, and to send elsewhere some which had already arrived at Annapolis. He urged him to offer a truce to the insurgents to prevent further bloodshedding, and said : " I respectfully suggest that Lord Lyons [the British Minister] be requested to act as mediator between the contending parties of our country." To these degrading propositions Secretary Seward replied, in behalf of the President, in which he expressed the deepest regret because of the public disturbances, and assured the Governor that the troops sought to be brought through Maryland were " intended for nothing but the defense of the Capital." He reminded his Excellency that the route chosen by the General-in-chief for the march of troops absolutely needed at the Capital, was farthest removed from the populous cities of the State ; and then he administered the following mildly drawn but stinging rebuke to the chief magistrate of a State professing to hold allegiance to the Union, who had so far forgotten his duty and the dignity of his Commonwealth as to make such suggestions as Governor Hicks had done. " The President cannot but remember," he said, " that there has been a time in the history of our country [1814] when a General [Winder] of the American Union, with forces designed for the defense of its Capital, was not unwelcome anywhere in the State of Maryland, and certainly not at Annapolis, then, as now, the capital of that patriotic State, and then, also, one of the capitals of the Union. If eighty years could have obliterated all the other noble sentiments of that age in Maryland, the President would be hopeful, nevertheless, that there is

---

[1] Mayor Brown's report of the interview.

one that would ever remain there as everywhere. That sentiment is, that no domestic contention whatever, that may arise among the parties of this Republic, ought in any case to be referred to any foreign arbitrament, least of all to the arbitrament of a European monarchy."[1]

Still another embassy, in the interest of the secessionists of Baltimore, waited upon the President. These were delegates from five of the Young Men's Christian Associations of that city, with the Rev. Dr. Fuller, of the Baptist Church, at their head. The President received them cordially, and treated them kindly. He met their propositions and their sophisms with Socratic reasoning. When Dr. Fuller assured him that he could produce peace if he would let the country know that he was "disposed to recognize the independence of the Southern States—recognize the fact that they have formed a government of their own; and that they will never again be united with the North," the President asked, significantly, "And what is to become of the revenue?" When the Doctor expressed a hope that no more troops would be allowed to cross Maryland, and spoke of the patriotic action of its inhabitants in the past, the President simply replied, substantially, "I *must* have troops for the defense of the Capital. The Carolinians are now marching across Virginia to seize the Capital and hang me. What am I to do? I *must* have troops, I say; and as they can neither crawl under Maryland, nor fly over it, they must come across it." With these answers the delegation returned to Baltimore. The Government virtually declared that it should take proper measures for the preservation of the Republic without asking the consent of the authorities or inhabitants of any State; and the loyal people said Amen! Neither Governor Hicks, nor the Mayor of Baltimore, nor the clergy nor laity of the churches there, ever afterward troubled the President with advice so evidently emanating from the implacable enemies of the Union.

The National Capital and the National Government were in great peril, as we have observed, at this critical juncture. The regular Army, weak in numbers before the insurrection, was now utterly inadequate to perform its duties as the right arm of the nation's power. Twiggs's treason in Texas had greatly diminished its available force, and large numbers of its officers, especially of those born in Slave-labor States, were resigning their commissions, abandoning their flag, and joining the enemies of their country.[2]

Among those who resigned at this time was Colonel Robert Edmund Lee, of Virginia, an accomplished engineer officer, and one of the most trusted and beloved by the venerable General-in-chief. His patriotism had become weakened by the heresy of State Supremacy, and he seems to have been easily

---

[1] Letter of Secretary Seward to Governor Hicks, April 22, 1861.

[2] Notwithstanding a greater number of those who abandoned their flag and joined the insurgents at that time were from the Slave-labor States, a large number of officers from those States remained faithful. From a carefully prepared statement made by Edward C. Marshall, author of *The History of the Naval Academy*, it appears that in 1860, just before the breaking out of the war, there were seven hundred and forty-seven graduates of the United States Military Academy at West Point, to which might be added seventy-three who graduated in June, 1861, making a total of eight hundred and twenty. These were all officers. At the close of 1861, the number of graduates who had resigned or had been dismissed within the year was only one hundred and ninety-seven, leaving six hundred and seventeen graduates who remained loyal. The number of graduates from the Slave-labor States was three hundred and eleven, of whom one hundred and thirty-three remained loyal. The remainder were disloyal. To these add nineteen who were born in Free-labor States, and we have the total of only one hundred and ninety-seven, of the eight hundred and twenty graduates, who were unfaithful.

seduced from his allegiance to his flag by the dazzling offers of the Virginia conspirators. So early as the 14th of April, he was informed by the President of the Virginia Convention that that body would, on the nomination of Governor Letcher, appoint him commander of all the military and naval forces of the Commonwealth.[1] When, on the 17th, the usurpers, through violence and fraud, passed an ordinance of secession, he said, in the common phrase of the men of easy political virtue, "I must go with my State;" and, on the 20th, in a letter addressed to General Scott, from his beautiful seat of "Arlington House," on Arlington Hights, opposite Washington and

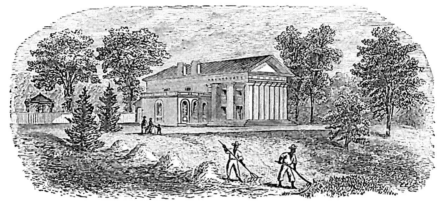

ARLINGTON HOUSE IN 1860.[2]

Georgetown, he proffered the resignation of his commission in terms of well-feigned reluctance.[3] He then hastened to Richmond, and offered his services to the enemies of his country. He was received by the Convention [a] with profound respect, for he was the representative of one of the most distinguished families of the State, and brought to the conspirators an intimate knowledge of General Scott's plans, and the details of the forces of the National Government, with which he had been fully intrusted. Alexander H. Stephens, Lieutenant Maury of the National

[a] April 22, 1861.

---

[1] Richmond Correspondence of the *Charleston Mercury*.

[2] This view of Arlington House, the seat of the late George Washington Parke Custis, the adopted son of Washington, and father-in-law of Colonel Lee, was drawn by the author in 1860.

[3] The following is a copy of Colonel Lee's letter to General Scott:—

"ARLINGTON HOUSE, April 20, 1861.

"GENERAL:—Since my interview with you on the 18th inst., I have felt that I ought not longer to retain my commission in the Army. I therefore tender my resignation, which I request you will recommend for acceptance. It would have been presented at once, but for the struggle it has cost me to separate myself from a service to which I have devoted all the best years of my life and all the ability I possessed.

"During the whole of that time—more than a quarter of a century—I have experienced nothing but kindness from my superiors and the most cordial friendship from my comrades. To no one, General, have I been so much indebted as to yourself for uniform kindness and consideration, and it has always been my ardent desire to merit your approbation. I shall carry to the grave the most grateful recollections of your kind consideration, and your name and fame will always be dear to me.

"Save in defense of my native State, I never desire again to draw my sword. Be pleased to accept my most earnest wishes for the continuance of your happiness and prosperity, and believe me, most truly yours,

"R. E. LEE.

"Lieutenant-General WINFIELD SCOTT, *Commanding United States Army*."

At that time, according to the correspondent of the *Charleston Mercury*, Lee knew that he was to be the General-in-chief of the Virginia forces, and had necessarily resolved to draw his sword not only in defense of his native State, but against the National Government, whenever the conspirators should order him to do so.

Observatory,[1] Governor Letcher, and others who were present, joined in the reception of Lee, standing. He was then greeted by the President, who made a brief speech, in which he announced to the Colonel that the Convention had, on that day, on the nomination of Governor Letcher, appointed him General-in-chief of the Commonwealth; to which the recipient replied in a few words, accepting the so-called honor.[2] In time, Lee became the General-in-chief of all the armies in rebellion against his Government, at whose expense he had been educated, and whose bread he had eaten for more than thirty years.[3]

No man had stronger inducements to be a loyal citizen than Robert E. Lee. His ties of consanguinity and association with the founders of the Republic, and the common gratitude of a child toward a generous and loving foster-parent, should have made him hate treason in its most seductive forms, instead of embracing it in its most hideous aspect. He was a grandson of the "Lowland Beauty," spoken of by the biographer as the object of Washington's first love. He was a son of glorious "Legion Harry Lee," who used his sword gallantly in the old war for independence and the rights of man, in New York, New Jersey, Pennsylvania, and especially in the Southern States, and who was the leader of an army to crush an insurrection.[4] He was intimately associated with the Washington family, having married the daughter of an adopted son of the Father of his Country (George Washington Parke Custis); and his residence, "Arlington House," was filled with furniture, and plate, and china, and pictures, from Mount Vernon, the consecrated home of the patriot. It was one of the most desirable residences in the country. Around it spread out two hundred acres of lawn, and forest, and garden; and before it flowed the Potomac, beyond which, like a panorama, lay the cities of Washington and Georgetown.

A charming family made this home an earthly paradise. The writer had been a frequent guest there while the founder of Arlington House (Mr. Custis) was yet alive. He was there just before the serpent of secession beguiled the later master. It was his ideal of a home that should make the possessor grateful for the blessings, political and social, that flow from our beneficent Government, under which all rights are fully secured to every citizen. War came and wrought great changes in the relations of men and things. The writer visited Arlington House again with two traveling companions (F. J. Dreer and Edwin Greble, of Philadelphia), not as a guest, but as an observer of events that sadden his heart while he makes the record. It was just before sunset on a beautiful day in early May, 1865, when the possessor of Arlington[5] had been engaged for four years in endeavors to

---

[1] See note 3, page 394.

[2] *Richmond Enquirer*, April 24, 1861.

[3] He was graduated at West Point Military Academy. in June, 1825.

[4] The "Whisky Insurrection" in Western Pennsylvania.

[5] The Arlington estate was not the actual property of Colonel Lee. The late Mr. Custis, by his Will, left it to his daughter, Mrs. Lee, during her life, when it was to become the property of her eldest son, who also became a general in the army in rebellion against his Government. The property, therefore, was not liable to confiscation. It came into the possession of the Government when it was sold to liquidate a claim for unpaid taxes. The grounds near the mansion were dedicated by the Government as the resting-place of the remains of soldiers, a few of whom belonged to the Confederate Army. Among them were the remains of a large number of colored soldiers. The whole number of graves at that time was a little more than seven thousand.

On another part of the estate was a freedman's village, containing about one hundred neat dwellings, a church, and a school-house. There were residing the families of freedmen who were mostly employed on the Government

destroy his Government, and to build upon its ruins a hideous empire founded upon human slavery. How altered the aspect! The mighty oaks of the fine old forest in the rear of the mansion had disappeared, and strewn thickly over the gently undulating ground, and shaded by a few of the smaller trees that the ax had spared, were the green graves of seven thousand of our countrymen—many of them of the flower of the youth of the Republic—who had died on the battle-field, in the camp, or in the hospital. It was a vast cemetery, belonging to the National Government, having long graveled lanes among the graves. Even in the garden, and along the crown of the green slope in front of the mansion, were seen little hillocks, covering the remains of officers. In the midst of this garner of the ghastly fruits of the treason of Lee and his associates—fruits that had been literally *laid at his door*—were the beautiful white marble monuments erected to the memory of the venerable Custis and his life-companion—the founders of "Arlington House" and the parents of Lee's wife. On that of the former we read the sweet words of Jesus, "*Blessed are the merciful, for they shall obtain mercy.*" Then we thought of Belle Island, in the James River, which we had just visited, and of the hundreds of our starved countrymen held there as prisoners in the blistering summer's sun and the freezing winter's storm, into whose piteous faces, where every lineament was a tale of unutterable suffering vainly pleading in mute eloquence for mercy, Robert E. Lee might have looked any hour of the day with his field-glass from the rear gallery of his elegant brick mansion on Franklin Street, in Richmond. It seemed almost as if there was a voice in the air, saying, "Vengeance is mine, I will repay."[1]

While army and navy officers were abandoning their flag, it was painfully evident to the President and his Cabinet that Washington City was full of resident traitors, who were ready to assist in its seizure. Many of the District militia, who had been enrolled for the defense of the Government, were known to be disloyal;[2] and when, on the 18th of April, word came to some guests—true men—at Willard's Hotel, that a large body of Virginians were to seize Harper's Ferry and its munitions of war, and the rolling stock of the Baltimore and Ohio Railway, that evening, and, during the night, make a descent upon the Capital, while secessionists in Washington were to rise in rebellion, set fire to barns and other combustible buildings, and, in the confusion and terror that conflagration would produce, join the invaders, and make the seizure of the President and his Cabinet, the archives of the Government, and public buildings an easy task, it seemed as if the prophecy of Walker, at Montgomery,[3] was about to be fulfilled. It was one of those

---

farms in the neighborhood. A greater portion of the one thousand acres of the Arlington estate was then under excellent cultivation as such farms. The village originated in an order from the Secretary of War, directing the then commandant at Arlington to supply the aged negroes on the estate with subsistence. Mr. Custis, in his Will, directed that his slaves should all be set free five years after his decease, which occurred in October, 1857. It is said that when Colonel Lee abandoned his home and his flag to make war on his Government, he took with him all the slaves excepting the aged and infirm. The writer saw some of the latter whom he had known when Mr. Custis was master of Arlington House. Among these was Ephraim, the butler ; Daniel, the coachman ; and "Aunt Eleanor," who was the nurse of Mrs. Lee in her infancy. These were all over seventy years of age, and were well cared for by their true friends, the officers of the Government.

[1] St. Paul's Epistle to the Romans, xii. 19.

[2] The regular Army oath was administered to these troops by Adjutant-General Thomas, when many refused to take it, and were dismissed. Some of these, then ready to betray the Government into the hands of its enemies, afterward joined the ranks of the insurgents.

[3] See page 339.

moments upon which have hung the fate of empires. Happily, the men at
Willard's at that time, to whom the startling message came, comprehended
the magnitude of the danger and had nerve to meet it. They assembled in
secret all the loyal guests in that house, and, forming them into committees,
sent them to the other hotels to seek out guests there who were known to be
true, and invite them to a meeting in a church on F Street, in the rear of
Willard's,[1] that evening. A large number assembled at the appointed hour.
They took a solemn oath of fidelity to the old flag, and signed a pledge to do

every thing in their power in defense of
the Capital, and to be ready for action
at a moment's warning, when called by
General Scott. Cassius M. Clay, the
distinguished Kentuckian, was among
them. He was appointed their leader,
and thus was formed the notable CAS-
SIUS M. CLAY BATTALION, composed of
some of the noblest and most distinguished men in the country, in honor,
wealth, and social position. They chose
efficient officers; and all that night they
patroled the streets of the city to guard
against incendiaries, and prevent the
assembling of the secessionists. Another
party, commanded by General Lane, of

CASSIUS M. CLAY.

Kansas, went quietly to the "White House"—the Presidential mansion—to
act as a body-guard to his Excellency. They made the great East Room
their quarters, where they remained until the danger was passed. The principal passages of the Treasury building were guarded by howitzers. The
Pennsylvanians, as we have observed, occupied the Halls of Congress, in the
Capitol; and General Scott took measures to make that building a well
garrisoned citadel. Thither stores and munitions of war were carried, and in
it howitzers were planted; and behind the massive walls of that magnificent
structure, with a few hundred men as defenders, the President and his Cabinet and the archives of the nation would have been safe until the thousands
of the men of the loyal North, then aroused and moving, could reach and
rescue them.

Although the President and his Cabinet were not actually compelled to
take refuge in the well-guarded Capitol, yet for several days after the affair
in Baltimore, and the interruption of communication with the Free-labor
States, they and the General-in-chief were virtually prisoners at the seat of
Government. Soldiers from the Gulf States and others below the Roanoke,
with those of Virginia, were pressing eagerly toward the Capital, while the
Minute-men of Maryland and the secessionists of Washington were barely
restrained from action by the Pennsylvanians and the *Cassius M. Clay Battalion*, until the speedy arrival of other troops from the North gave absolute present security to the Government.

---

[1] This church had lately been attached to Willard's Hotel for the purpose of a concert room, and was the
hall in which the Peace Convention assembled a few weeks before. See page 236.

The massacre in the streets of Baltimore,[a] and the dangers that threatened the isolated Capital, produced the most intense anxiety and excitement throughout the Free-labor States, while the conspirators and insurgents were jubilant, because they regarded the stand taken by the secessionists of that city as a sure promise of the active

[a] April 19, 1861.

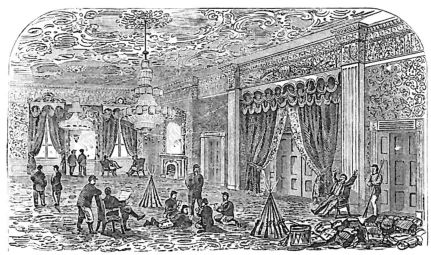

THE EAST ROOM.[1]

and effective co-operation of all Marylanders in the work of seizing the Capital.[2] That massacre seemed to the loyal people as an imperative call to patriotic duty, and like one of the repetitions of history. It was on the 19th of April, 1775, that the blood of the citizen soldiery of Massachusetts, the

---

[1] This is the great room in the Presidential mansion in which the attendants upon the public receptions of the President are assembled. It is so called, because it is in the extreme eastern portion of the White House. It is an elegantly finished and furnished room.

[2] " The glorious conduct of Maryland," said the *Richmond Enquirer*, "decides the contest at hand. With a generous bravery, worthy of her ancient renown, she has thrown herself into the pathway of the enemy, and made of her body a shield for the South. She stands forth in our day the leader of the Southern cause. . . . The heart of all Maryland responds to the action of Baltimore, and that nursery of fine regiments, instead of being the camping-ground of the enemy, preparing to rush upon the South, will speedily become the camping-ground of the South, preparing to cross the line of Mason and Dixon. . . . To have gained Maryland is to have gained a host. It insures Washington City, and the ignominious expulsion of Lincoln from the White House. It transfers the line of battle from the Potomac to the Pennsylvania border. It proclaims to the North that the South is a unit against them, henceforth and forever. It gives us the entire waters of the Chesapeake. It runs up the Southern seaboard to the mouth of the Delaware. It rounds out the fairest domain on the globe for the Southern Confederation."

In a speech at Atlanta, in Georgia, on the 30th of April, on his return to Montgomery from his mission to Richmond, Alexander H. Stephens said:—" As I told you when I addressed you a few days ago, Lincoln may bring his seventy-five thousand soldiers against us; but seven times seventy-five thousand men can never conquer us. We have now Maryland and Virginia and all the Border States with us. We have ten millions of people with us, heart and hand, to defend us to the death. We can call out a million of people if need be; and when they are cut down, we can call out another, and still another, until the last man of the South finds a bloody grave, rather than submit to their foul dictation. But a triumphant victory and independence, with an unparalleled career of glory, prosperity, and progress await us in the future. God is on our side, and who shall be against us? None but His Omnipotent hand can defeat us in this struggle." And so this conspirator went from place to place, deceiving the people with false hopes, arousing their baser passions, and precipitating them into the gulf of a horrid rebellion, to endure woes unutterable.

first that was shed in that revolution in which the liberties of the American people were secured, moistened the green sward at Lexington; now, on the 19th of April, 1861, the blood of the citizen soldiery of Massachusetts was the first that was shed in defense of those liberties endangered by a malignant internal foe.   The slain at Lexington, in 1775, and the slain in Baltimore, in 1861, were regarded as equal martyrs; and with the hot indignation that burned in every loyal bosom was mingled a reverential recognition of the dignity and significance of that sacrifice, for thoughtful men read in it a prophecy of the purification and strengthening of the nation by the good providence of God.

LUTHER C. LADD.

Luther C. Ladd, a young mechanic of Lowell, only a little more than seventeen years of age; Addison O. Whitney, another young mechanic of Lowell, but twenty-one years of age; and Charles A. Taylor, a decorative painter, of Boston, who were killed outright,[1] and Sumner H. Needham, of Lawrence, a plasterer by trade, who was mortally wounded, were the slain of the New England troops in Baltimore.   "I pray you, cause the bodies of our Massachusetts soldiers, dead in battle," telegraphed Governor Andrew to Mayor Brown, "to be immediately laid out, preserved in ice, and tenderly sent forward by express to me.   All expenses will be paid by this Commonwealth."   The Mayor promised acquiescence in the request; reminded the Governor that the Massachusetts troops were considered invaders of the soil of Maryland; told him that the wounded were "tenderly cared for," and said: "Baltimore will claim it as her right to pay all expenses incurred."   The Governor thanked the Mayor for his kind attention to the wounded and dead, and then, with rebukeful words that will ever be remembered, he exclaimed: "I am overwhelmed with surprise that a peaceful march of American citizens over the highway to the defense of our common Capital, should be deemed aggressive to Baltimore.   Through New York the march was triumphal."

It was several days before the bodies of the young martyrs reached Boston.   On the 6th of May,[a] those of Ladd and Whitney arrived at Lowell by a special train.   The day was dark and stormy. All the mills of the city were stopped running, the stores were closed, and all business was suspended.   The bodies were received by a great concourse of citizens and six military companies just organized for the war, and escorted to Huntington Hall, which was draped in black.   There funeral services were held, during which, the Rev. W. R. Clark, of the Methodist Church, preached an impressive sermon before the authorities of the city and the people;[2] and then the two bodies were laid in a vault

[a] 1861.

---

[1] Ladd was pierced by several bullets, and Whitney by only one, which entered his breast and passed downwards in his body.   It evidently came from a window above him.

[2] All denominations engaged in the services.   The Scriptures were read by the Rev. W. C. Himes, *Episcopalian;* the Rev. Dr. Cleaveland, *Congregationalist,* prayed; an original hymn was read by the Rev. J. J

in the Lowell Cemetery. A little more than four years afterward, the remains of these "first martyrs" were laid beneath a beautiful monument of Concord granite, erected, to commemorate their history, in Merrimack Square, in Lowell. It was formally dedicated on the 17th of June, 1865, in the presence of nearly twenty thousand people, who were addressed by the same chief magistrate of the Commonwealth who had besought the Mayor of Baltimore to send the bodies of the young men "tenderly" to him. In the mean time Maryland had disappointed the hopes of the conspirators, and dissipated the cloud that then hung over her like a pall. Baltimore had soon attested and vindicated its loyalty and attachment to the Union; and Maryland had not only spurned the traitors, but had purged her soil of the evil root of slavery,[1] for the perpetuation of which they had taken up arms. And more. At the conclusion of the consecrating ceremonies at the tomb of the young martyrs in Lowell, Lieutenant-Colonel Morris, of the staff of Governor Bradford, of Maryland, presented to Governor Andrew, as the representative of Massachusetts, a beautiful National banner, made of silk, and wrought by

MARTYRS' MONUMENT.[2]

Twiss, *Universalist;* the closing prayer was by the Rev. D. Mott, *Baptist;* and the benediction was pronounced by the Rev. F. Hinckley, *Unitarian.* Over the rostrum were displayed the words:—

"APRIL 19, 1775; APRIL 19, 1861."

[1] By the act of a Convention of the people in the autumn of 1862, and by the ratification of the Amendment to the Constitution of the United States, abolishing Slavery, by act of the Maryland General Assembly, February 3, 1865.

[2] The monument is of Concord granite, and its entire hight twenty-seven feet six inches. The plan is cruciform, the larger arms measuring fifteen feet, and the shorter, twelve feet. It consists of a central shaft placed upon a plinth, with a high base, upon two sides of which, forming the longer arms, are two sarcophagi, having on each side, respectively, the names of the young martyrs. Inserted in the ends are raised laurel wreaths. The cornices of the sarcophagi are ornamented with thirteen raised stars each. Upon the other two sides of the base, forming the shorter arms, are two plinths, the same hight as the sarcophagi, with inscriptions. On the Merrimack Street side are the words:—

"ADDISON O. WHITNEY, BORN IN WALDO, ME., OCT. 30, 1839; LUTHER C. LADD, BORN IN ALEXANDRIA, N. H., DEC. 22, 1843; MARCHED FROM LOWELL IN THE SIXTH M. V. M. TO THE DEFENSE OF THE NATIONAL CAPITAL, AND FELL MORTALLY WOUNDED IN THE ATTACK ON THEIR REGIMENT WHILE PASSING THROUGH BALTIMORE, APRIL 19TH, 1861. THE COMMONWEALTH OF MASSACHUSETTS AND THE CITY OF LOWELL DEDICATE THIS MONUMENT TO THEIR MEMORY."

"APRIL 19, 1865."

On the Moody Street side are the following words:—

"NOTHING IS HERE FOR TEARS, NOTHING TO WAIL OR KNOCK THE BREAST; NO WEAKNESS, NO CONTEMPT, DISPRAISE OR BLAME; NOTHING BUT WELL AND FAIR, AND WHAT MAY QUIET US IN A DEATH SO NOBLE."

"1861."

The horizontal lines are merged into the vertical ones by fluted trusses, with raised stars resting upon the four arms, and above these is a plinth, on two sides of which are bronzed medallions of the arms of Massachusetts and the city of Lowell. The engraving is from a photograph kindly sent to me by Major-General Butler.

This monument was dedicated on the 17th of June, 1865, with imposing ceremonies by the Masonic frater-

the loyal women of Baltimore for the purpose. It was of regimental size, and surmounted by a carved eagle holding thunderbolts in its talons, and an olive-branch in its beak. On the polished black-walnut staff was a silver plate, bearing an engraving of the arms of Maryland and of Massachusetts, and the words, "MARYLAND TO MASSACHUSETTS, APRIL 19, 1865. MAY THE UNION AND FRIENDSHIP OF THE FUTURE OBLITERATE THE ANGUISH OF THE PAST." This was the crowning evidence of the sorrow of true Marylanders for the wrongs inflicted on citizens of Massachusetts in their commercial capital, and a desire to obliterate the feelings occasioned by them. Only a few months after the occurrence, and when the Union men of the State had obtained partial control of the public affairs of the Commonwealth, the Legislature took steps^a to "wipe out," as they expressed it, "the foul blot of the Baltimore riot;" and on the 5th of March, 1862, the General Assembly appropriated seven thousand dollars, to be disbursed, under the direction of the Governor of Massachusetts, for the relief of the families of those who were then injured. To-day Massachusetts and Maryland cordially embrace each other as loving sisters in the great family of the Nation.

^a December, 1861.

"Through New York the march [of Massachusetts troops] was triumphal," said Governor Andrew. It was so. The patriotism of the people of that great city and of the State had been thoroughly aroused, as we have observed, by the attack on Fort Sumter; and now, when the National Government was struggling for life in the toils of the conspirators, with no ability to make its perils known to the loyal people, they put forth the strong arm of their power without stint. Already the Legislature had authorized the Governor to enroll thirty thousand troops for two years, instead of for three months, and appropriated three millions of dollars for war purposes. Now, the citizens of the metropolis, in concert with General Wool, performed services of incalculable value, which the General-in-chief afterward declared had been mainly instrumental in saving the Capital from seizure, and the Republic from ruin.[1] They heard the call of the President for seventy-five thousand men with profound satisfaction. On the same evening some gentlemen met at the house of an influential citizen, and resolved to take immediate measures for the support of the Government. On the following day,^b they invited, by a printed circular letter, other citizens to join them, for the purpose of making arrangements for a public meeting of men of all parties, "to sustain the Federal Government in the present crisis."[2] The arrangements were made, and the

^b April 16, 1861.

---

nity, a large number of military companies, and citizens, and the Otto (Singing) Club. Governor Andrew delivered an oration, after which Lieutenant-Colonel Thomas J. Morris presented the Maryland flag mentioned in the text. There was a collation at Huntington Hall, where toasts were given and speeches made. Among the speakers was Major-General Butler, whose military experience in Maryland, just after the riot in Baltimore, made him a deeply interested participant in the ceremonies. He paid a fine tribute to the volunteer soldiers, and to the Navy.

[1] Speech of General Scott before the Union Defense Committee of New York, November 8, 1861. See the published *Reports, Resolutions, and Documents* of that Committee.

[2] The following is a copy of the circular:—"SIR: At a meeting held at the house of R. H. McCurdy, Esq., you were appointed member of a Committee to make arrangements for a public meeting of citizens, of all parties, to sustain the Federal Government in the present crisis. You are earnestly requested to attend a meeting of said Committee, for the above-named purpose, at the rooms of the Chamber of Commerce, corner of William and Cedar Streets."

great meeting at Union Square, already mentioned,[1] was held on the 20th of April, when a Committee of Safety was appointed. It was composed of some of the most distinguished citizens of New York, of all parties. They organized that evening, with the title of THE UNION DEFENSE COMMITTEE.[2]

Intelligence had already gone over the land of the attack on the Massachusetts troops in the streets of Baltimore, and the isolation and perils of the Capital; and the first business of the Committee was to facilitate the equipment and outfit of regiments of volunteer militia, and their dispatch to the seat of Government. So zealously and efficiently did they work, that within ten days from the time when the President made his call for troops, no less than eight thousand well-equipped and fully armed men had gone to the field from the city of New York. Already, before the organization of the Committee, the celebrated Seventh Regiment of the National Guard of New York, Colonel Marshall Lefferts, had left for Washington City; and on the day after the great meeting (Sunday, the 21st), three other regiments had followed, namely, the Sixth, Colonel Pinckney; the Twelfth, Colonel Butterfield; and the Seventy-first, Colonel Vosburg.

Major-General Wool, next in rank to the General-in-chief, and the Commander of the Eastern Department, which comprised the whole country eastward of the Mississippi River, was then at his home and head-quarters at Troy, New York. When he heard of the affair at Baltimore, he hastened to Albany, the State capital, to confer with Governor Morgan. While he was there, the Governor received an electrograph, urging him to send troops forward to Washington as speedily as possible. At the same time he received an offer of the regiment of Colonel Ellsworth, whose skillfully executed and picturesque Zouave tactics had lately excited the attention and admiration of the country. These volunteers were accepted, and the Governor determined to push forward troops as fast as possible. General Wool at once issued orders[a] to Colonel Tompkins, the United States Quartermaster at New York, to furnish all needful transportation; and Major Eaton, the Commissary of Subsistence, was directed to issue thirty days' rations to each soldier that might be ordered to Washington.

[a] April 20, 1861.

Governor Morgan went to New York on the evening of the 20th, and was followed by General Wool on the 22d. The veteran made his head-quarters at the St. Nicholas Hotel, and there he was waited upon by the Union Defense Committee on the 23d, when a plan of operations for the

---

[1] See page 354.

[2] The Committee was composed of the following citizens:—John A. Dix, *Chairman;* Simeon Draper, *Vice-Chairman;* William M. Evarts, *Secretary;* Theodore Dehon, *Treasurer;* Moses Taylor, Richard M. Blatchford, Edwards Pierrepont, Alexander T. Stewart, Samuel Sloane, John Jacob Astor, Jr., John J. Cisco, James S. Wadsworth, Isaac Bell, James Boorman, Charles H. Marshall, Robert H. McCurdy, Moses H. Grinnell, Royal Phelps, William E. Dodge, Greene C. Bronson, Hamilton Fish. William F. Havemeyer, Charles H. Russell, James T. Brady, Rudolph A. Witthaus, Abiel A. Low, Prosper M. Wetmore, A. C. Richards, and the Mayor, Controller, and Presidents of the two Boards of the Common Council of the City of New York. The Committee had rooms at No. 30 Pine Street, open all day, and at the Fifth Avenue Hotel, open in the evening. The original and specific duties assigned to the Committee, by the great meeting that created it, were, "to represent the citizens in the collection of funds, and the transaction of such other business, in aid of the movements of the Government, as the public interests may require."

During the existence of this Committee, which continued about a year, it disbursed almost *a million of dollars,* which the Corporation of New York had appropriated for war purposes, and placed at its disposal. It assisted in the organization, equipment, &c., of forty-nine regiments, or about forty thousand men. For military purposes, it spent, of the city fund, nearly seven hundred and fifty-nine thousand dollars, and for the relief of soldiers' families, two hundred and thirty thousand dollars.

salvation of the Capital was arranged between them. No communication could be made to the Government, as we have observed. The General-in-chief could not speak to a single regiment outside of the District of Columbia; and General Wool was compelled, in order to act in conformity to the demands of the crisis and desires of the loyal people, to assume great responsibilities. He did so, saying :—"I shall probably be the only victim; but, under the circumstances, I am prepared to make the sacrifice, if thereby the Capital may be saved." Day and night he labored with the tireless energy of a strong man of forty years, until the work was accomplished. Ships were chartered, supplies were furnished, and troops were forwarded to Washington with extraordinary dispatch, by way of Chesapeake Bay and the Potomac River. The transports were convoyed by armed steamers to shield them from pirates; and one of them—the *Quaker City*—was ordered to Hampton Roads, to prevent the insurgents transporting heavy guns from the Gosport Navy Yard with which to attack Fortress Monroe, the military key to Virginia. To that immensely important military work, Wool sent gun-carriages, ammunition, and provisions, that it might be held, and command the chief waters of Virginia. A dozen State Governors applied to him, as the superior military officer that could be reached, for advice and for munitions of war, and he assisted in arming no less than nine States.[1] In reply to Governor Yates, of Illinois, asking for five thousand muskets and a complement of ammunition, he directed him to send a judicious officer, with four or five companies, to take possession of the Arsenal at St. Louis, which he believed to be in danger of seizure by the secessionists of Missouri. He also telegraphed to Frank P. Blair, of St. Louis (afterward a major-general in the National Army), to assist in the matter. By judicious management, twenty-one thousand stand of small arms, two field-pieces, and one hundred and ten thousand rounds of ammunition were transferred from St. Louis to Illinois. Wool also ordered heavy cannon, carriages, *et cætera*, to Cairo, Illinois, which speedily became a place of great interest, in a military point of view. He authorized the Governors of New Hampshire and Massachusetts to put the coast defenses within the borders of their respective States in good order, and approved of other measures proposed for the defense of the seaport towns supposed to be in danger from the pirate vessels of the "Confederacy," then known to be afloat. He also took the responsibility of sending forward to Washington Colonel Ellsworth's Zouave Regiment, composed principally of New York firemen, who were restrained, for the moment, by official State authority.[2]

---

[1] General Wool ordered the following ordnance and ordnance stores to be issued to the Governors of the following States:—PENNSYLVANIA, 16,000 muskets, 640,000 cartridges, 150,000 caps, 3,080 muskets for six Ohio regiments, and 117,889 cartridges for the same. OHIO; 10,000 muskets and 400,000 cartridges, and 5,000 muskets from Illinois. INDIANA, 5,000 muskets and 200,000 cartridges, with caps. ILLINOIS, 200,000 cartridges. MASSACHUSETTS, 4,000 stand of arms. NEW HAMPSHIRE, 2,000 muskets and 20,000 cartridges. VERMONT, 300 rifles. NEW JERSEY, 2,880 muskets with ammunition. In addition to these, he ordered the issue of 10,000 muskets and 400,000 cartridges to General Patterson, then in command in Pennsylvania; 16,000 muskets to General Sandford, of New York, and forty rifles to General Welch.

[2] While General Wool was reviewing this regiment, when on its march to embark for Washington, an order was received from the Governor of the State, acting under authority of law, forbidding their embarkation, unless the regiment, which was of maximum number, should be reduced to seventy-seven men to a company. No part of the regiment would go without the remainder, and, fortunately for the public good, General Wool took the responsibility of ordering them forward as a whole. They were escorted to the water by five thousand firemen.

Troops and subsistence so promptly forwarded to Washington by the Union Defense Committee, under the direction of General Wool, and with the cordial co-operation of Commodores Breese and Stringham, saved the Capital from seizure.[1] Fortress Monroe, made secure by the same energetic measures, held, during the entire war, a controlling power over all lower and eastern Virginia and upper North Carolina; and the possession of the arms in the St. Louis Arsenal by the friends of the Government, at that time, was of the greatest importance to the National cause in the Mississippi Valley. We shall consider this matter presently.

JOHN ELLIS WOOL.

When the troops sent forward had opened the way to Washington, the first communication that General Wool received from his superiors was an order from the General-in-chief[a] to return to his head-quarters at Troy, for "the recovery of his health, known to be feeble." The General's health was

[a] April 30, 1861.

perfect. He, and the Union Defense Committee (who appreciated his services, and heartily thanked him for them), and the people, were surprised. The Secretary of War was asked[b] by the veteran why he had been sent into retirement at that critical juncture of affairs. A month later,[c] the minister replied:—"You were ordered to return to your head-quarters at Troy, because the issuing of orders by you,

[b] May 9.

[c] June 7.

on the application of the various Governors, for arms, ammunition, et cœtera, without consultation, seriously embarrassed the prompt and proper administration of the Department." This sentence in the letter seemed more extraordinary than the order of the General-in-chief. The Government, during the time alluded to, could not be consulted. It was, as it were, shut up in prison, and its rescue from imminent peril had been effected only by the employment of unauthorized measures, less grave than the Government itself was compelled to resort to for its own preservation—measures which it afterward asked Congress to sanction by special act.[2] The people were

---

[1] "I remember how you sustained the Government by forwarding troops for the defense of the National Capital; how, by your zeal in equipping and sending forward, with the means at your disposal, large bodies of patriotic and excellent troops, which came in good time, the tide of rebellion, which commenced at Baltimore, was turned against the enemies of our country. The Government had not the means of defending itself, when they were most needed. This Committee came forward and applied the remedy, and averted the danger."— *Speech of General Scott before the Union Defense Committee*, November 8, 1861. Before the close of the year 1861, one hundred and seven volunteer regiments had gone to the field from the State of New York, sixty-six of which were aided by the Union Defense Committee. Of these regiments, ninety were infantry, ten were cavalry, five were artillery, one of engineers, and one a coast-guard.

[2] On the 31st of April, 1861, the Union Defense Committee, by unanimous vote, adopted the following resolutions:—

"*Resolved*, That this Committee regard it as an incumbent duty to express their high appreciation of the wisdom, energy, and patriotism of Major-General John E. Wool, commanding this Military District, evinced in moments of critical emergency in the affairs of the country.

"*Resolved*, As the deliberate judgment of this Committee, that the zeal, activity, and patriotism of General Wool have been eminently conspicuous in the arrangements made by him for expediting the transport of troops and supplies to the scene of action; and especially so in assuming the responsibility of dispatching the

not satisfied, and, they complained.   Their murmurs were heeded ; and, a few
weeks[a] later, General Wool was called from his retirement and

[a] August 17, 1861.
placed in command of the *Department of Southeastern Virginia*,
which had been recently created, with his head-quarters at
Fortress Monroe.   He succeeded General Butler, who was assigned to another field of active duty.

---

fine regiment of New York Fire Zouaves, commanded by Colonel Ellsworth, thus avoiding the delays which
might otherwise have detained them for several days.

"*Resolved*, That this Committee desire to express in these resolutions their grateful sense of the distinguished services rendered by General Wool since entering upon his duties in this city; and their acknowledg-
ments to the War Department for affording this community the great advantage of his military skill and long
experience in the service of his country.

"*Resolved*, That while the organization of the Western Department of the United States, comprising within
its limits the National Capital, under the able, judicious, and patriotic management of Lieutenant-General
Scott, Commanding General of the Army, insures public confidence and the protection of the National honor,
the Committee deem it fortunate for the country that the President has exercised the sagacious discretion of
placing the Eastern Department under the control of an officer worthy of all the confidence reposed in him.

"*Resolved*, That this Committee desire most emphatically to express their gratitude to Major-General Wool
for the promptness and readiness with which he has yielded to their wishes and requests, and assumed great
and heavy responsibilities, which the exigency of the case and the difficulties of communicating with the Government rendered necessary; and they most earnestly request the War Department and the President of the
United States to ratify and approve the conduct and action of Major-General Wool in these particulars; and
also, that he may be continued in command in this city and of this Department.

"*Resolved*, That copies of the preceding resolutions, properly authenticated, be transmitted to the President
of the United States, Lieutenant-General Scott, and Major-General Wool."

UNION GENERALS

CHAPTER XVIII.

THE CAPITAL SECURED.—MARYLAND SECESSIONISTS SUBDUED.—CONTRIBUTIONS BY THE PEOPLE.

T has been observed that the Seventh Regiment of New York left that city for Washington on the memorable 19th of April. It was the favorite military corps of the metropolis, and was composed mostly of young men, a large majority of them connected with families of the higher social positions. It was known that they were to leave in the afternoon, and all New York appeared to turn out to see them depart, and bid them God speed.

The regiment was formed on Lafayette Place, where an immense National flag was waving over the Astor Library. Just as it was about to march, it received intelligence of the attack on the Massachusetts Sixth, in the streets of Baltimore. Forty-eight rounds of ball-cartridges were served out to each man, and then they moved through Fourth Street into Broadway, and down that great thoroughfare to Courtlandt Street and the Jersey City Ferry. The side-walks all the way were densely packed with men, women, and children. Banners were streaming everywhere.

"Banners from balcony, banners from steeple,
Banners from house to house, draping the people;
Banners upborne by all—men, women, and children,
Banners on horses' fronts, flashing, bewild'ring!"

The shipping at the ferry was brilliant with flags. Already the Eighth Massachusetts Regiment, Colonel Timothy Monroe,[1] accompanied by General Benjamin F. Butler, one of the most remarkable men of our time, had passed through the vast throng that was waiting for the New York Seventh, and being greeted with hearty huzzas and the gift of scores of little banners by the people. At sunset all had gone over the Hudson—the New York Seventh and Massachusetts Eighth—and crossed New Jersey by railway to the banks of the Delaware. It had been a day of fearful excitement in New York, and the night was one of more fearful anxiety. Slumber was wooed in vain by hundreds, for they knew that .

PRIVATE OF THE SEVENTH REGIMENT.

[1] See pages 401 and 402.

their loved ones, now that blood had been spilt, were hurrying on toward great peril. Regiment after regiment followed the Seventh in quick succession,[1] and within ten days from the time of its departure, full ten thousand men of the city of New York were on the march toward the Capital.[2]

The Massachusetts regiment had been joined at Springfield by a company under Captain H. S. Briggs, and now numbered a little over seven hundred men. It reached Philadelphia several hours before the New York Seventh arrived there, and was bountifully entertained at the Girard House by the generous citizens. There Butler first heard of the attack on the Sixth, in Baltimore. His orders commanded him to march through that city. It was now impossible to do so with less than ten thousand armed men. He counseled with Major-General Robert Patterson, who had just been appointed commander of the "Department of Washington," which embraced the States of Pennsylvania, Delaware, and Maryland, and the District of Columbia, and whose head-quarters were at Philadelphia. Commodore Dupont, commandant of the Navy Yard there, was also consulted, and it was agreed that the troops should go by water from Perryville, at the mouth of the Susquehanna River, to Annapolis, and thence across Maryland to Washington City. Butler was ordered to take that route, seize and hold Annapolis and Annapolis Junction, and open and thoroughly guard a military pathway to the Capital.[3]

---

[1] "The enthusiasm of the people—of the young men in particular—was wonderful. Sometimes several brothers would enlist at the same time. The spirit of our women, who were animated by the same patriotic feelings, is well illustrated by a letter written by a New York mother of five sons who enlisted, to her husband. She was absent from home at the time. 'Your letter,' she said, 'came to hand last evening. I must confess I was startled by the news referring to our boys, and, for the moment, I felt as if a ball had pierced my own heart. For the first time I was obliged to look things full in the face. But although I have always loved my children with a love that none but a mother can know, yet, when I look upon the state of my country, I can not withhold them; and in the name of their God, and their mother's God, and their country's God, I bid them go. If I had ten sons instead of five, I would give them all sooner than have our country rent in fragments. . . . I hope you will provide them each with a Bible, and give them their mother's love and blessing, and tell them our prayers will accompany them, and ascend on their behalf, night and day."—*The History of the Civil War in America:* by J. S. C. Abbott, i. 108.

In contrast with this was the letter of a Baltimore mother to her loyal son, a clergyman in Boston, who, on the Sunday after the attack on Fort Sumter, preached a patriotic discourse to his people. The letter was as follows:—

"BALTIMORE, April 17, 1861.

"MY DEAR SON:—Your remarks last Sabbath were telegraphed to Baltimore, and published in an extra. Has God sent you to preach the sword, or to preach Christ?   YOUR MOTHER."

The son replied:—

"BOSTON, April 22, 1861.

"DEAR MOTHER:—'God has sent' me not only to 'preach' the sword, but to *use* it. When this Government tumbles, look amongst the ruins for   YOUR STAR-SPANGLED BANNER SON."

[2] John Sherman, now (1865) United States Senator from Ohio, was then an aid-de-camp of General Patterson. He was sent by that officer to lay before General Scott the advantages of the Annapolis route, suggested by General Patterson. The route was approved of by the Lieutenant-General. See *A Narrative of the Campaign in the Valley of the Shenandoah:* by Robert Patterson, late Major-General of Volunteers.

[3] In the midst of the wild tumult, caused by the call to arms—the braying of trumpets and the roll of drums—the representatives of a sect of exemplary Christians, who had ever borne testimony against the practices of war, met in the City of New York (April 23), and reiterated that testimony. That sect was the Society of Friends, or Quakers. They put forth an Address to their brethren, counseling them to beware of the temptations of the hour, and to pray for divine blessings on their country. They were a loyal "Peace party" for conscience' sake. "We love our country," they said, "and acknowledge, with gratitude to our Heavenly Father, the many blessings we have been favored with under its Government, and can feel no sympathy with any who seek its overthrow; but, in endeavoring to uphold and maintain it, as followers of the Prince of Peace, we must not transgress the precepts and injunction of the Gospel."—*Address to the Members of the Religious Society of Friends within the limits of the New York Yearly Meeting.* Signed, "WILLIAM WOOD, *Clerk.*" Similar testimony was borne by the Quakers elsewhere; yet the homily was practically unheeded by a large number of the younger members, who, with many of their seniors, held that the war was an exceptional one— a holy war of Righteousness against Sin. They were, as a body of Christians, universally loyal to the flag, even in

Late in the evening General Butler summoned all of his officers, thirteen in number, to his room. It was a singular council of war. On his table lay thirteen revolvers. "I propose," said the General, substantially, "to join with Colonel Lefferts, of the Seventh Regiment of New York, sail for Annapolis from Havre de Grace, arrive there to-morrow afternoon at four o'clock, occupy the capital of Maryland, and call the State to account for the death of Massachusetts men, my friends and neighbors. If Colonel Lefferts thinks it best not to go, I propose to take this regiment alone." Then, taking up one of the revolvers, he said: "I am ready to take the responsibility. Every officer willing to accompany me will please take a pistol." Not one hesitated; and then the General sketched a plan of his proposed operations, to be sent to Governor Andrew after his departure. He proposed to hold Annapolis as a means of communication, and, by a forced march with a part of his command, reach the Capital in accordance with his orders. He telegraphed to the Governor to send the Boston Light Battery to Annapolis to assist in the march on Washington.[1]

Colonel Lefferts did not feel at liberty to accept General Butler's proposition, and the latter made preparations to go on with the Massachusetts troops alone. The President of the Philadelphia, Wilmington, and Baltimore Railway Company placed their great steam ferry-boat *Maryland*, at Perryville, at his disposal; and two companies were ordered to go forward early in the morning and take possession of it. Word came meanwhile that the insurgents had already seized and barricaded it, and Butler resolved to push on with his whole force and capture it. "If I succeed," he wrote to Governor Andrew, "success will justify me. If I fail, purity of intention will excuse want of judgment, or rashness.[2]

Butler left Philadelphia at eleven o'clock in the morning,[a] and   [a] April 20, 1861. when near the Susquehanna his troops were ordered from the cars, placed in battle order, and marched toward the ferry, in expectation of a fight. Rumor had been untrue. There were no insurgents in arms at Perryville or Havre de Grace; and there lay the powerful ferry-boat in the quiet possession of her regular crew. The troops were soon embarked, and at six o'clock in the evening the huge vessel—with a captain who seemed to need watching by the vigilant and loyal eyes of the soldiers, lest he should run them into Baltimore or aground—went out toward Chesapeake Bay. Making good time, she was off the old capital of Maryland at a little past midnight, when, to Butler's surprise, Annapolis and the Naval Academy were lighted up, and the people were all astir. The town and the Academy were in possession of the secessionists. They were expecting some insurgents from Baltimore, and they intended, with united force, to seize the venerable frigate *Constitution*, then moored there as a school-ship, and add her to the "Confederate navy." For four days and nights her gallant commander,

---

North Carolina; and while they avoided, as far as possible, the practices of war, which their conscience and Discipline condemned, they aided the Government in every other way, such as services in hospitals, and other employments in which non-combatants might engage. A large number of their young men, however, bore arms in the field, and acted in compliance with the spirit of the alleged injunction of the Philadelphia mother:—
"Let thy musket not hold a silent meeting before the enemy."

[1] *General Butler in New Orleans*, &c.: by James Parton, page 71.
[2] Report of the Adjutant-General of Massachusetts, December 31, 1861, page 22.

Captain Blake, Superintendent of the Academy, had kept her guns double-shotted, expecting an attack every moment.

The arrival of the Massachusetts troops was just in time to save the *Constitution*. Communication was speedily opened between General Butler and Captain Blake, and a hundred of the troops, who were seamen at home, with the Salem Zouaves as a guard, were detailed to assist in getting the *Constitution* from the wharf, and putting her out beyond the bar in a place of safety. With the help of the *Maryland*, acting as a tug, this was accomplished. That venerable vessel, in which Hull, and Bainbridge, and Stewart had won immortal honors in the Second War for Independence, was built in Boston, and was first manned by Massachusetts men; now she was preserved to the uses of the Government, for whose sovereignty she had gallantly fought, by the hands of Massachusetts men. "This," said General Butler, in an order thanking the troops for the service, "is a sufficient triumph of right; a sufficient triumph for us. By this the blood of our friends, shed by the Baltimore mob, is so far avenged." We will add, that the *Constitution* was soon afterward taken to New York; and when the naval school was removed to Newport, Rhode Island, she became a school-ship there.

In assisting to get out the *Constitution*, the *Maryland* grounded on a sand-bank. The suspected captain was confined, and the vessel was put under the management of seamen and engineers from among the Massachusetts troops.[1] There she lay helpless all that day and the next night, to the great discomfort of her passengers. Her water-casks were nearly emptied, and their provisions were almost exhausted. In the mean time Governor Hicks, who was in Annapolis, and still under the malign control of the secessionists, was urging Butler not to land "Northern troops." "The excitement here is very great," he said; "and I think that you had better take your men elsewhere." Butler, in reply, spoke of his necessities and his orders, and took the occasion to correct the Governor's sectional phraseology by saying of his force: "They are not '*Northern* troops;' they are a part of the whole militia of the United States, obeying the call of the President." This was the root of the matter. Therein was the grand idea of nationality as opposed to State Supremacy, in which the General acted throughout with the clearest advantage.

Butler now went ashore, and had a personal conference with the Governor and the Mayor of Annapolis. "All Maryland," they said, "is at the point of rushing to arms. The railway is broken up, and its line guarded by armed men. It will be a fearful thing for you to land and attempt to march on Washington."—"I *must* land," said the General, "for my troops are hungry."—"No one in Annapolis will sell them any thing," replied these authorities of the State and city. Butler intimated that armed men were not always limited to the necessity of *purchasing* food when famishing; and he gave both magistrates to understand that the orders and demands of his Government were imperative, and that he should land and march on the Capital as speedily as possible, in spite of all opposition. At the same time

---

[1] The composition of this regiment was very remarkable. It contained men skilled in almost every trade and profession; and Major Winthrop, who went out with the New York Seventh Regiment, was nearly right when he said, that if the words were given, "Poets, to the front!" or "Painters, present arms!" or "Sculptors, charge bayonets!" there would be ample responses.

he assured them that peaceable citizens should not be molested, and that the laws of the State should be respected. And more. He was ready to co-operate with the local authorities in suppressing a slave insurrection, or any other resistance to law. The Governor contented himself with simply protesting against the landing of troops as unwise, and begged the General not to halt them in Annapolis.

All the night of the 21st, the *Maryland* lay aground, and immovable by wind or tide. At dawn on the 22d, another steamer appeared approaching. It was the *Boston*, bearing the New York Seventh Regiment. Colonel Lefferts had become convinced that he could not pass through Baltimore, so he chartered this steamer at Philadelphia with the intention of going to Washington by way of the Potomac. They embarked at four o'clock in the afternoon.[a] Only April 20, 1861. a few officers were intrusted with the secret; the men had no knowledge of their route. Quietly they passed down the Delaware to the ocean, on a beautiful April evening, and entered the waters of Virginia between its great Capes, Charles and Henry. Informed of batteries near Alexandria, and

MARSHALL LEFFERTS.

finding no armed vessel to convoy the *Boston*, Colonel Lefferts deemed it prudent to follow General Butler to Annapolis; so they went up the Chesapeake, and came in sight of the grounded *Maryland* at dawn. The Seventh cheered the old flag seen at her fore, and the two regiments soon exchanged greetings.

The *Boston* now attempted to get the *Maryland* from the ground. For many hours both regiments worked faithfully, but in vain. The Massachusetts

LANDING AT THE NAVAL ACADEMY[1] GROUNDS.

troops were without a drop of liquid of any kind to drink for twelve hours, and were suffering intensely. Finally it was agreed that the *Boston* should land the Seventh at the Naval Academy's wharf, and then take the Eighth from the *Maryland* and put them ashore at the same place. This was done,

[1] In this view the buildings of the United States Naval Academy are seen.

and in the course of the afternoon both regiments were landed and quartered in the buildings of the Academy (the National property), when the members of the Seventh hastened to share their rations with their famished friends. The threat of the secessionists, that if Butler should land with the intention of passing over the railway to Washington, the track should be destroyed, was carried out. The rails were removed and hidden, and locomotives were taken in pieces and concealed.

Terrible stories of the gathering of insurgents at Annapolis Junction, and other places on the route to Washington, now came to the ears of General Butler and Colonel Lefferts. The former did not believe half that was told him. He had positive information that the secessionists had torn up much of the railway between Annapolis and the Junction, and carried off the materials, and that bitterness of spirit prevailed everywhere; yet he resolved to move forward at once and rebuild the road, for over it supplies, and also other troops, must follow him. He again invited Colonel Lefferts to join him. At first that prudent commander declined, thinking it best to wait for reenforcements.[1] He changed his mind, and early the next morning the two regiments joined hands in vigorous preparations for that strange, eventful march on the Capital, which has no parallel in history.

In the mean time, two companies of the Massachusetts troops had seized the railway station, and there found a locomotive engine disabled and concealed. "Does any one know any thing about this machine?" inquired General Butler. "Our shop made that engine, General," said Charles Homans, of the Beverly Light Guard, as he looked sharply at it. "I guess I can put her in order and run her."—"Do it," said the General; and it was soon done, for that regiment was full of engineers, workers in metal, and mechanics of all kinds. It seemed like a providential organization, made expressly, with its peculiar leader, for the work in hand. Such impediments of civil authority, hostile feeling, armed resistance, and destructive malignity, would have appalled almost any other man and body of men; but Butler generally exhibited an illustration of the truth of the saying, "Where there's a will there's a way," and the Massachusetts Eighth was an embodiment of the axiom. The engine was speedily repaired; the rails hidden, some in thickets, and some in the bottom of streams, were hunted up, and on the evening of the 23d, the troops were nearly ready for a forward movement, when General Butler formally took military possession of the Annapolis and Elkridge Railway. Governor Hicks protested against such occupation, on the ground that it would prevent the assembling of the Legislature, called to meet at Annapolis on the 26th. General Butler reminded the Governor that his Excellency had given as a reason why the troops should not land, that they could not pass over the road because "the Company had taken up the rails, and they were private property. It is difficult to see," said the General, "how it can be, that if my troops could not pass over the railroad one way, the members of the Legislature could pass the other way."[2] He told the Governor that he was there to maintain the laws, and, if possible, protect the road from destruction by a mob. "I am endeavoring," he said, "to save and

[1] Letter of Colonel Lefferts to General Butler, Monday night, April 22, 1861.
[2] Correspondence between General Butler and Governor Hicks, April 23, 1861.

not to destroy; to obtain means of transportation, so that I can vacate the capital prior to the sitting of the Legislature, and not be under the necessity of encumbering your beautiful city while the Legislature is in session." This logic and this irony were unanswerable, and the General was never again troubled with the protests of the Maryland Executive.

On the morning of the 24th, the combined regiments moved forward at the rate of about a mile an hour, laying the track anew and building bridges. Skirmishers went ahead and scouts on the flanks. The main column was led by a working party on the road, behind which followed a car with a howitzer loaded with grape-shot, in charge of Lieutenant Bunting. It was a hot April morning, and the men suffered much from heat and fatigue. They had a stretch of twenty-one miles to go over between Annapolis and the Junction. A shower in the afternoon, and balmy air and bright moonlight in the evening, with the freshness of early spring, gave them pleasure in the midst of their toil. All night long they moved forward, keeping very vigilant eyes upon the surrounding country, but falling in with none of those terrible Marylanders which the Governor and the Mayor of Annapolis had predicted would be upon them. These braves seemed to have a wholesome fear of the "Yankees," and made their observations, if at all, at a safe distance. The country appeared to be depopulated. The inhabitants had fled or hidden, with the evident expectation of an invasion by almost savage men. "I know not," said a member of the Seventh,[1] "if I can describe that night-march. I have a dim recollection of deep cuts through which we passed, gloomy and treacherous-looking, with the moon shining full on our muskets, while the banks were wrapped in shade, each moment expecting to see the flash and hear the crack of the rifle of the Southern guerrillas. . . . On all sides dark and lonely pine woods stretched away, and, as the night wore on, the monotony of the march became oppressive."

The troops reached Annapolis Junction on the morning of the 25th, when the co-operation of the two regiments ceased, the Seventh New York going on to Washington, and the Eighth Massachusetts remaining to hold the road they had just opened. Before their departure from Annapolis, the *Baltic*, a large steamship transport, had arrived there with troops, and others speedily followed. General Scott ordered General Butler to remain there, hold the town and the road, and

ANNAPOLIS JUNCTION IN 1861.

superintend the forwarding of troops to the Capital. The "Department of Annapolis," which embraced the country twenty miles on each side of the railway, as far as Bladensburg, was created, and General Butler was placed in

---

[1] Fitz James O'Brien, a young and brilliant writer, who afterward gave his life to the cause.

command of it, with ample discretionary powers to make him a sort of military dictator. This power, as we shall observe presently, he used with great efficiency.

The railway from Annapolis Junction to Washington was uninjured and unobstructed, and the Seventh Regiment reached the Capital early in the afternoon of the 25th, where they were heartily welcomed by the loyal people. They were the first troops that arrived at the seat of Government after the sad tragedy in Baltimore six days before,[a] and they were hailed as the harbingers of positive safety for the Capital. Although they were wearied and footsore, they marched up Pennsylvania Avenue with the firm and united step which always characterized their parade marches in Broadway, and halted only when they arrived at the front of the "White House," whither they went to pay homage to the President, whom they had come to protect and support. Their discipline and fine appearance were a' marvel, and loyal crowds followed them to the President's house, and filled the air with vociferous cheering.[1] Then they marched to the Capitol, and made their quarters there; and that night the anxious loyal citizens of Washington went to rest with a sense of positive security. That security was well assured the next day, when the Seventh, Twelfth, and Seventy-first New York Volunteer Regiments arrived, and reported the Fifth, Eighth, and Sixty-ninth at Annapolis.

* April 19, 1861.

Baltimore, in the mean time, had become firmly grasped by the secessionists; and the authorities there, civil and military, had prepared to dispute the passage of any more loyal troops through their city. Armed men flocked into the town from the country, with all sorts of weapons, scarcely knowing for what purpose; while the secessionists in the city were organized for treasonable work under Colonel J. R. Trimble and others.

WINANS'S STEAM-GUN.

On Sunday, the 21st, cannon were exercised openly in the streets. A remarkable piece of ordnance, called a steam-gun, invented by Charles S. Dickinson, and manufactured by Ross Winans, a wealthy iron-worker of Baltimore, was purchased by the city authorities at the price of twenty-five hundred dollars. Much was expected of this invention, for it was claimed that it could throw two hundred balls a minute a distance of two miles. It was supposed to be ball-proof, and admirably adapted to the purposes of city defense.[2] Marshal Kane, under the direction of a city ordinance, passed

---

[1] This is the almost universal testimony. There is one dissenting voice. In a letter to the author, dated "Arlington House, May 1, 1861," the writer says:—"I was in Washington the day the Seventh Regiment arrived, the one most entitled perhaps to a warm reception here, and their march through the city resembled a funeral procession. Not a *single cheer* was raised from even a small boy among the motley crowd that followed them, and the countenances of the citizens were dark and sad. I saw tears in the eyes of several. When the regiment reached the President's house, there was some cheering from men *hired* for the purpose, I am told. These are plain *facts* and speak for themselves."

[2] This gun was protected by a ball-proof cone of iron, and, with its motive-power apparatus, mounted on

by the Common Council, ordered the National flag to be humbled for thirty days, by forbidding its display during that time, under the pretense that it would cause " a disturbance of the public peace." The old flag suddenly disappeared, and on the day when the order went forth, only a single banner was seen in the harbor of Baltimore, and that was a secession ensign floating over the steamer *Logan*. For a few days, it seemed as if all patriotism, all national feeling had suddenly died out in Maryland, and the exasperation felt toward the city of Baltimore in the Free-labor States was intense and universal. The stand taken by its authorities was perilous to its very existence. That action was considered a national insult; and, so long as that gate stood barred across the great highway to the Capital against the passage of troops summoned for its protection, the nation was dishonored. The people could hardly be restrained from banding in thousands and tens of thousands, for the purpose of opening that way. "Turn upon it the guns of Fort McHenry!" cried one.—"Lay it in ashes!" cried another.—"Fifty thousand men may be raised in an hour," exclaimed a third, " to march through Baltimore."

> " Bow down in haste thy guilty head!
>   God's wrath is swift and sore:
> The sky with gathering bolts is red—
> Cleanse from thy skirts the slaughter shed,
> Or make thyself an ashen bed,
>   O Baltimore!"

wrote Bayard Taylor. And an active citizen of New York (George Law), in a letter to the President, in which he declared that the people of the Free-labor States demanded of the Government measures to open and establish lines of direct communication with the Capital, said: "Unless this is done, they will be compelled to take the matter into their own hands, let the consequences be what they may, and let them fall where they will." The same sentiment animated the Government as soon as

RAILWAY BATTERY.

it felt assured of its own safety by the presence of many troops, and measures were speedily adopted for taking military possession of Baltimore. Preparations were made to repair the burnt bridges between Havre

---

four wheels, so as to be quickly moved from place to place. It could be made to project missiles of any size, from a bullet to a 100-pound cannon-ball. It was believed that one of these, of musket-ball caliber, would be terribly destructive in front of an army, mowing down regiments like grass. It was specially recommended for sea-fights. Its efficiency was never tested. It was captured from the insurgents in less than a month after the city of Baltimore purchased it, by Colonel Jones, of the Sixth Massachusetts Regiment, when on its way to the insurgent camp at Harper's Ferry, and was placed in position to guard the viaduct over the Patuxent of the Washington Branch of the Baltimore and Ohio Railway.

de Grace and Baltimore; and a singular railway battery was constructed in Philadelphia, to be used for the protection of the men engaged in the work. It was a car made of heavy boiler iron, musket-proof, with a 24-pound cannon mounted at one end, on a gun-carriage. This was to fire grape, canister, and chain shot, while a garrison of sixty men inside would have an opportunity to employ musketry, through holes pierced in the sides and ends for the purpose.

General Scott planned a grand campaign against Baltimore. "I suppose," he said, in a letter to General Butler, General Patterson, and others,[a] "that a column from this place [Washington] of three thousand men, another from York of three thousand men, a third from Perryville, or Elkton, by land or water, or both, of three thousand men, and a fourth from Annapolis, by water, of three thousand men, might suffice." Twelve thousand men, it was thought, might be wanted for the enterprise. They were not in hand, for at least ten thousand troops were yet needed at the capital, to give it perfect security. The Lieutenant-General thought some time must elapse before the expedition could be undertaken against the rebellious city.

[a] April 29, 1861.

General Butler had other views. He had become satisfied that the secession element in Baltimore was numerically weak, and that the Union men, with a little help, might easily reverse the order of things there. He hastened to Washington to consult with General Scott. He did not venture to express any dissent to the plans of the General-in-chief. He simply asked permission to take a regiment or two from Annapolis, march them to the Relay House, on the Baltimore and Ohio Railway, nine miles from Baltimore, and hold it, so as to cut the secessionists off from facile communication with Harper's Ferry. It was granted. He then inquired, what were the powers of a General commanding a Department. "Absolute," replied the Lieutenant-General; "he can do whatever he thinks best, unless restricted by specific orders or military law." Butler ascertained that Baltimore was within his Military Department, and, with a plan of bold operations teeming his brain, he returned to Annapolis.

At the close of April, General Butler had full ten thousand men under his command at Annapolis, and an equal number were guarding the seat of Government. Already the Unionists of Maryland were openly asserting their rights and showing their strength. An extraordinary session of the Legislature, called by Governor Hicks at Annapolis, was not held there, for obvious reasons, but was opened on the 27th,[b] at Frederick, about sixty miles north of Baltimore, and far away from National troops. In his message to that body, the Governor said it was his solemn conviction that the only safety for Maryland lay in its maintaining a neutral position in the controversy, that State having "violated no right of either section." He said: "I cannot counsel Maryland to take sides against the General Government, until it shall commit outrages upon us which would justify us in resisting its authority. As a consequence, I can give no other counsel than that we shall array ourselves for Union and peace, and thus preserve our soil from being polluted with the blood of brethren. Thus, if war

[b] April.

---

must be between the North and the South, we may force the contending parties to transfer the field of battle from our soil, so that our lives and property may be secure."

The secessionists in the Legislature, doubtful of gaining control of Maryland by constitutional means, if not made circumspect by a threat, said to have been made by General Butler, that he would arrest them all if they should pass an Ordinance of Secession, changed their tactics. They procured a vote against the secession of the State, and then proceeded to appoint a State Board of Public Safety, which was invested with full powers to control the organization and direction of all the military forces in the commonwealth, and to " adopt measures for its safety, peace, and defense." The members of the Board were all active secessionists, excepting Governor Hicks. They were not required to take the usual oath to support the Constitution of the United States, and were left free to act in accordance with their revolutionary proclivities. It was evident from the composition of the Board, and the character of the men who established it—men who openly advocated the secession of Maryland, and uniformly denounced the acts of the National Government as tyrannical—that it was to be used as a revolutionary machine, fraught with immense power to do mischief. The loyal people of the State, perceiving with amazement the practical patriotism of the inhabitants of the Free-labor States, and feeling the tread of tens of thousands of armed men hurrying across Maryland to the defense of the Government, recovered, in the presence of this new danger, from the paralysis produced by the terrible events of the 19th, and were aroused to action. A Home Guard of Unionists was formed in Frederick, under the direct observation of the disloyal Legislature. Similar action was taken in other parts of the State, especially in the more northern portion; and, on the evening of the 4th of May, an immense Union meeting was held in Baltimore, whereat the creation of the Board of Public Safety and other revolutionary acts of the Legislature were heartily condemned. On the same day, Otho Scott, Robert McLane, and W. J. Ross, a Committee of that Legislature, were in Washington, remonstrating with the President and Secretary of War against the military occupation, by National troops, of the capital of Maryland and of some of the railways of the State. They returned to their constituents " painfully confident," they said, " that a war was to be waged to reduce all the seceding States to allegiance to the United States Government, and that the whole military power of the Federal Government would be exerted to accomplish that purpose."[1]

General Butler was aware of the latent force of the Unionism of Maryland, and of its initial developments, and felt that it was time for him to move. He had proposed to himself to do at once, with a few men, what the Lieutenant-General, with more caution, had proposed to do at some indefinite time in the future, with twelve thousand men, namely, seize and hold the city of Baltimore. Accordingly, on Saturday afternoon, the 4th of May, while the Commissioners of the Maryland Legislature were protesting before the President against Butler's occupation of their political capital, he issued orders for the Eighth New York and Sixth Massachusetts regiments, with Major A. M. Cook's battery of the Boston Light Artillery, to be ready to march at two o'clock the next morning. These troops were in Washington City. At dawn on the 5th, they left the Capital in thirty cars; and about two hours later they alighted at the Relay House, within nine

THE RELAY HOUSE IN 1864.

miles of Baltimore, seized the railway station there, spread over the hills in scouting parties, and prepared to plant cannon so as to command the Washington Junction of the Baltimore and Ohio Railway at the great viaduct over the Patapsco Valley, and the roads leading to Baltimore and Harper's Ferry. General Butler accompanied the troops, and established a camp on the hills, a quarter of a mile from the Relay House, near the residences of P. O'Hern and J. H. Luckett. The writer visited this interesting spot late in 1864. Brigadier-General John R. Kenly, whose meritorious services in Baltimore will be noticed presently, was then in command there. On the hights back of the Relay House, near which General Butler encamped, was a regular earthwork, called Fort Dix, and a substantial block-house built of timber, which is seen in our little picture. It was a commanding position, overlooking the narrow valley of the Patapsco above the viaduct toward Ellicott's mills, up which passes the railway to Harper's Ferry, and the expanding valley and beautifully rolling country below the viaduct, wherein may be seen, nestling at the foot of hills, the ancient village of Elkridge Landing, to which, in former days, the Patapsco was navigable. Near here, on a range of lofty hills running northward from Elk-

GREAT VIADUCT AT THE WASHINGTON JUNCTION.

ridge, are the residences of several gentlemen of wealth, among them J. H. B. Latrobe, a distinguished citizen of Maryland, whose house may be observed on the wooded hills seen beyond the viaduct in the little accompanying picture.

General Butler remained a little more than a week at the Relay House, preparing to carry out his plan for seizing Baltimore. Meanwhile General Patterson, anxious to vindicate the dignity and honor of his Government, and to teach the secessionists of Maryland a practical lesson of its power, and compel them to submit to lawful authority, sent the First Pennsylvania Volunteer Artillery (Seventeenth in the line) and Sherman's Battery, in all nine hundred and thirty men, under the command of his son, Francis E. Patterson, to force a passage through Baltimore. These troops left Philadelphia on the 8th of May, and on the following morning, accompanied by a portion of the Third Infantry Regiment of regulars from Texas, embarked on the steamers *Fanny Cadwalader* and *Maryland*, and went down Chesapeake Bay. The whole force under Colonel Patterson was about twelve hundred. They debarked at Locust Point, near Fort McHenry, under cover of the guns of the *Harriet Lane* and a small gunboat, at about four o'clock in the afternoon of the same day, in the presence of the Mayor of Baltimore, the Police Commissioners, and Marshal Kane and a considerable police force.[1] A counter-revolution in public sentiment was then making the Unionists of Maryland happy. The presence of troops at the Relay House was promoting and stimulating the Union feeling amazingly, and these troops landed and passed through the city on their way toward Washington without molestation. The wharves were crowded with excited citizens when the debarkation took place, and hundreds of these gave the Pennsylvanians hearty shouts of welcome. These were the first of that immense army that streamed through Baltimore without hinderance, thousands after thousands, while the great war that ensued went on.

General Butler was visited at the Relay House by many Unionists from Baltimore, who gave him all desired information; and he received such communications from General Scott, on application, that he felt warranted in moving upon the town. He had informed Scott of the increasing power of the Unionists in Baltimore; reminded him that the city was in the Department of Annapolis; and expressed the belief that, with his force in hand at the Relay House, he could march through it. Colonel (afterward General) Schuyler Hamilton, who had accompanied the New York Seventh to Washington, was then on the staff of the General-in-chief. He had learned the metal of General Butler, and was not inclined to cast any obstacles in his way. The orders of General Scott, prepared by him, gave Butler permission to arrest secessionists in and out of Baltimore, prevent armed insurgents from going to join those already in force at Harper's Ferry, and to look after a large quantity of gunpowder said to be stored in a church in Baltimore for the use of the secessionists. To do this, Butler must use force; and as no word that came from the General-in-chief forbade his going into Baltimore with his troops, he prepared to do so. Already a party of the Sixth Massachusetts had performed good service, in connection with a company of the New York Eighth and two guns of the Boston Light Artillery, all under Major Cook, in capturing Winans's steam-gun at Ellicott's Mills,[a] together with Dickinson,[2] the inventor. Butler had promised Colonel Jones, of the Sixth, which had fought its way through Bal-

a May 10. 1861.

---

[1] It is related that when the troops landed, Marshal Kane, with a false pretense of loyalty, approached Major Sherman of the battery, and said: "Can I be of any assistance to you, Major?"—"Who are you, Sir?" inquired Sherman.—"I am Marshal of the Police of Baltimore," he replied, "and would render any assistance."—"O, yes," Sherman replied, "we have heard of you in the region from whence we came; we have no need of you. We can help ourselves." The Marshal retired, with all his force, an object of supreme contempt.

[2] See page 440. Winans was an aged man, a thorough secessionist, and worth, it was estimated, about

timore on the 19th of April, that his regiment should again march through that city, and now it was invited to that duty.

Toward the evening of the 13th, the entire Sixth Massachusetts Regiment, and a part of the New York Eighth, with the Boston Light Artillerymen and two field-pieces—about one thousand men in all—and horses belonging to the General and his staff, were on a train of cars headed toward Harper's Ferry. Before this train was a short one, bearing fifty men, who were ordered up to Frederick to arrest Winans. When these trains moved up along the margin of the Patapsco Valley, a spy of the Baltimore conspirators started for that city with two fast trotting horses, to carry the important information. The trains moved slowly for about two miles, and then backed as slowly to the Relay House, and past it, and at twilight had backed to the Camden Street Station in Baltimore. Intensely black clouds in the van of an approaching thunder-storm were brooding over the city, threatening a

FEDERAL HILL IN MAY, 1861.[1]

fierce tempest, and few persons were abroad, or aware of this portentous arrival. The Mayor was informed of it in the course of the evening, and at once wrote a note to General Butler, saying that the sudden arrival of a large body of troops would create much surprise, and he would like to know whether the General intended to remain at the station, that the police might be notified, and take proper precautions for preserving the peace. Butler and his troops had disappeared in the gloom when the messenger with this note arrived at the Station; but the inquiry was fully answered, to the astonishment of the whole city, loyal and disloyal, early the next morning, by a proclamation from the General in the columns of the faithful *Clipper*, dated "Federal Hill, Baltimore, May 14, 1861," in which it was announced that a detachment under his command occupied the city, "for the purpose, among other things, of enforcing respect and obedience to the laws, as well of the

---

fifteen millions of dollars. It was reported that he contributed largely in aid of the revolutionists; and that, among other things for their use, he manufactured five thousand pikes in his iron-works. He was arrested on a charge of treason, but the lenient Government released him.

[1] This is a view of Federal Hill before General Butler occupied it. It was so named, because, upon its summit, there was a grand celebration in honor of the final ratification of the "Federal" or National Constitution, in 1788. It overlooks the harbor; and upon it was a telegraphic station, the old-fashioned semaphoric apparatus being used. It is seen toward the left of the picture.

State, if requested thereto by the civil authorities, as of the United States laws, which are being violated within its limits by some malignant and traitorous men; and in order to testify the acceptance by the Federal Government of the fact, that the city and all the well-intentioned portion of its. inhabitants are loyal to the Union and the Constitution, and are to be so regarded and treated by all."

How came Butler and his men on Federal Hill? was a question upon thousands of lips on that eventful morning. They had moved stealthily from the station in the gloom, at half-past seven in the evening, piloted by Colonel Robert Hare, of Ellicott's Mills, and Captain McConnell, through Lee, Hanover, Montgomery, and Light Streets, to the foot of Federal Hill. The night was intensely dark, made so by the impending storm. The flashes of lightning and peals of thunder were terrific, but the rain was withheld until they had nearly reached their destination. Then it came like a flood, just as they commenced the ascent of the declivity. "The spectacle was grand," said the General to the writer, while on the *Ben Deford*, lying off Fort Fisher one pleasant evening in December, 1864. "I was the first to reach the summit. The rain was falling in immense volumes, and the lightning flashes followed each other in rapid succession, making the point of every bayonet in that slow-moving column appear like a tongue of flame, and the burnished brass cannon like sheets of fire."

BUTLER'S HEAD-QUARTERS ON FEDERAL HILL.

Officers and men were thoroughly drenched, and on the summit of the hill they found very little shelter. A house of refreshment, with a long upper and lower piazza, kept by a German, was taken possession of and made the General's head-quarters; and there, dripping with the rain, he sat down and wrote his proclamation, which appeared in the morning. His men had procured wood when the storm ceased, lighted fires, and were making themselves comfortable. At eight o'clock, long after his proclamation had been scattered over the town, he received the Mayor's message of the previous evening. Important events had transpired since it was written, twelve hours before. The Massachusetts Sixth had again marched through Baltimore, not, as before, the objects of assault by a brutal mob, but as a potential force, to hold that mob and all others in subserviency to law and order, and welcomed as deliverers by thousands of loyal citizens.

So confident was General Butler in the moral and physical strength of his position, and of the salutary influence of his proclamation, in which he promised security to the peaceful and true, punishment to the turbulent and false, and justice to all, that he rode through the city with his staff on the day after his arrival, dined leisurely at the Gillmore House, and had conferences with friends. In that proclamation he forbade transportation of supplies to the insurgents; asked for commissary stores, at fair prices, to the amount of forty thousand rations, and also clothing; forbade all assemblages of irregular military organizations; directed State military officers to report to him; offered aid to the corporate authorities of Baltimore, in the due administration of law; forbade the display of any secession flags or banners; and assured the people that he had such confidence in their loyalty that of the many thousands of troops which he might immediately concentrate there, he had come with scarcely more than a guard. He made some important seizures of materials of war intended for the insurgents;[1] cast Ross Winans into Fort McHenry, in accordance with orders from Washington, and was preparing to try him by court-martial for his alleged crimes, when a letter, bearing a sting of reproof, came from General Scott, saying:—"Your hazardous occupation of Baltimore was made without my knowledge, and, of course, without my approbation. It is a God-send that it was without a conflict of arms. It is also reported that you have sent a detachment to Frederick, but this is impossible. Not a word have I heard from you as to either movement. Let me hear from you."

The operations of a night with a thousand men and a ready pen had made a future campaign with twelve thousand men, which the General-in-chief had planned, unnecessary. The Lieutenant-General thought that the Brigadier had used too daringly the "absolute" power accorded to a "commander of a department," unless "restricted by specific orders or military law," and overlooking, for the moment, the immense advantages gained for the Government by such exercise of power, he insisted upon the recall of General Butler from Baltimore. It was done. Viewed in the light of to-day, that recall appears like an almost fatal mistake. "I always said," wrote Mr. Cameron, then Secretary of War, from St. Petersburg, many months afterward, "that if you

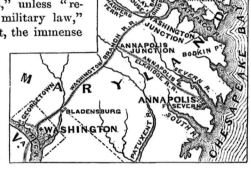

THE DEPARTMENT OF ANNAPOLIS.

had been left in Baltimore, the rebellion would have been of short duration."[2]

There was no rebuke in President Lincoln's recall of General Butler

---

[1] General Butler ascertained that a large quantity of arms, in charge of the city authorities, were stored in a warehouse on the corner of Gay and Second Streets, and he sent Colonel Hare, with thirty-five soldiers, to demand their surrender into his custody. This force reached the warehouse at about four o'clock in the afternoon, where three policemen were found in charge. Hare demanded the surrender of the building and its contents, in the name of the National Government. The policemen refused compliance, until they should receive orders to that effect from Marshal Kane, to whom word was immediately sent. A large crowd rapidly collected at the spot, but were quiet. Kane soon appeared, with a deputy marshal and several policemen, when Hare, in the name of General Butler, repeated the demand for a surrender. Kane replied that he could not do so without the sanction of the Police Commissioners. In the mean time, Commissioner J. W. Davis had arrived, and, after consultation, he hastened to the office of the Board of Police, when that body determined to surrender the arms under protest, and they did so. The doors of the warehouse were then opened, and thirty-five drays and furniture wagons were employed in carrying away the arms. They were in boxes, ready for shipment to the insurgents in Virginia or elsewhere, and consisted of two thousand two hundred muskets, and four thousand and twenty pikes or spears, manufactured by Winans. While the vehicles were a-loading, the crowd, which had become large, were somewhat agitated by persons who desired a collision, but there was very little disturbance of any kind. The arms were taken to Federal Hill, and from there to Fort McHenry.

[2] Parton's *General Butler at New Orleans*, page 117.

from Baltimore, in compliance with the wishes of General Scott. On the contrary, it had the appearance of commendation, for he immediately offered him the commission of a Major-General of Volunteers, and the command of a much more extended military district, including Eastern Virginia and the two Carolinas, with his head-quarters at Fortress Monroe. He was succeeded in command at Baltimore by General Cadwalader, of Philadel-- phia, and the troops were temporarily withdrawn. Afterward the Fifth New York Regiment (Zouave), Colonel Abraham Duryèe, occupied Federal Hill, and thereon built the strong earthwork known as Fort Federal Hill, whose cannon commanded both the town and Fort McHenry.

The 14th of May was a memorable one in the annals of Maryland, as the time when the tide of secession, which for weeks had been threatening to ingulf it in revolution, was absolutely checked, and the Unionists of the State were placed upon solid vantage-ground, from which they were never driven a line, but were strengthened every hour. On that day General Butler broke the power of the conspirators, by the military occupation of Baltimore and the promulgation of his proclamation, which disarmed treason. On that day the dangerously disloyal Legislature adjourned, and Governor Hicks, relieved of the pressure of rampant treachery around him, and assured by the Secretary of War that Maryland troops would not be ordered out of the State, issued a proclamation calling for the four regiments named in the Secretary's requisition for militia as the quota of that Commonwealth. Thenceforth the tongues of loyal Marylanders were unloosed, and treason became weaker every hour; and their State was soon numbered among the stanchest of loyal Commonwealths, outstripping in practical patriotism Delaware, Kentucky, and Missouri. On that eventful 14th of May, the veteran Major W. W. Morris, in command at Fort McHenry, near Baltimore (which had lately been well garrisoned), first gave practical force to the suspension of the privilege of the writ of *habeas corpus*, which the exigency of the times seemed to give constitutional sanction for.[1] A man claiming to be a soldier of the Maryland State Militia, was imprisoned in Fort McHenry. Judge Giles, of Baltimore, issued a writ of *habeas corpus* for his release, which Major Morris refused to obey. His letter to the Judge was a spirited protest against the treasonable practices around him, and seemed to be a full justification of his action. "At the date of issuing your writ," he said, "and for two weeks previous, the city in which you live, and where your court has been held, was entirely under the control of revolutionary authorities. Within that period United States soldiers, while committing no offense, had been perfidiously attacked and inhumanly murdered in your streets;* no punishment had been awarded, and, I believe, no arrests had been made for these atrocious crimes;* supplies of provisions intended for this garrison had been stopped; the intention to cap-

          * April 19, 1861.

---

[1] The second clause of the ninth section of the first Article of the National Constitution says:—"The privilege of the writ of *habeas corpus* shall not be suspended, unless when in cases of rebellion or invasion the public safety may require it."

[2] In the Maryland Legislature, S. T. Wallis moved—"That the measures adopted and conduct pursued by the authorities of the City of Baltimore, on Friday, the 19th of April, and since that time, be, and the same are hereby, made valid by the General Assembly." This would cover the conspirators and their tools, the mob, from punishment. In furtherance of this project for shielding the guilty, T. Parkins Scott proposed, in the same body, a bill to suspend the operations of the criminal laws, and that the Grand Jury should be stopped from finding indictments against any of the offenders.—*Baltimore Clipper*, June 23, 1861.

ture this fort had been boldly proclaimed; your most public thoroughfares were daily patrolled by large numbers of troops, armed and clothed, at least in part, with articles stolen from the United States; and the Federal flag, while waving over the Federal offices, was cut down by some person wearing the uniform of a Maryland soldier.[1] To add to the foregoing, an assemblage elected in defiance of law, but claiming to be the legislative body of your State, and so recognized by the Executive of Maryland, was debating the Federal compact. If all this be not rebellion, I know not what to call it. I certainly regard it as sufficient legal cause for suspending the privilege of the writ of *habeas corpus*." He added :—"If, in an experience of thirty-three years, you have never before known the writ to be disobeyed, it is only because such a contingency in political affairs as the present has never before arisen."

Since the 19th of April, the Government had felt compelled to resort to extraordinary measures for its preservation, and much was done "without due form of law," excepting what the exercise of the war powers of the President might justify. On the day after the massacre at Baltimore, the

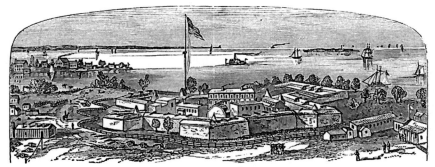

VIEW OF FORT M'HENRY.

original dispatches in the telegraph offices in all the principal cities in the Free-labor States, received during a year previously, were, by order of the Government, issued on the 19th,[a] seized by the United States Marshals at the same hour, namely, three o'clock in the

* April, 1861.

afternoon. The object was, to obtain evidence of the complicity of politicians in those States with the conspirators. Every dispatch that seemed to indicate such complicity was sent to Washington, and the Government was furnished with such positive evidence of active sympathy with the insurgents that the offenders became exceedingly cautious and far less mischievous. At about the same time, the necessity for arresting and imprisoning seditious persons in the Free-labor States seemed clear to the apprehension of the Government, and such were made on simply the warrant of the Secretary of State. These offenders were confined in Fort McHenry, at Baltimore; Fort Lafayette, near New York, and Fort Warren, in Boston harbor. Writs of *habeas*

---

[1] This was also done on Federal Hill, a few days before the arrival of General Butler, by order of Marshal Kane. A bold Union boy, standing near when the work was accomplished, exclaimed:—" Why don't you try your hand on *that* flag?" pointing to the one floating over Fort McHenry. The boy saved himself from punishment by the secessionists by superior fleetness of foot.

corpus were issued for their release. At first some of them were obeyed, but finally, by order of the Government, they were disregarded, and their issue ceased. The most notable of these cases, at the beginning, was that of John Merryman, a member of the Maryland Legislature, who was cast into Fort McHenry late in May. The Chief-Justice of the United States (R. B. Taney), residing in Baltimore, took action in the matter, but General Cadwalader, the commander of the department, refused to obey the mandates of this functionary, as well as that of the inferior judge, and the matter was dropped, excepting in the form of personal, newspaper, and legislative discussions of the subject, the chief questions at issue being, Which branch of the Government has the power to suspend the privilege of the writ? and Do circumstances warrant the exercise of that power? We will not discuss that question here. Many arrests were made; among them a large number of the members of the Maryland Legislature, the Mayors of Baltimore and Washington, Marshal Kane and the Police Commissioners of Baltimore, and a number of other prominent men throughout the country. Within the space of six months after the tragedy in Baltimore, no less than one hundred prisoners of state, to whom the privilege of the writ of *habeas corpus* was denied, were confined in Fort Lafayette alone.

The Government not only resorted to these extreme measures, but made greater preparations for a conflict of arms, plainly perceiving that *insurrection* was rapidly assuming the proportions of formidable and extended *rebellion*. By a proclamation on the 27th of April, the blockade[1] was extended to the ports of North Carolina and Virginia; and by another proclamation on the 3d of May, the President called into the service of the United States forty-two thousand volunteers for three years; ordered an increase of the regular Army of twenty-two thousand seven hundred and fourteen officers and enlisted men, for not less than one year nor more than three years; and for the enlistment of eighteen thousand seamen for the naval service. This was the first call for *volunteers*, the former requisition being for the militia of the several States,[2] full one hundred and fifty thousand of whom were organized or were forming at the close of April. The response to this was equally if not more remarkable. The enthusiasm of the people was unbounded. Money and men were offered in greater abundance than the Government seemed to need. The voluntary contributions offered to the public treasury, and for the fitting out of troops and maintaining their families, by individuals, associations, and corporations, amounted, at the beginning of May, to full *forty millions of dollars!*

Six weeks earlier than this, that sagacious Frenchman, Count Agénor de Gasparin, one of the few foreigners who seemed to comprehend the American people, and the nature and significance of the impending struggle, wrote, almost prophetically, saying:—"At the present hour, the Democracy of the South is about to degenerate into demagogism. But the North presents quite a different spectacle. Mark what is passing there; pierce beneath appearances, beneath the inevitable wavering of a *début*, so well prepared for

---

[1] See page 372.
[2] The Act of 1795, under the authority of which the President called for seventy-five thousand militia, restricted their service to three months. See notes 2 and 3, page 336.

by the preceding Administration, and you will find the firm resolution of a people uprising. Who speaks of the end of the United States? This end seemed approaching but lately, in the hour of prosperity; then, honor was compromised, esteem for the country was lowered, institutions were becoming corrupted apace; the moment seemed approaching when the confederation, tainted with Slavery, could not but perish with it. Now, every thing has changed in aspect. The friends of America should take confidence, for its greatness is inseparable, thank God! from the cause of justice. *Justice can not do wrong.* I like to recall this maxim, when I consider the present state of America."[1]

At the middle of May, Washington City was safe, for thousands of well-armed loyal men were within its borders. Troops were quartered in the immense Patent Office building. The Capitol was a vast citadel. Its legislative halls, its rotunda, and other rooms were filled with soldiery, and its basement galleries were converted into store-rooms for barrels of beef, pork, and other materials for army rations in great abundance. Under the direction of Lieutenant T. J. Cate, of the Massachusetts Sixth, the vaults under the broad

GOVERNMENT BAKERIES AT THE CAPITOL.

terrace on the western front of the Capitol were converted into bakeries, where sixteen thousand loaves of bread were baked every day. The chimneys of the ovens pierced the terrace at the junction of the freestone pavement and the grassy slope of the glacis, as seen in the picture; and there, for months, smoke poured forth in dense black columns like the issues of a smoldering volcano. Before the summer had begun, Washington City was an immense garrisoned town, and strong fortifi-

---

[1] *The Uprising of a Great People :* by Count Agénor de Gasparin. Translated by Mary L. Booth. These sentences were written in March, 1861, just after President Lincoln's Inaugural Address reached Europe, and when the legislative proceedings and public meetings in the Free-labor States were just made known there, and gave assurance that the great body of the Nation was loyal and would sustain the incoming Administration. Speaking of the departure of Mr. Lincoln for Washington, and the farewell to his friends and neighbors, mentioned on page 275, the Count exclaims : "What a *début* for a Government! Have there been many inaugurations here below of such thrilling solemnity ? Do uniforms and plumes, the roar of cannon, triumphal arches, and vague appeals to Providence, equal these simple words, ' Pray for me!' ' We will pray for you.' Ah! courage, Lincoln ! the friends of freedom and of America are with you. Courage! you hold in your hands the destinies of a great principle and of a great people. Courage! you have to resist your friends and to face your foes; it is the fate of all who seek to do good on the earth. Courage! you will have need of it to-morrow, in a year. to the end ; you will have need of it in peace and in war; you will have need of it to avert the compromise, in peace or war, of that noble progress which it is your charge to accomplish, more than in conquests of Slavery ! Courage! your *rôle*, as you have said, may be inferior to no other, not even to that of Washington : to raise up the United States will not be less glorious than to have founded them."

cations were rapidly growing upon the hills around it.   And yet the conspirators still dreamed of possessing it.   Two days after their Convention at Montgomery adjourned to meet in Richmond on the 20th of July, Alexander H. Stephens, in a speech at Atlanta,[a] in Georgia, after referring to the occupation of the National edifices at Washington   ^{a May 23, 1861.} by the soldiery, said :—"Their filthy spoliation of the public buildings and the works of art at the Capitol, and their preparations to destroy them, are strong evidences to my mind that they do not intend to hold or defend that place, but to abandon it, after having despoiled and laid it in ruins.   Let them destroy it, savage-like, if they will.   We will rebuild it.   We will make the structures more glorious.   Phenix-like, new and more substantial structures will rise from its ashes.   Planted anew, under the auspices of our superior institutions, it will live and flourish throughout all ages."

At the beginning of May, by fraud, by violence, and by treachery, the conspirators and their friends had robbed the Government to the amount of forty millions of dollars ; put about forty thousand armed men in the field, twenty-five thousand of whom were at that period concentrating in Virginia ; sent emissaries abroad, with the name of Commissioners, to seek recognition and aid from foreign powers ; commissioned numerous pirates to prey upon the commerce of the United States ; extinguished the lights of light-houses and beacons along the coasts of the Slave-labor States, from Hampton Roads to the Rio Grande,[1] and enlisted actively in their revolutionary schemes the Governors of thirteen States, and large numbers of leading politicians in other States.   INSURRECTION had become REBELLION; and the loyal people of the country, and the National Government, beginning to comprehend the magnitude and potency of the movement, accepted it as such, and addressed themselves earnestly to the task of its suppression.

---

[1] The light-houses and beacons seized, and lights extinguished, commencing with that on Cape Henry, in Virginia, and ending with Point Isabel, in Texas, numbered one hundred and thirty-one. Of these, thirteen were in Virginia, twenty-seven in North Carolina, fourteen in South Carolina, thirteen in Georgia, eighteen in Florida, eight in Alabama, twenty-four in Louisiana, and fourteen in Texas.

CHAPTER XIX.

EVENTS IN THE MISSISSIPPI VALLEY.—THE INDIANS.

HILE thousands of the loyal people of New England and of the other Free-labor States eastward of the Alleghanies were hurrying to the field, and pouring out their wealth like water in support of the Government, those of the region westward of these lofty hills and northward of the Ohio River were equally patriotic and demonstrative. They had watched with the deepest interest the development of the conspiracy for the overthrow of the Republic, and when the President's call for the militia of the country to arrest the treasonable movements reached them, they responded to it with alacrity by thousands and tens of thousands and hundreds of thousands.

The Legislature of Ohio, as we have observed, had spoken out early,[1] and pledged the resources of the State to the maintenance of the authority of the National Government. This pledge was reiterated, in substance, on the 14th of March, when that body, by vote, declared its high approval of President Lincoln's Inaugural Address. On the day when Fort Sumter was attacked,[a] an act of the Legislature, providing for the enrollment of the militia of the State, became a law; likewise another, for the regulation of troops to be mustered into the National service. Provision was also made for the defense of the State, whose peace was liable to disturbance by parties from the Slave-labor States of Virginia and Kentucky, between whom and Ohio was only the dividing line of a narrow river. Appropriations for war purposes were made on a liberal scale; and when the twenty days, allowed by the President in his proclamation for the insurgents to lay down their arms,[2] had expired, a stirring order went out from the Adjutant-General of the State (H. B. Carrington), for the organization of one hundred thousand men as a reserved force; for sagacious observers of the signs of the times, like Governor Dennison, plainly perceived that a great war was impending. The people contributed freely of their means, for fitting out troops and providing for their families. George B. McClellan, who had held the commission of captain by brevet after meritorious services in Mexico, but was now in civil service as superintendent of the Ohio and Mississippi Railway, was commissioned a major-general by the Governor, and appointed commander of all the forces of the State. Camps for rendezvous and instruction were speedily formed, one of the most important of which was Camp Dennison, on the line of the Cincinnati and Columbus Railway, and occupying a position on the pleasant slopes of the hills that skirt

Note in margin: a April 12, 1861.

the Miami Valley, about eighteen miles from Cincinnati. So Ohio began to prepare for the struggle.

The people of Indiana moved as promptly and vigorously as those of Ohio. In March, the vigilant Governor Morton, seeing the storm gathering,

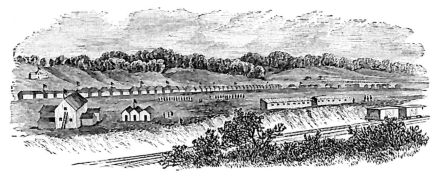

CAMP DENNISON.

went to Washington and procured about five thousand second-class muskets. These and a few others formed all the means at his command for arming the State, when the President's call reached him on Monday, the 15th of April. The militia of the State were unorganized, and there was no Adjutant-General to whom he might turn for aid, for the incumbent of that office refused to act. At that time there was an energetic young lawyer residing at Crawfordsville, who had served in Mexico at the age of nineteen years, and was well versed in military affairs. In the State Senate, of which he had been a member, he had vainly urged the adoption of measures for organizing the militia of the State. Fond of military maneuvers, he had formed a company and drilled them in the tactics of the Zouaves, several weeks before the famous corps of "Ellsworth's Zouaves" was organized. This lawyer was Lewis Wallace, who became a Major-General of Volunteers at an early period of the war that ensued.

O. P. MORTON.

Governor Morton called Wallace to his aid. A dispatch summoning him to Indianapolis reached him on Monday evening,[a] while he was trying a cause in Clinton County. He reported to the Governor the next morning. "The President has called on Indiana for six regiments to put down a rising rebellion," said Morton. "I have sent for you to assist me in the business. I want to appoint you Adjutant-General."—"Where is the Adjutant-General's office?" inquired Wallace.—"There is none," responded the Governor.—"Where are the books?"—"There are none."—"How many independent companies are there in the State?"—"I know of but three—

[a] April 15, 1861.

two here in Indianapolis, and your own."—"Where is the law defining the duties of the Adjutant-General?"—"There is no law on the subject—nothing pertaining to military organization."—"Well, then," said Wallace, "your immediate business is the raising of six regiments."—"That is it," said the Governor.—"Have you objections to giving me one of them after they are raised?" inquired Wallace.—"None at all; you shall have one of them," was the answer.

This brief conversation gives an idea of the absolute want of preparation for war on the part of Indiana when the rebellion broke out—a State that afterward sent about two hundred thousand troops to the field. It occurred on Tuesday morning succeeding the attack on Fort Sumter, and *April 19, 1861. on the following Friday night* Wallace reported to the Governor the sixty companies for the six regiments, complete, and in " Camp Morton," adjoining Indianapolis. He reported, in addition, more than eighty surplus companies, organized and ready to move. With the report he sent in his resignation, and a request for permission to go out and organize his own regiment. It was given, and within the next twenty-four hours he reported the " Eleventh Regiment Indiana Volunteers " (Zouaves), which did admirable service in Western Virginia a few weeks later, as organized, armed, and ready for marching orders.[1] Within four days after the President's call was promulgated from Washington, more than ten thousand Indianians were in camp. So Indiana, one of the younger States of the Union, also prepared for the struggle.

Illinois, under the vigorous leadership of Governor Yates, was early upon the war-path. At the beginning of April, Yates saw the clouds of most alarming difficulty surely gathering, while many others perceived nothing but a serene sky. On the 12th he issued a call for an extraordinary session of the Legislature on the 23d. On receiving the President's call for troops on the 15th, he issued a stirring appeal to the people, and in less than twenty-four hours afterward, four thousand men reported themselves ready and anxious for service. The quota of the State (six thousand) was more than filled by the 20th; and, pursuant to the request of the General Government, Yates sent two thousand of these State troops to possess and hold Cairo, at the confluence of the Ohio and Mississippi Rivers, a point of great strategic importance at that time, as we shall observe presently.

The Legislature of Illinois met at Springfield on the 23d, and two days afterward it was addressed by the distinguished United States Senator, Stephen A. Douglas, the rival of Mr. Lincoln for the Presidency of the Republic. When Treason lifted its arm to strike, Mr. Douglas instantly offered himself as a shield for his country. He abandoned all party alle-

---

[1] Wallace's regiment was a fair type of the Indiana Volunteers who composed her quota. It was an assemblage of mechanics, farmers, lawyers, doctors, and clergymen. They were all young and full of life, and ambitious, quick, shrewd, and enterprising. The regiment adopted the Zouave costume of Colonel Wallace's Crawfordsville Company. The color was steel gray, with a narrow binding of red on their jackets and the top of a small cap. The shirt was of dark blue flannel. The *Zouaves*, from whom they derived their name, were a body of Algerine soldiers, whom the French incorporated into their army after the conquest of Algeria. They were a wild, reckless set of men, in picturesque costume, and marked for their perfect discipline and particularly active tactics. The native Zouaves finally disappeared from the French army, but their costume and tactics were preserved. When French Zouave regiments performed eminent service in the Crimea, and gained immense popularity, Wallace and Ellsworth introduced the costume and system of maneuvers into this country, and at the beginning of the civil war large numbers of the volunteers assumed their garb and name.

giance, put away all political and personal prejudices, and, with the spirit and power of a sincere patriot, became the champion of the integrity of the Union.[1] As soon as he was relieved from his senatorial duties at Washington, he hastened to Illinois and began battle manfully. His speeches and conversation on the way had foreshadowed his course. To the Legislature of his State he addressed arguments and exhortations, powerful and persuasive. In Chicago he did likewise. Alas! his warfare was brief. He arrived at his home in Chicago on the 1st of May, suffering from inflammatory rheumatism. Disease assumed various and malignant forms in his system, and on the 3d of June he died.[2] His loss seemed to be peculiarly inauspicious at that time, when such men were so few and so much needed. But his words were living and of electric power. They were oracles for thousands, whose faith, and hope, and patriotism were strengthened thereby.[3] His last coherent utterances were exhortations to his children and his countrymen to stand by the Constitution and the Government.

STEPHEN A. DOUGLAS.

The Legislature of Illinois appropriated three millions of dollars for war purposes, and authorized the immediate organization of the entire militia force of the State, consisting of all able-bodied men between the ages of eighteen and forty-five years. Michigan was equally aroused by the call of the President. He asked of her one regiment only. Ten days afterward she

---

DOUGLAS LYING IN STATE.

[1] In his last speech, made at Chicago, at the beginning of May, he said:—"This is no time to go into a discussion of the causes that have produced these results. The conspiracy to break up the Union is a fact now known to all. Armies are being raised and war levied to accomplish it. There can be but two sides to this controversy. *Every man must be on the side of the United States or against it.* There can be no neutrals in this war. There can be none but traitors and patriots."

[2] The funeral of Senator Douglas was an imposing spectacle. His body was embalmed, and it lay in state in Bryan Hall, Chicago, where it was visited by thousands of sincere mourners. It was dressed in a full suit of black, and, the entire lid of the burial-case being removed, the whole person was exposed. The coffin was placed under a canopy or catafalque, in the center of the hall. The canopy was supported by four columns, and both were heavily draped in black. It was surmounted by an eagle, whose talons grasped the flag of the Union in a manner to allow it to lie, outspread, over a portion of the canopy. Each pillar was also surmounted by an eagle. At the foot of the coffin was a broken or truncated column, denoting the termination of a life in the midst of usefulness. At the head stood a vase of many kinds of flowers.

[3] One of the last letters written by Mr. Douglas was addressed to Mr. Hicox, Chairman of the Illinois State Democratic Committee, in reply to one addressed to him on the great topic of the hour. It was full of suggestions of great moment and patriotic sentiments. In it he said:—" I know of no mode by which, a loyal citizen may so well demonstrate his devotion to his country as by sustaining the flag, the Constitution, and the Union, under all circumstances, and under any administration (regardless of party politics), against all assailants at home and abroad. The course of Clay and Webster toward the administration of General Jackson, in the days of nullification, presents a noble and worthy example for all true patriots." He said in conclusion, "If we hope to regain and perpetuate the ascendency of our party, we should never forget that a man can not be a true Democrat unless he is a loyal patriot." This letter was dated May 10, 1861.

had five regiments ready for the field, and nine more were forming. Governor Blair called the Legislature together on the 7th of May, when that body made liberal appropriations for war purposes. The Legislature of Wisconsin, under the lead of Governor Randall, was equally liberal. That of Iowa and Minnesota followed the patriotic example. The enthusiasm of the people everywhere was wonderful. Before the close of the year (1861), Minnesota sent more men to the field than its entire population numbered in 1850.[1]

The position of the inhabitants of Kentucky, as a professedly loyal State, was peculiar and painful at this time. We have observed with what insulting words her Governor (Magoffin) responded to the President's call for troops,[2] and the fierce denunciations of that call by the *Louisville Journal*.[3] These demonstrations in high places against the war policy of the President, were followed by a great Union meeting in Louisville on the evening of the 18th of April,[a] over which James Guthrie[4] and other leading politicians of the State held controlling influence. At that meeting it was resolved that Kentucky reserved to herself " the right to choose her own position; and that, while her natural sympathies are with those who have a common interest in the protection of Slavery, she still acknowledges her loyalty and fealty to the Government of the United States, which she will cheerfully render *until that Government becomes aggressive, tyrannical, and regardless of our rights in Slave property*." They declared that the States were the peers of the National Government; and gave the world to understand that the latter should not be allowed to use " sanguinary or coercive " measures to " bring back the seceded States." They also resolved that they looked to the young men of the " Kentucky State Guard " as the " bulwark of the safety of the Commonwealth," and begged those who composed that Guard to remember that they were " pledged equally to fidelity to the United States and to Kentucky."

a 1861.

This meeting delighted the conspirators, for *conditional* Unionism was the best auxiliary they could have in loyal States, in their schemes for destroying the nationality of the Republic. If it could prevail—if it could be made the settled policy of a commonwealth—if it could stifle the enthusiasm of the people, and circumscribe their aspirations and their action within the limits of their own State, and the service of the single dominating class and interest for whose benefit and conservation the conspirators were making war, it would go far toward keeping the sword of the Republic in its scabbard, and to invite its enemies to plunder and destroy without stint.

The indorsement of the State Guard as the " bulwark of the Commonwealth," was a particularly hopeful sign of success for Governor Magoffin and his friends. That Guard had been formed under his auspices, for the ostensible purpose of defending the State against, What? It was hard to answer. Simon B. Buckner, a captain in the National Service, and a traitor without excuse, and then, evidently, in the secret service of the conspirators at Montgomery, was placed at the head of the Guard, and used his position effectively in seducing large numbers of the members from their allegiance to the old flag, and sending them as recruits to the armies of Jefferson Davis.

---

[1] Message of Governor Ramsay to the Minnesota Legislature.
[2] See page 337.
[3] See page 339.
[4] See page 233.

In this work the Governor gave him all the aid in his power. He tried to induce the Legislature to appropriate three millions of dollars to be used by himself and Buckner in "arming the State"—in other words, as the sequel shows, for corrupting the young men of the Commonwealth, and preparing the State for an armed alliance with the conspirators. Sustained by the declarations of the Conditional Unionists, and by resolutions of the lower house of the Legislature, which approved of the Governor's refusal to furnish troops to the National Government, and declared that the State should remain neutral during the impending contest,[1] Magoffin issued a proclamation of neutrality, in which he denounced the war as "a horrid, unnatural, and lamentable strife," and notified "all other States, separate or united, especially the United States and Confederate States," that he not only forbade either of them invading the soil of Kentucky, but also forbade its own citizens making "any hostile demonstrations against any of the aforesaid sovereignties."

Notwithstanding the position taken by the Legislature, that body, unwilling to assume so high a stand as the Governor, refused to indorse his proclamation, or to make the required appropriation of three millions of dollars. On the contrary, they so amended the militia law as to require the State Guard to swear allegiance to the National Government as well as to Kentucky; and Senator Rousseau (afterward a Major-General in the National Army) and others denounced the disunionists and their schemes in unmeasured terms.[2] As Buckner could not conscientiously allow his guard to take the new oath, it was not long before he led a large portion of them into the camp of the rebellion, and became a major-general in the "Confederate" army. Then the *Louisville Journal*, the organ of the "Conservatives," as the Conditional Unionists were called, indignantly cursed him,[a] saying :—" Away with your pledges and assurances— [a] September 27, 1861. with your protestations, apologies, and proclamations, at once and altogether ! Away, parricide ! Away, and do penance forever !—be shriven or be slain !

SIMON BOLIVAR BUCKNER.

—away ! You have less palliation than Attila—less boldness, magnanimity, and nobleness than Coriolanus. You are the Benedict Arnold of the day ! You are the Catiline of Kentucky ! Go, thou miscreant !" And when, in

---

February, 1862, Buckner and many of the Kentucky "State Guard" were captured at Fort Donelson, and he was sent a prisoner to Fort Warren, many of those who were deceived by the belief that the Guard was "the bulwark of the Commonwealth," demanded his delivery to the civil authorities of Kentucky, to be tried for treason against the State.

It has been claimed that the position taken by the Conditional Unionists in Kentucky at that time, saved the State from "drifting into secession." The President, estimating the importance of preserving the attachment of the Border Slave-labor States to the Union, at that crisis, and especially the populous and powerful Commonwealth of Kentucky, accepted the plea of expediency as sufficient, and acted accordingly for a long time. It was alleged and believed that a more decided and radical course would alienate the sympathies of the predominating slaveholding class in particular from the Union, and possibly drive them into alliance with their political and social affinities, the insurgents of the Cotton-growing States; and that only by assuming the attitude of neutrality, in deference to the slaveholders, could the State be kept out of the vortex of revolution. On the other hand, it is argued that such a course was not only not necessary, but unwise and mischievous. That the Unconditional Unionists in Kentucky and throughout the Slave-labor States were disheartened by that neutrality of leading politicians, cannot be denied; and that it amazed, disappointed, and perplexed the loyalists of the Free-labor States, is well known. It is alleged that it hurtfully restrained the patriotism of the great mass of the people of Kentucky, at the outset of the struggle, who showed their loyalty to the Union by giving a majority of fifty thousand votes in its favor at an election, in May, for delegates to a Border State Convention.[1] It is alleged that the Unconditional Unionists had the pledges of the Governors of Ohio, Indiana, and Illinois, to give them all needful military aid to keep their State out of the hands of its enemies; and that had the patriotic instincts of the people been allowed full play, regiment after regiment of loyal troops would have sprung into existence at the President's call, shortened the period of the war, and spared the State the sacrifice of millions of treasure and the more precious lives of thousands of her sons—the flower of her youth. It is declared that

---

[1] That election was held on the 4th of May. At a special election of Congressmen, held on the 20th of June, when only four-sevenths of the total vote of the State was cast, the Unionists had a majority of over fifty thousand. They elected *nine* representatives, and the secessionists only *one*. That one was Henry C. Burnet, who afterward joined the "Confederates." The Border State Convention was proposed by Virginians, and was held at Frankfort, Kentucky, on the 27th of May. It was a failure. There were no delegates present from Virginia, and only five beside those of Kentucky. Four of these were from Missouri and one from Tennessee. John J. Crittenden presided. The convention was as "neutral" as possible. It very properly deprecated civil war as terrible and ruinous to every interest, and exhorted the people to hold fast "to that sheet-anchor of republican liberty," the right of the majority, whose will has been constitutionally expressed, to govern. The wrongs of "the South," and the "sectionalism of the North," were spoken of as chief causes of the trouble at hand; but while it condemned the rebellion, it failed to exhort the loyal people to put it down. It recommended a voluntary convention of all the States, and to ask Congress to propose "such constitutional amendments" as should "secure to the slaveholders their legal rights, and allay their apprehensions in regard to possible encroachments in the future." They regarded this result—the National protection and fostering of the Slave system—as "essential to the best hopes of our country;" and in the event of Congress refusing to propose such amendments, then a convention of all the States should be held to effect it.

It is a notable fact that while the National Government, on no occasion, ever exhibited the slightest intention to interfere with the rights of the slaveholders, or of any other class of citizens, the Conditional Unionists assumed that the Government was, or was about to be, an aggressor on the rights of that class in a minority of the States, who seemed to think that *their* interest was paramount to all others; even to the life of the nation. This obeisance to the selfish demands of that interest was the stumbling-block in the way of many a true patriot in every part of the Republic.

the Conditional Unionists bound the stalwart limbs of her Samson—her National allegiance—while it was reposing its head trustfully in the lap of Delilah—the Slave power; and that they came near being instrumental (though not intentionally) in putting out its eyes, and making it grind ignobly in the prison-house of the "Confederate" Philistines. Perhaps the records of the war in Kentucky, that may be found in future pages of this work, may aid us in forming a correct judgment in the matter. It is certain that the record contains some very instructive lessons concerning the danger to a free people of class legislation and class domination. Whenever a single interest overshadows all others, and is permitted to shape the public policy of a subordinate commonwealth, or a great nation, the liberties of the people are in danger.

While the zealous loyalists of Kentucky were restrained and made comparatively inactive by what they deemed an unwise and mischievous policy, those of Missouri were struggling manfully to keep the State from revolution and ruin. We have observed how strongly the people declared for the Union in their election of delegates to the State Convention, which assembled at Jefferson City on the 28th of February. In that Convention there was

JEFFERSON CITY IN 1861.

not a single openly avowed disunionist, but there were a few secret ones and many Conditional Unionists.[1] Notwithstanding the slaves in Missouri were less than one-tenth of the population, and the real and best interests of the State were in close affinity with free labor, the Slave power, which embraced a large number of active politicians, was potential. These politicians were mostly of the Virginia and South Carolina school, and through their exertions the disloyal Claiborne F. Jackson was elected Governor of the State.[2]

On the second day of its session the Missouri Convention adjourned to St. Louis, where it reassembled on the 4th of March,[a] in the Mercantile Library Hall, with Sterling Price as President, and　　[a] 1861. Samuel A. Lowe as Secretary. Price, who had been Governor of Missouri, and who afterward became one of the most active generals in the "Confederate" service in the Southwest, had obtained his election to the Convention under the false pretense of being a Unionist, and hoped, no doubt, to find a sufficient number of disloyal men in that body to enable him and his political friends to precipitate Missouri into revolution. He was mistaken, and was

---

[1] The Convention consisted of one hundred and four members, of whom fifty-three were lawyers. One-quarter of them were natives of Virginia, and only fourteen of them were born in Missouri. Thirteen were from Kentucky, and three were natives of Europe.

[2] See page 201.

made conscious of the fact at the beginning of the session, not only from conversation with the members, but from the reception given to a communication, written and verbal, from Luther J. Glenn, an accredited "Commissioner" from Georgia, and who was allowed to address the Convention on the subject of his mission on the first day of its session in St. Louis.[a] In his written communication and in his speech he strongly urged Missouri to join the "Southern Confederacy."[1] The atmosphere of St. Louis, in and out of the Convention, was not congenial to such seditious sentiments. The population of that city was made up largely of New Englanders and Germans, who were loyal, while immigrants from the Slave-labor States, and especially from Virginia, composed the great body of the secessionists. The spectators in the Convention greeted Glenn's remarks with hisses and hootings; and subsequently the Convention itself, through a committee to which the "Commissioner's" communication was referred, assured him that his views were not acceptable to that body, whose proceedings throughout were characterized by great dignity, and acts and expressions that gave cheerfulness to the loyal men of the country.

> [a] March 4, 1861.

The Committee of the Convention on Federal Relations, through its chairman, H. R. Gamble, reported at length, on the 9th of March, in a manner to assure the country of the loyalty of the Convention. In that report the great topics of the hour were temperately discussed. It was declared that "the people of the Southern States" had a right to complain "of the incessant abuse poured upon their institutions by the press, the pulpit, and many of the people of the North;" and then enumerated some of the alleged "aggressions on the rights of the South," so commonly found at that time in the newspapers of the Slave-labor States, and the speeches of politicians. Yet it was declared truly, that "heretofore there has been no complaint against the action of the Federal Government in any of its departments, as designed to violate the rights of the Southern States." The Slavery question was reviewed, and the possession of the Government by "a sectional party, avowing opposition to the admission of Slavery into the Territories of the United States," was "deeply regretted," because it threatened dangerous sectional strife; but, after all, the Committee thought that the history of the country taught that there was not much to be feared from political parties in power. The value of the Union to Missouri was pointed out, with forcible illustrations; and the report closed with seven resolutions, which declared that there was then no adequate cause to impel Missouri to leave the Union, and that she would labor for its security; that

---

[1] Mr. Glenn's communication to the Convention was referred to a Committee, whereof John B. Henderson was chairman. That Committee reported on the 21st of March. They regretted that the Commissioner from Georgia, who invited Missouri to withdraw from the Union, had "no plan of reconciliation" to offer. The Committee reviewed the causes of difference between "the North" and "the South," and concluded with a series of five resolutions, in which it declared its disapproval of secession as a right or a necessity; that a "dissolution of the Union would be ruinous to the best interests of Missouri;" and that "no efforts should be spared to secure its continued blessings to her people." The fourth resolution was a pointed rebuke for all disturbers of the peace of the Republic. "This Convention," it said, "exhorts Georgia and the other seceding States to desist from the revolutionary measures commenced by them, and unite their voice with ours in restoring peace. and cementing the Union of our fathers." Judge Birch, of the same Committee, offered a minority report, in the form of resolutions, less offensive to the slaveholders. The two reports were laid on the table, and, by a vote of fifty-six against forty, the subject was made the special order for the third Monday in December following, to which time it was proposed to adjourn the Convention when it should adjourn.

the people of Missouri were devotedly attached to the institutions of the country, and earnestly desired a fair and amicable adjustment of all difficulties; that the Crittenden Compromise was a proper basis for such adjustment; that a convention of the States, to propose amendments to the Constitution, would be useful in restoring peace and quiet to the country; that an attempt to "coerce the submission of the seceding States, or the employment of military force by the seceding States to assail the Government of the United States," would inevitably lead to civil war; and earnestly entreated the Government and the conspirators to "withhold and stay the arm of military power," and on no pretense whatever bring upon the nation the horrors of such war.

On the 19th of March the report of the Committee was considered, and substantially adopted. An amendment was agreed to, recommending the withdrawal of the National troops "from the forts within the borders of the seceded States, where there is danger of collision between the State and Federal troops." So the Convention declared that the State of Missouri would stand by the Government on certain conditions; and after appointing delegates to the Border State Convention,[1] and giving power[a] to a committee to call another session whenever it might seem necessary,[2] the Convention adjourned to the third Monday in December.

[a] March 21, 1861.

The Legislature of Missouri was in session simultaneously with the Convention. Governor Jackson could not mold the action of the latter to his views, so he labored assiduously to that end with the former. He determined to give to the secessionists control of the city of St. Louis, the focus of the Union power of the State, and the chief place of the depository of the National arms within its borders. He succeeded in procuring an Act for the establishment of a metropolitan police in that city, under five commissioners to be appointed by the Governor.[3] This was an important step in the way of his intended usurpation; and he had such assurances from leading politicians throughout the State of their power to suppress the patriotic action of the people, that when the President's call for troops reached him he gave the insolent answer already recorded.[4] The *Missouri Republican*, a newspaper in St. Louis, which was regarded as the exponent of the disloyal sentiments of the State, raised the standard of revolt on the following day[b] by saying, editorially, "Nobody expected any other response from him. They may not approve of the early course of the Southern States, but they denounce and defy the action of Mr. Lincoln in proposing to call out seventy-five thousand men for the purpose of coercing the seceded States of the Union. Whatever else may happen, he gets no men from the Border States to carry on such a war."

[b] April 16, 1861.

---

[1] See page 460. The delegates from Missouri consisted of one from each Congressional district. The following named gentlemen were chosen:—Hamilton R. Gamble, John B. Henderson, William A. Hall, Jas. H. Moss, William Douglass, Littlebury Hendrick, William G. Pomeroy.

[2] This Committee was composed of the President of the Convention, who should be *ex-officio* chairman, and one from each Congressional district.

[3] The Commissioners appointed were the political friends of the Governor. Among them was Basil Duke, afterward the noted guerrilla chief under the notorious John Morgan.

[4] See page 388.

Jackson followed up this revolutionary movement by calling [a] the Legislature to assemble in extraordinary session at Jefferson City on
[a] April 22, 1865. the 2d day of May, "for the purpose," he said, " of enacting such laws and adopting such measures as may be deemed necessary and proper for the more perfect organization and equipment of the militia of this State, and to raise the money and such other means as may be required to place the State in a proper attitude for defense." The Governor was acting under the inspiration of a disloyal graduate of the Military Academy at West Point, named Daniel M. Frost, a native of New York, who was then bearing the commission of a brigadier-general of the Missouri militia, and was commander of the St. Louis District. So early as the 24th of January preceding, we find Frost giving the Governor assurances, in writing, of his treasonable purposes, and of the complicity with him of Major William Henry Bell, a native of North Carolina, who was then commander of the United States military post at St. Louis, and having in charge the Arsenal there.[1] On the day when [b] April 15. the President called [b] for troops, Frost hastened to remind the Governor that it was time to take active measures for securing the co-operation of Missouri in the disunion scheme. He suggested that the holding of St. Louis by the National Government would restrain the secession movement in the State ; and he recommended the calling of the Legislature together ; the

DANIEL M. FROST.

sending of an agent to Baton Rouge to obtain mortars and siege-guns ; to see that the Arsenal at Liberty should not be held by Government troops ; to

---

[1] General Frost informed the Governor that he had just visited the Arsenal, and said :—" I found Major Bell every thing that you or I could desire. He assured me that he considered that Missouri had, whenever the time came, *a right to claim it* [the Arsenal], as being upon her soil. . . . He informed me, upon the honor of a gentleman, that he would not suffer any arms to be removed from the place, without first giving me *timely information,* and I, in turn, promised him that I would use all the force at my command to prevent him being annoyed by irresponsible persons. I, at the same time, gave him notice that if affairs assumed so threatening a character as to render it unsafe to leave the place in its comparatively unprotected condition, that I might come down and quarter a proper force there to protect it from the assaults of any persons whatsoever, to which he assented. In a word, the Major is with us, where he ought to be, for all his worldly wealth lies here in St. Louis (and it is very large) ; and then, again, his sympathies are with us." Frost then proceeded to inform the Governor that he should keep a sharp eye upon " the sensationists," that is, the Unionists ; that he should be " thoroughly prepared, with proper force, to act as emergency may require," and that he would use force, if any attempt at "shipment or removal of the arms " should be attempted. " The Major informs me," he said, " that he has arms for forty thousand men, with all the appliances to manufacture munitions of every kind." He continued :—" This Arsenal, if properly looked after, will be every thing to our State, *and I intend to look after it,* very quietly, however." Then again, referring to Major Bell, he said :—" He desired that I would not divulge his peculiar views, which I promised not to do, *except to yourself.* I beg, therefore, that you will say nothing that might compromise him eventually with the General Government, for thereby I would be placed in an awkward position, whilst he would probably be removed, which would be *unpleasant* to our interests."—*Letter of D. M. Frost to C. F. Jackson, Governor of Missouri,* January 24, 1861. See Appendix to the "*Journal of the Senate, Extra Session of the Rebel Legislature,*" called together by a proclamation of Governor Jackson, and held at Neosho, Missouri, in October, 1861. It was published by order of the House of Representatives of the General Assembly of Missouri, in 1865. This *Journal,* in MS., was captured by the Forty-ninth Missouri Volunteers, in the State of Alabama.

publish a proclamation to the people, warning them that the President's call for troops was illegal, and that they should prepare to defend their rights as citizens of Missouri, and to form a military camp at or near St. Louis, whereat the commander might be authorized to "muster military companies into the service of the State, erect batteries," *et cætera*.[1]

In accordance with General Frost's advice, the Governor, on the day when he issued his call for the meeting of the Legislature, caused his Adjutant-General (Hough) to send orders to the militia officers of the State to assemble their respective commands on the 3d of May, and go into encampment for a week, the avowed object being for the militia "to attain a greater degree of efficiency and perfection in organization and discipline." In all this the treasonable designs of the Governor were so thinly covered by false pretense that few were deceived by them. The intention clearly was to give to the Governor and his friends military control and occupation of the State, that they might, in spite of the solemn injunctions of the people, expressed in their Convention, annex Missouri to the "Southern Confederacy." Had evidence of his treasonable designs been wanting, the Governor's Message to the Legislature on the 2d of May would have supplied it. "Our interests and our sympathies," he said, "are identical with those of the Slaveholding States, and necessarily unite our destiny with theirs. The similarity of our social and political institutions, our industrial interests, our sympathies, habits, and tastes, our common origin and territorial contiguity, all concur in pointing out our duty in regard to the separation which is now taking place between the States of the old Federal Union." He denounced the President's call for troops as "unconstitutional and illegal, tending toward a consolidated despotism." He said all that he dared, short of calling the people to arms in set terms, to overthrow the Republic. The Legislature obsequiously acquiesced in the demands of the

UNITED STATES ARSENAL AT ST. LOUIS.[2]

Governor, and he began at once to work the machinery of revolution vigorously.

The capture of the United States Arsenal at St. Louis, with its large supply of munitions of war, and the holding of that chief city of the State and of the Mississippi Valley, formed a capital feature in the plan of the conspirators. Already an unguarded Arsenal at Liberty, ° April 20, 1861. in Clay County, had been seized° and garrisoned by the secessionists, under the direction of the Governor, and its contents dis-

---

[1] Letter of D. M. Frost, Brigadier-General commanding Military District of Missouri, dated "St. Louis, April 15, 1861."

[2] The grounds of the Arsenal slope to the river, and on two sides have a sort of terraced wall. It is south of the city; and near the river a railway passes through the grounds. Connected with that wall at the railway, a battery was established.

tributed among the disloyal inhabitants of that region capable of bearing
arms. The Arsenal at St. Louis could not be so easily taken. It was
guarded by a garrison of between four and five hundred regular troops,
under Captain Nathaniel Lyon, one of the bravest and best men in the
Army, who had lately been appointed commandant of the post, in place of
Major Bell. Lyon caused earthworks to be thrown up for the protection of
this important depository of arms.

For weeks before the President's call for troops, the secessionists of St.
Louis held secret meetings in the Bethold Mansion, belonging to one of the
oldest French families in the State, where they were drilled in the use of
fire-arms, and were so bold as to fling out a secession flag during a portion
of the sittings of the State Convention. They were furnished with State
arms; and many of them there received commissions from the Governor, and
were secretly sworn into the military service of the State. They were
closely watched from the beginning by a few vigilant Unionists, who met in
secret in the law office of Franklin A. Dick.[1] There Captain Lyon frequently
met them in consultation; and when it was evident that the secessionists
were preparing to seize the Arsenal and the city, they made first Washington
Hall and then Turners' Hall (both belonging to the Germans) places for rendezvous for the Unionists of St. Louis. These (who were mostly Germans)
were formed into military companies, drilled in the use of fire-arms, and
thus were fully prepared to resist the traitors. Finally, when the President's call for troops came, they drilled openly, made their hall a citadel with
barricaded entrance, established a perpetual guard, and kept up continual
communication with the Arsenal. They were denounced by the secessionists
as outlaws, incendiaries, and miscreants, preparing to make war on Missouri;
and it was with the greatest difficulty that they were recognized by the Government at Washington. They were finally relieved of much anxiety and
embarrassment by an order issued by the President, on the 30th of April, for
Captain Lyon to enroll in the military service of the United States the loyal
citizens of St. Louis, in number not exceeding ten thousand. This order was
procured chiefly through the instrumentality of Colonel (afterward Major-
General) Frank P. Blair, who, within ten days after the call of the President
for troops was received, had raised and organized a regiment of Missourians,
and assisted in the primary formation of four others. On him Captain Lyon
leaned much in this emergency.

In the mean time General Wool's timely order to Governor Yates, to send
a force from Illinois to hold the St. Louis Arsenal,[2] had been acted upon.
Yates sent Captain Stokes, of Chicago, on that delicate mission. He found
St. Louis alive with excitement, and, after consultation with Captain Lyon
and Colonel Blair, it was thought best to remove a large portion of the arms
secretly to Illinois. This was done between midnight and daylight on the
morning of the 26th of April. They were taken to Alton in a steamboat,
and from thence to Springfield by railway.

---

[1] The gentlemen who attended these meetings were James S. Thomas, now (1865) Mayor of St. Louis; Frank
P. Blair, Oliver D. Filley, James D. Broadhead, Samuel J. Glover, Benjamin Farrar, B. Gratz Brown, Franklin
A. Dick, Peter L. Foy, Henry T. Blow, Giles F. Filley, John D. Stevenson, John Doyle, Henry Boernstein,
Samuel T. Gardner, and Samuel Sinews.

[2] See page 480.

The Governor and the secessionists of St. Louis were unsuspicious, or at least uninformed, of the removal of so many arms from the Arsenal, and, under orders for the establishment of camps of instruction, they prepared to seize it with its valuable contents. The Governor's zealous adviser, General Frost, formed a camp in Lindell's Grove,[1] in the suburbs of St. Louis, on the designated day,[a] and there was collected a considerable force of State troops. He called the place of rendezvous " Camp Jackson," in honor of the Governor; and in compliment to the chief civil and military leader of the rebellion, he named two of the principal avenues formed by tents, " Davis " and " Beauregard." To deceive the people, he kept the National flag waving over this camp of disloyalists.

[a] May 3, 1861.

Captain Lyon, in the mean time, had been very watchful. Under the orders of the President, of the 30th of April, he enrolled a large number of volunteers. These occupied the Arsenal grounds, and some of them, for want of room thereon, were quartered outside of them. The latter movement brought the metropolitan police into action, and they demanded the return of the troops to the Government grounds, because they were " Federal soldiers violating the rights of the Sovereign State of Missouri," which had " exclusive jurisdiction over her whole territory." Lyon saw no force in their argument, and paid little attention to their folly, but continued his preparations to defend and hold the Arsenal. To make his little force appear stronger than it really was, he sent out squads of soldiers in disguise during the hours of night, while the secessionists slept, with orders to rendezvous at a distant point, and march back to the Arsenal the next morning in uniform, with drums beating and flags flying.[2]

On the morning of the 19th, word came to Captain Lyon that heavy cannon and mortars in boxes, marked " Marble,"[3] and shot and shell in barrels, had been landed at St. Louis from the steamer *J. C. Swan*, and taken to Camp Jackson on drays. Reports concerning the matter were contradictory, and the commander resolved to make a personal reconnoissance of the secession camp. Disguised as a woman closely veiled, he rode in a carriage up to and around the camp unsuspected,[4] and was convinced that the time for vigorous action had arrived. Frost had become uneasy, and on the morning of the 10th he wrote to Lyon, saying that he was constantly in receipt of information that an attack on his camp was contemplated, because of the impression that had gone abroad that he was about to attack the Arsenal. Then, with the most adroit hypocrisy, he solemnly declared that he had no hostile designs against the property of the United States or its representatives, and that the idea of such hostility had never been entertained by him nor by any one else in the State. He was acting, he said, only in accordance with his constitutional duties. In support of his assertion he pointed to the fact, that he had offered the services of the troops under his command for

---

[1] This grove was in an inclosure of about sixty acres, bounded on the north by Olive Street, and extending west along Grand Avenue.

[2] *Life of Nathaniel Lyon :* by Ashbel Woodward, page 244.

[3] Proclamation of General W. S. Harney, May 14, 1861.

[4] On that occasion Captain Lyon wore the dress, shawl, and bonnet of Mrs. Andrew Alexander, a daughter of Governor George Madison, of Kentucky, whose bravery was conspicuous at Frenchtown, on the River Raisin, early in 1813. The carriage was driven by William Roberts, a colored man; and Captain J. J. Witzig was Lyon's guide.

the protection of the public property. He desired to know "personally" from Captain Lyon whether the rumor of his intended attack on Camp Jackson was true.

Lyon refused to receive Frost's note, but the traitor was answered by the vigilant commander "personally" that day, in a way to silence all further inquiries. Early in the afternoon, Lyon, by a quick movement, surrounded Camp Jackson with about six thousand troops and heavy cannon, so placed as to command the entire grove.[1] Guards were placed so as to prevent any communication between the town and the camp. Then Lyon sent a note to General Frost, demanding an immediate surrender of the men and munitions of war under his command, and giving him only thirty minutes for deliberation.

In the mean time, information of this movement had spread over the town. Rumors of an attack on Camp Jackson had been exciting the people for two days, and now a portion of the population, who sympathized with the rebellion, were in a state of frenzy, and, armed with whatever weapon they could find—rifles, pistols, knives, clubs—they hurried toward Lindell's Grove to assist the State troops. They found the south side of the camp open, and many of them forced their way into it and joined their friends. They were too late. Frost perceived by the array of armed men around his camp that resistance with his twelve hundred militia would be useless, and he surrendered before the half hour allowed him for deliberation had expired. With his men Frost surrendered twenty cannon, twelve hundred new rifles, several chests of muskets, and large quantities of ammunition. The most of these materials of war had been stolen from the Arsenal at Baton Rouge.

Lyon offered to release the State troops, who were now prisoners, on condition of their taking an oath of allegiance to the National Government, and promising not to take up arms against it. Nearly all of them declined the offer, and toward sunset they were marched out of the camp between two regiments (Blair's and Boernstein's), followed by the excited crowd, who yelled and cursed like madmen, as they were. They huzzaed for Jefferson Davis and the Southern Confederacy. Women waved their handkerchiefs in token of friendship for the prisoners; and upon the German Unionists in the ranks the most insulting epithets were poured out. At length, just as the last of the prisoners and guard were leaving the camp, some of the rabble in the grove fired upon some of Boernstein's command.[2] The Germans returned the attack in kind. More than twenty of the crowd were wounded, including some women and children, some of them mortally. Lyon in-

---

[1] The regiments of Missouri Volunteers, under Colonels Boernstein, Franz Sigel (afterward Major-General), and Blair, were drawn up on the north and west sides of the camp; the regiment of Colonel Nicholas Schüttner, with a company of United States Regulars and a battery of artillery, under Lieutenant Lathrop, were placed on the east side of the camp; and a company of Regulars, under Lieutenant Saxton, and a battery of heavy guns were on the north side of the camp. Lyon's staff consisted of Franklin A. Dick, Samuel Simmons, Bernard G. Farrar, and Mr. Conant. Mr. Dick was afterward Provost-Marshal General of the Department of Missouri under General S. R. Curtis, with the rank of colonel.

[2] Captain Blandowski, of Boernstein's regiment, was mortally wounded, and died a few days afterward, when he was buried with the honors of war. Captain Lyon was present at his death, and he remarked to the victim's widow:—"Madam, since my boyhood, it has always been my highest wish to die as your husband has died." That wish was soon afterward gratified.

stantly ordered the firing to cease, and at twilight the prisoners in hand were conveyed to the Arsenal. Many had escaped.

The night of the 10th[a] was a fearful one in St. Louis. The secessionists were determined on revenge. They gathered in excited throngs in the streets, and were alternately inflamed by incendiary speeches, and quieted by judicious harangues by distinguished citizens. [a] May, 1861. They marched in procession with significant banners; broke open a gun-store, and seized some of the arms in it; and all night long the air was resonant with the shouts of an excited multitude. Toward dawn, through the exertion of the Mayor and police, the populace dispersed to their homes, with hearts filled with deep-seated hatred of the Union troops, especially of the Germans, who formed a greater portion of the "Home-Guard." This hatred was violently exhibited toward the evening of the 11th, when some of these troops were entering the town from the Arsenal. A great crowd had gathered on Fifth Street and showered insults upon them; and at the corner of Fifth and Walnut Streets, a boy in the crowd fired a pistol at the soldiers. Their rear line turned and fired, and immediately the whole column was broken, and bullets from their guns flew thick among the people on the sidewalk and in the streets. Several were killed and wounded, and a number of the soldiers themselves suffered from the wild firing of their exasperated comrades. Mayor Taylor and a heavy police force soon appeared, and quiet was restored.

General William S. Harney, of the National Army, had arrived at St. Louis from the East during the excitement, and on the 12th, he resumed the command of the Department of the West, of which he was the head. The hot indignation of the populace was smothered, and, with one or two exceptions,[1] the city of St. Louis (which remained under Union control) was spared from other scenes of bloodshed during the war.[2] When all the facts became known, the conduct of Captain Lyon was approved by his Government, and by the loyal people of the country. By his promptness and skill, and with the assistance of hosts of loyal and zealous men, he saved the Arsenal and the city of St.

W. S. HARNEY.

Louis from the grasp of the conspirators, and so consolidated and encouraged the Union sentiment of the Commonwealth, that Missouri was saved from the disgrace of being rightfully called a "seceded State."

---

[1] On the 18th of June the city was violently agitated by a fearful occurrence on Seventh Street, between Olive and Pine Streets. As some troops were passing, a pistol-shot was fired among them from a fire engine-house. They were alarmed and confused, and commenced firing upon the people in the street, in all directions. Several persons were killed and others were wounded. Quiet was soon afterward restored.

[2] Statements made to the author by Colonel F. A. Dick, John Coleman, Jr., and other eye-witnesses: *Oration,* by Charles D. Drake, on the Anniversary of the capture of Camp Jackson, May 11, 1863. *Proclamation* of General W. S. Harney, May 14, 1861. *Life of General Lyon:* by Ashbel Woodward, M. D.

The capture of Camp Jackson produced great consternation among the secessionists at Jefferson City, the capital of the State, where the Legislature was in session. A military bill was immediately passed, by which a fund for war purposes was decreed. The Governor was authorized to receive a loan of five hundred thousand dollars from the banks, and to issue State bonds to the amount of one million dollars. He was also authorized to purchase arms; and the whole military power of the State was placed under his absolute control, while every able-bodied man was made subject to military duty. A heavy extraordinary tax was ordered; and nothing was left undone in preparations for actual war.

Soon after General Harney returned to his command, he issued a proclamation,[a] in which he characterized this military bill as an indirect secession ordinance, even ignoring the forms resorted to by the politicians of other States, and he told the people of Missouri that it was a nullity, and should be regarded as such by them. Yet he was anxious to pursue a conciliatory policy, to prevent war. He entered into a compact[b] with Sterling Price (President of the late Convention, and then a General of the State militia), which had for its object the neutrality of Missouri in the impending conflict. Price, in the name of the Governor, pledged the power of the State to the maintenance of order; and Harney, in the name of his Government, agreed to make no military movement, so long as that order was preserved. The loyal people were alarmed, for they well knew the faithlessness to pledges of the Governor and his associates, and they justly regarded the whole matter as a trick of Jackson and other conspirators to deceive the people, and to gain time to get arms, and pre-

STERLING PRICE.

[a] May 12, 1861.

[b] May 21.

pare for war. Fortunately for the State and the good cause, the National Government did not sanction this compact. Captain Lyon had been commissioned a brigadier-general[c] in the mean time, by an order dated the 16th of May, several days before this treaty with Price. General Harney was relieved of command, and on the 29th he was succeeded by Lyon, who bore the title of Commander of the Department of Missouri. Most of the prisoners taken at Camp Jackson had concluded to accept the parole first offered them, and they were released.

[c] May 17, 1861.

Governor Jackson paid no attention to the refusal of the National Government to sanction the compact between Harney and Price, but proceeded as if it were in full force. The purse and the sword of Missouri had been placed in his hands by the Legislature, and he determined to wield both for the benefit of the "Southern Confederacy." He issued a proclamation, in which he declared that "the people of Missouri should be permitted, in peace and security, to decide upon their future course," and that "they could not be subjugated." Finally, on the 11th of June, General Lyon, Colonel Blair, and Major H. A. Conant held a four hours' interview with Governor Jackson, General Price, and Thomas L. Smead, the latter being the Governor's private secretary. Jackson demanded, as a vital condition of pacification, that throughout the State the Home-Guards, composed of loyal citizens, should be disbanded, and that no National troops should be allowed to tread the soil of Missouri. Lyon peremptorily refused compliance, and Jackson and his associates returned to Jefferson City that night. On the following day [a] the Governor issued a proclamation,   [a] June 12, 1861. calling into active service fifty thousand of the State militia, "for the purpose of repelling invasion, and for the protection of the lives, liberty, and property of the citizens."

NATHANIEL LYON.

In this proclamation he told the people, that while it was their duty to "obey all of the constitutional requirements of the Federal Government," it was equally his duty to advise them, that their "first allegiance was due to their own State, and that they were under no obligations whatever to obey the unconstitutional edicts of the military despotism which had enthroned itself at Washington, nor to submit to the infamous and degrading sway of its minions in this State." At the same time two important railway bridges between St. Louis and Jefferson City were burnt, and the telegraph wires were cut, under the direction of a son of the Governor. So the disloyal Chief Magistrate of Missouri inaugurated civil war in that State; and those movements of troops within its borders immediately began, which continued during almost the entire period of the conflict, with the most disastrous results to the peace and prosperity of the Commonwealth.

While the loyalists and disloyalists of Missouri were grappling in their first struggles for supremacy, the National Government was busy on the Southeastern borders of that Commonwealth, in making preparations for securing its capital city, St. Louis, from the armed occupation of the insurgents, and also from invasion of southern Illinois and Indiana, by the banded enemies of the Republic. The possession of the mouth of the Ohio River, where it pours its tribute into the Mississippi, was of importance, as that point was the key to a vast extent of navigable waters, whose control would give great advantage to the party who should be allowed to exercise it. Both Governor Yates and the Government at Washington had been early informed of a conspiracy to seize Cairo, a small village in Illinois, on the low marshy point at the confluence of those two great rivers, and the lower portion of the Illinois Central Railway, that terminated there. By this means they hoped to control the navigation of the Mississippi to St. Louis, and of the Ohio to Cincinnati and beyond; and also to cut off all communication with the interior of Illinois. They further hoped that their permanent possession of that point, which gave them absolute control of the navigation of the Mississippi below, whose stream traversed a Slave-labor territory exclusively, would cause the Northwestern States of the Union to join hands with the insurgents, rather than lose the immense commercial advantages which the free navigation of that great stream afforded. The scheme was foiled by the vigilance of the Government and the patriotism of the people in the Northwest; and, as we have observed, Governor Yates, under directions from the Secretary of War, sent Illinois troops, at an early day, to take possession of and occupy Cairo.[1] The secessionists, especially of Kentucky and Missouri, were alarmed and chagrined by this important movement, and never ceased to lament it.

By the middle of May there were not less than five thousand Union volunteers at Cairo, under the command of the experienced B. M. Prentiss, who had just been commissioned a brigadier-general. They occupied the extreme point of land within the *levee*

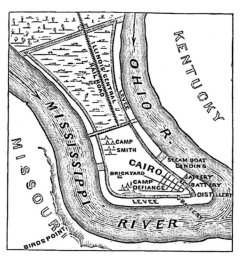

MILITARY POSITION AT CAIRO.

or dike that keeps out the rivers at high water, at the confluence of the Ohio and Mississippi. There they cast up fortifications, and significantly called the post Camp Defiance. A smaller one, called Camp Smith, was established in the rear of it; and troops occupied other points near, on the banks of the two rivers. Heavy ordnance was forwarded from Pittsburg, and 42-pounder cannon commanded the two streams, and bade every steamer and other craft to round to and report to the military authorities there. Before the close of May, the post at Cairo was considered impregnable against any force the Confederates were likely to bring. It soon became a post of immense importance to the Union cause, as a point where some of those land and naval expeditions which performed signal service in the Valley of the Mississippi were fitted out, as we shall observe hereafter.

Adjoining Missouri on the South was the Slave-labor State of Arkansas, in which, as we have seen, attachment to the Union was a prevailing sentiment of the people at the beginning of the year.[a] Unfortunately for them, the Governor and most of the leading politicians of the State were disloyal, and no effort was spared by them to obtain the passage of an ordinance of secession by a Convention of delegates who met on the 4th of March.[b] That Convention was composed of

<small>a 1861.</small>

<small>b 1861.</small>

---

[1] See page 456. Cairo is one hundred and seventy-five miles below St. Louis. It is situated on a boot-shaped peninsula, which has been formed by the action of the two rivers. At high water it is usually overflowed to a great extent; and embankments, twenty or thirty feet in height, along the rivers, called *levees*, had been thrown up to keep out the waters. These *levees* are forty feet above ordinary low water, and rise about ten feet above the natural level of the land. The ground in the rear of the city is lower than that on which the town stands, and, during overflows, the only dry communication with the country is by the causeway of the Illinois Central Railway, which extends up into the immense prairies of Illinois.

seventy-five members, forty of whom were regarded as Unionists. These were so decided and firm, that no ordinance of secession could be passed. The conspirators were disheartened, and, for a while, despaired of success. At length they accomplished by a trick, what they could not gain by fair means. A self-constituted Committee, composed of "Secessionists" and "Co-operationists," reported an ordinance providing for an election, to be held on the 17th of August following, at which the legal voters of the State should decide by ballot for "Secession" or "Co-operation." If a majority of the votes then cast should be for "Secession," that fact was to be considered in the light of instruction to the Convention to pass an ordinance to that effect; if for "Co-operation," then measures were to be used, in conjunction with the Border Slave-labor States "yet in the Union," for the settlement of existing difficulties. To this fair proposition the Unionists in the Convention agreed, and the vote on the question was unanimous. Taking advantage of the excitement caused by the attack on Fort Sumter, the President's call for troops, and the events at Baltimore, Governor Rector

VIEW AT CAIRO, ON THE OHIO RIVER FRONT, IN 1861.

(whose election had been gained by the influence of the "Knights of the Golden Circle"[1]) and his disloyal associates adopted measures immediately for arraying Arkansas on the side of the conspirators without consulting the people.

We have already observed the insulting response of the Governor to the President's call.[2] This was followed by a high-handed measure on the part of the President of the Convention, who professed to be a loyal man. In violation of the pledge of that body, that the whole matter should be submitted to the people in August, he issued a call for the Convention to reassemble on the 6th of May. It met on that day. The number of delegates present was seventy. An Ordinance of Secession, previously pre-

---

[1] See page 187.   [2] See page 337.

pared, was presented to it at three o'clock in the afternoon, when the hall in which the delegates met was densely crowded by an excited populace. It was moved that the "yeas" and "nays" on the question should be taken without debate. The motion was rejected by a considerable majority, but the President declared it to be carried. Then a vote on the Ordinance was taken, and a majority appeared against it. The conspirators were determined not to be foiled. The President, who seems to have been a plastic instrument in their hands, immediately arose, and in the midst of the cheers of the people, vehemently urged the Unionists to change their votes to "ay" immediately. It was evident that a large number of that crowd were prepared to compel them to do so, and the terrified Unionists complied, with only one exception, and that was Isaac Murphy, who was compelled to fly for his life. He was rewarded for his fidelity by the Unionists, who elected him Governor of the State in 1864.

Thus, by fraud and violence, Arkansas was placed in the position of a rebellious State. The Convention then authorized the Governor to call out sixty thousand men, if necessary, for military duty. The State was divided into two military divisions, eastern and western. General Bradley was appointed to the command of the Eastern Division, and General Pearce, late of the National Army, was made commander of the Western Division. An ordinance was also passed confiscating all debts due from citizens of Arkansas to persons residing in the Free-labor States, and all the personal property belonging to such persons in Arkansas at the time of the passage of the Ordinance. A system of terrorism was at once commenced. Unionists were everywhere shamefully persecuted. They were exiled, imprisoned, and murdered. Confederate troops from Texas and Louisiana were brought into the State to occupy it and overawe the loyalists; and Arkansas troops, raised chiefly by fraud and violence, were sent out of the State, for the conspirators would not trust them.

Not content with this usurpation at home, Governor Rector and his associates, acting under the directions of the arch-conspirators at Montgomery, took measures to attach to their cause, by persuasion or coercion, the powerful civilized Indians residing in the Territory adjoining the western boundaries of Arkansas and northern Texas. These were the Cherokees, Choctaws, and Chickasaws, numbering at that time about forty thousand souls.[1] There were also in that region a remnant of the Creek Nation who formerly inhabited Alabama, and some Senecas and Shawnoese from the North, who had lately gone there on a visit. It was believed that a band of efficient warriors might be drawn from these nations, whose very name would be terrible; and through the resident agents, who were secessionists, and by other means, the work of corruption and coercion was vigorously commenced among them.

_{a 1861.} A brother of Governor Rector was then Government agent among the Cherokees, and used all his influence to seduce them from their allegiance. When, in May,[a] Jefferson Davis ordered three regi-

---

[1] The Cherokees numbered twenty-two thousand, the Choctaws about eighteen thousand, and the Chickasaws about five thousand. A large proportion of these were engaged in the pursuits of civilized life, especially the Cherokees, who had many flourishing schools.

ments of these Indians to be formed, he commissioned Albert Pike,[1] a poet of some pretensions, who was a native of New England, but had long resided in Arkansas, to make a treaty with them to that effect.

ALBERT PIKE.

Pike went into the Indian country, where he met them in council. He succeeded with the less civilized Choctaws and Chickasaws, and by virtue of a treaty made with them, they were entitled to the privilege of having two of their number occupy seats as delegates in the "Congress" of the conspirators at Montgomery. Two regiments of these Indians were raised, and, under Pike, who was commissioned a brigadier-general, they joined the army of the conspirators. A third regiment was organized before the close of 1861. We shall meet Pike and his dusky followers hereafter, among the Ozark Mountains.

The Cherokees and Creeks were not so easily moved. The venerable John Ross, who for almost forty years had been the principal Chief of the Cherokees, took a decided stand against the secessionists, and resisted them so long as he had the power. On the 17th of May[a] he issued a proclamation, in which he reminded his people of their treaty obligations to the United States, and urged them to be faithful in the observance of them. He exhorted them to take no part in the exciting

a 1861.

FORT SMITH, ARKANSAS.

events of the day, but to attend to their ordinary avocations; and not to be alarmed by false reports circulated among them by designing men, but to cultivate peace and friendship with the inhabitants of all the States. He

---

[1] Pike was a remarkable man. He was a native of Boston, and was then fifty-one years of age, with long gray flowing locks. He dressed himself in gaudy costume and wore an immense plume to please the Indians. He seems to have gone into the rebellion heartily, forgetful of the warnings of his own remarkable prophecy, which he put in the following words, toward the close of a poem entitled *Dissolution of the Union*, written before the war. After describing civil war and its effects, he says to the deceived people:—

> "Where are your leaders? Where are they who led
> Your souls into the perilous abyss?
> The bravest and the best are lying dead,
> Shrouded in treason and dark perjuries:
> The most of them have basely from you fled,
> Followed by Scorn's unending, general hiss;
> Fled into lands that Liberty disowns,
> Encrouched within the shadow of tall thrones."

earnestly urged them to observe a strict neutrality, and to maintain a trust that God would not only keep from their borders the desolation of war, but stay its "ravages among the brotherhood of States."

But Ross and his loyal adherents among the Cherokees and Creeks were overborne by the tide of rebellion, and were swept on, powerless, by its

JOHN ROSS.

tremendous current. The forts on the frontier of Texas (Gibson, Arbuckle, and Washita), used for their defense, had, as we have observed, been abandoned by United States troops, in consequence of the treason of Twiggs, and the Indians were threatened by an invasion from that State. Fort Smith, on the boundary-line between Arkansas and the Indian Territory,[1] had also been evacuated, and was now in possession of the insurgents. Their immediate neighbors, the Choctaws and Chickasaws, with wild tribes westward of them, were rallying to the standard of the conspirators; and the National troops in Missouri were unable to check the rising rebellion there. Isolated and weak, and perceiving no hope for relief by their Government, the chief men of the Cherokees held a mass meeting at Tahlequah in August,[a]

[a] August 2, 1861.

and with great unanimity declared their allegiance to the "Confederate States." Ross still held out, but, finally yielding to the force of circumstances and the teachings of expediency, he called on the Council of the Cherokee Nation to assemble at Tahlequah on the 20th of the same month, when he sent in a message, recommending the severance of their connection with the National Government, and an alliance with the "Confederates." Four days afterward,[b] he sent a note[2] to an

[b] August 24.

officer of the insurgent forces, covering dispatches to Ben McCulloch, under whom the Indians and some Texan troops were to act, informing him that the Cherokee Nation had espoused the cause of the conspirators. The wife of Ross, a young and well-educated woman, still held out; and when an attempt was made to raise a "Confederate" flag over the Council

---

[1] The boundary-line runs through the fort. It is at the confluence of the Arkansas and Poteau Rivers, and near it is the city of Fort Smith, at which an immense trade with the Indians and New Mexicans was carried on before the war. It was next to Little Rock, the capital of the State, in population.

[2] The following is a copy of Ross's note:—

"EXECUTIVE DEPARTMENT, }
"PARK HILL, C. N., August 24, 1861. }

"To Major G. W. CLARK, A. Q. M., C. S. A.:

"SIR:—I herewith forward to your care dispatches for General McCulloch, C. S. A., which I have the honor to request you will cause to be forwarded to him by earliest express. At a mass meeting of about four thousand Cherokees, at Tahlequah, on the 21st inst., the Cherokees, with marked unanimity, declared their allegiance to the Confederate States, and have given their authorities power to negotiate an alliance with them. In view of this action, a regiment of mounted men will be immediately raised, and placed under command of Colonel John Drew, to meet any emergency that may come. The dispatches to General McCulloch relate to the subject, and contain a tender from Colonel Drew of his regiment, for service on our northern border. Having espoused the cause of the Confederate States, we hope to render efficient service in the protracted war which now threatens the country, and to win the liberal confidence of the Confederate States.

"I have the honor to be, Sir, very respectfully, your obedient servant,   JOHN ROSS,
"*Principal Chief Cherokee Nation.*"

House, she opposed the act with so much spirit, that the insurgents desisted. Equally spirited was the head Chief of the Creeks. After fighting the insurgents in the field, he was driven into Kansas, where he died in 1864.

During the civil war, the Cherokees suffered terribly, at times, from the depredations of guerrilla bands of rebels, who infested the western borders of Missouri and Arkansas and Upper Texas, roaming through the Indian country, and committing violence and robberies everywhere. Three of the most noted of the leaders of these robber bands were named, respectively, Taylor, Anderson, and Tod, who gave to the bravest of their followers a silver badge, star-shaped, and bearing their names.

The secessionists would not trust Chief Ross. Indeed, his loyalty to his country was so obvious that they were about to arrest him, when he fled to the North with some National troops who penetrated the Cherokee country in 1862. About fifty of his relations escaped with him. During the remainder of the war he and his family resided in Philadelphia, where the writer had a long and interesting interview with him early in 1865. Mr. Ross had in his possession one of the guerrilla badges just mentioned, of which an engraving, the size of the original, is given below. He was then seventy-four years of age. He was of medium hight, compactly built, with abundant white hair, and having only one-eighth of Indian blood in his veins, he had every appearance of a purely white man. His life, as principal Chief of the Cherokees during their emergence from Paganism, their persecutions and sufferings while eastward of the Mississippi, and their settlement and advancement in their new homes westward of the Father of Waters, had been an exceedingly interesting one.

CHAPTER XX.

COMMENCEMENT OF CIVIL WAR.

T the close of April,[a] Jefferson Davis and his confederates were satisfied that the Government and the loyal people of the country were resolved to maintain the nationality of the Republic at all hazards, and they put forth extraordinary efforts to strike a deadly blow before it should be too late. The possession of Washington City being the chief object to be first obtained, troops were hurried toward it, as we have seen, from all points of the Slave-labor States, with the greatest possible haste and in the greatest possible numbers. At the beginning of May there were sixteen thousand of them on their way to Virginia or within its borders, and, with the local troops of that Commonwealth, were pressing on toward Washington, or to important points of communication with it. At the same time measures were on foot at Montgomery for organizing an army of one hundred thousand men.[1]

[a] 1861.

The enthusiasm among the young men of the ruling class in the South was equal to that of the young men of the North. Notwithstanding the proclamation of the President, calling for seventy-five thousand men, was read by crowds, " on the bulletin-boards of the telegraph-offices in every town, with roars of laughter and derision, and cheers for the great rail-splitter Abraham," as one of their chroniclers avers, and few believed that there would be war, " companies were formed on the spot, from among the wealthiest of the youths, and thousands of dollars were spent on their organization, drill, and equipment ; indeed, had Jefferson Davis so desired, he could have had two hundred thousand volunteers within a month for any term of service."[2] The enthusiasm of the young men was shared by the other sex. " Banners of costly material," says the same writer, " were made by clubs of patriotic young ladies, and delivered to the companies with appropriate speeches—the men, on such occasions, swearing that they would perish rather than desert the flag thus consecrated. Subscriptions for arms and accouterments poured in, and an emissary was dispatched northward, post-haste, to get the requisites." Regarding the whole matter as a lively pastime in prospect, many of the companies prepared to dress in costly attire, and bear the most expensive rifles ; but those who knew better than they what kind of an entertainment the Southern youth were invited to, gave them some sound lessons at the beginning. " The young gentlemen of your company," wrote Jefferson

---

[1] " Message " of Jefferson Davis to the " Congress of the Confederate States of America," April 29, 1861.
[2] *Battle-Fields of the South :* by an English Combatant. Page 4.

Davis to a Mississippi captain, "must be thoroughly infused with the idea that their services will prove to be in hardships and dangers; the commonest material, therefore, will be the most desirable; and as for arms, we must be content with what we have; the enemy will come superabundantly provided with all things that money and ingenuity can devise. We must learn to supply ourselves from them." He recommended that all volunteers should be dressed in gray flannels and light blue cotton pantaloons.[1]

MISSISSIPPI RIFLEMAN.[2]

The grand rallying-place of the "Confederates," preparatory to a march on the Capital, was Manassas Junction, a point on the Orange and Alexandria Railway, where another joins it from Manassas Gap in the Blue Ridge, about twenty-five miles west from Alexandria, and thirty in a direct line from Washington City. This was a most important strategic point in the plans of the conspirators, as it commanded the grand Southern railway route, connecting Washington and Richmond, and another leading to the fertile valley of the Shenandoah, beyond the Blue Ridge. General Butler had already suggested to General Scott the propriety of sending National troops to occupy that very position before a "Confederate" soldier had appeared,[3] knowing that Washington City could be more easily defended at that distance from it, than by troops and batteries on Arlington Hights, just across the Potomac, within cannon-shot of the Capital. The General-in-chief disagreed with Butler; and while the veteran soldier was slowly

---

[1] *Battle-Fields of the South*, page 5.—This writer, speaking of the company to which he was attached, says:—" The ambition of all was to bear a musket in the holy war for independence," and added, " that his company was composed of men representing property, in the aggregate, of not less than twenty millions of dollars." Then, " to show the spirit of those about to fight for the freedom of their country," he says:—"A commissioned (company) officer, having donned his gray uniform and gilded shoulder-straps, began to strut about camp and assume 'airs,' eager to show his 'little brief authority' on all occasions. This unfortunate fellow disgusted those who elected him; and although the men were desirous of learning their duty thoroughly and expeditiously, he seized upon every opportunity to 'blackguard' his former associates. He was frequently told how obnoxious his assuming manner was; but, not heeding the admonition, several threatened to take him out and 'whale' him. Laughing at these suppressed remarks, he dared to lift his sword to slap one of the men when on parade: he was told what the immediate consequence would be, and foolishly raised the weapon again, and slapped one across the shoulders; when, in an instant, the rifle was dropped, a bowie-knife flashed, and the officer lay dead on the turf, stabbed five or six times in as many seconds. The company did not stir, but looked on and applauded; the culprit quietly wiped his knife, resumed his place in the ranks, and dress-parade proceeded as if nothing had happened. Courts-martial could not—or at all events *did* not—attempt to exercise any jurisdiction in this or similar cases; they were reckoned affairs of self-defense, or 'honor.'"

[2] The Mississippi Riflemen were renowned as destructive sharp-shooters during the war. In addition to their rifle, they carried a sheath-knife, known as the bowie-knife, in their belt. This is a formidable weapon in a hand-to-hand fight, when wielded by men expert in its use, as many were in the Southwestern States, where it was generally seen in murderous frays in the streets and bar-rooms. Its origin is

BOWIE-KNIFE AND SHEATH.

connected with an incident in the life of Colonel Bowie, who was engaged in the revolt of Texas against Mexico, in 1835 and 1836. His sword-blade was broken in an encounter, when he converted the remainder into a stout sharp-pointed knife, and the weapon became very popular. See note 1, page 266.

[3] Parton's *Butler in New Orleans*, page 105.

preparing for a defensive campaign, the enemies of the Government, moving aggressively and quickly, had taken full possession, unopposed, of one of the most important positions for the accomplishment of their object. They attempted to do more. Under Colonel Lee, the late occupant of Arlington House, they were preparing to fortify Arlington Hights, where heavy siege-guns would absolutely command the cities of Washington and Georgetown. Fortunately for the country, this movement was discovered in time to defeat its object. That discovery revealed the necessity of an immediate advance of National forces beyond the Potomac. The advantages gained by the insurgents in having possession of the railways in that region was painfully apparent. Already " Confederate" pickets were occupying Arlington Hights and the Virginia shore of the Long Bridge, which spans the Potomac at Washington City; and engineers had been seen on those hights selecting eligible positions for batteries.[1]

A crisis was evidently at hand, and the General-in-chief was now persuaded to allow an immediate invasion of Virginia.[2] Orders were at once issued[a] for the occupation of the shores of the Potomac opposite, and also the city of Alexandria, nine miles below, by National troops. General Mansfield was in command of about thirteen thousand men at the Capital. Toward midnight, these forces in and around Washington were put in motion for the passage of the river, at three different points. One column was to cross at the Aqueduct Bridge, at Georgetown; another at the Long Bridge, at Washington; and a third was to proceed in vessels, and seize the city of Alexandria.

a May 23, 1861.

The three invading columns moved almost simultaneously. The one at Georgetown was commanded by General Irvin McDowell. Some local volunteers crossed first, and drove the insurgent pickets from the Virginia end of the Aqueduct Bridge. These were followed by the Fifth Massachusetts; the Twenty-eighth New York, from Brooklyn; Company B of the United States Cavalry; and the Sixty-ninth New York, which was an Irish regiment, under Colonel Michael Corcoran. Their march across that lofty structure, in the bright light of a full moon, was a beautiful spectacle. Thousands of anxious men and women saw the gleaming of their bayonets and the waving of their

---

[1] James D. Gay, mentioned in note 1, page 418, visited the steamship *Monticello* on the 23d of May, then discharging Government stores at Georgetown, and while viewing Arlington Hights, not far from the Aqueduct Bridge, through a telescope, discovered Lee (according to his description) and some subordinate officers, apparently engaged, in the partial concealment of bushes and irregularities of the ground, in laying out fortifications. After satisfying himself that preparations were being made by the insurgents to plant batteries on Arlington Hights, Gay hastened to the head-quarters of General Mansfield and told him what he had seen, in detail. The General, not doubting that a battery would be built on Arlington Hights that night, went immediately to the War Department with his information. The order went out at once for the troops to move into Virginia and occupy Arlington Hights before the insurgents should gain absolute possession there. The success of the National troops on that occasion was a very severe blow to the conspirators. The loss of that opportunity to gain a position that would doubtless have secured their possession of Washington City, was at the time, and frequently afterward, spoken of in the Richmond press as one of the greatest of misfortunes.

[2] On the previous day (May 22) a large National flag, purchased by the clerks of the Post-Office Department, in testimony of their loyalty, was raised over the General Post-Office, in Washington City, by the hand of President Lincoln. The air was almost motionless, and the banner clung ominously sullen to the staff and the halliards. In a few moments a gentle breeze came from the North, and displayed the Stripes and Stars in all their beauty and significance to the assembled crowd. "I had not thought to say a word," said the President when he observed the incident, "but it has occurred to me that a few weeks ago the 'Stars and Stripes' hung rather languidly about the staff, all over the nation. So too with this flag, when it was elevated to its place. At first it hung rather languidly, but the glorious breeze from the North came, and it now floats as it should. And we hope that the same breeze is swelling the glorious flag throughout the whole Union."

banners, and heard the sounds of their measured foot-falls borne on the still night air, with the deepest emotions, for it was the first initial act of an opening campaign in civil warfare, whose importance no man could estimate.

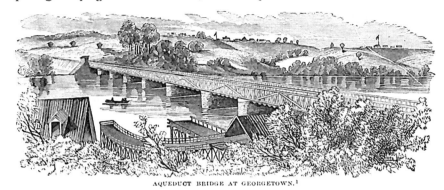

AQUEDUCT BRIDGE AT GEORGETOWN.[1]

Two miles distant from this passing column was another crossing the Long Bridge. It consisted of the National Rifles under Captain Smead, and a company of Zouaves under Captain Powell, who drove the insurgent pickets toward Alexandria, and took position at Roach's Spring, a half a mile from the Virginia end of the bridge. These were immediately followed by the Constitutional Guards of the District of Columbia under Captain Digges, who advanced about four miles on the road toward Alexandria. At two o'clock in the morning, a heavy body, composed of the New York Seventh Regiment; three New Jersey regiments (Second, Third, and Fourth), under Brigadier-General Theodore Runyon, and the New York Twelfth and Twenty-fifth, passed over. The New York troops were commanded by Major-General Charles W.

THEODORE RUNYON.

Sandford, who, at the call of the President, had offered his entire division to the service of the country.

The New York Seventh Regiment was halted at the end of the Long

---

BLOCK-HOUSE.

[1] This is a view of the Aqueduct Bridge at Georgetown, over which flow the waters of the Chesapeake and Ohio Canal, in its extension to Alexandria, after having traversed the valley of the Potomac from the eastern base of the Alleghany Mountains. The picture is from a sketch made by the writer in the spring of 1865, from the piazza in the rear of the *Cumberland House*, which was the residence of Francis S. Key, author of "The Star-Spangled Banner," at the time when that poem was written. See Lossing's *Pictorial Field-Book of the War of* 1812. Arlington Hights are seen beyond the Potomac, with Fort Bennett on the extreme right, the flag of Fort Corcoran in the center, and three block-houses on the left, which guarded the Virginia end of the bridge. Several of these block-houses were built on Arlington Hights early in the war, all having the same general character of the one delineated in the annexed engraving. They were built of heavy hewn timber, and were sometimes used as signal-stations.

Bridge. One New Jersey regiment took post at Roach's Spring, near which a redoubt was cast up, and named Fort Runyon, in honor of the Commanding General under whose direction it was constructed. It crossed the road leading from the Long Bridge to Alexandria, near its junction with the Columbia Turnpike. The remainder of the troops, including the New York Seventh and a company of cavalry under Captain Brackett, now joined those who crossed the Aqueduct Bridge, and these forces combined took possession of and commenced fortifying Arlington Hights.

NEW JERSEY STATE MILITIA.

In the mean time, the New York Fire Zouave Regiment,[1] under Colonel Ephraim E. Ellsworth, who had been encamped on the east branch of the Potomac, near the Navy Yard, were embarked on two schooners and taken to Alexandria; while the First Michigan Regiment, Colonel Wilcox, accompanied by a detachment of United States cavalry commanded by Major Stoneman, and two pieces of Sherman's battery[2] in charge of Lieutenant Ransom, marched for the same destination by way of the Long Bridge. The troops moving by land and water reached Alexandria at about the same time. The National frigate *Pawnee* was lying off the town, and her commander had already been in negotiation for the evacuation of Alexandria by the insurgents. A detachment of her crew, bearing a flag of truce, now hastened to the shore in boats, and leaped eagerly upon the wharf just before the Zouaves reached it. They were fired upon by some Virginia sentries, who instantly fled from the town. Ellsworth, ignorant of any negotiations, advanced to the center of the city, and took possession of it in the name of his Government, while the column under Wilcox marched through different streets to the Station of the Orange and Alexandria Railway, and seized it, with much rolling stock. They there captured a small company (thirty-five men) of Virginia cavalry, under Captain Ball. Other Virginians, who had heard the firing of the insurgent pickets, escaped by way of the railroad.

ELLSWORTH ZOUAVES.

Alexandria was now in quiet possession of the National troops, but there

---

[1] See page 429.

[2] Sherman's Battery, which, as we have observed, accompanied the Pennsylvania troops under Colonel Patterson (see page 445), consisted of six pieces. The whole battery crossed the Long Bridge on this occasion, but only four of the pieces were taken to Arlington Hights.

were many violent secessionists there who would not submit. Among them was a man named Jackson, the proprietor of an inn called the Marshall House. The Confederate flag had been flying over his premises for many days, and had been plainly seen from the President's house in Washington.[1] It was still there, and Ellsworth went in person to take it down. When descending an upper staircase with it, he was shot by Jackson, who was waiting for him in a dark passage, with a double-barreled gun, loaded with buckshot. Ellsworth fell dead, and his murderer met the same fate an instant afterward, at the hands of Francis E. Brownell, of Troy, who, with six others, had accompanied his commander to the roof of the house. He shot Jackson through the head with a bullet, and pierced his body several times with his saber-bayonet. The scene at the foot of that staircase was now appalling. Immediately after Jackson was killed, a woman came

THE MARSHALL HOUSE.

rushing out of a room, and with frantic gestures, as she leaned over the body of the dead inn-keeper, she uttered the wildest cries of grief and despair. She was the wife of Jackson.

Ellsworth's body was borne in sadness to Washington by his sorrowing companions, and funeral services were performed in the East Room of the White House, with President Lincoln as chief mourner. It was then taken to New York, where it lay in state in the City Hall, and was afterward carried in imposing procession through the streets before being sent to its final resting-place at Mechanicsville, on the banks of the upper Hudson. Ells-

EPHRAIM ELMORE ELLSWORTH.

worth was a very young and extremely handsome man, and was greatly beloved for his generosity, and admired for his bravery and patriotism. His death produced great excitement throughout the country. It was the first of

---

[1] On the preceding day (May 23d) a Confederate flag, flying in Alexandria, had attracted the attention of the troops in Washington City. Just at evening, William McSpedon, of New York City, and Samuel Smith, of Queen's County, Long Island, went over and captured it. This was the *first flag taken from the insurgents.*

note that had occurred in consequence of the National troubles; and the very first since the campaign had actually begun, a few hours before. It intensified the hatred of rebellion and its abettors; and a regiment was raised in his native State (New York) called the Ellsworth Avengers.

Intrenching tools were sent over the Potomac early on the morning of the 24th, and the troops immediately commenced casting up intrenchments and redoubts, extending from Roach's Spring, on the Washington and Alexandria Road, across Arlington Hights, almost to the Chain Bridge. The brawny arms of the Sixty-ninth (Irish) Regiment soon piled up the banks of Fort Corcoran, on the Arlington estate, while the less vigorous men of the New York Seventh,

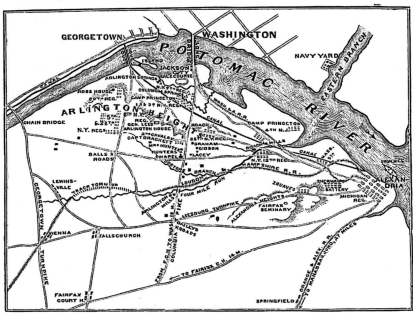

MAP SHOWING THE FIRST DEFENSES OF WASHINGTON.

a greater portion of whom were unaccustomed to manual labor, worked with surprising zeal and vigor in the trenches with their more muscular companions in arms. Fort Corcoran was the first to assume a regular form, and when partly finished a flag-staff was raised, and the National banner was unfurled from it with imposing ceremonies.[1] That and Fort Runyon were the first regular works constructed by the National troops at the beginning of the civil war, and the first over which the flag of the Republic was flung out. At that point a small detachment of cavalry, under Lieutenant Tompkins, who had crossed the Chain Bridge, was stationed. Other fortifications were speedily constructed; and in the course of a few days there was a line

---

[1] On that occasion a group of officers stood around the flag-staff. Among them was Colonel Corcoran, the commander, Colonel (afterward Major-General) David Hunter, and Captain (afterward Brigadier-General) Thomas Francis Meagher. At the request of Corcoran, John Savage, his aid, the well-known Irish poet, sang a song, entitled *The Starry Flag*, which he had composed on the war-transport *Marion*, on the 13th of May, while on her perilous voyage with the regiment up the Potomac, exposed to the masked batteries planted by the Confederates on the Virginia shore. This song may be found in a collection of a few of Mr. Savage's poems, entitled *Faith and Fancy*. It is full of stirring sentiment.

of strong intrenchments extending from the Potomac toward Arlington House, across the Columbia Turnpike, and the railway and carriage-road leading to Alexandria; also detached batteries along Arlington Hights almost to the Chain Bridge, which spans the Potomac five or six miles above Washington. These, well manned and mounted, presented an impregnable barrier against any number of insurgents that might come from Manassas Junction, their place of general rendezvous. A reference to the map on the preceding page will show the position of the National troops on this the first line of the defenses of Washington, at the beginning of June.[1]

General Sandford, of the New York militia, took temporary command of the forces on Arlington Hights; and when he ascertained that the family of Colonel Lee had left Arlington House a fortnight before, he made that fine mansion his head-quarters, and sent word to Lee, then at Richmond, that he would see that his premises should receive no harm. He issued a proclamation,[a] in which he assured the frightened inhabitants of Fairfax County that no one, peaceably inclined, should be molested, and   [a] May 25, 1861.
he exhorted the fugitives to return to their homes and resume their accustomed avocations. Two days afterward,[b] he was succeeded by   [b] May 27.
General McDowell, of the regular Army, who was appointed to the command of all the National forces then in Virginia. Colonel Wilcox, who was in command at Alexandria, was succeeded by Colonel Charles P. Stone, who, as we have observed, had been in charge of the troops for the protection of Washington City during the latter part of the winter and the spring of 1861. Stone was soon recalled to the District, and was succeeded by the veteran Colonel S. P. Heintzelman, of the regulars, who, by order of General Scott, took special care for the protection of the estate of Mount Vernon from injury, and the tomb of Washington from desecration. It is a pleasant thing to record, that while the soldiers of both parties in the contest during the struggle were alternately in military possession of Mount Vernon, not an act is known to have occurred there incompatible with the most profound reverence for the memory of the Father of his Country.

NEW YORK STATE MILITIA.

The conspirators, alarmed by these aggressive movements, and by others in Western Virginia, took active measures to oppose them. The whole military force of Virginia, of which Robert E. Lee was now chief commander, was, as we have observed, placed, by the treaty of April 24, under the absolute control of Jefferson Davis;[2] and by his direction, his Virginia lieutenant, Governor Letcher, issued a proclamation on the 3d of May, calling out the militia of the State to repel apprehended invasion from "the Govern-

---

[1] This map was copied from one published early in June, 1861, and suppressed by the Government, because it afforded valuable information to the insurgents.

[2] See page 383.

ment at Washington." He designated no less than twenty places in the State as points of rendezvous for the militia. One-fourth of these places were westward of the mountains. At the same time the insurgents strengthened the garrison at Harper's Ferry, and erected batteries on the Virginia bank of the Potomac, below Washington, for the purpose of obstructing the navigation of that stream, and preventing supplies for the army near the Capital being borne upon its waters. This speedily led to hostilities at the mouth of Acquia Creek, fifty-five miles below Washington City, and the terminus of the Richmond, Fredericksburg, and Potomac Railway, where the insurgents had erected batteries to command the river: one at the landing, and two others, with a line of intrenchments, on the hights in the rear. The guns of these batteries had been opened upon several vessels during the few days that the National troops had occupied the Virginia shore, when they were responded to by Captain J. H. Ward, a veteran officer of the Navy, who had been in the service almost forty years.

^a May 16, 1861. At the middle of May,^a Ward had been placed in command of the Potomac flotilla, which he had organized, composed of four armed propellers, of which the *Thomas Freeborn* was his flag-ship, and carried 32-pounders. He was sent to Hampton Roads to report to Commodore Stringham. Before reaching that commander he had an opportunity for trying his guns. The insurgents who held possession of Norfolk and the Navy Yard had been constructing batteries on Craney Island and the main, for the protection of those posts, by completely commanding the Elizabeth River. They had also erected strong works on Sewell's Point, at the mouth of the Elizabeth;¹ and at the middle of May they had three heavy rifled cannon in position there, for the purpose of sweeping Hampton Roads. This battery was masked by a sand-hill, but did not escape the eye of Captain Henry Eagle, of the National armed steamer *Star*, who sent several shot among the workmen on the Point, on the 19th. The engineers in charge, supported by a company of Georgians and some Norfolk volunteers, sent several shot in response, five of which struck the *Star*, and she was compelled to withdraw.² That night almost two thousand of the insurgent troops were sent from Norfolk to Sewell's Point, and these were there on the morning of the 20th, when Commander Ward opened the guns of the *Freeborn* upon the redoubt. The battery was soon silenced, and the insurgents were driven away.

Ward reported to Stringham, and proceeded immediately toward Washington with his flotilla. On his way up the Potomac, and when ^b May 29, 1861. within twenty-five miles of the Capital, he captured^b two schooners filled with fifty insurgent soldiers. He then proceeded to patrol the river, reconnoitering its banks in search of batteries; and on the 31st of the month he attacked those at Acquia Creek, in which service the *Freeborn* was assisted by the gunboats *Anacosta* and *Resolute* of his flotilla. For two hours an incessant discharge upon the batteries was kept up, when all the ammunition of the flotilla suitable for long range was exhausted. The three

---

¹ See map on page 399.
² The insurgents magnified this withdrawal, caused by a lack of ammunition, into a repulse, and claimed a victory for themselves. "This is the first encounter in our waters, and the victory remains with us," said a writer at Norfolk. No one seems to have been hurt, on either side, in this engagement.

batteries had been silenced.   On the slackening of Ward's fire, the two on the hights began again, and for nearly an hour they poured volleys of heavy shot on the flotilla like hail, but only wounding one man.   Unable to reply at that distance with effect, Ward withdrew his vessels, but resumed the conflict on the following day,[a] in company with the sloop-of- war *Pawnee*, of eight guns, Captain S. C. Rowan.   For more than five hours, a continuous storm of shot and shell assaulted the works on shore. This cannonade and bombardment were briskly responded to by the insurgents, who seemed to have an ample supply of munitions of war.   Twice their batteries were silenced, but their fire was resumed whenever that of the flotilla

[a] June 1, 1861.

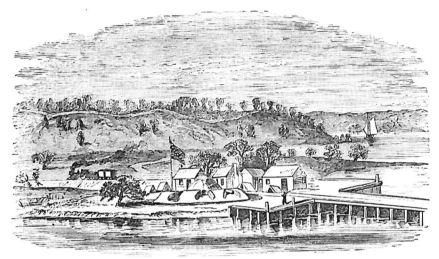

VIEW AT ACQUIA CREEK LANDING AT THE TIME OF THE ATTACK.[1]

ceased.   The *Pawnee* became the chief object of their attention.   She was hulled four times, and nine shots in all struck her ; and yet, neither on board of this vessel nor of those of Ward's flotilla was a single person killed or seriously injured.[2]   During the engagement, the large passenger and freight house near the landing was destroyed by fire.

At about this time, another aggressive movement was made by the United States forces.   It was important to gain information concerning the advance of the insurgents, said to be at Fairfax Court House at the close of May. Lieutenant Charles H. Tompkins, with seventy-five of Company B. of the Second Regiment of United States Cavalry, stationed, as we have seen, on Arlington Hights, was sent on a scout in that direction.   He left Fort Corcoran at half-past ten in the evening of the 31st,[b] and reached Fairfax Court House at about three o'clock the next morning, where Colonel (afterward General) Ewell, late of the United States

[b] May, 1861.

---

[1] This picture is from a sketch made by Mr. E. Forbes, an excellent artist, then accompanying the National forces.   Acquia Creek Landing, with the shore battery, is seen in the foreground, with the bluffs rising back of it.   The spectator is looking toward the northwest, up Acquia Creek, at the mouth of which is seen a sloop. The line of intrenchments is seen on the bluffs back of the landing.

[2] Report of Commander Ward to the Secretary of the Navy, May 31 and June 1, 1861.   Report of Commander Rowan to Secretary Welles, June 2, 1861.

Dragoons, was stationed with several hundred insurgents. Tompkins captured the pickets and then dashed into the town, driving a detachment of the insurgents before him. These were re-enforced, and a severe skirmish occurred in the street. Shots were fired upon the Union troops from windows. Finding himself greatly outnumbered by his enemy, Tompkins retreated in good order, taking with him five fully armed prisoners[1] and two horses. He lost one man killed, one missing, and four who were wounded. He also lost twelve horses and their equipments. It is estimated that about twenty of the insurgents were killed or wounded. Among the killed was Captain John Q. Marr, a highly esteemed citizen of Virginia, who had been a member of the late Secession Convention. "He has been the first soldier of the South," said the *Nashville Union*, " to baptize the soil of the Old Dominion with patriotic blood."

This gallant dash of Tompkins gave delight to the loyal people, and made the insurgent leaders at Manassas and its vicinity very vigilant and active. They were expecting an attack from the direction of Washington City, and were alarmed by military movements already commenced in Western Virginia. Troops from the more Southern States were still crowding in, and it was estimated that these, with the Virginians under arms, comprised about forty thousand men, in the camp and in the field, within the borders of the Old Commonwealth on the 1st of June, prepared to fight the troops of the Government.

There was a civil and political movement in Northwestern Virginia at this time, in opposition to the conspirators, really more important and more alarming to them than the aspect of military affairs there. It commanded the profound attention of the Government, and of the loyal and disloyal people of the whole country.

The members of the Virginia Secession Convention from the western portion of the State, as we have observed, could not be molded to suit the will of the conspirators, and they and their colleagues defied the power of the traitors who controlled the Convention. Before the adjournment of that Convention, the inhabitants of Northwestern Virginia were satisfied that the time had come when they must make a bold stand for the Union and their own independence, or be made slaves to a confederacy of traitors whom they abhorred; and Union meetings were called in various parts of the mountain region, which were largely attended. The first of these assembled at Clarksburg, in Harrison County, on the line of the Baltimore and Ohio Railway, on the 22d of April, when resolutions, offered by John S. Carlile, a member of the Convention yet sitting in Richmond, calling an assembly of delegates of the people at Wheeling, on the 13th of May, were adopted. The course of Governor Letcher was severely condemned, and eleven citizens were chosen to represent Harrison County in the Convention at Wheeling. Meetings were held elsewhere. One of these, at Kingwood, in Preston County,[a] evinced the most determined hostility to the conspirators, and declared that the separation of Western from Eastern Virginia was essential to the maintenance of their liberties. They

[a] May 4, 1861.

---

[1] Among the prisoners was W. F. Washington, son of the late Colonel John Marshall Washington, of the United States Army. He was sent to General Mansfield, at Washington City, with the other prisoners, where he took the oath of allegiance and was released.

also resolved to elect a representative in the National Congress. Similar sentiments were expressed at other meetings, especially in a mass convention held at Wheeling on the 5th of May, where it was resolved to repudiate all connection with the conspirators at Richmond. A similar meeting was held at Wheeling on the 11th, when the multitude were addressed by Mr. Carlile and Francis H. Pierpont.

The Convention of delegates met at Wheeling on the 13th. A large number of counties were represented by almost four hundred Unionists. The inhabitants of Wheeling were mostly loyal; and when the National flag was unfurled over the Custom House there, in token of that loyalty, with public ceremonies, it was greeted with loud acclamations of the people, and the flinging out, in response, of the flag of the Union over all of the principal buildings in the city.

The chief topic discussed in the Convention was the division of the State and the formation of a new one, composed of the forty or fifty Counties of the Mountain region, whose inhabitants owned very few slaves and were enterprising and thrifty. A division of the State had been desired by them for many years. The Slave Oligarchy eastward of the mountains and in all the tide-water counties wielded the political power of the State, and used it for the promotion of their great interest, in the levying of taxes and the lightening of their own burdens, at the expense of the labor and thrift of the citizens of West Virginia. These considerations, and their innate love for the Union, produced a unanimity of sentiment at this crisis that made the efforts of secret emissaries of the conspirators, and open recruiting officers of the military power arrayed against the Government, almost fruitless. This unanimity was remarkable in the Wheeling Convention, which, too informal to take definite action on the momentous question of the dismemberment of the State, contented itself with passing resolutions condemnatory of the Secession Ordinance, and calling a Provisional Convention to assemble at the same place on the 11th day of June following, if the obnoxious ordinance should be ratified by the voice of the people, to be given on the 23d of May. A Central Committee was appointed,[1] who, on the 22d of May, issued an argumentative address to the people of Northwestern Virginia.

These proceedings thoroughly alarmed the conspirators, who expected a revolt and an appeal to arms in Western Virginia, under the auspices of the National Government; and on the 25th of May, Governor Letcher wrote a letter to Colonel Porterfield, who was in command of some State troops at Grafton, at the junction of the Baltimore and Ohio and the Northwestern Railway, ordering him to "take the train some night, run up to Wheeling, and seize and carry away the arms recently sent to that place by Cameron, the United States Secretary of War, and use them in arming such men" as might "rally to his camp." He told him that it was "advisable to cut off telegraphic communication between Wheeling and Washington, so that the disaffected at the former place could not communicate with their allies at head-quarters." "Establish a perfect control over the telegraph, if kept up," he said, "so that no dispatch can pass without your knowledge and inspec-

---

[1] That Committee consisted of John S. Carlile, James S. Wheat, C. D. Hubbard, F. H. Pierpont, G. R. Latham, Andrew Wilson, S. H. Woodward, James W. Paxton, and Campbell Farr.

tion before it is sent.   If troops from Ohio or Pennsylvania shall be attempted
to be passed on the railroad, do not hesitate to obstruct their passage by all
means in your power, even to the destruction of the road and bridges."

The people in all Eastern Virginia, under the pressure of the bayonet, as
we have observed,[1] ratified the Ordinance of Secession, and gave a majority
of the votes of the State in its favor, while the vote in Western Virginia
was overwhelmingly against it.   A Convention was accordingly held at

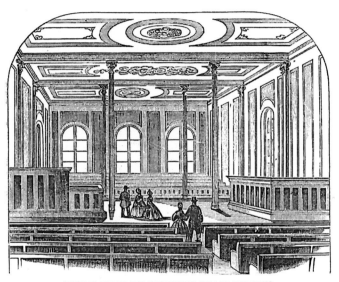

Wheeling on the
11th of June,
in which about
forty counties of
the mountain re-
gion were repre-
sented.   It met
in the Custom
House; and each
delegate, as his
credentials were
accredited, took
a solemn oath of
allegiance to the
National   Con-
stitution and its
Government.[2]

The Conven-
tion was organ-
ized by the ap-
pointment   of

ROOM IN WHICH THE CONVENTION MET AT WHEELING.

Arthur J. Boreman, of Wood County, as permanent President, and G. L.
Cranmer, Secretary.   The President made a patriotic speech on taking the
chair, and found the delegates in full union with him in sentiment.   The
Convention then went to work in earnest.   A committee was appointed to
draw up a Bill of Rights, and on the following day it reported through its
chairman, John S. Carlile.   All allegiance to the "Southern Confederacy"
was totally denied in that report, and it recommended a declaration that the
functions of all officers in the State of Virginia who adhered to it were suspended, and the offices vacated.   Resolutions were adopted, declaring the
intention of the people of Virginia never to submit to the Ordinance of
Secession, but to maintain the rights of the Commonwealth in the Union;
also, calling upon all citizens who had taken up arms against the National
Government to lay them down and return to their allegiance.

On the third day of the session,[*] an ordinance was reported
for vacating all the offices in the State held by State officers acting
in hostility to the General Government, and also providing for a Provisional

* June 13,
1861.

---

[1] See page 384.
[2] The delegates all took the following oath:—" We solemnly declare that we will support the Constitution
of the United States, and the laws made in pursuance thereof, as the supreme law of the land, any thing in the
Ordinance of the Convention that assembled at Richmond on the 13th day of February last to the contrary
notwithstanding. So help me God."

Government and the election of officers for a period of six months; also, requiring all officers of the State, counties, and towns to take the oath of allegiance. This movement was purely revolutionary. There was no pretense of secession from Virginia, but a declaration of the people that Governor Letcher and other State officers then in an attitude of rebellion against the National authority had "abdicated government," and were formally deposed, and that a new government for Virginia was formed. Governor Letcher had, by his acts, made war upon the people, and placed himself in the attitude of George the Third when he made war upon the Colonies, and thus, as they expressed it, he "abdicated government here, by declaring us out of his protection and waging war against us."[1] The Convention adopted a Declaration of Independence of the old government on the 17th, which was signed by all the members present, fifty-six in number, and on the 19th the ordinance for the establishment of a Provisional Government was adopted. The Convention had already considered the propriety of forming a new State, separate from the old one; and on the 20th there was a unanimous vote in favor of the ultimate separation of Western from Eastern Virginia. On that day, the new or "restored Government" was organized. Francis H. Pierpont, of Marion

FRANCIS H. PIERPONT.

County, was, on the nomination of the venerable Daniel Lamb, chosen Provisional Governor, with Daniel Polsley, of Mason County, as Lieutenant-Governor, and an Executive Council of five members. The unanimous voice of the Convention was given for these officers.

Governor Pierpont was a bold, patriotic, and energetic man. His first official act was to notify the President of the United States that the existing insurrection in Virginia was too formidable to be suppressed by any means at the Governor's command, and to ask the aid of the General Government. He organized the militia, and very soon no less than twelve regiments of the loyal mountaineers of Northwestern Virginia had rallied beneath the standard of the Union. Money was needed. There was no treasury, and the Governor borrowed, on the pledge of his own private fortune, twelve thousand dollars for the public service. In every way he worked unceasingly for the permanent establishment of the "restored government," and succeeded, in defiance of the extraordinary efforts of the conspirators at Richmond to crush the new organization, and bring the loyal people into subjection. A Legislature was elected, and they were summoned to a session at Wheeling on the 1st of July.[a] Soon after its assembling, it chose John S. Carlile and Waitman G. Willie to represent the restored Commonwealth in the Senate of the United States.

In the course of time the long desired dismemberment of Virginia occurred. The Convention reassembled on the 20th of August,[b]

a 1861.

b 1861.

_____

[1] The Declaration of Independence, July 4, 1776.

and passed an ordinance for the erection of a new State, in which Slavery was prohibited, to be called KANAWHA, the name of its principal stream. This ordinance was submitted to the people of the counties represented in the Convention on the 24th of October ensuing, when the vote was almost unanimous in its favor.   At a subsequent session of the Convention, on the 27th of November, the name was changed to WEST VIRGINIA, and a State Constitution was formed.   On the 3d of May following the people ratified it, and on the same day the Legislature, at a called session, approved of the division of the State, and the establishment of a new Commonwealth. All of the requirements of the National Constitution now having been complied with, West Virginia was admitted as a State of the Union on the 3d of June, 1863, by an Act of Congress, approved by the President on the 31st

SEAL OF WEST VIRGINIA.

of December, 1862.[1]   A State seal, with appropriate inscriptions and device, was adopted,[2] and the new Commonwealth took its place as the Thirty-fifth State of the Union, covering an area of twenty-three thousand square miles, and having a population, in 1860, of three hundred and ninety-three thousand two hundred and thirty four.

At the beginning of the efforts of the loyal men of Northwestern Virginia to lay the foundation of a new and Free-labor State, they found it necessary to prepare for war, for, as we have observed, the conspirators were forming camps of rendezvous in their midst, and preparing to hold them in subjection to the usurpers at Richmond.   Thousands of loyal men secretly volunteered to fight for the Union; and the National Government made preparations in Pennsylvania and beyond the Ohio River to co-operate with them at a proper moment.   Both the Government and the loyal citizens of Virginia abstained from all military movements on the soil

---

[1] The conspirators denounced the action of Congress and the President as usurpation, and a violation of the third section of the fourth Article of the Constitution, which says:—

"New States may be admitted by the Congress into this Union; but no new State shall be formed or erected within the jurisdiction of any other State, nor any State formed by the junction of two or more States or parts of States, without the consent of the Legislatures of the States concerned, as well as of the Congress."

Let us see how this matter will endure the constitutional test.   The loyal people of Virginia, and who alone constituted the State as a part of the Republic, deposed Governor Letcher and his fellow-traitors in regular form, and reorganized the Government of the Commonwealth, making Francis H. Pierpont chief magistrate.   The Legislature forming a part of this newly organized government agreed that a new State should be made out of a portion of the old one.   One part of the Constitutional requirement was thus complied with.   The other part was complied with when Congress, on the 31st of December, gave its consent to the transaction.

At midsummer, 1863, Virginia presented a curious political aspect.   Its deposed Governor, Letcher, at Richmond, claimed jurisdiction over all the State.   Governor Pierpont, at Alexandria, rightfully claimed authority over the whole State, excepting the fifty-one counties that composed the new State; and Governor Boreman, at Wheeling, legitimately exercised authority in that new State.

[2] The above picture represents the lesser seal of West Virginia, which bears the same words and devices as the great seal.   The latter is two inches and one-half in diameter.   On one side are the words, "STATE OF WEST VIRGINIA," and "MONTANA SEMPER LIBERI"—that is to say, "Mountaineers are always free."   In the center of the seal is seen a rock, on which ivy is growing, symbolizing stability and continuance, and bearing the inscription, "JUNE 20, 1863," the date of the organization and foundation of the State.   On the right of the rock is seen a farmer dressed in the hunting-shirt worn in that region, his right hand resting on a plow-handle, and on his left is reposing a woodman's ax, indicating the great business of the people to be the clearing of the forest and cultivating the soil.   There is also a sheaf of wheat and a corn-stalk near.   On the left of the rock is seen a miner with his pickax, with barrels and lumps of minerals at his feet.   An anvil and sledge-hammer are also seen, typical of the mechanic arts.   Two rifles lie in front, their junction covered by the Phrygian hood, or Cap of Liberty, indicating that the independence of the State was won and will be maintained by arms.

of that State before the votes of the people had been given on the Ordinance of Secession, on the 23d of May, for it was determined that no occasion should be afforded for a charge, which the conspirators would be quick to make, that the votes had been influenced by the presence of military power.   The reverse of this policy, as we have seen, had been pursued by the conspirators, and while the entire vote of the State showed a large majority in favor of the Ordinance, that of Western Virginia was almost unanimously against it. This verdict of the people on the great question relieved the Government and the loyal Virginians from all restraints ; and while Ohio and Indiana troops were moving toward the border, the patriots of Western Virginia, and especially of the river counties, rushed to arms.   Camp Carlile, already formed in Ohio, opposite Wheeling, was soon full of recruits, and the First Virginia Regiment was formed.   B. F. Kelley, a native of New Hampshire, but then a resident of Philadelphia, was invited to become its leader. He had lived in Wheeling, and had been commander of a volunteer regiment there.   His skill and bravery were appreciated, and in this hour of need they were required. He hastened to Wheeling, and, on the 25th of May, took command of the regiment.

George B. McClellan had been called to the command of the Ohio troops, as we have observed.   He was soon afterward commissioned a Major-General of Volunteers,[a] and assigned to the command of the Department of the Ohio, which included Western Virginia.

[a] May 14, 1861.

He was now ordered to cross the Ohio River with the troops under his charge, and, in conjunction with those under Colonel Kelley and others in Virginia, drive out the "Confederate" forces there, and advance on Harper's Ferry.   He visited Indianapolis on the 24th of May, and reviewed the brigade of Indianians who were at Camp Morton, under Brigadier-General T. A. Morris.   In a brief speech at the Bates House, he assured the assembled thousands that Indiana troops would be called upon to follow him and win distinction.[1] Two days afterward,[b] he issued an address to the Union

[b] May 26, 1861.

GEORGE B. M'CLELLAN.

citizens of Western Virginia, in which he praised their courage and patriotism, and warned them that the "few factious rebels" in their midst, who had lately attempted to deprive them of their rights at the polls, were seeking to "inaugurate a reign of terror," and thus force them to "yield to the schemes and submit to the yoke of the treacherous conspiracy dignified by the name of the 'Southern Confederacy.'"   He assured them that all their rights should be respected by the Ohio and Indiana troops about to march upon their soil, and that these should not only abstain from all interference with the slaves, but would, "on the contrary, with an iron hand, crush any attempt at insurrection on their part."   At the same time he issued a stirring address

---

[1] *Indiana's Roll of Honor:* by David Stevenson, Librarian of Indiana, page 39.

to his soldiers, telling them that they had been ordered to " cross the frontier;" that their mission was "to protect the majesty of the law, and secure our brethren from the grasp of armed traitors." He knew they would respect the feelings of the Virginians and their rights, and preserve perfect discipline. He believed in their courage. He begged them to remember that their only foes were "armed traitors;" and he exhorted his soldiers to show them mercy when they should fall into their hands, because many of them were misguided. He told them that when they had assisted the loyal men of Western Virginia until they could protect themselves, then they might return to their homes "with the proud satisfaction of having preserved a gallant people from destruction."

McClellan's addresses were read in Camp Carlile on the evening of the 26th, and Colonel Kelley and his regiment, full eleven hundred strong, immediately thereafter crossed over to Wheeling and moved in the direction of Grafton, where Colonel Porterfield was in command, with instructions from

VIRGINIA VOLUNTEER INFANTRY.

General Lee to gather volunteers there to the number of five thousand. His recruits came in slowly, and he had written to Lee, that if re-enforcements were not speedily sent into Northwestern Virginia, that section would be lost to the "Confederates."

On the evening of the 27th, Kelley reached Buffalo Creek, in Marion County, when Porterfield, thoroughly alarmed, fled from Grafton with about fifteen hundred followers, and took post at Philippi, a village on the Tygart's Valley River, a branch of the Monongahela, about sixteen miles southward from Grafton. He had destroyed two bridges in Kelley's path toward Grafton, but these were soon rebuilt by the loyal Virginians, who, under their commander, entered the deserted camp of Porterfield on the 30th. On that day, the latter issued a frantic appeal from Philippi to the

people of Northwestern Virginia, begging them to stand by the "legally constituted authorities of the State," of which he was the representative, and assuring all Unionists that they would be treated as enemies of the Commonwealth. He told the people that he came to protect them from "invasion by foreign forces," and secure to them the enjoyment of all their rights. "It seems to me," he said, most inappropriately, "that the true friend of National liberty cannot hesitate" to defend Virginia. "Strike for your State!" he exclaimed. "Strike for your liberties! Rally! rally at once in defense of your mother." His appeal had very little effect upon the sturdy people of the mountain region, and his efforts were almost fruitless.

While Colonel Kelley was pressing toward Grafton, the Ohio and Indiana troops were moving in the same direction. A part of them crossed the Ohio River at Wheeling, and another portion at Parkersburg; and they were all excepting two regiments (the Eighth and Tenth Indiana), at or near Grafton on the 2d of June, on which day General Morris arrived. Kelley was on the point of pursuing Porterfield. His troops were in line. Morris sent for him, and a new plan of operations was agreed to, by which Porterfield and his command at Philippi might be captured rather than dispersed. Kelley's troops returned to camp, and the impression went abroad that the National forces would not leave the line of the Baltimore and Ohio Railway. Word to this effect was sent to Porterfield by the secessionists in Grafton, and thus aid was unintentionally given to the "invaders" of Virginia.

The new plan was immediately executed. The forces at Grafton were arranged in two columns, commanded respectively by Colonels Kelley, of Virginia, and E. Dumont, of Indiana. Kelley's column was composed of his own regiment (the First Virginia), the Ninth Indiana, Colonel Milroy, and a portion of the Sixteenth Ohio, under Colonel Irwin. Dumont's column consisted of eight companies of his own regiment (the Seventh Indiana) ; four companies of the Fourteenth Ohio, commanded by Lieutenant-Colonel Steedman; four companies of the Sixth Indiana, under Colonel Crittenden, and a detachment of Barnet's Ohio Artillery, under Lieutenant-Colonel Sturgis. Dumont's column was accompanied by the gallant Colonel F. W. Lander, who was then a volunteer aid on General McClellan's staff, and represented him.

The two columns were to march upon Philippi by converging routes. Both left Grafton on the afternoon of the 2d ; Kelley's for Thornton, a few miles eastward, and Dumont's for Webster, a few miles westward. Kelley was to strike the Beverly Road above Philippi, in the rear of Porterfield, and Dumont was to appear at the same time on the hights overlooking that village, and plant cannon there. The hour appointed for the attack, simultaneously by both columns, was four o'clock on the dawn of the 3d.[a] Kelley had to march twenty-two miles, and Dumont twelve miles. The day was very hot, and the night was excessively dark, because of a heavy rain-storm, that commenced at sunset and continued until morning. In that darkness and in the drenching rain the two columns moved toward Philippi, over rugged hills, along slippery slopes, through humid valleys, and across swollen streams.

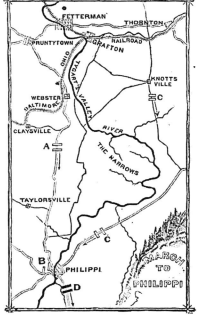

[a] June, 1861.

At the appointed time Dumont's column approached its destination. It was discovered by a woman, who fired a pistol twice at Colonel Lander, who was riding ahead of the column, and then sent her boy to alarm Porterfield. The boy was caught and detained ; and while Porterfield's camp was in commotion, on account of the report of the woman's pistol, Dumont's column took position on the hights, with his cannon commanding the bridge over the river, the village, and the insurgent camp, a fourth of a mile distant, when they were fired upon by Porterfield's pickets. Kelley had not arrived. His long march was a most wearisome one, yet he was not far off. Lander had taken command of the artillery, and fearing Porterfield might escape unhurt, should there be any delay, he ordered the opening of the heavy guns upon the insurgents. At the same time Dumont's infantry swept down the winding road to the bridge, where the insurgents had gathered in force to dispute their passage. They advanced at a double-quick, drove in the pickets, dashed across the bridge, and carried a fatal panic into the ranks of their opponents.

Kelley was hurrying on. The booming of Lander's cannon had invigorated his men. His guide was treacherous, and instead of leading him out from the hills in the rear of Porterfield's camp, he had brought him from the mountain road upon the flank of the now flying insurgents. He pushed rapidly over a ridge, and fell furiously upon the fugitives, who were driven in wild confusion through the town and up the Beverly Road. They were pursued by the columns, which had joined in the main street of Philippi, for about two miles, when the insurgents, abandoning their baggage-train, escaped, and halted only at Beverly, the capital of Randolph County, twenty-five or thirty miles farther up Tygart's Valley.[1] Porterfield's troops, about fifteen hundred strong, were one-third cavalry, and all were fresh.[2] Among the spoils of victory were the commander's official papers, a large quantity of baggage, three hundred and eighty stand of arms, and a regimental flag.[3]

BENJAMIN F. KELLEY.

The only serious casualty sustained by the Union forces in this engagement was the wounding of Colonel Kelley, who was shot through the right breast by a pistol-ball, while he was gallantly leading his troops through the town in the pursuit. He continued to press forward and urge on his men, when he fainted from loss of blood, and fell into the arms of some of his soldiers. It was believed that he was mortally hurt, and for a long time his recovery seemed almost impossible. "Say to Colonel Kelley," telegraphed General McClellan from Cincinnati to General Morris, on the day of the battle, "that I cannot believe that one who has opened his career so brilliantly can be mortally wounded. In the name of his country I thank him for his conduct, which has been the most brilliant episode

---

[1] Report of Colonel Dumont to General Morris, June 4, 1861; Grafton Correspondent of the *Wheeling Intelligencer*, June 3, 1861; *Sketch of the Life of Brigadier-General B. F. Kelley;* by Major John B. Frothingham, Topographical Engineers, serving on his staff.

[2] For the purpose of intimidating the inhabitants and suppressing all Union manifestations, Porterfield had reported his force to be twenty-five hundred in number. It did not exceed fifteen hundred, according to the most authentic estimates.

[3] Among the prisoners captured by Kelley's command was Captain J. W. Willey, on whom papers of considerable importance were found. The flag captured at Philippi was taken by men of Captain Ferry's company of the Seventh Indiana, and the National flag of that regiment, presented by the women of Aurora, was hoisted in its place.

THE UNION GENERALS

of the war, thus far. If it can cheer him in his last moments, tell him I cannot repair his loss, and that I only regret that I cannot be by his side to thank him in person. God bless him!" General Morris also sent to Kelley a cordial recognition of his bravery and valuable services; but when both messages were delivered to him, he was so weak that he could answer only with tears. A devoted daughter watched over him incessantly, and he recovered; and he soon bore the commission and the insignia of a brigadier-general.[1]

Colonel Dumont assumed the command of the combined columns after the fall of Kelley, and, assisted by Captain Henry W. Benham, the Engineer-in-chief of McClellan's army, he prepared to secure the approaches to Philippi, with a view of holding that position. Scouts, chiefly under J. W. Gordon, of the Ninth Indiana, were sent out to observe the position and number of the insurgents among the mountains, with a view to the pursuit

VIEW OF GRAFTON.[2]

of Porterfield up Tygart's Valley to Beverly. Guided by information thus obtained, and considering his lack of wagons and other means for transportation, General Morris thought it prudent to recall his troops from Philippi to Grafton, rather than to send them at that moment, and so ill prepared, on a most perilous expedition among the mountains. For a time Grafton became the head-quarters of the National troops in Northwestern Virginia.

---

[1] His commission as brigadier was dated May 17, 1861, or sixteen days earlier than the battle in which his gallantry won the reward.

[2] This village is situated among the hills, with the most picturesque scenery around it. Here the Baltimore and Ohio Railway, leading to Parkersburg, on the Ohio River, and the Northwestern Railway, leading to Wheeling, have a connection. It was an important military strategic point.

CHAPTER XXI.

BEGINNING OF THE WAR IN SOUTHEASTERN VIRGINIA.

HILST the campaign in Northwestern Virginia was opening with vigor, important events were occurring at and near Fortress Monroe, on the southeastern borders of that State, where General Benjamin F. Butler was in chief command. He had been sent thither, as we have observed, after he incurred the displeasure of the General-in-chief by the seizure of Baltimore, without orders to do so, and in a manner contrary to a proposed plan.[1] The President was not offended by the act, and he gave Butler the commission of a Major-General of Volunteers, on the 16th of May, the first of the kind that was issued from his hand.[2] With this he sent him to Fortress Monroe, to take command of the rapidly-gathering forces there, and to conduct military affairs in that part of Virginia.

Butler arrived at Fortress Monroe on the morning of the 22d of May, and was cordially received by Colonel Justin Dimick, of the regular Army, who was commander of the post. From the beginning of the rebellious movements in Virginia, that faithful officer, with only a small garrison—"three hundred men to guard a mile and a half of ramparts—three hundred to protect some sixty-five broad acres within the walls'"[3]—had kept the insurgents

---

[1] See page 448.

[2] The commissions of McClellan and Frémont were issued later, but antedated. Theirs are dated May 14. Those of Dix and Banks, bearing the same date as Butler's, were issued later, and antedated.

The following is the form of a Major-General's commission, with a representation of the seal of the War Department, which is attached to each :—

"THE PRESIDENT OF THE UNITED STATES. To all who shall see these presents, Greeting: Know ye that, reposing special trust and confidence in the patriotism, valor, fidelity, and abilities of —— ——, I have nominated, and by and with the advice and consent of the Senate, do appoint him Major-General of Volunteers, in the service of the United States, to rank as such from the — day of ——, eighteen hundred and sixty-one. He is therefore carefully and diligently to discharge the duty of Major-General, by doing and performing all manner of things thereunto belonging. And I do strictly charge and require all officers and soldiers under his command to be obedient to his orders as Major-General. And he is to observe and follow such orders and directions, from time to time, as he shall receive from me, or the future President of the United States for the time being. Given under my hand, at the city of Washington, this — day of ——, in the year of our Lord one thousand eight hundred and sixty-one, and in the eighty—— year of the Independence of the United States.

"*By the President,*   ABRAHAM LINCOLN.

"SIMON CAMERON, *Secretary of War.*"

SEAL OF THE WAR DEPARTMENT.

At the top of this commission is a large engraving of a spread eagle, and the words, "E PLURIBUS UNUM;" and at the bottom a trophy group, composed of flags and implements of war. The seal is an inch and seven-eighths in diameter, and impressed on colored paper.

[3] Major Theodore Winthrop, in the *Atlantic Monthly.*

at bay. He had quietly but significantly turned the muzzles of some of his great guns landward; and, unheeding the mad cry of the politicians, that it was an act of war, and the threats of rebellious men in arms, of punishment for his insolence, he defied the enemies of his country. Those guns taught Letcher prudence, and Wise caution, and Lee circumspection, and Jefferson Davis respectful consideration. The immense importance of the post was

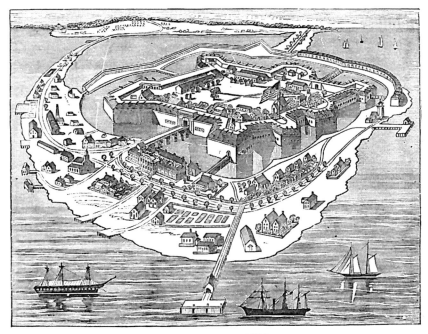

FORTRESS MONROE IN 1861.[1]

apprehended by them all, and its possession was coveted by them all; but there was Dimick, late in May, with the great fortress and its almost four hundred cannon—the massive key to the waters of Maryland, Virginia, and Upper North Carolina—firmly in his possession—" a fine old Leonidas at the

---

[1] This was the most extensive military work in the country. It was commenced in 1819, and was completed at a cost of two millions five hundred thousand dollars. It was named in honor of President Monroe. Its walls, faced with heavy blocks of granite, are thirty-five feet in thickness, and casemated below. It is entirely surrounded by a deep moat filled with water; and the peninsula, known as Old Point Comfort, on which it is constructed, is connected with the main by a narrow isthmus of sand, and by a bridge in the direction of the village of Hampton. The picture is a bird's-eye view of the fort and its surroundings in 1861. Beginning at the top of the picture, we see, on the extreme left, the Chesapeake Female Seminary, and toward the right, Camp Hamilton. Over and beyond us is the village of Hampton. Beginning at the isthmus, on the right, we see the grand water-battery. Next to it is the light-house, and the old wharf. Next are seen buildings, with trees in front, for the accommodation of the Government officers. There is seen the Quartermaster's, or Baltimore Wharf, near which are several buildings for Government use. Near there a railway commences which extends across the bridge to the main, to near Hampton Bridge. Farther to the left is seen the United States Hospital building, with wharves in front; and near by, the main entrance to the fort, across a drawbridge. Farther to the left are a church and the Ordnance Department. Within the fort, at the right of the flag, is seen the Commanding General's quarters, and not far from it, crossed by the perpendicular flag-staff, is the chapel. Across the parade from the church, are the barracks—a long building. The aspect of the place, outside of the fort, was much changed during the war.

head of the three hundred," when General Butler arrived and took the chief command, with troops sufficient to insure its safety against the attacks of any force at the disposal of the conspirators.

General Butler's first care was, after making Fortress Monroe secure from capture, to ascertain the condition of affairs in his department. He knew that it was the desire of the Government and the people to seize and hold Richmond, which the conspirators had chosen for their future and permanent head-quarters. The troops then in and around Washington City were barely sufficient to keep the hourly increasing host of the insurgents at Manassas in check; and the easiest and most expeditious route to Richmond seemed to be by way of the York and James Peninsula, and the James River, from Fortress Monroe. With the capture of Richmond in view, Butler shaped all of his movements.

On the day after his arrival, the Commanding General sent out Colonel Phelps, at the head of some Vermont troops, to reconnoiter the vicinity of Hampton. They were confronted at the bridge over Hampton Creek by the blazing timbers of that structure, which the insurgents had fired. The Vermonters soon extinguished the flames, crossed the stream, entered Hampton, and drove what few armed opponents they found there out upon the roads leading toward Yorktown and Newport-Newce.[1] They found the white inhabitants in sullen mood, but the negroes were jubilant, for they regarded the troops as their expected deliverers. Colonel Phelps did not linger long in Hampton, but recrossed the bridge, and on the Segar farm he selected a place for an encampment, which was at once occupied by the Vermont regiment and another from Troy (the Second New York), under Colonel Carr, and named Camp Hamilton. On the same day a small redoubt for two guns was cast up at the Fortress Monroe end of Hampton Bridge, so as to command that passage. This was the first military work made by Union troops on the soil of Virginia.

On the evening of the 24th,[a] a circumstance occurred at Fortress Monroe which had a very important bearing upon the contest then opening. In the confusion caused by Colonel Phelps's dash into Hampton, three negroes, claimed as the property of Colonel Mallory of that village, escaped to the Union lines, and declared that many of their race and class were employed by the insurgents in building forti-

[a] May, 1861.

---

[1] There has been some discussion and considerable research concerning the true orthography of this locality and the origin of its name. The commonly received explanation is that, at one time, when the English colony at Jamestown was in a starving condition, the supply ships of Captain Newport were first seen off this point, and gave the beholders the good news of food at hand; hence the place was called Newport's News. History does not seem to warrant the acceptance of this theory, but furnishes a better. In 1619 Governor Yeardley established a representative government in Virginia, with simple machinery, and laid the political foundations of that State. This government was strengthened by his successor, Governor Wyatt, under whom were proper civil officers. In instructions to Wyatt occurs the following sentence:—" George Sandis is appointed Treasurer, and he is to put into execution all orders of Court about staple commodities; to the Marshal, Sir William Newce, the same." This settles the point that there was a leading man in Virginia at that time named Newce—" Captain Nuse," as Captain Smith wrote the name. A writer in the *Historical Magazine* (iii. 347) says, that on earlier maps of Virginia, which he has seen, he finds the point called Newport *Neuse*, which, he argues, is only another way of spelling Newce, and that the name given is a compound of the name of the celebrated navigator and the Virginia marshal, namely, Newport-Newce. This compounding of words in naming places was then common in England, and became so in this country, as Randolph-Macon, Hampton-Sidney, and Wilkes-Barré. In Captain Smith's map of Virginia, the place is called Point Hope. That map was made after the alleged discovery of Newport with his supplies. Believing that the name was originally a compound of those of Captain Newport and Marshal Newce, the author of this work adopts the orthography given in the text—Newport-Newce.

fications, and that they themselves were about to be sent to North Carolina for the same purpose. They were taken before General Butler. He needed laborers on field-works, which he expected to erect immediately. Regarding these slaves, according to the laws of Virginia, as much the property of Colonel Mallory as his horses or his pistols, and as properly seizable as they, as aids in warfare, and which might be used against the National troops, Butler said:—"These men are contraband of war; set them at work." This order was scarcely pronounced before Major Carey, of the "Virginia Volunteers," sought an interview with the General respecting the fugitives, representing himself as the agent of Colonel Mallory in "charge of his property." The interview was granted, when the Major wished to know what the General intended to do with the runaways. "I shall detain them as contraband of war," was the reply; and they were held as such.

Other slaves speedily followed those of Colonel Mallory, and General Butler wrote to the Secretary of War concerning them, relating what he had done, on the assumption that they were the property of an enemy used in warfare, and asking for instructions. The General's action was approved by his Government; and thenceforward all fugitive slaves were considered as "contraband of war," and treated as such. On the spot where the first African who was sold as a slave in America first inhaled the fresh air of the New World, the destruction of the system of slavery, which had prevailed in Virginia two hundred and forty years, was thus commenced.[1] That master-stroke of policy was one of the most effective blows aimed at the heart of the rebellion; and throughout the war the fugitive slave was known as a *contraband.* "An epigram," prophetically wrote the brilliant Major Winthrop, of Butler's staff, who fell in battle a few days later—"an epigram abolished slavery in the United States."

THEODORE WINTHROP.

Thoroughly convinced that Fortress Monroe was the proper base for operations against Richmond; for the severance of Virginia from the other Southern States; and for the seizure of the great railway centers of that Commonwealth, Butler made his plans and dispositions accordingly. On the 27th of May he sent Colonel Phelps in the steamer *Catiline,* with a detachment, to occupy and fortify the promontory of Newport-Newce, where the United States steamer *Harriet Lane* lay to protect them. He was accompanied by Lieutenant John T. Greble, of the Second Regiment of Artillery, an accomplished young officer, educated at West Point, whom he appointed Master of Ordnance, to superintend the construction of the works. Greble had under his command two subalterns and twenty men of the regular Army. Camp Butler was at

---

[1] The peninsula on which Fortress Monroe stands was the first resting-place of the early emigrants to Virginia, after their long and perilous voyage, and was named by them Point Comfort. There the crew of a Dutch vessel, with negroes from Africa, landed in August, 1620, and a few days afterward sold twenty of their human cargo to the settlers at Jamestown. So negro Slavery was begun on the domain of the United States.

once established ; and in the course of a few days a battery was planted at Newport-Newce that commanded the ship-channel of the James River and the mouth of the Nansemond, on one side of which, on Pig Point, the insur gents had constructed a strong redoubt, and armed it well with cannon from the Gosport Navy Yard. It was a part of Butler's plan of campaign to

capture or turn that redoubt, pass up the Nansemond, and seize Suffolk ; and, taking possession of the rail-way connections between that town and Petersburg and Nor-folk, menace the Wel-don Road—the great highway between Vir-ginia and the Caro-linas. To do this re-quired more troops and munitions of war,

NEWPORT-NEWCE LANDING.

and especially of means for transportation, than General Butler had then at his command ; and he was enabled only to take possession of and hold the important strategic point of Newport-Newce at that time. In order to ascertain the strength of the Pig Point Battery, he sent Captain John Faunce, with the United States armed steamer *Harriet Lane*, to attack it.[a]

a June 5, 1861. The water was so shallow that Faunce was compelled to open fire at the distance of eighteen hundred yards. In the course of forty-five minutes he threw thirty shot and shell at the redoubt, most of which fell short. With guns of longer range, and more effective, the com-mander of the battery returned the fire. The *Harriet Lane* was struck twice, and five of her men were wounded. Satisfied that the battery was a dangerous one, her commander withdrew.[1]

On the day after Colonel Phelps's departure, Colonel Abraham Duryée, commander of a well-disciplined regiment of Zouaves, composing the Fifth New York Volunteers, arrived at Fortress Monroe, and was at once assigned to the command of Camp Hamilton, as acting brigadier-general. His regi-ment had preceded him a few days. He at once issued a proclamation to the inhabitants of that portion of Virginia, friendly in tone, and assuring them that the rights and property of all peaceable citizens should be re-spected. The troops in his charge consisted of the First, Second, Third, Fifth, Tenth, and Twentieth New York Volunteers, and the Pennsylvania Seventy-first, known as the California Regiment, under Colonel Baker, a member of the United States Senate.[2] Duryée was succeeded a few days afterward by Brigadier-General E. W. Peirce, of Massachusetts, Butler's senior in rank in the militia of that State, who had generously yielded his claims to higher position for the sake of his country. He was a brave and

1 Report of Captain Faunce to flag-officer J. G. Pendergrast, in command of the *Cumberland*, June 5, 1861.
2 See pages 227 and 355.

patriotic man, and was willing to serve the cause in any capacity. He came from the command of the principal rendezvous for Massachusetts troops, at Fort Warren, and entered upon his duties, as the leader of the forces at Camp Hamilton, on the 4th of June.

The forced inaction of the troops at Fortress Monroe, and the threatening aspect of affairs at Newport-Newce, which Greble was rendering impregnable, made the armed insurgents on the Peninsula, who were commanded by Colonel J. Bankhead Magruder[1] (who had abandoned his flag), bold, active, and vigilant. Their principal rendezvous was Yorktown, which they were fortifying, and from which they came down the Peninsula, to impress the slaves of men who had fled from their farms into service on the military works, to force Union residents into their ranks, and on some occasions to attack the Union pickets.

Major Winthrop, Butler's aid and military secretary, whose whole soul was alive with zeal in the cause he had espoused, was continually on the alert, and he soon learned from a "contraband," named George Scott, that the insurgents had fortified outposts at Great and Little Bethel (the names of two churches), on the road between Yorktown and Hampton, and only a few miles from the latter place. With Scott as guide, Winthrop

J. BANKHEAD MAGRUDER.

reconnoitered these positions, and was satisfied that Magruder was preparing to attempt the seizure of Newport-Newce and Hampton, and confine Butler to Fortress Monroe. The latter resolved upon a countervailing movement, by an attack upon these outposts by troops moving at midnight in two columns, one from Fortress Monroe and the other from Newport-Newce. Among Major Winthrop's papers was found a rough draft of the details of the plan, in his own handwriting, which the biographer of Butler says was "the joint production of the General and his Secretary," and which "was substantially adopted, and orders in accordance therewith were issued."[2]

At noon on Sunday, the 9th of June, General Peirce received a note from General Butler, written with a pencil on the back of an address card, summoning him to Fortress Monroe. Peirce was too ill to ride on horseback, and was taken by water in a small boat. There he found a plan minutely arranged for an attack upon the insurgents at the two Bethels, on the York-

---

[1] Magruder, who became a "Confederate general," was an infamous character. He was a lieutenant-colonel of the artillery in the National Army, and, according to a late writer, professed loyalty until he was ready to abandon his flag. "Mr. Lincoln," he said to the President, at the White House, at the middle of April, "every one else may desert you, but *I* never will." The President thanked him, and two days afterward, having done all in his power to corrupt the troops in Washington City, he fled and joined the insurgents. See Greeley's *American Conflict*, i. 506.

[2] Parton's *Butler in New Orleans*, page 142. In that plan Winthrop put down, among other items, the following:—"George Scott to have a shooting-iron."—"So," says Parton, "the first suggestion of arming a black man in this war came from Theodore Winthrop. George Scott *had* a shooting-iron." In one of his last letters to a friend, Winthrop wrote:—"If I come back safe, I will send you my notes of the plan of attack, part made up from the General's hints, part my own fancies."

town Road, and received orders to command the expedition. He was directed to lead Duryée's Fifth and Townsend's Third New York Volunteers from Camp Hamilton to a point near Little Bethel, where he was to be joined by a detachment from Colonel Phelps's command at Newport-Newce. These latter consisted of a battalion of Vermont and Massachusetts troops (the latter of Wardrop's Third Regiment), under Lieutenant-Colonel Washburne;

EBENEZER W. PEIRCE.

Colonel Bendix's Germans (the Seventh New York), known as the Steuben Rifle Regiment, and a battery of two light field-pieces (6-pounders), in charge of Lieutenant Greble, who was accompanied by eleven artillerymen of his little band of regulars. As the expedition was to be undertaken in the night, and there was to be a junction of troops converging from two points, General Butler ordered the watchword, "Boston," to be given to each party, and that they should wear on their left arms a white rag or handkerchief, so as to be known to each other. The column at Camp Hamilton was to start at midnight, and that at Newport-Newce a little later, as its line of march would be shorter. The troops at Camp Hamilton were ordered to shout "Boston," when they should charge the insurgents; and other precautions were taken to prevent blunders, into which inexperienced soldiers were liable to fall.

Duryée and his Zouaves left Camp Hamilton at near midnight,[a] preceded by two companies of skirmishers, under Captains Bartlett and Kilpatrick. Hampton Bridge had been so much injured by the fire that it might not be safely crossed in darkness, so the troops were ferried over the creek in surf-boats, after considerable delay. Colonel Townsend's Albany Regiment, with two mountain howitzers, marched an hour later to support Duryée. The latter was directed to take a by-road, after crossing New Market Bridge, over the southwest branch of Back River, and, getting between the insurgent forces at Big and Little Bethel, fall upon those at the latter place, and, if successful there, push on and attack those at the former.

[a June 9, 1861.]

Bartlett and Kilpatrick reached New Market Bridge at one o'clock in the morning,[b] where they awaited the arrival of the Zouaves at three o'clock. They then pushed on toward the new County Bridge at Big Bethel, and at a little before daylight captured an insurgent picket-guard near there. In the mean time Lieutenant-Colonel Washburne had advanced from Newport-Newce, followed by Bendix with his Germans, and Greble with his battery and artillerymen, as supports. Butler had directed the march of both columns to be so timed as to make a simultaneous attack at Little Bethel just at dawn; and to prevent mistakes he ordered the troops that might first attack to shout "Boston." Every thing was working admirably, according to instructions, when an unfortunate circumstance ruined the expedition.

[b June 10.]

Duryée, as we have observed, was pressing on to get in the rear of Little

Bethel, followed by Townsend. Washburne, at the same time, was pushing on toward the same point, followed by Bendix and the artillery. Townsend and Bendix approached the point of junction, in front of Little Bethel, in a thick wood, at the same moment. Townsend's men, dressed similar to the insurgents, wore their white badges, and were ready to shout the watchword. Bendix's men had no badges, and were ignorant of the watchword. Butler's aid, who was sent to Newport-Newce with orders for the advance, had neglected to give the watchword or order the wearing of the badges. Bendix knew that the insurgents, with proper precaution, had worn white bands on their hats. Seeing, in the dim starlight and a slight mist, just before the

DURYÉE'S ZOUAVES.[1]

dawn, similar badges on the arms of an approaching column of men, clad something like the enemy, he mistook them for his foe,[2] and ordered an attack. The Germans at once opened upon Townsend's column with musketry and one cannon. The other cannon was with Lieutenant Greble, who had pushed eagerly forward a mile or more in advance.[3] Townsend's men shouted " Boston " lustily, while Bendix's men shouted " Saratoga." The shots of the Germans were returned irregularly, when the assailed party,

---

[1] The costume of Duryée's corps was that of the Second Regiment of the French Zouaves, composed of a blue jacket trimmed with red, and blue shirt trimmed with the same; full scarlet trowsers with leather leggins, and scarlet cap with blue tassel, partly arranged in turban form.

[2] It is said that Bendix was also deceived by the fact that General Peirce and Colonel Townsend, with their respective staff officers, who were riding in front of the column, were mistaken for cavalry, and as there was none with the expedition, it was supposed to be that of the insurgents.

[3] For want of horses, one hundred men had drawn one of Greble's cannon from Newport-Newce, and two mules the other. With the latter, he was pressing on toward Duryée's column.

supposing they had fallen into an ambush of insurgents, retreated to the fork of the road, when the dreadful mistake was discovered. Townsend lost two men killed and several wounded in the affair. Captain Haggerty, the officer who forgot to give the order for the badges and the watchword, was greatly distressed by the consequences of his remissness, and exclaimed, " How can I go back and look General Butler in the face !"[1]

Hearing the firing in their rear, both Duryée (who had just surprised and captured an outlying guard of thirty men) and Washburne, and also Lieutenant Greble, thinking the insurgents had fallen upon the supporting columns, immediately reversed their march and joined the sadly confused regiments of Townsend and Bendix. In the mean time, General Peirce, who knew that the insurgents at Great Bethel had been warned of the presence of National troops by this firing, had sent back for re-enforcements. The First New York, Colonel William H. Allen, and the Second New York, Colonel Carr, were immediately sent forward from Camp Hamilton, the former with directions to proceed to the front, and the latter to halt for further orders at New Market Bridge. The insurgents at Little Bethel, not more than fifty in number, had fled to the stronger post at Big Bethel, four or five miles distant,

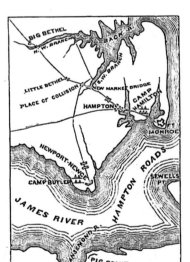

FROM PIG POINT TO BIG BETHEL.

and the National troops speedily followed, after destroying the abandoned camp of the fugitives.[2]

The insurgents at Big Bethel, about twelve miles from Hampton Bridge, were on the alert. Their position was a strong one, on the bank of the northwest branch of Back River, with that stream directly in front, which was there narrow and shallow, and spanned by a bridge, but widening on each flank into a morass, much of the time' impassable, according to the testimony of George Scott, the negro guide. They had erected a strong earthwork on each side of the road, which commanded the bridge, and a line of intrenchments along the bank of the wooded swamp on their right. Immediately in the rear of their works was a wooden structure known as Big Bethel Church. Behind these works, which were masked by green boughs, and partly concealed by a wood, were about eighteen hundred insurgents[3] (many of them cavalry), under Colonel Magruder, composed of Virginians and a North Carolina regiment under Colonel D. H. Hill. They were reported to be four thousand strong, with twenty pieces of heavy cannon ; and such was Kilpatrick's estimate, after a reconnoissance.[4]

[1] Statement of General Peirce to the author.
[2] Near Little Bethel, a wealthy insurgent, named Whiting, came out of his mansion and deliberately fired on the Union troops. Retaliation immediately followed. His large house, filled with elegant furniture and a fine library, was laid in ashes.
[3] Pollard's *First Year of the War*, page 77.   [4] Kilpatrick's Report.

Notwithstanding this reputed strength of the insurgents, and the weariness of his troops, who had been up all night, and had marched many miles in the hot sunbeams, General Peirce, after consultation with his officers, resolved to attack them. The whole force under his command pressed forward, and by half-past nine o'clock in the morning they reached a point within a mile of the foe, where disposition was made for battle.

To Duryée's Zouaves was assigned the duty of leading in the attack. Skirmishers, under Captains Kilpatrick, Bartlett, and Winslow, and all under the command of Lieutenant-Colonel G. K. Warren, of the Zouaves (who was acquainted with the ground), were thrown out on each side of the road leading to the bridge, closely followed by Duryée, and three pieces of artillery under Lieutenant Greble.[1] On the right of the advancing force was a wood that extended almost to the stream, and on the front and left were an orchard and corn-field. Into the orchard and corn-field Duryée advanced obliquely, with Townsend as a support on his right and rear. Greble, with his battery, continued to advance along the road, with Bendix as a support, whose regiment deployed on the right of the highway, in the wood, toward the left flank of the insurgents, with three companies of Massachusetts and Vermont troops of Washburne's command.

The battle was opened by a Parrott rifled cannon fired from the insurgent battery to the right of the bridge, by Major Randolph, commander of the Richmond Howitzer Battalion. This was answered by cheers from the Union troops, who steadily advanced in the face of a heavy fire, intending to dash across the stream and storm the works. Most of the shot passed over their heads at first. Very soon the firing became more accurate; men began to fall here and there; and at length the storm of shot and shell was intolerable. The skirmishers and Zouaves withdrew from the open fields to the shelter of the wood on the right of the road, whilst Greble, still advancing, poured a rapid and effective shower of grape and canister shot from his battery upon the works of the insurgents, at a distance, finally, of not more than two hundred yards. That position he held for almost two hours, while the remainder of the army was resting and preparing for a general assault. He had only an ordinary force of gunners at first, but Warren managed to send him relief, and by a skillful use of his guns, and limited supply of ammunition, he kept the insurgents within their works.

All things being in readiness, at about noon a charge was sounded, and the troops moved rapidly forward, with instructions to dash across the morass, flank the works of the insurgents, and drive out the occupants at the point of the bayonet. Duryée's Zouaves moved to attack them on their left, and Townsend's New York Third started for like duty on their right, while Bendix, with the New York Seventh and the rest of the Newport-Newce detachment, should assail them on their left flank and rear. Greble, in the mean time, kept his position in the road on their front.

Kilpatrick, Bartlett, and Winslow charged boldly on the front of the foe, while Captain Denike and Lieutenant Duryée (son of the Colonel) and some of Townsend's regiment as boldly fell upon their right. The insurgents were driven out of their battery nearest the bridge, and a speedy victory for the

---

[1] One of Townsend's mountain howitzers had been added to Greble's battery of two guns.

Union soldiers seemed inevitable.   The Zouaves were then advancing through
the wood to the morass, but, believing it to be impassable, their commander
ordered them to retire.   Town-

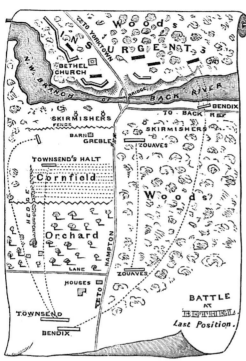

send was pressing vigorously
on toward the right of the foe,
but was suddenly checked by
a fatal blunder.   In the haste
of starting, two companies of
his regiment had marched unobserved on the side of a
thickly hedged ditch opposite
the main body, and, pushing
rapidly forward, came up a
gentle slope at some distance
in the front, where the smoke
was thick, to join their companions.   Their dress, as we
have observed, was similar to
that worn by the insurgents,
and they were mistaken for a
party of Magruder's men outflanking the New Yorkers.
Townsend immediately halted,
and then fell back to the point
of departure.   At that moment, General Peirce had
placed himself at the head
of the Zouaves, to lead them
to an attack, and Bendix and

BATTLE AT BIG BETHEL.

the rest of the Newport-Newce detachment were pressing forward, in obedience to orders.   Some of them crossed the morass, and felt sure of victory,
when they were driven back by a murderous fire.   The insurgents, having
been relieved on their right by the withdrawal of Townsend, had concentrated their forces at the battery in front of this assaulting party.   Major
Winthrop was with the Newport-Newce troops at this time, and had pressed
eagerly forward, with private Jones of the Vermont regiment, to a point
within thirty or forty yards of the battery.   He sprang upon a log to get
a view of the position, when the bullet of a North Carolina drummer-boy
penetrated his brain, and he fell dead.   •
     Townsend's retirement, the repulse on the right, and the assurance of
Colonel Duryée, that his ammunition was exhausted, caused General Peirce,
with the concurrence of his colonels, to order a retreat.   Greble was still at
work, but with only one gun, for he had only five men left.   On receiving
the order, he directed Corporal Peoples to limber up the piece and take it
away.   At that moment a shot from the insurgents struck a glancing blow
upon his right temple, and he fell dead, with the exclamation, " Oh! my
God!"   Thus perished, at the very opening of the civil war, one of the most
promising of the young officers who had hastened to the field in obedience
to the call of the President.   He was the first officer of the regular Army

who gave his life to his country in the great struggle; and was one of a class of graduates of the West Point Military Academy, which furnished several distinguished general officers for the war that ensued.[1] Generous, brave, and good, he was greatly beloved by all who knew him, and was sincerely mourned by the nation. His name will forever be associated, in the minds and hearts of his countrymen, with all the brave men who fought in that struggle for Nationality and Right, as the beloved young martyr.[2] So, too, will the memory of Winthrop, the gentle, the brilliant, and the brave, be cherished by a grateful people.

JOHN TROUT GREBLE.

General Butler, as we have observed, had sent Colonel Allen with the First, and Colonel Carr with the Second New York Regi-

---

[1] There were forty-six graduates of his class of one hundred, of whom twenty-three remained true to the Union, and fourteen joined the insurgents when the war broke out. At that time, seven of them were known to be dead. Ten of the fourteen disloyal ones became generals in the "Confederate" army, namely, G. W. C. Lee, Jas. Deshler, John P. Pegram, J. E. B. Stuart, Archibald Gracie, S. D. Lee, W. D. Pender, J. B. Villepigue, J. T. Mercer, and A. B. Chapman. Only four of the loyal graduates were raised to the rank of general, namely, Henry L. Abbot, Thomas E. Ruger, O. O. Howard, and S. H. Weed. Of the forty-six graduates, it is known that twelve were killed in battle, and, up to this time (December, 1865), eight have died.

[2] Lieutenant Greble's body was borne to Fortress Monroe by the sorrowing Zouaves, in the chapel of which it was laid, and received the administration of funeral rites before it was conveyed to his native city of Philadelphia. His father, accompanied by an intimate friend, had just arrived at Fortress Monroe, on a visit to his son, taking with him delicacies from home and tokens of affection from his young wife, when news of the battle, and the death of the hero, was communicated to him. Sadly they returned, bearing with the body the following touching letter to his wife, daughter of the Rev. J. W. French, his senior Professor at West Point:—"May God bless you, my darling, and grant you a happy and peaceful life. May the good Father protect you and me, and grant that we may live happily together long lives. God give me strength, wisdom, and courage. If I die, let me die as a brave and honorable man; let no stain of dishonor hang over me or you. Devotedly, and with my whole heart, your husband." This was written with a pencil, and evidently after arriving on the field. He seemed to have had a presentiment that he should not survive the expected battle. To a brother officer he said, on starting, "This is an ill-advised and badly arranged movement. I am afraid no good will come of it; and as for myself, I do not think I shall come off the field alive."

Lieutenant Greble's body received military honors in Philadelphia. It lay in state in Independence Hall, at the request of the City Councils, on the 14th of June, where it was visited by thousands of citizens. It was then borne in solemn procession to his father's residence, escorted by Captain Starr's company of militia, and followed by officers of the Army and Navy, the city authorities, and a large body of military and citizens. From there it was conveyed to Woodland Cemetery, in the vicinity of Philadelphia, when his father-in-law read the final funeral service, and he was buried with military honors. Over his remains his family erected a beautiful and unique monument of white marble, bearing the following inscriptions:—On the concave side, "John T. Greble, First Lieutenant, U. S. A. Born January 12, 1834; killed at Great Bethel, June 10, 1861." On the convex side, seen in the engraving, "John T. Greble, First Lieutenant, U. S. A. Blessed are the pure in heart, for they shall see God."

GREBLE'S MONUMENT.

The City Councils of Philadelphia adopted a series of resolutions relative to his death; and a portrait of the martyr, painted by Marchant, was presented to the corporation. The officers at Fortress Monroe had already, by resolution, on the 11th of June, borne testimony of their appreciation of their companion-in-arms; and Lieutenant-Colonel (afterward Major-General) Warren said: "His efficiency alone prevented our loss from being thrice what it was, by preventing the opposing batteries from sweeping the road along which we marched; and the impression which he made on the enemy deterred them from pursuing our retreating forces, hours after he had ceased to live."

ment, as re-enforcements. These arrived while the battle was going on. Peirce ordered them to the front, as if to renew the conflict, and they served as a cover to the wearied troops in their retreat. That retreat was in good order. The dead and wounded, and arms and munitions were all borne away. Lieutenant-Colonel Warren carried off the body of Lieutenant Greble, but that of Winthrop remained for a time with the insurgents.[1] Kilpatrick, who was badly wounded by a shot through his thigh, was rescued and borne away by Captain Winslow.[2] The insurgent cavalry pursued about six miles, when they returned; and on the same day Magruder and his whole party withdrew to Yorktown. The loss of the National troops was reported at sixteen killed, thirty-four wounded, and five missing. That of the insurgents was trifling. The number of the National force at Great Bethel was about twenty-five hundred, and that of the insurgents eighteen hundred.

As soon as General Butler was informed of the action he proceeded to Hampton, for the purpose of sending forward wagons and ambulances for the sick and wounded, and to join the expedition in person. His horse swam Hampton Creek, while he crossed in a boat. Tidings soon came that the battle was over, and he remained at Hampton to receive the disabled, who were sent by water to the hospital at Fortress Monroe.[3]

The battle at Bethel, with its disastrous results, surprised and mortified the nation, and the assurance of the Department Commander, that " we have gained more than we have lost," was not accepted at the time as a fair conclusion. " Our troops," he said, in support of his inference, " have learned to have confidence in themselves under fire; the enemy have shown that they will not meet us in the open field, and our officers have learned wherein their organization and drill are inefficient." But the people were not satisfied. Their chagrin must be appeased. It was felt that somebody was to blame, and the offender on whom to lay the responsibility was earnestly sought. The Department Commander, the chief leader on the field, and the heads of regiments, were all in turn censured, while the bravery of the troops was properly extolled. So thoroughly were Butler's services at Annapolis and Baltimore overshadowed and obscured by this cloud of disaster, that the confirmation of his appointment to a major-generalship was secured in the Senate by only two votes, and these through the exertions of Senator Baker, who was soon to fall a sacrifice to incompetency or something worse. The heaviest weight of responsibility finally rested, in the public comprehension of the affair, on General Peirce; but, we are satisfied, after careful investiga-

[1] The bravery of Winthrop was extolled by the foe. They gave his body a respectful burial at Bethel, and it was disinterred a few days afterward and taken to New York. "On the 19th of April," says his friend George W. Curtis, in a beautiful sketch of his life, " he left the armory-door of the Seventh, with his hand upon a howitzer—on the 21st of June, his body lay upon the same howitzer, at the same door, wrapped in the flag for which he gladly died, as the symbol of human freedom."—*The Fallen Brave :* edited by J. G. Shea, LL. D., page 41.

[2] In his report, Kilpatrick said, after speaking of the engagement, and of a number of men being killed :—" Having received a grape-shot through my thigh, which tore off a portion of the rectangle on Colonel Duryée's left shoulder, and killed a soldier in the rear, I withdrew my men to the skirts of the wood. . . . I shall ever be grateful to Captain Winslow, who rescued me after our forces had left."

[3] This account of the battle at Bethel is prepared from a written statement of General Peirce to the author, in February, 1865; Report of General Butler to the General-in-chief, June 10, 1861; Reports of Colonels Duryée and Allen, and Captain Kilpatrick, June 11, 1861; Orders of General Peirce, June 9, 1861, and letter of the same to the editor of the *Boston Journal,* August 3, 1861 ; Report of Colonel D. H. Hill to Governor Ellis, of North Carolina, June 11, 1861; and Report of Colonel Magruder, June 12, and correspondence of the *Richmond Despatch,* June 11, 1861.

tion, without justice. During the remainder of his three months' service, when he held command at Hampton, he bore the load of odium with suffering that almost dethroned his reason, but with the dignity of conscious innocence. Then he entered the service for three years as a private soldier. He arose quickly to the position of a commander of a regiment, and performed signal service in Maryland, Virginia, Kentucky, Tennessee, and Mississippi. In one of the severe battles fought on the Virginia Peninsula, which we shall consider hereafter, he was chosen by General Richardson to perform most perilous duty in front of a heavy battery of the foe, then hurling a hundred shot a minute. Whilst waving his sword, and shouting to his regiment, "At the double-quick! Follow me!" his right arm was torn from his shoulder by a 32-pound ball, that cut a man in two just behind him. Peirce was a gallant and faithful soldier during the whole war, and deserves the grateful thanks of his countrymen.

In contemplating the battle at Bethel in the light of contemporary and subsequent events, the historian is constrained to believe that the disaster on that day was chargeable more to a general eagerness to do, without experience in doing, than to any special shortcomings of individuals.

VIEW IN THE MAIN STREET OF HAMPTON IN 1864.[1]

The writer visited the battle-ground at Great Bethel early in December, 1864, in company with the father of Lieutenant Greble and his friend (F. J. Dreer), who was with him when he bore home the lifeless body of his son. We arrived at Fortress Monroe on Sunday morning,[a] and after breakfasting at the Hygeian Restaurant, near the Baltimore wharf, we called on General Butler, who was then the commander [a December 11, 1864.] of the Department of Virginia and North Carolina. He was at his quarters in the fortress, and was preparing to sail on the memorable expedition against the forts at the mouth of the Cape Fear River, and the town of Wilmington, so famous as the chief port for blockade-runners. We were invited by General Butler to accompany him, and gladly embraced the opportunity to become spectators of some of the most stirring scenes of the war. Whilst waiting two or three days for the expedition to sail, we visited the battle-ground at Big Bethel, the site of Hampton, and the hospitals and schools in the vicinity of Fortress Monroe.

[1] This is a view from the main street, looking northwest toward the old church, whose ruins are seen toward the left of the picture, in the back-ground. The three huts in front occupy the sites of the stores of Adler. Peake, and Armistead, merchants of Hampton. The one with the wood-sawyer in front was a barber's shop

Sixteen years before,[a] the writer, while gathering up materials for his *Pictorial Field-Book of the Revolution*, visited Hampton and the fortress,

a 1848. and traveled over the road from Yorktown to the coast, on which the battle at Great Bethel occurred. The aspect of every thing was now changed. The country, then thickly settled and well cultivated, was now desolated and depopulated. The beautiful village of Hampton, which contained a resident population of about fourteen hundred souls when the war broke out, had been devoured by fire; and the venerable St. John's Church, built in far-back colonial times, and presenting a picturesque and well-preserved relic of the past, was now a blackened and mutilated ruin, with the ancient brick wall around the yard serving as a part of the line of fortifications cast up there by the National troops. The site of the town

was now covered with rude cabins, all occupied by negroes freed from bondage; and the chimney of many a stately mansion that was occupied in summer by some of the wealthiest families of Virginia, who sought comfort near the seaside, now served the same purpose for a cabin only a few feet square. Only the Court House and seven or eight other buildings of the five hundred that comprised the village escaped the conflagration lighted by General Magruder just

RUINS OF ST. JOHN'S CHURCH.[1]

after midnight on the 7th of August, 1861, when the National troops had withdrawn to the opposite side of Hampton Creek. In that Court House, which had been partly destroyed, we found two young women from Vermont earnestly engaged in teaching the children of the freedmen. In the main street of the village, where we remembered having seen fine stores and

dwellings of brick, nothing was now to be seen but miserable huts, their chimneys composed of the bricks of the ruined buildings. It was a very sad sight. The sketches on this and the preceding page, made by the writer at the time, give an idea of the desolate appearance of the once flourishing town, over which the chariot of war rolled fearfully at the beginning of the struggle.

On Monday, the 12th of December, a cold, blustering day, we visited the Bethel battle-field, in company with Doctor Ely McClellan, of Philadelphia, then the surgeon in charge of the hospitals at Fortress Monroe, and Assistant Medical Director of the post. In a light wagon, drawn by two lively horses belonging to the doctor, we made a journey of about twenty-five miles during the short

CABIN AND CHIMNEY.   afternoon, attended by two armed outriders to keep off the "bushwhackers" or prowling secessionists with which the desolated country was infested. The road was fine, and passed over an

---

[1] This is a view from the Yorktown Road, and shows the front entrance to the church. Close by that entrance we observed a monument erected to the memory of a daughter of the Rev. John McCabe, the rector of the parish when the writer visited Hampton in 1853.

almost level country, gradually rising from the coast. Doctor McClellan was well acquainted with that region, and pointed out every locality of interest on the way. A few miles out from Hampton we passed a small freedmen's village. Then we came to the place, in a wood, where the collision between Bendix and Townsend occurred; and a mile or so onward we came to the site of Little Bethel and the ruins of Whiting's mansion.[1] A few miles farther brought us to the spot where the Union troops formed the line of battle for the final attack on the insurgents at Great Bethel. Near there was a brick house, used by General McClellan for head-quarters for a day or two in 1862; and by the road-side was a more humble dwelling, occupied by some colored women, one of whom was over eighty years of age. They lived near there at the time of the battle. "Law sakes alive!" said the old woman, " we was mighty skeered, but we reckoned all de time dat it was de Lord come to help us."

BIG BETHEL BATTLE-FIELD.[2]

Half a mile farther on we came to the County Bridge at Great Bethel, where the stream, widening into a morass on each side, is only a few feet in width. We visited the remains of Magruder's redoubts and intrenchments, and of Big Bethel Church; and from the embankments of the principal redoubt, westward of the bridge, made the accompanying sketch of the battle-field. Returning we took the Back River road, which passed through a

---

[1] See note 2, page 506.
[2] In this view is seen the place of the County Bridge, occupied by a rude temporary structure. In the foreground are seen the remains of the redoubt, and on the right a wooded morass. In the road, to the right of the tall tree, near the center of the picture, was the place of Greble's battery, and to the left is seen the wood in which the Union troops took shelter. In the middle of the sketch the open battle-field is seen, on which Townsend was checked by a misapprehension; and in the distance, the chimney of a house destroyed by a shell sent from the battery from which this view was taken.

pleasant country, with fine-looking houses and cultivated fields, that seemed to have suffered but little from the effects of war. The twilight had passed when we reached the Southwest Branch, and the remainder of the journey we traveled in the light of an unclouded moon.

We spent Tuesday among the ruins at Hampton and vicinity, and in visiting the schools and hospitals, and making sketches. Among these was

REMAINS OF THE REDOUBT AT HAMPTON BRIDGE.[1]

a drawing of the two-gun redoubt (erected, as we have observed, by order of General Butler, at the eastern end of Hampton Bridge), including a view of the desolated town. Near the bridge, on that side of the creek, were the summer residences of several wealthy men, then occupied for public uses. That in which Doctor McClellan resided belonged to Mallory, the so-called " Confederate Secretary of the Navy." A little below it was the house of Ex-President Tyler; and near it the spacious and more ancient looking mansion of Doctor Woods, who was then with the enemies of the Government, in which several Quaker women, from Philadelphia, had established an Orphan's Home for colored children. Tyler's residence was the home of several of the teachers of the children of freedmen, and others engaged in benevolent work.

JOHN TYLER'S SUMMER RESIDENCE.

On our return to Fortress Monroe in the evening, we received orders to go on board the *Ben Deford*, a stanch ocean steamer, which was to be General Butler's head-quarters in the expedition about to depart. At near noon the following day we left the wharf, passed out to sea with a large fleet of transports, and at sunset were far down the coast of North Carolina, and in full view of its shores. Our military company consisted of Generals Butler, Weitzel, and Graham, and their respective staff officers, and Colonel (afterward General) Comstock, General Grant's representative. We were the only civilians, excepting Mr. Clarke, editor of a newspaper at Norfolk. A record of the events of that expedition will be found in another volume of this work.

---

[1] In this view the new Hampton Bridge and the remains of the old one are seen, with the ruined village beyond. It was sketched from the gallery of a summer boarding-house near the bridge.

After the battle at Big Bethel, nothing of great importance occurred at Fortress Monroe and its vicinity during the remainder of General Butler's administration of the affairs of that department, which ended on the 18th of August,[a] excepting the burning of Hampton on the 7th of that month. It was now plainly perceived that the insurgents were terribly in earnest, and that a fierce struggle was at hand. It was evident that their strength and resources had been underrated. Before any advance toward Richmond, or, indeed, in any other direction from Fortress Monroe might be undertaken, a great increase in the number of the troops and in the quantity of munitions of war would be necessary; and all that General Butler was enabled to do, in the absence of these, was to hold his position at Newport-Newce and the village of Hampton. On the 1st of July that village was formally taken possession of, and General Peirce was placed in command of the camp established there. Under his direction a line of intrenchments was thrown up, extending from Hampton Creek across to the marshes of Back River, a part of which, as we have observed, included the old church-yard walls. On these intrenchments the large number of fugitive slaves who had fled to the Union lines were employed. Troops from the North continued to arrive in small numbers, and the spacious building of the

[a] 1861.

"Chesapeake Female Seminary," standing on the edge of the water, and overlooking Hampton Roads, was taken possession of and used as a hospital.

"CHESAPEAKE FEMALE SEMINARY."

Butler began to have hopes of sufficient strength to make some aggressive movements, when the disastrous battle at Bull's Run[b] occurred, and blasted them. The General-in-chief drew upon him for so many troops for the defense of Washington, that he was compelled to reduce the garrison at Newport-Newce, and to abandon Hampton. The latter movement greatly alarmed the "contrabands" there, under the protection of

[b] July 21, 1861.

the Union flag; and when the regiments moved over Hampton Bridge, during a bright moonlit evening,[c] these fugitives followed — men, women, and children—carrying with them all of their earthly effects. "It was a most interesting sight," General Butler wrote to the Secretary of War, "to see these poor creatures, who trusted to the protection of the arms of the United States, and who aided the troops of the United States in their enterprise, thus obliged to flee from their homes, and the homes of their masters who had deserted them, and become fugitives from fear of the return of the rebel soldiery, who had threatened to shoot the men who had wrought for us, and to carry off the women who had served us to a worse than Egyptian bondage." It was in this letter[d] that General Butler asked the important questions, "*First*, What shall be done with these fugitives? and, *second*, What is their state

[c] July 26.

[d] July 30.

and condition?" Then followed the consent of the Government to have them considered "contraband of war," already noticed.[1]

We have observed that the loyal people of the country were greatly disappointed and mortified by the affair at Great Bethel. That disappointment and chagrin were somewhat relieved by a victory obtained over insurgent troops at Romney, in Hampshire County, Northwestern Virginia, achieved on the following day by a detachment of the Eleventh Indiana (Zouaves),

commanded by Colonel Wallace, whose speedy organization of the first volunteer regiments of that State we have already observed.[2] That regiment, in material, deportment, drill, and discipline, was considered one of the best in the State. Its colors had been presented by the women of Indiana with imposing ceremonies,[3] and anticipations concerning its services had been raised which were never disappointed.[4] It expected to accompany the Indiana and Ohio troops whom General McClellan sent to Western Virginia, but was ordered instead to Evansville, on the Ohio, in Southern Indiana, to act as a police force in preventing supplies and munitions of war being sent to the South, and to protect that region from threatened invasion. The regiment chafed in its comparatively inactive service, with an earnest desire for duty in the field, and it was delighted by an order

ELEVENTH INDIANA REGIMENT.

issued on the 6th of June, by the General-in-chief, to "proceed by rail to Cumberland, Maryland, and report to Major-General Patterson," then moving from Pennsylvania toward Harper's Ferry, where the insurgents were in strong force under General Joseph E. Johnston. This order was the result of the urgent importunities of Colonel Wallace and his friends, to allow his fine regiment an opportunity for active duties. During the few weeks it had encamped at Evansville, it had been thoroughly drilled by the most severe discipline.

On the day after the receipt of the order, Wallace and his regiment were passing rapidly through Indiana and Ohio by railway, and were everywhere greeted by the most hearty demonstrations of good-will. At Grafton, it received ammunition; and on the night of the 9th, it reached the vicinity of

---

[1] See page 501. [2] See page 456.

[3] The presentation of colors took place in front of the State House at Indianapolis. The ladies of Terre Haute presented the National flag, and those of Indianapolis the regimental flag. Each presentation was accompanied by an address, to which Colonel Wallace responded. He then turned to his men, reminded them of the unmerited stain which Jefferson Davis had cast upon the military fame of Indianians in connection with the battle of Buena Vista, and exhorted them to remember that vile slander, and dedicate themselves specially to its revenge. He then bade them kneel, and, with uncovered heads and uplifted hands, swear "To stand by their flag, and remember Buena Vista!" They did so, as one man. It was a most impressive scene. The whole affair was spontaneous and without preconcert. The huzzas of the vast multitude of spectators filled the air when they arose from their knees; and "Remember Buena Vista!" became the motto of the regiment.

[4] A large majority of the members of this regiment became officers in the war that ensued; and every member of the *Montgomery Guards*—Wallace's original Zouave Company, who accompanied him on this tour of duty—received a commission. These commissions ranged from that of second lieutenant to major-general.

Cumberland,[a] where it remained, near the banks of the Potomac, until the next day. Its advent astonished all, and gave pleasure to the Unionists, for there was an insurgent force at Romney, only a day's march south from Cumberland, said to be twelve hundred strong; while at Winchester there was a much heavier one. General Morris, at Grafton, had warned Wallace of the proximity of these insurgents, and directed him to be watchful. Wallace believed that the best security for his troops and the safety of the railway was to place his foes on the defensive, and he resolved to attack those at Romney at once. He procured two trusty guides at Piedmont, from whom he learned that there was a rude and perilous mountain road, but little traveled, and probably unguarded, leading from New Creek Station, westward of Cumberland, to Romney, a distance of twenty-three miles. That road he resolved to traverse at night, and surprise the insurgents, before he should pitch a tent anywhere.

[a] June, 1860.

LEWIS WALLACE.

For the purpose of deceiving the secessionists of Cumberland, Wallace went about on the 10th with his staff, pretending to seek for a good place to encamp, but found none, and he told the citizens that he would be compelled to go back a few miles on the railway to a suitable spot. All that day his men rested, and at evening the train took them to New Creek, where Wal-

ROMNEY BATTLE-GROUND.[1]

lace and eight hundred of his command left the cars, and pushed on toward Romney in the darkness, following their guides, one of whom was afterward caught and hanged for his "treason to the Confederacy." It was a perilous and most fatiguing march, and they did not get near Romney until about

[1] In this view are seen Romney Bridge and the brick house of Mr. Gibson, between which and the bridge the skirmish occurred. Nearly over the center of the bridge, at a point indicated by a small figure, was the battery of the insurgents, and on the brow of the hill beyond is seen the village of Romney.

eight o'clock in the morning.[a]   In a narrow pass, half a mile from the bridge
which there spans the south branch of the Potomac, the advance-
guard was fired upon by mounted pickets, who then dashed ahead
and alarmed the camp of the insurgents, on a bluff near the village,
where they had planted a battery of field-pieces.   The guard followed,
crossed the bridge on a run, and drew several shots from a large brick
dwelling-house near the bank of the stream, which was used as a sort of
citadel.   Wallace immediately led a second company across, drove the foe
from the house to the shelter of the mountains, and then pushed four companies, in skirmish order, directly up the hill, to capture the battery.   This
was unexpected to the insurgents, who supposed the assailants would follow
the winding road, and they fled in terror to the forest, accompanied by all
the women and children of the village, excepting negroes, who seemed to
have no fear of the invaders.   Having no cavalry with which to pursue the
fugitives, and knowing that at a hundred points on the road between Romney and New Creek a small force might ruin or rout his regiment, Wallace
at once retraced his steps, and returned to Cumberland.   In the space of
twenty-four hours he and his men had traveled eighty-seven miles without
rest (forty-six of them on foot), engaged in a brisk skirmish, and, " what is
more," said the gallant Colonel in his report, " my men are ready to repeat
it to-morrow."[1]

This dash on the insurgents at Romney had a salutary effect.   It in-
spirited the loyal people in that region, thrilled the whole country with joy,
and, according to the Richmond newspapers, so alarmed Johnston by its
boldness, and its menaces of his line of communication with Richmond, and
Manassas (for he believed these troops to be the advance of a much larger
force), that he forthwith evacuated Harper's Ferry, and moved up the Valley
to a point nearer Winchester.

[a] June 11, 1861.

---

[1] Colonel Wallace's Report to General Patterson, June 11, 1861.

CHAPTER XXII.

THE WAR ON THE POTOMAC AND IN WESTERN VIRGINIA.

HE fulfillment of the prediction, that "Poor old Virginia will have to bear the brunt of battle,"[1] had now commenced. The clash of arms had been heard and felt within her borders. The expectations of her conspirators concerning the seizure of the National Capital had been disappointed; and thousands of armed men were marching from all parts of the Free-labor States, to contend for nationality upon her soil with herself and her allies whom she had invited to her aid.

Since the 19th of April, the important post of Harper's Ferry, on the Upper Potomac, had been occupied by a body of insurgents,[2] composed chiefly of Virginia and Kentucky riflemen. A regiment of the latter, under Colonel Blanton Duncan, took position on Maryland Hights, opposite the

KENTUCKY RIFLEMAN.

STOCKADE ON MARYLAND HIGHTS.

Ferry, where they constructed a stockade and established a fortified camp. Early in June,[a] the number of troops at *a 1861.* and near the confluence of the Potomac and Shenandoah Rivers was full twelve thousand, composed of infantry, artillery, and cavalry.

On the 23d of May, Joseph E. Johnston took the command of the insurgent forces at Harper's Ferry and in the Shenandoah Valley. He was a veteran soldier and meritorious officer, having the rank of captain of Topographical Engineers under the flag of his country, which he had lately abandoned. He now bore the commission of brigadier in the service of the conspirators, and was charged with the duty of holding Harper's Ferry (which was the key to the Shenandoah Valley, in its relation to the Free-labor States), and opposing the advance of National troops, both from Northwestern Virginia and from Pennsylvania, by whom it was threatened. Major-General McClellan was throwing Indiana and Ohio troops into that portion of Virginia; and Major-General Robert Patterson, a veteran of two wars, then at the head of the Department of Pennsylvania,[1] was rapidly gathering a large force of volunteers at Chambersburg, in that State, under General W. H. Keim.[2]

General Patterson took command at Chambersburg, in person, on the 3d of June. His troops consisted mostly of Pennsylvania militia, who had cheerfully responded to the call of the President, and were eager for duty in the field. The General had proposed an attack on the insurgents on Maryland Hights, and his plan was approved by General Scott. He was about to move forward for the purpose, when the cautious General-in-chief ordered him[a] to wait for re-enforcements. These were soon in readiness to join him, when Scott sent Patterson a letter of instruction,[b] in which he informed him what re-enforcements had been sent, and that he was organizing, for a diversion in his favor, "a small side expedition, under Colonel Stone," of about two thousand five hundred men, including cavalry and artillery, who would take post on the Potomac, opposite Leesburg, and threaten Johnston's rear. He directed Patterson to take his measures with circumspection. "We must sustain no reverses," he said. "But this is not enough," he continued; "a check or a drawn battle would be a victory to the enemy, filling his heart with joy, his ranks with men, and his magazines with voluntary contributions. . . . Attempt nothing without a clear prospect of success, as you will find the enemy strongly posted, and not inferior to you in numbers."[3]

FIRST PENNSYLVANIA REGIMENT.

a June 4, 1861.

b June 8.

Patterson advanced from Chambersburg with about fifteen thousand men. Already the insurgents, as we have seen, had been smitten at Philippi,[c] and, just as this movement had fairly commenced,

c June 3.

---

[1] When the war broke out there were only two military departments, named respectively the Eastern and the Western. By a general order issued on the 27th of April, 1861, three new departments were created, namely, the Department of Washington, Colonel J. K. F. Mansfield, Commander; the Department of Annapolis, Brigadier-General B. F. Butler, Commander; and the Department of Pennsylvania, Major-General Robert Patterson, Commander.

[2] General Patterson comprehended the wants of the Government, and while the National Capital was cut off from communication with the loyal States, he took the responsibility of officially requesting [April 25, 1861] the Governor of Pennsylvania to direct the organization, in that State, of twenty-five regiments of volunteers, in addition to the sixteen regiments called for by the Secretary of War. The Governor promptly responded to the call, but the Secretary of War, even when the term of the three months' men was half exhausted, declined to receive any more regiments. Fortunately for the country, Governor Curtin induced the Legislature to take the twenty-five regiments into the service of that State. This was the origin of that fine body of soldiers known as the Pennsylvania Reserves, who were gladly accepted by the Secretary of War after the disastrous battle of Bull's Run, and who, by hastening to Washington, assisted greatly in securing the National Capital from seizure immediately thereafter.　　[3] General Scott's *Letter of Instruction to General Patterson*, June 8, 1861.

the blow struck by Wallace at Romney[a] had filled them with alarm.   Johnston clearly perceived that he could not safely remain at Harper's Ferry, and he took the responsibility of abandoning that post.   He withdrew his troops from Maryland Hights,[b] and blocked up the railway and canal near the Ferry, by casting down by gunpowder blasts immense masses of stone that overhung them, including the famous Bolman's Rock, which always attracted the attention of tourists and of travelers on that road.   At five o'clock the next morning, with fire and gunpowder, he destroyed the great bridge of the Baltimore and Ohio Railway Company at the Ferry, a thousand feet in length, and much other property belonging to that corporation and the National Government.   Then he spiked the heavy guns that could not be taken away, burned another Potomac bridge a few miles above, and, on the 15th, marched up the Valley toward Winchester, and encamped near Charlestown.   On that day Patterson, who had received intimations from the General-in-chief that he was expected to cross the Potomac

[a] June 11, 1861.

[b] June 13.

BOLMAN'S ROCK.

after driving Johnston from the Ferry, was at Hagerstown, in Maryland, a few miles from that stream.   He pushed his columns forward, and on the following day (Sunday) and the next,[c] about nine thousand of his troops crossed the river, by fording, at Williamsport, twenty-six miles above Johnston's late encampment.   These troops consisted of two brigades (the First and Fourth), led by Brigadier-General George Cadwalader, at the head of five companies of cavalry.   The Potomac had been slightly swollen by recent rains, and the foot-soldiers were often breast-deep in the flood.   Eye-witnesses described the scene as most exciting.   The soldiers took to the water in high glee, singing popular songs, in the chorus of which the voices of whole regiments were heard.[1]

[c] June 16 and 17.

While this movement was going on, General Patterson received from General Scott[d] three dispatches by telegraph in quick succession, which surprised and embarrassed him.   The first inquired what movement in pursuit of the fugitives from Harper's Ferry he contemplated, and if none (and he recommended none), then " send to me," he said, " at once, all the regular troops, horse and foot, with you, and the Rhode Island [Burnside's] Regiment."   Patterson replied, that on that day and the next, nine thousand of his troops would be on the Virginia side of the Potomac, there to await transportation, and to be sent forward toward Winchester in detachments, well sustained, as soon as possible.   He requested that the Regulars might remain ; and he expressed a desire to make Harper's Ferry his base of operations ; to open and maintain a free communication along the Baltimore and Ohio Railway ; to hold, at Harper's Ferry, Martinsburg, and

[d] June 16.

---

[1] The favorite song among the soldiers at the beginning of the war was one entitled, *John Brown's Soul is Marching on !*

Charlestown a strong force, gradually and securely advancing a portion of them toward Winchester, and with a column from that point, operate toward Woodstock, thus cutting off all the communication of the insurgents with

ROBERT PATTERSON.

Northwestern Virginia, and force them to retire and leave that region in the possession of the loyal people. By that means he expected to keep open a free communication with the great West, by the Baltimore and Ohio Railway. The General-in-chief disapproved the plan; repeated the order to send to Washington the designated troops; told Patterson that McClellan had been ordered to send nothing across the mountains to support him, and directed him to remain where he was until he could satisfy his Chief that he ought to go forward. This was followed by another, saying: "You tell me you arrived last night at

Hagerstown, and McClellan writes that you are checked at Harper's Ferry. Where are you?" Early the next morning[a] the Chief telegraphed again, saying:—"We are pressed here. Send the troops I have twice called for, without delay."

[a] June 17.

This order was imperative, and was instantly obeyed. The troops were sent, and Patterson was left without a single piece of available artillery, with only one troop of raw cavalry, and a total force of not more than ten thousand men, the most of them undisciplined. A larger portion of them were on the Virginia side of the Potomac, exposed to much peril. Cadwalader had marched down toward Harper's Ferry as far as Falling Waters, to cover the fords; and Johnston, with full fifteen thousand well-drilled troops, including a considerable force of cavalry and twenty cannon, was lying only a few miles off.[1] Patterson had only the alternative of exposing the greater part of his army to destruction, or to recall them. He chose the latter, mortifying as it was, and they re-crossed the river at Williamsport, with the loss of only one man. Patterson was severely censured by the public, who did not know the circumstances, for not pushing on against the insurgents; but the welfare of the cause compelled him to keep silence and bear the blame.[2]

At that time there was an indescribable state of feverish anxiety in Washington City. It was shared by the Government and the General-in-chief. Exaggerated accounts of immense forces of insurgents at Manassas were continually reaching the Capital. It was known that General Beauregard, whose success at Charleston had made him famous, had been placed in command of the troops at Manassas at the beginning of June; and there was a general

[1] Report of the Joint Committee on the Conduct of the War, ii. 78, 79, and 80. Narrative of the Campaign in the Valley of the Shenandoah: by Major-General Robert Patterson.

[2] John Sherman, a representative of Ohio in Congress, was on General Patterson's staff at that time. On the 30th of June, he wrote to the General from Washington, saying:—"Great injustice is done you and your command here, and by persons in the highest military positions. I have been asked, over and over again, why you did not push on to Martinsburg, Harper's Ferry, and Winchester. I have been restrained, by my being on your staff, from saying more than simply that you had executed your orders, and that, when you were prepared to advance, your best troops were recalled to Washington."

belief that, under instructions from Davis, he would attempt the seizure of Washington City before Congress should meet there, on the 4th of July.[1] It was well known that the secessionists, then swarming in the Capital, were in continual communication with Beauregard, and it was believed that they were ready to act in concert with him in any scheme for overturning the Government. The consequence was, that credence was given to the wildest rumors, and the Government and the General-in-chief were frequently much alarmed for the safety of the Capital. It was during one of these paroxysms of doubt and dread that General Scott was constrained to telegraph to Patterson :—" We are pressed here. Send the troops I have twice called for, without delay."

The danger was, indeed, imminent. It is now known that, at about that time, a proposition was made to L. P. Walker, the so-called Secretary of War of the conspirators, to blow up the National Capitol with gunpowder, some time between the 4th and 6th of July, at a time when both Houses of Congress should be in session therein, and when Mr. Lincoln, it was hoped, would be present. This infernal proposition to murder several hundred men and women (for on such occasions the galleries of the halls of Congress were generally filled with spectators of both sexes) so pleased the conspirators, that directions were given for a conference between the assassin and Judah P. Benjamin, the so-called Attorney-General of the " Confederacy."[2] Thus early in the conflict, the plotters against their Government were ready to employ agencies in their wicked work such as none but the most depraved criminals would use. The records of the war show that Jefferson Davis, and his immediate accomplices in the Great Crime of the Ages, were participants in plans and deeds of wickedness which every right-minded man and woman who was misled into an adhesion to their cause should be eager to disavow, and, by genuine loyalty to their beneficent Government, to atone for.

General Patterson was compelled to remain on the Maryland side of the Potomac until the beginning of July. In the mean time the General-in-chief had asked him[a] to propose to him a plan of operations, without delay. He did so. He proposed to fortify Maryland Hights, and   [a] June 20, 1861. occupy them with about two thousand troops, provisioned for twenty days ; to remove all of his supplies to Frederick, and threaten with a force to open a route through Harper's Ferry ; and to send all available forces to cross the Potomac near the Point of Rocks, and, uniting with Colonel Stone at Leesburg, be in a position to operate against the foe in the Shenandoah Valley, or to aid General McDowell when he should make his proposed march, with the main army near Washington, on the insurgents at Manassas. This would have placed him in a better position to prevent Johnston, at Winchester, from joining Beauregard at Manassas, than if stationed between Williamsport and Winchester. These suggestions were not heeded ; and a few days afterward, while Patterson was begging earnestly for cannon and transportation, to enable him to well guard the fords of the river, and take position on the Virginia side, he received a dispatch   [b] June 25. from the General-in-chief,[b] directing him to remain " in front of the enemy, between Winchester and the Potomac," and if his (Patterson's)

---

[1] See the Proclamation of the President, April 15, 1861, on page 336.   [2] See note 1, page 232.

force was " superior or equal" to that of Johnston, he might " cross and offer him battle." The conditions would not warrant a movement then, and the disabilities were laid before the Chief. Two days afterward,[a] Scott telegraphed to Patterson that he expected he was " crossing the river that day in pursuit of the enemy."

a June 27, 1861.

Patterson was eager to advance, notwithstanding his foe was greatly his superior in numbers and equipment; and when, on the 29th,[b] harness for artillery horses arrived, he made instant preparations to go forward.[1] A reconnoissance in force was made on the 1st of July,[c] and on the 2d the whole army crossed the Potomac, at the Williamsport Ford, and took the road toward Martinsburg, nineteen miles northwest of Harper's Ferry. Near Falling Waters, five miles from the ford, the advance-guard, under Colonel John J. Abercrombie, which had crossed the river at four o'clock in the morning, fell in with Johnston's advance, consisting of about three thousand five hundred infantry, with cannon (Pendleton's battery of field artillery), and a large force of cavalry, under Colonel J. E. B. Stuart, the whole under the command of the heroic leader afterward known as " Stonewall" Jackson. Abercrombie

b June.

c 1861.

THOMAS J. ("STONEWALL") JACKSON.

immediately deployed his regiments (First Wisconsin and Eleventh Pennsylvania) on each side of the road; placed Hudson's section of Perkins's battery, supported by the First Troop Philadelphia City Cavalry, in the highway, and advanced to the attack, in the face of a warm fire of musketry and artillery. A severe contest ensued, in which McMullen's Philadelphia company of Independent Rangers participated. It lasted less than half an hour, when Lieutenant Hudson's cannon had silenced those of the insurgents, and Colonel George H. Thomas's brigade was coming up to the support of Abercrombie. Perceiving this, Jackson fled, hotly pursued about five miles, to the hamlet of Hainesville, where the chase was abandoned. Having been reenforced by the arrival of General Bee and Colonel Elzy, and the Ninth Georgia Regiment, Johnston had sent a heavy force out to the support of Jackson, and the Unionists thought it prudent not to pursue further. Jackson halted and encamped at Bunker's Hill, on the road between Martinsburg and Winchester. The skirmish (which is known as the Battle of Falling Waters) and the chase occupied about two hours. It was a brilliant little affair, for the insurgents considerably outnumbered the Union troops, and were sheltered by a wood in a chosen position; but by greater operations, that soon followed, it was almost totally obscured.

d July 3.

On the following day,[d] General Patterson and his army entered Martinsburg, where he was joined on the 8th by the Nine-

---

[1] On that day a party of insurgents dashed into Harper's Ferry village, drove out the Union men there, destroyed what was left of the railroad bridge and trestle-work in front of the army, and crossed the river and broke up or carried away all the boats they could find there.

teenth and Twenty-eighth New York Regiments, under Colonel Stone, and on the following day by the Fifth and Twelfth New York Regiments, under General Sandford. Thus strengthened, Patterson immediately issued orders for an advance on Winchester, when it was found that the troops of Stone were too weary and footsore to be of efficient service. The order was countermanded, and on the following morning[a] Patter-   ^a July 9, 1861. son held a council of officers at his quarters, a small house in the village, when he was advised not to advance at the present.[1] The wisdom of that advice will be apparent here-

PATTERSON'S QUARTERS AT MARTINSBURG.

after. Patterson acted in accordance with it, and remained almost a fortnight at Martinsburg, waiting for re-enforce-ment, supplies, and means for transporta-tion.

While these movements were in pro-gress in the vicinity of Harper's Ferry, others equally important were occurring elsewhere, and at points far distant from each other. In Missouri, the fires of civil war were blazing out; and in West-ern Virginia the opposing forces were carrying on quite an active campaign. Nearer Washington City blood began to flow. From their grand encampment at Manassas Junction the insurgents were continually sending out reconnoiter-ing parties, all having reference to the seizure of the Capital. These were frequently seen along the line of the Potomac from Leesburg to the Chain Bridge, within five or six miles of Washington City; while others were establishing batteries below Alexandria for the blockade of the river.

At the middle of June the insurgents were hovering along the line of the railway between Alexandria and Leesburg, and on the 16th they fired upon a train of cars on that road, at the little village of Vienna, fifteen miles from Alexandria. General McDowell immediately ordered the First Ohio Regi-ment, Colonel A. McD. McCook, to picket and guard the road. These troops left their encampment near Alexandria on the 17th, accompanied by Briga-dier-General Robert C. Schenck, and proceeded cautiously in cars and on trucks in the direction of Vienna. Detachments were left at different points along the road, one of which was the village of Falls Church, which became a famous locality during the earlier years of the war. When the train ap-proached Vienna, only four companies, comprising less than three hundred men, were on the train, and these were on open platforms or trucks.

In the mean time a detachment of Beauregard's army was waiting for them in ambush. These consisted of six hundred South Carolina infantry, a company of artillery, and two companies of cavalry, under Colonel Maxcy Gregg.[2] They had been on a reconnoissance up the Potomac region as far

---

[1] Report of General Patterson to Lieutenant-General Scott. Report of the *Committee on the Conduct of the War*, volume ii.

[2] Gregg was a leading member of the South Carolina Secession Convention (see pages 103 and 107). He entered the army, was promoted to brigadier-general, elected Governor of South Carolina, and was killed at Fredericksburg. Fort Gregg, on Morris Island, near Charleston, was named in his honor.

as Dranesville, and, having come down to Vienna, had just torn up some of the railway and destroyed a water-tank, and were departing, when they heard the whistle of a locomotive engine below the village. They hastened to the curve of the railway, in a deep cut a quarter of a mile from the village, and there planted two cannon so as to sweep the road, and masked them.

Unsuspicious of danger, McCook and his men entered the deep cut. Contrary to orders, the engineer had run up to that point quite rapidly, and there had been no opportunity for reconnoitering. The engine was behind the train, and was pushing it up. When the whole train was fairly exposed to the masked cannon, they opened fire, and swept it from front to rear with

grape and canister shot. Fortunately, the shot went high, and most of the soldiers were sitting. The frightened engineer, instead of drawing the whole train out of the peril, uncoupled the engine and one passenger-car, and fled with all possible speed toward Alexandria. The troops leaped from the train, fell back along the railway, and rallied in a grove near by, where they maintained so bold a front, under a shower of shell and other missiles, that the assailants believed them to be the advance of a heavier force near. With that belief they soon retired, and hastened to Fairfax Court House, leaving the hand-

ROBERT C. SCHENCK.

ful of Ohio troops, whom they might have captured with ease, to make their way leisurely back, carrying their dead and wounded companions on litters

SOUTH CAROLINA FLAG.

and in blankets. The Union loss was five killed, six wounded, and thirteen missing.[1] That of the insurgents is unknown. The latter destroyed the portion of the train that was left in the deep cut, and captured a quantity of stores. When they ascertained that the National troops were not in force in that vicinity, they returned and took possession of Vienna and Falls Church Village. On that occasion, the flag of the "Sovereign State of South Carolina"[2] was displayed, for the first time, in the presence of National troops out of that State.

We have observed that the insurgents were endeavoring to blockade the Potomac. Ten days after the affair at Vienna, there were some stirring scenes connected with that blockade at Matthias Point, a bold promontory in King George's County, Virginia, jutting out into the river, and giving it a short sharp turn. That point was covered with woods, and there the insurgents commenced erecting a battery which might completely destroy the

---

[1] Report of General Schenck to Lieutenant-General Scott. Correspondence of the *Louisville Courier*, June 29, and *New York Tribune*, June 20.

[2] The flag was composed of blue silk, with a golden Palmetto-tree on a white oval center-piece, and a silver crescent in the left upper corner. Partly surrounding the white oval were the words of the motto of the State: —"ANIMIS OPIBUSQUE PARATI." See picture of the Seal of South Carolina, on page 105.

water communication with the Capital. Captain Ward, of the Potomac flotilla, was with the *Freeborn*, his flagship, below this point, when information of the presence of an insurgent force on the promontory reached him.

He determined to drive them off, and on the evening of the 26th of June,[a] ^{a 1861.} he requested Commander Rowan, of the *Pawnee*, then lying near Acquia Creek, to send to him, during the night, two boatloads of marines, well equipped, with a competent leader. They were accordingly sent in charge of Lieutenant Chaplin. Ward's plan was to land, drive off the insurgents,

FALLS CHURCH IN 1865.[1]

and denude the Point of trees, so that there might be no shelter for the aggressors from the observation of cruisers on the river.

On the morning of the 27th,[b] the *Freeborn*, with the boats from the *Pawnee*, went up to Matthias Point, when the former commenced firing shot and shell into the woods. Under cover of this fire, ^{b June, 1861.} Lieutenant Chaplin and his party, with others from the *Freeborn*, landed at about ten o'clock. Captain Ward accompanied them. Skirmishers were thrown out, and these soon encountered the pickets of the insurgents, who fired and fled. Just then a body of four or five hundred of the foe were seen coming over a hill. Ward hastened back to the *Freeborn*, to renew the shelling, while Chaplin and his men took to their boats. The insurgents were checked, and, in the course of fifteen minutes, Chaplin was again ordered to land, and to throw up a breastwork of sand-bags. This was nearly ready for the guns that were to be sent ashore to arm them when a signal was given for him to retire, for the insurgents were too many for them. Before the men could reach their boats, the foe fired upon them with muskets. They safely embarked. Chaplin was the last to leave. The boats

---

[1] This is a view of the ancient church which gives the name to the village, mentioned on page 526, as it appeared when the writer visited and sketched it, at the close of April, 1865. The church is a cotemporary with Pohick Church, near Mount Vernon, built before the Revolution, of brick, and in a style similar to the latter. It is about eight miles north of Alexandria, and the same distance west of Washington City. The village that has grown up around the church was built chiefly by Massachusetts people who had settled there, but the congregation of this church (Episcopalians) were chiefly native Virginians, and were nearly all secessionists. Their rector, a secessionist, afraid to pray for the President of the United States or for Jefferson Davis, when the war broke out, took the safe course of praying for the Governor of Virginia. The church is now (1865) a ruin, made so by the National troops, who took out all of its wood-work for timber and fuel, and had commenced taking the brick walls for chimneys to huts. The latter depredation was immediately checked.

had drifted away. Unwilling to call the men back to an exposed position, the Lieutenant swam out to the nearest one, carrying on his back a soldier (and his musket) who could not swim.

Only one man of the party who landed was injured; but a sad event

JAMES HARMAN WARD.

occurred on the deck of the *Freeborn*. The gunner was wounded in the thigh, when Captain Ward took charge of the piece. While sighting it, a well-aimed Minié ball came from the shore and mortally wounded him by entering the abdomen. As he fell he was caught by one arm of Harry Churchill, the boatswain's mate, who used his other hand with the string to fire the well-aimed cannon, whose round shot struck plump among the insurgents. Ward lived only forty-five minutes. The ball had passed through the intestines and liver. His was the only life sacrificed on the occasion, on the Union side.[1]

This attack on the works of the insurgents on Matthias Point, and those on the batteries at Sewell's and Pig Point, and at Acquia Creek, convinced the Government that little could be done by armed vessels, without an accompanying land force, competent to meet the foe in fair battle.

While these events were transpiring in the region of the Potomac, others equally stirring and important were occurring in Northwestern *a* June 11, Virginia. For a month after the dash on Romney,*a* Colonel Wallace and his regiment were placed in an important and perilous position at Cumberland, in Western Maryland. When the insurgents recovered from the panic produced by that dash, which made them flee sixteen miles without halting, and found that Wallace had fallen back to Cumberland, they took heart, advanced to Romney, four thousand strong, under Colonel McDonald—infantry, cavalry, and artillery—and, pushing on to New

---

[1] Captain Ward was the first naval officer who was killed in the war. His body was taken to the Washington Navy Yard, and thence to New York, where, on the deck of the *North Carolina*, at the Brooklyn Navy Yard, it lay in state, and was visited by many persons. It was then conveyed to Hartford, where funeral services were performed by the Roman Catholic Bishop of that diocese, in the Cathedral. It was buried with imposing ceremonies.

The *Pawnee* became so obnoxious to the insurgents that they devised many schemes for her destruction. Among other contrivances was a torpedo, or floating mine, delineated in the accompanying sketch. It was picked up in the *Pawnee*, a few yards from the *Pawnee*, on the evening of the 7th of July, 1861. The following is a description :—1, 1, Oil-casks, serving for buoys. 2, 2, Iron tubes, four feet six inches long, and eighteen inches in diameter, charged with gunpowder. 3, A 3-inch rope, with large pieces of cork two feet apart. 4, 4, Boxes on top of casks with fuses. 5, 5, Gutta-percha tubing connected with capped tubes. 6, 6, Brass tops on the torpedoes. 7, 7, Copper tubes running through the casks. 8, Wooden platform in center of cask, on which the fusee was coiled and secured. 9, Fusee. This infernal machine was to be set afloat with the tide in the direction of the vessel to be destroyed, after the fusee or slow match was lighted. This was the beginning of the use of torpedoes, which the insurgents employed very extensively during the war.

TORPEDO.

Others will be hereafter delineated and described.

Creek, destroyed the bridge of the Baltimore and Ohio Railway at that place. Then they passed on to Piedmont, five miles farther westward, where they cut the telegraph-wires, and destroyed all communication between Cumberland and Grafton. Fortunately, the advance of the insurgents upon Piedmont was known in time to send all the rolling stock of the railway there to Grafton, and save it from seizure.

Wallace was now completely isolated, and expected an immediate attack upon his camp at Cumberland. He had no cannon, no cavalry, and very little ammunition. For twenty-one days his men had only ten rounds of cartridges apiece. He could not hold Cumberland against the overwhelming force of the insurgents, so he prepared for a retreat, if necessary, to Bedford, in Pennsylvania. He sent his sick and baggage in that direction, and after advising the Union people in Cumberland to keep within their houses, he led his regiment out upon the same road, to the dismay of the loyal inhabitants and the chagrin of his men, who did not comprehend his design. It was soon made apparent. He halted, changed front, and prepared for battle. Believing that when the insurgents should enter Cumberland they would scatter in search of plunder, he prepared to rush in, attack them in the streets, and defeat them in detail.

When the insurgents under McDonald reached Frostburg, only six miles from Cumberland, they were informed of Wallace's bold stand, and ventured no farther, but remained at that place until evening, when they turned southward and hastened to Romney. Wallace returned to Cumberland, and was joyfully received. He appealed to both Morris and McClellan at Grafton, and to Patterson at Hagerstown, for re-enforcements and supplies, but neither of them had any to spare. There was danger at all points and weakness at all points. Only the Governor of Pennsylvania could afford relief. He sent Wallace some ammunition, and ordered two regiments of the Pennsylvania Reserves,[1] under Colonel Charles J. Biddle, with a field-battery under Captain Campbell, to take post on the frontier of Maryland, but not to step over the line unless the Indianians should be attacked.[2] That frontier line was only five or six miles from Cumberland.

During that month of peril, while the Indiana regiment was engaged in independent duty, and successfully guarding the railway for about a hundred miles each way from Cumberland, it was subjected to the most trying and exhausting services. Wallace succeeded in impressing thirteen horses into his service, and on these scouts were mounted, whose performances, night and day, crowded that month's history of the Zouaves with the most exciting events. The insurgents felt a wholesome dread of these Zouaves; and their appearance created many a sudden flight of a much superior force. The foot-soldiers of the Eleventh were equally active. The Potomac was everywhere fordable, and both parties crossed and re-crossed it at their pleasure,

---

[1] See note 2, page 520.

[2] The Pennsylvanians were restive under the restraints of this portion of the order. "Campbell," says Dr. Stevenson, "ascertained exactly where the line of division ran, and camping his men close by, with cutting practical sarcasm, planted his guns so that the wheels were in Pennsylvania and the muzzles in Maryland."— *Indiana's Roll of Honor*, page 100. The order was in accordance with the deference then felt for the jurisdiction of the respective States. The Reserves were Pennsylvania State troops, and it was felt that they had no right upon the soil of Maryland.

and often engaged in little skirmishes. Finally, on the 26th,[a] a spirited affair occurred near Frankfort, on the road between Cumberland and Romney, in which thirteen picked men of the regiment, mounted on the thirteen impressed horses, were engaged. They were sent on a scout, led by Corporal D. B. Hay, one of their number. They boldly attacked forty-one mounted insurgents, killing eight of them, chasing the remainder two miles, and capturing seventeen of their horses. The leader of the scouts was severely wounded, but was saved. On their way back, they were attacked by seventy-five mounted men of the command of the afterward famous Ashby, near the mouth of Patterson's Creek. They fell back across a portion of the stream to Kelley's Island, at the mouth of the creek, where they had a terrible hand-to-hand fight with their assailants, that ceased only with the daylight. It ended at nightfall, with a loss to the Zouaves of only one man killed. The remainder made their way back to camp in the darkness.[1] Their bravery elicited the highest praise of both Patterson and McClellan. The former, in general orders,[2] commended their example to his troops; and the latter thanked them for their noble services, and said to Colonel Wallace:[b]—"I more than ever regret that you are not under my command. I have urged General Scott to send up the Pennsylvania regiments. I begin to doubt whether the Eleventh Indiana needs re-enforcements."[3]

[a] June, 1861.

[b] June 28.

On the 8th of July, by order of General Patterson, Wallace's regiment broke camp at Cumberland, and joined the forces under their chief at Martinsburg; and they were engaged on duty in that vicinity until after the battle of Bull's Run,[c] notwithstanding the term of their three months' enlistment had expired. For his eminent services in this three months' campaign, Wallace was rewarded with the commission of a brigadier.

[c] July 21.

Whilst the Baltimore and Ohio Railway—the great line of communication with the West—was thus held by the National troops, attempts were made by the insurgents to occupy the country in Western Virginia south of it. We have observed that Colonel Porterfield had notified the authorities at Richmond that a large force must be immediately sent into that region, or it would be lost to the " Confederacy."[4] A plan of campaign in that direction was immediately formed and put in execution. Porterfield was succeeded in command in Northwestern Virginia by General Robert S. Garnett, a meritorious officer, who served on the staff of General Taylor, in Mexico, and was breveted a major for gallantry in the battle of Buena Vista. He made his head-quarters at Beverly, in Randolph County, a pleasant village on a plain, traversed by Tygart's Valley River. It was an important point in operations to prevent McClellan pushing through the gaps of the mountain ranges into the Shenandoah Valley. Garnett proceeded at once to fortify places on the roads leading from Beverly through these mountain passes.

---

[1] The following are the names of the thirteen brave men :—D. B. Hay, E. H. Baker, E. Burkett, J. C. Hollenback, T. Grover, J. Hollowell, T. Brazier, G. W. Mudbargar, L. Farley, F. Harrison, P. M. Dunlap, R. Dunlap, and E. P. Thomas.

[2] Dated Hagerstown, June 30, 1861.

[3] Letter from General McClellan to Colonel Wallace, dated Grafton, June 28, 1861.

[4] See page 494.

He collected a considerable force at that place, and had outlying detachments at Bealington, Buckhannon, Romney, and Philippi. Ex-Governor Henry A. Wise, with a brigadier's commission, had been organizing a brigade in the Great Kanawha Valley, beyond the Greenbrier Mountains, for the purpose of holding in subjection the loyal inhabitants of the fertile regions of that river. He was now ordered to cross the intervening mountains around the head-waters of the Gauley River, and co-operate with Garnett; and every measure within the means of the "Confederates" was used for the purpose of checking the advance of McClellan's forces, and preventing their junction with those of Patterson in the Shenandoah Valley.

General McClellan took command of his troops in person, at Grafton, on the 23d of June, and on that day he issued a proclamation to the inhabitants of Western Virginia, similar in tenor to the one sent forth from Cincinnati a month earlier.[a] He severely condemned the guerrilla warfare in which the insurgents were engaged, and threatened the offenders with punishment, "according to the severest rules of military law." He also told the disloyal people of that section that all who should be found acting in hostility to the Government, either by bearing arms or in giving aid and comfort to its enemies, should be arrested. To his soldiers he issued an address two days afterward, reminding them that they were in the country of friends, and not of enemies, and conjuring them to behave accordingly. He denounced the insurgents as outlaws, who, without cause, had rebelled, and seized public property, and "outraged the persons of Northern men merely because they came from the North, and Southern men merely because they loved the Union;" and he exhorted his soldiers to pursue a different course. He concluded by saying :—" I now fear but one thing—that you will not find foemen worthy of your steel."

a May 23, 1861.

The entire force of Ohio, Indiana, and Virginia troops, now under the command of McClellan, numbered full twenty thousand men, and he resolved to advance. He sent a detachment, under General J. D. Cox, into the Kanawha Valley, to meet Wise and keep him in check, while his main body, about ten thousand strong, led by himself, advanced from Clarksburg, on the Baltimore and Ohio Railway, twenty-two miles west of Grafton, in the direction of Buckhannon, to attack Garnett at Laurel Hill, near Beverly. At the same time a detachment of about four thousand men,[1] under General Morris, moved from Grafton toward Beverly, by way of Philippi ; and another body, commanded by General Hill, was sent to West Union, eastward of Philippi, toward St. George, in Tucker County, to prevent the escape of the insurgents by that way over the Alleghany Mountains, to join Johnston at Winchester.

Morris was instructed not to attack Garnett, but to thoroughly reconnoiter the country, make such feints as would deceive the insurgents with the belief that they might expect the main attack from that officer, and to keep them employed until McClellan should gain their rear. Morris carried out the plan faithfully. He advanced to Bealington, within a mile of Garnett's camp, which was on a wooded slope on the eastern side of the Laurel

---

[1] This force was composed of the Sixth, Seventh, and Ninth Indiana, the Sixth and Fourteenth Ohio, the First Virginia, and Burnett's Artillery, of Cleveland, Ohio.

Hill range of mountains, between Leedsville and Beverly, where he had about eight thousand men strongly intrenched.[1] These were chiefly East Virginians, Georgians, Tennesseans, and some Carolinians.[2] In front of these intrenchments continual and heavy skirmishing was carried on daily, chiefly by the Seventh and Ninth Indiana Regiments, commanded respectively by Colonels E. Dumont and Robert H. Milroy. The troops were so eager for conflict that Morris found it difficult to restrain them. The scouting parties

were so earnest, vigilant, and bold, that when McClellan approached Beverly, each position of the insurgents and their works in all that region was perfectly known. A thousand deeds of daring, worthy of record, were performed during those few days. Those of the Ninth Indiana were so notable that the insurgents gave them the name of "Swamp Devils."

McClellan reached Buckhannon on the 7th of July, and advanced to Roaring Run, on the road to Beverly. He ascertained that a large force of insurgents, about fifteen hundred strong, under Colonel John Pegram, was occupying a heavily

T. A. MORRIS.

intrenched position in the rear of Garnett, in Rich Mountain Gap, of the Laurel Hill Range, about four miles from Beverly, where his forces commanded the important road over the mountains to Staunton, and the chief highway to Southern Virginia. Pegram boasted that his position could not be turned, because of the precipitous hills on his flanks ; but he was mistaken. McClellan sent the Eighth, Tenth, and Thirteenth Indiana Regiments, and the Sixteenth Ohio Regiment, with Burdsall's troop of cavalry, all in light marching order, under the command of Colonel (afterward General) W. S. Rosecrans, to do what Pegram thought impossible. They were accompanied by Colonel Lander, who was with Dumont at Philippi,[3] and were piloted by a young man named Hart, son of the owner of the mountain farm on which Pegram was encamped. They started

a July 11, 1861.

at three o'clock in the morning,[a] made a wide *détour* through the mountains in a heavy rain-storm, along most perilous ways, pathless, slippery, and rough, a distance of about eight miles, and at noon were on the summit of a ridge of Rich Mountain, high above Pegram's camp, and a mile from it. Just as they reached the Staunton road, near Hart's, they were furiously assailed by musket and cannon shot, bullets, grape, canister, and shells.

---

[1] Garnett's position was a very strong one by nature, and was made stronger by art. On a mountain slope, masked by woods, and commanding one of the most important passes in all that region, he had a line of intrenchments a mile in extent, stretching on each side of the main road that runs up from Philippi to Beverly. Within these were other works for final defense, if assailed. Outside of all was a strong abatis, formed of felled trees ; also numerous rifle-pits, the earth thrown up so as to make a breastwork for each man. These works extended up the slopes on each side of the narrow valley ; and on the summits of two elevations were two redoubts made of logs and earth, with embrasures for six cannon, and also loop-holes for musketry. See map on page 536.

[2] General McClellan's Dispatch to Adjutant-General Townsend, July 13, 1861.

[3] See page 495.

Rosecrans supposed his movements were unknown to the insurgents. He was mistaken. A courier sent after him by McClellan had been captured by Pegram's scouts, and the march of Rosecrans was revealed.[1] Pegram immediately sent about nine hundred men, with two cannon, up the mountain road in his rear, to meet him. They hastily cast up works of logs and earth near Hart's, and masked their cannon, and from these came the unexpected volley.

Rosecrans had no cannon, but he had men eager for conflict. He formed the three Indiana regiments in battle order, held the Ohio regiment as a reserve, and sent forward his skirmishers. They engaged in desperate fighting while the main body lay concealed in the grass, the shot of the insurgents passing over them. Finally, Pegram's men came out from their works and charged across the road. The Indianians sprang to their feet, and at a given order they fired, fixed their bayonets, and with a wild shout charged upon the foe. A sharp conflict ensued, when the latter gave way and fled in wild confusion down the declivities of the mountain to Pegram's main camp. Re-enforcements sent from Garnett's reserves at Beverly, then on their way, hearing of the disaster to their friends, fell back. Rosecrans recalled his men in pursuit of the fugitives, and prepared for another encounter.

This engagement, known as the BATTLE OF RICH MOUNTAIN, commenced at about two o'clock in the afternoon, and occupied less than an hour and a half. The Union troops in action numbered about eighteen hundred, and those of the insurgents about nine hundred. The loss of the former was eighteen killed, and about forty wounded. The latter lost about one hundred and forty killed, and a large number wounded and made prisoners. Their entire loss was more than four hundred, including several officers. For his gallantry on this occasion, Rosecrans was commissioned a brigadier-general.

The position of Rosecrans was now perilous. Pegram was immediately before him with an overwhelming force, and he was separated from the main army by the rough mountain over which he had passed with the greatest difficulty. Fortunately for him, McClellan, who, at his camp at Roaring Run, had heard the cannonading, advanced that evening to a position directly in front of Pegram's main camp, and prepared to assail it in the morning with twelve cannon. Pegram did not wait for the assault, but stole off during the night, and tried to make his way with the remnant of his troops to Garnett's camp. This movement exposed Garnett's rear, and he, too, under cover of the night, abandoned his camp and all in it—cannon, tents, and many wagons—and in light marching order pushed on toward Beverly, hoping to pass it before McClellan could reach it, and so escape over the mountains by Huttonsville, toward Staunton. He was too late. McClellan had moved rapidly on Beverly, and fugitives from 'Pegram's camp informed him that his advance was already there. Garnett turned back, and taking the road toward St. George, through a gap near Leedsville, he plunged into the wild mountain regions of the Cheat Range, taking with him only one cannon. His reserves at Beverly fled over the mountains, by way of Huttonsville, as far as Monterey, in Highland County, and the re-en-forcements that had been sent to Pegram, as we have observed, scattered over the Laurel Hill Range. Rosecrans entered Pegram's abandoned camp the next morning; while the latter, with about six hundred followers, weary, worn, and dispirited, were vainly seeking a way of escape. They had been without food for nearly two days. Seeing no hope of relief, Pegram offered to surrender to McClellan; and on Sunday morning, the 14th,[a] he and his followers were escorted into the camp of the chief at Beverly by some Chicago cavalry.

[a] July, 1861.

When it was discovered that Garnett had fled, McClellan ordered a hot pursuit. He sent a detachment from his own column, under Captain H. W. Benham, his Chief Engineer, to join that of General Morris, and the united forces started eagerly after the fugitives, who had about twelve hours the start of them. The recent rains had made the roads very muddy, and swelled the mountain streams. The fugitives, in their anxiety to escape, left knapsacks, provisions, camp furniture, and every thing that might impede their flight, along the way, and these were continual clews to their route, which frequently deviated from the main road along rough mountain paths. Broken and abandoned wagons were found in many places, and in narrow gorges the insurgents had felled trees and cast down rocks to obstruct the pursuit.

Both parties rested on the night of the 12th, and resumed the race in the morning. The pursuers gradually gained on the fugitives; and at about noon, while a driving rain-storm was drenching them, the advance of the former, composed of the Seventh and Ninth Indiana, Fourteenth Ohio, and a section of Burnett's Ohio Battery, came in sight of the flying insurgents at Kahler's Ford of a branch of the Cheat River. They were evidently preparing to make a stand there. The pursuing infantry dashed into the stream, which was waist deep, and halted under shelter of the bank until the artillery came up. A single cannon-shot set the insurgents in motion, for they were only the rear-guard of Garnett's force, the main body of which was some distance in advance. The exciting chase was renewed, and its interest was hightened by a sort of running fight for about four miles to another ford of the same stream, known as Carrick's, where the banks were high and steep, and the land a rolling bottom about a mile in width between the mountains.

After crossing the stream Garnett made a stand. The Fourteenth Ohio (Colonel Steedman) of the advance was close upon him, and rushed down to the Ford in pursuit, when it was met by a volley of musketry and cannon-shot from a single heavy gun, under Colonel Taliaferro, of the Twenty-third Virginia Regiment. The Ohio troops stood their ground bravely. The Seventh and Ninth Indiana and Burnett's battery hastened to their aid; and Captain Benham, who was in command of the advance, ordered Colonel Dumont and a detachment of his regiment to cross the deep and rapid stream above the ford, and gain the rear of the foe. The opposite shore was too precipitous for them to scale, and they were ordered to wade down in the bed of the stream hidden by the bank, and, under cover of fire of cannon and musketry, charge the insurgents in front. The order was quickly executed, and while the Indianians were struggling up the bank among the laurel bushes, the insurgents broke and fled. They had fought bravely against great odds, and yielded only when their ammunition was almost exhausted. Garnett tried to rally them to make another stand, and while trying to do so he was shot dead.[1] A youthful Georgian, who was among the few around the General at that moment, fell dead at his side. The insurgents fled to the mountains, and were pursued only about two miles. The

CARRICK'S FORD.[2]

main body of Morris's force soon came up, and the victors slept near the Ford that night. They had lost two killed and ten wounded, two of them mortally. The insurgents lost thirty men killed, a much larger number wounded, and many who were made prisoners. They also lost their cannon, many wagons, and forty loads of provisions. The body of their fallen General fell into the hands of the victors, and was tenderly cared for and sent to his friends.[3] This is known as the BATTLE OF CARRICK'S FORD.

Whilst the stirring events which we have just considered were transpiring, General McClellan, at Beverly, sent cheering dispatches to his Government; and, when he heard of the dispersion of Garnett's forces at Carrick's Ford, he expressed his belief that General Hill, then at Rowlesburg, on the Cheat River, where the Baltimore and Ohio Railway crosses that stream, would certainly intercept the fugitives at West Union or St. George. He

[1] Major Gordon, who accompanied the Ninth Indiana, had joined the Seventh in the water. He jumped upon a stump to cheer on his comrades, when Garnett directed several of his men (Tompkins's Richmond Sharp-shooters) to fire on him. They did so, but without effect. He discovered Garnett, and directed Sergeant Burlingame, of the Seventh, to shoot him. The General almost instantly fell.—See Stevenson's *Indiana's Roll of Honor*, page 58.

[2] This view of Carrick's Ford is from a drawing by Edwin Forbes, an artist who accompanied the expedition. The name of the Ford was derived from that of the person who owned the land there.

[3] Stevenson (page 59) cites the following description of Garnett, who was a graduate of West Point, of the class of 1841:—"In form he was about five feet eight inches, rather slenderly built, with a fine, high, arching forehead, and regular and handsome features, almost classic in their regularity, and mingled delicacy and strength of beauty. His hair, almost coal black, as were his eyes, he wore long on the neck, in the prevailing fashion of the Virginia aristocracy. His dress was of fine broad-cloth throughout, and richly ornamented. The buttons bore the coat of arms of the State of Virginia, and the star on his shoulder-strap was richly studded with brilliants."

was so confident of this result, that on the night of the 14th he telegraphed, saying:—"Our success is complete, and I firmly believe that secession is

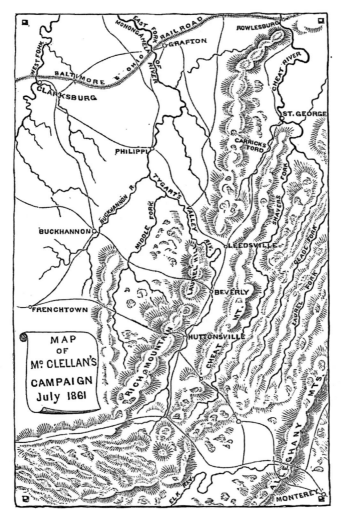

MAP OF McCLELLAN'S CAMPAIGN July 1861

SEAT OF WAR IN WESTERN VIRGINIA.

killed in this section of the country." He was disappointed. The fugitives were rallied by Colonel Ramsay, and turning short to the right near West Union, they fled over the Alleghanies and joined "Stonewall" Jackson at Monterey, Highland County, Virginia.

On the morning after the conflict at Carrick's Ford, General Morris returned to his camp at Bealington,[1] while detachments from McClellan's force pursued the fugitives from Beverly, under Major Tyler, to the summit of the Cheat Mountain Range, on the road toward Staunton, where the Fourteenth Indiana, Colonel Kimball, was left as an outpost.

A camp was established at the eastern foot of the mountain, and detachments were posted at important points along the eastern slopes of the Alleghanies.

On the 19th,[a] McClellan issued an address to his troops, from Huttonsville, telling them that he was "more than satisfied" with their conduct; that they had annihilated two armies well intrenched among mountain fastnesses; recounted the results of the campaign, and praised their courage and endurance without stint. The campaign

^{a July, 1861.}

---

[1] The three months' term of enlistment of these troops had now expired, and they returned to their homes, a greater portion of them to re-enlist for "three years or the war."

had been successful, and McClellan thus summed up the results in a dispatch to the War Department: "We have completely annihilated the enemy in Western Virginia. Our loss is about thirteen killed, and not more than forty wounded; while the enemy's loss is not far from two hundred killed; and the number of prisoners we have taken will amount to at least one thousand. We have captured seven of the enemy's guns in all."

General Cox had been successful in the Kanawha Valley. He crossed the Ohio at the mouth of the Guyandotte River, captured Barboursville [a] after a slight skirmish, and pushed on to the Kanawha River. [a July 12, 1861.] Wise was then in the valley of that stream, below Charleston, the capital of Kanawha County, and had an outpost at Scareytown, composed of a small force under Captain Patton. This was attacked by fifteen hundred Ohio troops under Colonel Lowe, who were repulsed. That night, the assailed insurgents fled up the valley to Wise's camp, and gave him such an alarming account of the numbers of the invaders, that the General at once retreated, first to Charleston, then to Gauley Bridge (which he burnt), near the mouth of the Gauley River,[b] and did not make a permanent halt until he reached Lewisburg, the capital of Greenbrier County. [b July 29.] The news of Garnett's disaster, and Wise's own incompetence, had so dispirited his troops, that large numbers had left him. At Lewisburg, he was re-enforced and outranked by John B. Floyd, late Secretary of War, who had a brigadier's commission.

The war in Western Virginia seemed to have ended with the dispersion of Garnett's forces, and there was much rejoicing over the result. It was premature. The "Confederates" were not disposed to surrender to their enemy the granaries that would be needed to supply the troops in Eastern Virginia, without a severer struggle. General Robert E. Lee succeeded Garnett, and more important men than Wise and Floyd took the places of these incompetents. Rosecrans succeeded McClellan, [c July 22.] who was called to the command of the Army of the Potomac,[c] and the war in the mountain region of Virginia was soon renewed, the most prominent events of which will be recorded hereafter.

CHAPTER XXIII.

THE WAR IN MISSOURI.—DOINGS OF THE CONFEDERATE "CONGRESS."—AFFAIRS IN
BALTIMORE.—PIRACIES.

ET us turn for a moment from the contemplation of
the aspect of affairs in Virginia, and in the immediate
vicinity of the National Capital, to that of the course
of events in the great valley of the Mississippi, and
especially in Missouri, where, as we have observed,
the loyalists and disloyalists had begun a sharp
conflict for the control of the State, early in May.
The first substantial victory of the former had been
won at St. Louis, in the loyal action of the State Convention,[1] and in
the seizure of Camp Jackson;[2] and its advantages, imperiled by the treaty
for pacification between Generals Harney and Price,[3] were secured by the
refusal of the Government to sanction that arrangement, and of General
Lyon to treat with the disloyal Governor Jackson. The latter plainly saw
the force of this advantage, and proceeded immediately to array the State
militia, under his control, in opposition to Lyon and his troops and the
General Government, and, by the violence of immediate war, to sever Missouri from the Union.

As we have observed,[4] Governor Jackson, by proclamation, called "into
the service of the State "[a] fifty thousand of the militia, "for the
purpose of repelling invasion," et cœtera; in other words, he
called into the service of the disloyal politicians of Missouri a
host of men to repel the visible authority of the National Government, in
the form of United States troops and regiments of loyal citizens of the Commonwealth. The Legislature worked in harmony with him, and various
moneys of the State, such as the School Fund, the money provided for the
payment of the July interest of the State debt, and other available means, to
the amount of over three millions of dollars, were placed at the disposal of
the conspirators, for military purposes. Jackson declared in his proclamation
that his object was peace; that he had proposed the fairest terms for conciliation, but they were rejected, and that now nothing was left for him to do
but to resist "invasion" by force of arms. At Jefferson City, the capital of
the State, he raised the standard of revolt, with General Sterling Price as
military commander.

General Lyon promptly took up the gauntlet cast down by the Governor.
He had already taken measures for the security of the important post at

* June 12,
1861.

---

[1] See page 461.   [2] See page 468.   [3] See page 469.   [4] See page 471.

Cairo, by sending a regiment of Missouri volunteers, under Colonel Shüttner, to occupy and fortify Bird's Point opposite.[1] That point is a few feet higher than Cairo, and a battery upon it perfectly commanded the entire ground

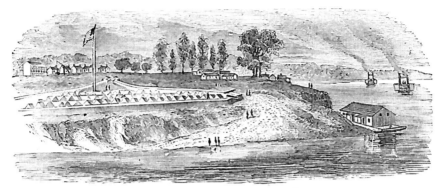

CAMP OF THE MISSOURI VOLUNTEERS ON BIRD'S POINT.

occupied by the National troops at the latter place. Captain Benham, of the Engineers,[2] who constructed the works there, called attention early to the importance of occupying that point, for its possession by the insurgents would make Cairo untenable. Shüttner so strongly fortified his camp, that he was in no fear of any force the insurgents were likely to assail it with. But he was there none too early, and cast up his fortifications none too soon, for General Pillow, who was collecting a large force in Western Tennessee for the capture of Cairo, made Bird's Point the most important objective in his plan.

Pillow worked diligently for the accomplishment of his purpose, efficiently aided by B. F. Cheatham, a more accomplished soldier of Tennessee, who served with distinction under General Patterson in the war in Mexico. He was among the first of his class in Tennessee to join the insurgents, and was now holding the commission of a brigadier-general in the service of the conspirators. Pillow was superseded in command by Leonidas Polk, a graduate of the Military Academy at West Point, and Bishop of the Protestant Episcopal Church of the Diocese of Louisiana. Early in July, Polk accepted the commission of major-general in the "Provisional Army of the Confederate States of America," and was appointed to the command of a department, which extended from the mouth of the Arkansas River, on each side of the Mississippi as far as the northern boundary of the "Confederacy." He made his head-quarters

BENJAMIN F. CHEATHAM.

at Memphis, in Tennessee; and, in his first general order, issued on the 13th of July, he showed great bitterness of feeling. He declared that the "invasion of the South by the Federal armies comes bringing with it a contempt for constitutional liberty, and the withering influence of the infidelity of New England and Germany combined."

General Lyon's first movement against Jackson and Price was to send ° the Second Missouri Regiment of Volunteers, under Colonel *June 12, (afterward General) Franz Sigel, to occupy and protect from injury the Pacific Railway, from St. Louis to the Gasconade River, preparatory to an advance toward the southern portion of the State,

LEONIDAS POLK.

by way of Rolla, to oppose an invasion by Ben McCullough, the Texas Ranger,[1] who had crossed the border from Arkansas with about eight hundred men, and was marching, with rapidly increasing numbers, on Springfield. On *June 13. the following day,[b] Lyon left St. Louis in two river steamers (*Iatan* and *J. C. Swan*), with about two thousand men well supplied for a long march, their immediate destination being the capital of the Commonwealth, on the Missouri River, and their first business to drive Jackson and Price, with their followers, out of it. These troops were composed of Missouri volunteers, under Colonels Blair and Boernstein; regulars, under Captain Lathrop; and artillery, under Captain James Totten. The expedition reached the capital on the afternoon of the 15th. Jackson and Price, with their armed followers, had fled westward by way of the railroad, destroying the bridges behind them, and, turning northward, took post ° June 16. a few miles below Booneville, on the Missouri, forty miles from Jefferson City. Lyon followed them the next day,[c] leaving Colonel Boernstein, with three companies of his regiment, to hold the capital. Contrary to the expectation of the insurgents, Lyon went by water, in three steamers (*A. McDonnell, Iatan,* and *City of Louisiana*), and the destruction of bridges availed the insurgents nothing.

At Rocheport, at dawn on the 17th, Lyon ascertained that the insurgents were encamped a few miles below Booneville. Pressing into his service a ferry-boat there, he pushed forward a short distance, when he discovered a *June 18. battery on a bluff, and scouts hastening to report his approach. He at once disembarked[d] on low ground, on the south side of the river, formed in column, sent forward his skirmishers, and soon found his foes. They were encamped on the high ground, and were under the command of Colonel J. S. Marmaduke, of the State forces, General Price having gone on in a boat to Lexington, on account of alleged illness. On the near approach of Lyon, the frightened Governor had ordered that no resistance should be made; but the braver Marmaduke, feeling strongly posted, had resolved to fight. A troop of his cavalry and a battalion of infantry occupied the road. Some of his troops had made a citadel of a strong brick house on

---

[1] See page 267.

his left; and in a lane in his rear, leading to the river, was the main body of his left wing. His main right wing was posted behind a fence, between a wheat and corn field, and in these fields were detached and unorganized squads of men.[1]

Lyon led his troops up a gently rolling slope for half a mile, and when within three hundred yards of his foe, he made dispositions for battle. He posted the regulars, with Colonel Blair's troops, on the left, and some German volunteers of Boernstein's regiment, under Lieutenant-Colonel Shaeffer, on the right. Totten's artillery occupied the center, and they opened the conflict by firing a shell from a 12-pounder in the midst of the insurgents in the road. Another shell immediately followed, and scattered the men in the wheat-field, when Lyon's column advanced, and the battle began. It continued for a short time with great spirit on both sides. The insurgents were forced back by the pressure of the Union infantry, and the round shot, and shell, and grape, and canister, from Totten's cannon. Two of his shells entered the brick house and drove out the inmates; and twenty minutes later, Lyon's men occupied it, and had full possession of the battle-field.

The insurgents made a stand at the edge of a wood near their camp, but were soon driven from their rallying-point. They now fled in confusion, for they found themselves attacked on their flank by a cannonade from the river. Captain Richards, with some infantry, and a small company of artillery, under Captain Voester, who had been left in charge of the transports, had moved up the river and captured a shore-battery of two guns, with which the insurgents intended to sink the vessels of their pursuers. They also took twenty prisoners, several horses, and a considerable amount of military stores. They then moved forward to co-operate with the land force; and it was the shot from a howitzer on the *City of Louisiana*, and the missiles from Totten's guns, falling simultaneously among the insurgents, that produced a panic and a flight. Their camp, which Lyon took possession of immediately afterward, showed evidences of hasty departure.[2]

---

[1] These were new recruits just sent in from Camp Vest, about four miles from Booneville. That camp had been established on the 14th, and Marmaduke had sent out urgent appeals to the inhabitants of the surrounding country to rally to his standard. "Hurry on, day and night," he said. "Everybody, citizens and soldiers, must come, bringing their arms and ammunition. Time is every thing." As they came into the camp, they were sent to the front in squads.

[2] An eye-witness wrote, that the breakfasts of the men were found in course of preparation. Half-baked bread was in the heat of fires, and hams had knives sticking in them. Pots of coffee were on the fires; and in various ways there was evidence that the flight of the occupants of the camp had been most precipitate. Lyon's loss was two killed, two wounded, and one missing. That of the insurgents is unknown. It was estimated at more than fifty killed and wounded, and a considerable number made prisoners. The latter were nearly all young men, who declared that they had been deceived and misled by the conspirators. They were very penitent, and Lyon released them. The whole number of insurgents was about three thousand, of whom nine hundred were half-disciplined cavalry, and the remainder raw militia, six-sevenths of them armed with the rifles, shot-guns, and knives which they had brought from their homes. The Union troops numbered less than two thousand; and not a third of either party was in the engagement at one time.

WEAPONS OF THE INSURGENTS.

The accompanying illustration represents weapons found in the camp of the insurgents near Booneville. The knife was made, evidently, by a common blacksmith, in the form of the Bowie [see note 1, page 266], but very rudely. The sheath below it was made of common stiff leather. The dagger, also, was the work of a blacksmith. The handle of each was made of hickory wood. Weapons of this kind were in common use among the insurgent troops from the Mississippi region during the earlier period of the war.

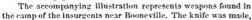

Leaving a company to hold the camp, Lyon pressed on to Booneville, where the loyal inhabitants received him with joy, and the town was formally surrendered to him. The insurgents had continued their flight. Some of them went directly southward, but a large portion of them, including most of the cavalry, fled westward toward Lexington, whither, as we have observed, General Price had gone. The Governor, who had kept at a safe distance from the battle, fled, with about five hundred men, to Warsaw, on the Osage River, eighty miles southwest of Booneville, pursued

^a June, 1861. some distance by Totten. There he was joined, on the 20th,^a by about four hundred insurgents, under Colonel O'Kane, who, before dawn on the 19th, had surprised, dispersed, and partially captured about the same number of Home Guards, under Captain Cook, who were asleep in two barns, fifteen miles north of Warsaw, at a place of rendezvous called Camp Cole.

Jackson and his followers continued their retreat fifty miles farther southwest, to Montevallo, in Vernon County, on the extreme western borders of Missouri, where he was joined by General Price,^b with

^b July 3. troops gathered at Lexington and on the way, making the whole force there about three thousand. At the same time, General G. J. Rains, a

graduate of the Military Academy at West Point, was hurrying forward to join Jackson with a considerable force of insurgents, closely pursued by Major Sturgis, of the regular Army, who was leading a body of Kansas volunteers, who were eager to be avenged on Jackson for sufferings which they alleged he had caused them a few years before, when they were struggling with invaders from Missouri, called "Border Ruffians," of whom the now fugitive Governor was a conspicuous leader. Satisfied that the northern part of the State was lost to the cause of Secession, for the time, Jackson now endeavored to concentrate all of the disloyal Missouri troops, with

GABRIEL JAMES RAINS.

McCullough's men, in the southwestern part of the Commonwealth, preparatory to the speedy "deliverance of the State from Federal rule."

In the camp of the insurgents, near Booneville, Lyon found ample evidence of the hypocrisy of Jackson and Price, who had proclaimed to the world that they earnestly desired peace and reconciliation, but that it was denied them by the National Government and its servants, while, at the same time, they were preparing to wage a cruel and relentless war in favor of the rebellion. To counteract the effect of the false allegations of the

^c July 18. Governor in his proclamation,¹ Lyon issued an address, at Boonevville,^c to the inhabitants of Missouri, plainly stating the intentions of the Government to be nothing more than the maintenance of its authority, and the preservation of the life of the Republic. On the day

¹ See page 470.

before, Colonel Boernstein, who was holding the capital to obedience with a mild but firm hand, had issued a proclamation, addressed to the inhabitants of that immediate region, assuring them of protection in the enjoyment of all their rights, and that "slave property" should not be interfered with, nor the slaves encouraged to be unfaithful; at the same time warning all disloyal men that he would not allow the enemies of the Government to work mischief openly. These proclamations quieted the fears of the people, and strengthened the cause of the Government. Assured of military protection, and encouraged by the aspect of affairs favorable to the maintenance of the National authority in the Commonwealth, the State Convention was called to reassemble at Jefferson City on the 22d of July.

General Lyon remained at Booneville about a fortnight, making preparations for a vigorous campaign against gathering insurgents in the southwestern part of the State. He now held military control over the whole region northward of the Missouri River, and east of a line running south from Booneville to the Arkansas border, thus giving to the Government the control of the important points of St. Louis, Hannibal, St. Joseph, and Bird's Point, as bases of operations, with railways and rivers for transportation. On the 1st of July there were at least ten thousand loyal troops in Missouri, and ten thousand more might be thrown into it, in the space of forty-eight hours, from camps in the adjoining State of Illinois. And, at the same time, Colonel Sigel, already mentioned, an energetic and accomplished German liberal, who had command-

ed the republican troops of his native state (the Grand Duchy of Baden) in the revolution of 1848, was pushing forward with eager soldiers toward the insurgent camps on the borders of Kansas and Arkansas, to open the campaign, in which he won laurels and the commission of a brigadier. That campaign, in which Lyon lost his life, will be considered hereafter.

There was now great commotion all over the land. War had begun in earnest. The drum and fife were heard in every city, village, and hamlet, from the St. Croix to the Rio Grande. Propositions for compro-

FRANZ SIGEL.

mises and concessions were no longer listened to by the opposing parties. The soothing echoes of the last "Peace Convention," held at Frankfort, in Kentucky, on the 27th of May,[1] were lost in the din of warlike preparations; and it was evident that the great question before the people could only be settled by the arbitrament of the sword, to which the enemies of the Republic had appealed.

As we look over the theater of events connected with the secession movement at the beginning of July, 1861, we perceive that the Insurrection had then become an organized Rebellion, and was rapidly assuming the dignity and importance of a Civil War. The conspirators had formed a confed-

[2] See page 460.

eracy, civil and military, vast in the extent of its area of operations, strong
in the number of its willing and unwilling supporters, and marvelous in its
manifestations of energy hitherto unsuspected.   It had all the visible forms
of regular government, modeled after that against which the conspirators
had revolted; and through it they were wielding a power equal to that of
many empires of the globe.   They had been accorded belligerent rights, as a
nation struggling for its independence, by leading governments of Europe,
and under the sanction of that recognition they had commissioned embassadors to foreign courts, and sent out upon the ocean armed ships, bearing
their chosen ensign, to commit piracy, as legalized by the law of nations.
They had created great armies, and were successfully defying the power of
their Government to suppress their revolt.   Henceforth, in this chronicle, the
conflict will be treated as a civil war, and the opposing parties be designated
respectively by the titles of *Nationals* and *Confederates.*

We have already noticed the meeting of the Confederate " Congress,"
so-called, in second session, at Montgomery, on the 29th of April,[a]
[a] 1861.   and the authorization thereby of the issuing of commissions for
privateering; also for making thorough preparations for war on the land.[1]
That " Congress" worked diligently for the accomplishment of its purposes.
It passed an unlimited Enlistment Act, it being estimated that arms for one
hundred and fifty thousand men could be furnished by the Confederacy.
That Act authorized Jefferson Davis to "accept the services of volunteers
who may offer their services, without regard to the place of enlistment,
either as cavalry, mounted riflemen, artillery, or infantry, in such proportion
of their several arms as he may deem expedient, to serve for and during the
existing war, unless sooner discharged."[2]   Acts were passed for the regulation of telegraphs, postal affairs, and the mints;[3] and on the 16th of May an
Act was approved authorizing the issuing of bonds for fifty millions of dollars, at an annual interest not to exceed eight per cent., and payable in
twenty years.   Made wiser by their failure to find a market for their bonds
authorized in February,[4] and offered in April, the conspirators now devised
schemes to insure the sale of this new issue, or to secure money by other
means.   The Act gave the Secretary of the Treasury, so-called, discretionary
power to issue in lieu of such bonds twenty millions of dollars in treasury
notes, not bearing interest, in denominations of not less than five dollars,
and "to be receivable in payment of all debts or taxes due to the Confederate States, except the export duty on cotton, or in exchange for the bonds
herein authorized to be issued.   The said notes," said the Act, "shall be payable at the end of two years from the date of their issue, in specie."[5]

---

[1] See page 372.
[2] Approved May 8, 1861. See *Acts and Resolutions of the three Sessions of the Provisional Congress of the Confederate States:* Second Session, page 5.
[3] The Act directed that the operations of the mints at New Orleans, in Louisiana, and Dahlonega, in Georgia, should be suspended. They had no other dies for coin than those of the United States, and the conspirators saw, in the scheme for issuing an irredeemable paper currency, without limit, no use for coin.
[4] See page 263.
[5] Act approved May 16, 1861. See *Acts and Resolutions of the Confederate Congress:* Second Session, pages 32 to 34. A *fac-simile* of one of these treasury notes, issued at Richmond after that city became the seat of the Confederate Government, is given on page 545. After this issue, the terms of redemption were changed. A note before me, dated " Richmond, September 2d, 1861," reads as follows:—" Six months after the ratification of a Treaty of Peace between the Confederate States and the United States, the Confederate States of America

Another scheme for raising money, in connection with the issue of bonds, is found in an act approved on the 21st of May, which forbade the debtors to individuals or corporations in the Free-labor States from making payments of the same " to their respective creditors, or their agents or assignees, pending the existing war."[1] Such debtors were authorized by the act to pay the amount

will pay to the bearer Five Dollars. Richmond, September 2d, 1861. Fundable in eight per cent. Stock or Bonds of the Confederate States of America. Receivable in payment of all dues except export duties." Hundreds of millions of dollars in these notes were issued during the war. The bonds issued by the conspirators, from time to time, in different denominations, also to the amount of hundreds of millions of dollars, were in the usual form of such evidences of debt, and contained various devices, most of them of a warlike character, and several of them with a portrait of Memminger, the so-called Secretary of the Treasury. These bonds and notes, and the checks of the Confederate Government, are all much inferior in execution to those issued by our Government. On the notes, green and blue inks were used to prevent counterfeits.

[1] This Act excepted in its operations the Slave-labor States not in the Confederacy, namely : Delaware, Maryland, Kentucky, and Missouri, and the District of Columbia.

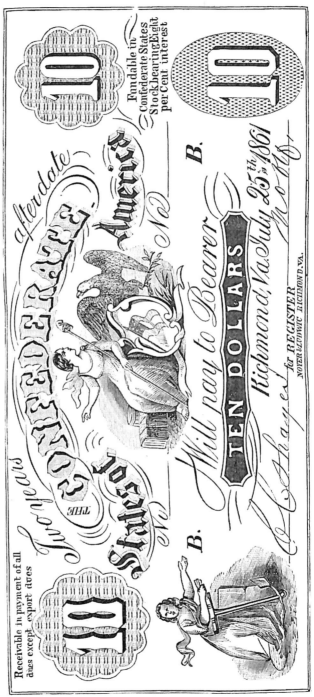

CONFEDERATE TREASURY NOTE.

of their indebtedness "into the treasury of the Confederate States, in
specie or treasury notes," and receive for the same the treasurer's certificate, which should show the amount paid in, and on what account, and
the rate of interest to be allowed. These were to be " redeemable at the
close of the war and the restoration of peace, in specie or its equivalent."[1]
It was estimated that the aggregate of the indebtedness of the business men
within the lines of the so-called Confederate States to those of the Free-labor
States, at that time, was about two hundred millions of dollars. All honorable debtors gave no countenance to the proposed scheme of villainy, and
not only refrained from reporting their indebtedness and paying the amount
into the treasury of the conspirators, but took every favorable opportunity
to liquidate the claims of Northern creditors. There was a large class who
favored secession because by its means they hoped to avoid paying their
debts. These, too, kept away from the Secretary of the Treasury ; and this
notable scheme gave the craving coffers of the conspirators very little relief.

Still another scheme for insuring the sale of the bonds was planned. To
recommend them to the confidence of the people, it was necessary for them
to have some tangible basis for practical purposes, in the absence of specie.
The conspirators could not calculate upon a revenue from commerce, for the
blockading ships of the Government were rapidly closing the seaports of
States in which rebellion existed to regular trade. It was therefore proposed to make the great staple of the Confederacy—cotton—the main basis
for the credit of the bonds, with other agricultural products in a less degree.
The blockade was, of necessity, diminishing the commercial value of the
surplus of these products, for, without an outlet to the markets of the
world, they were useless. The experiment was tried; and while the conspirators realized very little money, almost every thing required for the
consumption of their armies, for a while, was supplied. The plan was, that
the planters should subscribe for the use of the government a certain sum of
money out of the proceeds of a certain number of bales of cotton, when
sold, the planter being allowed to retain the custody of his cotton, and the
right to choose his time for its sale. When sold, he received the amount of
his subscription in the bonds of the Confederacy. The people had little
confidence in these bonds, but were willing to invest in them the surplus of
their productions, which they could not sell; and it was announced by the
so-called Secretary of the Treasury of the Confederates, when the " Congress " reassembled at Richmond, late in July, that subscriptions to the
Cotton Loan amounted to over fifty millions of dollars.[2] Bonds, with cot-

[1] *Acts, &c., of the Confederate Congress:* Second Session, page 88.

[2] Alexander H. Stephens assumed the office of expounder of the principles, intentions, and effects of this Cotton Loan. The object of the scheme was, he said, to avoid taxing the people, if possible. But he told the inhabitants of Georgia, plainly, that if it should be necessary to tax the people, the taxes would be levied, and they would be compelled to pay them. "I tell you the government does not intend to be subjugated," he said, "and if we do not raise the money by loans, if the people do not contribute, I tell you we intend to have the money, and taxation will be resorted to, if nothing else will raise it. Every life and dollar in the country will be demanded rather than you and every one of us shall be overrun by the enemy. On that you may count." He then proceeded to speak of the great value of the bonds, which bore eight per cent. interest, payable semi-annually, and declared that if the Confederacy was not defeated, they would be the best government bonds in the world, and would doubtless command a premium of fifteen or twenty per cent. At the same time he frankly told them (what came to pass) that if the schemes of the conspirators did not succeed, " these bonds will not be worth a dime."—*Speech of Alexander H. Stephens to a Convention of Cotton-growers at Augusta,* July 11, 1861. These planters well understood the tenor of his demands. They well knew that an omission to subscribe to the loan would be constructive treason to the " Confederate States Government," which would soon

ton as a basis of promises of redemption, to the amount of fifteen millions of dollars, were disposed of in Europe, chiefly in England. We shall hereafter further consider this Cotton Loan.

In retaliation for an order issued by Mr. Chase, the Secretary of the Treasury, on the 2d of May, directing all officers in the revenue service, on the Northern and Northwestern waters of the United States, to seize and detain all arms, munitions of war, provisions, and other supplies, on their way toward States in which rebellion existed—in other words, establishing a blockade of the Mississippi and the railways leading southward from Kentucky—the Confederates forbade the exportation of raw cotton or cotton yarn, "excepting through" seaports of the Confederate States, under heavy penalties, expecting thereby to strike a heavy blow at manufactures in the Free-labor States.[1] By an order of John H. Reagan, the so-called Postmaster-General of the Confederates, caused by an order of Postmaster-General Blair for the arrest of the United States postal service in States wherein rebellion existed, after the 31st of May, the postmasters in those States were ordered to retain in their possession, after the 1st of June, "for the benefit of the Confederate States, all mail-bags, locks and keys, marking and other stamps," and "all property connected with the postal service."

The Confederate "Congress" adjourned on the 21st of May, to reassemble at Richmond on the 20th of July following,[2] after providing for the removal thither of the several Executive Departments and their archives, and authorizing Davis, if it "should be impolitic to meet in Richmond" at that time, to call it together elsewhere. He was also authorized to proclaim a Fast Day, which he did on the 25th, appointing as such the 13th of June. In that proclamation he said : "Knowing that none but a just and righteous cause can gain the Divine favor, we would implore the Lord of Hosts to guide and direct our policy in the paths of right, duty, justice, and mercy ; to unite our hearts and our efforts for the defense of our dearest rights ; to strengthen our weakness, crown our arms with success, and enable us to secure a speedy, just, and honorable peace."

On Sunday, the 26th,[a] Davis left Montgomery for Richmond, with the intention, it is said, of taking command of the Confederate troops in Virginia in person,[3] accompanied by his favorite aid, Wigfall, of Texas,[4] and Robert Toombs, his "Secretary of State." His journey was a continuous ovation. At every railway station, men, women, and children greeted him with cheers and the waving of handkerchiefs. "When the flute-like voice of Davis," said a reporter of the *Richmond*

[a] May, 1861.

---

feel the force of a penalty, and so they subscribed, with a feeling akin to that of Englishmen in the case of the levying of ship-money by Charles the First; a proceeding that cost him his head, and his heir a kingdom.

[1] Act approved May 21, 1861.

[2] In a speech at Atlanta, Georgia, on the day after the adjournment, Howell Cobb gave reasons for the adjournment to Richmond:—"I will tell you why we did this," he said. "The Old Dominion, as you know, has at last shaken off the bonds of Lincoln, and joined her noble Southern sisters. Her soil is to be the battle-ground, and her streams are to be dyed with Southern blood. We felt that her cause was our cause, and that if she fell, we wanted to die by her. We have sent our soldiers into the posts of danger, and we wanted to be there to aid and counsel our brave boys. In the progress of the war, further legislation may be necessary, and we will be there, that when the hour of danger comes, we may lay aside the robes of legislation, buckle on the armor of the soldier, and do battle beside the brave ones who have volunteered for the defense of our beloved South." This was the open pretense. The speaker, with wise caution, refrained from avowing the real reason to be, to keep war from the households of the Montgomery conspirators, who well knew that one grand objective of the National Army would be the possession of the seat of the Confederate "Government."

[3] Speech of Alexander H. Stephens at Atlanta, Georgia, May 23, 1861.   [4] See pages 81 and 326.

Enquirer, who had been sent to chronicle the journey, "arose upon the air, hushed to silence by the profound respect of his auditors, it was not long before there was an outburst of feeling which gave vent to a tornado of voices. Every sentiment he uttered seemed to well up from his heart, and was received with the wildest enthusiasm." The modesty of Wigfall on the occasion was most remarkable. "In vain," says the chronicler, "he would seek some remote part of the cars; the crowd hunted him up, and the welkin rang with rejoicings, as he addressed them in his emphatic and fervent style of oratory." Toombs was likewise modest. "He, too," said the chronicler, "sought to avoid the call, but the echo would ring with the name of Toombs! Toombs! and the sturdy Georgia statesman had to respond." At Golds-boro', in North Carolina, Davis was received at the cars by the military (a

NORTH CAROLINA MOUNTED RIFLEMAN.

part of which were some of the mounted riflemen of that State, then on their way to Virginia), who escorted him to the hotel, where he supped. "The hall," says the chronicler, "was thronged with beautiful girls, and many were decking him with gar-lands of flowers, while others fanned him. It was a most interesting occasion." After declaring that the confidence of the people showed "that the mantle of Washington" fell "gracefully upon the shoulders" of the arch-conspirator, the historian of the journey said: "Never were a people more enraptured with their chief magistrate than ours are with President Davis, and the trip from Mont-gomery to Richmond will ever be remembered with delight by all who witnessed it."[1]

Davis and his party were met at Peters-burg by Governor Letcher and the Mayor (Mayo) of Richmond; and he was escorted into his future "capital" by soldiers and civilians, and out to the "Fair Grounds," where he addressed a great crowd of people,[a] and de-clared that, to the last breath of his life, he was wholly their own.

[a] May 28, 1861.

On the evening of the 31st he was serenaded, when he took the occasion to utter that memorable speech, so characteristic of the orator when-ever he was impressed with a sense of power in his own hands, which gave the people of the Free-labor States an indication of the spirit that ani-mated the conspirators, and with which the opening war would be waged. He said that upon the Confederates was laid the "high and holy responsi-bility of preserving the constitutional liberty of a free government." "Those with whom we have lately associated," he said, "have shown themselves so incapable of appreciating the blessings of the glorious institutions they in-herited, that they are to-day stripped of the liberty to which they were born. They have allowed an ignorant usurper to trample upon all the prerogatives of citizenship, and to exercise powers never delegated to him; and it has

---

[1] *Richmond Examiner*, May 28, 1861.

been reserved to your State, so lately one of the original thirteen, but now, thank God! fully separated from them, to become the theater of a great central camp, from which will pour forth thousands of brave hearts, to roll back the tide of this despotism. Apart from that gratification we may well feel at being separated from such a connection, is the pride that upon you devolves the task of maintaining and defending our new government. I believe that we shall be able to achieve this noble work, and that the institutions of our fathers will go to our children as safely as they have descended to us. In these Confederate States, we observe those relations which have been poetically ascribed to the United States, but which never there had the same reality—States so distinct that each existed as a sovereign, yet so united that each was bound with the other to constitute a whole—'Distinct as the billows, yet one as the sea.' Upon every hill which now overlooks Richmond you have had, and will continue to have, camps containing soldiers from every State in the Confederacy; and to its remotest limits every proud

DAVIS'S RESIDENCE IN RICHMOND.

heart beats high with indignation at the thought that the foot of the invader has been set upon the soil of Old Virginia. There is not one true son of the South who is not ready to shoulder his musket, to bleed, to die, or to conquer in the cause of liberty here. . . . We have now reached the point where, arguments being exhausted, it only remains for us to stand by our weapons. When the time and occasion serve, we shall smite the smiter with manly arms, as did our fathers before us, and as becomes their sons. To the enemy we leave the base acts of the assassin and incendiary.[1] To them we leave it to insult helpless women; to us belongs vengeance upon man." He had ceased speaking, and was about to retire, when a voice in the crowd shouted: "Tell us something about Buena Vista," when he turned and said: " Well, my friends, I can only say we will make the battle-fields in Virginia another Buena Vista, and drench them with blood more precious than that which flowed there."

The Virginians were so insane with passion at that time, that instead of rebuking Davis for virtually reiterating the assurance given to the people of the more Southern States, "You may plant your seed in peace, for Old Virginia will have to bear the brunt of battle,"[2] they rejoiced because upon every hill around their State capital were camps of " soldiers from every State in

---

[1] See the proposition to destroy the National Capitol, with Congress in session, on page 523.
[2] See note 1, page 344.

the Confederacy;" and the citizens of that capital purchased from James A. Seddon (afterward Confederate "Secretary of War") his elegant mansion, on the corner of Clay and Twelfth Streets, and presented it, sumptuously furnished, to the "President" for a residence.[1]

In successful imitation of his chief, Beauregard, who arrived at Richmond on the 1st of June,[a] and proceeded to take command of the Confederate troops in the "Department of Alexandria," issued a proclamation from "Camp Pickens, Manassas Junction," to the inhabitants of that region of Virginia, which has forever linked his name with those of the dishonorable men of his race.[2] The obvious intention of Davis and Beauregard, and the authors of scores upon scores of speeches at political gatherings, from pulpits, and to soldiers on their departure for the seat of war, poured forth continually at that time in all parts of the Confederacy, was, by the most reckless disregard of truth, and the employment of the most incendiary language, to "fire the Southern heart," and make the people and the soldiers believe that they were called upon to resist a horde of cut-throats and plunderers, let loose by an ignorant usurper, for the sole object of despoiling the Slave-labor States. Every thing that malignity could imagine and language could express, calculated to cast discredit upon the National Government, abase the President in the opinions of the Southern people, and make them hate and despise their political brethren in the Free-labor States,

[a] 1861.

---

[1] The view of the residence of Davis in Richmond, given on the preceding page, is from a sketch made by the writer just after that city was evacuated by the Confederates, in April, 1865. It was a brick house, painted a stone color. On the corner diagonally opposite was the residence of A. H. Stephens. In front of the residence of Davis is seen a sentry-box, and beyond it the stables belonging to the establishment. The house was occupied, at the time of the writer's visit, by General Ord, who had there the table on which Lee and Grant had signed articles of capitulation a few days before. A picture of it will be found in another part of this work. A small black-and-tan terrier dog that belonged to Mrs. Davis was left in the house when the "President" hastily fled from Richmond, at midnight, early in April, 1865.

[2] The following is a copy of Beauregard's proclamation:—"A reckless and unprincipled tyrant has invaded your soil. Abraham Lincoln, regardless of all moral, legal, and constitutional restraints, has thrown his Abolition hosts among you, who are murdering and imprisoning your citizens, confiscating and destroying your property, and committing other acts of violence and outrage too shocking and revolting to humanity to be enumerated. All rules of civilized warfare are abandoned, and they proclaim by their acts, if not on their banners, that their war-cry is 'Beauty and Booty.' All that is dear to man—your honor, and that of your wives and daughters, your fortunes, and your lives—are involved in this momentous contest. In the name, therefore, of the constituted authorities of the Confederate States—in the sacred cause of constitutional liberty and self-government, for which we are contending—in behalf of civilization itself—I, G. T. Beauregard, Brigadier-General of the Confederate States, commanding at Camp Pickens, Manassas Junction, do make this my proclamation, and invite and enjoin you, by every consideration dear to the hearts of freemen and patriots, by the name and memory of your Revolutionary fathers, and by the purity and sanctity of your domestic firesides, to rally to the standard of your State and country, and, by every means in your power compatible with honorable warfare, to drive back and expel the invaders from your land. I enjoin you to be true and loyal to your country and her legal and constitutional authorities, and especially to be vigilant of the movements and acts of the enemy, so as to enable you to give the earliest authentic information at these head-quarters, or to officers under my command. I desire to assure you that the utmost protection in my power will be given to you all."

The reader will comprehend the infamy and shamelessness displayed in this proclamation, by considering that it was from a man who, at the head of several thousand troops, had, almost two months before, when there was no war in the land, assailed a garrison of seventy men in Fort Sumter, and when its interior was all on fire, inhumanly allowed, if not directed, his gunners to fire red-hot shot and heavy bombshells with increased rapidity into that furnace where the little band of defenders were almost roasting; also, by considering the fact that at the time this proclamation was issued, the only National troops in Virginia (excepting in the loyal western counties) were those who were holding, as a defensive position in front of Washington, Arlington Hights and the shore of the Potomac to Alexandria, and the village of Hampton, near Fortress Monroe. It must be remembered, also, that the only "murders" that had been committed at that time were inflicted on the bodies of Massachusetts soldiers by his associates in Baltimore, and on the body of Colonel Ellsworth by one of his confederates in treason in Alexandria. It must also be remembered that the superiors of the author of this proclamation, at about the same time, entertained a proposition for wholesale murder at the National Capital. See page 523. Beauregard was noted, throughout the war, for his official misrepresentations, his ludicrous boastings, and his signal failures as a military leader, as the record will show.

was, as we have already observed, continually thrust upon the notice of that people through the most respectable as well as the most disreputable of their public speakers and journals. The Richmond papers, published under the inspiration of Davis and his fellow-conspirators, were especially offensive. Sufficient has been cited from these journals, and others in the Slave-labor States, to show how horribly the minds of the people were abused; and yet what we have given is mild in sentiment and decent in expression compared with much that filled the newspapers of the Confederacy and was heard from the lips of leaders.

The speech of Davis and the proclamation of Beauregard were applauded by the secession leaders in Washington City and in Baltimore, as exhibiting the ring of true metal, and gave a new impulse to their desires for linking the fortunes of Maryland with the Confederacy, and renewed their hopes of a speedy consummation of their wishes. The temporary panic that seized them when Butler so suddenly took military possession of Baltimore had quickly subsided after he was called away; and under the mild administration of martial law by General Cadwalader, his successor, they became daily more bold and defiant, and gave much uneasiness to the Government. It was known that the majority of the members of the Maryland Legislature were disloyal, and that secretly and openly they were doing all they could to array their State against the National Government. A committee of that body [1] had addressed a sympathizing epistle to Jefferson Davis, in which he was unwarrantably assured that the people of Maryland coincided with the conspirators in sentiment; for at the elections for members of Congress,[a] to represent the State in the extraordinary session to begin on the 4th of July, so loyal was the great mass of the people of that State, that not a single sympathizer with secession was chosen.

[a June 13, 1861.]

In the city of Baltimore was the head of the secession movements in the State; and it was made apparent to the Government, early in June,[b] that there was a powerful combination there whose purpose was to co-operate with the armed insurgents in Virginia in attempts to seize the National Capital, by preventing soldiers from the North passing through that city, and by arming men to cross into Virginia to swell the ranks of the insurgents there. The Government took energetic steps to avert the threatened danger. N. P. Banks, Ex-Governor of Massachusetts, who had lately been appointed a Major-General of Volunteers, was assigned to the command of the Department of Annapolis, with his head-quarters at Baltimore; and on the 10th of June he succeeded Cadwalader, who joined the expedition under General Patterson.[2] It soon became so evident to Banks that the Board of Police, and Kane,[3] the Chief of that body, were in active sympathy, if not in actual complicity, with the conspirators, that he reported to his Government his suspicions of the dangerous character of that organization, suspicions which subsequent events showed to be well founded.

[b 1861.]

After satisfying himself of the guilt of certain officials, General Banks ordered a large body of soldiers, armed and supplied with ball-cartridges, to march from Fort McHenry into the city just before daybreak on the 27th

---

[1] The Committee consisted of Messrs. McKaig, Yellott, and Harding.
[2] See page 521.
[3] See page 281.

of June, and to proceed to the arrest of Marshal Kane, and his incarceration in that fort. He at once gave to the people, in a proclamation, his reasons for the act. He told them it was not his intention to interfere in the least with the legitimate government of the citizens of Baltimore or of the State ; on the contrary, it was his desire to " support the public authorities in all appropriate duties. But unlawful combinations of men," he continued, " organized for resistance to such laws, that provide hidden deposits of arms and ammunition, encourage contraband traffic with men at war with the Government, and, while enjoying its protection and privileges, stealthily wait an opportunity to combine their means and force with those in rebellion against its authority, are not among the recognized or legal rights of any class of men, and cannot be permitted under any form of government whatever." He said that such combinations were well known to exist in his department, and that the Chief of Police was not only believed to be cognizant of those facts, " but, in contravention of his duty and in violation of law," was, " by direction or indirection, both witness and protector to the transaction and parties engaged therein." Under such circumstances, the Government could not " regard him otherwise than as the head of an armed force hostile to its authority, and acting in concert with its avowed enemies." He further pro-

claimed that, in accordance with instructions, he had appointed Colonel (afterward Brigadier-General) John R. Kenly, of the First Maryland Volunteers, provost-marshal in and for the city of Baltimore, "to superintend and cause to be executed the police laws" of the city, "with the aid and assistance of the subordinate officers of the police department." He assured the citizens that whenever a loyal man among them should be named for the performance of the duty of chief of police, the military would at once yield to the civil authority.

Colonel Kenly was well known and highly respected as an influential citizen and thorough loyalist ; and he entered upon the important duties of his office with promptness and energy. The Police Commissioners[1] had met as soon as Banks's proclamation appeared, and protested against his act as illegal, and declared

FIRST MARYLAND REGIMENT.

that the " suspension of their functions suspended at the same time the operations of the police laws," and put the subordinate officers and men off duty. This declaration filled the citizens with the liveliest excitement, caused by indignation and alarm. They felt that they were given over to the power of the worst elements of society, with no law to protect them.

a June 27, 1861.   Banks hastened, by the publication *a* of instructions to Kenly, to disabuse and quiet the public mind. He therein declared that the functions of the police officers and men, and the operations of police

---

[1] These Commissioners were Charles Howard, *President*, and William H. Gatchell, Charles D. Hincks, and John W. Davis, with George W. Brown, the Mayor, who was *ex-officio* a member of the Board.

laws, were in full force, excepting so far as the latter affected the Commissioners and the Chief of Police; and he authorized Kenly, in the event of a refusal of any of the police force to perform their duty, to select, in conjunction with such of the public authorities as would aid him, "good men and true," to fill their places.

Kenly worked with energy. He chose to select new men for a police force. Before midnight, he had enrolled, organized, and armed such a force, two hundred and fifty strong, composed of Union citizens whom he could trust, and had taken possession of the head-quarters of the late Marshal and Police Commissioners, in the Old City Hall, on Holliday Street. In that building he found ample evidence of the guiltiness of the late occupants. Concealed beneath the floors, in several rooms, were found a large number of arms, con-

JOHN R. KENLY.

sisting of muskets, rifles, shot-guns, carbines, pistols, swords, and dirk knives, with ample ammunition of various kinds; also, in the covered yard or wood-room in the rear, in a position to command Watch-house Alley, leading to Saratoga Street, were two 6-pound and two 4-pound iron cannon, with suitable cartridges and balls. In that building was also found the cannon-ball sent from Charleston to Marshal Kane, delineated on page 322. These discoveries, and others of like character in other parts of the city, together with the rebellious conduct of the Board of Police, who continued their sittings daily, refused to acknowledge the new policemen, and held the old force subject to their orders, seemed to warrant the Government in ordering their arrest. They were accordingly taken into custody, and were confined in Fort Warren, in Boston Harbor, as prisoners of State.

These vigorous measures secured the ascendency of the Unionists in Maryland, which they never afterward lost. It was thenceforward entitled to the honor of being a

OLD CITY HALL, BALTIMORE.[1]

loyal State, and Baltimore a loyal city. The secessionists were silenced; and, at the suggestion of many Unionists of Baltimore, George R. Dodge, a citizen and a civilian, was appointed [a] marshal of police in place of Colonel Kenly, who, with his regiment, soon after-

a July 10, 1861.

---

[1] This is a view of the building as it appeared when the writer sketched it, in the autumn of 1864, from Holliday Street, near Saratoga Street. Adjoining it is seen the yard of the German Reformed Church, and in the distance the spire of Christ Church. The City Hall was built of brick, and stuccoed.

ward joined the Army of the Potomac. When the necessity for their presence no longer existed, Banks withdrew his troops from the city, where they had been posted at the various public buildings and other places; and, late in July, he superseded General Patterson in command on the Upper Potomac, and his place in Baltimore was filled by General John A. Dix. A few days later, Federal Hill was occupied, as we have observed, by the Fifth New York regiment (Zouaves), under Colonel Duryée (who was appointed a brigadier on the 31st of August), and by their hands the strong works known as Fort Federal Hill were constructed.

The turn of affairs in Maryland was disheartening to the conspirators. They had counted largely upon the active co-operation of its citizens in the important military movements about to be made, when Johnston should force his way across the Potomac, and with their aid strike a deadly blow for the possession of the National Capital in its rear. These expectations had been strongly supported by refugees from their State who had made their way to Richmond, and these, forming themselves into a corps called The Maryland Guard, had shown their faith by offering their services to the Confederacy. These enthusiastic young men, blinded by their own zeal, assured the conspirators that the sympathies of a greater portion of the people of their State were with them. This was confirmed by the arrival of a costly " Confederate " banner for the corps, wrought by women of Baltimore, and sent clandestinely to them by a sister secessionist. This was publicly presented to the Guard [a] on Capitol Square, in front of the monument there erected in honor of Washington and the founders of Virginia.[1] Ex-Senator Mason made a speech on the occasion, in which the hopes of the conspirators concerning Maryland were set forth. " Your own honored State," he said, " is with us heart and soul in this great controversy. . . . We all know that the same spirit which brought you here actuates thousands who remain at home." He complimented Chief Justice Taney for his sympathies with the conspirators, as one (referring to his action in the case of Merryman [2]) who had " stood bravely in the breach, and interposed the unspotted arm of Justice between the rights of the South and the malignant usurpation of power by the North." In conclusion, after hinting at a contemplated Confederate invasion of Maryland, in which the troops before him were expected to join,[3] he told them they were to take the flag back to Baltimore. " It came here," he said, " in the hands of the fair lady who stands by my side, who brought it through the camps of the enemy with a

[a] June 8, 1861.

---

[1] The *Richmond Despatch* of June 10 thus announced the event:—"Mrs. Augustus McLaughlin, the wife of one of the officers of the late United States Navy, who brought the flag from Baltimore, concealed as only a lady knows how, was present, and received the compliments of a large number of ladies and gentlemen who surrounded her upon the steps of the monument."—Moore's *Rebellion Record*, vol. i., Diary, page 96.

On the banner were the following words:—" The Ladies of Baltimore present this flag of the Confederate States of America to the soldiers comprising the Maryland Regiment now serving in Virginia, as a slight testimonial of the esteem in which their valor, their love of right, and determination to uphold true constitutional liberty are approved, applauded, and appreciated by the wives and daughters of the Monumental City."

[2] See page 451.

[3] A correspondent of the *Charleston Mercury*, writing at Richmond, on the 4th of July, said:—"Every thing depends upon the success and movements of General Johnston. If he has orders from President Davis to march into Maryland, and towards Baltimore, the game commences at once. Lincoln will find himself encompassed by forces in front and rear. Cut off from the North and West, Washington will be destroyed, and the footsteps of the retreating army, though tracked in blood across the soil of Maryland—as they assuredly will be, in such an event—may possibly pave the way to an honorable peace."—Duyckinck's *War for the Union*, i. 249.

woman's fortitude and courage and devotion to our cause; and you are to take it back to Baltimore, unfurl it in your streets, and challenge the applause of your citizens." For more than three years the conspirators were deceived by the belief that Maryland was their ally in heart, but was made powerless by military despotism; and her refugee sons were continually calling with faith, in the spirit of Randall's popular lyric:—

> "Dear Mother! burst the tyrant's chain,
> Maryland!
> Virginia should not call in vain,
> Maryland!
> She meets her sisters on the plain;
> ' *Sic Semper*,' 'tis the proud refrain
> That baffles minions back again,
> Maryland!
> Arise in majesty again,
> Maryland! my Maryland!" [1]

The delusion was dispelled when, in the summer of 1863, Lee invaded Maryland, with the expectation of receiving large accessions to his army in that State, but lost by desertion far more than he gained by recruiting.

At about this time, a piratical expedition was undertaken on Chesapeake Bay, and successfully carried out by some Marylanders. On the day after the arrest of Kane,[a] the steamer *St. Nicholas*, Captain Kirwan, that plied between Baltimore and Point Lookout, at the mouth of the Potomac River, left the former place with forty or fifty passengers, including about twenty men who passed for mechanics. There were also a few women, and among them was one who professed to be a French lady. When the steamer was near Point Lookout, the next morning, this "French lady," suddenly transformed to a stout young man, in the person of a son of a citizen of St. Mary's County, Maryland, named Thomas, and surrounded by the band of pretended mechanics, all well armed, demanded of Captain Kirwan the immediate surrender of his vessel. Kirwan had no means for successful resistance, and yielded. The boat was taken to the Virginia side of the river, and the passengers were landed at Cone Point, while the captain and crew were retained as prisoners. There one hundred and fifty armed accomplices of the pirates, pursuant to an arrangement, went on board the *St. Nicholas*, which was destined for the Confederate naval service. She then went cruising down the Chesapeake to the mouth of the Rappahannock River, where she captured three brigs laden respectively with coffee, ice, and coal. With her prizes, she went up the Rappahannock to Fredericksburg, where the pirates sold their plunder, divided the prize-money, and were entertained at a public dinner by the delighted citizens of that town, then suffering from the blockade, when Thomas appeared in his costume of a "French lady," and produced great merriment.

A few days after this outrage, officers Carmichael[2] and Horton, of Kenly's Baltimore police force, were at Fair Haven, on the Chesapeake, with a cul-

a June 28, 1861.

---

[1] Written by James R. Randall, at Point Coupee, Louisiana, on the 26th of April, 1861. It contains nine stanzas, and was very popular throughout the "Confederacy." It was successfully parodied by a loyal writer, after Lee's invasion of Maryland.

[2] This was Thomas Carmichael, who was afterward marshal of the police of Baltimore, and, with officer D. P. West, arrested a number of the members of the Maryland Legislature on a charge of disloyalty.

prit in charge. They took passage for home in the steamer *Mary Washington*, Captain Mason L. Weems. On board of her were Captain Kirwan and his fellow-prisoners, who had been released; also Thomas, the pirate, and some of his accomplices, who were preparing, no doubt, to repeat their bold and profitable achievement. Carmichael was informed of their presence, and directed Weems to land his passengers at Fort McHenry. When Thomas perceived the destination of the vessel he remonstrated; and, finally, drawing his revolver, and calling around him his armed associates, he threatened to throw the officers overboard and seize the vessel. He was overpowered by superior numbers, and word was sent to General Banks of the state of the case, who ordered an officer with a squad of men to arrest the pirates. Thomas could not be found. At length he was discovered in a large bureau drawer, in the ladies' cabin. He was drawn out, and, with his accomplices, was lodged in Fort McHenry.

Piratical operations on a more extended scale and wider field, under the sanction of commissions from the conspirators at Montgomery, were now frightening American commerce from the ocean. We have already mentioned the issuing of these commissions by Jefferson Davis,[1] the efforts of the conspirators to establish a navy, and the fitting out of vessels for the purpose, which had been stolen from the National Government, or purchased. Among the latter, as we have observed, was the *Lady Davis*, the first regularly commissioned vessel in the Confederate Navy. When the National Congress met in extraordinary session, on the 4th of July, more than twenty of these ocean depredators were afloat and in active service;[2] and at the close of that month, they had captured vessels and property valued at several millions of dollars. Their operations had commenced early in May, and at the beginning of June no less than twenty vessels had been captured and sent as prizes into the port of New Orleans alone.

The most notable of the Confederate pirate vessels, at that early period of the war, were the *Savannah*, Captain T. H. Baker, of Charleston, and the *Petrel*, Captain William Perry, of South Carolina; one of which was captured by an armed Government vessel, and the other was destroyed by one.

The *Savannah* was a little schooner which had formerly done duty as

---

[1] See page 372. The terms *pirate* and *piratical* are here used considerately, when speaking of the so-called privateering under commissions issued by Jefferson Davis and Robert Toombs (See note 4, page 37). The lexicographer defines a pirate to be "A robber on the high seas;" and piracy, "The act, practice, or crime of robbing on the high seas: the taking of property from others by open violence, and without authority, on the sea." The acts of men commissioned by Davis and Toombs were in exact accordance with these conditions. These leading conspirators represented no actual government on the face of the earth. The Confederacy of disloyal men like themselves, formed for the purpose of destroying their Government, had been established, as we have observed, without the consent of the people over whom they had assumed control, and whose rights they had trampled under foot. They had no more authority to issue commissions of *any* kind, than Jack Cade, Daniel Shays, Nat. Turner, or John Brown. Hence, those who committed depredations on the high seas under their commissions, did so "without authority." And privateering, authorized by a regular government, is nothing less than legalized piracy, which several of the leading powers of Europe have abolished, by an agreement made at Paris in 1856. To that agreement the United States Government refused its assent, because the other powers would not go further, and declare that all private property should be exempt from seizure at sea, not only by private armed vessels, but by National ships of war. The governments of France and Russia were in favor of this proposition, but that of Great Britain, a powerful maritime nation, refused its assent. It also refused its assent to a modification of the laws of blockade, saying, "The system of commercial blockade is essential to our naval supremacy."

[2] A full account of the operations of the Confederate Navy, domestic and foreign, will be given in another part of this work.

pilot-boat No. 7, off Charleston harbor. She was only fifty-four tons burden, carried one 18-pounder amidships, and was manned by only twenty men. At the close of May she sallied out from Charleston, and, on the 1st of June, captured the merchant brig *Joseph*, of Maine, laden with sugar, from Cuba, which was sent into Georgetown, South Carolina, and the *Savannah* proceeded in search of other prizes. Three days afterward,[a] she fell in with the National ^{a June 3, 1861.} brig *Perry*, which she mistook for a merchant vessel, and approached to make her a prize. When the mistake was discovered, the *Savannah* turned and tried to escape. The *Perry* gave hot pursuit, and a sharp fight

THE SAVANNAH.

ensued, which was of short duration. The *Savannah* surrendered; and her crew, with the papers of the vessel, were transferred to the war-ship *Minnesota*, the flag-ship of the Atlantic Blockading Squadron, and the prize was sent to New York in charge of Master's Mate McCook. She was the first vessel bearing the Confederate flag that was captured, and the event produced much gratification among the loyal people.

The captain and crew of the *Savannah* were imprisoned as pirates, and were afterward tried[b] as such, in New York, under the proclamation of the President of the 19th of April.[1] In the mean time, ^{b October, 1861.} Jefferson Davis had addressed a letter[c] to the President, in ^{c July 8.} which he threatened to deal with prisoners in his hands precisely as the commander and crew of the *Savannah* should be dealt with. He prepared to carry out that threat by holding Colonel Michael Corcoran, of the Sixty-ninth New York (Irish) Regiment, who was captured near Bull's Run, and others, as hostages, to suffer death if that penalty should be inflicted on the prisoners of the *Savannah*.[2] Meanwhile the subject had been much discussed at home,[3] and commanded attention abroad, especially

1 See page 372.

2 Corcoran was treated with great harshness He was handcuffed and placed in a solitary cell, with a chain attached to the floor, until the mental excitement produced by this ignominious treatment, combining with a susceptible constitution, and the infectious nature of the locality (Libby Prison), brought on an attack of typhoid fever. See Judge Daley's public letter to Senator Harris, December 21, 1861.

3 On the 21st of December, Charles P. Daley, Judge of the Court of Common Pleas in the city of New York, addressed a letter to Ira Harris, of the United States Senate, in discussion of the question, "Are Southern Privateersmen Pirates?" in which he took the ground, first, that they were on the same level, in the grade of guilt, with every Southern soldier, and that if one must suffer death for *piracy*, the others must suffer the same for *treason ;* and, secondly, by having so far acceded to the Confederates the rights of belligerents as to exchange prisoners, the Government could not consistently make a distinction between prisoners taken on land and those taken on the sea. He strongly recommended, as a measure of expediency, that the President should treat the " privateersmen," who had been convicted, and were awaiting sentence, as prisoners of war. He also pleaded in extenuation of the rebellious acts of the people of the South, that, through their want of information concerning the people of the North, they had "been hurried into their present position by the professional politicians and large landed proprietors, to whom they had hitherto been accustomed to confide the management of their public affairs."

in England, where it was assumed that Davis was at the head of an actual government, to whom the British authorities had officially awarded belligerent rights. With that assumption, and that opinion of the character of the Confederates, it was argued in the British Parliament that the captives were not pirates, but privateers, and ought to be treated as prisoners of war. The United States Government, on the contrary, denied that Jefferson Davis represented any government, and hence his commissions were null, and the so-called privateers were pirates, according to the accepted law of nations; but, governed by the dictates of expediency and a wisely directed humanity, it was concluded to treat them as prisoners of war, and they were afterward exchanged.

The *Petrel* was more suddenly checked in her piratical career than the *Savannah*. She was the United States revenue-cutter *Aiken*, which had been surrendered to the insurgents at Charleston, in December, 1860, by her disloyal commander.[1] She was now manned by a crew of thirty-six men, who were mostly Irishmen, picked up in Charleston while seeking employment. She evaded the blockading squadron off Charleston harbor, and went to sea on the 28th of July, when she was discovered by the National frigate *St. Lawrence*, that was lying behind one of the islands on that coast. The *St. Lawrence* was immediately made to assume the appearance of a large merchant vessel. Her heavy spars were hauled down, her ports were closed, and her people sent below. The *Petrel* regarded her as a rich prize, and bore down upon her, while the *St. Lawrence* appeared to be crowding sail so as to escape. As the *Petrel* approached, she sent a warning shot across the *St. Lawrence*, but the latter kept on her course, chased by the pirate. When the *Petrel* came within fair range, the *St. Lawrence* opened her ports, and gave her the contents of three heavy guns. One of them—a Paixhan—was loaded with an 8-inch shell, known as the " Thunderbolt,"[2] which exploded in the hold of the *Petrel*, while a 32-pound solid shot

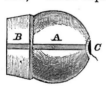

THUNDERBOLT SHELL.

struck her amidships, below water-mark. These made her a total wreck in an instant, and she went to the bottom of the ocean, leaving the foaming waters over her grave thickly strewn with splinters and her struggling crew. Four of her men were drowned, and the remainder, when brought out of the water, were so amazed and confused that they scarcely knew what had happened. A flash of fire, a thunder-peal, the crash of timbers, and engulfment in the sea, had been the incidents of a moment of their experience. The rescued crew were sent to Philadelphia and placed in Moyamensing Prison, to answer the charge of piracy. They, like the crew of the *Savannah*, were finally admitted to the privileges of prisoners of war, and were exchanged.

While the piratical vessels of the Confederates were making war upon

---

[1] See page 138.

[2] This shell was invented by William Wheeler Hubbell, counselor at law, of Philadelphia, in the year 1842, and for which he received letters patent in 1856. It was introduced into the service in 1847, under an agreement of secrecy, by Colonel Bomford, the inventor of the columbiad (see page 123), then the Chief of the Ordnance Department. This shell was the most efficient projectile in use when the war broke out. Its appearance is shown by the annexed illustration, of which *A* is the shell; *B*, the sabot, or shoe of wood, and *C*, the fuse. The peculiar construction of this shell will be hereafter mentioned, when noticing the various projectiles used in the war.

commerce, and the conspirators were encouraged by foreign powers, who had conceded to them belligerent rights, to increase their number, Secretary Welles was putting forth, in full measure, all the instrumentalities at his command for increasing the strength and efficiency of the National Navy. The blockade of ports along almost three thousand miles of coast, with its numerous harbors and inlets,[1] had been declared, and must be made as perfect as the law of nations, as they

GIDEON WELLES.

were then construed, required, to command respect. There was no time for the building of vessels for the purpose; so the Secretary purchased various kinds of craft, and converted them into warriors as speedily as possible.

We have seen how inefficient and scattered was the Navy at the accession of the new Administration, at the beginning of March;[a] *a 1861.* now, at the beginning of July, four months later, there were forty-three armed vessels engaged in the blockade service, and in defense of the coast on the eastern side of the continent. These were divided into two squadrons, known respectively as the Atlantic and the Gulf Squadron. The former, under the command of Flag-officer Silas H. Stringham, consisted of twenty-two vessels, and an aggregate of two hundred and ninety-six guns and three thousand three hundred men; the latter, under command of Flag-officer William Mervine, consisted

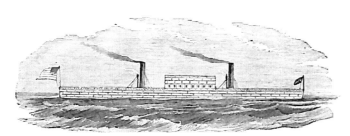

STEVENS'S IRON-CLAD FLOATING BATTERY.

of twenty-one vessels, with an aggregate of two hundred and eighty-two guns and three thousand five hundred men.[2] And before the close of the year, the Secretary purchased and put into commission no less than one hundred and thirty-seven vessels, and had contracted for the building of a large number of steamships of a substantial class, suitable for performing continuous duty off the coast in all weathers.

The Secretary, in his Report, called attention to the important subject of

---

[1] Report of Gideon Welles, Secretary of the Navy, July 4, 1861.

[2] Report of the Secretary of the Navy, July 4, 1861. The commanders of the squadrons had been instructed to permit the vessels of foreigners to leave the blockaded ports within fifteen days after such blockade was established, and their vessels were not to be seized unless they attempted, after being once warned off, to enter an interdicted port.

iron-clad vessels, and recommended the appointment of a competent board to inquire into and report on the subject. Already there had been spent more than a million of dollars in the construction of an immense iron-clad floating battery, for harbor defense, by Messrs. Stevens, of Hoboken, New Jersey, most of it by the Government, and yet it was not completed. He recommended a special inquiry concerning that battery, before the large sum asked for its completion should be appropriated.[1]

The call for recruits for the Navy was promptly complied with, and for the want of them no vessel was ever detained more than two or three days. Since the 4th of March, two hundred and fifty-nine officers had resigned their commissions or had been dismissed from the service for disloyalty; and several vessels were sent to sea at first without a full complement of officers. The want was soon supplied. Many who had retired to civil pursuits now patriotically came forth promptly to aid their country in its struggle for life, and were re-commissioned;[2] while many masters and masters' mates were appointed from the commercial marine.[3] The Naval School and public property at Annapolis, in Maryland, had been removed to Newport, Rhode Island, because it was unsafe, in the state of public affairs in Maryland, to continue the school there. Fort Adams, near Newport, was tendered by the War Department for the temporary accommodation of the school.

[1] Until just before the war, this structure had been shut in from the public eye. It was to be seven hundred feet long, covered with iron plates, so as to be proof against shot and shell of any kind. It was to be moved by steam-engines of sufficient power to give it a momentum that would cause it to cut in two any ship-of-war then known, when it should strike it at the waist. It was intended to mount a battery of sixteen heavy rifled cannon, in bomb-proof casemates, and two heavy columbiads for throwing shells. The latter were to be on deck, fore and aft. The smoke-stack was to be constructed in sliding sections, like a telescope, for obvious purposes; and the vessel was to be so constructed that it might be sunk to the level of the water. Its burden was to be rated at six thousand tons. It is yet (1865) unfinished.

[2] The following is the form of the naval commissions:—"THE PRESIDENT OF THE UNITED STATES OF AMERICA, To all who shall see these presents, Greeting: Know ye, that reposing special Trust and Confidence

NAVY DEPARTMENT SEAL.

in the Patriotism, Valor, Fidelity, and Abilities of —— ——, I have nominated, and, by and with the advice and consent of the Senate, do appoint him a ——, from the —— day of ——, 18—, in the service of the United States. He is therefore carefully and diligently to discharge the Duties of ——, by doing and performing all Manner of Things thereto belonging. And I do strictly charge and require all Officers, Seamen, and Marines, under his command, to be obedient to his Orders as ——. And he is to observe and follow such Orders and Directions, from time to time, as he shall receive from me, or the future President of the United States, or his Superior Officer set over him, according to the Rules and Discipline of the Navy. This Commission to continue in force during the pleasure of the President of the United States for the time being. Given under my hand at Washington, this —— day of ——, in the year of our Lord One Thousand Eight Hundred and Sixty-one, and in the Eighty-fifth year of the Independence of the United States.

" ABRAHAM LINCOLN.

"GIDEON WELLES, *Secretary of the Navy.*"

These commissions are printed on parchment. At the top is seen a spread eagle on a rock in the ocean, on which is a mariner's compass, the fasces and olive-branch, with sailing vessels-of-war in the distance. At the bottom, Neptune and the Goddess of Liberty, in a shell drawn by horses and surrounded by Tritons; and below this the seal, surrounded by a wreath, and military and naval trophies.

[3] Report of the Secretary of the Navy, July 4, 1861.

CHAPTER XXIV.

THE CALLED SESSION OF CONGRESS.—FOREIGN RELATIONS.—BENEVOLENT ORGANI-
ZATIONS.—THE OPPOSING ARMIES.

N Thursday, the 4th of July, 1861, which was the eighty-fourth anniversary of the Declaration of the Independence of the United States, the Thirty-seventh Congress assembled in the Capitol at Washington City, in extraordinary session, in compliance with the call of the President.[a] No Congress since the First—by which the *a April 15, 1861.* policy of the new government in its domestic and foreign relations had to be determined, the practical foundations of the Nation established, and the machinery of law put in motion—had been burdened with such momentous duties and such grave responsibilities as this. The delicate and difficult task of preserving, by the strong arm of absolute power, the life of the Nation, imperiled by internal foes, without usurping the constitutional prerogatives of the people, was imposed upon it. Its members were elected when the country seemed to be in a state of profound peace and great prosperity; they now came together, a few months later, to legislate, when the country was rent by violence and its industrial energies were paralyzed—when the fires of civil war were madly blazing over an area of more than three-quarters of a million of square miles of the Republic, and were, in a special manner, menacing the seat of government and the national archives with utter desolation. Large armies, destined for the overthrow of the Government, were within the sound of cannon of the Capital; and secret assassins, it is believed, intrusted with errands of deadliest mischief by conspirators, were prowling about the halls of Congress and the house of the Chief Magistrate. At such a time, the representatives of the people went up to the National Capital, charged with the duty of preserving the Republic from harm; and, as we shall observe, the great majority of them wisely, patriotically, and efficiently performed that duty.

In the Senate, twenty-three States, and in the House of Representatives, twenty-two States and one Territory were represented. There were forty senators and one hundred and fifty-four representatives present on the first day of the session. Ten States, in which the politicians had adopted ordinances of secession, were not represented.[1] In both houses, there was a large majority of Unionists.

---

[1] These were Virginia (the eastern portion, controlled by the conspirators at Richmond), North and South Carolina, Georgia, Florida, Alabama, Mississippi, Louisiana, Arkansas, and Texas. Four Slave-labor States, namely, Delaware, Maryland, Kentucky, and Missouri, were represented. Tennessee had not then held its

The proceedings of the Senate, over which Hannibal Hamlin, the Vice-President of the United States, presided, were opened by prayer by the Rev. Byron Sunderland, D. D., and those of the House of Representatives

by the Rev. T. H. Stockton, chaplain of the last House.[1] This was the first session of this Congress, and the House of Representatives was organized by the election of Galusha A. Grow, of Pennsylvania, to be speaker or presiding officer.

On the second day of the session,[a] President Lincoln sent into Congress, by the hands of his private secretary, J. G. Nicolay, a message, devoted almost exclusively to the consideration of the important subject which occasioned the assembling of that body in extraordinary session. He recited the many and grave offenses of the con-

HANNIBAL HAMLIN.

[a] July 5, 1861.

spirators, such as the seizure and appropriation of public property, the preparations for war, and the seeking of recognition by foreign powers, as an independent nation; and then he gave an outline history of events connected with Fort Sumter, already recorded in this volume. Speaking of the assault on that work, he said that it was in "no sense a matter of self-defense upon the part of the assailants,"[2] for they "knew that the garrison in the fort could by no possibility commit aggression upon them." By the affair at Fort Sumter, he said, " the assailants of the Government began the conflict of arms, without a gun in sight or in expectancy to return their fire, save only the few in the fort, sent to that harbor years before for their own protection, and still ready to give that protection in whatever was lawful. In this act, discarding all else, they have forced upon the country the distinct issue, 'immediate dissolution or blood.' And this issue embraces more than these United States. It presents to the whole family of man the question, whether a constitutional republic or democracy—a government of the people by the same people—can or can not maintain its territorial integrity against its own domestic foes. It presents the question, whether discontented individuals, too few in number to control administration according to organic law, in any case, can always, upon the pretenses made in this case, or on any other pretenses, or arbi-

---

elections for members of Congress. When they were held, five weeks later, only three districts in East Tennessee chose representatives. One of these, Thomas A. R. Nelson, while on his way to Washington City, was arrested by the insurgents and taken to Richmond, where he secured his personal liberty by an open profession of allegiance to the "Southern Confederacy" of conspirators. Andrew Johnson, of Tennessee, appeared and took his seat in the Senate.

[1] See page 65.

[2] The excuse of the conspirators for their revolutionary act alluded to by the President, like all others, was only a pretext, and so transparent that no well-informed person was deceived by it. Such was, evidently, the Peace Convention (see page 235) at Washington, planned by the Virginia conspirators. Such, also, was the mission of Forsyth and Crawford (see page 300), who were sent by Jefferson Davis to Washington to say that they were "intrusted with power, in the spirit of humanity, the civilization of the age," et cetera, to offer to the National Government the olive-branch of peace (see page 303), when it is known that while they were in the Capital, these "peace ambassadors" made large contracts with Northern manufacturers (to the shame of these contractors be it recorded!), for arms and ammunition, in preparation for war.

trarily, without any pretense, break up their government, and thus practically put an end to free government upon the earth. It forces us to ask, ' Is there in all republics this inherent and fatal weakness? Must a government, of necessity, be too strong for the liberties of its own people, or too weak to maintain its own existence?' So viewing the issue, no choice was left but to call out the war-power of the Government, and so to resist force employed for its destruction by force for its preservation."

The President then reviewed the conduct of the Virginia conspirators and secessionists after the attack on Fort Sumter, and condemned the policy of " armed neutrality " proposed in some of the Border Slave-labor States, as a policy that recognized "no fidelity to the Constitution, no obligation to maintain the Union."[1] He then noticed the call for troops to put down the insurrection, and the wonderful response; the action of the executive government in the matter of the writ of *habeas corpus ;* the attitude of foreign nations toward the Government, and the necessity for vindicating its power; and then said, " It is now recommended, that you give the legal means for making this contest a short and decisive one; that you place at the control of the Government, for the work, at least four hundred thousand men and four hundred millions of dollars.[2] . . . A right result, at this time, will be worth more to the world than ten times the men and ten times the money. The evidence reaching us from the country leaves no doubt that the material for the work is abundant, and that it needs only the hand of legislation to give it legal sanction, and the hand of the Executive to give it practical shape and efficiency. In other words, the people will save their Government, if the Government itself will do its part only indifferently well."

The President spoke of the methods used by the conspirators to stir up the people to revolt, already noticed,[3] and then argued, at considerable length, against the existence of State Sovereignty and the right of a State to secede;[4] and he questioned whether, at that time, there was a majority of the legally qualified voters of any State, excepting South Carolina, who were in favor of disunion. " This is essentially a people's contest," he said; and he was happy in the belief that the " plain people " comprehended it as such. He then noticed the remarkable fact, that while large numbers of the officers of the Army and Navy had proved themselves unfaithful, " not one common soldier or common sailor is known to have

---

[1] Although the President made no allusion to Slavery, as the inciting cause of the rebellion, he stated the significant fact, that "None of the States, commonly called Slave States, except Delaware, gave a regiment, through regular State organizations," for the support of the Government. "A few regiments," he said, "have been organized within some others of those States, by individual enterprise, and received into the Government service."

[2] Four hundred thousand men constituted only about one-tenth of those of proper age for military service "within the regions where," the President said, "apparently all are willing to engage;" and, he added, the sum of four hundred millions of dollars "is less than a twenty-third part of the money value owned by the men who seem ready to devote the whole."

[3] See page 40.

[4] "The States have their *status* in the Union," he said, "and they have no other legal *status.* If they break from this, they can only do so against law and by revolution. The Union, and not themselves separately, procured their independence and their liberty. By conquest or purchase, the Union gave each of them whatever of independence or liberty it has. The Union is older than any of the States, and, in fact, it created them as States. Originally, some dependent colonies made the Union, and, in turn, the Union threw off their old dependence for them, and made them States, such as they are. Not one of them ever had a State Constitution independent of the Union. Of course, it is not forgotten that all the new States framed their constitutions before they entered the Union; nevertheless, dependent upon and preparatory to coming into the Union."

deserted his flag. . . . This is the patriotic instinct of plain people. They understand, without an argument, that the destroying of the Government which was made by Washington means no good to them."

The President concluded by assuring the people that it was with the deepest regret that he found himself compelled to employ the war-power in defense of the Government, and that the sole object of its exercise should be the maintenance of the National authority and the salvation of the life of the Republic. "And having so chosen our course, without guile and with pure motives," he said to Congress, after expressing a hope that the views of that body were coincident with his own, "let us renew our trust in God, and go forward without fear and with manly hearts."

The President's Message was accompanied by important reports from heads of Executive Departments. Mr. Cameron, the Secretary of War, recommended the enlistment of men for three years, with a bounty of one hundred dollars for the additional regiments of the regular Army; that appropriations be made for the construction, equipment, and current expenses of railways and telegraphs for the use of the Government; also, for the furnishing of a more liberal supply of approved arms for the militia of the several States and Territories, and other measures necessary in a state of war. He also recommended the appointment of an Assistant Secretary of War, and an increase of the clerical force of his department.

SALMON P. CHASE.

Mr. Chase, the Secretary of the Treasury, whose management of the financial affairs of the country during a greater portion of the period of the war was considered eminently wise and efficient, asked for two hundred and forty millions of dollars for war purposes, and eighty millions of dollars to meet the ordinary demands for the fiscal year ending on the 30th of June, 1862. He proposed to raise the eighty millions, in addition to the sum of nearly sixty-six millions of dollars already appropriated, by levying increased duties on specified articles, and also by certain internal revenues, or by the direct taxation of real and personal property. To raise the amount asked for war purposes, he proposed a National loan of not less than one hundred millions of dollars, to be issued in the form of treasury notes, bearing an annual interest of seven and three-tenths per centum, or one cent a day on fifty dollars, in sums from fifty dollars to five thousand dollars. He proposed to issue bonds, or certificates of debt, in the event of the National loan proving to be insufficient, to the amount of not exceeding one hundred millions of dollars, to be made redeemable at the pleasure of the Government, after a period not exceeding thirty years, and bearing an interest not exceeding seven per cent. He further recommended, for the supply of the full amount, the issue of another class of treasury notes, not exceeding in the aggregate fifty millions of dollars (some of small denominations), bearing an interest of three and sixty-five one-hundredths per cent., and exchangeable at the will of the holders for the treasury notes of the first-named issue.

The Secretary of the Navy, who had been compelled to employ extraordinary measures to meet the demands imposed by treason, asked Congress to sanction his acts, and recommended various measures for the increase of the efficiency of his department. He also recommended the appointment of an Assistant Secretary of the Navy; an increase of the clerical force of the department; and the appointment of commissioners to inquire into the expediency of iron-clad steamers or floating batteries.

With the President's Message and the reports of Cabinet ministers before it, Congress prepared to enter upon its solemn and important duties with industry and vigor, after disposing of several claims for seats in dispute in the House of Representatives. And in that chamber, one of the first acts was to provide for checking irrelevant discussion, by the adoption of a resolution that only bills relating to the military, naval, and financial affairs of the Government at that crisis should be considered, and that all other business should be referred to appropriate committees, to be acted upon at the next regular session.

It was very important that Congress should confine its efforts to the one great object of furnishing the Executive with ample powers for suppressing the rebellion speedily, for its magnitude and promises of success were so great and hopeful, that a recognition of the independence of the " Confederate States," and armed interference in their favor by powerful foreign governments, seemed to be not only possible but probable. From the time when South Carolinians declared their State withdrawn from the Union,[a] there had been observed in most of the European courts, and in [a] December 20, 1860. the public journals in their interest, an unfriendliness of spirit toward the National Government, and a willingness to encourage its enemies in their revolutionary measures. At these courts, and at the ear of these journals, emissaries of the conspirators had already been engaged in magnifying the strength of the Slave-labor States; in promising great benefits to European friends and helpers; and in misrepresenting the character, temper, and resources of the National Government. And at the powerful French court, the source of much of the political opinion of the ruling classes of Continental Europe, Charles J. Faulkner, of Virginia, the American Minister Plenipotentiary, it was believed, was an efficient accomplice of the conspirators in the work of misrepresenting their Government, and maturing plans for securing the recognition of the independence of the " Seceded" States. This suspicion of Mr. Faulkner was unfounded in truth.

When, during the month of January, the politicians of several of the Slave-labor States declared those States separated from the Union, and, early in February, proceeded to form a League of so-called Seceded States, Europe was prepared to accept the hopeless dissolution of the Republic as a fact accomplished. This belief was strengthened by the dispatches of most of the foreign ministers at Washington to their respective governments, early in February, who announced the practical dissolution of the Union; and some affected to be amazed at the folly of Congress in legislating concerning the tariff and other National measures, when the Nation was hopelessly expiring!

It is not to be wondered at that foreign governments and publicists should have made this grave mistake. They had been for a quarter of a century taught by a certain class of leading politicians, in all parts of the Union, that the States were sovereign, and formed only a league by compact, without having more than a few dissenting opinions from the expounders of the Constitution in Congress and out of it; and the practical conclusion was, what some of the conspirators boldly asserted, that secession was a " reserved right " of the States. When, therefore, the positive and irrevocable dissolution of the Union, by the secession of several States, was announced on the floor of Congress and in leading newspapers, by men of every portion of the Union, what other conclusion could ill-informed or misinformed foreigners arrive at than that the war was unrighteous, and that, instead of being waged by the National Government in vindication of its own rightful and supreme authority over all the States, and for the preservation of its integrity, it was a war of sections—a war of States against States? This fundamental error prevailed during the entire period of the war, and was for a long time a stumbling-block in the way of many earnest friends of our Government abroad.

So early as the close of February, Mr. Black, the Secretary
^{a February 28, 1861.} of State under Mr. Buchanan,[1] addressed ^a a circular letter to the American ministers abroad, informing them of the state of public affairs at home, directing them to endeavor to counteract the efforts of the agents of the conspirators at foreign courts, and assuring them that the Government had not " relinquished its constitutional jurisdiction within the States " wherein rebellion existed, and did " not desire to do so."
^{b March 9.} This was followed, a few days afterward,^b by a circular letter from Mr. Seward, the Secretary of State under Mr. Lincoln, conjuring them to use all diligence to " prevent the designs of those who would invoke foreign intervention to embarrass and overthrow the Republic." More than a month later, when Jefferson Davis had offered commissions for depredating on the commerce of the United States, and Mr. Lincoln had declared that such depredators should be treated as pirates,[2] Mr. Seward addressed another circular to American ministers at the principal European courts, in which he reviewed recent measures tending to the abolition of the practice of privateering, and instructed the American minister at the British court to seek an early opportunity to propose to that government an agreement on the subject, on the basis of the declarations of the Congress at Paris, in 1856, with an additional agreement that should secure from seizure on the high seas, under all circumstances, private property not contraband of war. Charles Francis Adams, a son of John Quincy Adams, had just been appointed to fill the station of minister at the court of St. James,[3] which had been held by his father and grandfather; and to him the proposed negotiation was intrusted. Mr. Adams had already been instructed[4] concerning the manner in which he should oppose the efforts of the agents of the con-

---

[1] See page 70.   [2] See page 372.
[3] Mr. Adams succeeded the late George M. Dallas, of Pennsylvania, as embassador at the British court. Mr. Dallas was a highly accomplished and patriotic gentleman, whose voice was heard, on his return home, in wholesome denunciations of the conspirators against the life of the Republic.
[4] See Mr. Seward's *Letter of Instructions to Mr. Adams*, April 10, 1861.

spirators. He was directed to acknowledge the appreciation of the American people and Government of the late expressions of good-will by the Queen and her ministers;[1] at the same time, he was warned not to "rely upon any mere sympathies or national kindness,"[2] but to stand up manfully as the representative of his *whole* country, and that as a powerful nation, asking no favors of others.[3] The high position taken by Mr. Seward, in the name of his Government, in that able letter of instructions to Mr. Adams, was doubtless one of the most efficient causes, together with the friendly attitude assumed by Russia toward the United States, of the fortunate delay of Great Britain in the matter of recognizing the independence of the Confederates, until the strength and resources of the Republic were made so manifest that common prudence compelled all foreign powers unfriendly to that Republic to act with great circumspection.

CHARLES FRANCIS ADAMS.

But whilst it seemed inexpedient for the British crown to formally recognize the independence of the Confederates, the ministry, evidently sympathizing most thoroughly with the political objects of the conspirators, procured in their behalf the powerful assistance of a Proclamation of Neutrality by the Queen,[a] by which a Confederate Government, as existing, was acknowledged, and belligerent rights were accorded to the insurgents.[4] Already an understanding existed between the British Government and the French Emperor, that they were to act together in regard to American affairs. They had even gone so far as to

a May 13, 1861.

---

[1] Reference is here made to an expression in the Queen's speech from the throne on the 5th of February, 1861, in which she declared her "great concern" at the events then taking place in the United States, and a "heart-felt wish that the differences that then distracted the country might be susceptible of a satisfactory adjustment." For these humane expressions, Mr. Toulmin Smith, the conductor of the Parliamentary Remembrancer (vol. iv., page 3), reproved his Sovereign. "These last loose words," he said, "are characteristic of the very loose notions that are common in England on the subject of what used to be the United States of North America. It is, from the very nature of the facts, no other than impossible that the 'differences' can be 'susceptible' [whatever that means] of satisfactory adjustment." He then went on to say: "Already the honor of the Northern States has been seriously imperiled; and it has been proclaimed that many of them are so given up to the worship of the 'almighty dollar,' that every great principle will be cheerfully sacrificed by them, if only the States of the South will be so good as to remain in the Union, which the Northern States take to be rather profitable, in a commercial sense, to themselves." This reads strangely in the light of subsequent events.

[2] "There can be no greater error than to expect or calculate upon real favors from nation to nation. 'Tis an illusion which experience must cure—which a just pride ought to discard."—*Washington's Farewell Address.*

[3] "You will, in no case," said Mr. Seward, "listen to any suggestions of compromise by this Government, under foreign auspices, with its discontented citizens. If, as the President does not at all apprehend, you shall unhappily find Her Majesty's Government tolerating the application of the so-called Seceding States, or wavering about it, you will not leave them to suppose for a moment that they can grant that application and remain the friends of the United States. You may even assure them promptly, in that case, that if they determine to recognize, they may at the same time prepare to enter into an alliance with the enemies of this Republic. You alone will represent your country at London, and you will represent the whole of it there. When you are asked to divide that duty with others, diplomatic relations between the Government of Great Britain and this Government will be suspended, and will remain so until it shall be seen which of the two is most strongly intrenched in the confidence of their respective nations and of mankind."

[4] A motion, with the view of recognizing the independence of the so-called "Confederate States," was made in Parliament by Mr. Gregory, at the beginning of May, and, in reply to a question from him on the 6th

apprise other European governments of this understanding, with the expec‹ tation that they would concur with them, and follow their example, whatever it might be.[1] Thus, at this early stage of our difficulties, these two professedly friendly powers had clandestinely entered into a combination for arraying all Europe on the side of the insurgents, and giving them moral, if not material aid, in their efforts to destroy our Republic.

This action of a professedly friendly power, from whom the American people felt that they had reason to expect the kindest consideration on all occasions, seemed almost inexplicable to them, for they had been taught by British statesmen, orators, and publicists, that Great Britain felt deeply the wrongs of Slavery, and could have no sympathy with men rebelling against a humane Government for the avowed purpose of perpetuating those wrongs. They were loth to believe that these professions of philanthropy were not sincere. They were unwilling to believe that the assertion of Montesquieu, made more than a hundred years before, that England, unlike all other countries, allowed commerce to regulate its politics,[2] was still so true, that its government and people would be willing to sacrifice a great principle, and falsify the most solemn and abounding professions of Christian benevolence, for the sake of securing the advantages of free trade, so largely promised by the agents of the conspirators, as their most costly and coveted bribe;[3] and they were disposed to regard the famous epigram of the London

---

of that month, Lord John Russell, the Minister for Foreign Affairs, gave the first authoritative statement of the position which the Government intended to take. "The Attorney and Solicitor-General and the Queen's Advocate and the Government," he said, "have come to the opinion that the Southern Confederacy of America, according to those principles which seem to them to be just principles, must be treated as a belligerent." Following the Queen's Proclamation, was a debate on the subject of blockades and privateering, in all of which the sovereignty of the States and the right of secession, according to the doctrines of the Calhoun school, were assumed, and it was fairly concluded that, the Confederates having formed a government, privateers commissioned by Davis could not be treated as pirates. But while belligerent rights were accorded to them, one of which was that of privateering, the British Government, by an order in council on the 1st of June, deprived the conspirators of the chief advantage to be derived from that pursuit, namely, the prohibition of the disposal of prizes in British ports. France took the same ground, and the rule was applied equally to the parties in conflict.

[1] *Letter of Secretary Seward to Minister Adams*, May 21, 1861.

[2] Speaking of the spirit of the English people with respect to commerce, Montesquieu said:—"Supremely jealous with respect to trade, they bind themselves but little by treaties, and depend only on their own laws. Other nations have made the interests of commerce yield to those of politics; the English, on the contrary, have ever made their political interests give way to those of commerce."—*Spirit of the Laws*, fifth English edition, ii. 8.

[3] The agents of the conspirators offered to the governments of Europe, as a bribe for recognition, free trade; and as the National Government had just imposed a heavy tariff on many foreign products, that offer had great force. Their boastings and their sophisms so far blinded the foreign traders and statesmen, that they actually regarded the commerce with the Cotton-growing States as of more value to them than that of all the rest of the Union. Even the usually well-informed *London Economist*, after stating that the "population of the seceding States is eight millions," said, that England, in her consideration of the rebellion, must look upon that portion of the United States as "furnishing an ample market for her manufactured goods." At that very time, the proof was abundant, that of the little more than nine millions of inhabitants in those States, nearly one-half of them did not consume British goods to the amount of half a million of dollars annually. These included the slaves and the poor and laboring white people, called by the Oligarchy "white trash." These two classes, who were the most numerous in the population of the States alluded to, were chiefly clad throughout the year in coarse domestic goods, and did not in reality consume foreign goods, of any and all kinds, to the extent of twenty-five cents a head. Of the bulk of the white population in those States, two-thirds of them wore no foreign goods whatever. The Northern and Western States were the main consumers of British goods. The total white population of the "seceding" States at that time was only about five millions two hundred and thirty-one thousand, and of the "non-seceding" States, twenty-two millions two hundred and forty-five thousand. When we consider that, during the ten years preceding the rebellion, the United States were the market for about one-fifth of the total exports of British goods to all foreign countries, and that the inhabitants of the Free-labor States, who were loyal to the Government, were the purchasers of the much greater portion of those goods, the madness and folly of the British statesmen, traders, and manufacturers, in espousing the cause of the few insurgents, for the sake of free commercial intercourse with them, at the risk of losing the custom of the great bulk of the Nation, are most amazing. For a full exposition, from official reports, of the commerce

Punch as a good-natured slander, uttered for the sake of the wit.[1] Only a few months before, the people of the Free-labor States, who were loyal to their Government, had shown the most cordial good-will toward the British Queen, in the almost affectionate attentions which they gave to her son, the Crown Prince of the realm, on the occasion of his visit to the United States, and thereby certified their friendship for the English people.[2] Thinking of this, and of the heritage of the two nations in common, of historic traditions, language, literature, and laws, and the intimate relations of their commerce, they were amazed at the unseemly haste displayed in the recognition of the insurgents as belligerents, for the Queen's Proclamation appeared before the representative of the assailed Republic, under the new Administration, had been formally received at Court. It was a proceeding so "precipitate and unprecedented," as Mr. Adams afterward said,[3] that it made a most unfavorable impression upon right-minded statesmen and philanthropic Christians everywhere.[4]

The Proclamation of the Queen was followed in the British Parliament, and in most of the newspapers in the interest of the government, and the ruling classes in Great Britain and her colonies, by the most dogmatic assertions that the Republic of the West was hopelessly crumbling into ruins, and was unworthy of respectful consideration. In addition to affected indifference to the fate of the Nation, British legislators, orators, publicists, and journalists were lavish of causeless abuse, not· only of the Government, but of the people of the Free-labor States who were loyal to that Government.

---

with Great Britain of the Free and Slave-labor States, and the comparative insignificance of the latter as a market for British goods, see a paper entitled, *A Few Plain Words to England and her Manufacturers:* by J. SMITH HOMANS, editor of *The Bankers' Magazine and Statistical Register,* in which it appeared at the beginning of 1862.

[1] The following is the epigram, entitled: *Shop and Freedom :*—

"Though with the North we sympathize,
   It must not be forgotten
That with the South we've stronger ties,
   . Which are composed of cotton,
Whereof our imports 'mount unto
   A sum of many figures;
And where would be our calico,
   Without the toil of niggers?
	"The South enslaves those fellow-men
	   Whom we love all so dearly;
	The North keeps commerce bound again,
	   Which touches us more nearly.
	Thus a divided duty we
	   Perceive in this hard matter—
	Free trade, or sable brothers free?
	   Oh, will we choose the latter!"

[2] It has been asserted, and not denied, that the late Prince-Consort (Albert), who was the ever-trusted confidential adviser of the Queen, entertained feelings of the most cordial friendship toward the Government and people of the United States, and that such remained the sentiments of Her Majesty during the whole war. As parents, they could not forget the kindness bestowed upon their child; and it is believed that the Queen's influence was very powerful in restraining the eagerness of her ministers and the ruling classes of Great Britain to recognize the independence of the so-called " Confederate States."

[3] Mr. Adams to Earl Russell, the Foreign Secretary, May 20, 1865.

[4] Two months before, the astute Count de Gasparin, observing the unfriendly tone of English leaders of opinion, and aware of the seductive character of the bribe of free trade in cotton, which the agents of the conspirators were offering, said :—" Let England beware! It were better for her to lose Malta, Corfu, and Gibraltar, than the glorious position which her struggle against Slavery and the Slave-trade has secured her in the esteem of nations. Even in our age of armed frigates and rifled cannon, the chief of all powers, thank God! is moral power. Wo to the nation that disregards it, and consents to immolate its principles to its interests! From the beginning of the present conflict, the enemies of England, and they are numerous, have predicted that the cause of cotton will weigh heavier in her scales than the cause of justice and liberty. They are preparing to judge her by her conduct in the American crisis. Once more, let her beware!"—*The Uprising of a Great People;* Miss Booth's translation, page 250.

A year later, De Gasparin wrote, when considering the unprecedented precipitancy with which leading European powers recognized the insurgents as belligerents:—" Instead of asking on which side were justice and liberty, we have hastened to ask on which side were our interests; then, too, on which side were the best chances of success." He said England had a legal right to be neutral, but had no moral right to withhold her sympathies with a nation struggling for its existence and universal justice against rebels intent on crimes against humanity.—*America before Europe:* translated by Mary L. Booth.

That abuse was often expressed in phrases so unmanly and ungenerous, and even coarse and vulgar at times, that high-minded Englishmen blushed with shame. Only here and there throughout the kingdom, for a long time, was heard a voice of real sympathy for a great and enlightened nation struggling for existence, which had, in a measure, sprung from the loins, as it were, of the English people. Those few voices were pleasant to the ears of the earnest champions of the Republic and universal freedom, during the conflict; and the memory of the utterers will be ever cherished in the heart of hearts of a grateful and generous people, who can, with the magnanimity of true nobility, forgive the arrogant and the misinformed in other lands, who, failing to comprehend the dignity of the cause for which the loyal Americans were contending, treated them unkindly in the hour of their greatest distress. How powerfully the conspirators were aided by the British Government and British subjects, under the overshadowing wing of the Queen's Proclamation of Neutrality, and so prolonged the war at least two years, will be observed hereafter.

The French Emperor, to whose court William L. Dayton, of New Jersey,

WILLIAM L. DAYTON.

was sent, by the new Administration, to succeed Faulkner, of Virginia,[1] was cautious and astute. While expressing the most friendly feelings toward the Government and people of the United States, he followed the British Queen in according belligerent rights to the insurgents, by a decree issued on the 11th of June;[a] and, as we shall observe hereafter, he entered into political combinations and military enterprises, at about the same time, for the aggrandizement of his empire, and the propagation of imperialism on the American Continent, with the belief that the days of the Great Republic were

[a] 1861.

numbered, and its democratic forces hopelessly paralyzed. The Queen of Spain also hastened to proclaim the neutrality of her government,[b] and to combine with the French Emperor in replanting the seeds of monarchical institutions in the New World, now that the menacing Republic was expiring. The King of Portugal also recognized[c] the insurgents as belligerents; but the enlightened Emperor of Russia, who was about to strike the shackles from almost forty millions of slaves in his own dominions,[2] instructed his chief

[b] June 17, 1861.

[c] July 29.

---

[1] In his instructions to Mr. Dayton (April 22, 1861), Mr. Seward took the same high ground as in those to Mr. Adams. "The President neither expects nor desires intervention, or even favor," he said, "from the Government of France, or any other, in this emergency. Whatever else he may consent to do, he will never evoke nor even admit foreign interference or influence in this or any other controversy in which the Government of the United States may be engaged with any portion of the United States." On the 4th of May, Mr. Seward instructed Mr. Dayton to say to M. Thouvenal, the French Minister for Foreign Affairs, that "the thought of dissolution of this Union, peaceably or by force, has never entered into the mind of any candid statesman here, and it is high time that it be dismissed by statesmen in Europe."

[2] This was accomplished in the spring of 1863, when over sixteen millions of crown serfs and twenty-two millions belonging to private owners were emancipated by proclamation of the Emperor Alexander.

minister to say to the imperial representative at Washington, " In every event, the American Nation may count upon the most cordial sympathy on the part of our august master during the important crisis which it is passing through at present."[1] The Russian Emperor kept his word ; and the powers of Western Europe, regarding him as a promised ally of the Republic, in case of need, behaved prudently.

Congress followed the President's suggestions with prompt action. On the first day of the session,[a]
Mr. Wilson, Chairman of [a] July 4, 1861.
the Committee on Military
Affairs of the Senate, gave notice
that on the following day he should
ask leave to introduce six bills, having
for their object the suppression of the
rebellion.[2] These, and others origin-
ating in the Lower House, were soon
brought to the consideration of Congress, and elicited much debate. It
was manifest at the outset of the session, that there were a few among the
Opposition, in Congress, whose sympathies were with the secessionists,
and who were disposed to withhold

HENRY WILSON.

from the Executive the means necessary for the preservation of the Republic. The leader of this faction in the Senate was the late Vice-President, John C. Breckinridge, of Kentucky, who, soon after the close of the session, en- tered the military service of the conspirators ; and, in the House of Repre- sentatives, Clement L. Vallandigham, of Ohio, was regarded as the ablest opponent of the war-measures.

When, on the 10th of July, a loan-bill, authorizing the Secretary of the Treasury to borrow two hundred and fifty millions of dollars, for the support of the Government and to prosecute the war, was before the House of Repre- sentatives, Vallandigham made an elaborate speech against the measure, and the entire policy of " coercion "—in other words, the vindication of the National authority by force of arms, if necessary. He charged the President with usurpation, in calling out and increasing the military and naval forces of the country, blockading ports, suspending the privilege of the writ of *habeas corpus,* and other acts which the safety of the Government had re- quired him to perform, and all these without the authority of Congress. He declared that the first projects for disunion were found in New England, at the beginning of the century ;[3] and that the civil war in which the country

[1] Letter of Prince Gortschakoff to Baron de Stoeckl, dated July 10, 1861.

[2] These were, 1. To ratify and confirm certain acts of the President for the suppression of insurrection and rebellion. 2. To authorize the employment of volunteers to aid in enforcing the laws and protecting public property. 3. To increase the present military establishment of the United States. 4. Providing for the better organization of the military establishment. 5. To promote the efficiency of the Army. 6. For the organization of a volunteer militia force, to be called the National Guard of the United States.

[3] The plainest facts in our history teach us that in Virginia, and not in New England, threats of disunion were first made, and made so earnestly, that they alarmed Washington and his compatriots. It was there offered by political doctors as the grand panacea for the evils endured by wounded State and family pride. See note 1, page 17, and note 1, page 63.

was involved, had been brought about by the "violent and long-continued denunciations of Slavery and the Slave-holders, especially since 1835," by the Abolitionists.[1] He reviewed the conduct of the Republicans in the last Congress, as indicating the determination of the party to have war instead of peace; denounced the revenue law known as the Morrill Tariff, as injurious to the cotton-growers; charged the Administration with having adopted a war policy merely for party purposes; and declared that in the train of usurpations already enacted would follow a host of others, such as the denial of the right of petition, and the freedom of religion, whose holy temples had been already defiled, and "its white robes of a former innocency trampled under the polluting hoofs of an ambitious and faithless or fanatical clergy."[2] This was the first trumpet-blast, clear and distinct, for the marshaling of the hosts for battle of the great Peace Party, which soon became a power in the land, and played a most important part in the drama of the civil war, but touched no sympathizing chord in the hearts of the great body of the people.

The loan-bill was passed under the previous question, on the 10th;[3] and on the following day an Army appropriation bill was acted upon, when Vallandigham moved to add a proviso, that "no part of the money hereby appropriated shall be employed in subjugating, or holding as a conquered province, any sovereign State, now, or lately, one of the United States; nor in abolishing or interfering with African Slavery in any of the States." This proviso was rejected, and the bill, appropriating one hundred and sixty-one millions of dollars, was passed. Already a resolution had been adopted in the same House,[a] that it was "no part of the duty of the soldiers of the United States to capture and return fugitive slaves."[4]

[a] July 9, 1861.

The Senate took measures at an early day to purge itself of treasonable members. On the 10th,[b] on motion of Mr. Clark, of New Hampshire, it expelled ten Senators who were named,[5] because of their being engaged "in a conspiracy for the destruction of the Union and the Government." The resolution for expulsion received the required vote of two-thirds of the Senate (thirty-two against ten); and, on the 13th,

[b] July.

[1] See page 65, and note 2, page 65; also note 1, page 66.

[2] *Congressional Globe*, July 10, 1861.

[3] The vote was one hundred and fifty ayes and five noes. The latter were Burnett, of Kentucky; Norton and Reid, of Missouri; Vallandigham, of Ohio; and Benjamin Wood, of New York. The first three named joined the rebels soon after the close of the session. While Vallandigham, in the lower House, was abusing the President, and avowing his determination to thwart the Government in its attempts to put down rebellion, Senator Baker, of Oregon, was eloquently appealing to the other House to come up to the help of the Executive with the most generous aid. He declared his approval of every measure of the President in relation to the rebellion, and said:—"I propose to ratify whatever needs ratification. I propose to render my clear and distinct approval not only of the measure, but of the motive which prompted it. I propose to lend the whole power of the country—arms, men, and money—and place them in his hands, with authority almost unlimited, until the conclusion of this struggle. He has asked for four hundred millions of dollars. We propose to give him five hundred millions of dollars. He has asked for four hundred thousand men. We propose to give him half a million; and, for my part, if, as I do not apprehend, the emergency should be still greater, I will cheerfully add a cipher to either of these figures." A hundred days later, the speaker gave his life to his country, at Ball's Bluff, on the Potomac.

[4] This was proposed by Mr. Lovejoy, of Illinois, and was passed by a vote of ninety-two against fifty-five.

[5] James M. Mason and Robert T. M. Hunter, of Virginia; Thomas L. Clingman and Thomas Bragg, of North Carolina; James Chesnut, Jr., of South Carolina; A. O. P. Nicholson, of Tennessee; William K. Sebastian and Charles B. Mitchell, of Arkansas; and John Hemphill and Louis T. Wigfall, of Texas.

the places of Hunter and Mason were filled by John S. Carlile and Waitman T. Willey,[1] who appeared with proper credentials. On the same day[a] John B. Clark, of Missouri, was, on motion of F. P. Blair, expelled from the House of Representatives as a traitor.

[a] July 13, 1861.

When a bill providing for the calling out half a million of men for the war was under consideration, on the 13th,[b] Vallandigham offered a proviso that the President, before he should have the right to summon any more troops to the field, should appoint seven commissioners, who should accompany the army in its marches, with authority to receive from Jefferson Davis proposals looking to an armistice, or obedience to the National Government. The proviso was rejected, and the bill was passed. Two days afterward,[c] Benjamin Wood, of New York, proposed that Congress should take measures for the assembling of a convention of all the States, at Louisville, Kentucky, in September following, to devise measures for restoring peace to the country. It was tabled, and on the same day, Allen, of Ohio (opposition), moved that when " the States now in rebellion " should desist, it was the duty of the Government to suspend the further prosecution of the war; and that it was not the object of the war to interfere with Slavery. This was ruled out of order, when Vallandigham offered a long series of resolutions, in tenor like his speech on the 10th, condemning nearly every important act of the President, in resisting the conspirators, as unconstitutional. These were tabled, and a bill, introduced by Hickman, of Pennsylvania, for defining and punishing conspiracies against the United States, was passed, with only seven dissenting voices. On motion of McClernand, of Illinois (opposition), the House pledged itself[d] to vote for any amount of money, and any number of men, which might be necessary for the speedy suppression of the rebellion. This was passed with only five dissenting voices.[2]

[b] July.

[c] July 15.

[d] July 15.

A spirited and able debate arose in the Senate, on the 18th,[e] by an addition to the bill providing for the reorganization of the Army, offered by Powell, of Kentucky, which declared, that no part of the Army or Navy should be employed in "subjecting or holding as a conquered province any sovereign State now, or lately, one of the United States." Sherman, of Ohio, offered as a substitute a clause, declaring that the purposes of the military establishment provided for in the Act were "to preserve the Union, to defend the property, and to maintain the constitutional authority of the Government." This was adopted, with only four dissenting voices;[3] when Breckinridge moved as an additional amendment the substance of Powell's proposition, and the words, " or to abolish Slavery therein "—that is, in any State " lately one of the United States." This was rejected; and the bill, as it came from the Committee of the Whole, was adopted. On the following day the venerable John J. Crittenden, who was now a member of the House of Representatives, offered a joint resolution, "That the present deplorable civil war has been forced upon the country by the Disunionists of the Southern States now in revolt against the constitu-

[e] July.

[1] They had been appointed by the Legislature of reorganized Virginia. See page 491.
[2] Burnett and Grider, of Kentucky; Norton and Reid, of Missouri; and Benjamin Wood, of New York.
[3] Breckinridge and Powell, of Kentucky; and Johnson and Polk, of Missouri.

tional Government, and in arms around the Capital; that in this National emergency, Congress, banishing all feeling of mere passion or resentment, will recollect only its duty to its country; that this war is not waged, on our part, in any spirit of oppression, nor for any purpose of conquest or subjugation, nor purpose of overthrowing or interfering with the rights or established institutions of those States; but to defend and maintain the supremacy of the Constitution, and to preserve the Union, with all the dignity, equality, and rights, of the several States unimpaired; and as soon as these objects are accomplished, the war ought to cease."

This resolution, so consonant with the feelings of the great body of the loyal inhabitants of the Republic, was laid over until Monday, the 22d. During that interval, momentous events had occurred. The first great battle of the war had been fought, within thirty miles of the Capital, which is known in history as the BATTLE OF BULL'S RUN. Let us see how it was brought about.

When Congress met, at the beginning of July, there were about three hundred thousand Union troops enrolled. About fifty thousand of these were in arms in the vicinity of the Potomac River, designed for the defense of the Capital, or an attack upon the Confederates at Manassas,[1] as circumstance might require. The enthusiasm of the people was at fever-heat. In their patriotic zeal for the overthrow of the rebellion, they did not stop to consider the necessity for military discipline and thorough organization; and because the troops lingered along the line of the Potomac week after week, in seeming inactivity, they became impatient. There was a burning desire for the seizure and occupation of Richmond by the National forces before the so-called Confederate Government should be established there, on the 20th of July; and because the President and his Cabinet and the General-in-chief were still holding back the army when Congress met, they were censured without stint, and the loyalty of General Scott, who was born in Virginia, was actually questioned. In public speeches, in the newspapers, and everywhere among the people, there was a mad cry of *Forward to Richmond!* which finally impelled the General-in-chief to order the army to move in that direction.[2]

In the mean time the loyal people at home—men, women, and children—had been making earnest preparations for assisting the soldiers in the field, and alleviating their sufferings when in hospitals. The call for troops, on the 15th of April, electrified the women of the land; and individuals and small groups might be seen every day, in thousands and tens of thousands of households—women and children—with busy fingers preparing lint and bandages for wounds, and hospital garments for the sick and maimed, and shelters for the heads and necks of the soldiers, when marching in the hot sun, known as *havelocks.*[3] The movement was spontaneous and universal. The necessity

[1] See page 479.
[2] The *New York Tribune,* a daily paper of immense circulation throughout the Free-labor States, and of great influence, first raised this war-cry in its columns, on the 26th of June, and kept the paragraph in a conspicuous place among its editorials until the 3d of July. Its words were as follows:—
"THE NATION'S WAR-CRY.—*Forward to Richmond! Forward to Richmond! The Rebel Congress must not be allowed to meet there on the 20th of July.* BY THAT DATE THE PLACE MUST BE HELD BY THE NATIONAL ARMY."
[3] The name of *havelock* was derived from Sir Henry Havelock, an eminent English commander in the East

for some systematic plan for the collection and distribution of these products of busy fingers was immediately apparent; and at a meeting of fifty or sixty women, in the city of New York, on the 25th of April,[a] a Central Relief Association was suggested. A plan was formed, and the women of New York were addressed by a committee, and invited to assemble in council, at the Cooper Institute, on the morning of the 29th. The response was ample. No such

THE HAVELOCK.

[a] 1861.

gathering of women had ever been seen in this country. David Dudley Field presided, and the object of the meeting was explained by H. W. Bellows, D. D., when the assemblage was addressed by Mr. Hamlin, Vice-President of the United States, and others. Then a benevolent organization was effected, under the title of *The Women's Central Association for Relief*, with the late venerable Dr. Valentine Mott as President, Dr. Bellows, Vice-President, G. F. Allen, Secretary, and Howard Potter, Treasurer. Auxiliary associations of women were formed in all parts of the Free-labor States; and when wounds and sickness appealed for relief, a few weeks later, a general system for the purpose was so well organized that all demands were, at first, promptly met. It was soon discovered, however, that a more perfect system, to have an official connection with the Medical Department of the Government, and under the sanction of the War Department, was needed, and, after much effort, THE UNITED STATES SANITARY COMMISSION was organized, and entered upon its great and beneficent labors. A fuller history of the organization and labors of this Commission, and also of its kindred society, the sturdy offspring of the Young Men's Christian Association, called THE UNITED STATES CHRISTIAN COMMISSION, will be found in another part of this work.

Before any of these propositions or efforts for giving aid to the sick and wounded were publicly made, a woman who for many years, Howard-like, had been laboring unceasingly for the poor, the unfortunate, and the afflicted, had obtained the sanction of the War Department for the organization of military hospitals, and the furnishing of nurses for them. That woman was Miss Dorothea L. Dix, whose name was familiar to the people throughout the land. She offered her services gratuitously to the Government, and they were accepted. So early as the 23d of April, or only eight days after the President called for troops to put down the rebellion, the Secretary of War issued a proclamation, announcing the fact of such acceptance;[1] and on the 1st of May, the Surgeon-General (R. C. Wood), "cheerfully and thankfully

DOROTHEA L. DIX.

Indies during the rebellion of the Sepoys, in 1857, who caused his soldiers to be furnished with these protectors against the heat of the sun. They were made of white cotton cloth, and covered the military cap and the neck with a cape. Our soldiers soon discarded them, as being more uncomfortable, by the exclusion of air, than any rays of the sun to which they were exposed. They had been sent to the army by thousands.

[1] The following is a copy of the proclamation or order:—" Be it known to all whom it may concern, that the

recognizing the ability and energy of Miss D. L. Dix in her arrangements for the comfort and welfare of the sick soldiers in the present exigency," requested all women who offered their services as nurses to report to her. Like an angel of mercy, this self-sacrificing woman labored day and night throughout the entire war for the relief of the suffering soldiers, without expecting or receiving any pecuniary reward. She went from battle-field to battle-field, when the carnage was over; from camp to camp; and from hospital to hospital, superintending the operations of the nurses, and administering with her own hands physical comforts to the suffering, and soothing the troubled spirits of the invalid or dying soldier with a voice low, musical, and attractive, and always burdened with words of heart-felt sympathy and religious consolation. The amount of happiness that resulted from the services of this woman of delicate frame, which seemed to be incapable of enduring the physical labor required of it, can never be estimated. The true record is only in the great Book of Remembrance. Yet she was not the only sister of charity engaged in works of mercy. She had hundreds of devoted, earnest, self-sacrificing co-workers of the gentler sex all over the land, serving with equal zeal in the camps and hospitals of the National and Confederate armies; and no greater heroism was displayed by soldiers in the field than was exhibited by these American women everywhere.

Working in grand harmony with those more extended organizations for the relief of the soldiers, were houses of refreshment and temporary hospital accommodations furnished by the citizens of Philadelphia. That city lay in the channel of the great stream of volunteers from New England, New York, and New Jersey, that commenced flowing abundantly early *a* 1861. in May.*ᵃ* These soldiers, crossing New Jersey, and the Delaware River at Camden, were landed at the foot of Washington Avenue, where, wearied and hungry, they often vainly sought for sufficient refreshments in the bakeries and groceries in the neighborhood before entering the cars for Washington City. One morning, the wife of a mechanic living near, commiserating the situation of some soldiers who had just arrived, went out with her coffee-pot and a cup, and distributed its contents among them. That generous hint was the germ of a wonderful system of relief for the passing soldiers, which was immediately developed in that city. Some benevolent women, living in the vicinity of this landing-place of the volunteers, imitated their patriotic sister, and a few of them formed themselves into a Committee[1] for the regular distribution of coffee on the arrival of soldiers. Gentlemen in the neighborhood interested themselves in procuring other supplies, and for a few days these were dispensed under the shade of trees in front of the cooper-shop of William M. Cooper, on Otsego Street,

---

free services of Miss D. L. Dix are accepted by the War Department, and that she will give, at all times, all necessary aid in organizing military hospitals for the care of all the sick or wounded soldiers, aiding the chief surgeons by supplying nurses, and substantial means for the comfort and relief of the suffering; also, that she is fully authorized to receive, control, and disburse special supplies bestowed by individuals or associations for the comfort of their friends or the citizen soldiers from all parts of the United States." Dated April 23, 1861, and signed SIMON CAMERON, Secretary of War.

On the 4th of May, Miss Dix issued a circular letter to the large number of women who were offering their services as nurses, giving them information and directions, and then commenced her beneficent labors with great assiduity.

[1] This Committee was composed of Mrs. William M. Cooper, Mrs. Grace Nickles, Mrs. Sarah Ewing, Mrs. Elizabeth Vansdale, Mrs. Catharine Vansdale, Mrs. Jane Coward, Mrs. Susan Turner, Mrs. Sarah Mellen, Mrs. Catharine Alexander, Mrs. Mary Plant, and Mrs. Captain Watson.

near Washington Avenue. Then this shop—generously offered for the purpose by Mr. Cooper—was used for refreshing the soldiers; and very soon whole regiments were fed there at tables supplied by the contributions of citizens of Philadelphia, and waited upon by the wives and daughters of those in the neighborhood. The first of the entire regiments so supplied was Colonel Blenker's (German Rifles), more than a thousand strong, who partook of a coffee breakfast there on the morning of the 27th of May.

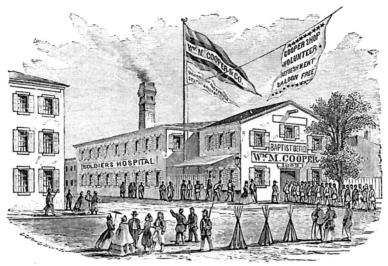

THE COOPER-SHOP VOLUNTEER REFRESHMENT SALOON AND HOSPITAL IN 1864.

The cooper-shop was not spacious enough to accommodate the daily increasing number of soldiers, and another place of refreshments was opened on the corner of Washington Avenue and Swanson Street, in a building formerly used as a boat-house and riggers' loft. Two Volunteer Refreshment Saloon Committees were formed, and known respectively as the "Cooper-Shop" and the "Union." The former was organized on the 26th and the latter on the 27th of May.[1] They worked in harmony and generous rivalry,

---

[1] The following were the Officers and Managers of the two Associations, respectively:—

THE COOPER-SHOP.—President, William M. Cooper; Vice-President, C. V. Fort; Recording Secretary, Wm. M. Maull; Corresponding Secretary, E. S. Hall; Treasurer, Adam M. Simpson; Storekeeper, Sam. W. Nickles; Hospital Committee, Philip Fitzpatrick, R. G. Simpson, L. W. Thornton; General Committee, Henry W. Pearce, Wm. H. Dennis, George M. Flick, R. H. Ransley, Captain R. J. Hoffner, H. H. Webb, Fitzpatrick Horety, Jacob Plant, Henry Dubosq, L. W. Thornton, R. G. Simpson, Wm, Sprole, J. Coward.

THE UNION.—Chairman, Arad Barrows; Recording Secretary, J. B. Wade; Treasurer, B. S. Brown; Steward, J. T. Williams; Physician, E. Ward; Corresponding Secretary, Robert R. Corson.

Committee of Gentlemen.—Arad Barrows, Bazilla S. Brown, Joseph B. Wade, Isaac B. Smith, Sr., Erasmus W. Cooper, Job T. Williams, John W. Hicks, George Flomerfelt, John Krider, Sr., Isaac B. Smith, Jr., Charles B. Grieves, James McGlathery, John B. Smith, Curtis Myers, Dr. Eliab Ward, Chris. Powell, Captain W. S. Mason, Charles S. Clampitt, Leopold M. J. Lemmens, D. L. Flanagan, Richard Sharp, Charles H. Kingston, Robert R. Corson, Samuel B. Fales, James Carroll, John T. Wilson.

Committee of Ladies.—Mrs. Mary Grover, Mrs. Hannah Smith, Mrs. Priscilla Grover, Miss Sarah Holland, Mrs. Margaret Boyer, Mrs. Eliza J. Smith, Mrs. Anna Elkinton, Mrs. Ellen B. Barrows, Mrs. Mary L. Field, Mrs. Ellen J. Lowry, Mrs. Martha V. R. Ward, Mrs. Eliza Plumer, Mrs. Emily Mason, Mrs. Mary Green, Miss Catharine Baily, Mrs. Eliza Helmbold, Miss Amanda Lee, Mrs. Elizabeth Horton, Mrs. Sarah Femington, Mrs. Kate B. Anderson, Miss Anna Grover, Miss Martha B. Krider, Miss Annie Field, Miss Mary Grover, Mrs. Mary E. Cassedy.

all through the period of the war, in doing good. Both saloons were enlarged as necessity required, and both had temporary hospitals attached to them. To the immortal honor of the citizens of Philadelphia it must be recorded, that they liberally supplied these saloons with ample materials to give a bountiful meal, during the four years of the war, to almost twelve hundred thousand Union soldiers. In the Union Volunteer Saloon, alone, seven hundred and fifty thousand soldiers were fed; forty thousand were accommodated with a night's lodging; fifteen thousand refugees and freed-

THE UNION VOLUNTEER REFRESHMENT SALOON IN 1861.

men were cared for, and employment found for them; and, in the hospital attached, the wounds of almost twenty thousand soldiers were dressed. The women who devoted themselves to the service of preparing the meals, and waiting upon this vast host of the defenders of the Union, deserve the choicest blessings their country can bestow. At all hours of the day and night, these self-sacrificing heroines, when a little signal-gun, employed for the purpose,[1] announced the approach of a regiment or a company, would repair to the saloons, and, with the greatest cheerfulness, dispense the generous bounties of their fellow-citizens. These saloons, in which such an abounding work of love and patriotism had been displayed, were formally closed in August, 1865, when the sunlight of Peace was reilluminating the land, and the Flag of the Republic—

" That floating piece of poetry,"

as Dr. Francis Lieber so appropriately called it in his song, " Our Country and Flag," was waving, unmolested, over every acre of its domain.

    Philadelphia was also honored by another organization for the good of the volunteers, known as the Firemen's Ambulance System, which was wholly the work of the firemen of that city, who also contributed largely from their body to the ranks of the Union army. When sick and wounded

---

[1] This little cannon, made of iron, has a notable history. It was cast at the Armory in Springfield, Massachusetts, and was a part of the ordnance in the army of General Taylor on the Rio Grande, in 1846, where it was captured, placed on a Mexican privateer, and, while on duty in the Gulf of Mexico, was recaptured by a United States cruiser. It was finally lodged, for a while, in the Navy Yard at Philadelphia, and then put on board of the receiving-ship *Union*, which was scuttled by ice one night, and went to the bottom. It was afterward raised, and when the rebellion broke out, was sent down on service to Perryville, while the secessionists held Baltimore. Soon after its return to Philadelphia, it was mounted on a clumsy carriage captured in the Castle of San Juan de Ulloa, at Vera Cruz, in 1847, and placed at the disposal of the Union Volunteer Refreshment Committee, as a signal-gun for the purpose mentioned in the text.

SIGNAL CANNON.

soldiers began to be brought in transports from camps and battle-fields to Philadelphia, to be placed in the admirable military hospitals that were established there, the Medical Department found it difficult to procure proper vehicles to convey them from the wharves to their destination. Delays and inconvenient conveyances caused much distress, which the sympathetic firemen attempted to remedy. An arrangement was made for the Chief of the Department to announce the arrival of a transport by a given signal, when the firemen would turn out with wagons, and repair to the landing-place. Finally, the Northern Liberties Engine Company had a splendid ambulance constructed. More than thirty other engine and hose companies followed its example, and the suffering soldiers were conveyed from ship to hospital with the greatest tenderness. These ambulances cost, in the aggregate, over thirty thousand dollars, all of which sum was contributed by the firemen. They also gave their personal ser-

PHILADELPHIA FIREMEN'S AMBULANCE.

vices freely, unmindful of their private interests. The number of disabled soldiers who were conveyed in these ambulances, during the period of the war, was estimated at more than one hundred and twenty thousand. Without disparagement to other cities (for all did noble work), it may, with propriety, be said, that in labors of genuine benevolence and generous giving for the comfort of the soldiers of the great Union Army, the citizens of Philadelphia stand peerless.

While the people at home were working with unceasing diligence for the comfort of the soldiers, and were contributing the means for making the contest, as the President desired it to be, " short and decisive," those soldiers were eager for action. A large portion of those near the Potomac had enlisted for only three months, and their terms would expire before the close of July. They were anxious to move against the insurgents at Manassas, and to win the victory which they felt certain of achieving. It was important that such movement should be made, for various reasons, before the regiments of early volunteers should be dissolved. These volunteers would be so disheartened by the inglorious and almost inactive campaign in which they had been engaged, that they would be tardy in volunteering for the war. Those who might fill their places would be almost wholly ignorant of discipline and the rudiments of the military art which the first had acquired; and in the confusion incident to the substitution of new recruits for the three-months' men, the well-organized and well-officered insurgents might, by a sudden and concentrated movement, overwhelm the Union forces, seize the Capital, and, with the *prestige* thus obtained, secure for the Confederacy the recognition of its independence by foreign governments. This real danger was before the mind of the people and their representatives, and intensified the cry of " *Forward to Richmond!*" while the earlier troops had yet some time to serve. That cry found a sympathetic response in the Army and in Congress; and at the middle of July, the General-in-chief gave orders for a forward movement upon the foe at Manassas. An earlier day[a] had been fixed upon for the beginning of the movement, but the new regiments came in so slowly that it was not deemed safe to break camp before the 15th.

[a] July 8, 1861.

Lieutenant-General Scott was too infirm to take command of the Army in the field. He was afflicted with dropsy and vertigo; and for four months he had not been able to mount a horse. He chose Brigadier-General Irvin McDowell for that responsible posi-

IRVIN M'DOWELL.

tion. That officer was a native of Ohio; a graduate[b] of the Military Academy at West Point; an excellent soldier, who had seen service under General Wool, in Mexico, and was then in the prime of life. He had been appointed[c] to the command of the Department of Virginia, with his head-quarters at Arlington House, as we have observed;[1] and for several weeks he had been actively engaged in the reception of materials for, and the organization of, what was afterward known as the Army of the Potomac. This work was but im-

[b] 1834.

[c] May 27, 1861.

perfectly accomplished, when public opinion bore upon the authorities with such fearful pressure, that the Army, such as it was, was moved forward, with McDowell as its chief.[2]

The relative position of the forces now to be brought into contact, each

---

[1] See page 485.

[2] The people who were shouting "*Forward to Richmond!*" had no conception of the time and labor required to organize, equip, and provide for the feeding of an army sufficient for the emergency. When the war broke out, the preparations for it by the Government, as we have observed, were very meager. Every thing had to be provided—created, as it were—with inadequate means for doing the work. The armories and the armorers were few. The materials for making cannon and small-arms and munitions of war had to be collected. Agents had been sent to Europe to purchase arms for use until they could be manufactured at home. None of these had yet arrived; and the only ordnance that had crossed the ocean, for use by the National troops, was a battery of six Whitworth cannon, which were sent over and presented to the Government by loyal Americans residing in England. They were 12-pounders, and each bore the inscription:—"From Loyal Americans in Europe to the United States Government, 1861." The funds for their purchase were collected chiefly by R. G. Moulton, then residing in Manchester, England. The cost of the six guns, including the freight, was twelve thousand dollars. They were purchased of the Whit-

WHITWORTH CANNON.

worth Ordnance Company of Manchester. They were each nine feet long, and were loaded at the breech; and the weight of each was eleven hundred pounds. The bore was three inches, and rifled, and the ball was a double cone of iron, nine inches long. The charge required to throw the ball five miles was two pounds and one-half of powder.

In addition to a lack of arms was a want of means for transportation. The men who fight must be fed; and it required seven hundred and fifty wagons, three thousand horses, and almost a thousand teamsters, to carry provisions, tents, intrenching tools, *et cætera*, for an army of fifty thousand men, such as was ordered to engage in the business of going forward to Richmond. These wagons had to be made, and the horses purchased, and the teamsters engaged, before that army could move efficiently, for it was going into an enemy's country. Only about ten weeks had been allowed for these preparations to be made, when "*Forward to Richmond!*" was the war-cry of the people.

of which was divided, was as follows: The main body of the National army, under McDowell, about forty-five thousand in number, occupied a line, with the Potomac at its back, extending from Alexandria, nine miles below Washington City, almost to the Chain Bridge, about six miles above the Capital. The remainder, under General Patterson, about eighteen thousand strong, was at Martinsburg, beyond the Blue Ridge, also with the Potomac at its back, as we have observed.[1] There were three important bridges spanning the Potomac in the vicinity of Washington City, which were well guarded. The Upper, or Chain Bridge, where the banks of the

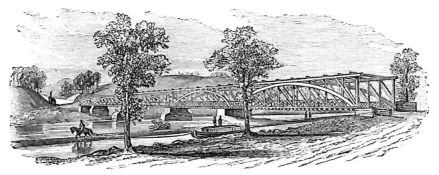

CHAIN BRIDGE.[2]

river are high and precipitous, was beyond the Union lines at that time, on the Virginia side, but on the Maryland, or District side, it was well guarded by two batteries—one at the bridge, and the other on the high bank above it—and both thoroughly commanding it. In addition to these batteries, a heavy two-leaved gate was constructed at the center of the bridge, which was covered on the Virginia side with heavy iron plates, and was pierced for

musketry. At Georgetown was the Aqueduct Bridge,[3] which was well guarded by Fort Corcoran and block-houses on Arlington Hights, and a battery on Georgetown Hights, north of the city. At Washington City, at the junction of Maryland Avenue and Fourteenth Street, was the Long Bridge, a mile in length, whose Virginia end was commanded by three forts, named, respectively, Jackson, Runyon, and Albany. They were built chiefly of earth. Fort Jackson

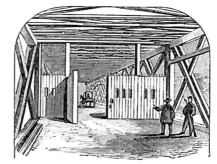

GATE ON CHAIN BRIDGE.

was close by the river, with heavy pickets and picket-gate crossing the railway which there passes over the Long Bridge, and connects Washington

---

[1] See page 525.
[2] This is from a sketch made at the close of April, 1865, from the Maryland or District of Columbia side of the river. The Chesapeake and Ohio Canal is seen in the foreground. The Potomac is here broken into rapids called the Little Falls. [3] See page 481

City with Alexandria. Other fortifications, as we have observed, extended along the line of Arlington Hights, and guarded every approach to positions which commanded the National Capital and Georgetown.

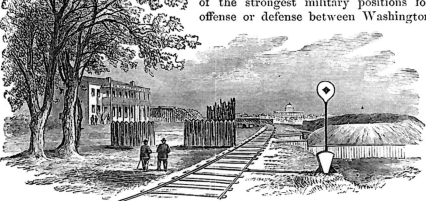

The main Confederate army, under the command of Beauregard, supposed to have been a little less than McDowell's in number (forty-five thousand), was at and near Manassas Junction, then considered one of the strongest military positions for offense or defense between Washington

REMAINS OF FORT JACKSON, AT THE LONG BRIDGE.[1]

MARINE ARTILLERY-MAN AT MANASSAS.

and Richmond. It is about half way between the eastern range of the Blue Ridge and the Potomac at Alexandria, and was connected by railway with Richmond and the fertile Shenandoah Valley, as we have observed. The main portion of the army was on an elevated plateau in the crotch formed by the Occoquan River and its main tributary, Bull's Run. The bed of each stream, canal-like, was cut through horizontal strata of red stone, making it difficult for an attacking army to approach the Confederate works.[2] A succession of broken, wooded hills around the plateau, composed strong natural fortifications; and Beauregard's engineers had cast up formidable artificial ones there. Among these, the most noted was the Naval Battery, composed of the heaviest Dahlgren guns, which the insurgents seized at the Gosport Navy Yard, and manned by seamen, commanded by officers of the National Navy who had abandoned their flag.

---

[1] This is from a sketch made by the author at the close of April, 1865, and shows the embankments of Fort Jackson on the right, and the remains of the pickets, with the railway, in the foreground. On the left is a public house of entertainment, and just beyond it is seen a portion of the Long Bridge. The Capitol is seen in the distance.   [2] *The C. S. A. and the Battle of Bull Run :* by Major J. G. Barnard.

Beauregard's force was mostly composed of Virginians, South Carolinians, Alabamians, Mississippians, and Louisianians.

Another Confederate army, about as strong in numbers as Beauregard's actually was, was in the Shenandoah Valley, under General Johnston, his superior in rank, whose head-quarters were at Winchester, around which he had caused to be cast up heavy intrenchments, under the directions of Major W. H. C. Whiting, his Chief of Engineers. Johnston was charged with the duty, as we have observed, of checking the advance of Patterson, and preventing the junction of the troops under that officer with those under McClellan among the Alleghany ranges. Among the most active of his infantry force was a corps of Tennessee riflemen or "sharp-shooters." These had been raised in West Tennessee, where the people were mostly disloyal. They were among the earliest of the troops of that State who made their way into Virginia, after the treaty was concluded for

TENNESSEE SHARP-SHOOTER.

the annexation of that Commonwealth to the Confederacy,[1] and the control of its military affairs was placed in the hands of Jefferson Davis. Tennessee and Kentucky were well represented in the Army of the Shenandoah.

---

[1] See page 387.

CHAPTER XXV.

THE BATTLE OF BULL'S RUN,

HE long-desired forward movement of the greater portion of the National Army that lay in the vicinity of the
Capital, full fifty thousand in number, began on the
afternoon of Tuesday, the 16th of July,[a]
leaving about fifteen thousand, under General
Mansfield, to guard the seat of Government. The advancing troops consisted chiefly of volunteers from New
England, New York, and New Jersey, and some from
Western States. A greater portion of them had enlisted for only three
months, and their terms of service were nearly ended. The remainder were
chiefly recent volunteers for "three years or the war," who were almost
wholly undisciplined; and when the army moved, some of the regiments
were not even brigaded. There were also seven or eight hundred regular
troops (the fragments of regiments), and a small cavalry force, and several
light batteries. With the exception of the regulars, the only troops on whom
McDowell might rely were the three-months men. He had only seven companies of regular cavalry in his army, and two of these were left for the defense of Washington City.[1]

McDowell's forces were organized in five divisions,[2] commanded respec-

[a] 1861.

---

[1] *History of the United States Cavalry:* by Albert C. Brackett, page 212.

[2] This army was composed of excellent material, in a very crude state. With the exception of the regulars, the men were instructed in only the rudiments of military tactics and discipline, and a large portion of
their officers were no wiser than they. The cardinal virtue of a thorough soldier, *obedience*, had yet to be
acquired. Officers and men, in many cases, had been social companions, and the latter were restive under restraints imposed by the former. In comparison with the same army two years later, McDowell's force appears
little better than a huge mob, with noble instincts, but having no adequate conception of the grave duties laid
upon it.*

---

* The composition of this first great American army was as follows :—

McDowell's Staff.—Captain James B. Fry, Assistant Adjutant-General; Aids-de-camp—First Lieutenant Henry W. Kingsbury, Fifth
United States Artillery, and Majors Clarence S. Brown and James S. Wadsworth, New York State Artillery; Acting Inspector-General—
Major William H. Wood, Seventeenth United States Infantry; Engineers—Major John G. Barnard and First Lieutenant Frederick E.
Prime; Topographical Engineers—Captain Amiel W. Whipple, First Lieutenant Henry L. Abbot, and Second Lieutenant Haldimand S.
Putnam; Quartermaster's Department—Captain O. H. Tillinghast; Commissary of Subsistence—Horace F. Clark; Surgeon—William S.
King; Assistant Surgeon—David L. Magruder.

First Division.—General Tyler. Four brigades. The *First* Brigade, commanded by Colonel Erasmus D. Keyes, of the Eleventh
United States Infantry, was composed of the First, Second, and Third Regiments of Connecticut Volunteers, the Fourth Maine Volunteers,
Captain Varian's New York Battery, and Company B of the Second United States Cavalry. The *Second* Brigade, under Brigadier-General
R. C. Schenck, consisted of the First and Second Ohio Volunteers, the Second New York Volunteers, and a light battery with a part of
Company E of the Third United States Artillery. The *Third* Brigade was commanded by Colonel William T. Sherman, of the Thirteenth
United States Infantry, and was composed of Colonel Corcoran's Irish Regiment (Sixty-ninth New York Militia), Colonel Cameron's
Scotch Regiment (Seventy-ninth New York Militia), the Thirteenth New York Volunteers, Second Wisconsin Volunteers, and a light
battery with a part of Company E United States Artillery. The *Fourth* Brigade, under Colonel J. B. Richardson, of the Michigan Volunteers, embraced the Second and Third Michigan, First Massachusetts, and the Twelfth New York Volunteers.

Second Division.—Colonel David Hunter. Two brigades. The *First* Brigade was commanded by Colonel Andrew Porter, of the Sixteenth United States Infantry, and was composed of a battalion of regular Infantry, the Eighth and Fourteenth New York Militia, a
squadron of the Second United States Cavalry, consisting of Companies G and L, and a light battery of the Fifth United States Artillery.
The *Second* Brigade was commanded by Colonel Ambrose E. Burnside, of the Rhode Island Volunteers, and consisted of the First and

tively by Brigadier-Generals Daniel Tyler and Theodore Runyon, and Colonels David Hunter, Samuel P. Heintzelman, and Dixon S. Miles. The Confederate force against which this army was to move was distributed along Bull's Run,[1] from Union Mill, where the Orange and Alexandria Railway crosses that stream, to the Stone Bridge of the Warrenton Turnpike, the interval being about eight miles.[2] The run formed an admirable line of defense. Its steep, rocky, and wooded banks, and its deep bed, formed an almost impassable barrier to troops, excepting at the fords, which were a mile or two apart. They had reserves at Camp Pickens, near Manassas Junction, a dreary hamlet before the war, on a high, bleak plain, and composed of an indifferent railway station-house and place of refreshments and a few scattered cottages. Near there, at Weir's house, at the junction of the Centreville and Union Mill roads, Beauregard had his head-quarters. The Confederates had an outpost, with fortifications, at Centreville, and strong pickets and slight fortifications at Fairfax Court House, a village, ten miles from the main army, in the direction of Washington City. General Johnston, as we have observed, was strongly intrenched at Winchester, in the Shenandoah

DANIEL TYLER.

---

[1] This is an inconsiderable stream, which rises in the range of hills known as Bull's Run Mountains. See map on page 586. It empties into the Occoquan River about twelve miles from the Potomac.

[2] The disposition of the Confederate forces was as follows:—

Ewell's brigade occupied a position near the Union Mill Ford, and was composed of the Fifth and Seventh Alabama, and Fifth Louisiana Volunteers, with four 12-pound howitzers of Walton's battery of the Washington Artillery of New Orleans, and three companies of Virginia cavalry. D. R. Jones's brigade was in the rear of McLean's Ford, and was composed of the Fifth South Carolina and the Fifteenth and Eighteenth Mississippi Volunteers, with two brass 6-pounders of Walton's battery, and one company of cavalry. The brigade of James Longstreet covered Blackburn's Ford. It was composed of the First, Eleventh, and Seventeenth Virginia Volunteers, with two brass 6-pounders of Walton's battery. M. L. Bonham's brigade, stationed at Centreville, covered the approaches to Mitchell's Ford. It consisted of the Second, Third, Seventh, and Eighth South Carolina Volunteers, two light batteries, and four companies of Virginia cavalry under Colonel Radford. Cocke's brigade held a position below the Stone Bridge and vicinity, and consisted of, the Eighteenth, Nineteenth, and Twenty-eighth Virginia Volunteers, a company of cavalry, and a light battery. Colonel Evans, with the Fourth South Carolina, a special Louisiana battalion under Colonel Wheat, four 6-pounders, and a company of Virginia cavalry, guarded the Stone Bridge; and Early's brigade, composed of the Seventh and Twenty-fourth Virginia, and Seventh Louisiana Volunteers, with three rifled cannon of Walton's battery, held a position in the rear of Ewell's brigade.—*Beauregard's Report to Adjutant-General Cooper.*

Second Rhode Island Volunteers, the Seventy-first New York Militia, the Second New Hampshire Volunteers, and a battery of the Light Artillery of the Second Rhode Island. See page 402.

Third Division.—Colonel Samuel P. Heintzelman, of the Seventeenth United States Infantry. Three brigades. The *First* Brigade, commanded by Colonel W. B. Franklin, of the Twelfth United States Infantry, was composed of the Fourth Pennsylvania Militia, Fifth and Eleventh Massachusetts Militia, First Minnesota Volunteers, Company E of the Second United States Cavalry, and a light battery with Company 1 of the First United States Artillery. The *Second* Brigade, led by Colonel O. B. Wilcox, of the Michigan Volunteers, was composed of the First Michigan Volunteers, Eleventh New York Volunteers, and a light battery with Company D of the Second United States Artillery. The *Third* Brigade, commanded by Colonel O. O. Howard, of the Maine Volunteers, included the Second, Fourth, and Fifth Maine, and Second Vermont Volunteers.

The Fourth and Fifth Divisions constituted the reserves, and were composed as follows:—

Fourth Division.—General Theodore Runyon, of the New Jersey Militia. One brigade, composed of the First, Second, Third, and Fourth New Jersey three-months Militia, and the First, Second, and Third New Jersey three-years Volunteers.

Fifth Division—Colonel Dixon S. Miles, of the Second United States Infantry, contained two brigades. The *First* Brigade, commanded by Colonel Louis Blenker, of the New York Volunteers, consisted of the Eighth and Twenty-ninth New York Volunteers, the New York Garibaldi Guard, and the Twenty-fourth Pennsylvania Volunteers. The *Second* Brigade was commanded by Colonel Thomas A. Davies, of the New York Volunteers, and was composed of the Sixteenth, Eighteenth, Thirty-first, and Thirty-second New York Volunteers, and a light battery with Company G of the Second United States Artillery. The foregoing was compiled from the General Orders of the Commander-in-chief, dated 8th of July, 1861.

Valley; and General Patterson was at Martinsburg, a few miles below him, charged with the duty of keeping Johnston from re-enforcing Beauregard at Bull's Run. The subjoined map indicates the theater of operations on which the four armies were about to perform.

Orders for the advance were given on the 15th,[a] and at half-past

[a] July, 1861.

two o'clock in the afternoon of the next day, Tyler's column, forming the right wing, went forward to Vienna, and encamped for the night. At sunrise the next morning,[b] the whole army moved

[b] July 17.

in four columns. The men were in light marching order, with cooked provisions for three days in their knapsacks. The village of Fairfax Court House was their destination,

BEAUREGARD'S HEAD-QUARTERS AT MANASSAS.

where, it was expected, the Confederates would offer battle.

Tyler, with the right wing, moved along the Georgetown Road. Hunter, with the center, advanced by the Leesburg and Centreville Road; and a portion of the left wing, under Heintzelman, went out from near Alexandria, along the Little River Turnpike. Another portion, under Miles, proceeded by the old "Braddock Road," that passes through Fairfax Court House and Centreville, where it becomes the Warrenton Turnpike. They found the roads obstructed by felled trees near Fairfax Court House, but no opposing troops. These had fallen back to Centreville. The impediments were soon removed. At noon, the National Army occupied the deserted village, and the National flag, raised by some of Burnside's Rhode Islanders, soon occupied the place of a Confederate one found flying over the Court House. The Commanding General and Tyler's division moved on two miles farther, to the little village of German-town, where it encamp-

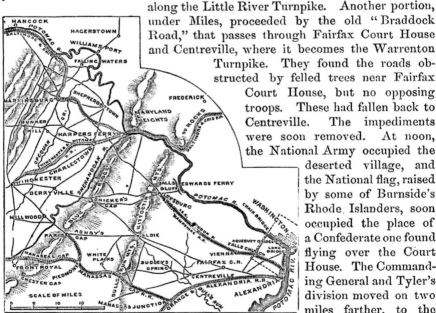

THE FIELD OF OPERATIONS.

ed. The conquest had been so easy, that the troops, in high spirits, and under the inspiration of a belief that the march to Richmond was to be like a pleasure excursion, committed some excesses, which the commander promptly rebuked. He reminded them that they were there "to fight the

·enemies of the country, not to judge or punish the unarmed and defenseless, however guilty they may be." The excesses were not repeated.[1]

General McDowell, pretty well informed concerning the strong position of the Confederate force, intended to turn its right flank at Manassas by a sudden movement to his left, crossing the Occoquan River below the mouth of Bull's Run, and, seizing the railway in the rear of his foe, compel both Beauregard and Johnston to fall back from their positions, so menacing to the National Capital. With this view, he made a reconnoissance on the morning of the 18th, while Tyler moved forward with his division, and at nine o'clock marched through Centreville without any opposition, and halted in a little valley between it and Bull's Run. This movement was intended as a feint, but ended in a sharp engagement.

Centreville was a small village on the west side of a ridge running nearly parallel with the general course of Bull's Run, which was west of it five or six miles, and near it the Confederates had erected strong earthworks. These were occupied by a brigade of South Carolinians under General Bonham, who fled, at the approach of Tyler, to the wooded banks of Bull's Run. Several roads, public and private, led to that stream from Centreville. One was the War-

THE STONE BRIDGE.[2]

renton Turnpike, that crossed at the Stone Bridge, a structure of a single arch that spanned the Run; another led to Mitchell's Ford, midway between Centreville and Manassas Junction; and still another led to Blackburn's Ford, over which General James Longstreet was watching.

Toward noon, Tyler went out on a reconnoissance toward Blackburn's

<hr />

[1] Many of the inhabitants abandoned their houses and fled in terror at the approach of the troops. Some of these houses were entered and plundered by the National soldiers, and some barns and other out-houses on the outskirts of the village were burnt, one of the troops, it was said, having been shot by a man concealed in one of them. Some of the soldiers appeared in the streets in the evening, dressed in women's apparel, which they had found in the houses; and one man, with the gown and bands of a clergyman, which he had found, went through the streets with an open book, reading the funeral service of the "President of the Southern Confederacy." These shameful scenes were soon ended when the conduct of the soldiers was reported to the officers. General McDowell issued a stringent order, and threatened the severest penalties for a violation of it.

[2] This is a view of the Stone Bridge and its vicinity, as it appeared after the battle there on the 21st of July, and, with pictures of several buildings mentioned in connection with that event, was kindly given to me by Mr. Gardner, the well-known photographer of Washington City, who took them from nature.

Ford, taking with him Richardson's brigade, a squadron of cavalry, and Ayres's battery, and holding Sherman's brigade in reserve. He found the Confederates in heavy force. Beauregard, who had been informed of all of McDowell's movements by spies and traitors,[1] was there, and had ordered up from Manassas some North Carolina and Louisiana troops, who had just arrived there on their way to Winchester. The woods were so thick that his forces were mostly concealed, as well as his batteries, excepting one on an open elevation. Hoping to draw their fire and discover their position, Ayres's battery was placed on a commanding eminence, and a 20-pound cannon, under Lieutenant Edwards, was fired at random. Only the battery in view responded, and grape-shot from it killed two cavalry horses and

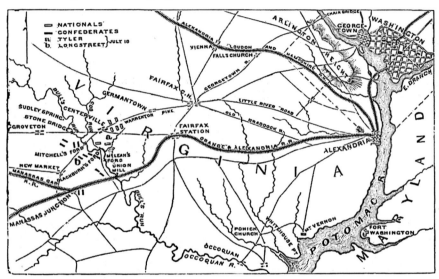

THE FIELD OF OPERATIONS FROM JULY 16 TO JULY 19.[2]

wounded two men. Richardson now sent forward the Second Michigan regiment as skirmishers. They were soon engaged in a severe contest in the woods, on a level bottom near the Run. The Third Michigan, First Massachusetts, and Twelfth New York were pushed forward to support the advance, and these, too, were soon fighting severely. The cavalry and two howitzers were now sent forward, and were furiously assailed by musketry in the woods, and at the same time a severe enfilading fire came from a concealed battery on a ridge six hundred yards in front of the Ford. In the mean time, Longstreet had called up some re-enforcements from Early's

---

[1] Washington City, as we have observed, was filled with spies and traitors. Even Cabinet secrets were made known to the Confederates. Information seemed to go out to them regularly from the head-quarters of the General-in-chief. For example, a military map of the region west of Washington had been completed at the War Department only two days before Tyler's advance on Centreville. When the Confederates left there in haste, they left many things behind them. Among these was a copy of that map, which was supposed to be known only to some of the higher officers in the Army.

[2] This map shows a geographical plan of the country between Washington City and Manassas Junction. with the roads traversed by the troops, and the relative position of the opposing forces in the skirmish on the 18th of July.

brigade, and the Nationals, greatly outnumbered, withdrew behind Ayres's battery on the hill. In this movement, a part of the New York Twelfth were thrown into confusion, but were soon rallied. Just then, Sherman with his brigade came up, having Colonel Corcoran's New York Sixty-ninth in front, when Ayres's battery again opened fire, and an artillery duel was kept up for an hour, the Confederates responding gun for gun. It was now four o'clock in the afternoon. McDowell had just returned from his reconnoissance, satisfied that his plan for turning the Confederate position was impracticable; and he ordered the whole body to fall back to Centreville.[1] This severe skirmish was called by the Confederates the BATTLE OF BULL'S RUN, and was claimed by them as a victory. The loss of the combatants was about equal, that of McDowell being seventy-three, and of Beauregard, seventy.[2]

CORCORAN'S SIXTY-NINTH NEW YORK.

The affair at Blackburn's Ford elated the Confederates and depressed the Nationals. The loss of life saddened the soldiers and the people at home. Yet the result of that reconnoissance was important and useful, in revealing the strength and excellent equipment of the Confederates, which had been much underrated, and caused that circumspection which prevented the Nationals from being allured, by the appearance of weakness and timidity on the part of their foes, into a fatal snare. It appears to have been a part of Beauregard's plan to entice McDowell, by skirmishes and retreats, across Bull's Run, and when he had placed that stream at the back of his antagonist, to fall upon him, front and flank. For this purpose, he carefully concealed his batteries.

McDowell felt the pressing necessity for an immediate and vigorous attack on the Confederates. In the course of a few days he might lose full ten thousand of his best troops, in consequence of the expiration of their term of service, while Beauregard's army was daily increasing. He concentrated all of his forces at and around Centreville on the 18th, and made instant preparations for an advance. He had thirty thousand men there, and five thousand more, under Runyon, were within call, guarding his communications with Washington. He caused a thorough reconnoissance to be made on the 19th with the intention of attacking his foe on Saturday, the 20th.

---

[1] Beauregard had made his head-quarters, during the engagement, at the house of Wilmer McLean, near McLean's Ford. Soon after this, when military occupation made that region almost untenable, Mr. McLean went with his family to another part of Virginia, near Appomattox Court House, hoping for quiet. There came the same armies, after a lapse of almost four years, and under his roof Grant and Lee signed articles of capitulation early in April, 1865, for the surrender of the Confederate forces under the latter.

[2] Report of Colonel Richardson to General Tyler, July 19, 1861; Report of General Tyler to General McDowell, July 27, 1861; Report of General Beauregard to Adjutant-General Cooper, August, 1861; *The C. S. A. and The Battle of Bull's Run: a Letter to an English Friend:* by Major J. G. Barnard, who was with Tyler's division. The Nationals lost nineteen killed, thirty-eight wounded, and twenty-six missing; the Confederates lost, according to Beauregard's Report, fifteen killed, fifty-three wounded (several of them mortally), and two missing.

But his needful supplies did not arrive until Friday night, and he was compelled to remain at Centreville a day longer than he expected to. On that evening, his army began to melt away. The term of service of the Fourth Pennsylvania and Varian's battery of the New York Eighth expired that day, and neither the persuasions of the Commanding General, nor those of the Secretary of War, who was at head-quarters, could induce them to remain. They turned their faces homeward that evening, and a few hours later they heard the thunders of the battle at their backs, in which their brave companions were engaged. On the evening of the 20th, McDowell's force consisted of about twenty-eight thousand men and forty-nine cannon.

The reconnoissance on the 19th satisfied McDowell that an attack on the Confederate front would not be prudent, and he resolved to attempt to turn their left, drive them from the Stone Bridge, where they had a strong battery, force them from the Warrenton Turnpike, and, by a quick movement, seize the Manassas Gap Railway, and thus sever the most important connection between Beauregard and Johnston. For this purpose, Tyler was to move along the Warrenton Turnpike, and open fire on the Confederate left at the Stone Bridge, while Hunter and Heintzelman, with about fifteen thousand men, should make a circuit by a forest road, cross Bull's Run at fords near Sudley Church, and fall upon the flank and rear of the Confederates at the Stone Bridge, where Colonel Evans was in command, with his head-quarters at Van Pelt's. In the mean time, Richardson's brigade was to be temporarily attached to Miles's division, which was left, as a reserve, at Centreville, with orders to strengthen the intrenchments there, and see that the Confederates did not cross Bull's Run, and, by a flank movement, capture the supplies and ammunition of the Nationals there, and cut off their line of

retreat. Richardson kept almost the exact position occupied by him on the 18th during the artillery duel.

Fully informed of McDowell's force and position by spies and traitors, Beauregard was contemplating an attack upon the Nationals at Centreville at the same time. The orders for an advance and attack by McDowell and Beauregard were dated on the same day.[a] The latter ordered the brigades of Ewell and Holmes to cross Bull's Run at Union Mill Ford, to be ready to support the attack on Centreville. The brigades of Jones and Longstreet were directed to cross at McLean's Ford, for the same purpose; while those of Bonham and Bartow were to cross at Mitchell's Ford, and those of Cocke and Evans at the Stone Bridge, and make the direct attack on Centreville.

a July 20, 1861.

GRAYSON DARE-DEVILS.

The brigades of Bee and Wilcox, with Stuart's cavalry (among whom was a dashing corps known as the Grayson Dare-devils), with the whole of Walton's New Orleans Battery, were to form a reserve, and to cross at Mitchell's Ford when called for. Confident of success, Beauregard ordered the Fourth and Fifth Divisions of his army "to advance to the attack of Fairfax Court House by way of the Old Braddock Road," "after the fall of Centreville."[1]

McDowell issued specific orders on the 20th,[a] for the advance and method of attack by the three divisions chosen for the work. The troops were supplied with three days' rations. The columns were to move at about two o'clock in the morning of Sunday, the 21st. Tyler was to be in position at four o'clock, or daybreak, to menace the Confederate left at the Stone Bridge, while the real attack was to be made by Hunter and Heintzelman, about two hours later. Every thing was in readiness by midnight. The camp-fires of forty regiments were burning dimly all around Centreville. The full moon was shining brightly. The air was fresh and still. Never was there a midnight more calm and beautiful; never did a Sabbath morning approach with gentler aspect on the face of nature.

a July, 1861.

McDowell, fearful of unforeseen obstacles, proposed to make a part of the march toward Bull's Run on the evening of the 20th, but he was, unfortunately, overruled by the opinions of others. He was satisfied that Beauregard's army, on the 19th, was inferior to his own; and he had no information of his having been re-enforced. He believed Patterson was holding Johnston at Winchester;[2] and whilst he felt extremely anxious under the weight of responsibility laid upon him, he did not permit himself to entertain a doubt of his success, if his orders as to time and place should be promptly executed.

But important circumstances, of which McDowell was ignorant, had occurred. When he advanced to Fairfax Court House on the 17th, Beauregard informed the Confederate War Department of the fact, and orders were immediately telegraphed to Johnston for the Army of the Shenandoah to join that of the Potomac at Manassas at once. Johnston received the dispatch at one o'clock on the morning of the 18th. It was necessary to fight

JOSEPH E. JOHNSTON.

and defeat General Patterson or to elude him. The latter was accomplished, and Johnston, with six thousand infantry, reached Manassas Junction at about noon on the 20th. His whole army, excepting about two thousand of his sick and a guard of militia, who had been left at Winchester, had marched by the way of Millwood through Ashby's Gap to Piedmont,[3] whence the infantry were conveyed by railway, while the cavalry and artillery, because of a lack of rolling stock[4] on the road, were compelled to continue their march as before. Johnston's six thousand made Beauregard's army stronger

---

[1] Beauregard's special and confidential orders, dated "Head-Quarters Army of the Potomac, July 20, 1861."
[2] See map on page 586.
[3] See map on page 586. Beauregard sent Colonel Chisholm, one of his aids, to meet Johnston, and suggest the propriety of his sending down a part of his force by the way of Aldie, to fall upon the flank and rear of the Nationals at Centreville. Lack of transportation prevented that movement. See Beauregard's Report, August 26, 1861.
[4] This technical term means the engines and cars, with their appurtenances.

than McDowell's by at least four thousand men. He was the senior officer, and took the chief command of the army. He approved of Beauregard's plan for an attack on the left wing of the Nationals; and both generals, before daybreak on the morning of the 21st, made active preparations for its execution. A few hours later the Confederates, instead of being the aggressors, were fighting on the defensive on their side of Bull's Run.

The general disposition of the Confederate army on the 21st[a] was nearly the same as on the 18th.[1] The arrival of re-enforcements, and preparations for the attack on the National left, had made some changes. The detachments of the brigades of Bee of South Carolina, and Bartow of Georgia, that came from the Shenandoah Valley with Johnston, about three thousand in number, had been placed in reserve between McLean's and Blackburn's Fords; and Colonel Cocke's brigade, with which were connected two companies of cavalry and a battery of four 6-pounders, occupied a line in front of Bull's Run, below the Stone Bridge, to guard Island, Ball's, and Lewis's Fords. Three hundred of Stuart's

[a] July 1861.

FOURTEENTH VIRGINIA CAVALRY.

cavalry, of the Army of the Shenandoah, and two companies of Radford's cavalry, were in reserve not far from Mitchell's Ford. Near them was a small brigade under General Holmes, and some cavalry.[2]

The three divisions of the National army moved from Centreville in the bright moonlight at the appointed hour.[b] They advanced slowly, for raw troops were difficult to handle. After crossing Cub Run, Hunter and Heintzelman turned into the road to the right that led through the "Big Woods," whilst Tyler moved along the Warrenton turnpike directly toward the Stone Bridge, with the brigades of Schenck and Sherman, leaving Keyes to watch the road that came up from Manassas, and Richardson to co-operate with Miles in keeping ward over Blackburn's Ford and vicinity, on the extreme

[b] July 21, 1861.

left. Tyler's division was accompanied by the batteries of Ayres and Carlisle; and its first business was to make a feigned attack near the bridge at dawn, to deceive the foe and divert his attention until Hunter and Heintzelman should fall upon the flank and rear of his left wing. McDowell, who was ill, had followed the columns from Centreville in a carriage, and he took a position at the junction of the turnpike and the forest road, where he might be in quick communication with all his forces.

These movements were all much slower than had been calculated upon, and the mistake in not making an advance the previous evening was soon painfully apparent. The advantage of a surprise was lost. It was half-past six o'clock, when the sun had been shining on the Stone Bridge nearly two hours, before Tyler was ready to open fire on the Confederates there; and

1 See note 2 on page 585.   2 Beauregard's Report, August 26, 1861.

the forest road was so rough and obscure, and the distance so much greater than was expected, that Hunter and Heintzelman were four hours behind the appointed time, when they crossed Bull's Run at and near Sudley's Ford. McDowell had become exceedingly impatient of delay, and at length he mounted his horse, and with his escort, composed of Captain A. G. Brackett's company of United States Cavalry, he rode forward, and overtook and passed Hunter and Heintzelman. McDowell and his attendants were the first in the open fields that became a battle-ground, and were the targets for the first bullets fired by the Confederates.

Tyler placed Schenck's brigade on the left of the turnpike, in a position that menaced the Confederate battery at the Stone Bridge, and Sherman's was posted on the right, to be in a position to sustain Schenck or to cross Bull's Run, as circumstances might require. When this disposition was made, a shell was hurled from a 30-pounder Parrott gun of Edwards's Fifth Artillery battery (then attached to Carlisle's, and stationed in the road, under the direction of Lieutenant Haines) at a line of Confederate infantry seen in a meadow beyond Bull's Run. This was the herald of the fierce battle on that eventful day. It exploded over the heads of the Confederates, and scattered their ranks. Other shells were sent in quick succession, but elicited no reply. This silence made McDowell suspect that the Confederates were concentrating their forces at some point below, to strike his left wing. He therefore held one of Heintzelman's brigades (Howard's) in reserve for a while, to assist Miles and Richardson if it should be necessary.

Colonel Evans, commanding at the Stone Bridge, believing Tyler's feint to be a real attack, sent word to Beauregard that the left wing of their army was strongly assailed. Re-enforcements were ordered forward, and Cocke and Evans were instructed to hold the position at the bridge at all hazards. At the same time, hoping to recall the troops in front of Evans, Johnston ordered an immediate, quick, and vigorous attack upon McDowell's left at Centreville; and his force was so strong on his right, that he and Beauregard confidently expected to achieve a complete victory before noon. The movement miscarried, as Ewell soon informed them; and crowding events changed their plans. From an eminence about a mile from Mitchell's Ford, the two commanders watched the general movements, and waited for tidings of the battle that soon began, with the greatest anxiety. A cloud of dust, seen some distance to the northward, gave Johnston apprehensions that Patterson was approaching, not doubting that he had hastened to re-enforce McDowell as soon as he discovered that the Army of the Shenandoah had eluded him.

Before we consider the conflict, let us take a glance at the topography of the region about to become a sanguinary battle-field :—

Near the Stone Bridge the general course of Bull's Run is north and south, and the Warrenton turnpike crossed it there nearly due west from Centreville. On the western side of the Run the road traversed a low wooded bottom for half a mile, and then, passing over a gentle hill, crossed, in a hollow beyond, a brook known as Young's Branch. Following the little valley of this brook, the road went up an easy slope to a plain in the direction of Groveton, about two miles from the Stone Bridge, where a road from Sudley's Spring crossed it. Between that road and the Stone Bridge, Young's Branch, bending northward of the turnpike, forms a curve, from the outer edge of which the ground rises gently to the northward, in a series of undulating open fields, dotted with small groves. On that slope was the scene of the earliest sharp conflict on the eventful 21st of July. From the inner edge of the curve of Young's Branch, southward, the ground rises quite abruptly to an altitude of about a hundred feet, and spreads out into a plateau, an irregular ellipse in form, a mile in length from northeast to

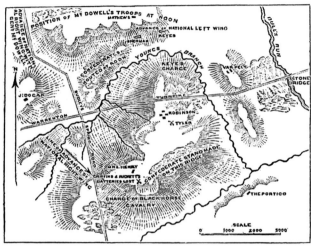

TOPOGRAPHY OF THE BATTLE-FIELD.

southwest, and half a mile in width from northwest to southeast. It contained about two hundred acres of cleared land, with a few clumps of oak and pine trees. On the eastern and southern sides of the plateau was a dense wood of small pines; and on the western edge of the fields was a belt of oaks, through which the Sudley's Spring road passed. A short distance from this was the house of Judith Henry, a widow and an invalid, confined to her bed; and nearer the turnpike, on the northern edge of the plateau, were the house and out-houses of a free colored man, named Robinson. This table-land, which is bounded on three sides by a stream of water, was the theater of the principal struggle on the day in question.

Whilst the three brigades were operating against the Confederate left, Colonel Richardson, and Colonel T. A. Davies, of Miles's division, with their respective brigades and batteries, under Lieutenants Green and Benjamin, and Major Hunt, were making a strong demonstration on the Confederate right to distract him. Before nine o'clock, Evans had become satisfied that Tyler's attack, as well as the cannonade below, was only a feint, and that the real assault would be on his flank

SUDLEY CHURCH.[1]

and rear. He had been informed of the moving of the heavy columns through the forest toward Sudley's Ford, two miles above him, and he took immediate steps to oppose them. At about half-past nine, when the head of Hunter's column, led by Burnside, was crossing at Sudley Church, and the men were filling their canteens with fresh water from Bull's Run, Evans was posting his troops in a commanding

---

[1] This church, built of brick, and belonging to the Methodists, stood on the wooded right bank of Bull's Run, at Sudley's Ford, about two miles above the Stone Bridge.

position on the north side of the Warrenton turnpike, within the curve of Young's Branch. The re-enforcements ordered by Johnston had not reached him when he commenced this movement. He sent word to General Bee, who commanded the reserves nearest to him, to hurry forward in support, and leaving four of his fifteen regiments to guard the Stone Bridge, he hastened with the remaining eleven, composed of South Carolinians under Sloan, and Louisianians under Wheat, with two field-pieces of Latham's battery, to confront the approaching foe. He formed his line not far from the Pitt-sylvania Mansion of the Carter family, with the battery behind a house, his right covered by a grove, and his left sheltered by shrubbery along the road.

It was half-past ten before the head of Hunter's column, led by Burnside, came in sight of Evans. The division had rested half an hour at the ford, and, being well supplied with water, was quite refreshed. The Second Rhode Island, Colonel John Slocum, led. As they approached the open fields he threw out skirmishers, and very soon his regiment, with Marston's Second New Hampshire, and Martin's Seventy-first New York, with Griffin's battery, and Major Reynolds's Marine Artillery, of Rhode Island, opened the battle. Evans was soon so hard pressed that his line was beginning to waver, when General Bee, who had advanced with the detachments of his own and Bartow's Georgia brigade, and Imboden's battery, to the northern verge of the plateau, just described, perceiving the peril, hurried down the slope, crossed Young's Branch valley, and gave the Confederates such strength that the Nationals were in turn sorely pressed. These re-enforcements consisted of two Georgia regiments (Seventh and Eighth), under Bartow, the Fourth Alabama, and some Mississippians, while Imboden's battery, on the plateau, poured a destructive fire upon the Nationals.

GEORGIA HEAVY INFANTRY.

Burnside called for help; and Colonel Andrew Porter, whose brigade was marching down the Sudley's Spring Road, immediately furnished it, by sending a battalion of regulars under Major Sykes, of the Third Infantry, to his aid. These made the National line firm, and while the battle was raging with equal vigor on both sides, Colonel Hunter was so severely wounded that he was compelled to leave the field.[1] Colonel Slocum, of the Second Rhode Island, fell mortally wounded soon afterward, and his Major, Sullivan Ballou, had his leg crushed by a cannon-ball that killed his horse.[2]

<hr />

[1] Isaac N. Arnold, a member of the National House of Representatives, was a volunteer aid to Colonel Hunter, and remained on the field until that officer was wounded, when he devoted himself to having the wounded removed, and in attention to their wants.

[2] Major Ballou was taken to Sudley Church, which was used as a hospital, and there soon afterward died, at the age of thirty-two years. He was buried near the church. In March, 1862, the bodies of Slocum, Ballou, and Captain Tower, of the same regiment (the latter was killed at the beginning of the battle), were disinterred and conveyed to Rhode Island. When their remains reached New York, General Sandford detailed the Sixty-ninth, Seventy-first, and Thirty-seventh New York Regiments to act as an escort.

Porter was next in rank to Hunter, but his position was such, with his brigade, that the battle was directed by Burnside, who was ably assisted by Colonel Sprague, the youthful Governor of Rhode Island, who took the immediate command of the troops from his State.

The conflict had been going on for about an hour, and the result was doubtful, when Porter came up and poured a heavy fire upon Evans's left, which made his whole column waver and bend. Just then a strong force was seen coming over a ridge, in the direction of Bull's Run, to the assistance of the Nationals, and the head of Heintzelman's division, which had not reached the ford above when the battle commenced, was coming upon the field. The

column on the left was Sherman's brigade, from Tyler's right wing, led by Colonel Corcoran, with his New York Sixty-ninth, sixteen hundred strong. Using a high tree for an observatory, an officer of Tyler's staff had watched the movements of the columns of Hunter and Heintzelman from the moment when they crossed Bull's Run; and when there seemed danger that the tide of battle might be turned against the attacking force of his division, Tyler promptly ordered Sherman to cross just above the Stone Bridge to their assistance. He did so without much molestation, when his advance (the Sixty-ninth) soon encountered some of the Confederates flying before Hunter's forces.

MICHAEL CORCORAN.

Sherman's approach was timely. Those in conflict, having been on their feet most of the time since midnight, and having fought for an hour in the scorching sun, were much exhausted. Sherman's troops were fresh, and the Confederates knew it. Menaced by these on their right, heavily pressed by Burnside and Sykes on their center, and terribly galled by Porter on their left, they gave way, and their shattered column fled in confusion up the slopes of the plateau and across it, beyond the Robinson and Henry houses. The final blow that broke the Confederate line into fragments, and sent them flying, was a furious charge directly on their center by the New York Twenty-seventh, Colonel Henry W. Slocum.[1]

The fugitives found General T. J. Jackson, with Stanard's battery, on the plateau. He was in command of reserves next behind Bee, and had just arrived and taken position on the eastern edge of the table-land. When Bee hurriedly exclaimed, "They are beating us back!" Jackson calmly replied, "Well, Sir, we will give them the bayonet." This firmness encouraged Bee, and he tried to rally his men. "Form! form!" he cried. "There stands Jackson like a stone wall." The force of that idea was wonderful. The flight was checked, and comparative order was soon evolved out of the direst con-

---

[1] The troops engaged in this first severe conflict of the day were the First and Second Rhode Island, Second New Hampshire, Eighth, Fourteenth, and Twenty-seventh New York, Sykes's battalion of Regulars, Griffin's battery, and Major Reynolds's Rhode Island Marine Artillery.

fusion. From that time, the calm leader that stopped the flight was known as "Stonewall Jackson."

It was noon when Bee and Evans fled from the first field of close conflict, with their comrade, Colonel Wheat, desperately wounded, and joined Jackson on the plateau, while the Nationals were pressing closely in pursuit. Johnston and Beauregard, alarmed by the heavy firing, and by intelligence that reached them of the strength and movements of the Nationals, sent orders for Generals Holmes, Early, and Ewell to move with their troops with all possible speed in the direction of the sound of the battle, and for Bonham to send forward two regiments and a battery. They then hurried at a rapid gallop from their position, four miles distant, to the plateau, where they found the whole Confederate force to be only about seven thousand men, including Jackson's brigade. They were in a strong position, well sheltered by the thicket of pines already mentioned, and had thirteen cannon, most of them masked in shrubbery, in position to sweep the whole table-land with grape and canister. Pendleton, Johnston's Chief of Artillery, had been ordered to follow him with a battery. But the Nationals, who were then pressing hard upon them, greatly outnumbered them. It was a moment of intense anxiety for the Confederate commanders. They had little hope for victory unless their expected re-enforcements should speedily arrive.

There was not a moment to lose. Johnston comprehended the danger and sought to avert it. Placing himself by the colors of the Fourth Alabama Regiment, he proceeded to reorganize the broken columns of Bee, Bartow, and Evans; and Beauregard formed them in battle-line near the edge of the plateau, where the first shock of an impending attack might be felt. That leader, in a few hurried words, told his troops that the fate of the day depended on their holding their position on that commanding eminence.

When order was restored, Johnston left Beauregard in command on the battle-field, while he withdrew and made his head-quarters at the house of Mr. Lewis, known as "The Portico," on an eminence south of, and even higher than the plateau, from which he had a comprehensive view of the region beyond Bull's Run toward Centreville, the approaches to the Stone Bridge, the field of battle, and the valley far away toward Manassas, whence

ALABAMA LIGHT INFANTRY.

his re-enforcements came. There he exercised a general supervision of the army, and forwarded reserves and re-enforcements. Near his new quarters, Colonel Wade Hampton, who had come up from Richmond by railway that morning, with six infantry companies of his legion, had taken position as a reserve; and other re-enforcements were now beginning to arrive. When, between one and two o'clock in the afternoon, the struggle for the plateau commenced, the Confederates had on the field about ten thousand men, horse, foot, and artillery, and twenty-two heavy guns.

Whilst these movements were in progress on the west side of Bull's Run, General Schenck, with his brigade and Carlisle's battery, and a part of Ayres's, had been vainly endeavoring to turn or silence a Confederate battery opposite Tyler's extreme right. In this attempt the Second New York suffered severely. In the mean time, Keyes's brigade had followed Sherman's across the run, eight hundred yards above the Stone Bridge, taken a position on his left, and joined in the pursuit of the broken column of the Confederates. Their batteries near the bridge were soon withdrawn, and between two and three o'clock, Captain Alexander, of the Engineers, with a company of ax-men, proceeded to cut a passage through the abatis that obstructed the road. By three o'clock, there were no impediments in the way of the advance of re-enforcements from Centreville; for at one o'clock the National forces had possession of the Warrenton Turnpike from near the bridge westward, which was one of the grand objectives of the movement against the Confederate left.

"THE PORTICO."

But there was a formidable obstacle in the way of the complete execution of the design. The Confederates were on the commanding plateau, too near the turnpike and the bridge to make an attempt to strike the Manassas Gap Railway a safe operation. To drive them from it was the task now immediately in hand. To accomplish it, five brigades, namely, Porter's, Howard's, Franklin's, Wilcox's, and Sherman's, with the batteries of Ricketts, Griffin, and Arnold, and the cavalry under Major Palmer, were sent along and near the Sudley's Spring Road, to turn the Confederate left, while Keyes was sent to annoy them on the right. The brigade of Burnside, whose ammunition had been nearly exhausted in the morning battle, had withdrawn into a wood for the purpose of being supplied, and was not again in action. Eighteen thousand Nationals were on the west side of Bull's Run, and thirteen thousand of them were soon fighting the ten thousand Confederates on the plateau.

Up the slope south of the Warrenton Turnpike, the five brigades, the batteries, and the cavalry moved, accompanied by McDowell, with Heintzelman (whose division commenced the action here) as his chief lieutenant on the field. They were severely galled by the batteries of Imboden, Stanard, Pendleton, Alburtis of the Shenandoah Army,

WADE HAMPTON.

and portions of Walton's and Rogers's batteries of the Army of the Potomac. Yet they pressed forward, with the batteries of Ricketts and Griffin in front, and, outflanking the Confederates, were soon in possession of the western portion of the plateau. There was a swell of ground westward of the Henry house occupied by the Confederates, the possession of which was very important. Whoever held it could command the entire plateau. Ricketts and Griffin were ordered to seize it, and plant their batteries there. The Eleventh New York (Ellsworth's Fire Zouaves), Colonel Farnham, were assigned to their immediate support; and· the Twenty-seventh New York, Fifth and Eleventh Massachusetts, the Second Minnesota, and Corcoran's Sixty-ninth New York, were moved up to the left of the batteries.

The Artillery and the Zouaves went boldly forward in the face of a severe cannonade, until an ambushed Alabama regiment suddenly came out from a clump of pines partly on their flank, and poured upon them a terrible shower of bullets. This hot and unexpected attack made the Zouaves, who had never been under fire, recoil, when two companies of the fine corps of Stuart's horsemen, known as the Black Horse Cavalry (Carter's and Hoge's), dashed furiously upon their rear from the woods on the Sudley's Spring Road. A portion of the Zouaves' line now broke in some confusion, and the cavalry went entirely through their shattered column. Farnham

VIRGINIA ARTILLERY.—ROCKINGHAM BATTERY.

and his officers displayed great coolness. They rallied most of the regiment, under the immediate eye of McDowell, and, with a part of Colburn's United States Cavalry, and led by Colonel J. H. Ward, of Wilcox's brigade, they attacked the Confederate horsemen and dispersed them. The Zouaves, as a compact regiment, did not again appear in the battle; but a larger portion of them, under their Colonel, and others who attached themselves to different regiments, did valiant service wherever they found work to do.

It was now about two o'clock. Keyes's brigade, on the left, had been arrested by a severe fire from a battery of eight guns on the hill near Robinson's buildings, and shelled by them from the National batteries on their left. Tyler ordered him to capture it. He assigned the Third Connecticut, Colonel

BLACK HORSE CAVALRY.[1]

Chatfield, and the Second Maine, Colonel Jamieson, to that perilous duty. They charged directly up the northern slope of the plateau, and drove the

---

[1] This corps received its name from the fact that all the horses were black. The corps was composed chiefly of the sons of wealthy Virginians; and their whole outfit was of the most expensive kind.

Confederates from Robinson's buildings; but the battery was too well defended by infantry and riflemen to be taken by them. They instantly found themselves exposed to a terrible fire from breastworks in their rear, which threatened their speedy annihilation. They withdrew; and under the brow of the hill, and sheltered by the pine thicket, Keyes led his brigade in search of some favorable spot to charge upon the Confederate left, but without success. This march, which led Keyes a mile or more from the hottest of the battle on the western edge of the plateau, caused the Confederates to retire from the Stone Bridge, and gave Captain Alexander the opportunity to make a passage through the abatis, as we have observed.

The struggle for the possession of the plateau, in the mean time, had been fearful. When the Zouaves gave way, Heintzelman ordered up the First Minnesota Regiment, Colonel Gorman, to the support of the batteries, which were directed to take position on the extreme right. The infantry and the artillery did so at the double quick, when they found themselves suddenly confronted by troops less than a hundred feet from them. The Nationals were embarrassed, for an instant, by doubt whether they were friends or foes. Heintzelman himself was uncertain, and he rode in between the two lines. The problem was solved a moment afterward, when the colors of each were seen. Then a blaze of fire flashed from each line, and terrible slaughter ensued. Both batteries were disabled by the first volley, for, it prostrated a greater portion of the cannoneers and one-half of the horses. Captain Ricketts was wounded, and Lieutenant D. Ramsay was killed. The Confederates were there in overwhelming numbers. The Minnesota regiment was compelled to retire. The First Michigan and Fourteenth New York were likewise repulsed. The Confederates, too, were often pushed back, and both sides fought with the greatest bravery. "Stonewall Jackson" had dashed forward and attempted to carry off the guns, but was driven back by the Thirty-eighth New York and the Zouaves, and the latter dragged three of Ricketts' pieces away, but not far enough to save them.

In the mean time, McDowell had ordered Sherman, who occupied the center of the National force, to charge the batteries of the Confederates with his entire brigade, and sweep them from the hill. Placing the riflemen of Quimby's Thirteenth New York in front, he ordered the Second Wisconsin, Lieutenant-Colonel Peck, the Seventy-ninth (Scotch) New York, Colonel Cameron, and the Sixty-ninth (Irish) New York, Colonel Corcoran, to follow in battle order. The brigade dashed across the Warrenton Turnpike and up the slopes of the plateau to the left of the Sudley's Spring Road, in the face of a galling artillery fire, toward the point where Ricketts' Battery was so severely cut up. They saw the Zouave and other regiments hurled back, but, steadily advancing, had reached the brow of the hill, when the Wisconsin regiment received a severe fire from the Confederates. They withstood it for a while, returning it with spirit, when they broke and fled down the hill in confusion. Being dressed in gray, like the great bulk of the Confederate army, they were fired upon by the Nationals. They rallied, pushed up to the brow of the hill, and were again repulsed. The Seventy-ninth New York then closed up, and pressed forward in the face of a murderous fire from rifles, muskets, and cannon. Headed by Cameron (who was brother of the Secretary of War), they charged across the hill, and fought desperately with the Confederates, who were there in much greater force than was expected. The gallant Cameron was killed,[1] and for the third time they were repulsed. Then Corcoran led his Sixty-ninth to the charge, and the roar of cannon and musketry was incessant. The regiment received and repelled a furious charge of the Black Horse Cavalry, whose ranks were terribly shattered by the murderous fire of the Irish and some Zouaves who had joined them. They held their position for some time, but were compelled at length to give way before fresh troops in overwhelming numbers, who were pouring in and turning the tide of battle. At that moment, Corcoran was some distance in front, and becoming separated from his troops by the falling of his horse, which was shot dead, he was made prisoner. It was now half-past three o'clock.

Now was the crisis of the battle. The slaughter had been fearful. For an hour, dead and wounded men of both sides had been carried from the field in large numbers. The Confederates had lost many officers. Bee and Bartow had fallen near each other, not far from Mrs. Henry's. Hampton, at the head of his legion, had been wounded during the charge of the Seventy-ninth, and Lieutenant-Colonel Johnston of his corps had been killed. Beauregard had placed himself at the head of the Legion, and led it gallantly against his foe, when he was slightly wounded by a shell that cut off the head of his horse and killed two others on which his aids were riding. Jackson had been wounded, but did not leave the field.

At that time the Confederates were sorely pressed, and Johnston, at "The Portico," with full knowledge of the situation, began to lose heart. Victory seemed about to perch on the National standard. He believed the day was lost. Why did not Early come with his three fresh regiments? He had sent him word at eleven o'clock to hurry forward, and now it was

CAVALRY OF HAMPTON'S LEGION.

three. By some mischance, the order did not reach him until two. He was on the way; but would he be up in time? "Oh for four regiments!" cried Johnston to Colonel Cocke, in the bitterness of his soul.[2] His wish was soon more than satisfied.

Just then, a cloud of dust was seen in the direction of the Manassas Gap Railway. Johnston had already been informed that United States troops were on that road. He believed Patterson had outmarched his oncoming

[1] The biographer of Colonel Cameron says: "No mortal man could stand the fearful storm that swept them. As they fell back, Cameron again and again led them up, his 'Scots, follow me!' ringing above the din of battle, till at last Wade Hampton, who had marked his gallant bearing, and fired rifle after rifle at him, as his men handed them up, accomplished his murderous purpose." He was buried near the house of Mr. Dogan.
[2] Statement of an eye and ear witness, in a letter to the *Richmond Despatch*, dated July 22, 1861.

Army of the Shenandoah, and with fresh troops would easily gain a victory for the Nationals. The story was untrue. They were Johnston's own troops, about four thousand in number, under General E. Kirby Smith, of Connecticut. They had come down by the Manassas Gap Railway; and when Smith heard the thunder of cannon on his left, he stopped the cars, and leaving them, he hurried across the country with his troops in the direction of the conflict, with three regiments of Elzy's Brigade. Johnston received him at "The Portico" with joy, and ordered him to attack the right flank of the Nationals immediately. In doing so he fell, severely wounded, when Colonel Elzy executed the order promptly.

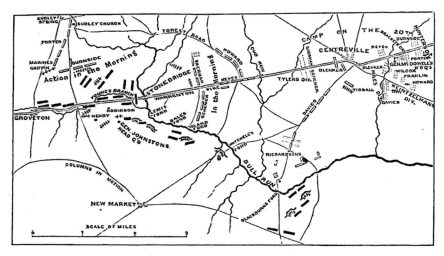

MAP ILLUSTRATING THE BATTLE OF BULL'S RUN.

When Johnston saw his re-enforcements coming, he ordered Colonel Cocke's brigade up from Bull's Run, to join in the action, and within a half an hour the South Carolina regiments of Cash and Kershaw, of Bonham's brigade, with Fisher's North Carolina regiment, were also pressing hard upon the right of the Nationals. With all these re-enforcements, Beauregard's army of twelve regiments, with which he began the battle, had been increased to the number of twenty-five. These were now all concentrating on the right and rear of McDowell's forces. The woods on his flank and rear were soon swarming with Confederates, who were pouring destructive volleys of musketry and cannon-shot upon him. The blow was sudden, unexpected, heavy, and overpowering. In the course of fifteen minutes, the National army, expectant of victory, was swept from the plateau and its slopes. There was no time for Burnside's rested brigade to come up, nor for Schenck's to cross Bull's Run. As regiment after regiment gave way, and hurried toward the turnpike in confusion, others were seized with panic, and joined in the race from danger. At four o'clock, a greater portion of the National Army was moving rapidly toward Sudley's Ford and other passages of Bull's Run, toward Centreville. With many of the regiments it was not a retreat, nor an orderly flight, but a rout, absolute and uncontrollable. It was seen with the greatest exultation by Jefferson Davis, who had left Richmond that morning, arrived at Manassas Junction at four o'clock, and hastened on horseback to the head-quarters of Johnston. From the Junction, that night,[a] he telegraphed to his "Congress," which had convened in Richmond the day before—"Night has closed upon a hard-fought field. Our forces were victorious. The enemy was routed,

[a] July 21, 1861.

BULL'S RUN BATTLE-GROUND.[1]

and fled precipitately, abandoning a large amount of arms, ammunition, knapsacks, and baggage. The ground was strewed for miles with those killed, and the farm-houses and the ground around were filled with wounded. . . . Our force was fifteen thousand; that of the enemy estimated at thirty-five thousand."[2]

Why did not Patterson hold Johnston at Winchester, or re-enforce McDowell at Bull's Run? was a question asked by the people with the severest earnestness, when it was known that to the presence of the former and his troops must be, in a great degree, attributed the disasters that had befallen the National arms. With better information than the public then possessed, the question may now be answered, with the sanction of official and semi-official records, in these few words :—Because his force was greatly inferior in numbers and appointment to that of Johnston ; because he was posi-

---

[1] This is from a drawing by Mr. Forbes, already mentioned, made after the evacuation of Manassas by the Confederates, in the spring of 1862. It was taken from near the center of the battle-field, and shows the ruins of Mrs. Henry's house, and to the right of them, through an opening in the distance, looking southeast, is seen Manassas Junction. In the foreground is seen a portion of a small marble monument erected to the memory of General Bee, whose body was buried on that spot. Other graves are seen near; and turkey buzzards, which uncovered many bodies that were put in shallow graves, are seen feasting on the carcass of a horse.

Mrs. Henry, it is said, was confined to her bed, and remained in her house during the battle. Shot and shell went through it, and she was wounded two or three times. She died soon afterward. Robinson was yet occupying his house, with his family, at the close of 1865.

[2] This was not only an exaggeration but a misrepresentation. From the most reliable authorities on both sides, it appears that, in the final struggle, the Nationals had about thirteen thousand men and the Confederates about twenty-seven thousand. The latter had been receiving re-enforcements all day, while not a man crossed Bull's Run after twelve o'clock to re-enforce the Nationals.

tively instructed not to fight without a moral certainty of success;[1] because his army had commenced dissolving, by the expiration of the terms of enlistment of the three-months regiments, and when Johnston started for

Manassas[a] Patterson could not have brought ten thousand effec-

a July 18, 1861. tive men into action; and because, by some strange mischance,

he was for five days, at the most critical time, namely, from the 17th to the 22d of July, when McDowell was moving upon Manassas and fighting the Confederates, without the slightest communication from the General-in-chief, whilst he (Patterson) was anxiously asking for information

and advice. He had been informed by General Scott on the 12th,[b]

b July. that Manassas would be attacked on Tuesday, the 16th. On the

13th, he was directed by his Chief to make demonstrations to keep Johnston at Winchester, if he (Patterson) did not feel strong enough to attack him. Patterson made the demonstration, accordingly, on the day when Manassas was to be attacked, and drove Johnston's pickets within their intrenchments. On the following day he moved his army to Charlestown, where he could more easily re-enforce McDowell, if called to do so; and at the same time he re-

ceived a dispatch from Scott,[c] saying—"McDowell's first day's

c July 17. work has driven the enemy beyond Fairfax Court House. To-

morrow, probably, the Junction will be carried."

Johnston was still at Winchester, with full thirty thousand troops, and Patterson, supposing that the work at Manassas would be completed on the morrow, felt a satisfaction in having accomplished what he was ordered to do. He was too weak to attack Johnston, but he had held him, he believed,

until Beauregard was smitten. On the following morning,[d] at the

d July 18. hour when Johnston received orders to hasten to Manassas, Pat-

terson telegraphed to Scott the relative forces of the opposing armies in the Valley, showing his to be greatly inferior, but asking, "Shall I strike?" To this he received no reply; and when, on the 20th, he telegraphed to the Chief that Johnston, with a greater part of his army, had moved off southwestward, and he received no orders in reply, he supposed that McDowell had been victorious at Manassas, and that the Confederates, in numbers too overwhelming to make it prudent for him to follow, were flying from the Valley for safety. The first knowledge that he received of the battle, fought three days later than was intended, was conveyed to him in a newspaper from Philadelphia.[2] Patterson seems to have done all that was possible for a prudent and obedient soldier to do, under the circumstances. If he did not prevent the disaster at Bull's Run, he undoubtedly prevented a greater, by keeping Johnston and his heavy force from a meditated invasion of Maryland, and the capture of Washington City by assault in the rear.

The flight of the National army back to the defenses of Washington, and the attending circumstances, afforded one of the most impressive, picturesque, and even ludicrous episodes in history. The determination, the strength, and the resources of the Confederates had been greatly underrated, and there was perfect confidence in the public mind that the impending

---

[1] See page 520.

[2] For a full elucidation of this matter, see volume ii. of the *Report of the Committee on the Conduct of the War;* and *Narrative of the Campaign in the Shenandoah Valley:* by Major-General Robert Patterson.

battle near Manassas would result in absolute and crushing victory for the National arms. It was expected to be the finishing blow to the rebellion. The skirmish of the 18th had cast only a passing cloud over the otherwise serene sky of expectation; and it was dispelled in the course of twenty-four hours.

It became known at Washington on Saturday that McDowell was to attack Beauregard on the line of Bull's Run on Sunday, and scores of men, and even women—Congressmen, officials of every grade, and plain citizens —went out to see the grand spectacle, as the Romans went to the Coliseum to see the gladiators fight. They had tickets of admission to the amphitheater of hills near Bull's Run, in the form of passes from the military authorities; and early on Sunday morning Centreville was gay with civilians. The headquarters of Colonel Miles was crowded with guests, where wine and cigars were used prodigally. The Hights during the day were covered with spectators and the soldiery enjoying the new sensation of the sight of clouds of smoke over the battle-field in the distance, and the roar of heavy guns far and near, whose booming was heard even at Alexandria and Washington City. As the battle waxed hotter, and the interest became more intense,

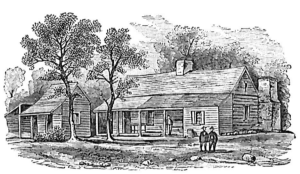

MILES'S HEAD-QUARTERS AT CENTREVILLE.

some, more courageous or more curious than others, pushed on toward the Stone Bridge, some distance beyond Cub Run, where they could hear the scream of shells, and see the white puffs of smoke when they exploded in the air. The excitement was delicious whilst danger was distant; but before sunset, cheeks that glowed with exhilaration at noon, were pale with terror. Then the actors and the audience were commingled in wild disorder, in a flight from the scenes of the bloody drama as precipitate as that from a theater on fire.

When the right of the National army gave way, Johnston, hoping to cut off their retreat, ordered Ewell to cross Bull's Run in heavy force, and attack the left at Centreville. Ewell instantly made the attempt, but his columns were so severely smitten by a storm of grape and canister, from the heavy guns of the gallant Colonel Davies, that they recoiled, and fled back in confusion. The enterprise was abandoned, and thereafter the left was unmolested. Davies was the senior of Richardson in rank, and commanded the detachment which all day long had been watching the lower fords, and annoying passing columns of the Confederates beyond Bull's Run with shot and shell from the batteries of Green, Hunt, Benjamin, and Tidball, the latter belonging to Colonel Blenker's brigade.

Whilst the left was standing firmly, the vanquished right was moving from the field of strife, in haste and much disorder, towards the passages of

Bull's Run, from the Stone Bridge to Sudley's Ford, pursued by Confederates of all arms, who made many prisoners. Still greater would have been the number of captives, had not many of the troops been free from panic, and in condition to cover the retreat and give encouragement to the disordered mass. When McDowell perceived that the day was lost, and retreat inevitable, his first care was to protect his army in its flight. For this purpose he detailed Colonel Porter and his regulars, with the cavalry. He also sent word to Miles to order a brigade to the Warrenton Road, at Cub Run, for the same purpose, and Blenker was sent. McDowell himself hastened to the left, where he found much confusion that might prove dangerous, caused by orders and counter-orders of Miles and his brigade commanders. He was informed that Miles had been intoxicated nearly all day, and playing the buffoon, to the disgust of his officers and men. So he took command of the division himself, for Miles could not be trusted.

Porter performed his duties admirably. He kept the Confederates in check; and after the retreat had fairly begun, according to orders, there was not much panic or confusion visible, until those who crossed at and near the Stone Bridge, and others at the fords above, met in converging streams (one along the Warrenton Turnpike, and the other down the forest road traversed by Hunter and Heintzelman in the morning) near the bridge over Cub Run, which was barricaded by a caisson [1] that had been overturned on it by a solid shot from the pursuers. Schenck's Brigade had already crossed, and gone on to Centreville, but many civilians in his rear were caught here by the hurrying mass of soldiers. The excitement was intense. The number of the pursuers was magnified by fear from five hundred to five thousand, and they were not far behind. Shots from their Flying Artillery were coming too near to be harmless. Frightened teamsters cut their horses loose, mounted them, and scampered away, leaving their wagons to block the road. The drivers of artillery horses did the same, and left their cannon behind to be seized by the Confederates. Full one-third of the artillery lost that day was left between Cub Run and the Stone Bridge. [2]

The caisson on the bridge was soon removed, and onward the excited mass pressed. Blenker's protecting brigade, lying across the road, opened and let them pass; and at twilight the fugitives were all behind the lines at Centreville, where the Fifth Division, intact, formed a strong protecting force. Ignorant of the number and exact position of McDowell's reserves, only five hundred cavalry of the pursuing force crossed Bull's Run that even-

---

[1] A caisson is an ammunition-chest on wheels, for the service of artillery in battle.

[2] The Nationals lost twenty-seven cannon, ten of which were captured on the field, and the remainder were abandoned during the flight to Centreville. They had forty-nine pieces in all, of which twenty-eight were rifled. All but two were fully horsed and equipped. Only twenty-eight of the forty-nine pieces crossed Bull's Run before the battle, and only one was brought safely back to Centreville. Besides these cannon, the Nationals lost a large amount of small arms, ammunition, stores, provisions, and clothing. A large number of the knapsacks and blankets that were lost had been laid aside by the soldiers before going into battle, on account of the heat of the day.

Beauregard reported his spoils of victory to be twenty-eight field-pieces captured, with over one hundred rounds of ammunition for each gun: also thirty-seven caissons; six forges; four battery-wagons; sixty-four artillery horses completely equipped; five hundred thousand rounds of small arms ammunition; four thousand five hundred sets of accouterments, and over five thousand muskets. His engineer-in-chief, Captain E. P. Alexander, reported in addition as captured, a large number of intrenching, carpenters', and blacksmiths' tools; camp and cooking utensils; clothing and blankets; twenty-two tents, and a large quantity of medicines and hospital supplies.

ing; and when, at dusk, these encountered some of Blenker's pickets in the gloom, they wheeled and hastened back to the Stone Bridge, when some of his brigade went boldly forward, and brought away two of the cannon abandoned near Cub Run.[1] In the mean time a part of Beauregard's reserves, which had been ordered up, had arrived.

At Centreville, McDowell held a brief and informal council with his officers, when it was determined to continue the retreat to the defenses of Washington, for the shattered and demoralized army was in no

STONE CHURCH, CENTREVILLE.

condition to resist even one-half of the Confederates known to be at Manassas. They had been on duty almost twenty-four hours, without sleep, without much rest, and many of them without food; and during seven or eight hours of the time, a greater portion of those who came over Bull's Run had been fighting under a blazing sun. They needed rest; but so dangerous did it seem to remain, that the soldiers cheerfully obeyed the order to move forward. Indeed, large numbers of them had already done so. Leaving the sick, and wounded, and dying, who could not be removed, under proper caretakers in a stone church at Centreville (which was used a long time as a hospital), the army moved forward at a little past ten o'clock, with Colonel Richardson's brigade as a rear-guard. Most of them reached the camps near Washington, which they had left in high spirits on the 16th,[a] before daylight. Richardson left Centreville at two o'clock

MONUMENT ON BULL'S RUN BATTLE-GROUND.

[a] July, 1861.

in the morning, when all the other troops and batteries had retired, and twelve hours afterward he was with his brigade on Arlington Hights. The survivors of the conflict had left behind them not less, probably, in killed, wounded, and prisoners, than three thousand five hundred of their comrades,

---

[1] Beauregard, in his official report, gives as the reason for relinquishing the pursuit, a report that McDowell's reserves, "known to be fresh and of considerable strength," he said, "were threatening the position of Union Mills Ford," near which lay the forces under Ewell.

though the official report made the number somewhat less. The Confederates, who held the field, lost not less, it is believed, than twenty-five hundred, though Beauregard in his Report gave the number about nineteen hundred.[1]

Such was the immediate and most dreadful result of this first great conflict of the Civil War, known as the BATTLE OF BULL'S RUN.[2] We shall hereafter observe its effects upon public sentiment—how it increased the arrogance of the conspirators, and the number of their adherents—how it quickened into powerful and practical action the feeling of nationality and intense love for the Union latent in the hearts of all loyal Americans—how it produced another and more important uprising of the faithful People in defense of the Republic, and how it made the enemies of the Union in Europe hopeful that it would utterly perish in the struggle then earnestly begun.

---

[1] In the compilation of this account of the BATTLE OF BULL'S RUN, I have drawn the materials chiefly from the various official Reports of Generals McDowell, Beauregard, and Johnston, and their subordinate commanders. McDowell reported his loss at four hundred and eighty-one killed, and one thousand and eleven wounded. Of the missing, many of whom afterward re-appeared, and a large portion were prisoners, he made no report. They were estimated at about fifteen hundred, which would make the total National loss two thousand nine hundred and ninety-two. Beauregard reported his loss three hundred and seventy-eight killed, one thousand four hundred and eighty-nine wounded, and thirty missing—in all, one thousand eight hundred and ninety-seven. His estimate of missing is much below the mark. More than one hundred, captured during the day, were sent to Washington.

Among the killed of the National Army were Colonel James Cameron, of the Seventy-ninth New York (Highlanders); Colonel John Slocum and Major Ballou, of the Second Rhode Island; and Lieutenant-Colonel Haggerty, of the New York Sixty-ninth (Corcoran's Irish Regiment). Among the wounded were Colonels Hunter, Heintzelman, Wilcox, Gilman, Martin, Wood, H. W. Slocum, Farnham, and Corcoran, and Major James D. Potter. Wilcox, Corcoran, and Potter, were made prisoners.

[2] The Confederate commanders, and the writers in their interest, call it the BATTLE OF MANASSAS. It was fought much nearer Bull's Run than Manassas, and the title above given seems the most correct. About four years after the battle, when the war had ceased, National soldiers erected on the spot where the conflict raged most fiercely, a very few yards southward from the site of Mrs. Henry's House, a substantial monument of stone, in commemoration of their compatriots who fell there. A picture of it is given on the preceding page. It is made of ordinary sandstone, found near Manassas Junction. Its total hight is twenty-seven feet, including the base, and it stands upon an elevated mound. On each corner of the base is a block of sandstone, on which rest elongated conical 100-pounder shells, the cone pointing upward. The top of the shaft is also surmounted by one. On one side of the monument are these words:—"IN MEMORY OF THE PATRIOTS WHO FELL AT BULL RUN, JULY 21, 1861." On the other side:—"ERECTED JUNE 10, 1865." It was constructed by the officers and soldiers of the Sixteenth Massachusetts Light Battery, Lieutenant James McCallom (who conceived the idea), and the Fifth Pennsylvania Heavy Artillery, Colonel Gallup. Generals Heintzelman, Wilcox, and others, who fought in the battle, were present at the dedication of the monument at the date above named. The picture is from a photograph by Gardner, of Washington City. A hymn, written for the occasion by the Rev. John Pierpont, then eighty years of age, was sung. The services were opened by Rev. Dr. McMurdy, of Kentucky; and several officers made speeches.

CPSIA information can be obtained at www.ICGtesting.com
Printed in the USA
BVOW041904191112

305966BV00001B/12/P